A CASE STUDY OF MAINSTREAM PROTESTANTISM

A Case Study
of Mainstream Protestantism

The Disciples' Relation to American Culture,
1880–1989

Edited by

D. Newell Williams

WILLIAM B. EERDMANS PUBLISHING COMPANY
GRAND RAPIDS, MICHIGAN

CHALICE PRESS
ST. LOUIS

Copyright © 1991 by Wm. B. Eerdmans Publishing Co.
First published 1991 jointly by
Wm. B. Eerdmans Publishing Co.,
255 Jefferson Ave. S.E., Grand Rapids, Mich. 49503
and Chalice Press, P.O. Box 179,
St. Louis, Mo. 63166.

Printed in the United States of America

Library of Congress Cataloging-in-Publication Data

A Case study of mainstream Protestantism: the Disciples' relation to
   American culture, 1880-1989 / edited by D. Newell Williams.
     p.   cm.
   Essays based on drafts presented at a conference entitled
"Twentieth-Century Disicples" held 15-18 April, 1989 at Christian
Theological Seminary.
   Includes bibliographical references.
   1. Christian Church (Disciples of Christ) — Congresses.
2. Protestant churches — United States — Influence — Case
studies — Congresses.   I. Williams, D. Newell.
BX7305.C37   1991
286.6'73 — dc20   91-13552
                                 CIP

Eerdmans ISBN: 0-8028-0540-X
Chalice Press ISBN: 0-8272-0460-4

Contents

V. STRUCTURE

VI. THEOLOGICAL, MORAL, AND SOCIAL PROFILE

VII. ECOLOGY OF GROWTH AND DECLINE

VIII. CONCLUSION

Preface: The Disciples as a Case Study of Mainstream Protestantism

The Disciples, officially known since 1968 as the Christian Church (Disciples of Christ), and other "mainstream" Protestant denominations have declined numerically since the mid-1960s and have suffered significant losses of influence in American culture. In response to the changing status of the Disciples and other mainstream Protestant denominations, the Lilly Endowment awarded Christian Theological Seminary a grant to facilitate an examination of the Christian Church (Disciples of Christ) as a case study of mainstream Protestantism. The essays in this volume represent one segment of this project. The purpose of these essays is to help the Disciples and other mainstream Protestant denominations to better understand their current situation and make appropriate responses to their changing status in American society.

The terms *mainstream* and *mainline* have been used in recent scholarship in relation to religious bodies in at least two ways. William R. Hutchison has used the term *mainline* to refer to a religious "establishment" identifiable both as a group of denominations and a network of leaders related to those denominations that existed *within* American Protestantism. He notes that when historians have used the term *mainline* with regard to nineteenth-century religion, they have almost always meant Congregationalists, Episcopalians, Presbyterians, and the white divisions of the Baptist and Methodist families. He further notes that the Disciples have usually been included, along with the United Lutherans, only for the decades *since* 1900, while the southern segment of the Baptists has been seen as intentionally distancing itself from the mainline churches during this later period. This establishment has generally been described as having exercised a dominant religious influence on American culture during the first half of the twentieth century.[1] The churches included in this definition of mainline

---

1. Hutchison, *Between the Times: The Travail of the Protestant Establishment in America, 1900-1960*, ed. William R. Hutchison (Cambridge: Cambridge University Press, 1989), pp. 3-4.

have all declined numerically and suffered a loss of influence in American culture since the mid-1960s.

Sociologists Wade Clark Roof and William McKinney have defined mainstream religious groups as those that "identify with and contribute to the definition of the society's core values."[2] This allows them to suggest that the Disciples joined the mainline *before* 1900 and to include the Southern Baptists and other groups that have grown since the mid-1960s in their discussion of contemporary mainline religion. According to Roof and McKinney, mainstream groups may be classified along a liberal to conservative spectrum according to religious, social, and political views. On the left is the Jewish community. Just to the right of the Jewish community are liberal Protestants, identified as Episcopalians, Presbyterians, and the United Church of Christ. In the center are Catholics and moderate Protestants, identified as the Methodists, Lutherans, Northern Baptists, the Reformed churches, and the Disciples. To the right of the center are Black Protestant denominations. To their right are conservative Protestants, such as Southern Baptists, Churches of Christ, Nazarenes, Assemblies of God, and Churches of God.[3] According to this classification, only the moderate and liberal mainline groups have declined numerically and suffered a loss of influence in American culture since the mid-1960s.

The year 1880 was chosen as the starting point for this study for two reasons. First, in 1880 James A. Garfield, a Disciples preacher and educator who had served for seventeen years in the U.S. Congress, was elected president of the United States. The election of a Disciples preacher to the highest office in the land clearly suggests that by 1880 Disciples were viewed — at least by the American electorate — as identifying with and contributing to "society's core values." According to the criteria offered by Roof and McKinney, this means that the Disciples were a mainstream denomination in 1880. (Two other Disciples have since been elected president: Lyndon Johnson and Ronald Reagan.) More importantly, however, by 1880 the Disciples were clearly in the process of joining the mainstream according to the narrower definition of that term given by Hutchison. This study of the Disciples will help us to see how a denomination that has identified with and contributed to society's core values since at least 1880 eventually became part of the group of churches *within* American Protestantism that have been identified by historians as having exercised a dominant religious influence on American culture during the first half of the twentieth century — an influence that is widely recognized as having diminished more recently.

The essays in this volume examine the socioeconomic status of the Disciples and explore how and why the Disciples have changed in their beliefs,

2. Roof and McKinney, *American Mainline Religion: Its Changing Shape and Future* (New Brunswick, N.J.: Rutgers University Press, 1987), p. 236.

3. Roof and McKinney, *American Mainline Religion,* pp. 223-28. See also Bruce Greer's essay in this volume, "Active and Inactive Disciples, Presbyterians and Southern Baptists: A Comparative Profile," pp. 386-415).

mission, educational programs, organization, geographical distribution, and growth rate over the past one hundred years. They also consider the current theological and moral positions of Disciples ministers and laity. Because of the Disciples' historic relationships to the Presbyterians and the Baptists (most of the early Disciples congregations were either Presbyterian or Baptist in origin) and because of contemporary similarities and differences among Disciples, Presbyterians, Northern Baptists, and Southern Baptists, several of the essays compare the Disciples to Presbyterians and/or Baptists.

In the introductory chapter of this volume I offer an explanation of how and why the Disciples have changed in relation to American culture since 1880 and an assessment of their current situation based on my interpretation of the chapters that follow. In the concluding chapter I offer recommendations to the Christian Church (Disciples of Christ) based on my interpretation of the findings of this study. I have included these two chapters in the hope that they will provoke discussion of the findings in this study. I concede that the materials of this study are open to other interpretations, and indeed that any of the other contributors to this study might have written these two chapters differently.

The design of this volume began to emerge at a conference in Indianapolis held 13-14 December 1987 for the purposes of identifying key areas for research and the names of scholars who might contribute to the study. The forty persons who attended the conference included theologians, historians, sociologists, and Disciples pastors, regional ministers, and general church executives. In addition, thirty-two members of Indianapolis-area Disciples congregations joined the conference participants in a two-hour session devoted to identifying the perspectives of Disciples laity regarding the changing status of the Disciples.

Based on the conclusions of the 1987 conference, I prepared and widely disseminated a call for research proposals. After a number of proposals had been accepted, James O. Duke and Wade Clark Roof provided valuable counsel by identifying gaps in the emerging study and scholars who might be invited to pursue specific topics and issues.

The writers of this volume met in Indianapolis 3-5 December 1988 to mutually criticize and discuss their research.

Early drafts of the essays were presented 15-18 April 1989 to a conference at Christian Theological Seminary (CTS) entitled "Twentieth-Century Disciples: Appraising a Mainstream Denomination and Its Future Prospects." The conference, which gathered 197 participants, was divided into six working groups, each of which heard and discussed three or four of the essays. Both ordained and lay Disciples leaders served as moderators of the groups and presented formal responses to the papers. A response from each of the working groups was drafted by a CTS student, approved by the working group as a whole, and presented to the concluding session of the conference. These responses have been included in this volume.

James M. Washington of Union Theological Seminary in New York, who was to have been a contributor to this volume, presented remarks at the April 1989 conference entitled "Peculiar Restorationism of African-American Disciples and Baptists." Unfortunately, Professor Washington did not submit an essay for inclusion in this volume.

Four other papers presented to the conference could not be included because of constraints on the length of this volume. These essays, which complement the chapters that follow, are to be published elsewhere: Edwin L. Becker's "Yale Divinity School and the Disciples of Christ"; Judith Kaye Jones's "Changing Authority and Practice in Disciples Worship, 1880-1989"; William H. Brackney's "Disciples as Compared to American Baptists, 1880-1980: A Search for Denominational Integrity"; and John P. Marcum's "Family, Birth Control, and Sexuality in the Christian Church (Disciples of Christ): 1880-1980."

Kathleen Bell had major responsibilities in making arrangements for the 1989 conference and also assisted in innumerable ways in the administrative tasks of assembling a volume written by twenty-eight authors. Mary Lindop was a great help in the final stages of preparing the manuscript.

I would like to thank the people mentioned above and all others who participated in the conferences, helped to make them possible, or helped to identify scholars who have contributed to the project. I would also like to express my appreciation to C. Jones Russell, a Disciples elder who commented on early drafts of the introduction and conclusion of this volume.

A further word of appreciation is due to three other individuals. First, to Robert Wood Lynn, former vice president for religion of the Lilly Endowment, whose concern for the role of religious groups in American life stands behind this and numerous other studies of American religion. Second, to Richard D. N. Dickinson, president of Christian Theological Seminary, who requested funds for the Disciples Study and has been supportive of the project at every stage of its development. And, finally, I wish to express appreciation to my spouse, Mary Susan McDougal, my most supportive colleague in this as in so many other endeavors, and the one Disciples minister who more than any other helps me to keep in touch with a pastor's perspective on the joys and sorrows, frustrations and opportunities of leading a Disciples congregation.

D. Newell Williams

I. INTRODUCTION

How and Why the Disciples Have Changed in Relation to American Culture

D. Newell Williams

The Disciples have experienced three major shifts in their relation to American culture since 1880. With each of these shifts the Disciples have lost the ability to directly influence the culture of a significant segment of American society. The first shift in the relation of the Disciples to American culture occurred in the latter decades of the nineteenth century. It was directly related to the Disciples' first major division, which produced the separate body known as the Churches of Christ. The second shift occurred in the 1920s. It was directly related to the second major Disciples division, which produced the separate body known as the Christian Churches and Churches of Christ (often referred to by Disciples as the Independents or Independent Christian Churches). The third shift began in the 1960s. It has been marked by a sharp numerical decline that is largely attributable to the failure of the Disciples to appeal to the current generation of younger adults — the so-called "baby boomers."

The purpose of this chapter is to explain how and why the Disciples have changed in relation to American culture since 1880 and to show the relation of these changes to the Disciples' emergence as a "moderate" Protestant denomination. Each of the major shifts in the relation of the Disciples to American culture is related to major social developments in American history. At the same time, the diminishing cultural influence of the Disciples which has resulted from their shifts in relation to American culture can be attributed to theological and institutional failings. These failings, still evident in their corporate life, constitute a threat to their future prospects.

I. THE FIRST DIVISION: CHURCHES OF CHRIST

The first shift in the Disciples' relation to American culture is directly associated with the separation of the Disciples and the Churches of Christ. The

3

major issues in this division were the use of instrumental music in worship and the deployment of missionaries through missionary societies. Some Disciples opposed these practices on the grounds that they did not find them authorized by the teaching or example of the apostles as recorded in the New Testament. Other Disciples promoted these practices as mere "expedients" for achieving ends that all Disciples agreed were advocated by the apostles.

Disciples who were to become identified with the Churches of Christ refused Christian fellowship with the supporters of the disputed measures. Disciples who were to remain identified as Disciples advocated the disputed measures or at least chose to remain in Christian fellowship with those who did. Although the actual date of the separation is subject to debate, the existence of a separate body known as the Churches of Christ was officially recognized in the federal census of 1906.

The importance of social forces in the division of the Churches of Christ and the Disciples of Christ is indicated by the fact that roughly three-fourths of the membership of the Churches of Christ was located in the South.[1] David Edwin Harrell, whose work Clark Gilpin calls "one of the most important pieces of Disciples historiography of the past twenty-five years" (p. 272), has argued convincingly that the separation of the Churches of Christ from the Disciples reflected the different economic patterns in the North and South following the Civil War. After the war, the North entered a period of economic and industrial growth that resulted in the rapid development of cities and in an increase in the middle class, while the South remained largely agrarian and impoverished. Harrell provides strong evidence of an agrarian social class consciousness set against an urban, middle-class Christianity in early Churches of Christ literature opposing the use of instrumental music in worship and missionary societies. He also shows that, unlike the Churches of Christ, the Disciples in the South found their strength in the cities.[2]

From a theological perspective, the Disciples and the Churches of Christ divided because they could not identify a basis of Christian fellowship that would allow them to remain united despite differences on the use of instrumental music in worship and missionary societies. Both parties claimed that the only appropriate basis of Christian fellowship was conformity to the teachings of the New Testament. Unfortunately, the social groups to which they belonged following the Civil War seem to have significantly affected the way they interpreted the New Testament regarding the use of instrumental music in worship and missionary societies. Thus, their common claim that conformity to the teachings of the New Testament is the basis of Christian fellowship notwithstanding, the Churches of Christ and Disciples of Christ found it impossible to remain united.

1. See Roger W. Stump's essay in this volume, "Spatial Patterns of Growth and Decline among the Disciples of Christ, 1880-1980," pp. 451-53. Subsequent references to material in this volume will be cited parenthetically in the text, using page numbers only.

2. Harrell, *The Social Sources of Division in the Disciples of Christ: 1865-1900* (Atlanta: Publishing Systems, 1973), 323-50.

The schism of the Disciples and the Churches of Christ seems to have had little affect on the growth rate of the Disciples. The combined movement grew dramatically during the period from 1890 to 1906. Indeed, it was the fastest growing of the large Protestant denominations, increasing at a rate nearly twice that of all Protestants combined and more than twice that of the U.S. population. By 1906 they numbered over 1.1 million. Even after the separation of the Churches of Christ, the Disciples numbered nearly a million adherents and continued to grow (pp. 449, 451-53). Nevertheless, with the separation of the Churches of Christ, the Disciples lost their ties to a predominantly rural and agrarian population located primarily in the South. Thus, despite continuing numerical growth, the Disciples no longer influenced as broad a segment of American society and culture as they had before.

Ironically, the separation of the Churches of Christ and the Disciples was critical to the Disciples' eventual affiliation with the group of churches *within* American Protestantism that historians have identified as exercising a dominant religious influence on American culture during the first half of the twentieth century, the group of churches often referred to by historians as the "mainline churches." In addition to the Disciples, this group of churches includes the Episcopalians, Congregationalists, Presbyterians, Methodists, Northern Baptists, and United Lutherans.[3] All of these churches generally identified more with the urban and industrial segments than with the rural and agrarian segments of American society and culture that had emerged in the post–Civil War era. Thus, when the larger body of Disciples separated from the socially and culturally more rural and agrarian population of the Churches of Christ, it became a natural candidate for affiliation with the early twentieth-century Protestant establishment. To be a mainline Protestant denomination in the early years of the twentieth century was to be identified with the religious interests and aspirations of persons associated with the urban and industrial segments of American society and culture that had emerged in the post–Civil War era.

II. THE SECOND DIVISION: INDEPENDENT CHRISTIAN CHURCHES

Even as the Churches of Christ and the Disciples were separating along social and cultural lines, a second division of the Disciples was beginning to appear. This division resulted in the separate communion known as the Christian

3. For a discussion of the term *mainline*, see *Between the Times: The Travail of the Protestant Establishment in America, 1900-1960*, ed. William R. Hutchison (Cambridge: Cambridge University Press, 1989), pp. 3-6. These are churches that sociologists Wade Clark Roof and William McKinney, employing a broader definition of the term *mainline*, have identified as moderate to liberal Protestants (see the preface herein, p. x).

Churches and Churches of Christ (often referred to by Disciples as the Independents or Independent Christian Churches).

The major issue in the division of the Independents and the Disciples was recognition of "the denominations" as churches. All Disciples were opposed to "denominationalism." The nineteenth-century founders of the Disciples had called for the union of all Christians through a restoration of the faith and practice of apostolic or New Testament Christianity. The Disciples' distinctive practices of believer's immersion and weekly observance of the Lord's Supper (identified by the Disciples founders as apostolic practices) are part of the Disciples' restoration legacy.

The controversy over recognition of the denominations as churches concerned how best to oppose denominationalism. Some Disciples held that failure to recognize the denominations as churches amounted to de facto promotion of "denominationalism." Other Disciples argued that to recognize the denominations as churches was to condone denominationalism. In their view, genuine Christian union could be achieved only when Christians rejected their denominations in favor of the apostolic faith and practice revealed in the New Testament. To recognize the denominations was to abandon the Disciples' "plea" for Christian unity through the restoration of New Testament faith and practice. In particular, opponents of recognizing the denominations as churches were concerned that such recognition would result in a slighting of the Disciples' distinctive teaching on the New Testament practice of baptism. (On this, see the chapters by Dunnavant, Foster, and Toulouse herein.) Disciples who were to become identified as Independents refused to support organizations that employed leaders who favored recognition of the denominations as churches. Disciples who remained identified as Disciples favored recognition of the denominations as churches or were at least willing to support organizations that employed leaders who favored recognition of the denominations.

The division of the Independents and the Disciples took on major institutional form with the establishment of the North American Christian Convention as an alternative to the Disciples' International Convention in 1927, although Disciples and Independents ostensibly remained one body for another forty years. In 1968, after a plan for restructuring the Disciples' International Convention and related agencies was approved by the International Convention, more than a third of the congregations listed in the Disciples' yearbook formally withdrew from the denomination. This action was the result of a widely propagated false assertion that unless congregations formally withdrew from the Disciples by a certain time they would place themselves in jeopardy of losing control of their congregational property. Many of these congregations had not supported the "cooperative" program of the Disciples for many years. Over the next few years, many other congregations that had earlier stopped support for the Disciples' cooperative program also formally withdrew from the Disciples. In 1971 the Independents asked that they be listed as a separate body in the *Yearbook of American Churches*. It seems clear, however, that the actual division occurred much earlier.

The importance of social forces in the division of the Independents and the Disciples, as in the division of the Churches of Christ and the Disciples, is indicated by the demographic distribution of the two groups. The 1971 census shows that Disciples and Independents did not differ significantly in number, on the average, in either rural or suburban counties; however, the Disciples' total membership in urban counties exceeded the Independents' by fifty percent (p. 460).

The essays in this volume suggest that the separation of the Independents and the Disciples reflected differences between rural and urban life in late nineteenth- and early twentieth-century America. During this era urban Americans were exposed to social problems related to the increase in the urban poor that accompanied industrialization — problems that were foreign to the experience of most rural Americans. Though the Disciples were (and remain) largely a rural and small-town people, they could not long ignore the social problems of the era. By 1906, significant numbers of Disciples had already begun to appear in several major urban centers (p. 451). In these cities, Disciples were forced to respond to the social challenges associated with the increase in the urban poor.

The essays suggest that the separation of the Independents and the Disciples also resulted from differences in exposure to intellectual developments associated with the developmental hypothesis. This hypothesis posits that phenomena are the result of natural processes of development and growth. Applied to biology, it produced Darwinism or the theory of evolution. In history it translated as historicism, the idea that all events and even ideas are fashioned by historical forces. In the case of the Bible, the result was historical or "higher" criticism, which seeks to make sense of the variety of thought in the biblical literature in terms of a historical development of biblical religion. In all fields, the developmental hypothesis ignored or rejected nonnaturalistic (or *super*naturalistic) explanations. Thus, as applied to the Bible, it raised questions not only concerning the historicity of events described in the Bible but also concerning traditional views of the inspiration and authority of the Scriptures. In particular, it suggested that the teachings of the Bible, compiled over a long period of time and from different contexts, are not equally authoritative for modern readers. Furthermore, it suggested that revelation has not ceased, but continues.

Twentieth-century Disciples could not long ignore intellectual developments associated with the developmental hypothesis. The Disciples founders had valued education and honored free inquiry. By 1880 Disciples ministerial candidates were already seeking graduate education in major universities where faculty were beginning to apply the developmental hypothesis to history and the biblical literature. By 1900 twenty-seven Disciples had been enrolled in Yale Divinity School. The Divinity School of the

University of Chicago, founded in 1892, soon had a significant number of Disciples students as well.[4]

In response to the social and intellectual developments of the era, a new Disciples interpretation of Christianity began to emerge among university-educated Disciples professional leaders that had a direct bearing on the issue of recognition of the denominations. This new Disciples interpretation of Christianity saw Jesus as a moral teacher whose principles, if applied to contemporary social circumstances, would solve the problems of the cities. The Bible was understood as a library of "primary sources" that disclose the history of the moral and spiritual development of the human soul in relation to God. The life and teachings of Jesus were identified as the highest point in this development. To be a Christian was to follow Jesus by working for the application of his ideals to contemporary social problems. According to this understanding of Christianity, the goal of Christian union was to marshal the resources of the churches in order to effectively address the pressing social issues of the day.

Given the developmental view of history and the Bible, the organization of the apostolic church disclosed in the New Testament could no longer be viewed as a supernaturally established blueprint for the order of the church in all times and places but only as *a* form of organization adopted by the early Christians out of the resources of their own background and culture. Thus, old dividing issues based on differing interpretations of New Testament practice — such as the proper subject and mode of baptism — seemed much less significant than before. Based on the new Disciples interpretation of Christianity, there was an eminently good reason to recognize the denominations as churches (to join them in working to apply the principles of Jesus to pressing social problems) and no good reason for not recognizing the denominations as churches.

However, not all Disciples accepted the new Disciples interpretation of Christianity. Many Disciples preferred viewing Christ as the supernatural savior of individuals from personal sins who, by saving individuals, would save the world. They felt little attraction to the Christ whose moral principles, if applied to contemporary social circumstances, would solve the problems of the cities. These Disciples affirmed the Bible as the inerrant history of God in relation to humanity, every verse of which unambiguously mediates the will and purposes of God. They were not interested in a Bible that was seen as a collection of "primary sources" that disclose the history of the moral and spiritual development of the human soul in relation to God. Moreover, they tended to be concerned not so much with the social problems of the cities as with the ethical questions that exercised the mind of small-town America, such

---

4. For an extensive treatment of the relationship of Yale and the Disciples, see Edwin L. Becker, *Yale Divinity School and the Disciples of Christ* (Nashville: Disciples of Christ Historical Society, 1990).

as dancing, drinking, and divorce. The primary focus of their Christian ethical reflection was personal, not social. The goal of Christian union, according to this interpretation of Christianity, was to draw unbelievers to faith in Christ as the supernatural savior of individuals. Believing that the Bible does provide a supernaturally established blueprint for the order of the church, they argued that genuine Christian union could be achieved only when the denominations accepted the New Testament order as historically interpreted by the Disciples. Given this view, to recognize the denominations as churches would be to surrender the "plea" for Christian union. (On this, see the chapters by Boring, Foster, and Williamson and Blaisdell herein.)

The integral relation of recognition of the denominations to the new Disciples interpretation of Christianity indicates that the Disciples-Independent division must be understood as the Disciples version of the larger Protestant liberal-conservative controversy. In other denominations the controversy centered on the Social Gospel (the view that Jesus was a moral teacher whose principles, if applied to contemporary social circumstances, would solve the problems of the cities) and the higher criticism of the Bible (the application of the developmental hypothesis to the literature of the Bible). However, in all of the denominations involved in the liberal-conservative controversy, the question of relations with other denominations was at issue. For liberals — those who favored the Social Gospel and approved of the higher criticism of the Bible — closer relations with other denominations was seen as an important step toward establishing an earthly kingdom of God based on the social principles of Jesus. For conservatives — those who showed little interest in the Social Gospel and opposed the higher criticism of the Bible — closer relations with other denominations was viewed as betrayal of distinctive denominational teachings. (On this, see in particular Foster's discussion of Presbyterian reactions to the Ecumenical Movement, pp. 241-43). The fact that the Disciples-Independent division centered on recognition of the denominations rather than on the Social Gospel or higher criticism does not mean that the latter issues were unimportant in this context; rather, it reflects the fact that the Disciples' distinctive teachings concerned the means of achieving Christian union. Disciples conservatives were identified as "restorationists" because they were committed to preserving the Disciples' distinctive "plea" for the union of the church through the restoration of New Testament faith and practice.

In sum, the separation of the Disciples and the Independents, like the liberal-conservative controversy in other denominations, seems to have been the result of different responses to the social challenges associated with the increase in the urban poor that accompanied industrialization and different reactions to the intellectual challenges associated with the application of the developmental hypothesis to history and the study of the Bible. The fact that the Disciples' total membership in urban counties exceeded the Independents' by fifty percent indicates that urban location was an important social factor in determining how one responded to these issues. The concentration of liberals among university-educated Disciples professional leaders indicates that where one went to school — at least for ministers — was also an important social factor in determining one's response to these issues.

From a theological perspective, the separation of the Disciples and the Independents was the result of their failure to claim an understanding of the mission of the church that would allow them to cooperate in mission despite differences regarding the character of the Bible, the primary focus of Christian moral reflection (personal vs. social), and the purpose and means of achieving Christian union. Both parties claimed that their understanding of the mission of the church was founded on the New Testament. Unfortunately, urban versus rural location and differences in educational background seem to have significantly influenced their interpretation of the New Testament regarding the church's mission. As a result, the two parties, both of which claimed the New Testament as the standard for their understanding of the mission of the church, found it impossible to cooperate in mission.

The controversy over the Disciples version of liberalism may have been a factor in a reduction of their growth rate. From 1906 to 1952 Disciples increased to 1.8 million members with a growth rate about equal to that of the American population, though somewhat lower than that of other large Protestant groups, including Baptists, Methodists, and Lutherans (p. 453). But the reduction in the growth rate of the Disciples during this era may also be related to the fact that during these years the interior of the nation, where the Disciples had their greatest membership concentration, suffered a decline in population growth (p. 454). In any event, the de facto separation of the Independents in the 1920s marked the second major shift in the relation of the Disciples to American culture. By the end of the 1920s, the Disciples were no longer directly related to the culture of a predominately rural and suburban population who refused to cooperate religiously with the advocates of liberalism. Thus, the direct influence of the Disciples on American society and culture, already reduced by their separation from the culture of persons represented by the Churches of Christ, was further reduced to liberals and conservatives who were willing to support organizations that employed liberals as leaders.

The de facto separation of the Independents from the Disciples in the 1920s was critical to the Disciples' continued affiliation with the Protestant establishment. For the period following the liberal-conservative struggles of the early twentieth century, historians have typically classified churches as mainline only to the degree to which they cooperated with other churches that included liberals in positions of leadership. The de facto separation from the Disciples of a population that refused to support organizations that included liberals in positions of leadership allowed the larger body of Disciples to maintain and strengthen ties with the Protestant establishment formed in the early years of the twentieth century.

III. NUMERICAL DECLINE: THE LOST GENERATION

From 1952 to 1971 Disciples and Independents together declined by 70,000 members while the United States population grew by 35 percent (p. 457)! The first years that the Disciples and Independents together showed net losses were in the mid-1960s (membership figures for the Independents were not reported separately until 1971). Since 1971 the Disciples have continued to suffer net losses in membership — though the Independents have not. In 1989 the Disciples comprised fewer than a million participating members.

The essays by Greer, Hadaway, and Schumm, Hatch, Hevelone, and Schumm indicate that the Disciples' numerical decline since the mid-1960s is largely the result of their failure to appeal to the current generation of younger adults — people born during the post–World War II "baby boom" from 1945 to 1965. Schumm, Hatch, Hevelone, and Schumm found that people who switched from the Disciples to another denomination during the 1980s were younger than active Disciples (p. 547). Greer found that people who identify themselves in national surveys as Disciples but indicate that they attend church infrequently (and may, in fact, no longer appear on the membership roll of a Disciples congregation) are also younger than active Disciples (pp. 391-92). Hadaway reports that people who switched to the Disciples from another denomination are older than persons who switched from the Disciples to another denomination (pp. 505, 507, 508). Thus, a consistent pattern emerges: Disciples have failed to appeal to the current generation of younger adults. This failure represents the third shift in the Disciples' relation to American culture.

What is the cause of the Disciples' failure to appeal to the current generation of younger adults? Essays in this volume examine both contextual and institutional factors of denominational growth and decline. Contextual factors are those over which a congregation or denomination cannot be expected to exert much influence, such as major demographic patterns. Institutional factors are those over which a congregation or denomination can exert influence, such as its teaching and organization. The failure of the Disciples to appeal to members of the current generation of younger adults appears to be the result of both contextual and institutional factors.

It must first be noted, however, that not all Disciples *congregations* have declined in membership since the mid-1960s. Indeed, many congregations have shown significant growth during this period. Massa shows that in New York City Spanish and Haitian Disciples congregations have experienced dramatic growth while the numerical membership of Anglo congregations has declined. Schumm, Hatch, Hevelone, and Schumm note the growth of minority Disciples congregations in Los Angeles (pp. 553-54). Meyers and Olson report significant numerical growth among Black Disciples congregations between the years 1978 and 1982 (p. 516). Although the essays do not indicate the average age of the membership in Disciples congregations that have grown since the mid-1960s, presumably the congregations that have grown during this period have been successful in appealing to younger adults. Thus, the question seems to be why more Disciples congregations have not been successful in appealing to members of the baby boom generation.

A. CONTEXTUAL FACTORS

The growth of Disciples minority congregations in the face of declining Anglo memberships might suggest that the overall numerical decline of the denomination is related to upward social mobility of persons reared in Disciples congregations. As Hadaway shows, the Disciples are a decidedly middle-class denomination. The theory that Americans tend to change denominations or become religiously unaffiliated in accord with increases in social status has been widely supported in other studies. It could be hypothesized that one cause of the Disciples' numerical decline is that people reared among them have risen from their middle-class origins to the upper middle class or higher. However, Hadaway argues that the membership decline among the Disciples cannot be attributed to upwardly mobile Disciples switching to higher status denominations or to religious nonaffiliation (pp. 500-501, 508).

Stump shows that part of the answer to the question of the Disciples' numerical decline since 1971 is low population growth rates in areas of Disciples concentration, the continuing effects of the Disciples-Independent Christian Churches division, and the contextual factors that have been inhibiting the growth of other mainline denominations in particular geographical areas. Between 1971 and 1980 Disciples congregations were less likely to grow in counties where the population growth was less than the national median. Disciples were also less likely to grow in counties where Independent Christian churches were present. And Disciples were less likely to grow in counties where the combined membership of the United Methodist Church and the United Presbyterian Church declined. Nearly half of all Disciples in 1971 lived in counties having all three of these conditions, and three-fourths of Disciples lived in counties having at least two of these conditions. Meanwhile, fewer than four percent of all Disciples lived in counties characterized by none of these conditions (pp. 463-66).

B. INSTITUTIONAL FACTORS

Meyers and Olson found that Disciples congregations that experienced growth in membership from 1978 to 1982 showed evidence of increased commitment of members to the local program of the congregation *prior* to the onset of growth. Such commitment was measured in terms of per capita expenditures for local church programs and church school participation. These findings suggest that if more Disciples had demonstrated increased commitment to the local program of their congregations in these two ways, the denomination as a whole might have shown growth despite the disadvantages imposed upon them by low population growth rates in areas where their membership is concentrated, the continuing legacy of the Disciples-Independent division, and whatever contextual factors were generally inhibiting the growth of mainline denominations in particular geographical areas. Thus, the critical question in relation to the failure of the Disciples to appeal to baby boomers seems to be why more Disciples have not demonstrated increased commitment to the local program of their congregation.

1. Ministry-Laity Gap

This study suggests that one reason more Disciples have not demonstrated increased commitment to the local program of their congregation is that a gulf exists between the theological and moral views of Disciples ministers and active members of Disciples congregations. Guth and Turner found that Disciples ministers are quite liberal theologically and morally. Greer reports that Disciples who indicate that they attend church frequently are decidedly conservative theologically and morally. Given the wide difference between the theological and moral positions of pastors and active members, it is not surprising that pastors and active members, who may well have rather different interests as well as significantly different views on matters of common interest, have found it difficult to generate increased commitment to the local program of their congregations.

How is the difference between the theological and moral views of Disciples ministers and active members to be explained? Guth and Turner attribute the liberalism of Disciples ministers to their education. They found that among Disciples (and also Presbyterians and Southern Baptists who were studied as comparison groups), ministers become increasingly liberal with each advance in secular and (especially) theological education (p. 389). The vast majority of Disciples ministers attended Disciples colleges and seminaries, all of which produce theological and moral liberals in overwhelming numbers. They are joined by a minority of Disciples ministers who are even more liberal — those who have attended schools such as Yale, Vanderbilt, and Chicago. With few exceptions, the only conservative Disciples ministers are persons brought up in a more conservative denomination and/or educated in a conservative denomination's schools, older ministers who have attended a Bible college and perhaps a year or two of seminary at most, and licensed ministers with little or no formal theological education. Thus, Guth and Turner conclude that the gap between the views of Disciples ministers and the Disciples constituency results from the fact that the great majority of Disciples ministers have educational backgrounds quite unlike those of most of the Disciples membership (pp. 384-85).

Guth and Turner's conclusion that educational differences account for the gap in the views of Disciples ministers and the Disciples membership raises a critical question in view of the fact that Protestant ministers have historically been understood to be the teachers of the congregations. If the teachers (ministers) become liberal through their college and seminary studies, why do their students (the active laity) remain conservative?

One might hypothesize that the difference between the views of Disciples ministers and Disciples active members is merely the result of a time lag. That is, one would predict that Disciples active members will, under the continued instruction of Disciples ministers, eventually become liberal. But this hypothesis assumes that the liberalism of the Disciples ministry is a recent development. Although there are no comprehensive studies of the views of Disciples ministers prior to Guth and Turner's study, this does not seem likely. Dunnavant shows, that the Disciples' professional leadership assumed a liberal posture politically in the 1930s. Harrison shows that the oldest of the Disciples seminaries has been solidly liberal since the 1920s.

Thus, the question would seem to be how the endurance of the gap between the theological and moral positions of Disciples ministers and active members is to be explained. The essays in this volume suggest that the gulf has endured at least in part because of the failure of the Disciples to engage in serious and sustained dialogue regarding the issues that divide the ministers and active members. This failure, in turn, is related to at least six factors: the Disciples' indifference toward theology, the democratic polity of the Disciples, the gulf between college and seminary educators on the one hand and pastors and denominational leaders on the other, the quality of Disciples preaching, the character of Disciples congregational education, and the limited influence of Disciples-related higher education.

a. Indifference toward Theology

Twentieth-century Disciples have claimed that their unity is based on their common confession that Jesus is the Christ — a theological affirmation. At the same time, Disciples have been remarkably vague regarding the theological content of this affirmation. The underlying message has been that all theological positions are acceptable as long as unity is maintained and there is some prospect of the denomination serving as a force for good in the world. No doubt the separation of the Independents, who advocated a specific theological position but refused to support the cooperative program of the denomination, has contributed to the Disciples' tendency toward theological indifference (see below the discussion of Duke's conclusions regarding the report of the Panel of Scholars). The effect of this tendency has been to discourage serious and sustained discussion of theological issues.

b. Democratic Polity

The Disciples, more than some other denominations and more than the Disciples founders ever advocated,[5] allow the students (congregations) free rein to hire and *fire* the teachers (ministers). As a consequence, ministers who sense that they hold views more liberal than those of their congregations have been hesitant to advocate those views in the congregation. This conclusion is supported by Guth and Turner's finding that very few Disciples ministers report having publicly addressed the issues of pornography, abortion, gambling, prayer in schools, or homosexuality — the very issues on which Disciples ministers perceive the greatest gap between themselves and their congregations (p. 375). Faulkner's study of Disciples preaching in 1988 confirms the testimony of the ministers that they do not generally address these issues.

The same "democratic" structural dynamic was operative at the denominational or general level of the Disciples at least during the first part of the twentieth century. Toulouse shows that the leadership of the United Christian Missionary Society, compelled to maintain the support of the membership if they were to fund missionary efforts, refused to take a teaching role in the liberal-restorationist controversy over the requirements for Christian fellowship on the mission field. Rather, the leadership of the society, which seems to have been personally disposed to the liberal stance advocated by many of the missionaries, established policies meant to satisfy the conservative constituency of the denomination. In response to criticism of these actions by missionaries, society leaders responded that U.C.M.S. was a democracy and could change its policies when directed to do so by its constituency (pp. 213-20). However, some missionaries retorted that the society actively sought to suppress discussion of the issue. How was the mind of the constituency to be changed, they asked, if the issue was never discussed? Toulouse reports that as late as 1968, missionaries complained that the Society had failed to inform the membership of the true character of work on the field (pp. 220-24).

c. Separation of Career Tracks

The tendency of pastors and denominational leaders to avoid addressing issues on which they perceive that their views and the views of the constituency differ significantly — issues that seemingly *are* addressed in Disciples educational institutions — has been exacerbated by the separation of the career tracks of Disciples college and seminary educators from Disciples pastors and denominational leaders. Chaves shows that this separation occurred early in the twentieth century (pp. 347, 357). College and seminary teachers, having little pastoral or denominational leadership experience, may not have given sufficient attention to whether and how ideas advanced in the schools could be

---

5. See D. Newell Williams, *Ministry among Disciples: Past, Present, and Future* (St. Louis: Christian Board of Publication, 1985), pp. 8-10, 14-15.

taught to congregations and the church at large. Or ministerial candidates may have been influenced by their teachers' relative lack of pastoral and denominational leadership experience to dismiss their admonitions to teach certain ideas and their advice on how those ideas might be taught. In any event, most pastors have not shared the ideas they were taught in seminary with their congregations. And Disciples denominational leaders have been hesitant to call on Disciples educational leaders to serve as teachers of the laity (see Toulouse's discussion of correspondence between missionary executive Archibald McLean and C. C. Morrison regarding speakers for the Des Moines International Convention, pp. 220-21; see also Rowell and Seymour's comment regarding the limited role of academicians in the development of Disciples educational resources, p. 335, n. 51).

d. Quality of Preaching

Contemporary Disciples sermons are hard to follow, and with some notable exceptions, they do not prepare people to discuss the issues that divide Disciples ministers and active laity. This is the unhappy conclusion to which one is led by Faulkner's study of Disciples preaching in 1988. However, the poor quality of Disciples pulpit instruction described by Faulkner (failure to define theological terms, pointless illustrations, etc.) may be as much a matter of how priorities get established for Disciples ministers as it is a matter of their teaching qualifications. Given the high expectations of Disciples congregations for ministers to provide pastoral support (see p. 554) and the heavy load of administrative functions often assumed by Disciples pastors (due frequently to the lack of support staff and lay involvement), it may be that Disciples pastors simply do not devote much time to the preparation of their sermons.

e. Congregational Education

Rowell and Seymour report that Disciples were leaders in the progressive religious education movement. The goal of the "progressives" was to relate the church's educational work to research and scholarship in education and biblical criticism. The Disciples' Bethany Series was the paradigm of progressive curricula (pp. 322-25). Furthermore, it was widely used. The Christian Board of Publication reported that in 1954 congregations whose church school enrollment constituted 76 percent of the total Disciples church school enrollment used Bethany materials (p. 327). Nevertheless, Rowell and Seymour state that Disciples education has tended not to make explicit the use of scholarly insights, and especially the higher criticism, in curriculum resources and congregational programs (p. 335). In other words, the issue of the character of the Bible's authority (a critical issue separating liberals and conservatives) has simply not been addressed in Disciples congregational education resources. This helps to account not only for the failure of Disciples to engage in serious and sustained dialogue regarding the character of biblical authority but also for Greer's remarkable finding that six percent of active Disciples (members of a denomination that once prided itself as the "People of the Book") answer "Don't know" when asked whether they believe the Bible is the actual word of God, the inspired word of God but not inerrant, or a book of ancient fables and moral precepts (p. 399, Table 5)!

f. Disciples-Related Higher Education

Brereton argues that the Disciples tradition of honoring free inquiry and their perception of themselves as a people of the "frontier" (Gilpin includes an extensive discussion of the Disciples' understanding of themselves as a frontier people) has encouraged Disciples college and university leaders to accept new ideas and to develop new educational strategies. Nevertheless, she reports that there is little evidence of concern during the first part of the twentieth century for communicating the insights of higher criticism to undergraduates in the Disciples institutions she examined (pp. 315-16). The failure of early twentieth-century Disciples educational institutions to expose undergraduates to higher criticism helps to account for the failure of the denomination as a whole to have engaged in serious and sustained discussion of the issue of biblical authority.

However, even more critical with regard to the failure of the Disciples to have engaged in serious and sustained dialogue concerning the issue of biblical authority is the fact that only a small percentage of Disciples have attended Disciples schools. Historically Disciples have demonstrated a willingness to patronize state-supported institutions. Indeed, as early as 1920 the Board of Education of the Disciples reported that 6.87 percent of the students in fifteen large state universities were Disciples (p. 305). So, whatever the character of Disciples undergraduate biblical instruction may have been, only a small percentage of Disciples have received instruction in the Bible from a Disciples educational institution.

Brereton notes that the willingness of Disciples to patronize state-supported higher education has required the Disciples schools to seek students and funding from outside the denomination. This situation, along with the influence of secular accrediting associations, has led to the secularization of the Disciples colleges and universities. As a result, the teaching of Bible has become increasingly less central to the total curriculum of even Disciples institutions (pp. 315-17).

Thus, the bottom line regarding the relation of Disciples higher education to the failure of Disciples to have engaged in serious and sustained dialogue regarding the issue of biblical authority is that only a small percentage of Disciples have been exposed to the higher criticism of the Bible by a Disciples educational institution. Disciples who attended Disciples undergraduate institutions in the first part of the century do not seem to have received instruction in the higher criticism of the Bible. Disciples who have attended Disciples colleges and universities in more recent years have not been required to follow a curriculum centered on instruction in Bible. Moreover, *most* Disciples have not attended a Disciples education institution.

Nevertheless, it is worthy of note that Meyers and Olson found that from 1978 to 1982 Disciples congregations located near a Disciples educational institution were more likely to show growth (p. 516). There are many factors that may account for this finding, such as the location of Disciples-related schools in areas of greater Disciples numerical strength. However, it may be that the number of graduates in local churches and educational opportunities made available by these institutions to local churches have helped to foster dialogue regarding the issues that divide Disciples ministers and active members — dialogue that has served to narrow the gap in the views of Disciples ministers and active members or at least to enable mutual understanding and appreciation. Further research would be needed to test this hypothesis.

2. Theological Failure

The chapters by Schumm, Hatch, Hevelone, and Schumm and Williamson and Blaisdell suggest that the reason more Disciples have not demonstrated increased commitment to the program of their congregation since the 1960s is not attributable solely to a division in the views of Disciples ministers and active members: a religious or theological failure of the Disciples seems also to be involved.

Schumm, Hatch, Hevelone, and Schumm found that intrinsic religiosity is the most consistent predictor of commitment to a Disciples congregation as measured by attendance and giving (they did not distinguish, as did Meyers and Olson, between giving for the local program and giving for the larger denominational program). Intrinsically religious persons respond affirmatively to statements such as "I have often had a strong sense of God's presence" and "My religion is important to me because it answers many questions about the meaning of life." In contrast, extrinsically religious people report going to church mainly to enjoy seeing people whom they know rather than because of religious convictions (pp. 535-36). Schumm, Hatch, Hevelone, and Schumm state that "the importance of intrinsic religiosity within a congregation is not illogical. If a congregation is only existing to serve the purpose of a social club, why bother? There are too many competing organizations that may serve equally well as places of fellowship" (pp. 551-52). According to this view, the fact that more Disciples have not shown evidence of increased commitment to their congregation would seem to be a result of the failure of the Disciples to foster intrinsic religiosity.

How is this failure to be explained? Schumm, Hatch, Hevelone, and Schumm do not offer an answer to this question. They do show, however, that there is a negative relationship among Disciples between intrinsic religiosity and the affirmation of liberal theological and moral positions (p. 534). Essentially the same pattern can be observed among people who left the Disciples in the 1980s. People who simply dropped out of Disciples congregations, as distinguished from persons who switched from the Disciples to another denomination, were more liberal theologically (though not morally) than active Disciples. People who switched from the Disciples to another denomination tended to be highly committed to the program of a congregation as evidenced by attendance and giving and even more conservative (both theologically and morally) than active Disciples (pp. 545-49). These findings, combined with the observation that the rapidly growing Spanish and Haitian congregations in New York city described by Massa are theologically and morally more conservative than the numerically declining Anglo congregations in New York City, *might* suggest that intrinsic religiosity is dependent on the affirmation of conservative theological and moral positions. In this case, the Disciples' failure to foster intrinsic religiosity could be identified as the result of the liberal theological and moral positions of Disciples ministers.

However, the simple thesis that intrinsic religiosity is dependent on the affirmation of conservative theological and moral positions is refuted by the fact that the pool of intrinsically religious Disciples includes liberals as well as conservatives. Controlling for intrinsic religiosity, Schumm, Hatch, Hevelone, and Schumm found that there is no difference in attendance between Disciples liberals and Disciples conservatives and that Disciples liberals actually give slightly more than Disciples conservatives. Intrinsically religious Disciples liberals appear to be every bit as much committed to the program of their congregation as intrinsically religious Disciples conservatives. Schumm, Hatch, Hevelone, and Schumm conclude that despite the large percentage of conservatives among intrinsically religious Disciples, intrinsic religiosity is not dependent on the affirmation of conservative theological and moral positions (p. 543).

Williamson and Blaisdell's thesis regarding why Disciples have declined numerically accords well with the findings of Schumm, Hatch, Hevelone, and Schumm and, further, offers an explanation for the negative relationship between the affirmation of liberal theological views and commitment to the program of a congregation. In their view, the numerical decline of the Disciples is directly related to the work of the theologians who influenced the Disciples during the period from 1880 to 1953. How so?

Williamson and Blaisdell argue that any adequate Christian theology must meet three tests. First, it must present the Christian faith as intellectually credible. Standards of credibility can differ from one era to another and among different groups in a society. Second, it must present the Christian faith as morally responsible. Judgments regarding what constitutes moral responsibility can also differ from one era to another and among different groups in a society. And, finally, any adequate Christian theology must offer a distinctively Christian standard for judging theological statements and moral action (a norm of "appropriateness" to the Christian faith). Based on their interpretation of the work of theologians influential among the Disciples during the period from 1880 to 1953, they conclude that Disciples were offered two theological choices during this era. In their view, neither one of these choices provided a fully adequate Christian theology for a significant number of Disciples.

One option offered to Disciples, according to Williamson and Blaisdell, was to maintain a position that in light of the intellectual and social challenges of the age was no longer intellectually credible or morally plausible but did have the virtue of clearly stating a standard of appropriateness to the Christian faith. This was the position of the Disciples conservatives described above. These Disciples would not give up their belief in an infallible Bible (their norm of appropriateness to the Christian faith) despite intellectual challenges to that position. Neither, in the view of many Disciples, did they display much interest in addressing the pressing social challenges of urban America.

The other option offered to Disciples, according to Williamson and Blaisdell, was the Disciples version of liberalism discussed above. This was the option generally chosen by the Disciples' professional leadership. It was intellectually credible according to the new ideas of the era and morally plausible to people concerned with the social issues raised by the urbanization of American life, but it lacked a distinctively Christian norm for judging theological statements and moral action (pp. 137-38). To be sure, Disciples liberals asserted that Jesus represented the highest level of moral and spiritual development and insisted that all theological statements and moral actions were to be tested by his principles. Nevertheless, Williamson and Blaisdell argue that when one investigates the principles of Jesus as discerned by the liberal theologians, they turn out to be little more than a reflection of the "best" social thinking of the period rather than a set of distinctive theological and moral guidelines (pp. 116-19, 124-25, 128-29, 132-34).

According to Williamson and Blaisdell, one reason that more Disciples have not evidenced increased commitment to the program of their congregation is the failure of the liberal theology adopted by Disciples ministers in the first half of the twentieth century to identify a distinctively Christian standard for judging theological statements and moral action: "If we do not teach the Christian faith and communicate to people the excitement generated by understanding themselves in light of the gospel, can we blame them for finding that everything presented as 'Christian' is available elsewhere?" (p. 108).

Williamson and Blaisdell hypothesize that many people who are open to liberal theological and moral positions and who in fact may have once been attracted to the Disciples because of the liberal stance of their ministers have discovered that the liberal theology of Disciples ministers adds nothing distinctive to their lives. This hypothesis is supported not only by Schumm, Hatch, Hevelone, and Schumm's finding that people who simply dropped out of Disciples churches in the 1980s, as distinguished from persons who switched from the Disciples to another denomination, were more liberal theologically (though not morally) than active Disciples, but also by Greer's profile of the Disciples constituency. Greer reports that people who identify themselves as "Disciples" in national surveys but indicate that they attend church infrequently (and may in fact no longer be included on the membership roll of a congregation) are theologically and morally more liberal than Disciples who attend church frequently (pp. 398-400, 401-8).

It is important to note that the problem identified by Williamson and Blaisdell is not *liberal* theological and moral positions as such. Indeed, according to their scheme for judging the adequacy of any Christian theology, the liberal theologians who influenced Disciples ministers in the first half of the twentieth century were on the right track at two points. First, they understood that if a theology is to have power in one's life it must be intellectually credible. People who had been led by their formal education to accept the implications of the developmental hypothesis as applied to history and to the Bible could not be expected to find credible a version of Christianity that denied the implications of this hypothesis. Second, they understood that a convincing interpretation of Christianity must show that Christianity is morally responsible. A theology that would convince people who had become concerned about the social challenges presented by the urbanization of American life could not ignore those concerns. The weakness in the liberal theology adopted by Disciples ministers in the first half of the twentieth century was not its acknowledgment of contemporary intellectual and social concerns; rather, it was its failure to identify a distinctively Christian standard for judging theological statements and moral action. This isolation of the weakness in Disciples liberal theology accords well with Massa's suggestion that one of the components in the rapid growth of Spanish and Haitian Disciples churches in New York City is not their conservatism as such but the fact that these churches offer a *distinctive* message and identity (pp. 481, 488-90).

Williamson and Blaisdell's identification of the weakness in the liberal theology adopted by Disciples ministers in the first half of the twentieth century may also help to explain Schumm, Hatch, Hevelone, and Schumm's finding that some of the Disciples who demonstrate the greatest commitment to the program of their congregation are liberals. It may be hypothesized that these liberal Disciples have discovered a distinctively Christian norm for judging theological statements and moral action. Of course, more research on intrinsically religious Disciples liberals would be needed to test this thesis.

If Williamson and Blaisdell are correct regarding the results of the liberal theology influential among Disciples ministers in the first half of the twentieth century, one might expect to find that the Disciples growth rate picked up some in the 1960s as a result of mainstream Protestantism's theological renaissance of the 1950s. This movement, while advancing a spectrum of theologies, was sharply critical of the earlier type of theological liberalism for mistaking liberal social values and faith in the moral progress of humanity for the Christian gospel. Quite the opposite, of course, was the fact. The 1960s marked the beginning of the sharp numerical decline of the Disciples. How is the failure of the theological renaissance to have sparked Disciples numerical growth to be explained?

Two of the essays suggest that Disciples' participation in the theological renaissance was marginal. Rowell and Seymour note that while those who prepared the church school curriculum in some denominations sought to incorporate the insights of the theological renaissance into the development of new curricula, Disciples religious educators showed no interest in developing such materials (p. 325). Duke shows that Disciples theological scholars were discouraged from participating in the movement by leading Disciples intellectuals such as Edward Scribner Ames, who identified "theology" with the position of the Disciples conservatives or restorationists. The Disciples founders had rejected creeds as a means of achieving church union, and Ames asserted that in doing so they had rejected Protestant theology. Thus, to participate in a Protestant theological renaissance was to reject one's Disciples heritage (pp. 141-42)! Unfortunately, the mistaken notion that the Disciples founders had rejected Protestant theology was supported by the work of W. E. Garrison, the most influential of the twentieth-century historians of the Disciples. (Both strengths and weaknesses of Garrison's work are discussed in the chapter by Gilpin.)

Eventually Disciples did participate slightly in the theological renaissance. Duke states that the centerpiece of the theological renaissance for Disciples was the report of the Panel of Scholars published in 1963, which concluded that Disciples do have a tradition, the core of which is Jesus Christ as understood in the nineteenth-century Disciples slogan "No creed, but Christ." This assertion was understood as granting Disciples freedom and responsibility to express their faith in words (theology), deeds (program), and structure (a new polity) suitable to the contemporary world. However, Duke finds that the report as a whole is rather vague and uncertain regarding the distinctive meaning of the confession that Jesus is the Christ. Hence he concludes that the Panel failed to give full assurance that the Disciples tradition is in any sense a source or guide for formulating or reformulating church doctrine (pp. 146-49, 163). In other words, it would seem that the fundamental problem in the Disciples version of Protestant liberalism identified by Williamson and Blaisdell — the failure to identify a distinctively Christian norm — was not overcome by the report of the Panel of Scholars.

What, then, was achieved by the report of the Panel? Although Duke is careful to note its positive achievements (p. 149), his final conclusion suggests that the basic effect of this centerpiece of the Disciples participation in the theological renaissance of the 1950s was ironic. Duke states that by means of frequent warnings against pressing theological points too far and appeals for toleration of diversity, the Panel gave the impression that theological scholarship was actually not very important so long as the church remained a place for diversity of opinion and a force for good in the world. In other words, the basic result of the Panel's work was to reassure Disciples that their church could be at once diverse and relevant (pp. 149, 163). One can well imagine that such reassurance would have been welcome to the members of a church who knew their number to include both liberals and conservatives and who, due to the separation of the Churches of Christ and the refusal of the Independents to participate in the cooperative program of the denomination, understood themselves as identified by a willingness to accept diversity.

Duke's analysis of the work of Disciples theologians in the 1960s and 1970s suggests that despite some promising ventures by H. Jackson Forstman and Clark M. Williamson, the fundamental problem in the theology of Disciples liberals identified by Williamson and Blaisdell had not been overcome by 1980. Duke states that in the 1960s and 1970s most Disciples theologians set out on mainstream Protestantism's neoliberal quest for new linkages between Christianity and the modern world, fixing on some thing, persons, group, or cause as "the good" to which the church should lend full force. From a liberal social perspective, many of the projects advocated by the neoliberal theologies are worthy of support. Nevertheless, it seems clear that these thematic or programmatic theologies did not identify a distinctively Christian norm for judging theological statements and moral action.

Thus, it seems that in addition to the gulf between the theological and political views of Disciples ministers and active members, a primary reason that more Disciples have not demonstrated increased commitment to the program of their congregation is the fundamental failing of the theology most influential among their ministers — its failure to identify a distinctively Christian norm for judging theological statements and moral action.

3. Impact of the 1960s

Neither the gap between the views of Disciples ministers and active members nor the weakness in liberal Disciples theology were new to Disciples in the 1960s. Thus, it must be asked what happened in the 1960s to cause these two factors to have such a negative influence on the commitment of Disciples to the program of their congregations. The answer to this question is the social and cultural polarization of the 1960s.

Duke argues that the old-style liberalism had wanted to see "the best" of Christianity and "the best" of American culture established at home and abroad, while the various theologies advanced by the theological renaissance had sought to hold Christianity and American culture in dialectical tension. The result in both cases had been "an ethics of meliorism" — that is, an ethics rooted in the assumption that human society is improving and will continue to do so. Such an ethics affirmed working within the system as the appropriate means to promoting beneficial social change. In the 1960s, as national problems such as race relations, poverty, the war in Southeast Asia, the generation gap, and the counterculture became national crises, the ethics of meliorism gave way to a radical ethics that viewed human society less positively and called for confrontation of the system. In due course, meliorist ethics came to be seen by some mainline Protestants as not only inadequate but immoral. (This development is illustrated by Perdue's discussion of divinity school professor J. Philip Hyatt's "loss of honor" for working within the system at Vanderbilt in regard to the university's treatment of a black divinity school student involved in civil rights activities, pp. 102-4.) Duke states that once consensus broke down regarding what, if anything, was "the best" of American culture, the support holding mainstream Protestantism together was gone (p. 153).

This analysis helps to explain how the negative impact on commitment to the local program of a congregation resulting from the difference in the views of Disciples ministers and active laity has increased since the 1960s. As the fissure in mainstream Protestantism between liberals and conservatives has widened and has remained open, liberal ministers and conservative laity have no doubt found it more difficult than before to generate increased commitment to the program of their congregation.

Duke's analysis of what happened to mainstream Protestantism in the 1960s also helps to explain how the weakness in liberal Disciples theology has become increasingly evident since the 1960s and had a negative impact on commitments to congregational programs. As the Disciples, like other mainstream denominations, became a battleground over such issues as civil rights, the war in Vietnam, and later the women's movement, gay rights, and abortion, many liberal Disciples discovered that their Disciples theology added nothing distinctive to their lives. Disciples claiming equal allegiance to Jesus Christ were often on the other side of the issues. Meanwhile, support for liberal stands has often been found as easily if not more easily outside Disciples congregations. Hence, among Disciples liberals commitments to congregational programs have decreased.

Contemporary Disciples are theologically and morally divided with a liberal ministry on one side and a conservative active membership on the other. Moreover, their professional leadership says little to the culture that is not said outside of the church. In the context of the social and cultural polarization of American life since the 1960s these two factors seem to have prevented them from generating an increased commitment to the program of their congregations necessary to have appealed to the current generation of younger adults.

IV. THE CURRENT SITUATION

As a result of the three shifts in their relation to American culture, the Disciples are currently cut off from directly influencing the culture of large groups in contemporary American society. The first of the Disciples' divisions severed their ties with a predominantly rural and agrarian population located primarily in the South. Many of the descendants of this population have now moved to the cities and out of the South. Nevertheless, as a group they show little openness to direct cultural influence from the Disciples. The Disciples' second division severed their ties with a predominantly rural and suburban population that rejects affiliation with religious organizations that include liberals in positions of leadership. As a result of their failure to appeal to the present generation of younger adults, the Disciples currently have less direct influence on the culture of younger adults than ever before in their history or than is currently the case in conservative Protestant denominations. The primary causes of the narrowing cultural influence of the Disciples are (1) their failure to identify a basis for Christian union that can overcome social and cultural division (the fundamental theological cause of their two major divisions), (2) the difference between the views of their ministers and active laity, and (3) the failure of their professional leadership to identify a distinctively Christian norm for judging theological statements and moral action. The latter two of these causes seem to have hindered commitments to congregational programs especially since the mid-1960s. Throw in the disadvantages that the Disciples have suffered from the contextual factors associated with their geographical distribution identified by Stump, and it is little wonder that the Disciples have declined numerically since the mid-1960s and have a diminishing influence on American culture.

As previously noted, it was the separation of the Churches of Christ and the Independent Christian Churches from the Disciples that allowed the Disciples to become and remain identified as a mainline Protestant denomination. Clearly, the prominence of the mainline churches has been due not only to their former size but also to their identification with social classes related to the industrial and urban segments of American society and culture that have been ascendant in American society and culture since the Civil War. The failure of the Disciples and other mainline Protestant denominations to appeal to the current generation of younger adults has dramatically disclosed truths about the identity of the mainline churches throughout the twentieth century: the mainline churches have not represented "American Protestantism" but only one segment of a genuinely pluralistic social and religious order. For the past twenty-five years this segment of American Christianity has had difficulty reproducing itself, and now, not surprisingly, its role in American culture is diminishing.

In light of the analysis presented in this chapter, one might predict that the numerical decline of the Disciples and their loss of influence on American culture can only continue. The failure to appeal to the baby boomers alone would seem to significantly limit their future prospects. Nevertheless, based on the following essays and the responses of Disciples at the conference that reviewed early drafts of the material (also included in this volume), there is, in fact, good reason to believe that it is too early to write the obituary of the Christian Church (Disciples of Christ).

II. BIBLE AND THEOLOGY

The Disciples and Higher Criticism:
The Crucial Third Generation

M. Eugene Boring

INTRODUCTION

In the early nineteenth century, when the western regions of Pennsylvania and Virginia still represented the American frontier, where the vista of the future still stretched out with seemingly unlimited possibilities for new beginnings, Thomas and Alexander Campbell and a few other hardy pioneers set out to unite the fragmented church by restoring New Testament Christianity. They failed to unite the church. They did succeed, however, in restoring New Testament Christianity.[1] But what they restored was not the doctrine, practices, and polity of the early church, as they had hoped, but rather its social dynamics. The movement they founded underwent a series of internal transformations, at once theological and sociological, analogous to the transformations early Christianity experienced as it progressed from an eschatological movement within Judaism to a new and separate religious group self-consciously distinct from its parent religious body, with its own doctrines, institutions, and internal history and troubles.

Our internal history and troubles are reflected in the way we have handled the Bible. Since we have often claimed not to have a theology, the history of our biblical interpretation represents the history of our thought even more than is typical of Protestantism. Examine the role that the Bible has played in Disciples thought, and you have your hand on the pulse of the denomination's theology.[2]

1. Note the relation of unity and restoration on the title page of Alexander Campbell's *The Christian System: In Reference to the Union of Christians, and a Restoration of Primitive Christianity, as Plead in the Current Reformation* (Bethany, W. Va.: McVay & Ewing, 1839).

2. "Church history is the history of the exposition of Scripture" (Gerhard Ebeling, *The Word of God and Tradition* [Philadelphia: Fortress Press, 1968], p. 11). This statement by a Lutheran theologian who is not a Bible scholar and has no professional axe to grind may or may

Disciples theology has a variegated pattern, both longitudinally and latitudinally. Not only has our brief history of five generations embraced a vast variety, but each generation has included a broad spectrum of theological views. This makes writing a longitudinal history of Disciples thought, or the history of Disciples biblical interpretation, a difficult task. Not only the sweep of the generations but the scope of *each* generation must be taken into account. Nonetheless, there are representative figures in each generation who serve as legitimate points of orientation for Disciples thought of that generation. This does not mean, of course, that all Disciples, or even the majority of them, agreed with these representative figures. It does mean that they set the agenda for Disciples theology in their time, in both content and method, and thus shaped the way Disciples thought about the faith, themselves, and their role in the world.

FIVE GENERATIONS OF DISCIPLES BIBLICAL SCHOLARSHIP

We are a young denomination. We are only beginning the fifth generation of Disciples Bible scholars. Even these overlap, so that, for instance, young as I am, I have been personally acquainted with people who studied under J. W. McGarvey, who studied under Alexander Campbell.[3] With regard to the number of generations and people involved, it is not difficult to chart the history of biblical study within the Disciples. The five generations, divided unequally in terms of the major scholars concerned, are as follows:[4]

1. 1809-1866, the period of *Eden* (from the *Declaration and Address* to the death of Alexander Campbell). This creative period gave birth to the

---

not be considered true with regard to church history in general. I regard it as not only generally true but particularly true with reference to Disciples, who began their history with a claim to reject human tradition and to appeal to the Bible alone, who liked to refer to themselves as the "people of the Book," and who used such slogans as "Where the Scriptures speak, we speak, and where the Scriptures are silent, we are silent."

3. One such individual was Roger T. Nooe, who was minister emeritus at Vine Street Christian Church in Nashville, Tennessee, when I was a minister at First Christian Church, Paris, Tennessee, and a graduate student at Vanderbilt University.

4. Although I have worked out this periodization on the basis of the shifts in biblical hermeneutics in the Disciples tradition, it has a close analogy in the typical phases of the life cycle of an institution as charted by sociologists. See for example the adaptation of this pattern of institutional life to Disciples history by Peter M. Morgan, "The Christian Church (Disciples of Christ) in a Time for Revitalization, Lecture One: An Analysis" (unpublished lecture presented at the Oreon E. Scott Lectures at Bethany College, 11 April 1983), and "The Life Cycle of a Religious Community: A Sociological Model," in *Shaping the Coming Age of Religious Life*, by Lawrence Cada et al. (New York: Seabury Press, 1979), pp. 51-76.

Note also the periodization by Ronald E. Osborn in "Theology among the Disciples," in *The Christian Churches (Disciples of Christ): An Interpretative Examination in the Cultural Context*, ed. George G. Beazley, Jr. (St. Louis: Bethany Press, 1973), pp. 81-115: (1) The Founders, (2) Disciples Scholasticism, (3) Liberal Reformulation, (4) Neo-Orthodoxy and the Revival of Theology. Osborn puts McGarvey in (2) and Willett in (3).

grand vision and saw the formation of a hermeneutical tradition, represented by the biblical scholarship of Alexander Campbell.

2. 1866-1894, the period of *Ideology* (from the death of Alexander Campbell and founding of the *Christian Standard* to the death of B. W. Johnson). This period saw the development of an indigenous Disciples tradition, represented by the biblical study of Isaac Errett, Robert Milligan, and B. W. Johnson.

3. 1893-1929, the period of *Conflict* (from the death of B. W. Johnson and beginning of McGarvey's "Biblical Criticism" column in the *Christian Standard* to Willett's retirement from the University of Chicago). This period saw the encounter between the developing indigenous ecclesiastical tradition and the incursion of higher criticism from the academic world, represented by the conflicting positions of John W. McGarvey of the College of the Bible and Herbert L. Willett of the Disciples Divinity House of the University of Chicago.

4. 1929-1967, the period of *Secularization and Compartmentalization* (from Willett's retirement to the retirement of Stephen J. England from the Graduate Seminary of Phillips University). If progress is seen in moving from what is regarded as the dogmatic interpretation of a sect to what is regarded as the secularized atheological context of the academy as the base for biblical interpretation, then this period will be called the period of "independence" and "progress." From such a perspective, one might see this period as represented by the work of S. Vernon McCasland. In this period critical biblical study moved to the academy. But if one asks about the particular confessional stream of hermeneutics represented by Disciples tradition (still represented by both McGarvey and Willett in different ways), one will name J. Philip Hyatt of Vanderbilt and Stephen J. England of Phillips as representative figures and might consider it a period of "isolation" or even "sedimentation" rather than "independence." Both Hyatt and England were respected figures in the academy (especially Hyatt), but both saw their biblical scholarship as informed and complemented by their religious commitments, and both understood their scholarship to be interior to and in the service of Disciples tradition. In the midst of this period (or at its conclusion, depending on how one divides the generations) comes the *Panel of Scholars Reports.*[5] A panel of seventeen Disciples scholars worked five and a half years (1956-62) and published their results in three handsome volumes in 1963. Three of the seventeen were Bible scholars, one Old Testament (Hyatt) and two New Testament (England and William R. Baird, then of the College of the Bible). None of the three Bible scholars was a merely nominal or incidental Disciple; they

5. *The Renewal of Church: The Panel Reports,* 3 vols., ed. W. B. Blakemore (St. Louis: Christian Board of Publication, 1963).

were all thoroughly Disciples in orientation. Yet in the *Panel of Scholars Reports* taken as a whole, biblical scholarship came to be regarded as a separate discipline with a minimal relation to constructive theology. Disciples now had respectable Bible scholars of whose achievements in the academy they could be proud but whose influence on the way the denomination thought and interpreted its Bible was diminishing. For better or worse, the *Panel of Scholars Reports* shows that in the fourth generation biblical scholarship and Disciples theology were at least moving in different realms, perhaps in different directions.

5. 1967 — . The fifth generation is represented by the current crop of Disciples Bible scholars. I would designate this generation the period of *Quest*. At worst, this could simply mean we don't know what we are doing, that we have lost our way. Our latest official history characterizes us as a denomination "reexamining its heritage and searching for its identity."[6] There is still a tradition of confessionally oriented biblical scholarship among us, but it is difficult to identify, define, and analyze. When it occasionally comes into focus, contemporary Disciples Bible scholars are not clear as to whether we should deny it, be embarrassed by it as unwelcome vestiges of a bygone day we should have outgrown and sink into union with the SBL/AAR at large,[7] or whether we might better acknowledge it, nurture it, and attempt to reclaim it before it is too late.

These five generations correspond to the five chapters of a larger project, a comprehensive history of biblical interpretation in the Campbell tradition, in which I am only in the beginning stages. I am somewhat hesitant about the way I characterize sections 4 and 5 and the labels I have given them, and present them here only as the tentative framework for the segment of our history I wish to discuss more carefully — namely, the third generation. It is the third generation that I consider to be the crucial period for the way our history has unfolded, that has made us what we are and presented us with both the problems and challenges of the present situation.

THE THIRD GENERATION

The third generation was the crucial period for early Christianity, in which it self-consciously became a separate religious group. As documentation for the

6. William E. Tucker and Lester G. McAllister, *Journey in Faith: A History of the Christian Church (Disciples of Christ)* (St. Louis: Christian Board of Publication, 1975), p. 11.

7. The 1804 *Last Will and Testament of the Springfield Presbytery*, one of the founding documents of the Disciples, states, "We *will*, that this body die, be dissolved, and sink into union with the Body of Christ at large" (cited in *Historical Documents Advocating Christian Union*, ed. Charles Alexander Young [Joplin, Mo.: College Press, 1985], p. 20). SBL/AAR stands for Society of Biblical Literature/American Academy of Religion — two of the major scholarly societies in the field of religion.

"third generation" phenomenon in early Christianity, I would list Matthew, Luke-Acts, John, and particularly the Johannine epistles (though not by the same author as the Gospel), the Pastorals, Jude, and 2 Peter. For explicit reference to the *third* generation, see 2 Timothy 1:5.

The first generation had the new, magnificent vision. The second generation inherited and consolidated it but did not yet have enough internal history to recognize inherent problems in its own history. In the third generation, it was recognized that the group had its own history and that the vision had become tarnished. The charismatic leadership of the first generation was gone, and a set of traditions now functioned as the test of fellowship.[8] There was an internal struggle over who were the legitimate heirs and custodians of the first generation's insights and gains.[9] The distinction between orthodoxy and heresy developed and was applied. The enemy came to be seen not as merely "them" in the parent group ("the Jews"/"the sects"), but as an internal threat, members of one's own group who had become heretical in their effort to become "progressive." For the third generation of early Christianity, this is evident in the Pastorals, Jude, and 2 Peter 2 throughout; see specifically 1 John 2:18-19 for labeling the self-styled progressives as traitors who no longer belong to "us."

The Disciples' theological point of view prohibited the labels "orthodox" and "heretical" from being widely used, but identification of persons and ideas within the movement as having betrayed the faith appeared already in the second generation. Already in 1863 Lard spoke of the new ideas as a "degeneration" of the pure faith of the founding fathers.[10] This process was crystallized and polarized in the third generation when McGarvey spoke of his theological opponents within the church and within the Disciples movement as "infidels." The myth of the pure first generation developed, and fellow members of the group were accused of abandoning the faith once for all delivered to the saints in the first generation (Jude 3).[11] Those of false or perverted faith came to be seen as morally reprobate, not merely doctrinally mistaken: they were deceivers and hypocrites whose motives are impure. The Pastorals and Jude

8. The Disciples adopt a set of mottos that constitute the identifying marks of "our" people; "faithful sayings" emerge in the Pastorals (1 Tim. 1:15, 3:1, 4:9; 2 Tim. 2:11; Tit. 3:8).

9. Note the pseudonymous author's explicit reference to the recipient of the Pastorals, the fictitious "Timothy," as "my true [= 'legitimate'] child in the faith" (1 Tim 1:2). The rejection of others who claimed to be the heirs of the Pauline tradition comes to expression here. Likewise, in Disciples history, John W. McGarvey and Moses E. Lard considered the advocates of the new ideas and practices by the liberal (false) brethren to be illegitimate heirs, falsely claiming allegiance to the "restoration plea."

10. See *Lard's Quarterly* 1 (1863): 101, which speaks of the "degeneracy in our brotherhood" in reaction to Isaac Errett's "creed."

11. Although Paul's own letters indicate that Christians struggled with each other within the church before it had become clear what was to be the main stream of Christian orthodoxy, later admirers of Paul, Peter, and the first generation picture the first generation as pure and assert that false teaching entered the church only after their deaths. To be sure, Paul and Peter are said to have predicted this but not to have experienced it (see Acts 20:29; 1 Tim. 4:1-3; 2 Pet. 2).

provide examples of this in early Christianity.[12] The view that false faith necessarily both generates and proceeds from false morals was repeatedly taken up by McGarvey. It has often been noted that his vitriolic attacks and charges against his theological opponents do not correspond to his gentle personal manner.[13] The explanation can be found not in Jekyll-and-Hyde terms but in terms of the third generation of the first Christian century: heresy is not merely an intellectual misstep but an expression of sin; false faith is inevitably bound up with a false heart.

In three generations, early Christianity modulated from a renewal movement to a separate religious body. So did the Campbell-Stone movement, in each of the above respects. If the first generation of Disciples is represented in the New Testament by Paul, the third generation is a struggle between the author of the Pastorals on the one hand (McGarvey is much like the pastor in all the above respects) and the fourth Gospel on the other (Willett's favorite Gospel, understood in his own way, was John). The conflict over higher criticism can be understood within the context of this general pattern of sociological development and theological tension. It is an accident of history that higher criticism became an issue for Disciples during the third generation of our history, but it nevertheless cannot be considered as an isolated issue: it must be considered as an aspect of a complex process through which the adolescent denomination was proceeding.[14] The sociological and intellectual developments that conditioned this period of American history, including the Disciples response to higher criticism, are detailed elsewhere in this volume.

12. See for example 1 Tim. 1:19-20; 4:1-3; 2 Tim. 3:1-9; Tit. 1:10-16; Jude 4, 12-13, 17-19.

13. The following epithets are samples taken from the columns of his "Biblical Criticism" column in the *Christian Standard,* as reprinted in *Short Essays in Biblical Criticism* (Cincinnati: Standard Publishing, 1910): "destructive critics," p. 46; "the great unbeliever," p. 62; "infidel," p. 75; "Enemies — purpose of overthrowing the Christian faith," p. 236; "Device of the Unbelievers" (opinions that differ from his), p. 256; "not fair minded," p. 322; "lost in the fog of their own conceit," p. 380; "sapheads who wrote for newspapers," p. 385; "the crooked critics," p. 386; "the cranks who have discovered a mare's nest," p. 397; "critics consider themselves better than the apostles," p. 401; "their vaporing assumptions," p. 402; "their infidel theory," p. 403; "these crooked critics," p. 420; "all his hair-brained [*sic*] speculations," p. 434; "an apostasy unparalleled in the history of Christendom," p. 422.

14. After I had noticed and worked out this correspondence between the social dynamics of early Christianity and the early Disciples movement, I discovered that Willett had also posited a similarity between the theological development of early Christianity and the theological development of the whole later history of the church. He argued that just as early Christianity developed from the theology of Peter through Paul to that of John as the culmination and crown of early Christian thought, so prior to the Reformation Petrine theology dominated the church, the Reformation and afterward advanced to Paul's theology, but that John was to be the theologian for the future — specifically, the theologian of liberal Christianity to flower in "the Christian century" (see H. L. Willett and James M. Campbell, *The Teachings of the Books; or, The Literary Structure and Spiritual Interpretation of the Books of the New Testament* [New York: Fleming H. Revell, 1899], p. 78). We will return to Willett's judgment about the place of the Gospel of John in the New Testament and Christian theology.

Before proceeding, we must make a brief digression to discuss the meaning of the term "higher criticism." Experience shows that even in theologically sophisticated groups, one can not always assume this.[15] The term is not felicitous: *criticism* sounds negative, and *higher* sounds arrogant. No term, with the possible exception of *demythologizing,* could be calculated to excite more resistance and sarcasm from self-appointed defenders of the Bible. Felicitous or not, we seem to be stuck with it, and we would do well to explain it constructively to ourselves and others.

I do not know who was the first to use the adjective *critical* with reference to biblical study. It, and the related noun *criticism,* seems to have occasioned no great objection. *Criticism* was understood in its proper sense of "careful, analytical, discerning," in contrast to "uncritical," which is to say "naive." Books about the Bible with the word *criticism* in the title were used and commended by the first generation of Disciples without objection, and McGarvey called his own notorious column in the *Christian Standard* "Biblical Criticism" and considered himself a critical scholar of the Bible in the proper sense.[16] The objectionable connotations emerged after Johann Gottfried Eichhorn's division of biblical criticism into "lower" and "higher" criticism. The former has to do with the establishment of the original wording of the biblical texts from the variety of extant manuscripts. If we had the original manuscripts, there would be no need for lower criticism. This process of reconstructing the original wording of the text, and this alone, is called *textual criticism,* or, in Eichhorn's terminology, "lower criticism." He presumably chose this term because it is the foundational work for all else. The additional critical work that is constructed on this foundation, dealing with the formation of the books themselves (i.e., issues of historical background, authorship, date, sources, literary characteristics, genre, and historical reliability) — what is usually called historical criticism — Eichhorn called "higher criticism." Unfortunate as the label was, it stuck, and we are stuck with it. In the writings of the period we are studying, however, the term "higher criticism" often refers to more than simply the historical study of the Bible. Many American conservatives exploited the negative potential of the term (again, like "demythologizing" two generations later) to galvanize their constituency against the "higher criticism" now specifically identified with the methods and conclusions of the "radical" German critics.[17]

15. For example, there is the (rather uncritical) tendency to lump all the disciplines of critical study under the heading of "text criticism."

16. See the initial essay in this department of the *Christian Standard* for 7 January 1893, reprinted in *Short Essays in Biblical Criticism,* pp. 5-6.

17. McGarvey is not untypical when, on the first page of the announcement of his new colunm in the *Christian Standard* he identifies higher criticism with "the destructive criticism which originated in the rationalistic schools of Germany" (*Short Essays in Biblical Criticism,* p. 1).

McGARVEY AND WILLETT AS REPRESENTATIVE FIGURES

So far as the history of Disciples biblical interpretation is concerned, it is a helpful oversimplification to see the fork in the road the adolescent denomination faced at this juncture as represented by the two figures of John W. McGarvey and Herbert L. Willett. In their persons, writings, and careers, each embodied and projected into the future one of the major options available to Disciples as they faced the threat and challenge of the new intellectual currents.

John William McGarvey was an important figure whose significance is seldom fully appreciated because of the effectiveness of his later detractors' caricature of "McGarveyism." (It must be admitted, however, that certain features of his life — his ear trumpet, for example — clearly invited caricature.) McGarvey was born 1 March 1829 in Hopkinsville, Kentucky, and spent his youth in Hopkinsville and Tremont, Illinois, where his parents moved when he was ten years old. At the age of eighteen he entered Bethany College, where he became well acquainted with the Campbells. Untypical of the student body generally, he was faithful in attendance at Alexander Campbell's Bible lectures for the entire three and one half years he was at Bethany. These daily lectures were never less than an hour in length. As a guest in the Campbell home, he read the Bible to the blind and aged Thomas Campbell and so impressed Alexander Campbell with his interest and proficiency in biblical studies that he received an inscribed copy of the New Testament from Mrs. Campbell.[18] After graduating from Bethany 4 July 1850, he moved to Missouri, where his parents had relocated in the meantime. At first he taught school and then began pastoring a church, all the while preparing himself for his future work by engaging in a disciplined study of the text of the Bible and secondary works on biblical interpretation. In 1862, at the age of 33, he was called to be the pastor of the Main Street Christian Church in Lexington, Kentucky. Shortly thereafter, Kentucky University moved from Harrodsburg to Lexington, Robert Milligan became the president of its College of the Bible, and in 1865 J. W. McGarvey became its first professor of sacred history. Except for a brief period of expulsion, he had found the niche for which he had been preparing himself and continued as the dominant figure in the College of the Bible until his death in 1911. Almost single-handedly McGarvey planned and implemented the model that became the dominant force in Disciples ministerial education for two generations, the effects of which are still being felt.[19]

---

18. W. C. Morro, *"Brother McGarvey": The Life of President T. W. McGarvey of the College of the Bible of Lexington, Kentucky* (St. Louis: Bethany Press, 1940), p. 60.

19. In an article entitled "Ministerial Education" in the 1865 volume of *Lard's Quarterly* (pp. 239-50), McGarvey delineates the vision of the kind of Bible-centered ministerial education he had in mind for the Disciples. The implementation of this vision is documented in engaging detail by Dwight E. Stevenson in *Lexington Theological Seminary, 1865-1965* (St. Louis: Bethany Press, 1964), especially chaps. 1-5 and 9. If ever an institution was "the lengthened shadow of one man," this was true of the College of the Bible from 1865 to 1911.

In terms of pure chronology, McGarvey could be seen as belonging to the second generation of Disciples history.[20] I consider him a representative figure of the *third* generation because it was in this period that biblical criticism became an issue that brought his opposition to the fore, it was then that he debated his much younger contemporary Willett and the other leaders of the emerging new liberalism among Disciples,[21] it was then that the influential revised edition of his *Acts* commentary appeared (1892), and it was then that he launched the "Biblical Criticism" column in the *Christian Standard* with the explicit purpose of opposing the "destructive rationalistic higher criticism from the German universities" (1893, when McGarvey was sixty-four years old).

Herbert Lockwood Willett clearly belongs to the third generation.[22] Willett was born in 1864 in Ionia County, Michigan, into a family deeply influenced by Isaac Errett, pastor of the Ionia church. At the age of nineteen he entered Bethany College, from which he graduated with an A.B. in 1886 and an M.A. in 1887. The second generation of professors was in place in Bethany by then. Ironically, McGarvey, who became the champion of the conservative cause, studied at Bethany during the more dynamic first generation, while the future leader of liberal biblical study among the Disciples began his education under the second-generation faculty, some members of which were already becoming scholastic and reactionary in the face of the newer higher critical theories. Willett said he was taught to regard the Bible as inerrant — the standard position of all the mainline American denominations — and to reject biblical criticism.[23] But he also noted that in contrast to the advice being given graduates by "Presidents I. A. Hobbs of Drake, H. W. Everest of Eureka, E. V. Zollars of Hiram, and J. W. McGarvey of the Bible College at Lexington," he was encouraged by President Woolery to continue his education at one of the large eastern universities, preferably Yale.[24] Willett accepted this advice as valuable, but for financial reasons was not able to take advantage of it immediately. Instead, he pastored churches in Ohio. Then, in 1891, at the age of twenty-eight, he took a leave of absence from his congregation in Dayton to attend Yale Divinity School. Leo Perdue

20. See, for example, J. J. Haley, "History and Teaching of the Disciples of Christ: President John W. McGarvey, Conservative Leader of the Second Generation," *The Christian-Evangelist* 14 May 1914); and Richard O. N. Halbrook, "J. W. McGarvey: His Role in Communicating the Conservative Approach to Scripture during the Rise of Liberalism, 1865-1911" (M.A. thesis, Vanderbilt University, 1979), p. 1.

21. For example, he debated his old college friend Alexander Procter on the historical accuracy of the Old Testament at the Missouri Christian Lectureship in Paris, Missouri, in 1895. See Morro, *"Brother McGarvey,"* p. 59; and Halbrook, "J. W. McGarvey," p. 102.

22. For a more detailed portrayal of Willett, see Leo G. Perdue, "The Disciples and Higher Criticism: The Formation of an Intellectual Tradition," pp. 71-106 herein.

23. Willett, "The Corridor of Years: An Autobiograhical Record," manuscript in the holdings of the Disciples of Christ Historical Society, Nashville, p. 23. These issues had not yet emerged as "dangerous" when McGarvey was at Bethany thirty years previously.

24. Willett, "The Corridor of Years," p. 37.

has described in engaging detail Willett's transforming encounter at Yale with critical biblical scholarship, especially as embodied in W. R. Harper, and his subsequent move to Chicago, where he earned a doctorate at the new university founded by Harper on the German pattern of graduate education but devoted to the populist ideal of its founder.[25] Willett became the first dean of the Disciples Divinity House, in which for almost a generation, until his retirement in 1929, he played a role analogous to that of McGarvey at the College of the Bible.

In these two men, their institutions, writings, and careers, Disciples may see an embodiment and reflection of themselves and their possibilities at the turn of the century. A comparison and contrast of their lives, methods, perspectives, philosophies, and continuing influence might enable contemporary Disciples to recover something of their own past and understand something of their present.

GENERAL SIMILARITIES

BOTH WERE THOROUGHLY DISCIPLES

Both had been born and reared in homes that were thoroughly aware of and committed to the Disciples cause, homes in which the parents were in contact with significant figures in the Disciples movement. McGarvey's stepfather, Dr. Saltonstall, was a trustee of Bethany who had contributed $2,500 to the new college. Willett's parents were admirers of their local minister, Isaac Errett. Later, Errett's views of ministerial education would influence McGarvey.[26] Both McGarvey and Willett studied at Bethany, though in different generations.

The careers of both were spent in the service of the denomination, teaching in institutions oriented to preparing ministers for the denomination. Both published extensively in the denominational journals and wrote books published by the denominational publishing houses or with publishers closely associated with them. Both addressed the denomination, not the public in general.[27] The first course in Disciples history was taught by Willett in Chicago in 1894.[28]

Both had a "messianic vision" of the role of Disciples in the future of the church in America and the world. Their visions had different content, as we shall see, but both saw the Disciples as playing a grand role in the future history of the church and the world.

25. See Perdue, "The Disciples and Higher Criticism."

26. See Morro, *"Brother McGarvey,"* p. 226.

27. This is less true of Willett than of McGarvey. Yet neither wrote for the general academic world but for the people in the churches, especially the people in the Christian Churches (Disciples of Christ).

28. Osborn, "Theology among the Disciples," p. 104.

Both were interested in the *growth* of the Disciples. Each defended his theology and method of interpreting the Bible not merely in terms of its theological and intellectual integrity but in terms of its practical outworking in the growth of the church. The differences in *how* they understood this are discussed below, but they had this interest and perspective in common.

BOTH WERE SCHOLARS/EDUCATORS

Both Were Well-Read Scholars

Both McGarvey and Willett were well-read scholars who lived in the world of books. It is clear that Willett, a graduate of Yale and Chicago who did some postdoctoral study in Berlin, was a man of many books. But so was McGarvey. The great difference between them was not a matter of literacy. McGarvey has sometimes been caricatured as an ignoramus, but this is unfair. He had a large personal library to which he went at five o'clock in the morning and to which he returned in the evening after his classes at the College. He loved books, and said a touching good-bye to his library as he departed on the one great trip of his life.[29] In his commentary on the four Gospels he cites not only standard reference books but also more than eighty commentaries; in the revision of his Acts commentary he cites at least twenty books; and in his book on the text and canon of the New Testament he cites fifty sources.[30] While some of these are lightweights by contemporary standards, his writings are also polka-dotted with citations from the classics and the Church Fathers, often in the original languages, and it is clear that he read extensively in the radically critical works of Ferdinand Christian Baur, David Friedrich Strauss, and Ernst Renan.

Both Were Educators Who Trained Significant Leaders for the Denomination

Although both were ordained ministers who pastored churches and preached regularly, each thought of himself as standing within the Disciples educational tradition, which magnified the office of the teacher. Both held professorial appointments and spent the major portion of their time and energy in the specific task of ministerial education in the classroom.

29. McGarvey describes this six-month trip to the "Bible lands" of Palestine, Turkey, Greece, and Italy, via England and France, in *Lands of the Bible: A Geographical and Topographical Description of Palestine with Letters of Travel in Egypt, Syria, Asia Minor, and Greece* (Cincinnati: Standard Publishing, 1880). See also Morro, *"Brother McGarvey,"* pp. 155-64.

30. These figures are from John Clifton Trimble, "The Rhetorical Theory and Practice of John W. McGarvey" (Ph.D. diss., Northwestern University, 1966), p. 27.

BOTH WERE AUTHORS WHO WROTE EXTENSIVELY

Both men also wrote extensively.[31] In neither case was this a matter of publishing for the sake of ego, credentials, or career pressure; rather, it was an expression of the conviction each had regarding the power of the printed word to educate the pastors and laity of the church. Neither was a research scholar. Their primary intent was not to advance the frontiers of knowledge in the academic community but to relay the body of truth recognized in their respective worlds to the people to whom it belonged. Their writing, like their teaching and administration of their respective schools, was an expression of their common conviction regarding the value of education — especially of an educated ministry — for the growth of the Disciples. Once again, this common conviction came to expression differently in ways that will be discussed below.

Both Were Populists and Popularizers

This is to say that the grand Disciples populist tradition continued in both McGarvey and Willett. It is not the case that we have one sophisticated elitist and one popularizer. Neither was an elitist. Both were popularizers. Willett's devotion to Harper kept him from being an elitist. McGarvey modeled himself after Paul in an attempt to be the kind of scholar who reads the original languages but expresses himself in the vernacular.[32] Today, as James O. Duke's study of Disciples scholarship indicates, very few of those who write for their peers write for the church.[33] The popularizer aspect of Disciples scholarship has been almost lost.

BOTH WERE THEOLOGIANS AND SAW THEMSELVES AS SUCH

Both Saw Interpreting the Bible as the Way of Doing Theology

For McGarvey, as for Disciples tradition generally, what is usually called theology was "Bible study." He readily acknowledged that the College of the Bible was "in ordinary parlance, a theological seminary." Willett shared this characteristic Disciples point of view. Although he did not restrict himself to biblical exposition as the sole means of doing theology,[34] his biblical inter-

---

31. For a listing of their writings, see the appendix on pp. 66-70 herein.

32. See McGarvey, *Short Essays in Biblical Criticism,* pp. 46-47, 56-57.

33. See Duke, "Disciples Theologizing amid Currents of Mainstream Protestant Thought, 1940-1980: Sketchbook Observations," pp. 139-64 herein; and "Scholarship in the Disciples' Tradition," *Disciples Theological Digest* 1 (1986): 5-40.

34. For example, Willett wrote topically arranged theological works, such as his *Basic Truths of the Christian Faith* (Chicago: Christian Century Company, 1903), which passes for a simple populist "systematic theology." The chapter titles are "The Primacy of Christ," "The

pretations functioned theologically, just like those of McGarvey. That the theology was different goes without saying. But neither McGarvey nor Willett considered the theological task as a separate job to be done on exegesis after the Bible scholar had simply laid bare the historical meaning. This bifurcation had not entered the theological work of either scholar.

Both Dealt with the Whole Bible

When I began this study I knew that Willett had taken his Ph.D. in Semitics (i.e., "Old Testament"), and I had identified McGarvey as a New Testament scholar primarily on the basis of his famous *Commentary on Acts* and because Disciples are a "New Testament people," often accusing each other of being crypto-Marcionites. I was unaware at the time that I had retrojected the compartmentalization that has since become standard in theological faculties into this period. It does not fit. Willett, the "Old Testament scholar," wrote without apology on New Testament subjects and on the Bible as a whole. McGarvey, whose title at the College of the Bible was never "Professor of New Testament" but "Professor of Sacred History," taught courses from Genesis to Revelation every year of his career and wrote not only on Acts but on Deuteronomy.[35] There are far more articles in his "Biblical Criticism" column dealing with the Old Testament than with the New. In McGarvey's case, of course, this is partly due to the fact that it was the Old Testament over which the critical battles were being fought. "Destructive criticism" of the New Testament was not yet being taken seriously in this country. But this is only a partial explanation. It is also the case that both Willett and McGarvey represent a continuation of the holistic approach to the Bible that Alexander Campbell had developed at Bethany, where both of them had studied,[36] and that had become a part of Disciples approach to the Bible as represented in the classic work of the second generation, Robert Milligan's Genesis-to-Revelation *Scheme of Redemption*.[37]

Father," "The Scriptures," "The Value of Human Life," "The Redemptive Work of Christ," "The Death of Christ," "The Resurrection," "Present Proofs of Christianity," "Faith," "Repentance," "Baptism," and "The Programme of Christ." One may here note that Willett's topics represent a combination of generic liberal Christianity and his Disciples heritage, so that on this point of allowing his Disciples heritage to shape his theological agenda he is little different from McGarvey. It is true that McGarvey could never have dealt with these topics in the form of a "systematic theology," but he did deal with them in sermons and in biblical exposition.

    35. The only technical work written by either scholar was McGarvey's *Authorship of the Book of Deuteronomy with Its Bearing on the Higher Criticism of the Pentateuch* (Cincinnati: Standard Publishing, 1902).

    36. Cf. Boring, "The Formation of a Tradition: Alexander Campbell and the New Testament," *Disciples Theological Digest* 2 (1987): 8-13.

    37. Milligan, *An Exposition and Defense of the Scheme of Redemption as It is Revealed and Taught in Holy Scriptures* (St. Louis: Christian Board of Publication, 1868).

Both Were Apologists for the Faith

McGarvey saw himself not only as apologist in the sense of defender of the faith for the sake of the average church member who lacked the opportunity and skills to evaluate the onslaughts of destructive critics, but also in the classical sense of making a case for the truth of the faith to honest, thoughtful unbelievers and inquirers who were willing to listen. All McGarvey's writings had an apologetic slant, but he also tackled the subject directly. It may come as a surprise to contemporary readers — though it was no surprise to *his* contemporaries who understood Disciples tradition and presuppositions — to learn that McGarvey's *Evidences of Christianity* was not a philosophical defense of Christianity but a book about the New Testament. (The "evidences of Christianity" *are* the books of the New Testament.) The first volume of this two-volume work deals with "The Integrity of the New Testament Text," which McGarvey subdivided into issues of the "Integrity of the Text" (lower criticism) and "Genuineness" (higher criticism). The second volume also contains two parts, "The Credibility of the New Testament Books," dealing with objections to the historical veracity of New Testament events and explaining alleged contradictions, and "The Inspiration of the New Testament Books," arguing his theory of inspiration with regard to each of the New Testament documents. Thus McGarvey's "apologetic" turns out to be entirely biblicistic. Faith is belief of testimony, in good Disciples tradition. Despite the attacks of the higher critics, the New Testament is reliable testimony that will generate faith. There is a kind of "Barthian" approach here in that faith is bound up entirely with the word of God spoken in the Bible. Yet unlike Barth, and like the liberals he decries, McGarvey holds that an apology for the faith can be made to reasonable people. His content is different, but the form of his argument is not so different from that of his liberal opponents.

Willett also saw himself as an apologist for the faith and a defender of the Bible. But he considered both the conservative biblicists and their secular rationalistic opponents to be burdened with the same error — a level, homogenized Bible. Willett viewed higher criticism as an apologetic tool that lets us see the progressive development of revelation in the Bible; it is the method for putting the Bible back into the hands of those who thought they had to abandon it because of its inconsistencies and historical problems.

Both Were "Rationalistic" Thinkers Who Prized "Consistency"

It is not the case that here we have a rational thinker over against a nonthinker, reason over against dogma. Both Willett and McGarvey were "rationalists," true heirs of the nineteenth-century rationalist Disciples tradition that tended to exalt a certain kind of logic. Both McGarvey and Willett studied at Bethany while Richard Whately's syllogistic logic was the dominant mode of thought there. McGarvey especially was influenced by this mode of thought and its vocabulary, which is reflected throughout his writings. Early Disciples documents used "command" and "approved example" as their hermeneutical tool for extracting instruction for the contemporary church from the New Testament, but they had not yet discovered "necessary inference." This scholastic development had influenced the Disciples stream from which both McGarvey and Willett drank deeply.[38] There is certainly a difference in the way they appealed to reason, but the difference is not that one favored reason and the other opposed it.

Willett was indeed a liberal thinker who honored the core of biblical faith because it represented reason. He said, for example, that "One is Christian in virtue of his belief in the reasonableness and finality of Jesus' interpretation of life."[39] And "I believe in him because his way of life appeals to me as the most reasonable and convincing."[40] Perdue cites these quotations as evidence of the "centrality of Christ" in Willett's religion, which is reflective of the way Willett himself saw his theology.[41] I consider these references documentation for the centrality of reason in his religion, of which reason Jesus is then a good illustration. "It must not be understood that mere unreasoning obedience is ever demanded of any man," wrote Willett. "God's message to men is 'Come, now, let us reason together. . . .' "[42] He believed that human reason was the instrument by which the variety of biblical expressions could be sorted out and arranged in a developmental order that made sense, with the reasonable teaching of Jesus at the apex.

McGarvey used the term *rationalist* as a synonym for *unbeliever* and *higher critic,* and yet one of the features he shared with Willett was that he too was a consistent rationalist. If a tidy mind is a small mind, then McGarvey was a small-minded person. He believed that if you can prove something is inconsistent, you will have proven that it is untrue. To function as an authority in the church, the New Testament must therefore represent a consistent system of doctrine. For example, there is — and can be — no theological differences among the apostles. Professor Briggs and the Tübingen school alleged that there were doctrinal differences between Peter and Paul, and McGarvey responded, "Prove this proposition, and you will sweep away the very foundations of apostolic authority."[43]

McGarvey was not thought of as a logician or rationalist but as a "great Bible

38. See Michael Wilson Casey, "The Development of Necessary Inference in the Hermeneutics of the Disciples of Christ/Churches of Christ" (Ph.D. diss., University of Pittsburgh, 1986), which traces the shift from the inductive logic of the early Campbell to the deductive, syllogistic logic adopted by the later Campbell and propagated by Bethany College.

39. Willett, "The Corridor of Years," p. 156.

40. Willett, "The Corridor of Years," p. 157.

41. Cf. chap. 1 of Willett's *Basic Truths of the Christian Faith,* "The Primacy of Christ," and Perdue's "The Disciples and Higher Criticism."

42. "Obedience Better than Sacrifice," *Christian Century,* 16 July 1908, p. 355.

43. McGarvey, *Short Essays in Biblical Criticism,* p. 73.

scholar" because he seemed able to quote reams of the biblical text.[44] People are too easily impressed by this, then and now, just as they too easily dismiss a knowledge of the content of the Bible now. McGarvey was thought of as a person who "really knows the Bible," but in fact he was a rationalist who feared critical Bible study because it messed up his system.[45] McGarvey's studies of the Gospels are dominated by his effort to show the logical argument within each Gospel and the harmonious consistency of all four accounts.[46] He interprets "I believe; help my unbelief" as the report of contradiction and confusion found in the distraught mind of the father of an epileptic boy rather than profound Markan or church theology.[47] The resurrection of Jesus is "reasonable" — not the shattering of our expectations but the confirmation of our reasonable reflections.[48] McGarvey's equation of biblical authority with the authority of a consistent rationalistic system is illustrated by the occurrence on the same page of *Biblical Criticism* of statements asserting (1) that the Bible is the authority and (2) that the Bible is subject to "rational proof."[49] Therefore, "biblical authority" is "rational proof." Although McGarvey did not realize it, he considered the authority of the Bible to be established by — which is to say, subject to — the authority of reason.[50]

44. See Morro, *"Brother McGarvey,"* p. 232. There can be no doubt that McGarvey was thoroughly acquainted with the content of the Bible, an achievement not to be disdained, but the pious legends about his having memorized the text of the Bible are much exaggerated. Actually, McGarvey spent part of every class day rememorizing the chapters to be rehearsed that day.

45. See Morro, *"Brother McGarvey,"* p. 255.

46. As evidence for this see the following:

  (1) J. W. McGarvey, *Matthew and Mark,* New Testament Commentary, vol. 1 (St. Louis: Christian Board of Publication, 1875), *passim;*

  (2) J. W. McGarvey and Philip Y. Pendleton, *The Fourfold Gospel; or, A Harmony of the Four Gospels* (Cincinnati: Standard Publishing Co., 1905);

  (3) McGarvey's long section harmonizing alleged discrepancies in *Evidences of Christianity* (1886, 1891; reprint, Cincinnati: Standard Publishing, 1912), pp. 30-82;

  (4) McGarvey's many articles in his "Biblical Criticism" column in the *Christian Standard,* including, for example, his harmonization of the accounts of Passion Week (*Short Essays in Biblical Criticism,* pp. 405-7); and

  (5) the elaboration below, where I detail the difference from Willett's implementation of reason in the study of the Gospels.

47. McGarvey, *Matthew and Mark,* p. 318.

48. McGarvey, *Matthew and Mark,* p. 376.

49. McGarvey, *Short Essays in Biblical Criticism,* p. 226.

50. Two quotations from *Short Essays in Biblical Criticism* (p. 226) illustrate this (and could be duplicated many times):

The Scriptures are not to be tested by the science of chemistry, or that of astronomy, or that of geology, or that of mathematics, but they are to be tested by the science of logic. Demonstration is not the right word. Demonstrations are addressed to the eye. But scientific proof — that is, logical proof — is the test by which the Scriptures are to be tried; and no man is required to believe them except on such proof.

"Is reason the supreme guide in religion?" No. Reason must determine for us whether the Bible is from God; must detect and correct all mistakes and changes made by copyists, and must ascertain as best it can the meaning of all obscure passages; but here her work terminates. These questions being settled, the Bible itself is our sole guide and authority.

BOTH SHARED A CERTAIN BODY OF CRITICAL CONCLUSIONS

Willett accepted some of the results of the German and British higher criticism of the Old Testament, at least tentatively, and thus revised his date for the book of Daniel, his view of Mosaic authorship of the Pentateuch, and his view of the unity of Isaiah (three cardinal litmus tests of one's stance on Old Testament criticism). All of this McGarvey considered heresy. But regarding the New Testament, Willett's conclusions on such matters were not so different from McGarvey's during the period McGarvey was debating with him in the pages of the *Christian Standard.* He was completely traditional in his view of the authorship of the Gospels. A companion of Paul wrote Acts. Paul wrote all the letters attributed to him in the tradition (except Hebrews), writing the Pastorals during a postulated "second Roman imprisonment" according to the traditional, but not the critical, pattern of Paul's life. James the Lord's brother wrote the Epistle of James. Only about 2 Peter does he express doubts, and then does not pronounce against it but says it adds interest to read the epistle as from Peter, even if only in a secondary sense, and that the inspiration of the book is in any case unquestionable.[51] He even leans toward apostolic authorship of Revelation.[52] Willett and McGarvey had their differences, but it is not the case that Willett was the progressive critic who accepted the radical views of higher criticism's judgment on matters of authorship and date of New Testament books, while McGarvey was the reactionary who rejected them. They both rejected them, as did most proponents of biblical criticism in its American dress in their day,[53] and they would have stood together against the consensus of higher criticism today.

In the above respects, McGarvey and Willett were two peas from the same Disciples pod, true sons of the nineteenth-century Disciples tradition. But as the

51. Willett and Campbell, *The Teachings of the Books,* pp. 286, 294.

52. All the information on Willett's views is taken from *The Teachings of the Books,* published in 1899. Eighteen years later he changed his mind on the authorship of the Pastorals and accepted the critical consensus that 2 Corinthians was composite (see *Our Bible* [Chicago: Christian Century Press, 1917]). Twelve years later still, he was expressing doubts about the authorship of the fourth Gospel (*The Bible through the Centuries* [Chicago: Willett, Clark, & Colby, 1929]).

53. The International Critical Commentary was just beginning under the editorship of Driver of Oxford, Plummer of Durham, and Briggs of New York. Its Old Testament volumes conformed to the critical norms of the German universities, as Driver's own 1895 commentary on Deuteronomy makes clear. Despite McGarvey's total rejection of the critical theory espoused in it, he gave it a surprisingly moderate review in the 19 June 1897 issue of the *Christian Standard* (*Short Essays in Biblical Criticism,* pp. 206-7). But the early New Testament volumes were all conservative in their critical conclusions. Ezra Gould's 1896 commentary on Mark affirms the traditional authorship and has a rather straightforwardly conservative exposition.

Washington Gladden, outspoken liberal pastor and champion of the Social Gospel who became a target for McGarvey's attacks in the *Christian Standard,* also affirmed the traditional authorship of the New Testament Gospels, all of which he believed were written independently of each other by the authors whose names they bear (*Who Wrote the Bible?* [Boston: Houghton, Mifflin, 1892], pp. 237-66, esp. p. 245). This may be contrasted with the contemporary critical view at every point, as illustrated in such standard works as Francis W. Beare, *The Earliest Records of Jesus* (Nashville: Abingdon, 1962), and all standard introductions to the New Testament used in college courses.

twentieth century dawned, there were also manifest differences between them that represented the options before the denomination. We will first survey the general contrasts between the two men and their approaches to religion and theology and then explore their particular treatments of the Bible.

GENERAL DIFFERENCES

As everyone knows, the difference between McGarvey and Willett was that the former was a conservative and the latter was a liberal. But labels can be libels, and before these tags can be very helpful, they must be filled in with specific content. I will characterize the difference between McGarvey's conservatism and Willett's liberalism in relation to (1) their sociological and cultural background and setting, (2) their academic orientation, (3) their theological stance, (4) their general approach to the Bible, and (5) their different manners of responding to and appropriation of Disciples tradition.

SOCIOLOGICAL AND CULTURAL: DIFFERENCES RELATED TO THEIR BACKGROUND AND EDUCATION

Rural/Urban

McGarvey represented the conservative rural tradition and mindset of a country that was struggling to come to terms with the sweeping sociological changes it was experiencing. He grew up in the country, lived all his life in a rural setting, most of it in Lexington, the population of which was about ten thousand at the turn of the century. His one big trip was to the "lands of the Bible" in 1879. The mindset of rural America pervades his text. He often uses barnyard analogies.[54] He advised his students to "stay out of cities," and wrote for *Lard's Quarterly*, which contrasted its contents with the views of "the city pastors."[55] McGarvey started in the country, stayed there, and admonished the Disciples to do the same.

Willett also started in the country, but made the transition from rural Michigan to Bethany to Dayton to New Haven, Chicago, and Berlin. "When Fort Dearborn was incorporated as the village of Chicago in 1833, it was an ugly frontier outpost of seventeen houses. By 1900, though still ugly, it was a sprawling western metropolis of 1,698,575 people — the fifth largest city in the world."[56] One way to symbolize the difference between McGarvey and Willett is to think about the difference between Lexington and Chicago in 1900.

---

54. See, e.g., *Short Essays in Biblical Criticism*, pp. 72, 176.
55. *Lard's Quarterly* (1864): 141.
56. Sydney Ahlstrom, *A Religious History of the American People* (New Haven: Yale University Press, 1972), p. 735.

Regional/Cosmopolitan

Willett's background gave him a cosmopolitan perspective; he thought in terms of the world. He read German, had studied in Germany under Harnack, Weiss, and others, and knew personally some of the "destructive higher critics." These remained an impersonal list of names and positions for McGarvey, who, like Alexander Campbell, knew no German and read German works only in translation. McGarvey was thus able to share the anti-German feeling latent in some American circles at the turn of the century and exploit it polemically. In this context, to label higher criticism "German" was already to condemn it.[57]

McGarvey addressed himself to the ethical questions that exercised the mind of small-town America. These were individual and local: divorce, drinking, dancing, organ-playing in the church. He did not write about reconstruction, economic issues, or the Spanish-American War. Willett, on the other hand, already manifested the dawning of the Social Gospel conscience that was to characterize American liberalism.

Backward-Looking, Status Quo/Forward-Looking, Progressive

Willett shared the general forward-looking stance of liberalism. Faithfulness to God was willingness to grow and change, with one's eyes focused on the future. On the first page of his *Prophets of Israel* he explains that Israel was chosen by God not because they were better than other nations but because they had the least to unlearn and were thus able to grow and change.[58] On the other hand, Jesus rejected the scribes and Pharisees because they were fixed and rigid. Faithfulness to God and the Bible required Disciples to accept the new truth revealed in changing times rather than to attempt to restore a static truth from the past. As a famous hymn of liberal Christianity put it, "Time makes ancient good uncouth."[59]

McGarvey was the spokesperson for the majority of the denomination that looked back to the New Testament as a fixed pattern of truth and back to the first generation of Disciples as the model for apprehending and implementing it.

Absolute/Relative

This meant that for McGarvey truth was absolute, and discussions of the truth of the Christian faith were to be conducted in absolute terms. He tended to

---

57. Note the explicit anti-German statements in *Short Essays in Biblical Criticism*, pp. 1, 54, 55, 57, 75, 77, 105.

58. Willett, *The Prophets of Israel*, Bethany C. E. Reading Courses (Chicago: Fleming H. Revell, 1899), p. 11.

59. James Russell Lowell's "The Present Crisis," set to music and included in hymnals under its first line, "Once to Every Man and Nation."

pose all issues in yes/no, right/wrong, either/or terms. The difference between Christianity and other religions was an absolute difference. He criticized the great William Sanday of Oxford, whom he saw as a "conservative" critic, because Sanday thought the pagan religions of antiquity differed from Christianity "only in degree."[60]

Crisp Boundaries, Exclusive/Soft Boundaries, Inclusive

Mary Douglas would have a field day studying Christian communities who understood themselves as McGarvey did. His rigid categories meant that his doctrine of the church must make absolutely clear who is in and who is out, and the procedure for making the transition. McGarvey drew crisply defined boundaries that shut certain ones in and certain ones out. This was one element in his opposition to higher criticism, which in his view gave fuzzy edges to those things that had to be clear for his system to function.

Willett, on the other hand, in accord with the more vague soteriology characteristic of liberal theology in general, could not be so precise as to who was in and who was out of the Christian community, who would be saved and who would not be. He drew his circle larger and with less precision. Edwin Markham's ditty expressing the spirit of liberalism became popular about this time:

> He drew a circle that shut me out—
> Heretic, rebel, a thing to flout.
> But Love and I had the wit to win:
> We drew a circle that took him in.

It expresses an inherently noble spirit, but as a strategy it did not work, at least not on McGarveyites. The very point of view he considered an asset was placed on the liability side of the ledger by McGarvey.

ACADEMIC: DIFFERENCES RELATED TO THEIR GENERAL EDUCATIONAL PHILOSOPHY

Indoctrination/Education

In McGarvey and Willett, propaganda and education stand over against each other. *Propaganda* in its etymological and basic meaning is not necessarily an evil word. The Roman Catholic Church has had an office with this name in the title for some centuries, in the sense of propagation of the faith, evangelism. McGarvey believed that his basic documents, the sixty-six books of the Protestant Bible, were a once-for-all static revelation. Their

60. McGarvey, *Short Essays in Biblical Criticism*, pp. 55-56.

consistent system of doctrine was to be inculcated into receptive students, who were not to be troubled with alternative views. Ministers were to give one clear, authoritative answer to every question. Biblical criticism was the enemy of this. This was what higher criticism took away. It was therefore the enemy of all that Disciples stood for in McGarvey's view. Hence the passion (and vitriol) with which McGarvey defended his view of the Bible and opposed higher criticism. This was the peculiarly Disciples issue at stake in the battle over biblical criticism for both McGarvey and Willett. Willett saw biblical criticism as the liberating means of *attracting* people to the Bible, of showing them the variety in the Bible and its record of the growth and development of a religious community toward ever higher truth. *This* is what Willett wanted his students to see in the Bible. It was not a dogmatic theory about the Bible as such that bothered Disciples but a matter of how it affected their understanding of how the Bible is to be used in the propagation of the faith.

McGarvey believed that an uncritical apprehension of a homogeneous Bible provided the foundation for an authoritative approach to evangelism and indoctrination that made the church grow — and he believed that the history of the Disciples verified his position. And what he believed he taught. He made hardly any reference to secondary works on the Bible. Students who studied under McGarvey for four years of Bible class, two semesters per year, could not recall his having referred them to any books except the Bible and his own *Lands of the Bible*.[61] The College of the Bible library thus did not need to be large or up to date, and it was not, for it was barely used. "According to the librarian's report of June 2, 1905, The College of the Bible library was then subscribing to eight periodicals and had added fifty-six new books to its collection during the year. Over the same period only 240 books circulated."[62]

McGarvey was himself well-read, but he saw his function as teacher to serve as a guardian for the ministry and the church. He would read the critical studies, digest and respond to them, and deliver the results to his students and the church at large, which he did not encourage to read and think for themselves. McGarvey stood between the critics and the people to guard them, because he did not respect or trust them.[63] "Father McGarvey" might better express this paternalistic kind of populism than "Brother McGarvey." McGarvey's tone in his writings was caustic and sarcastic, oversimplifying

---

61. Dean Colby D. Hall of Texas Christian University, who studied under McGarvey, so reports in Morro, *"Brother McGarvey,"* p. 253.

62. Stevenson, *Lexington Theological Seminary,* p. 306.

63. Cf. McGarvey, *Short Essays in Biblical Criticism,* p. 3, and Morro, *"Brother McGarvey,"* passim. And see *Short Essays in Biblical Criticism,* p. 72, where McGarvey explicitly claims his role of guardian: "I only aim to stand in between the critics, some of whom I have had opportunity to study, and my brethren who have not enjoyed this opportunity, that I may give the latter the benefit of my readings, and guard them against being misled."

issues and allowing himself a manner of argument and use of evidence that he would not grant his opponents. McGarvey thought he had to be simplistic, hostile, and derogatory to hold the attention of laypersons.[64] His writings were a journalistic success in the same way that Hal Lindsey's and Jerry Falwell's are today. He made pronouncements with authority, leaving nothing open — in other words, using an essentially uncritical approach. He wrote to entertain and confirm, not to persuade, to readers who had already made up their minds.[65]

In Willett's classes at Chicago and in his writings, on the other hand, students were encouraged to explore a variety of sources in a large library, listen to a variety of points of view from their teachers, and make up their own minds. There was variety on the faculty at Chicago and the sort of disagreement that the students at Lexington would have found disturbing. Willett trusted the nonspecialists to evaluate the newer scholarship, and he wanted to share it with them. This is not to say that he simply listed a variety of scholarly opinions and left his readers to decide for themselves. His writings too are somewhat propagandistic, communicating the views of higher criticism in a positive way to his students and his lay readership. But this process of communication had built into it the variety of opinions inherent in the higher critical method and so was not merely the liberal counterpart to McGarvey's propaganda for a single, narrow point of view.

Both McGarvey and Willett thought their respective approaches led to church growth. McGarvey turned out to be right, in terms of numbers. Liberal *education* does in fact gain some that would otherwise be lost, but authoritative *indoctrination* on the basis of a monolithic Bible far outstripped this approach numerically.[66]

Antiscientific/Scientific

Willett attempted to come to terms with the dominant scientific view of his time, the new theory of evolution. Like the others in the small group of Disciples liberals, he accepted the theory and interpreted the Bible in relation to it.[67] Though he took pains not to be overly provocative, he expressed his understanding that God creates not "by sudden and catastrophic means, but by

64. See Morro, *"Brother McGarvey,"* pp. 179-80.
65. See Morro, *"Brother McGarvey,"* p. 203.
66. Even without Dean Kelley's *Why Conservative Churches Are Growing* (New York: Harper and Row, 1974), we would all observe that a clear, authoritarian, monolithic presentation of the faith has more market appeal than a liberal one.
67. On the early representatives of Disciples liberalism, see Joseph R. Jeter, Jr., "Alexander Procter, the Sage of Independence: Incipient Liberalism in the Nineteenth-Century American Pulpit" (Ph.D. diss., Claremont Graduate School, 1983), p. 281 and passim. Jeter cites Procter's statement in *The Witness of Jesus* that "I have been an evolutionist from the beginning and have not been at all afraid to avow it. . . . [By evolution] I mean the method by which God works" ("Alexander Procter," p. 281).

slow and often painful growth."[68] Willett saw evolution as true, but he did not view it as the kind of unwelcome, disruptive truth with which one must try to come to terms simply because one is honest; rather, he viewed it as the kind of truth to be welcomed as the key to many other truths. He understood the Bible and biblical religion in terms of progressive, developing evolution toward the highest form of life, climaxing in Jesus of Nazareth.

McGarvey saw evolution as the great evil, the key to many other evils. There was no room for the idea of development in either his idea of the origin of the world and the human race or his idea of the origin of the church. The world came into being fully formed during the six days described in Genesis 1. The church likewise came into being fully formed on the one day described in Acts 2. Both world and church have declined since their creation, and the Christian's task is to restore the original perfection. But neither evolved. There can be no compromise or accommodation between this theory, representing the science of the day, and biblical faith. A typical quote:

> Evolution, properly defined as a theory of the origin and growth of things, means development from within; and it excludes any and every force from without. This being true, to talk of theistic evolution is to use contradictory terms, and to talk nonsense. If God in any way exerts a power in the growth of matter external to matter as such, then the theory of evolution is false; and all this theorizing about theistic evolution is but a deceptive use of words. It is a delusion and a snare.[69]

In McGarvey's view, the theory of evolution was the lie that underlay the presuppositions of the higher critics and was therefore an unmitigated evil that had to be opposed.[70] This had the effect of forcing his students to choose between science and the Bible. This was precisely the choice McGarvey wanted to require, and to his way of thinking there was no doubt which choice they and the church should make.

Anticritic/Critic

On the one hand, McGarvey acknowledged that biblical criticism, both higher and lower, was a valid discipline, that biblical criticism was a part of the

---

68. Willett, *Basic Truths of the Christian Faith,* p. 27.

69. McGarvey, *Short Essays in Biblical Criticism,* p. 178.

70. McGarvey's opposition to the theory, usually represented by scorn rather than argument, appears incidentally throughout his later writings. See, for example, *Short Essays in Biblical Criticism,* pp. 140-42 (in which condemns Darwinism as the root of contemporary unbelief) and pp. 169-70 (in which he denounces Lyman Abbott's explanation of the miracles in terms of evolution as exactly the opposite of the truth). It is most clearly evident in his attack on James Lane Allen's novel *The Reign of Law* and in his clash with Burris A. Jenkins, president of Kentucky University, both of which are described in detail by Stevenson in *Lexington Theological Seminary, 1865-1965,* pp. 111-15, 130-34.

minister's equipment, and that he too was a critic.[71] In actual practice, however, McGarvey almost always restricted "criticism" to mean "the rationalistic destructive higher criticism of the Germans," and so he customarily denied that he was a critic. Although Willett acknowledged being a critic, McGarvey said that he made "no such pretension."[72] He stayed outside the critical process, reviewing the critical work of others from a safe distance and hurling Bible verses "they" didn't "believe."[73] While this was rhetorically effective with his readership, it had the effect of conceding the field of criticism to his opponents and driving an enormous wedge between a large body of Disciples and "higher criticism," giving them the choice of "believing the Bible or the higher critics." Although McGarvey himself produced a considerable amount of secondary source material to help people understand the Bible in the way he thought it should be understood, his rhetoric of "the Bible versus the critics" reinforced the latent anti-intellectualism in American culture and the tendency to regard the Bible as transparent, its meaning immediately available without benefit of clergy or hermeneutic. This was a retrogression from Alexander Campbell. But this legacy, and even this terminology, is still with us today.

Hebrew Text/English Bible

Although McGarvey himself could read Greek and Hebrew well, he explicitly designated himself Professor of English Bible. The expectation of linguistic competence present in the first generation of Disciples biblical scholarship was being diluted. Willett worked with the Hebrew and Greek text of Scripture. The grand linguistic tradition of the University of Chicago, an extension of the founder's enthusiasm for biblical languages, and the linguistic tradition of the Disciples reinforced each other in the developing Chicago version of the Disciples' tradition. At Lexington, this tradition did not wither, but under McGarvey it did not flourish. This was partly a matter of the difference between the expectations of a graduate school founded on the German model and a seminary that during McGarvey's time also included undergraduate students. In any case, the Greek and Hebrew scholarly tradition of biblical study was channeled more through Chicago than through Lexington.

71. In McGarvey's first "Biblical Criticism" column in the *Christian Standard* he gives good definitions of both lower and higher criticism and argues that even higher criticism is "a perfectly legitimate branch of study" and that "its pursuit must lead to the truth concerning the Bible" (*Short Essays in Biblical Criticism,* p. 6). In a programmatic essay entitled "Ministerial Education" in *Lard's Quarterly* for 1865 (p. 250) he includes "biblical criticism" as a part of the proposed curriculum in the ideal training school for ministers. In actual practice, McGarvey restricted biblical study to content during the first three years, a period in which he considered the students' ears to be too tender for criticism; he introduced critical issues, filtered through his own perspective, only in the fourth year.

72. McGarvey, *Short Essays in Biblical Criticism,* p. 72.

73. McGarvey, *Short Essays in Biblical Criticism,* pp. 272 and passim.

THEOLOGICAL: DIFFERENCES RELATED TO THEIR BASIC THEOLOGICAL STANCE

I will not attempt here an exhaustive theological comparison of McGarvey and Willett, much of which is implicit in the discussion of other issues in any case. However, three additional points on which their general theological approaches differ are important for our purposes here: their respective soteriologies, their views of revelation in history, and their interpretation of church history.

Soteriology: Conditional vs. Unconditional Salvation

Alexander Campbell rejected the doctrine of universal salvation.[74] But from their earliest days Disciples were also hospitable to the theology of universal salvation, an idea that was widespread and widely debated in nineteenth-century American Christianity.[75] Thomas Campbell declared that, while he was not a "restorationist," he defended the right of Aylett Raines to believe in universal salvation.[76] Elias Smith, one of the leaders of the New England "Christians" that formed one of the roots of the Disciples in their earliest history, drifted in and out of universalism.[77] Even the hyperorthodox Moses E. Lard, though not a consistent universalist, in 1879 wrote an extensive essay against the idea of eternal damnation.[78] The idea of universal salvation slum-

74. "Reconciliation is not universal, but partial," says Campbell in *The Christian System* (pp. 25, 27). He goes on to explain how the idea of a universal forgiveness is in conflict with the idea of the moral order of a universe governed by God. I am grateful to D. Newell Williams for pointing out sections of Campbell's writings which indicate that Campbell was not absolute in his insistence that only Christian believers will be saved, and that a contextual and nuanced understanding of Campbell's soteriology may be more biblical and profound than either Willett's or McGarvey's. (See Campbell's *Christian Baptism: With Its Antecedents and Consequences* [St. Louis: John Burns, 1882], p. 432; and *The Christian System*, pp. 16, 166, 203).

75. Some titles of eighteenth- and nineteenth-century works: *The Salvation of All Men Strictly Examined; Universalism False and Unscriptural; The Universal Restoration;* Charles Chauncy, *Salvation for All Men;* Samuel Mather, *All Men Will Not Be Saved Forever.* Alexander Hall, a member of the Disciples movement, published *Universalism against Itself* in 1846. Some indication of interest in the topic is given by the fact that 25,000 copies were sold.

76. Lester G. McAllister quotes Thomas Campbell as follows: "Brother Raines and I have been much together for the last several months, and we have mutually unbosomed ourselves to each other. I am a Calvinist, and he a Restorationist; and though I am a Calvinist, I would put my right arm into the fire and have it burned off before I would raise my hand against him. And if I were Paul, I would have Brother Raines in preference to any other young man of my acquaintance to be my Timothy" (*Thomas Campbell: Man of the Book* [St. Louis: Bethany Press, 1954], p. 201). Note that in 1828 "restoration" terminology self-evidently referred to the "restitution of all things" at the end of time (Acts 3:21, KJV) — which is to say, universal salvation, not to the "restoration of the New Testament church."

77. See J. A. Garrison and A. T. DeGroot, *The Disciples of Christ: A History,* 2d ed. (St. Louis: The Bethany Press, 1958), pp. 89-90.

78. Lard, *Do the Holy Scriptures Teach the Endlessness of Future Punishment?* (cited by Garrison and DeGroot in *Disciples of Christ,* p. 384).

bered during the second generation but revived within the emerging liberal movement represented by a small group of Disciples such as Alexander Procter.[79] But since all Disciples partook of the kind of commonsense rationalism that prohibited dialectical thought on the matter, supposing that the language of the Bible and theology about the ultimate destiny of human beings was objectively descriptive, referential language, everyone saw the issue in either/or terms to which a univocal answer in referential language could and should be given.

Since we might anticipate that the conservative McGarvey would believe in limited salvation and the liberal Willett would lean toward universalism, we may be surprised to discover that Willett and McGarvey had the same opinion on this controversial issue: both affirmed the idea of limited salvation, and they did so because they shared a rationalistic point of view. Willett did so because he saw no logical way that universal salvation would not eliminate human responsibility; since he could neither give up his conviction about human responsibility nor his faith in logical consistency as the final arbiter of truth, he explicitly rejected the idea of universal salvation.[80] Yet Willett's emphasis on God as the loving Father who wills the reconciliation of all would not allow him to have an explicit doctrine of future punishment for the unsaved. The result was that he was somewhat vague in his eschatological views. He held out the hope of a blessed immortality based on the love of God for his creatures, but he was not precise about who was included and excluded or how one transferred from one group to the other. He thus left himself open to the classic charge of being a fuzzy-thinking liberal, an opportunity McGarvey did not fail to exploit.

McGarvey himself represented the kind of rationalistic approach to the Bible that, when coupled with a clear doctrine of limited salvation, made it very important to be able to find a clear doctrine of the necessity of conversion and clear commands and examples on how conversion is to be accomplished. Conversion was crucial for McGarvey; it was not so important for Willett. Knowing the steps of conversion, the "plan of salvation," and having a biblical command, approved example, or necessary inference for each one was crucial for McGarvey; it was not so important for Willett, though his treatment of these themes was influenced both positively and negatively by their role in Disciples tradition.[81]

---

79. See Jeter, "Alexander Procter," p. 297.

80. "Nor again can it be said that the death of Christ was an act of such tremendous effectiveness that it at once relieves human life from all responsibility of attitude or conduct, and insures the salvation of all," wrote Willett. "No such teaching finds expression in the Holy Scriptures" (*Basic Truths of the Christian Faith,* p. 62).

81. Note the chapters on "Faith," "Repentance," and "Baptism" in his *Basic Truths of the Christian Faith.* Their presence there at all is testimony to the influence of Disciples tradition; the way in which these themes are handled is testimony to his reaction to/rejection of some dimensions of Disciples tradition.

Revelation in History: Positivistic, Static Revelation/Evolution; Progressive Revelation

For McGarvey, it was thus important that biblical revelation be understood in positivistic, static, factual terms. Development, change, or variety in the New Testament would get in the way of its primary function in his system. The threat of higher criticism for him was not a threat to some doctrine about the Bible that was important in itself as doctrine; the threat was posed by higher criticism's positing variety and development, which called in question the consistent "plan of salvation" as transmitted in what had become one of the central Disciples theologoumena. Although, like Campbell, he could handle the variety in the Bible as a whole by dividing it into "dispensations," in each dispensation there could be no development or variety: everything had to be there at the beginning.[82] Thus his study of Deuteronomy saw no development: all was already there with Moses. His study of Acts saw no development in the history of the early church: all was already there at Pentecost.

On the other hand, in the the critical, evolutionary scheme espoused by Willett, Deuteronomy and Acts were prime examples of the development of the religions of Israel and early Christianity, respectively.[83]

ANTI-*RELIGIONSGESCHICHTE*/ AFFIRMED *RELIGIONSGESCHICHTE*

Although Willett believed in special revelation in the history of Israel, Jesus, and the early church, he was in step with and attuned to the American history-of-religions school developing at Chicago. He referred readily to the "religion" of the Bible, and had a positive stance toward the study of the religions of Israel and the church in their *religionsgeschichtlich* context. He saw continuities between the revelation of God in the Bible and the revelation of God in other religions, and so he felt it important to study the thought, scriptures, and practices of these other religions.

McGarvey saw only discontinuity between the revelation of God in the Bible and the pagan religions. His interest in the religions of the biblical world was minimal and functioned only to highlight the distinctiveness of the biblical faith.[84] And despite his interest in "historical" exegesis, McGarvey did not read the texts in the light of the issues prevailing in their own religious context, but rather read his own questions into the text and answered them "only" from

82. On Disciples dispensationalism, see Boring, "The Formation of a Tradition," pp. 8-11.

83. Note the subtitle of one of Willett's major works: *The Moral Leaders of Israel: Studies in the Development of Hebrew Religion and Ethics* (Chicago: Disciples Publication Society, 1916).

84. For example, although McGarvey was well-grounded in the Greek and Latin classics from his study at Bethany and his personal study, he did not know Philo firsthand (*Short Essays in Biblical Criticism*, p. 71).

the text. He knew and cared nothing about the *con*text, that is, what was happening *beside* the text in the religious-historical situation of the Hellenistic world. This fed his exclusivity and clarity, making everything neater than it was: he only had to fit things into a logical system derived from *his* context rather than that of the text.

Church History as Decline, Apostasy/Church History as Progress

In Willett's view, the church had not only grown and developed in its insights into God's truth during the New Testament period but continued to do so in the history of the Disciples. In contrast, McGarvey regarded Christian truth as having been given once and for all in the Bible and viewed the history of the church as mainly a matter of decline, perversion, and apostasy.

DENOMINATIONAL: DIFFERENCES RELATED TO THEIR STANCE IN APPROPRIATING SPECIFIC ELEMENTS OF DISCIPLES TRADITION

Both McGarvey and Willett were heirs of the Disciples tradition, which they consciously affirmed, appropriated, and to which they responded — albeit in different ways.

Disciples History as Decline/Disciples History as Progress

McGarvey shared the third generation's myth of the pure first generation, the teachings of which were to be retained. The innovations of the higher critics represented only degeneration. Willett saw the history of Disciples as ever developing toward new insights.

DISCIPLES TRADITION AND METHODS/ ACADEMIC TRADITION AND METHODS

It is at this point in Disciples history that the divergence was beginning to develop between the churchly tradition developed within the Disciples' own schools, which were extensions of the church and propaganda centers for the inculcation of Disciples tradition, and the major universities where a nonchurchly academic tradition of biblical tradition was beginning to develop. Again, by *propaganda* I do not necessarily mean anything negative. Several of these schools, such as Bethany, offered a solid classical education. But they also offered religious and biblical instruction from within the tradition cultivated within the denomination.

McGarvey had only minimal contacts with other scholars, was practically self-taught, and did not develop his own views in dialogue with other scholars. Scholars and critics were always "them," off somewhere else in some large town or even a foreign country. He represented the populist Disciples tradition as he had learned it at Bethany and cultivated it in the rural churches of Missouri and Kentucky.

Willett had also drunk deeply at this well, but he represented the incursion of an external academic tradition into Disciples history, as it flourished both in "the denominations" and in the ecumenical and secular university. Is it at this point that the academic paradigm begins to impose itself on the populist-ecclesiastical paradigm previously dominant in Disciples history? Do we see here the point of the wedge between the churchly and secular hermeneutical paradigms appearing in Disciples tradition? By a "churchly" hermeneutical paradigm I mean an approach to Scripture that (1) is self-consciously confessional, (2) appropriates the biblical faith from within the community of faith's own tradition — which always means within the context of a particular tradition, (3) looks for the normative dimension of what it is interpreting, and (4) is more or less direct and immediate in its apprehension of the meaning of Scripture. By a "secular" hermeneutical paradigm, I mean an approach to the Bible that (1) is self-consciously objective, (2) appropriates the meaning of religious statements from a presumed spectator stance, (3) looks for descriptive, value-neutral ways to apprehend the material, and (4) tends to regard hermeneutics as a second, indirect step to be taken after the first historical and objective step has been made. Both McGarvey and Willett were deeply influenced by the Disciples churchly tradition. But in Willett we begin to see the secular academic tradition of biblical study making itself felt. Church and academy are beginning to be separated.

"Plan of Salvation" as Hermeneutical Handle/Other Handles

If one has a confessional approach to the interpretation of Scripture, acknowledged or not, one will tend to see the text in the light of subjects and issues that have been important to that religious tradition. Roman Catholics see texts in terms of how they deal with the status of Mary in a way that is foreign to Disciples. Lutherans filter the text through their perception of justification by faith. Liberal Protestants look for the bearing of each text on the "kingdom of God" and "social justice." Premillennial dispensationalists find amazing things related to the blueprint for the end of the world in texts which to other eyes have nothing to do with eschatology.

The eyes with which Disciples steeped in the denominational tradition read the Bible were more sensitive than others to certain issues that had played a key role in Disciples history and religious experience: the mode, subjects, and meaning of baptism; the role of the Holy Spirit in the process of conversion; the frequency of the Lord's Supper; church polity; status of ministers within the congregation; and Christian unity.

Disciples "Canonical Hermeneutic"

At some point between Campbell and McGarvey, I know not when or where, a structure for apprehending the contents of the New Testament became traditional for Disciples and was correlated with their emphasis on the "plan of salvation." It goes like this: the New Testament has Gospels to tell us about Jesus so we can believe in him, Acts to tell us how to become Christians, epistles to tell us how to live a Christian life, and Revelation to tell us to hold on to the end, so we can receive the crown of life. Put in a more sophisticated way now called "canonical criticism," the idea is that the Christian community put its Bible together in a theologically significant manner, so that the meaning of a text is influenced not only by its context within its own document but also by the context of the document within the structure of the canon as a whole.[85]

Appropriation of this Disciples theologoumenon is reflected in the hermeneutic of both McGarvey and Willett — in different ways, to be sure, but nonetheless in a manner that identifies them both as Disciples. Both, for instance, were typical Disciples in that they had little to do with the book of Revelation. McGarvey rarely mentioned Revelation, which he sometimes called by the common misnomer "Revelations."[86] Likewise Willett barely refers to Revelation in his survey of the whole Bible, and he devotes less space to Revelation than to Hebrews in his earlier, more detailed survey of the New Testament.[87]

The particular point of how the traditional Disciples "canonical hermeneutic" impacted the work of McGarvey and Willett, as well as several features of their different approaches to biblical interpretation already discussed, are evident in their handling of the Gospels and Acts. I will deal with each in turn, and utilize this discussion as a summary illustration of their two approaches.

McGARVEY ON THE GOSPELS

The Gospels are interpreted by McGarvey from a particularly Disciples point of view. Both the Gospels and the Disciples said a lot about "faith." Yet, a firm point in the Disciples "plan of salvation" was that "faith only" is not

---

85. One of the leaders of the contemporary school of canonical criticism is Brevard Childs of Yale. It is of more than passing interest to students of the history of Disciples hermeneutics that Childs understands the canonical function of Acts in a manner analogous to Disciples tradition as expressed in McGarvey's work. Childs, of course, does this with much more critical sophistication than does McGarvey, including an abandonment of the literal historicity of the Acts account. But for Childs too, Acts serves as the "canonical bridge between the fourfold Gospel collection and the apostolic letters" (*The New Testament as Canon: An Introduction* [Philadelphia: Fortress Press, 1984], p. 219). Childs is even similar to McGarvey when he argues that in Acts, "Indeed, the consistent and detailed outlining of the steps on the way to salvation appears almost as an *ordo salutis*" (p. 224)

86. For example, in *Matthew and Mark*, pp. iv, 290.

87. See *The Bible through the Centuries*, p. 227; and *The Teachings of the Books*, pp. 245-64 (Hebrews) and 320-37 (Revelation).

adequate; faith is only the "first step" in the "plan of salvation."[88] The Gospels are not adequate to instruct one in how to become a disciple of Jesus; they are only for the purpose of creating faith. They, like Jesus, belong to the "Jewish dispensation" and do not tell us how to become Christians or how to live as Christians. Christians can, in McGarvey's view, pray the Lord's prayer only after it has been corrected from a post-Pentecost perspective — namely, by omitting the prayer for the coming of the kingdom and by adding "in Jesus' name."[89] Since in the Disciples tradition faith is "the belief of testimony," the Gospels must be seen as transparent report, as history, not as containing interpretation of the events by the church or the evangelists. To be reliable witnesses that can generate faith as McGarvey had come to understand it from the Disciples tradition, the Gospels must be historically accurate. The four witnesses must harmonize if their testimony is to be convincing enough to generate faith. Harmonizing the Gospels, showing that they are all historically accurate, was the chief labor of his commentary work, replacing exegesis. He did not look for the meaning of the text but looked through the text to the event. The text's sole function was to mediate the event rather than to interpret it. All of these points can be illustrated ad nauseam or in very fascinating ways, depending on one's interests — especially the intricate ways in which McGarvey anticipated the objections of the "negative critics" and showed how all things harmonize.[90] McGarvey's harmonizing hermeneutic precludes his having a "favorite Gospel," for there is no variety or development within the Gospels. He always worked with all four Gospels at once, and finally, with P. Y. Pendleton, wrote *The Fourfold Gospel,* which spelled out what had always been his method of dealing with any one of them.

A number of features of McGarvey's hermeneutic are illustrated in his treatment of the healing of blind Bartimaeus in Mark 10:46-52 and parallels:

88. In some versions of "the plan of salvation," "hearing the word" was the first step, and "faith" was the second step (cf. Rom. 10:9-10).

89. McGarvey, *Matthew and Mark,* p. 64.

90. It should be noted, however, that McGarvey did not often go to the extremes of the current "evangelicals" whose harmonizing efforts insist on the infallibility of the Gospels as history. In an effort to preserve the veracity of the Gospels' varying reports of Peter's three denials of Jesus, Harold Lindsell, for example, proposes that there were actually six denials, with each Gospel reporting a selected three (*The Battle for the Bible* [Grand Rapids: Zondervan, 1976], pp. 174-76). McGarvey also counts six denials in the combination of all four accounts, but declares that "Peter's second denial was of a quadruple nature. He denied to four different parties, but in such quick succession that the event is regarded as one" (*The Fourfold Gospel,* p. 701). McGarvey was sometimes troubled by the variations in the Gospels' structure which locate the same event at different points in the chronology, and so he was not embarrassed to argue that Jesus cleansed the temple twice (*The Fourfold Gospel,* pp. 121-25, 582). But then he did not follow Osiander and the Protestant scholastics of the sixteenth century to the extreme of suggesting that Jairus's daughter was raised twice, though the report occurs at different points in the outlines of Matthew, Mark, and Luke (see H. K. McArthur, *The Quest through the Centuries* [Philadelphia: Fortress Press, 1966]). Here and elsewhere, the problem posed for McGarvey's theory by the text is passed over in silence (*The Fourfold Gospel,* p. 352).

1. *The Gospel genre is "report."* The account of the healing of Bartimaeus is merely a straightforward account of what happened. Blindness has no symbolic significance.

2. *The infallible nature of the text results in the necessity to harmonize.* Matthew has two such stories, with two blind men each (9:27-31; 20:29-34); Mark has only one story with one blind man. A different location, temporally and geographically, is given for the story in Luke 18. McGarvey is at pains to show that Matthew deals with two separate events, one of which was omitted by Mark, and that Jesus healed two blind men in each case, one of which was omitted by Mark. The different location (as Jesus left Jericho in Mark 10, as Jesus entered Jericho in Luke 18) McGarvey handles by having the blind man scurry through the town in order to appear at both sites as the procession goes by.

3. *"Faith only" is not enough.* McGarvey was obviously bothered by Jesus' concluding statement to Bartimaeus, "Your faith has made you well" (Mark 10:52), since he knew that the Greek text read "Your faith has *saved* you (ἡ πίστις σου σέσωκέν σε). This was too susceptible of being understood as salvation by faith alone. No, Bartimaeus had to act, and his actions can be reconstructed by combining Mark and Luke and seeing how much Bartimaeus had to *do* to show his faith: it was not mere faith as an inward trust but faith manifested in his hurrying across town, blind as he was, in order to meet Jesus as he exited through the city gate.[91]

McGARVEY ON ACTS

McGarvey's commentary on Acts is one of the classic documents of Disciples history. It has been reprinted many times and is still available through the publishers of the Independent Christian Churches and the Churches of Christ.[92] Though McGarvey considered his commentary a piece of unadorned exposition of the "simple" meaning of the Bible, it is correctly described by J. J. Haley as "a manual of Disciples teaching."[93] It symbolizes the transition from the epistles, especially Hebrews, as the center of the Disciples canon to Acts as the typical Disciples' favorite book. It is ironic that this shift from Campbell's discursive propositional language to the narrative of Acts merely involves a shift of emphasis from "direct command" to "approved example" as the means of extracting direction for the church from the text. Narrative is written

---

91. McGarvey, *The Fourfold Gospel,* pp. 332-33.

92. The impressive story of the survival of McGarvey's works in print is told in detail in Halbrook, "J. W. McGarvey." It is ironic but symbolic of their differing hermeneutics that McGarvey's works remain available while Willett's have long since gone out of print. Willett anticipated the growth in insight and understanding that would make his own publications obsolete. McGarvey and his successors believed in a static, once-for-all statement of truth, which has kept his books in print.

93. Haley, *Makers and Molders of the Reformation Movement* (St. Louis: Christian Board of Publication, 1914), p. 139.

for the imagination, of which McGarvey had no more than Campbell. But for McGarvey the purpose of the narrative was to deliver "facts," which then became material for logical inferences concerning the "plan of salvation." A nonfactual narrative was useless for McGarvey's hermeneutic. He was forced to regard as entirely factual not only everything in Acts but also every narrative in the Bible, including the Jonah story and all the parables of Jesus.

McGarvey's agenda for looking at Acts was set by one of the major concerns of Disciples tradition — namely, the "plan of salvation." Acts was the "book of conversions," intended to set forth the "conditions of pardon" by giving examples of how people become Christians.

An additional hermeneutical handle that made Acts important for McGarvey was its focus on the absoluteness of apostolic authority and inspiration, so necessary to a program of restoring the apostolic church. McGarvey was willing to surrender everything to this principle, accepting as actions which on their own merits might be objectionable or repulsive as legitimate if they are done by an inspired apostle. This principle is illustrated most clearly in McGarvey's defense not only of the apostolic participation in the death of Ananias but of the "seemingly" cruel way in which he was peremptorily buried without telling his wife, who was then "entrapped" into admitting the same crime before she too was struck dead.

McGARVEY ON THE "KINGDOM OF GOD" AS THE CHURCH

McGarvey realized, of course, that the burden of Jesus' message in the Gospels is the proclamation of the kingdom of God. But since he was thoroughly imbued with the "dispensational" view of biblical theology dominant in the Disciples tradition, he understood the kingdom as neither present in Jesus' life and ministry nor only an eschatological reality to appear in history at the parousia. The kingdom "was established" on Pentecost with the beginning of the church, as narrated in Acts. Jesus' ministry and proclamation of the kingdom as narrated in the Gospels meant that he was making preparations for the founding of the church. McGarvey virtually identified the kingdom with the church, understood in institutional and legal terms. In all this, "Jesus as example" or "Jesus as teacher of ethical principles" played only a negligible role.

WILLETT ON THE GOSPELS

Willett no longer accepted the traditional Disciples view of faith as the belief of testimony.[94] Hence he not only failed to be disturbed by the variations in the Gospels but in fact considered them a positive aspect of the Gospels, in

---

94. See chap. 9, "Faith," in *Basic Truths of the Christian Faith,* pp. 89-95.

that they demonstrated the development of the faith within early Christianity. Nor did he view the Gospels as merely a prelude to Acts. In Willett, we see the growing influence among Disciples of Protestant liberalism's predilection for the Gospels. For him, the Gospels replace Paul (Campbell) and Acts (McGarvey) as the central core of the canon. Willett explicitly argued that the history of the later church corresponds to the history of early Christianity — in its *development,* not in its *pattern.* Early Christianity moved from Peter to Paul to John as its culmination. The later church moved from Peter (prior to the Reformation) to Paul (the Reformation churches), and now, at the dawn of the liberal "Christian century," the church was moving to John as the culmination of the canon. John was the crowning achievement of early Christianity, and the Gospel of John was Willett's favorite New Testament book, because: (1) it is about Jesus, (2) it advocates a realized eschatology, (3) it is inward and spiritual, and (4) its λόγος theology manifests an orientation toward the wider world and all of history.

John, the author, himself embodied this development. It was important for Willett (at least in the early stage reflected in the 1899 *Teachings of the Books*) to hold on to Johannine authorship in order to illustrate in the person John the development from primitive Jewish beginnings to the broader spiritual perspective of the Fourth Gospel. John progressed from Judaism through Synoptic theology to the refined theology of the fourth Gospel, which, understood in Schleiermacherian terms, is the apex of the New Testament.

WILLETT ON ACTS

Willett seems to have been aware of the role Acts has played in Disciples tradition. He repeats the theologoumenon that Acts is the "one book in the New Testament devoted to the method of becoming a Christian."[95] Yet he consciously distances himself from this view, pointing out that (following the traditional Disciples categorization of the New Testament books) there is only one book of Acts, but twenty-one letters to tell us how to live a Christian life,[96] and so it would seem that the New Testament is more interested in Christian living than in conversion. If we apply this same criterion to Willett's own writings, Acts comes off rather poorly. He devotes only 17 of 337 pages of his survey of the New Testament to Acts (James gets 16!). While he affirms Acts as an important part of the Scripture, he does not give it the pride of place it received through McGarvey's popularization of Acts as *the* document exhibiting the New Testament "plan of salvation."

Nor does he consider Acts to portray a static "New Testament church" that is to be "restored." Acts is rather the record of the growth of the church

---

95. Willett, *The Basic Truths of the Christian Faith,* p. 121.
96. Willett, *The Basic Truths of the Christian Faith,* p. 122.

from a Jewish sect to a universal religion, a record of an infant church learning to outgrow its "literalizing tendencies" and "burst its Jewish shell."[97] Without naming McGarvey, Willett explicitly opposes his belief in the *dis*continuity between the Gospels and Acts, and reads Acts 1:1 as saying that the narrative of Acts continues the work described by the author in volume one, the Gospel of Luke.

WILLETT ON THE "KINGDOM OF GOD" AS THE CHURCH

There is nothing in Willett's work on Acts that suggests the story of the beginning of the church is the account of the "setting up of the kingdom." He makes a decisive break with the Campbellian talk of the kingdom, with its king, constitution, members, entrance requirements, laws, territory, subjects, and so on.[98] For Willett as for the Gospels and for Protestant liberalism, the kingdom of God is central because it was central in the message of Jesus. Yet he has his own way of making contact with the Disciples theologoumenon that identified the kingdom of God with the church by understanding it in terms of the inwardness of Protestant liberalism rather than institutionally. Kingdom-of-God language was one means by which Willett and other Disciples liberals were able to make the transition from Campbell's biblical theology oriented to the transcendence of God and salvation history to the more immanent God of liberalism whose revelation is not bound so closely with the Bible. The Bible was on the way to becoming a source book of illustrations for a theology that looked elsewhere for its legitimating authority.

CONCLUSION

McGARVEY'S PROGNOSIS

McGarvey's fears about what would happen if higher criticism were to become a prevalent method of biblical interpretation are stated in the announcement of his "Biblical Criticism" column in the *Christian Standard* for 1 January 1893:

> For years past I have observed with much solicitude and pain the increasing tendency, both in Great Britain and America, to adopt the methods of destructive criticism which originated in the rationalistic schools of Germany. This tendency has been conspicuous in the writings of many scholars of high repute, and it has spread like leaven among the masses of the reading and thinking young people

97. Willett, *The Teachings of the Books*, p. 92.
98. See Campbell, *The Christian System*, pp. 107-52.

of both countries. It has infected the minds of thousands of preachers, both old and young, and it threatens to bring about a radical revolution in the public estimate of the Bible. While this tendency has alarmed me, I have been at the same time constantly chafed as I have read the writings of these critics, and seen how much of the shallowest sophistry, and the baldest dogmatism, which they have published, is being taken for conclusive proof and profound learning. I have been alarmed, let it be understood once and for all, not for the Bible itself, as though it was in danger of perishing, but for the souls that are being led astray, and for the incalculable loss to the cause of truth and salvation which results from a weakening of the faith of those who preach the Word.

McGarvey could not be correct; his hermeneutic was wedded to an obsolete worldview. But is it more than accidental that the groups that have continued to advocate his hermeneutic have continued in the numerical growth that once characterized the whole Campbell tradition?

WILLETT'S EXPECTATIONS

Both Willett's love for the Bible as the church's book, and his evangelical liberal excitement about the value of higher criticism for interpreting it ring through these words published in 1929, the year he retired from the deanship of the Disciples Divinity House, and the year that the nineteenth century ended in America:[99]

> The work of Higher Criticism is not completed as yet, though the main lines of its affirmations have been established. It is largely in the region of details that work still remains to be done. Along the broad frontiers of biblical literature its results are accepted, and the great Christian public is well on its way toward complete conviction of its outstanding results and a calm and assured employment of its findings. It is difficult any longer to stir up controversy over the process. The odium once attached to those concerned with it has largely receded. On the foundations laid by the work of devout scholars in this field are building the impressive structures of a rational theology and religious education. The age of apprehension is passing. Our children will not have to fight the battle for freedom through which the present generation has been passing. The critical spirit that has given reasonable and convincing explanation of the physical universe has provided us with an equally satisfactory interpretation of the Word of God.
>
> The Higher Criticism has forever disposed of the fetish of a level Bible; it has destroyed the doctrine of verbal inspiration; it has set in proper light the

99. Liberal Christianity had thought of the nineteenth century as the last century before the dawn of the coming of the kingdom in the twentieth century through the "christianizing of the social order," which would make the twentieth century the "Christian century." In terms of the history of Christian thought, the nineteenth-century viewpoint extended to the beginning of the First World War in Europe and to the stock market crash and the beginning of the Great Depression in America.

partial and primitive ethics of the Hebrew people; it has relieved the church of the responsibility of defending ancient social abuses which received popular and even prophetic sanction in Old Testament times; it has made faith easier and more confident; it has helped the world to turn from the imperfect views of an adolescent stage of the race to the satisfying ideals of our Lord; it has enabled us to understand the varying testimonies to the life of Jesus and the divergent tendencies of the apostolic age; and most of all it has explained the seeming contradictions and conflicts of biblical statement which were in former periods the target of captious and often successful attack.

The work of Higher Criticism has its purposes and its limitations. It is a means to the better understanding of the Word of God. If it can make more vivid and convincing the pages of the Old Testament and the New it performs an admirable and gratifying service. Whatever helps to the intelligent appreciation of the Bible is of undoubted value, for as Mr. Gladstone wrote, "All the wonder of Greek civilization heaped together are less wonderful than this Book, the history of the human soul in relation to its Maker."[100]

Would that Willett had been correct! His hermeneutic was wedded to an illusory liberal view of the future. If the world had continued to progress as Willett and the liberals expected, this would have been the "Christian century," and the Disciples would have continued to grow along the lines he hoped, both in breadth and depth of vision, but also numerically.

The approach he espoused led, in the hands of others who were less steeped in the biblicism of the Disciples tradition, not to a revitalization of the Disciples' use of the Bible but to its decanonization. It resumed the iconic status it has had in the culture at large, which is to say that it is respected but no longer functions as the means of mediating God's will to the church and the world.

With the emergence of neo-orthodoxy, many in the nonfundamentalist stream of American Christianity found a way of affirming both the authority of the Bible and biblical criticism. But neo-orthodoxy passed the Disciples by.[101] What happened to the Bible among the Disciples in the fourth generation is a story yet to be told. But in the crucial third generation, many Disciples who did not remain devoted to McGarveyism lost their grip on the Bible. This was one of the factors in their statistical decline. Which is why the way forward from our own location in the fifth generation at the dawn of the twenty-first century is a matter for further reflection. But a responsible decision can hardly be made without reflecting on the response of our recent ancestors in the faith during the crucial period to which this study is dedicated.

---

100. Willett, *The Bible through the Centuries*, pp. 263-64.

101. For a more nuanced statement of this generalization, see Osborn, "Theology among the Disciples," pp. 108-13. See also Duke, "Disciples Theologizing amid Currents of Mainstream Protestant Thought."

Appendix: A Bibliography of the Works of J. W. McGarvey and Herbert L. Willett

Works by J. W. McGarvey

Books

Four Letters to Bishop McIlvaine on Christian Union. New York: Thomas Holman, 1865.

The Great Commission of Jesus Christ to His Twelve Disciples: Briefly Defined and Illustrated. Cleveland: Bethany Christian Education, 1873.

A Series of Fifty-Two Bible Lessons for the Use of Advanced Classes in the Sunday School. Lexington, Ky.: Transylvania Printing and Publishing, 1875?.

Matthew and Mark. Des Moines: Eugene S. Smith, 1875.
    St. Louis: Christian Board of Publishing, 1875.
    Cincinnati: Chase & Hall, 1875, 1876.
    Cincinnati: Central Book Concern, 1879.
    Delight, Ark.: Gospel Light Publishing, 1900.

Lands of the Bible: A Geographical and Topographical Description of Palestine with Letters of Travel in Egypt, Syria, Asia Minor, and Greece.
    Philadelphia: J. B. Lippincott, 1880, 1881.
    Cincinnati: Standard Publishing, 1880.
    St. Louis: John Burns, 1880.
    Louisville: Guide Printing & Publishing, 1890, 1893.
    Nashville: Gospel Advocate, 1957.

Commentary on the Gospel of Mark. Cincinnati: Central Book Concern, 1881.

A Commentary on Acts of the Apostles with a Revised Version of the Text.
    Cincinnati: Wrightson, 1863; 3d ed., 1864.
    Lexington, Ky.: Transylvania Printing and Publishing, 1863.
    Cincinnati: Central Book Concern, 1882.
    St. Louis: Christian Publishing, 1887.

Evidences of Christianity. Cincinnati: Guide Printing and Publishing, 1886, 1891.
> Cincinnati: Standard Publishing, 1912. (2 vols. in 1)
> Nashville: Gospel Advocate, 1956, 1964, 1974. Vol. 1: "The Text and the Canon, NT"; vol. 2: "Credibility and Inspiration."

New Commentary on Acts of Apostles, 2 vols. Cincinnati: Standard Publishing, 1892; reprinted 1930, 1960.
> Des Moines: Eugene S. Smith, 1900.

Class Notes on Sacred History, vol. 1: *The Pentateuch;* vol. 2: *From I Samuel to Nehemiah.* Bowling Green: John Marcrom, 1894. Vol. 3: *The Four Gospels.* Bowling Green: John Marcrom, 1893. Vol. 4: *Acts of Apostles.* Cincinnati: Standard Publishing, 1889.

Standard Eclectic Commentary on the International Sunday-School Lessons for 1894. Cincinnati: Standard Publishing, 1893.
> Cincinnati: Guide Printing and Publishing, 1893.

The Pentateuch, Joshua, Judges, Ruth and Job. Bowling Green: John Marcrom, 1893.

Sermons Delivered in Louisville, Kentucky, June-September 1893. Louisville: Guide Printing and Publishing, 1894.
> Cincinnati: Standard Publishing, 1894, 1918.
> Nashville: Gospel Advocate, 1958.

Jesus and Jonah. Cincinnati: Standard Publishing, 1896.

A Guide to Bible Study. Intro. by H. L. Willett. Cleveland: Bethany Christian Education, 1897.
> Chicago: Fleming H. Revell, 1897.
> St. Louis: Christian Publishing, 1897.

McGarvey, J. W. *The Authorship of the Book of Deuteronomy with Its Bearings on the Higher Criticism of the Pentateuch.* Cincinnati: Standard Publishing, 1902.

Short Essays in Biblical Criticism: Reprinted from the Christian Standard, 1893-1904. Cincinnati: Standard Publishing, 1910.

McGarvey, J. W., and Philip Y. Pendleton. *The Fourfold Gospel; or, A Harmony of the Four Gospels.* Cincinnati: Standard Publishing, 1914, 1950. First issued quarterly as Standard Bible Commentary.

McGarvey, J. W. and Philip Y. Pendleton. *Thessalonians, Corinthians, Galatians and Romans.* Cincinnati: Standard Publishing, 1916, 1940, 1960. First issued as Standard Bible Commentary.

The Autobiography of J. W. McGarvey, 1829-1911. Lexington: College of the Bible, 1960.

A Series of Fifty-Two Bible Lessons for the Use of Intermediate and Advanced Classes in the Sunday School. Cincinnati: Standard Publishing, n.d.

Midway Question Book. Cincinnati: Bosworth/Chase & Hall, n.d.

The Disciples of Christ. Cincinnati: A.C.M.S., n.d.

The Eldership. Cincinnati: Bosworth, n.d.

Articles

"The Witness of the Spirit." Pp. 327-38 in *The Living Pulpit of the Christian Church,* ed. W. T. Moore, 1867.

"The Indwelling Spirit." Pp. 10-15 in *Gems of Thought,* ed. J. H. Smart. St. Louis: Christian Publishing, 1883.

"Grounds on Which We Receive the Bible as the Word of God, and the Only Rule of Faith and Practice." Pp. 11-48 in *The Old Faith Restated,* ed. J. H. Garrison. St. Louis: Christian Publishing, 1891.

"Church Government; Preachers' Methods." Pp. 83-117, 188-209 in *The Missouri Christian Lectures,* vol. 2. St. Louis: John Burns, 1883, 1892.

"Biblical Criticism" (A Weekly Column), *The Christian Standard* 1893-1911.

"The Prints of the Nails." Pp. 41-43 in *On the Lord's Day,* ed. J. A. Lord, 1904.

Pamphlets

"Baptism. Vest-Pocket Series of Christian Tracts, 1:2." Cincinnati: Standard Publishing, 1900.

"Chapel Talks: Delivered before the Student Body of the College of the Bible in 1910 and 1911." Lufkin, Tex.: Gospel Guardian, 1956.

McGarvey, J. W.; F. G. Allen; et al. "What Shall We Do about the Organ?" Cincinnati: F. L. Rowe, n.d.

Works by Herbert L. Willett

Books

The Life and Teachings of Jesus. Chicago: Fleming H. Revell, 1898.
     St. Louis: Christian Publishing, 1898.
     Cleveland: Bethany Christian Education, 1898.

Willett, Herbert Lockwood, and James M. Campbell. *The Teachings of the Books; or, The Literary Structure and Spiritual Interpretation of the Books of the New Testament.* Chicago: Fleming H. Revell, 1899, 1901.

The Prophets of Israel. Chicago: Fleming H. Revell, 1899.
     St. Louis: Christian Publishing, 1899.

Our Plea for Union and the Present Crisis. Chicago: Christian Century Press, 1901.

The Ruling Quality: A Study of Faith as the Means of Victory in Life. Chicago: Fleming H. Revell, 1902.

Basic Truths of the Christian Faith. Chicago: Christian Century, 1903.

Studies in the First Book of Samuel: For the Use of Classes in Secondary

Schools and in the Secondary Division of the Sunday School. Chicago: University of Chicago Press, 1908.

The Call of Christ: A Study of the Challenge of Jesus to the Present Century. Chicago: Fleming H. Revell, 1912.

Willett, Herbert Lockwood, *The Moral Leaders of Israel. Studies in the Development of Hebrew Religion and Ethics I.* Chicago: Disciples Publication Society, 1916.

The Message of the Prophets of Israel to the Twentieth Century. Chicago: American Institute of Sacred Literature, 1916.
    Chicago: University of Chicago Press, 1919.

The Moral Leaders of Israel: Studies in the Development of Hebrew Religion and Ethics. Chicago: Disciples Publishing Society, 1916.

Our Bible: Its Origin, Character and Value. Chicago: Christian Century Press, 1917.

The Daily Altar: An Aid to Private Devotion and Family Worship. Chicago: Christian Century Press, 1918, 1924.
    New York: Harper & Brothers, 1918, 1924.
    New York: Willett & Clark, 1942.

The Bible through the Centuries. Chicago: Willett, Clark & Colby, 1929.
    Chicago: Willett, 1930.

The Jew through the Centuries. Chicago: Willett, Clark & Company, 1932.

The Corridor of Years, n.d. (copies are in the Herbert Lockwood Willett library of the Disciples Divinity House of the University of Chicago).

Articles

"Sunday School Lessons," *Christian Evangelist* 1897-99.
"Department of Biblical Problems," *Christian Century* 1908-9.
"International Sunday School Lessons," *Christian Century* 1908-11 (?).

Edited Books

Fallows, Samuel; Andrew C. Zenos; and Herbert Lockwood Willett, eds. *The Popular and Critical Bible Encyclopedia and Scriptural Dictionary: Fully Defining and Explaining All Religious Terms including Biographical, Geographical, Historical, Archaeological and Doctrinal Themes.* Chicago: Howard-Severance, 1902, 1903, 1904, 1906, 1908, 1910.

Willett, Herbert Lockwood; Orvis F. Jordan; and Charles M. Sharpe, eds. *Progress: Anniversary Volume of the Campbell Institute on the Completion of Twenty Years of History.* Chicago: Christian Century Press, 1917.

Willett, Herbert Lockwood, ed. *"That They May All Be One": Autobiography and Memorial of James M. Philputt, Apostle of Christian Unity.* St. Louis: Christian Board of Publication, 1933.

Introductions

Grafton, Thomas William. *Alexander Campbell, Leader of the Great Reformation of the Nineteenth Century.* Intro. by H. L. Willett. St. Louis: Christian Publishing, 1897.

McGarvey, J. W. *A Guide to Bible Study.* Intro. by H. L. Willett. Cleveland: Bethany Christian Education, 1897.
Chicago: Fleming H. Revell, 1897.
St. Louis: Christian Publishing, 1897.

Willett, Herbert L.; Orvis F. Jordan; and Charles M. Sharpe, eds. Intro. in *Progress.* Chicago: Christian Century, 1917.

The Disciples and Higher Criticism:
The Formation of an Intellectual Tradition

Leo G. Perdue

INTRODUCTION

This essay seeks to delineate the major features of the Disciples interpretation of the Old Testament by focusing on the work of two prominent scholars: Herbert Lockwood Willett of the University of Chicago and James Philip Hyatt of Vanderbilt University. In their day, they were considered to be among the leading biblical scholars in the academy. However, they directed their work not only to other members of the scholarly guild but also to clergy and laity in the churches. Thus they were equally well known for their education of ministers and laypeople for the churches. As scholars of the academy and theologians of the church, Willett and Hyatt helped to construct a distinctive Disciples hermeneutic for interpreting and appropriating the Old Testament.

Yet Willett and Hyatt were not content simply to develop a Disciples tradition for the interpretation of the Old Testament. They also recognized that the formation and transmission of a tradition required the development of institutions to shape and sustain it. Thus they worked to establish and give leadership to two Disciples Divinity Houses which became the necessary instruments for the formation and transmission of an interpretative tradition. This tradition and its institutional agency have had considerable influence on Disciples to the present period.

In addition to a Lilly Endowment grant administered by Christian Theological Seminary, research for this essay was made possible by the Institute for the Advanced Study of Religion at the University of Chicago Divinity School, and The Disciples Divinity House of the University of Chicago.

HERBERT LOCKWOOD WILLETT:
BIBLICAL INTERPRETATION AND THE LIBERAL VISION

INTRODUCTION

A protégé of William Rainey Harper, the noted Old Testament scholar and first president of the University of Chicago, Herbert Lockwood Willett was the most influential and articulate Disciples spokesperson for the scientific study of the Bible in the late nineteenth and early twentieth centuries. Perhaps more than anyone else, Willett was responsible for ushering Disciples into the modern world of intelligent discourse about the Bible and thereby into the religious mainstream of American liberal theology.

Yet Willett's prodigious accomplishments as scholar, professor, dean, and preacher were given their coherence and stimulus by his messianic vision for the Christian Church (Disciples of Christ). Willett believed that the primary purpose and mission of the Christian Church was to effectuate the unity of a divided Christianity. Willett understood church union to be an important and necessary dimension of the continuing inbreaking of the kingdom of God toward which creation and history were being divinely guided. Yet if Disciples were to fulfill their messianic mission in the age when the city was replacing the frontier as the context for American life and thought, Willett realized that they must forge an intellectual tradition that would engage constructively the challenges of a rapidly changing world. It was to this task that Willett committed his energy and work.

WILLETT: PROPHET OF TRANSFORMATION

Historical Setting

Willett (1864-1944) lived during a critical era of significant change in American life.[1] Rapid growth in the urban centers was accompanied by mounting and increasingly complex social problems and the need for reform. Child labor laws, unions, and antitrust legislation became part of the political response. Efforts to deal with social problems were accompanied by the development of movements for social justice: women's suffrage, temperance, and civil rights.

Significant social change was accompanied by dramatic intellectual developments which also required religious engagement: evolution, studies in

---

1. For surveys of Willett's life, see Charles Harvey Arnold, "The Illuminati: The Origins of Liberalism among the Disciples of Christ, 1866-1909," *Encounter* 43 (1982): 1-25; William Barnett Blakemore, *Quest for Intelligence in Ministry* (Chicago: Disciples Divinity House of the University of Chicago, 1970); and especially Willett's autobiography, *The Corridor of Years*, completed and supplemented by Herbert Lockwood Willett III, n.d. (copies are in the Herbert Lockwood Willett library of the Disciples Divinity House of the University of Chicago).

ancient and world religions, higher criticism, pragmatism, and relativism. These intellectual developments joined social changes in raising questions about a traditional worldview that had largely been shaped by evangelical Protestantism. A new social myth was called for and eventually provided by the liberal vision. But such a vision did not come without significant struggle.

Education

Ironically the first professional Bible scholar of the "New Testament church" was a specialist in Old Testament. Born in Ionia County, Michigan, 5 May 1864, to Disciples parents, Herbert Lockwood Willett received his B.A. (1886) and M.A. (1887) from Bethany College. At rural Bethany he was taught to regard the Bible as inerrant and to reject both biblical criticism and controversial scientific theories, especially evolution.[2] Thus his early life represented what had been typical for Disciples: life in a rural church on the frontier that was largely unaware or suspicious of intellectual and social developments in American cities and major universities.

After graduation Willett pastored churches in Ohio. Feeling the need for more education, he took a leave of absence from his congregation in Dayton to attend Yale Divinity School in 1891-1892, joining a small but growing number of other Disciples who began at this time to enter the major theological schools. At Yale Willett met the man who was to transform his life: William Rainey Harper, who had become the most famous biblical scholar in the country.[3] After explaining to Harper his plans to return to the ministry after finishing his B.D. at Yale, Willett remarked that Harper

> gave me the shock of my life by saying in the most peremptory manner, "You are going to do nothing of the kind. You are going into the Semitic Department and carry on the work you were doing with me at Lake Bluff [the location of Harper's Hebrew language institute]. Your people, the Disciples, need specialists in Old Testament studies, and you are going into that field." In that brief conversation of not over ten minutes my world turned quite around and a wholly new vista opened before me. That was one of the few decisive moments in my life.[4]

Willett soon followed Harper to Chicago. Matriculating in the spring quarter of 1893, he began graduate studies that led to a Ph.D. in 1896. In 1898 he joined the growing ranks of Americans who traveled to Germany to pursue graduate work. Taking up residence at the University of Berlin for a year, Willett studied under several of the giants of the theological world: Harnack, Pfleiderer, Kaftan, Weiss, and Gunkel.

2. *The Corridor of Years*, pp. 23-24.
3. See Thomas Wakefield Goodspeed, *William Rainey Harper* (Chicago: University of Chicago Press, 1928); and James P. Wind, *The Bible and the University: The Messianic Vision of William Rainey Harper* (Chico, Cal.: Scholars Press, 1987).
4. *The Corridor of Years*, p. 38.

Dean, Professor, Preacher, and Teacher

In 1894 Willett was named the first Dean of the newly incorporated Disciples Divinity House of the University of Chicago, a position he was to hold for the next twenty-seven years, albeit without pay. To earn a salary, he pastored Hyde Park Church of Christ. Even after joining the faculty of the university, Willett continued to pastor churches, including First Christian Church and Memorial Church of Christ in Chicago.

Willett joined the Department of Oriental Languages and Literature at the university in 1896 and rose through the ranks to full professor in 1915. It was in the university setting that he flourished as a respected member of the "Chicago School," joining the likes of Ernest DeWitt Burton, Shailer Matthews, Gerald Birney Smith, George Burman Foster, Shirley Jackson Case, Edgar J. Goodspeed, Winfried E. Garrison, and Edward Scribner Ames. Embodying the major characteristics of this school, Willett used higher criticism and other theories of scientific method to interpret the Bible and the history of Israel, to trace the development of the Judeo-Christian religion as a movement reacting to and shaped by social forces, to engage in the reformulation of the Christian tradition to bring about the unity of the churches, and to address pressing social issues of the day to improve the public good and to advance the kingdom of God.

As a scholar Willett chose the role of popularizer, presenting his studies primarily to lay audiences. He was a founding editor of the newly reincorporated *Christian Century,* wrote thirteen books and hundreds of essays, and helped establish the Willett and Clark publishing house which published many important Disciples books during the early part of the century. All of his writings had one goal in mind: the education of the laity in the liberal vision.

Upon retirement in 1929 as professor emeritus, Willett served the Union Church of Kenilworth, Illinois, for fifteen years until his death in 1944. He died of heart failure in Winter Park, Florida, where he was presenting a series of ten lectures on the Old Testament. His death occurred only three months before the Disciples Divinity House celebrated its fiftieth anniversary.

Willett's importance in American and Disciples religious history derives in the main from two factors. First, his integrative hermeneutic blended German higher criticism with classical liberal theology, the Social Gospel, and characteristically Disciples emphases on Christian unity, the Bible, and free and open inquiry. He shaped these existing currents into a comprehensive system of intelligent discourse that envisioned the inbreaking of the kingdom of God and set forth the role that biblical study and the Disciples would play in that eschatological drama. Second, Willett did not separate critical inquiry from personal faith and piety but rather approached his biblical work with the fervor of evangelical passion. He regarded the results of critical study not only as enlightening for scholars but also as essential for the shaping of spiritual life, moral existence, and Christian faith.[5] Inspired by Harper and committed to his Disciples heritage, Willett saw the critical study of the Bible, liberal theology, and the Disciples plea for unity as constituent elements of his own messianic vision of the kingdom of God.

WILLETT'S MESSIANIC VISION AND INTEGRATIVE HERMENEUTIC

The Impact of Biblical Criticism on American Religion

German higher criticism called into question the basic worldview that a previously unquestioned authoritative and inspired Bible had helped to construct. Nevertheless, some leading biblical scholars saw the new critical study of the Bible as relegitimating its role in the reconstruction of modern faith and the constitution of a new American social myth. Among these were William Rainey Harper and Herbert Lockwood Willett.

The Disciples' Responses to Higher Criticism

The impact that higher criticism began to have on American Protestantism in the years following the Civil War was even more significant for a community that prided itself on being "the people of the Book." The methodology raised difficult questions about inspiration, authority, diversity, and the plea to restore New Testament Christianity as the means to unite the denominations.[6]

With the application of historical criticism to the Bible, however, the doctrine of verbal inspiration and inerrancy faced serious challenges. And the question of authority became problematic, not only because of the demonstration of scientific and historical errors in the Bible but also because of the recognition of the historical development of biblical religion. What was especially threatening to many Disciples was the view of continuing revelation and the conception of progressive development beyond the New Testament into the future. The past, particularly its expression in New Testament Christianity, began to lose its privileged place in the matter of authority.

5. Editor's Note in reference to a series of articles on the Bible by Willett in the *Christian Century* ("Religion and Its Holy Books," *Christian Century* 34 [1917]: 8-10).

6. On the Disciples responses to higher criticism, see Anthony Ash, "Old Testament Scholarship and the Restoration Movement," *Restoration Quarterly* 25 (1982): 213-22; and William Edward Tucker, "Higher Criticism and the Disciples," *Discipliana* (Sept. 1962): 49-54, 59. This latter essay is a summary of part of Tucker's "James Harvey Garrison (1842-1931) and the Disciples of Christ: An Irenic Editor in an Age of Controversy" (Ph.D. diss., Yale University, 1960).

Willett and Higher Criticism

When Willett began to write the weekly Sunday School lesson for the *Christian Evangelist* in 1897, he set forth the major critical views of the Bible that were to become the center of debate for many years. These included the denial of Mosaic authorship of the entire Pentateuch[7] and the positing of a Maccabean date for the book of Daniel.[8] The open presentation of these critical views greatly intensified the controversy.

The opponents of higher criticism expressed their views mainly in the *Christian Standard.* Their champion was J. W. McGarvey, president of the College of the Bible in Lexington, who began his column "Biblical Criticism" in the *Standard* in 1893. With the appearance of Willett's essays in the *Christian Evangelist,* the Chicago "heresy" became the primary object of McGarvey's barbed attacks. McGarvey believed Moses wrote the Pentateuch, David the Psalms, and Daniel the book of Daniel. Jonah spent three days in the belly of a whale, and God created Eve from Adam's rib.[9]

For McGarvey the stakes were high. He considered criticism of the Bible to be destructive, concluding it impugned the veracity and therefore both the inspiration and authority of the Scriptures. He feared that without an authoritative and inspired Bible, the Disciples plea for restoration would become meaningless. And focusing on the diversity of Scripture rather than its unity would also undermine the plea for Christian union based on the New Testament. McGarvey attacked in an effort to defend what he saw as the legitimating basis of the Disciples and indeed the very foundation of Christianity itself.

Not surprisingly, Willett's view of inspiration bore the historical markings of higher criticism. He located inspiration not in the words of the Bible but in the history of the people of Israel and the early church.[10] Yet at the same time, he considered as inspired certain prophets, priests, and other leaders "whose lives were touched by the vision of truth."[11] That vision, for Willett,

7. Willett, "The Great Discovery," *Christian Evangelist,* 24 Nov. 1898, p. 669.

8. Willett, "The Genuineness of the Book of Daniel," *Christian Evangelist,* 31 Aug. 1899, p. 1100.

9. See, for example, McGarvey's "Biblical Criticism" columns of 9 Feb. 1895 (p. 131) and 23 Feb. 1895 (p. 179).

10. "These Scriptures are less the guaranteed and final words of men supernaturally safeguarded from error," wrote Willett, ". . . than the honest and urgent utterances of those who were sensitive to the divine will in their respective generations, and who contributed to the progress of that supreme religious movement which found its culmination in the life and teachings of our Lord" ("The Deeper Issues of Present Religious Thinking," *The Scroll* 10 [1914]: 6). The Bible was not mechanically inspired or infallible, but rather is "one record of the religious experience of a unique and elect people, and therefore marked by the limitations of the human lives which wrought it." Inspiration is evidenced by the lives of the people themselves ("My Confession of Faith in the Old Testament," *Christian Century,* 7 Nov. 1908, p. 639; cf. Willett's *Our Bible: Its Origin, Character and Value* (Chicago: Christian Century Press, 1917), pp. 15-17; and *The Bible through the Centuries* (Chicago: Willett, Clark, & Colby, 1929), p. 279.

11. Willett, *The Corridor of Years,* p. 160.

was the kingdom of God. He did not believe the Bible inerrant or infallible, especially in regard to its historical and scientific views, but he still argued that the religious content of the Bible, centered in the life and teachings of Jesus, served as the normative guide for faith and practice.

For Willett the authority of the Bible derived not from the premise of infallible, divine words but rather from the quality of two effects: its ability to produce "a better order of living," and its ability "to make clear the way of human fellowship with God."[12] Indeed, the authority of the Bible was to be demonstrated not by a blind appeal to a theological premise but by "the appeal which the Scriptures as a whole makes to the moral sense within humanity."[13] Furthermore, revelation for Willett was not limited to the past, to the sacred history captured in the Bible, but rather is an ongoing process. God continues to speak through the "stern lessons" of history, "human experience," and "the lives of choice and elect souls" who perceive the truth.[14]

Willett not only championed the critical interpretation of Scripture but also actively opposed approaches that he very strongly felt misused the Bible, subverted its integrity, and presented false interpretations of the kingdom. He viewed the blind and unyielding approach of the fundamentalists as more dangerous than that of skeptics who attacked Scripture. The uncritical, conservative reading of the Bible gave the infidels ammunition for attacking the integrity and value of Scripture, for they both followed the same premise of a level Bible that contained no factual, historical, or scientific errors. By contrast, critical study helped the intelligent Christian to come to a new and important view of the Bible. Therefore, Willett concluded, "The Bible as a result of these critical studies is not less divine but more human. It is seen to be less a supernaturally perfect record of history and science than a faithful and inspiring account of the most impressive movement of the divine activity in the world, written by men who were moved by the Spirit of God."[15]

The stakes in the "battle over the Book" were equally high for Willett. It was not simply a matter of intelligent discourse and the freedom of rational inquiry. Rather, the historical critical reading of the Bible allowed one to see the emergent and progressive development of the kingdom of God which reached its biblical apex in the teaching of the prophets and especially Jesus. Without higher criticism, the liberal vision of the advancing kingdom of God could not be biblically sustained.

---

12. Willett, *The Corridor of Years*, p. 160. See also "Religion and Its Holy Books," *Christian Century*, 11 Jan. 1917, pp. 8-10. For detailed discussions of inspiration and authority, see *Our Bible*, pp. 164-90.

13. Willett, *Our Bible*, p. 181.

14. Willett, *The Bible through the Centuries*, p. 300.

15. Willett, Introduction to *Progress: Anniversary Volume of the Campbell Institute on the Completion of Twenty Years of History*, ed. Herbert L. Willett, Orvis F. Jordan, and Charles M. Sharpe (Chicago: Christian Century Press, 1917), p. 14.

THE SPIRIT AND CONTENT OF LIBERAL THEOLOGY

Science and the Scientific Method

Liberal theology joined higher criticism as the second component of Willett's hermeneutic and messianic vision. Willett embraced the concept of evolution in the fields of science, history, and theology. In modern science, he noted, "the principle of growth in accordance with determinable laws and by means of resident forces is vindicated along the entire frontier of inquiry into natural phenomena."[16] He did not see the doctrine of creation and evolution as mutually exclusive; to the contrary, he embraced the idea of creative evolution: "Evolution is simply the best explanation of the way in which [God] has worked at the creation of the world."[17]

Willett not only considered evolution to be "the best explanation of the phenomena of life" but regarded it as "the principle which underlies all modern thought."[18] He recognized that the same principle was at work in the critical study of the Bible: "The critical spirit that has given reasonable and convincing explanation of the physical universe has provided us with an equally satisfactory interpretation of the Word of God."[19] Willett also correlated evolution with the development of thought and ethics (the "spiritual life") in the Bible and progressive revelation.[20] For him the Bible is "the record of and advancing disclosure of the divine purpose of the world as discerned by the most intuitive people of antiquity — the Hebrews—and as realized in a more complete degree in the life and teachings of Jesus Christ."[21] Yet historical progress in the development of religious ideas and virtues did not cease with Christ and the early church but continued into the future.

The stakes were high for Disciples who came to accept this view. Most important for their understanding of themselves was the implication that evolution and its incorporation into the worldview supported by the sciences and the humanities shifted the authoritative ground from origins and the past to

16. Willett, "The Deeper Issues of Present Religious Thinking," pp. 4-8; see also his Introduction to Progress.

17. Willett, "Biblical Problems," Christian Cemtury, 17 Sept. 1908, p. 501. In a later essay, Willett recommended to his readers two books on evolution and religion: E. Griffith-Jones's The Ascent through Christ and Lyman Abbott's The Theology of an Evolutionist.

18. Willett, "Prophets for the Time," The Scroll 5 (1907): 71. See also The Call of the Christ: A Study of the Challenge of Jesus to the Present Century (New York: Fleming H. Revell, 1912), pp. 197-98. Elsewhere he remarks, "The application of the scientific principle in the natural world led also to its recognition in the field of history and literature" (Introduction to Progress, p. 13). And see "Mr. Bryan's Last Word," Christian Century, 20 Aug. 1925, pp. 1048-50, a critique of William Jennings Bryan in which Willett refers to Bryan's "curious misreading of the entire meaning of evolution" and notes that he "made up in eloquence what he lacked in rigor and freshness of thinking" (p. 1048).

19. Willett, "The Higher Criticism," Christian Century, 15 March 1917, p. 11.

20. Willett, "The Higher Criticism," p. 71.

21. Willett, The Corridor of Years, p. 160.

the present and even more so to the future. Higher criticism could succeed in rediscovering the past and tracing its progress, but evolution denied to the past its singular normative status.

The Centrality of Christ

Christology was a central element in Willett's theology and consequently in his interpretation and application of Scripture to modern life.[22] It is the moral life and teachings of the historical Jesus, not the eschatological finality of God's action in Christ or the divinity of Christ that is the essence of Willett's understanding of christology. "One is Christian in virtue of his belief in the reasonableness and finality of Jesus' interpretation of life."[23] For Willett the *historical Jesus* could be discovered only through biblical criticism. Historical study not only kept the Jesus of history from being lost in the metaphysical Christ of faith but also re-presented the life and teachings of the one who is the central paradigm for Christian existence.

In Willett's view, Jesus did not call people to doctrines about or taught by him (including those of his messiahship or divinity), to forms of worship, or to organizations. He did not even have in mind the fashioning of a church. Rather the ethic of Jesus was grounded in divine love which resides at the heart of discipleship and stimulates progress in civilization and the kingdom of God.[24] Rejecting formalism and ritualism, Jesus taught that humanity's duty was to live in harmony with God and to love others. Indeed, divine love was the catalyst by which the kingdom of God progressed.[25] Jesus as apocalyptic seer had no place in Willett's christology.

In considering the nature of Jesus, Willett remarked that he had "no competent definition," though he was "unconvinced and puzzled" by expressions of Jesus' divinity. Jesus' authority resided not in a divine nature or in various roles (king, prophet, and priest) but rather in his life of righteousness which revealed "the character of God in terms of human experience."[26] Jesus was the Son of God by reason of being "intimately and ethically united with the life of God, and sustained by continual intercourse with him."[27]

---

22. Willett wrote two books on Jesus: *The Life and Teachings of Jesus,* Bethany C. E. Reading Courses (St. Louis: Christian Publishing Company, 1898); and *The Call of the Christ.* See also chap. 1 ("The Primacy of Christ") in his *Basic Truths of the Christian Faith* (Chicago: Christian Century, 1903), pp. 13-22.

23. Willett, *The Corridor of Years,* p. 156.

24. See *The Life and Teachings of Jesus,* pp. 99-103.

25. See *The Life and Teachings of Jesus,* pp. 134, 138.

26. Willett, *The Call of the Christ,* pp. 40-41.

27. Willett, *The Life and Teachings of Jesus,* p. 113.

The Fatherhood of God

While often speaking of God as the loving Father, Willett rejected any effort to define the divine nature.[28] Looking to the example of Jesus' relationship to the Father, Willett argued that Jesus' "companionship with the Father was his perennial inspiration and the secret of his undepleted vitality. He did not regard this relationship as unique or exclusive. He desired all his friends to share his experience of intimacy with the God he loved."[29]

For Willett God is not a mighty sovereign who rules the world as a royal despot. Rather "He is a sharer in the vast labor which is constructing the new order of the world."[30] As creator, God is constantly shaping reality and continuing to make humanity in the divine image. Central to God's character is love; all humans are the children of God who loves them.[31] And "through the passion of Christ, God suffers and reaches out in love to reclaim the human soul."[32]

God cannot be almighty, according to Willett, for if he were, the great tragedies in the world — significantly, the death and destruction wrought by the First World War — would incriminate him as either a direct participant or a passive bystander. In either case, God's goodness and justice would be impossible to maintain. Willett believed that while God was limited, he nevertheless engaged with humans in the slow but steady development of a better world. "If God is fighting his battles and needs our help, life becomes for us more worthful and significant." Indeed, humans must "join forces with God to bring things to the desired issue."[33] Thus God was ontologically related to the world, working through historical and natural process, albeit in hidden and mysterious ways, to bring about progressively the kingdom of God. For Willett, this formulation of divine presence and participation sanctioned the study of nature and history by means of scientific method. To understand the workings of nature and history was in some measure to discover the workings of God.[34]

The Kingdom of God

At the core of Willett's understanding of biblical religion, and thus his own vision of faith and guiding hermeneutic, was the kingdom of God construed

28. See Willett, *The Corridor of Years*, p. 158; "How to Pray," *Christian Evangelist*, 20 Jan. 1898, p. 38; and *Basic Truths of the Christian Faith*, pp. 23-32.

29. Willett, *The Corridor of Years*, p. 158.

30. Willett, "The War and the Kingdom of God," *Christian Century*, 12 Dec. 1918, pp. 6-7.

31. Willett, *The Life and Teachings of Jesus*, pp. 100-103.

32. Willett, *Basic Truths of the Christian Faith*, p. 65.

33. Willett, "The War and the Kingdom of God," pp. 6-7.

34. Willett considered the Trinity "an often unintelligible doctrine." He resolved the problem by regarding the Holy Spirit as "the indwelling, sanctifying, purifying spirit of Jesus in the lives of his people and in the ministries of his church" (*The Corridor of Years*, p. 161).

by and through the idea of progress. Stressing the leadership of the great prophets, Willett argued that Israel developed from a primitive tribe to an advanced civilization with lofty morals that reached their apex in the life and teachings of Jesus.[35] Yet the advance of the kingdom did not stop with the early church but continues to come into realization. He wrote that the Christian religion "is forever unsatisfied with present attainments, and is covetous of a social order wherein righteousness, justice, brotherliness and good will shall have the right of way — such an order as may truly be called the Kingdom of God."[36] Even the human carnage of the trench warfare in World War I did not dampen Willett's optimistic faith in progress, the continuing advance of the kingdom of God, and the increasing goodness of human nature. Contending that the end of the war signaled the emergence of a new social order, he asserted that it was the task of the church to carry out its programs and realize the ideals of the kingdom afforded by this period of new opportunity and challenge.

Suffering and the Advance of the Kingdom

Suffering for the advance of civilization, and hence for the kingdom of God, was central to Willett's liberal vision. Both Harper and Willett suffered physical ailments. After years of suffering, Harper died of stomach cancer in 1906, while Willett suffered many years from arthritis, an illness that interrupted his work more often in later life. But in Willett's case it was especially suffering for truth in withstanding the assaults of biblical obscurantists opposed to both critical thought and change that served as the most instrumental force in advancing the cause of civilization and therefore the kingdom of God. It was, after all, an age in which those discovered to harbor liberal religious views and to practice higher criticism were summarily dismissed from theological faculties. Some dismissals were accompanied by the ignominy of heresy trials. William Robertson Smith was deprived of his professorship at Oxford by the Church of England, while in the most famous of the heresy trials in America, C. A. Briggs was tried and initially acquitted by the presbytery of New York in 1892 only to be suspended by the General Assembly of the Presbyterian Church in 1893. Disciples experienced a similar purging: Oscar T. Morgan of Drake, Perry O. Powell of Albany, and Hiram van Kirk at Berkeley Bible Seminary were dismissed from their teaching posts while others were intimidated into silence.[37]

35. See Willett, *The Prophets of Israel* (Chicago: Fleming H. Revell, 1899), p. 11. As "pupils of the prophets," he wrote, the people of Israel received the instruction of God "with ever increasing fullness, until their partial disclosures of God were completed by the final revelation in the Christ" (p. 12).

36. Willett, *The Corridor of Years*, p. 160.

37. See Willett, *The Corridor of Years*, p. 151.

Willett's most strident critic was J. W. McGarvey, whom W. T. Moore described as the man who dipped his pen "in gall rather than in ink."[38] Surprisingly, Willett described his own personal relations with "Brother McGarvey" as "of the most friendly sort." While holding radically different positions on most key issues concerning the Bible, they nevertheless spent time in each other's homes for informal conversation. In 1908 the Congress of Disciples held in the Central Church of Indianapolis a debate between McGarvey and Willett that Willett later described as "a situation characterized by good will and lively interest." However, he did note it was "unfortunate that McGarvey's deafness made it impossible for him to hear most of the paper and discussion."[39]

The assault on Willett came to a head in 1909 when the program committee planning the centennial meeting celebrating the publication of the *Declaration and Address* asked Willett to address the convention on the life and work of Thomas Campbell. Led by Russell Errett, the owner of the *Christian Standard,* an intense and large-scale effort was launched to remove Willett from the program. The *Christian Century* rose to the occasion, publishing a series of articles and hundreds of letters in defense of Willett.[40] The journal also published three essays under the title "My Confession of Faith" in which Willett set forth in rather clear terms his own faith and understanding of the Bible and the program of the "fathers" of the Christian Church.[41] After a great

---

38. Moore, *A Comprehensive History of the Disciples of Christ* (New York: Fleming H. Revell, 1909), p. 743.

39. Willett, *The Corridor of Years,* p. 151.

40. The strongest defense of Willett came from Errett Gates, who used his "Christian Union" to respond to criticism of Willett, especially the harsh attacks by McGarvey. In referring to what Gates called McGarvey's "Lexington creed," which included the affirmation of the Mosaic authorship of the Pentateuch and literal reading of the Jonah story as tests of fellowship, Gates charged that "Lexington never seems to learn the lesson of tolerance and liberty, and sweet human charity, even from her own mistakes and lapses. Like Rome, she never changes, and never goes wrong" ("Questions for Prof. McGarvey," *Christian Century,* 9 Jan. 1909, p. 37). McGarvey's "Biblical Criticism" column in the *Christian Standard* was the forum for the attacks against Willett and critical study of the Bible in general. In response to this type of religious warfare, Gates argued that "The aim of the department of Biblical Criticism was to prevent the spread of the new ideas; it has resulted in preventing the spread of good will and unity among brethren, and has actually propagated the ideas it proscribed" ("Meaning of the Silence," *Christian Century,* 16 Jan. 1909, pp. 59, 64. What especially chafed Gates was what he perceived to be McGarvey's arrogant claims to absolute truth and supercilious castigation of Willett and other critics whom he described as infidels. Indeed, McGarvey took Willett's refusal to respond to the charges as proof that they were correct. Gates, referring to McGarvey as the theological *bete noir* of the Disciples, suggested that "No self-respecting Christian man will enter into contest with a disputant who persistently twists disagreement with his opinions into disloyalty to Christ and infidelity" ("Meaning of the Silence," p. 64; see also Gates, "Some Questions for Prof. McGarvey," *Christian Century,* 28 Nov. 1908, pp. 712, 722).

41. "My Confession of Faith," *Christian Century,* 31 Oct. 1908, p. 615; "My Confession of Faith in the Old Testament," *Christian Century,* 8 Nov. 1908, pp. 639-40; "My Confession of Faith in the New Testament," *Christian Century,* 14 Nov. 1908, pp. 663-64; and "My Confession of Faith — II. The Program of the Fathers," *Christian Century,* 21 Nov. 1908, pp. 687-88. Willett insisted that he would not have "one set of opinions for the class-room and another for the lecture-hall" ("My Confession of Faith in the Old Testament," p. 640).

deal of preconference controversy, Willett addressed an overflow audience at the convention.[42]

While the *Christian Standard* tried and convicted Willett in the press, two things spared him a heresy trial: the lack of any official Disciples organization empowered to carry out such a procedure and his employment by the University of Chicago, which was not a Disciples institution. Following his model of the suffering servant, Willett endured these assaults without responding in kind.

The Kingdom and the Social Gospel

The Social Gospel greatly impacted Willett's messianic vision. He joined those Christians who believed that the goal of Christianity was to transform the urban wilderness into the kingdom of God. Following the centennial meeting in Pittsburgh, Willett wrote, "We believe that the Disciples are awakening to a new sense of responsibility regarding the conditions of the laboring classes, the employers of labor, the housing of the poor, the saving of childhood, and the related questions which are becoming so imperious in our day."[43] He used the Bible to address these problems directly, and the Social Gospel became an important dimension of both his biblical and theological hermeneutic and his personal commitment.

Once again the moral leaders of Israel, the great prophets, and especially Jesus provided for Willett the message and the examples for the transformation of society into the kingdom of God. According to Willett, Jesus did not directly attack institutions and their abuses but rather sought to focus on the individual whose transformation would lay

> the foundations for a new conception of the dignity of human life which must issue presently in a new consciousness of social obligation. It is true that Jesus said nothing about the oppressive treatment of womanhood, of labour, of the slave and of the ruled class in the world of His day. But He laid down principles . . . which in the process of the centuries have emancipated womanhood, compelled the world to face the problem of the rights of man, woman and child in industry, to formulate the principles of good government and of clean city life, to emancipate the slave and to put war under the ban of increasing public disapproval.[44]

Indeed, the gospel should form the basis for a new and more esteemed place for women in society, for labor and capital relationships, for the temperance movement, and for the establishment of peace in international relations.[45]

---

42. For a transcript of the address, see "Thomas Campbell and the Principles He Promulgated," *Christian Century,* 21 Oct. 1909, 1043-46.

43. Willett, "Biblical Problems," *Christian Century,* 3 Feb. 1910, p. 103.

44. Willett, *The Call of the Christ,* pp. 206-7.

45. See Willett, *The Call of the Christ,* pp. 209-12.

DISCIPLES THEOLOGY: UNITY AND THE RESPONSE
TO CULTURE

The third and final component of Willett's hermeneutic was provided by the characteristic features of Disciples thought, which he succeeded in integrating with biblical criticism and liberal theology. In Willett's liberal vision, the Disciples were the key to Christian Union. This was their messianic mission. Their work for unity was to issue forth in the climatic inbreaking of the kingdom of God.

In commenting on the origins of the Disciples, Willett argued that "The great reformations in the history of the Christian faith have begun with a fresh interpretation of the Holy Scriptures."[46] In his view, these reformations followed three steps: protest, restoration, and evolution. Protesting against dogma and unyielding tradition, the reforming movements have sought to return to the original expression of the faith, and this is what the Disciples have attempted to do: "return to scriptural outlines of Christianity." "It was a return to the primal era of the faith."[47]

Yet Willett contended that the real goal of the early Disciples was not to restore the primitive order. They had recognized the progressive development in the Bible (e.g., the evolution of morality and understanding), he argued, and hence their true goal was the unity of Christendom that would lead to the climax of God's bringing into being the kingdom. It was toward the future that the founders ultimately turned; they had no desire to escape to the past.

Christian Unity

Christian unity was the compelling goal in Willett's thought and action. He believed that Christian unity had to be grounded in the life and teachings of Jesus, not in denominational creeds or in the literal restoration of New Testament Christianity. He believed that the only practical plan for union was to accept the ideals of the teachings of Jesus and those of his apostles expressed in the New Testament: an emphasis on love, the ordinances of baptism and the Lord's Supper, and joy in service to God.[48] Even more to the point, he maintained that faith was not propositional, but rather a matter of the transformed existence of Christians centered in the life, spirit, teachings, and love of Jesus.[49]

---

46. Willett, "Rightly Dividing the Word," in *The Scroll* 5 (1908): 243.

47. Willett, "Rightly Dividing the Word," p. 243.

48. See Willett, *Our Pleas for Union and the Present Crisis* (Chicago: Christian Century Press, 1901), p. 37; and "My Confession of Faith — II. The Program of the Fathers." He stressed variety even in these matters, urging that it should be left to the individual to decide between immersion or nonimmersion or church membership: the "individual must be responsible for this obedience of the Lord" (*Our Pleas for Union*, p. 126).

49. "In a word, the emphasis of early Christianity was placed not alone upon doctrine or ordinances but upon life, conduct, character, disposition, temper" (*Our Pleas for Union*, 116).

Unity and the Transformation of Culture

H. D. C. Maclachlan wrote in *The Scroll* in 1907 that the most significant issue facing Disciples was their attitude to modern culture: "The issue is simple: shall we or shall we not join hands with the great world forces that are fashioning our modern life." Included among these were progress, opportunity, and liberty.[50]

Willett grounded his argument for the Christian transformation of culture in two sources: Jesus' own progressive stance toward culture and the work of the early Disciples. Jesus was not limited by tradition but open to new insight. Likewise, the fathers of the Christian Church used, according to Willett, the results of biblical scholarship to criticize the orthodox world and its sectarian character.[51]

Willett discovered no timid bowing of the knee to cultural and religious orthodoxy but rather a prophetic transformation of past tradition in the early Disciples reformers.[52] Only the continuing transformation of the Christian Church would allow it to realize its messianic calling.

THE LIBERAL VISION AND INSTITUTIONAL AGENCY

In addition to a distinguished career as teacher and scholar, Willett became a leading associate of Harper and eventually became the de facto director of Harper's American Institute of Sacred Literature with its vast publishing and lecturing program for international lay education, reaching literally millions of people with the new critical study of the Bible. Following Harper's lead, Willett also lectured widely in the United States and abroad through the Lyceum and Chautauqua lectureships. And to transform Christian education by embracing the new philosophical theories of learning, Willett helped to found the Religious Education Association (1903).

Willett also was a leader in the establishment of ecumenical institutions, recognizing that the Disciples' plea for union could be realized only within an organizational structure that would bring churches together. Thus he partici-

50. Maclachlan, "The Disciples and Modern Culture," *The Scroll* 5 (1907): 1. Later in the same essay, he wrote, "We stand at the parting of the ways: On the one hand the spirit of progress is calling us to join the great forces that are everywhere leading men out of the fogs of ignorance and prejudice into the tonic atmosphere of clear thinking and exact endeavor. This is the spirit of free investigation, of reverence for truth, of humble waiting for the light, of unselfish aims and ideals, to be of which is to be borne along on the stream of time into larger spheres of usefulness. The alternative is the spirit of dogmatism, of sectarianism, the legalism of the letter, the dwarfing of vision, the pathetic rigidity of the death-mask. This is the mummification of faith, and to surrender to it can only mean for us that like the traveler lost in the desert, we shall keep aimlessly circling round our extinguished campfires, while the great world caravan moves on without us" (p. 4).

51. See Willett, "My Confession of Faith — II. The Program of the Fathers," 687-88.

52. Willett, Introduction to *Progress,* p. 17.

pated in the founding of the Church Federation of Greater Chicago, serving as one of its early presidents, and was a delegate at the founding meeting of the Federal Council of Churches of Christ in America (1908). Active in the Social Gospel movement, Willett promoted the "Social Settlement" plan among Disciples and sat on the Chicago Crime Commission.

Yet Willett also understood that to realize the liberal vision for Disciples he needed to establish educational and publishing organizations with which to forge for Disciples an intellectual tradition. Thus he was instrumental in setting up the Board of Education of the Christian Church in 1894 to upgrade standards for Disciples educational institutions, faculties, and ministers. He also helped to establish the Bible Chair movement, teaching in the first Bible Chair at the University of Michigan between 1893 and 1895. With Willett's help, the movement eventually spread to the University of Virginia, the University of Georgia, the University of Texas, the University of Missouri, and the University of Illinois.

One of Willett's most notable achievements was his involvement in the establishment of the Campbell Institute, which was designed to promote graduate education for the Disciples ministry and serve as a forum for intelligent discourse and study by Disciples who held advanced degrees. The Institute was to play an important role in the formation of an intellectual tradition for half a century.

But Willett's greatest achievement may have been the establishment and leadership of the Disciples Divinity House. An integral part of the University of Chicago Divinity School, the purpose of the house was to prepare young people for ministry. And it is here that Willett's dream of forging an intellectual tradition for Disciples has had its greatest success.

CONCLUSION

Willett did his work with a prophet's zeal. His strong emphasis on Christian and public education in religion was grounded in his belief that the unity of Christendom was to be achieved by means of both an intelligent appropriation of the teachings of the Bible and a zealous commitment to the advancing kingdom of God. The Christian Church was, for Willett, the effective and necessary instrument for the unity of a divided Christianity. In that respect, Willett assigned the Disciples a messianic role.

Willett's own personal transformation from a rural biblicist to an urban liberal reflected the course of many in that segment of the Stone-Campbell movement that became the Christian Church (Disciples of Christ). Through his enormous energy and influence he became a prophet of transformation, shaping the Disciples of Christ into a modern expression of mainline Protestantism that found its theological home in classical American liberalism. For Willett the Disciple, the critical study of the Bible stimulated this transformation both personally and in the church he served.

Willett's longtime friend and associate on the editorial staff of the *Christian Century,* Charles Clayton Morrison, called him "the most effective and fruitful public interpreter of the Scriptures which the American church had produced. . . . It is doubtful that the ministry of any other large denomination had been so profoundly impressed and changed by the influence of a single personality."[53]

FROM THE LIBERAL VISION TO CHRISTIAN REALISM: JAMES PHILIP HYATT AND VANDERBILT DIVINITY SCHOOL

INTRODUCTION

Depression, World War, and National Resurgence

The Great Depression and World War II brought an end to the steady optimism of American classical liberal theology and the indomitable faith in the steady progress toward the final realization of the kingdom of God.[54] The devastating toll exacted on social and economic life in America and the global community also fell on the churches. Yet the tremendous crisis of the age led to significant reflection on and involvement in the Social Gospel by Disciples.

Disciples moved into the era following the Great Depression and World War II with vision and energy. Indeed, the period immediately following the War was a time of great vitality and growth. The surging economic expansion accelerated both building and programs. Great optimism gripped both nation and church. Yet the period also ushered in the Cold War and one of America's most vicious internal reigns of terror, presided over by the junior senator from Wisconsin, Joe McCarthy. Two of his targets were the Revised Standard Version and its parent organization, the National Council of Churches. McCarthy suspected anyone associated with these of being a communist.

The Sixties and the Crisis of Faith

The turmoil of the sixties included assassinations (John F. Kennedy, his brother Robert Kennedy, and Martin Luther King, Jr.), the divisive war in Vietnam, and the struggle for civil rights. It was during this tumultuous time that Disciples hammered out the charter for restructure. But it did not come without cost: the obvious differences between independent and more progressive churches led to a second major split in the movement designed to unify the Great Church.

Perhaps the most distinguished Disciples interpreter of Scripture follow-

---

53. Morrison, in an appendix to *The Corridor of Years.*
54. See Lester McAllister and William Tucker, *Journey in Faith: A History of the Christian Church (Disciples of Christ)* (St. Louis: Christian Board of Publication, 1975), pp. 388-410.

ing World War II was James Philip Hyatt, whose career in many ways was caught up in the *Sturm und Drang* of social and historical processes in the larger world. For thirty-one years Hyatt served with distinction on the faculty of Vanderbilt University. A world-renowned Old Testament scholar, Hyatt not only engineered the development of a major ecumenical divinity school in the South but also succeeded in establishing a significant graduate program in religion. Just as important for Disciples, Hyatt helped to transform the Disciples Divinity Foundation in Nashville into a full-fledged house which became, after Chicago, the second major intellectual and community center for two generations of Disciples church leaders and scholars.

Hyatt's life and work were motivated by his vision of the inbreaking of the kingdom of God. Following in the footsteps of Willett, Hyatt also envisioned a messianic role for the Christian Church. The Disciples were to become the vehicle for church union in the New South, still torn and divided by entrenched sectionalism and rampant racism. But to accomplish this movement toward unity, both for the Church and the nation, the South in general and Southern Disciples in particular needed an intellectual tradition, shaped within the halls of a prominent divinity school. And Hyatt became a prophetic visionary to realize this dream. The driving force behind his ambition for a great Southern divinity school was his vision of the ecumenical and united church, to be achieved by the free and open discussion of the Christian religion. Public discourse and the effective impact of prophetic religion on public life, undertaken in the conservative South by a prominent Divinity School, was the practical means for unity. And the establishment of a house attached to the divinity school would provide Disciples with a community for the nurturing of their own theological tradition and eventual participation in the work of the kingdom.

The theological matrix for shaping Hyatt's vision of the kingdom was the Christian Realism of Reinhold Niebuhr. The liberal vision of the kingdom of God had not died for Hyatt but had been transformed by Niebuhr's recognition of the power of sin and the pervasive presence of evil in the world. In spite of many theological struggles and personal tragedies, Hyatt viewed the future with realistic hope. However, he learned that the kingdom would come not in peace but with a sword.

JAMES PHILIP HYATT: PROPHET OF HOPE

Birth and Education

James Philip Hyatt was born in Monticello, Arkansas, 16 February 1909. His parents were staunch Southern Baptists and instilled within their son a respect for God, Bible, and country. Graduating from Baylor with a Phi Beta Kappa key, Hyatt was ordained to the ministry of the Southern Baptist Church in 1929. He earned an A.M. from Brown in 1930 and a B.D. from Yale Divinity

School in 1933. In 1931-32 he was the Two Brothers Fellow of Yale, attending the American School of Oriental Research in Jerusalem. It was there that Hyatt developed a strong interest in biblical history and archaeology that directed him to the Department of Near Eastern Literatures and Languages at Yale when he returned for graduate work. In the summer of 1932, after his sojourn in Jerusalem, Hyatt studied at Marburg, where a Lutheran New Testament professor was beginning to shape a new and formidable theology that blended Lutheran confessionalism with Heideggerian existentialism. His name was Rudolf Bultmann. The new hermeneutic was *Entmythologizierung* ("demythology"), an approach that appealed to the young Hyatt at least in its first step of stripping away poetic metaphor and myth to return to the essence of the biblical message, even if the second stage, the reclothing in existentialist themes, did not carry such dramatic impact. Following his graduation from Yale Divinity School, Hyatt entered the Ph.D. program in the Department of Ancient Near Eastern Literatures and Languages, earning his Ph.D. in 1938.

Teaching Career

Following his first teaching appointment at Wellesley (1932-1941), Hyatt accepted an appointment as associate professor of Old Testament to teach in the School of Religion of Vanderbilt University. In 1944 he was appointed full professor and chair of the graduate department of religion, a post he was to hold for twenty years. In 1964 he stepped down from the chair to resume full-time teaching responsibilities.

Unable to adjust to the fundamentalism of Southern Baptists in Nashville, Hyatt sought out a new fellowship that would approximate the free-church tradition in which he was nurtured and yet provide the tolerance and open spirit of free and critical inquiry to which he had grown accustomed in his theological and graduate studies. He found this environment among the Disciples, joining Woodmont Christian Church in Nashville. He was to serve as a prophetic voice and active member for over thirty years. In 1946 Hyatt was ordained a Disciples minister.

Scholarly Works

A prolific and respected scholar, Hyatt wrote for both the academy and the church. His most significant work was the Interpreter's Bible commentary on Jeremiah, published in 1956. Hyatt's work on Jeremiah has been recognized as among the best of its day, and he pioneered several major positions that continue to draw scholarly interest.[55]

---

55. See Leo G. Perdue, "Jeremiah in Modern Research: Approaches and Issues," in *A Prophet to the Nations: Essays in Jeremiah Studies,* ed. Leo G. Perdue and Brian W. Kovacs (Winona Lake, Ind.: Eisenbrauns, 1984), pp. 1-32.

Hyatt's second major work was his commentary on the book of Exodus, which describes Israel's liberation from Egypt and tells of Israel's great prophetic redeemer and lawgiver Moses.[56] This choice was not simply a coincidence for Hyatt. He noted that the book of Jeremiah presents the prophet as the New Moses who shared with the lawgiver a common tradition. Both lived in periods of great crisis and yet also great opportunity. And both guided Israel to the experience of new liberation following a time of darkness and threatened oblivion. Not coincidentally, Hyatt's own life mirrored that of his prophetic models.

Hyatt's most significant collaborative effort was his editing of *The Bible in Modern Scholarship*, the collection of papers read by international scholars on the occasion of the celebration of the centennial of the Society of Biblical Literature (1964). Hyatt served on the program committee along with Samuel Sandmel, provost of Hebrew Union College–Jewish Institute of Religion, and John L. McKenzie, S.J., of Loyola University of Chicago.[57] This volume, largely the result of Hyatt's planning, is testimony to his commitment to biblical scholarship in all of its diversity as pursued by a collegium of scholars representing a rich diversity of institutional, ecumenical, interfaith, and international backgrounds.

Popular Works

Like Herbert Willett, Hyatt possessed the rare ability to communicate the best of technical and current scholarship in clear and understandable terms to both clergy and laity. The driving passion behind Hyatt's prolific writings and addresses for ministers and laypeople was his conviction of the Bible's relevance for modern life. This was especially true of his understanding of the Hebrew prophets. In the preface to *Prophetic Religion* he wrote, "I am sure that the prophets do have a profound and far-reaching message for our time, and that we should use all our resources of devotion, research, and insight to apply prophetic principles to our problems today. . . . I hope that some ministers may be inspired by these chapters to make their own ministry more prophetic, and that some laymen may be encouraged to allow their ministers to be prophets."[58]

Hyatt was active in the Academy, serving as the archaeological editor for the *Journal of Bible and Religion*, editor of the *Journal of Biblical Literature*, and editor of the Society of Biblical Literature's Monograph Series. In

56. Hyatt, *Exodus*, New Century Bible Commentary (London: Marshall, Morgan & Scott, 1971).

57. Also serving on the committee was Hyatt's longtime colleague and friend Kendrick Grobel of Vanderbilt Divinity School, who was executive secretary of the SBL. Grobel was to have coedited the volume with Hyatt, but he died before the task was completed. Hyatt edited the volume alone, but dedicated it to the memory of his deceased colleague.

58. Hyatt, *Prophetic Religion* (New York: Abingdon-Cokesbury, 1947), p. 8.

1956 the Society of Biblical Literature bestowed upon Hyatt its greatest honor, electing him president.

FROM LIBERAL THEOLOGY TO CHRISTIAN REALISM

Reinhold Niebuhr and the Disciples

Reinhold Niebuhr's Christian realism became one theological framework for construing Disciples theological thought in the period following World War II.[59] While Barthian theology, with its heavy emphasis on the depravity of human nature over against the radical sovereignty of God, began to make inroads into American theological thinking, most Disciples found it difficult to move so dramatically away from classical liberalism.[60] Reinhold Niebuhr's thought, however, was something of a compromise, taking seriously the difficulties of modern existence and the reality of sin, and yet providing a more positive view of humanity's ability to engage evil in ways that were more participatory.[61]

Niebuhr's influence on Disciples biblical scholars began to take hold as early as the 1940s. This was especially true of Hyatt. He had seen his youthful idealism, nourished by classical liberalism, fragment in the face of the grinding poverty of the Great Depression and the terrible destruction of life in the Second World War. Seeking new ways to express his faith and remain true to his critical training, Hyatt turned to the work of Reinhold Niebuhr. Niebuhr's Christian realism became a more acceptable compromise between the Old Liberals and Barth, requiring a rethinking of liberalism's uncritical idealism and natural theology and yet not abandoning authentic human participation in the enterprise of kingdom building.

59. See *The Essential Reinhold Niebuhr,* ed. Robert McAfee Brown (New Haven: Yale University Press, 1986); Gabriel Fackre, *The Promise of Reinhold Niebuhr* (Philadelphia: J. B. Lippincott, 1970); Charles W. Kegley and Robert W. Bretall, *Reinhold Niebuhr* (New York: Macmillan, 1956); Reinhold Niebuhr, *The Nature and Destiny of Man,* 2 vols. (New York: Scribner's, 1941, 1949); *Moral Man and Immoral Society* (New York: Scribner's, 1948); and *Love and Justice,* ed. D. B. Robertson (Philadelphia: Westminster Press, 1957).

60. "Barth's theology and teachings, while influencing many denominations, never really excited the Disciples. Due to the stimulus of the Depression, however, there was a revival in the 1930s of the social gospel" (McAllister and Tucker, *Journey in Faith,* p. 404).

61. See, e.g., Niebuhr's *Moral Man and Immoral Society* (New York: Scribner's, 1932). A formidable presence on Union's faculty, Niebuhr had several Disciples for students, including H. Jack Forstman and Walter Harrelson. "The theological renewal which began in the seminaries during the 1930s had barely begun to penetrate the ministry and the churches when World War II broke upon America. The task of theological reconstruction was delayed until after the war. The thought of Niebuhr did inform a sufficient number of American and Disciples ministers and churches so that the mistakes of World War I were avoided. American Christianity in general, and Disciples in particular, gave full support to the war effort, and looked upon the war not as a crusade of godly forces but as the lesser of two evils" (McAllister and Tucker, *Journey in Faith,* p. 405).

The Sovereignty of God

Hyatt found the radical sovereignty of God eloquently preached by the Hebrew prophets. This radical sovereignty of God included holiness, superiority over the human creature, majesty and transcendence, moral purity, and uncompromising demands for social justice.[62] Prophetic religion, Hyatt found, was especially God-centered, for God was "not primarily an object of thought and speculation but an object of intimately personal experience."[63] Yet God was also the one God, Yahweh, the judge of heaven and earth, who required of his human creatures faithful and obedient response. According to Hyatt's assessment of the prophets, God's very nature was moral, and therefore his requirements were ethical rather than ritual. Being moral and rational, God had the right to require morality and rationality of his human creatures.

As the one God, Yahweh was the Lord of history who controlled the human destinies of both individuals and nations. This Lord of history was the redeemer whose primal acts of deliverance were the Old Exodus in the time of Moses and the New Exodus during the period of 2 Isaiah. Yet God was also the Creator of heaven and earth, who ruled providentially and righteously over all creation.

This view of the sovereign Lord of history and creation was not for Hyatt a historical teaching locked within the prophetic corpus of the biblical past. To the contrary, the theology of the prophets was for Hyatt the compelling theology for the modern church.

Sin and the Need for Grace

Hyatt recognized the need for God's redemptive power to remove sin in order to move toward social justice. Hyatt's youthful optimism was replaced with a realistic appraisal of the deep-seated character of human sin, though not to the point of a more pessimistic Calvinistic position.[64] Hyatt did not believe in natural depravity, but he did locate the proclivity toward sin in human self-centeredness and the unrestrained free will of humans, even to disobey God.[65] Only divine grace and repentance leading to moral obedience would enable redemption and a reconstituted social order to come into being.

Hyatt believed that grace was grounded in God's love for humanity. He spoke of the concept of responsible love, grounded in the covenant between God and Israel. The New Israel, the church, has the commission to effectuate responsible love, grounded in the love of God, in deeds of kindness and justice for the neighbor who was not simply the Israelite or the Christian but also the stranger. This divine love, which humans are to emulate, is both conditional and

---

62. See Hyatt, *Meeting God through Isaiah* (Nashville: Upper Room, 1958), p. 4.
63. Hyatt, *Prophetic Religion*, p. 149.
64. See Hyatt, *Meeting God through Isaiah*, p. 15.
65. See Hyatt, *Jeremiah: Prophet of Courage and Hope* (Nashville: Abingdon Press, 1958), p. 92.

unconditional: "The love of God which is expressed in his election of Israel is a spontaneous and 'uncaused' love, not based upon the merit or goodness of Israel." Yet at the same time, the continuation of the covenant depends on the response of faithfulness and loyalty — in other words, *hesed* is required of human partners in covenant with their God.[66] Hyatt also recognized in Israel — and this had important implications for the church — that responsible love, structured within and by the covenant, found expression in obedient response to the law, especially the Decalogue. Divine love was not limited to Israel or even later the church. Rather, drawing on the preaching of the prophets, Hyatt argued that the prophets, followed later by Jesus, articulated a theology of universal ethical monotheism and would not "tolerate a narrowness of vision which was a practical denial of the sovereignty and goodness of God."[67]

Yet God's grace had to be accompanied by repentance if righteous and obedient faithfulness were to emerge from the human spirit. In looking at the prophets, Hyatt found that repentance meant the free turning away from evil toward the will of God revealed in divine instruction.[68] What was needed was a new heart, a transformation of will and character wrought by a free and open decision to follow God. For Jeremiah as well as for Hyatt, "Man is not naturally depraved; it should be a part of his nature to serve in gratitude the God who made him."[69]

Even so, the obedient response to God was not easy to formulate into faithful living. Finding his example in Jeremiah, Hyatt believed that faithful response to God involved wrestling with the divine will and even on occasion calling God to account for what seemed to be unfulfilled promises or uncaring abandonment.

The Reality of Sin

Like Niebuhr, Hyatt believed that sin was systemic, woven into the very fabric of human society. God as judge came to announce punishment through the prophets, who recognized the failures and corruptions of social life. God demanded that humans bring the entirety of their lives into subjection to the divine will. Sin is grounded primarily in human hubris, and expresses itself most openly in the rejection of the authority of God.[70]

The external agency to sin, which appeals to selfishness and pride within the human creature, is "the fascination with materialism and economic power,"

---

66. "The God of Love in the Old Testament," in *To Do and to Teach: Essays in Honor of Charles Lynn Pyatt*, ed. Roscoe M. Pierson (Lexington: College of the Bible, 1953), pp. 24-25.

67. Hyatt, *Prophetic Religion*, pp. 56-57.

68. See Hyatt, *Jeremiah: Prophet of Courage and Hope*, p. 94.

69. Hyatt, *Jeremiah: Prophet of Courage and Hope*, p. 113. "God made man for moral obedience, giving him freedom of the will that he might choose to obey or disobey; man has within his nature not only an inclination toward evil, but also an instinct for God" (p. 114).

70. Hyatt, *The Book of Jeremiah: Introduction and Exegesis*, in *Interpreter's Bible*, vol. 5 (Nashville: Abingdon Press, 1956), pp. 785-86.

which "exerts a strongly corrupting influence on men."[71] The prophets insisted that the social effects of wealth had a deleterious effect on human communities. "There is no denying that the prophets were generally more concerned with society as a whole, and with social systems and institutions, than with the individual." Social systems must conform to the divine requirements of mercy, justice, and humility.[72]

In regard to the matter of loyalty to country, an issue of considerable weight during the Cold War era, Hyatt affirmed the importance of taking a prophetic stance. While the prophets were not pacifists, they understood only too well the vanity of trusting in weapons: "They opposed militarism as a false confidence and denial of trust in God."[73]

> The prophetic definition of patriotism, then, does not affirm that one's state is always right and that one must be ready to defend its every action. Nationalistic patriotism was, to the prophets, utterly false. Real patriotism to them was international and spiritually founded. It sought the total welfare of the people of one's own country, not of selected groups with vested interests, but it did not seek their total welfare at the expense of men who happened to live in other states. The total welfare of foreign peoples, too, must be sought.[74]

The prophets, and Hyatt in their steps, believed wrong and unjust social relations were a denial of God's demand for Israel to be "the people of God."[75] Liberation from oppression came as a result of following the prophetic principles of social justice. And this life-giving liberation was to be experienced by oppressed nations, slaves, prisoners, the poor, and women. Hyatt believed that the Christian religion, promoted by the ideals of the prophets, served women well in the struggle for emancipation.

> In Christian lands, where the gospel has been taken seriously, women have been accorded more and more equality with men and given a higher status in society. Most of us who follow Christ no longer take literally the admonitions of the Apostle Paul concerning the place of women in the home and in the church. Yet, we can find in the Bible, especially in the teachings and attitude of Jesus, implications for giving women a higher status and for according to them treatment as individual persons in the sight of God.[76]

Christology

Like Willett before him, Hyatt often painted his portrait of Jesus with the strokes of classical liberal theology. Jesus was a great prophet who followed

71. Hyatt, *Prophetic Religion*, p. 61.
72. Hyatt, *Prophetic Religion*, pp. 74-75.
73. Hyatt, *Prophetic Religion*, p. 144.
74. Hyatt, *Prophetic Religion*, p. 148.
75. Hyatt, *Prophetic Religion*, p. 167.
76. Hyatt, *The Heritage of Biblical Faith* (St. Louis: Bethany Press, 1964), pp. 334-35.

in the line of Israel's classical prophets.[77] Yet Hyatt did not stop with the Jesus of the old liberals. Rather, he took the extra step of pointing to Jesus as Savior and Lord and the center of history: "To the Christian he [Jesus] is Saviour, Redeemer, Lord. And yet he is far more. None of our conventional categories are adequate to describe him; he broke through all categories, and he gives new meanings to them."[78] Proclaiming the gospel according to neo-orthodoxy, Hyatt wrote,

> For the Christian, Jesus Christ has become both the center and the criterion of history. . . . Jesus was the fulfillment of Old Testament prophecy, not in the sense that he mechanically conformed to all of its predictions, but in the sense that prophetic religion came to full fruition in him. But he was more than prophet, establishing a new era under a new covenant. The Christian finds in Christ both the culmination of the history of the chosen people and the criterion by which events in history are to be judged.[79]

BIBLICAL CRITICISM AND THE OLD TESTAMENT AS SCRIPTURE

Historical Method and Salvation History

Hyatt applied carefully and judiciously various developing methods in biblical scholarship to Scripture. Clear articulation of methods of inquiry and critical problems consistently characterizes his work. Even so, for Hyatt there was no "great ugly ditch" to jump over in moving from the present to the past. Indeed, the great course of human history and the positivistic assumption that events led to other events, all of which could be reconstructed and understood with some degree of clarity, cleared for Hyatt a sure and certain pathway back to Bible days.

Hyatt was thoroughly a historian who saw the turmoil of historical forces as the center of reality and the arena for the redemptive activity of God. Consequently he believed historical criticism was the method capable of tracing not only the redemptive history of Israel and the church but the grand sweep of history in general. For Hyatt it was the Hebrew prophets who first thought of God as the Lord of history, entering into space and time and controlling the destiny of peoples and nations. And it was Israel who became the elect, not through merit but through grace. Israel was no *Herrenvolk*, destined to rule the world; it was a servant people called to witness to and announce the enlightened rule of the God of heaven and earth.

Linear time was not a prison of despair from which to escape but rather a dwelling of hope whose door was open to future redemption. The same God

77. Hyatt, *Prophetic Religion*, p. 7.
78. Hyatt, *Prophetic Religion*, pp. 13-14.
79. Hyatt, *Prophetic Religion*, p. 87.

who liberated Israel from Egypt is also active to bring salvation to those who are oppressed in the present and is moving the history of redemption toward the future with purpose and power. Nevertheless, the prophets believed that "the promises made in the past could be fulfilled in the future only as men in their own day turned to God and sought to do his will."[80] Hyatt especially opposed the Calvinistic assumption of the millennialists that all of history is a stage and human beings are mere puppets whose strings are pulled by an all-powerful God with foreknowledge. He insisted to the contrary that humans possess the possibility of participating actively in bringing to completion the divine acts of redemption.

The Old Testament and the Christian Faith

Hyatt's scholarship did not begin and end with historical questions about the Bible and ancient Israel. Exegesis was only the beginning of the interpretative process. While he did not attempt to usurp the role and work of the contemporary theologian, he did not hesitate to deal with questions of modern import, especially as they related to the faith and practice of the church.

A major theological issue for the contemporary church has been the relevance of the Old Testament for Christian faith, and more to the point, the authority of the Old Testament. This issue has been even more problematic for Disciples who had inherited the theological mantle of Alexander Campbell. According to Campbell's dispensationalism, the Old Testament had no real authority over or relevance for the church. Even the Gospels, dealing as they do with the life and teachings of Jesus prior to the Christian dispensation, were denied normative value. Campbell's authoritative Bible begins with Acts and ends before Revelation. This canon within the canon was for Campbell a binding blueprint for Christian faith and practice.

Hyatt addressed this most problematic issue in his essay for the Panel of Scholars report.[81] He begins with a strong criticism of the Marcionite heresy implicit among many Christians who reject the Old Testament, and then seeks for it a more constructive role. Seeking to avoid the twin pitfalls of either Christianizing the Old Testament or overplaying Bultmann's principle of discontinuity, Hyatt proposes a more balanced view.[82]

To this end, Hyatt argues, first of all, that the modern church must honor the view that the entire Bible, both Old and New Testaments, constitutes the Christian canon. This is not to say that the entire Bible is equally authoritative

---

80. Hyatt, *Prophetic Religion,* p. 90.

81. The three volumes of the Panel of Scholars report were produced under the general editorship of W. B. Blakemore, dean of the Disciples Divinity House of the University of Chicago. Volume 2, edited by Ralph G. Wilburn, is entitled *The Reconstruction of Theology* (St. Louis: Bethany Press, 1963). Hyatt's essay, "The Place of the Old Testament in the Christian Faith" (pp. 47-64), appears in Part One, "Bible and Tradition for the Faith Today."

82. Hyatt, "The Place of the Old Testament in the Christian Faith," p. 55.

or inspired but that, in acknowledging the variety of perspectives inherent within Scripture, "we must seek to determine those points of view and those ideas which represent the highest, and are normative in the Bible as a whole."[83]

Hyatt felt it important to recognize that we need the Old Testament in order to understand the New and that Judaism and Christianity have a shared history and a common affirmation of revelation in history.[84] Moreover, Hyatt suggests that the Old Testament supplements and even serves to correct at times the New. For example, the stress on God as creator and the world as creation, while not absent in the New Testament, is obviously more prominent in the Old. And the communal faith of Israel tends to serve as an important corrective to the occasional one-sided emphasis on personal redemption in the New Testament.

Hyatt did not believe the Bible to be verbally inspired, and certainly not infallible or inerrant. Its various parts do not possess the same value and equal authority. However, read critically it opens up to modern humanity the possibility of encountering the God of Israel and the Christ of faith.[85]

DISCIPLES THOUGHT AND BIBLICAL INTERPRETATION

Freedom of Inquiry and Diversity of Understanding

Alexander Campbell's contention that reformation comes through critical and reasoned discussion was central to Hyatt's thinking. But in Hyatt's view, tolerance and support for diversity moved beyond simply affirming the principle of free and rational inquiry in the interpretation of Scripture to the recognition of the plurality of religious truth. He believed that God is active in many religions and cultures and has prophetic spokespersons in every culture and age who know the divine will and speak it clearly.[86] However, Hyatt was unwilling to abandon the commitment of Vanderbilt Divinity School to the training of Christian ministers for the church. Even in the sixties, when the winds of change blowing across university campuses led to the exchanging of traditional values for the attraction of the unusual, Hyatt remained adamant that theological education was for Christian ministry. The growth of interest in non-Christian cultures and expressions, including religion, the deprecation of traditional Christianity and its values, and the strong move toward ecumenism at the expense of negating or at least reducing the importance of denominational identity were strong forces. Yet Hyatt was a conservative in the best sense of the term — not in rejecting the new but in preserving what was best from the old.

---

83. Hyatt, "The Place of the Old Testament in the Christian Faith," p. 55.
84. See Hyatt, "The Place of the Old Testament in the Christian Faith," p. 58.
85. See Hyatt, *The Heritage of Biblical Faith*, p. 320.
86. See Hyatt, *Prophetic Religion*, p. 13.

The Rule of Reason

Hyatt was rationalist to the very core in his approach to interpreting the Bible and in his articulation of faith and practice. Even in understanding the revelatory experiences of the prophets, Hyatt argued that they received their messages, in the main, while possessing and using their rational faculties.[87] Yet rationalism was also key to the modern understanding of the Bible and to religious practice. The application of reason to the study of the Bible through the methods of Biblical criticism was second nature to Hyatt and was in keeping with the earlier Lockean rationalism used by the Campbells.

The Critique of Tradition: Von Rad's kleine Credo and Lutheran Confessionalism

A major object of Hyatt's criticism was the work of Gerhard von Rad, considered one of the real giants of Old Testament scholarship from just before the outbreak of World War II until his death in 1972, the same year that Hyatt died. Hyatt was especially critical of von Rad's understanding of history, for von Rad was one of the champions of *Überlieferungsgeschichte* ("Tradition-history"), which considers the faith of the Old Testament to be grounded in ancient creeds that were confessed during the great harvest festivals celebrated in the sanctuaries.

Disciple J. Philip Hyatt, who shrank at the very thought of creeds, would have none of this. Von Rad's ancient creed in Deuteronomy, he contended, was no more than a Deuteronomic summary of narratives that captured in essence primal historical events, while the Sinai event, which included at least the Mosaic covenant and ethical decalogue, if probably not the rituals and sacrifices, was a real and substantive component of Israel's earliest faith. Thus covenant and ethical laws were traced back to the early beginnings of Israelite faith.[88] This was also true of creation, as evidenced in the Yahwist, one of the earliest theologians of ancient Israel.

Hyatt believed that although the Old Testament contains much that is legendary and historically inaccurate, it is nonetheless a major resource for reconstructing the life and thought of ancient Israel. Hyatt saw in von Rad's tradition-history method not only unproven speculation but the subversion of history as event. Carried to its extreme, the method made faith lose its anchor in history.

---

87. See Hyatt, *Prophetic Religion*, p. 8.

88. See, for example, Hyatt, "Were There an Ancient Historical Credo in Israel and an Independent Sinai Tradition?" in *Translating and Understanding the Old Testament*, ed. Harry Thomas Frank and William L. Reed (Nashville: Abingdon Press, 1970), pp. 152-70.

Prophetic Criticism of Israelite Worship

Hyatt's strong free-church piety, nourished early in classical liberalism and given religious formulation in the staunchly antiritual posture of Baptists and Disciples, brought him into critical opposition to formal religious liturgy and ritual. This personal preference clearly came to expression in his reading of the Hebrew prophets. For Hyatt the great prophets were uniformly opposed to priestly religion, and indeed blamed the priests and their cultic religion for allowing, if not promoting, the moral decay of the nation.[89]

Hyatt saw these prophetic criticisms as striking directly at the heart of the false consciousness of modern religion. We prefer magic to judgment, self-interest to the will of God, familiarity with a personal God to the mystery of a transcendent Lord, and an aesthetically pleasing worship service to the righteous demands of social justice. As Hyatt saw it, the uniting element of prophetic religion is the sovereignty of God.[90]

The Unity of the Bible and the One Church

The unity of the Bible was for Hyatt a fundamentally important issue, for the discovery of unity within the diversity of Scripture pointed to the means for bringing together the divided churches into an ecumenical body. While the Bible was not a blueprint for restoration, Hyatt nevertheless believed a careful attention to its words, and not some theory about its interpretation, would lead to a common basis for interdenominational and interfaith dialogue.[91]

Hyatt also found a source for unity in the work of scholars whose use of and commitment to a common methodology led to many of the same general conclusions. He did not fail to note that there were many points of disagreement, but the common affirmation of many of the major results of scientific study of the Bible was a source of great satisfaction to one who was committed to unity in the midst of diversity.[92]

The search for the unity of all believers, so central to the Disciples, was the source of inspiration for Hyatt's life and work. Indeed, his attraction to Vanderbilt was in part due to the University's foundational mission in the promoting of the unity of a country still torn by Civil War and divided into a

89. See Hyatt, *Prophetic Religion,* pp. 124-32.

90. See Hyatt, *The Prophetic Criticism of Israelite Worship: The Goldenson Lecture of 1963* (Cincinnati: Hebrew Union College, 1963), p. 20. Hyatt believed true worship to be both cultic and moral, public and private. "We can worship God in synagogue or temple or church; yet we can worship also as we study, as we engage in commerce, as we live in our homes, and in all the activities of life, if we seek in all of them to serve God and his purposes" (p. 21).

91. See Hyatt, *Prophetic Religion,* p. 7.

92. See Hyatt's introduction to *The Bible in Modern Scholarship: Papers Read at the 100th Meeting of the Society of Biblical Literature, December 28-30, 1964,* ed. James Philip Hyatt (Nashville: Abingdon Press, 1965), a collection of essays written by scholars from substantially diverse backgrounds: "Perhaps the most amazing conclusion to which some readers will come is that the agreements among the writers outnumber their disagreements" (p. 11).

fiercely unrepentant sectionalism which damaged the prospects for the country's becoming once again "indivisible, with liberty and justice for all." Bishop McTyeire, whose tireless efforts eventually persuaded Cornelius Vanderbilt to put up the money to establish the university, said to his patron 17 March 1873, "I want to unite this country, and all sections of it, so all people shall be one, and a common country as they were before."[93] In following this founding vision, Hyatt believed it was only in the variety of Christian identities of both faculty and student body in the Divinity School that the quest for mutual respect and the forging of unity in diversity could be effectively carried through. The work of the RSV Committee (Hyatt was one of the original members of the committee that produced the first edition by 1952) represented the renewal of interest in the Bible in the postwar period. And its work was of special interest for the Disciple from Vanderbilt. Hyatt believed that a new and understandable version of the Bible in modern English would not only promote Bible study and understanding but also would aid the Disciples goal of effectuating the unity of all believers.

The Prophetic Vision of the Kingdom of God

For Hyatt the culmination of history "is the realization of God's sovereignty."[94] He found the images and theology for his own view of the kingdom of God in the texts of prophetic eschatology. Prophetic eschatology, pointing toward the kingdom of God as its center, bore no superficial optimism about an unchallenged entrance into the time and space of God's eternal reign. The true prophets combated the false prophets whose naive promises along these lines are as gladly received in our day as they were in theirs.

With their eye fixed on the future, the prophets always spoke with a sense of urgency. *The kingdom is at hand.* They believed that "the present moment is of critical importance, determining the future." "The present moment is always a moment of crisis. . . . An urgent moral demand, presented to nations and to individuals, is always an authentic and necessary element in prophetic religion."[95]

Yet it was Jesus who in Hyatt's view spoke most fervently of the inbreaking of the kingdom of God. "The view of the future held by Jesus of Nazareth centered around his teaching about the Kingdom of God. His gaze was almost entirely directed toward the future rather than the past."[96] According to Hyatt, Jesus was mainly concerned with spiritual preparation for entrance into the kingdom, breaking forth even during his public ministry. Thus repentance, humility, a childlike faith, watchfulness, and moral obedience were

93. Quoted by Bard Thompson in *Vanderbilt Divinity School: A History* (Nashville: Vanderbilt University, 1960), p. 5.
94. Hyatt, *The Heritage of Biblical Faith*, p. 112.
95. Hyatt, *Prophetic Religion*, p. 116.
96. Hyatt, *Prophetic Religion*, p. 111.

essential virtues for those who would see God. In essence, "The Kingdom of God meant above all the doing of God's will on earth."[97] Even so, Hyatt did not downplay the social requirements of the gospel or Jesus' own ministry of preaching and doing.

IN THE MIDST OF THE WHIRLWIND: SUFFERING FOR THE KINGDOM

Personal Tragedy and the Vision of the Kingdom

In fashion similar to William Rainey Harper and Herbert Lockwood Willett, Hyatt experienced the pain of physical suffering, emotional loss, and personal assault resulting from controversy.[98] Illness accompanied Hyatt through much of his adult life: bronchiectasis and spinal arthritis, followed by heart trouble. And devastating, at least for a time, was the death in 1960 of his oldest child, Lee, from pneumonia. But it was the assaults from his critics that opened the deepest wounds. The fundamentalists, on the one hand, saw in Hyatt and his work a dangerous threat to Christian faith and values. Liberal social activists, on the other hand, regarded Hyatt as a conservative Southerner.

In the Throes of Controversy: Joe McCarthy and the Revised Standard Version

Harvie Branscomb was appointed chancellor of Vanderbilt University in 1947 and served in this capacity until 1963, by far the most significant and tumultuous period in the history of the university. Branscomb was especially committed to the development of a prominent divinity school, having served as dean and professor of New Testament at Duke prior to accepting the post of chancellor at Vanderbilt. He also became Hyatt's close friend. Branscomb recognized that a distinguished faculty would have to be recruited if Vanderbilt were to achieve national prominence. And he turned to Hyatt in helping to bring scholars of national reputation to the Divinity School. Yet these faculty also became the object of great criticism from conservatives and fundamentalists.[99]

Hyatt himself came under heavy fire. A Southerner and a committed and active churchman, he was better equipped than most scholars for the task of defending the integrity of his work. Even so, Hyatt not only taught critical theories about the Bible in the middle of the Bible Belt but was a highly visible scholar. Fundamentalists accused him of destroying the inspiration and author-

---

97. Hyatt, *Prophetic Religion,* p. 113.

98. See the Preface to *Essays in Old Testament Ethics,* ed. James L. Crenshaw and John L. Willis (New York: Ktav, 1974), p. viii.

99. See Paul K. Conkin, *Gone with the Ivy: A Biography of Vanderbilt University* (Knoxville: University of Tennessee Press, 1985), p. 507.

ity of the Bible, denying the divinity of Jesus, and undermining the values of family and country. They also charged that the Revised Standard Version was written by subversive atheists determined to destroy the church by undermining its biblical authority and thus the country by attacking its biblical values. Hyatt had served on the committee from its inception. When the RSV appeared in its red cover edition, the fundamentalists literally saw red. Hyatt was defamed as a willing participant in a communist plot to destroy the Bible! Hyatt's resignation was demanded, and the criticism came to the attention of the board, already nervous and increasingly divided by the controversy surrounding liberal scholars in the Divinity School. To Branscomb's credit, he defended Hyatt from these attacks, emphasizing his evident churchmanship as proof of his strong belief in the Christian religion and its values for this country. At a later time, after much of the furor had subsided over the communist Bible, Hyatt wryly commented, "Early translators were burned to death; recently gentler critics have burned the new translations."[100]

James Lawson and the Civil Rights Movement

In the summer of 1956, Dean Benton died suddenly, and Hyatt found himself unexpectedly thrust into the job of acting dean. The search for a new dean led to the appointment in 1957 of J. Robert Nelson. Only thirty-six, he soon faced the most explosive period in the history of the Divinity School. In 1960, just as the Divinity School was moving into its new facility, thereby symbolizing its rise to academic prominence, a civil rights activist and senior divinity student named James Lawson was expelled by Chancellor Harvie Branscomb. As a result, Vanderbilt became the most criticized university in the country.[101]

Lawson, a Methodist pastor from Ohio and a graduate of Baldwin-Wallace, had been a student at the Oberlin School of Theology before entering Vanderbilt Divinity School in 1958.

He came to Nashville to finish his B.D. and to pursue his ministry as regional director of the Fellowship of Reconciliation. An able civil rights leader, Lawson was committed to Martin Luther King Jr.'s policy of nonviolence. A conscientious objector who was not granted a deferred status by his draft board, he refused induction in 1950 and received a three-year prison term. After eleven months he was paroled, went to work for a Methodist mission in India, and came under the influence of Gandhi.

After entering Vanderbilt in 1958, Lawson joined other black preachers in the Christian Leadership Council, which was affiliated with King's Southern Christian Leadership Conference. The civil rights movement in Nashville reached a dramatic point in 1960, when sit-ins in the segregated lunch counters were organized. Lawson was identified as a major ringleader and was accused

---

100. Hyatt, *The Heritage of Biblical Faith*, pp. 314-15.
101. For a brief discussion of the incident, see Conkin, *Gone with the Ivy*, pp. 502-3.

by the local authorities of breaking the law. The executive committee of the Vanderbilt board offered Lawson the choice of withdrawal or expulsion. Lawson chose expulsion.

Only the actions by the majority of the Divinity School faculty and students on behalf of Lawson preserved for Vanderbilt a degree of integrity. They asked for the readmission of Lawson to allow him to finish his degree. When Branscomb refused, nine divinity professors submitted their resignations. The very existence of the Divinity School now seemed in serious question, and a hostile and defiant Branscomb contemplated the closing of his most prestigious school.[102]

Two-thirds of the divinity faculty had resigned. Only two who had been at the Divinity School for a considerable period of time, George M. Mayhew, close to retirement, and James Philip Hyatt, the most distinguished member of the faculty, refused outright. Both were Southerners and both were Disciples. However, Hyatt recognized that his resignation could well signal the end of the Divinity School, since his personal friendship with Branscomb and considerable prestige with the board were the last link in any negotiations that might preserve a future. It is also clear from his personal papers that Hyatt lobbied behind the scenes on behalf of Lawson, supporting very strongly his admission to the Divinity School. But Hyatt received enormous criticism for refusing to resign.

In working out his own unilateral statement, without board support beforehand, Branscomb announced to the faculty that he would accept immediately Dean Nelson's resignation, allow Lawson to receive a B.D. by transfer of credit or written exams but not by readmission, give the divinity faculty ten days to withdraw their resignations, and then consider the matter closed. The board backed this action, but the fallout continued for many years.[103] On June 15, the divinity faculty, save for Bard Thompson, who was already leaving for another post, withdrew their resignations.

Hyatt suffered severely damaging criticism for his refusal to join in the resignations, and his relationships with several colleagues deteriorated. But he had believed that the very existence of the Divinity School was in peril. He had spent nearly twenty years of his life in transforming a small department of religion into a prominent divinity school and graduate school of religion.[104] Hyatt found himself caught up in the midst of a raging whirlwind. The very

---

102. See Conkin, *Gone with the Ivy,* p. 559.

103. See Conkin, *Gone with the Ivy,* p. 570. Lawson did not finish at Vanderbilt, but took his B.D. from Boston University, choosing to support Dean Nelson, who had resigned on his behalf.

104. Among the schools that had wooed Hyatt earlier were the University of Chicago Divinity School and (in the midst of the crisis) Texas Christian University. Conkin notes, "Dean Nelson had believed at the time of the dedication, and with some justification, that his school now ranked in the top five nationally. It also had become the brightest southern bastion of liberal Christianity and in 1960 was comparatively the strongest school in the whole university" (*Gone with the Ivy,* p. 501).

existence of the Divinity School, the honor of Vanderbilt, social justice for a wronged civil rights leader, and Hyatt's own personal career were at stake. It is here that the Christian realism of Reinhold Niebuhr impacted Hyatt's thoughts and actions. Theories of moral action in the abstract were one thing, but now the theoretical had become all too real. Action was demanded. To shrink from decision was to abandon all integrity and self-respect.

Hyatt, like William Rainey Harper, interpreted his suffering theologically through the lenses of the great prophets, especially the Servant of the Lord in 2 Isaiah and Jeremiah.[105] Suffering faithfully was the means by which a new reality was shaped. What gave Hyatt the courage to remain, even when other tempting offers came his way, was not only the conviction of his own integrity but a resolute hope for a new future for Vanderbilt, the Divinity School, and the church. He was unwavering in his conviction that he could help the Divinity School weather the current storm and eventually rebuild what had been torn asunder.[106]

PROPHETIC TRANSFORMATION AND INSTITUTIONAL AGENCY

Vanderbilt Divinity School

Hyatt had joined the Vanderbilt faculty in 1941. It was an auspicious year. That same year the School of Religion met all accreditation standards and the requirements of most denominations for training their pastors. The Southern Methodist Church approved Vanderbilt for training its ministers at the same level as its own seminaries. By 1941 the School of Religion was living from its own revenues, and "for the first time since 1914 the school seemed secure. Talk of suspension finally ended."[107]

The "Great Leap Forward" for Vanderbilt, as Conkin describes it, came during the period 1947-1963, the Branscomb years, and leading the way for this advance was the Divinity School. Conkin notes that it was Harvie Branscomb, then chancellor of Vanderbilt, who was the great ally of the Divinity School. Branscomb credited the Divinity School with keeping his own denomination, the Southern Methodist Church, out of the hands of the fundamentalists. Thus he supported the ambitions of Dean Benton to recruit outstanding professors and to expand programs.[108] Hyatt played the crucial role in bringing faculty of national reputation to Vanderbilt and in establishing a Ph.D. program.

---

105. See Hyatt, *Meeting God through Isaiah*, p. 21.
106. See Hyatt, *Jeremiah: Prophet of Courage and Hope*, pp. 98-107. "Hope gives us the conviction that the future will in some measure bring the fulfillment of our dreams and ambitions and see the fruition of some of our plans. For the Christian it means having faith that God will fulfill his promises" (p. 98).
107. Conkin, *Gone with the Ivy*, p. 389.
108. See Conkin, *Gone with the Ivy*, pp. 500-501.

The financial fortune that accelerated Vanderbilt to national prominence came from the Rockefellers. In 1955 John D. Rockefeller, Jr., an active Baptist, through one of his charities, the Sealantic Fund, awarded the Divinity School a $2.9 million endowment.[109] The proposal had been prepared by Hyatt and Roger L. Shinn. The "Hyatt-Shinn codex," as it was called, became the basis for receiving the award and setting its amount.

Yet the moment of Vanderbilt's greatest triumph also became the time of its greatest tragedy. A conservative board's abusive treatment of James Lawson seriously damaged the reputation and prestige of Vanderbilt, the Divinity School, and its most prominent scholar. It took several years for the situation to return to normal. However, Hyatt's decision to remain at Vanderbilt proved not only courageous but essential to the future chartering of the Divinity School's course.

Disciples Divinity House

The Disciples Divinity House of Vanderbilt Divinity School in Nashville came into existence in 1942 with a building on Grand Avenue. Hyatt served as dean, though without remuneration. In 1950 Herman A. Norton was hired to be dean of Disciples House and to continue as instructor of American church history in the Divinity School. A new building was constructed on Adelicia Avenue in 1958. Hyatt was on the board of directors at the time and worked hard for the construction of the new building. Following the lead of Herbert Willett, Hyatt realized that Disciples needed an institution attached to a major divinity school in order to train ministers and scholars. It was in keeping with his vision of the Disciples as a leading instrument for Christian union that Hyatt helped to establish and guide the house through the first thirty years of its existence.

Conclusions

Hyatt's own description of the prophets serves perhaps as the best memorial to his life and work:

> They did not live in ivory towers separated from the life of their time, though they did on occasion withdraw from the society of men for meditation and prayer. They were not automatons or puppets in the hand of an arbitrary Deity. God used them as his spokesmen without violating the integrity of their own personalities. He did not choose to send his word to the world through hollow tubes, but through living and struggling men who had dedicated themselves to his service.[110]

109. Conkin notes that Rockefeller gave $20 million for theological education, with the great bulk of the money going to the six major nondenominational seminaries — Union, Yale, Chicago, Harvard, Pacific School of Religion, and Vanderbilt (*Gone with the Ivy,* p. 501). Vanderbilt's gift was the largest, being a million dollars more than the next largest gift (Thompson, *Vanderbilt Divinity School,* p. 21).

110. Hyatt, *Jeremiah: Prophet of Courage and Hope,* p. 20.

And what enabled Hyatt to endure a period of great crisis and his own personal tragedy was his hope and faith in the future of Vanderbilt Divinity School, the Christian Church, and the kingdom of God: "Hope that is not ephemeral and illusory must be based upon the same kind of clear-eyed participation in life, and deep faith in God and man, which Jeremiah had. Such hope is not finally disappointed."[111]

EPILOGUE

Though living in different times, Willett and Hyatt shared many similar experiences and held many views in common. Both lived during critical periods of significant change in American history in general and the Christian Church in particular. Both lived in periods of dramatic growth, and sought to adapt the mission of the Disciples and the Bible to new and changing circumstances. These periods were times of great interest in the Bible, and perhaps this was one factor behind the growth. Both served as prophets of transformation and hope, leading the Disciples into a new and compelling vision of the kingdom of God and the role of the Christian Church in seeking to bring about the unity of the denominations.

Both recognized the need for Disciples to forge their own intellectual tradition, incorporating a distinctive hermeneutic that would bring together modern biblical scholarship, contemporary theology, and Disciples emphases on unity, reason, and the kingdom of God. They were major contributors toward this end. And to actualize this tradition, both helped to establish and lead the two major Disciples Divinity Houses which have provided the intellectual and spiritual community necessary for shaping future generations of Disciples leaders.

---

111. Hyatt, *Jeremiah: Prophet of Courage and Hope*, p. 115.

Disciples Contributions and Responses to Mainstream Protestant Theology, 1880-1953

Clark M. Williamson and Charles R. Blaisdell

INTRODUCTION

An apparently promising way of assessing Disciples' theological contributions and responses to the larger theological scene from 1880 to 1953 would be to identify those whom the church commissioned as professors of theology and simply find out what they published, whom they were reading and responding to, and the courses they taught. Yet, in sampling extant college and seminary records, those so identified can be counted on one hand. In most cases, when the term *theology* is used, what is meant is "moral theology" and the courses taught under this rubric were mostly nuts-and-bolts ministry courses.

And yet Disciples have clearly been *doing theology*. It is simply the case that their theological contributions and responses have been curiously mixed. In this "the critical period in American religious history," when American Protestants "came to grips with the impact of modernity on their psyches,"[1] Disciples displayed a grip that ranged from the oblivious to the facile and condescending to a wholehearted embrace. Just before the opening of our period of study, Robert Milligan's *Scheme of Redemption* was published (1878). To read it is to find no realization that Kant, Feuerbach, Strauss, or Darwin had come and gone. While J. W. McGarvey was reading "higher criticism," his uses of it often seem shallow and self-congratulatory.

Our thesis is that the roots of the present predicament in the Disciples of Christ can be traced back to its beginnings in the era 1880-1953. This predicament can be stated in several ways. Borrowing some metaphors from psychologist Robert Jay Lifton, we distinguish between two types of personal-

---

1. Arthur M. Schlesinger, Sr., quoted by Charles Harvey Arnold, in *Near the Edge of Battle: A Short History of the Divinity School and the "Chicago School of Theology," 1866-1966* (Chicago: Divinity School Association, 1966), p. 4.

ity, the protean and the closed-off. Protean people lack fixity or boundaries and are marked by fluidity. They lack fixed identities or centers. The opposite impulse is the tendency to develop a closed-off, tight personality structure. Closed-off people have a clear, if rigid, identity and a constricted self-process. They are reluctant to let any extraneous influence into their lives.[2]

Lifton's metaphors can be applied to churches. The Churches of Christ and the Independent Christian Churches reflect the closed-off structure of a constricted self. They have clear identities; they know who they are and what they believe. They are not involved in ecumenical conversation, nor do they manifest great concern for the liberation of people or the earth itself from various kinds of oppression.

Disciples might congratulate themselves on this difference if they did not also reflect the opposite, or protean, personality trait. Open to all influence from everywhere, virtually taking diversity as their norm, they lack identity and centeredness. Wanting to make nothing a "test of fellowship," they fail to recognize that some things are incompatible with the gospel. Averse to critical theological reflection, they fail to be authoritative teachers of the Christian faith. Overwhelmed by the flood of imagery and feelings flowing over them, they become walking affects.

No wonder such a church might shrink. Its members might discover that it adds little to the life of contemporary Americans. If we do not teach the Christian faith and communicate to people the excitement generated by understanding themselves in the light of the gospel, can we blame them for finding that everything presented as "Christian" is available elsewhere?

How did the Disciples get into this predicament? The roots of our present troubles can be found in this period and are either reflected in or created by what was said by those who were teachers of the Christian faith (theologians) in that era.

There were two "ideal types" of theologians influencing Disciples at this time: conservative and liberal. The Churches of Christ and the Christian Churches and Churches of Christ are the legatees of the conservative type of theology, as the Disciples are of the liberal. Conservative theologians do not find the claims of modernity to have any intrinsic theological relevance. Theologians are simply to give voice to an adequate understanding of the beliefs of their particular church tradition. Modern scientific, historical, and philosophical scholarship make no difference to the Christian faith's understanding of life.

The liberal theologian's commitments are to the basic cognitive claims and moral values of modernity, although these claims and values do not exhaust the liberal's commitment. As modernists, liberals value free and open inquiry, autonomous judgment, and critical method — a sort of "secular faith." Christianity needs to be rethought, cognitively and morally, to bring it into harmony

---

2. See Lifton, *Boundaries: Psychological Man in Revolution* (New York: Vintage Books, 1970), pp. 37-38, 43-44, 51.

with the vision and values of modernity. The liberal theologian is a self-consciously modern human being who reformulates the Christian tradition in accord with modern commitments and critiques.

We will look at the roots of both the protean and closed-off character of church life in this little more than seventy-year period. We will focus on those who most influenced the Disciples, as teachers, editors, or academics: J. W. McGarvey and J. H. Garrison from the earlier part of our period and E. S. Ames, C. C. Morrison, and D. C. Macintosh from the later part of our period. We have primarily concentrated on the available published works of these writers, especially their systematic or apologetic statements. Although other records would prove instructive (e.g., private correspondence), given our focus on the *public* theology of the day, such a methodological restriction seems appropriate.

J. W. McGARVEY

The Disciples of Christ movement has been called temperamentally and philosophically "empiricist." This temperament refers to an attitude, congruent with empiricist methodology, that finds value in the act of investigation despite the possibly discomforting results of such investigation. The empiricist attitude tends to regard fixed doctrines, claimed in advance of evidence, as either presumptuous or superfluous. The empiricist attitude also tends to produce a certain "metaphysical humility," with the realization that the world looks, at least ever so slightly (and sometimes ever so greatly), different from different perspectives. Hence, the number of perspective-invariant things that can plausibly be believed must be very few. Such an attitude was the legacy of the first generation of Disciples, providing the philosophical underpinnings for what has been known more formally as the "interpretation principle," the "unity principle," and the "restoration principle."[3] Given the manifold perspectives on things, what all "must" believe is relatively minimal (e.g., a belief in Christian unity via a restoration to New Testament *minima*), and the route to those beliefs and the paths leading from them are given interpretive latitude.

But this neat system fell apart. Increasing work in comparative religions, science, and philosophy suggested that the commonality in human experience lay in places other than New Testament ecclesiology. Concomitantly, critical work on the New Testament increasingly showed that "the" New Testament church, with its pattern of minimal "essentials," was a fiction. Therefore the triad of principles seemed inconsistent. Attempts to dissolve this inconsistency reached in at least two different directions: J. W. McGarvey, in essence, gave up the interpretation principle and the unity principle, substituting instead the

---

3. On the "interpretation principle," see Larry Bouchard, "The Interpretation Principle," in *Interpreting Disciples,* ed. L. Dale Richesin and Larry Bouchard (Fort Worth: Texas Christian University Press, 1987), pp. 7ff.

restorationist principle. McGarvey's strength was also his weakness: he clearly kept a set of *norms* for what was authentically Christian, but the very authenticity, intelligibility, and wider moral appropriateness of those norms was threatened. J. H. Garrison, on the other hand, embraced the interpretation and unity principles; yet by construing the restoration principle as focused on the figure of Jesus, he tended to lose any authentically Christian perspective, or at least the power to discriminate Christian from cultural norms.

The twenty years on either side of the turn of the century were a time of intense religious, scientific, and socioeconomic ferment. Higher criticism had been in full swing for more than half a century. The ideas of Darwin were now trickling down and being debated in certain quarters of the church. The ideas of Feuerbach, Kierkegaard, and Marx were powerful reminders that the truths of religion are inescapably tied to the truths of ideological commitments and psychological structures. Concomitant with these factors, the United States (outside the South) began a long period of economic and industrial growth, multiplying the number of city dwellers. Linked to such growth was a massive immigration to the U.S., and the majority of the new arrivals were eastern European, often non-Protestant, and inclined to be city dwellers. These factors changed the social context of theology at the same time developments in philosophy and science were changing its intellectual context. Homogeneity in the American religious scene began to disappear, and "validity structures" that had been implicit and taken for granted in theological thinking were now rendered both explicit and questionable.

We do not reduce theological assertions to the various conditions that help explain their plausibility; such a reduction would imply that theological assertions have no truth value but only degrees of meaningfulness in a given situation. Yet one ignores these broader conditions under which theology is done at the price of not fully comprehending them. McGarvey (1829-1911) — the lifelong resident of small towns, Southern in outlook, in the midst of a still agrarian and fairly homogeneous subculture, in a setting that could not be confused with an intellectual center — was both a product of his times and a reaction to the larger forces impinging on it.

McGarvey's theology poses a definitional problem, for his published works consist almost entirely of biblical criticism. Thus, even rudimentary distinctions between his apologetic, confessional, and systematic theologies are of little use. What theology is available in his writings does not "look like" theology. Yet there is one source, little noted in the secondary literature, in which McGarvey addresses "those who have made a thorough, systematic, and scientific investigation of *all the grounds* on which an intelligent faith may rest."[4] These words sound decidedly like an apologetic theological effort; indeed, they almost sound "liberal" in their invocation of "thorough, system-

4. McGarvey, "Grounds on Which We Receive the Bible as the Word of God, and the Only Rule of Faith and Practice," in *The Old Faith Restated,* ed. J. H. Garrison (St. Louis: Christian Publishing, 1891), p. 23; italics ours.

atic, and scientific investigation" and their tacit admission that religious faith rests on many "grounds." It would seem that an "intelligent faith" is the desideratum, a faith in which a reasonable evaluation of all the evidence will eventuate in a "scientifically" credible theology. In this essay McGarvey assembles a dozen or more arguments to show, in apparently apologetic fashion, that the Christian faith is true.

Yet this concession to apologetic theological norms is only apparent. It turns out that McGarvey summarizes a great deal of his thinking not in apologetic but in moral terms. McGarvey uses *"intelligent* faith" not as a functional or empiricist term but as a term of moral approbation, related to the correct *intent* of the theologian in question, not the results of his study. What is this "correct" intent? Belief in "the miraculous events recorded in the New Testament . . . is the crucial test of man's faith in Christ."[5] One is therefore "intelligent" if one starts theologizing from that point of view.

The opposite of "intelligent" faith is not stupid faith but immoral faith. McGarvey habitually refers to those critics of the Bible who did not start from this basis as "infidels." Those critics who were not "intelligent" possessed immoral motivations; McGarvey "believed that the critics had in large measure misused the science, with the evil intent of destroying the Bible and the faith associated with it."[6] William C. Morro has noted that McGarvey suspected a "bias on the part of the critics against instead of for the Bible."[7]

This moral equation of "intelligent" with "predisposed toward the Bible" is evident in the very structure of McGarvey's article. Apparently apologetic, McGarvey first seeks to respond to those whose faith is grounded in simple childhood teaching and who have seldom questioned their faith. Then he addresses those who have raised an occasional doubt under the influence of culture. Finally, he focuses on those who question systematically. He makes clear his belief that those who are most "intelligent," most moral, are the simple believers. Such individuals, he asserts, do not and need not question, because they experience the good fruits of their convictions in abundance. Because they are relatively uneducated, their belief, their "intelligence," has not been affected.[8] McGarvey considers it unfortunate that any further responses are needed, for such a need indicates that scholars have "unfavorably influenced" believers. "To him [McGarvey], the Bible was an inerrant revelation of God to man, plain, simple, and complete. Rejection of it, or any part of it, was rejection of God. Such was more than an error in judgment, it was moral delinquency."[9] Note the Newspeak going on here: to be "intelligent" is to be unquestioning; to intend to question is to be morally culpable.

5. McGarvey, "Grounds on Which We Receive the Bible," p. 32.
6. David H. Bobo, "John William McGarvey: A Biographical and Theological Study" (M.Th. thesis, Christian Theological Seminary, 1963), p. 364.
7. Morro, quoted by Bobo, in "John William McGarvey," p. 365.
8. See McGarvey, "Grounds on Which We Receive the Bible," pp. 12-15.
9. See William C. Morro, *Brother McGarvey* (St. Louis: Bethany Press, 1940), p. 32.

It should be obvious how McGarvey jettisoned the empiricist and inter- pretive motifs in Disciples thinking. He replaced them with the axiom that an intent to believe the Bible is categorically good. But what is the *content* of this intent that assumes such a foundational place in McGarvey's thinking? What does it mean to "uphold" the Bible? Again, we must infer much of what McGarvey's theological understanding of God is from his other statements about the Bible. If it is true, *pace* Bultmann, that every statement about God is also a statement about humanity and vice versa, it is also true that in McGarvey's thought every statement about the Bible implies a truth about God and vice versa. But even in this regard, McGarvey compounds the difficulty in assessing what he thinks about God: "I don't believe any . . . man knows what the reasoning of God was on this subject, by which he felt compelled, according to his own infinite nature, to refuse to pardon a single sin except through the blood of his son."[10] In other words, the Bible is the infallible but sometimes inscrutable record of an inscrutable God. Nevertheless, "all of its utterances are true . . . and . . . nothing else, as a matter of religious belief, is to be required of us."[11] Quite simply, "the fact that the Bible is from God makes it our duty to believe it."[12]

This also suggests that McGarvey's understanding of the role of God in humanity's affairs is precisely the *rule* of God. The New Testament functions as the infallible record of laws for Christian belief and behavior.[13] Given this understanding, McGarvey's theology contains "an emphasis on the legal and purposive aspects of God which are perhaps stronger than his stress upon God's fatherliness and forgiving compassion."[14] For example, in his *Commentary on Acts,* McGarvey's emphasis falls not upon God's inviting love and grace which justifies and saves but on the belief that "a man is justified by obedience."[15] Such obedience is most clearly symbolized in baptism, which, on the juridical understanding of God, is a "symbol of personal surrender."[16] Given this un- derstanding of the role and rule of God as perfectly manifest in the Bible, it is clear why anyone "who had been instructed in Bible truths and did not discover this revelation of God rested under a heavy guilt."[17]

Returning to the topic of intent, we would note that McGarvey consid- ered morally culpable any who questioned the Bible from a critical perspective. Nor can we leave this topic without commenting on McGarvey's arguments for the authority of the New Testament. In his article in *The Old Faith Restated,*

10. McGarvey, *McGarvey's Sermons* (Louisville: Guide Printing and Distribution, 1894), p. 51.

11. McGarvey, "Grounds on Which We Receive the Bible," p. 1.
12. McGarvey, "Grounds on Which We Receive the Bible," p. 44.
13. See McGarvey, "Grounds on Which We Receive the Bible," pp. 46-47.
14. Bobo, "John William McGarvey," p. 392.
15. Morro, *Brother McGarvey,* p. 103.
16. Morro, *Brother McGarvey,* p. 105.
17. Morro, *Brother McGarvey,* p. 32.

he offers fairly standard arguments ranging from the pragmatic (the "fruits of belief" in the lives of those who accept the Bible are so good that we can therefore trust its authority) to the popular and fallacious (since all attempts to disprove the authority of the Bible have failed, it must be authoritatively true).[18] But it is clear that McGarvey's entire edifice of belief rests on a circular argument: The writers of the New Testament are trustworthy because they were contemporaries of Jesus. How do we know they were contemporaries? Because they say so. And we can believe what they say because they were contemporaries of Jesus.[19]

How do we assess McGarvey's contributions and responses to mainstream theology? He was not unacquainted with theologians and biblical scholars of his day.[20] But his response to them tended to hinge on the question of whether they had the "proper" intent. Therefore McGarvey's responses to the theology of his day can be judged in many ways as increasingly irrelevant, especially as theology and biblical criticism sought the same sort of evidentiary and epistemological standards as other scholarly disciplines. Moreover, it is fair to say that given the ever-more-rigorous questioning of the foundations of all things religious, McGarvey's confusing of apologetics with a very narrow confessionalism increasingly made his thinking seem simply a *non sequitur.* He thought that the apologetic role of biblical criticism "is not to discover but to confirm."[21] And because he thought that there was nothing to be discovered (in any ordinary or scientific sense) about Christianity and the Bible, he could not respond to such discoveries.

What of his contributions? McGarvey had an enormous influence on the preachers whom he educated, including those in the Churches of Christ and what came to be the Christian Churches and Churches of Christ. But his contributions to mainstream theology were minimal. His writings were mostly ignored, "politely" commented on, or dealt with sarcastically.[22] When McGarvey published a book on Deuteronomy in which he upheld the Mosaic authorship of the book, a student of his requested that Harvard's George Foote Moore review it. Moore declined and instead wrote McGarvey a letter pointing out a number of factual errors and politely noting that McGarvey was "high minded." But Moore declined mainly because he and McGarvey simply had no common presuppositions from which to even begin a discussion.[23] J. H. Thayer echoed the same sentiments when, in declining to review McGarvey's work on Jonah, he wrote, "In the present case I imagine that you and I would have to begin our discussion too far back, and have to settle too many points . . . before we

18. See McGarvey, "Grounds on Which We Receive the Bible," pp. 15, 20-21.
19. See McGarvey, "Grounds on Which We Receive the Bible," pp. 32ff.
20. See, e.g., Morro, *Brother McGarvey,* pp. 190ff.; and Bobo, "John William McGarvey," pp. 363, 373.
21. Bobo, "John William McGarvey," p. 370.
22. See, e.g., Bobo, "John William McGarvey," p. 378.
23. See Bobo, "John William McGarvey," pp. 379-81.

could see eye to eye."[24] As these examples suggest, McGarvey was simply at odds with his theological times. Therefore his contribution to mainstream theology must be assessed as slight.

JAMES HARVEY GARRISON

Where J. W. McGarvey ended up rejecting the unity principle and sharply circumscribing the interpretation principle, J. H. Garrison (1842-1931) attempted persistently and irenically to retain the traditional Disciples threefold emphasis on unity, restoration, and interpretation. He is described by William Tucker as "basically . . . a theological moderate. He always sought to reflect the spirit of liberalism without giving up the 'fundamentals' of Christian faith, to live creatively in the present without disclaiming the past."[25] Yet, in many ways, such an attitude was increasingly untenable. Garrison never seemed to grapple seriously with the normative questions that science and criticism were raising with Christian theology; he failed to think through the serious challenges that modernity posed to the Disciples' "plea." As a result, he tended to confuse the norms of culture with those of the gospel. Believing in the "evolutionary and progressive" model of history and religion, he could find no basis from which to disentangle contemporary cultural norms from appropriate witness to the claims of the gospel. This tended to lead Garrison, in the spirit of irenic moderation, to read the Bible as a mirror of his own times. Where the claims of those times became too discomfiting to such eisegesis, Garrison simply defined them out of contention (e.g., with the question of evolution, or the assessment of history's ever-progressing character).

Sociology-of-knowledge considerations are again relevant. Whereas McGarvey was rural, nonintellectual, and provincial, Garrison spent his life in St. Louis and California, lived for a while in England, was conversant with the intellectual currents of the day, was in conversation with the Missouri liberalism in the Disciples in the latter 1800s, and mostly welcomed the increasing religious and cultural pluralism in American society (with one notable exception: Roman Catholicism). These considerations are suggestive: where McGarvey tended to define his message rigidly, Garrison tended to broaden his definition, with the result that it became increasingly hard to make appropriate normative discriminations.

Even with all that, we must judge Garrison's legacy as good. Theologically, he sought never to put limits on a God whom he conceived as being fundamentally a God of love. If such an attitude sometimes tended toward indiscriminate affirmation, it had the merit of remaining open to new truth.

It can be fairly said that Garrison sought to develop a Disciples plea for

---

24. Thayer, quoted by Bobo, in "John William McGarvey," p. 378.
25. Tucker, *J. H. Garrison and the Disciples of Christ* (St. Louis: Bethany Press, 1964), p. 134.

the modern era by recasting the restorationist principle. Where McGarvey sought the restoration of the church by identifying from the Scriptures a set of infallible laws to be obeyed, Garrison sought the restoration of the church in a focus on the *personal figure* of Jesus. For Garrison, restoration of the church (and with it the union of the church), as well as personal and social salvation, could be achieved by a belief in the salvific power of the personality of Jesus. All else was inessential, a matter of interpretation.

Given this shift in emphasis from the Bible to the figure of Jesus, Garrison could appear quite "liberal" (or quite like Luther!) in his treatment of the Bible. "Not even the scriptures are the object of Christian faith," he wrote.[26] "They are invaluable in their testimony concerning Christ, but they are no substitute for Christ."[27] But Garrison acknowledged that such an "intelligent treatment of the Biblical literature" had a cost. He held that one could treat the Bible in "modern" ways because it was an "evolutionary" document. The Bible is not "level"; it is "a progressive revelation as humans are able to take it in" (*HF*, p. 188). "Garrison argued that the scriptures did not uniformly disclose the true nature of God. Since God had to speak to and through man, he adapted his revelation to their circumstances."[28]

The price of such a view consistently carried through is that the entirety of the Hebrew Bible is dismissed as being irrelevant because primitive. The hermeneutical status of the Old Testament becomes simply that of "an index finger pointing towards" Christ.[29] Such a belief is not unusual in Christian history. What is new is the "evolutionary" motif.

Garrison never clearly thought through the implications of this idea. He argued that the Old Testament was given to the Hebrew people because of their "special fitness to receive" it (*HF*, p. 40), but unfortunately they were not fit *enough* to receive the full revelation of God because of their inferior evolutionary status. The revelation of Christ "divided all history into its two recognized divisions of B.C. and A.D." (*CW*, p. 11). It is not clear what this "evolutionary readiness" consisted of. Intertestamental culture was not morally "ready"; Garrison suggests that Christ came precisely at the time the cultures of Greece, Rome, and Israel were falling apart (*HF*, p. 45). Nor were the Hebrew people "ready": Garrison wrote that they "thought of [God] as a being of might and majesty, terrible in judgment and capable at times of extending mercy to those who had offended against His law" — which is to say that they envisioned a capricious God (*HF*, p. 68).

26. Garrison, *Helps to Faith: A Guide to Theological Reconstruction* (St. Louis: Christian Publishing, 1903), p. 112; subsequent references to this volume will be made parenthetically in the text, using the abbreviation *HF*.

27. Garrison, "Lessons from Our Past Experience," in *The Old Faith Restated*, ed. J. H. Garrison (St. Louis: Christian Publishing, 1891), p. 455.

28. Tucker, *J. H. Garrison and the Disciples of Christ*, pp. 144-45.

29. Garrison, *Christ the Way* (St. Louis: Bethany Press, 1926), p. 71; subsequent references to this volume will be made parenthetically in the text, using the abbreviation *CW*.

While Garrison initially suggested that God's self-revelation is given on the basis of readiness *qua* capability to receive, he later suggested that "readiness" for Christ was based on an evolving need. He asserted that if God were truly loving, he wouldn't allow "millions of His children . . . [to] sink into the irretrievable depth of sin and moral degradation without putting forth the highest possible effort to save them" (*HF*, pp. 72-73). And so he reasoned that if God were truly and completely loving, the incarnation was a "moral necessity" (*HF*, p. 44).

A question must be raised: How could people who were sinking in such moral degradation have the moral ability to recognize that Jesus "meets all our highest and worthiest conceptions of Godhood" (*HF*, p. 61)? And if the Hebrew people's "special fitness" had indeed continued to evolve, why would they stand in such moral need of Jesus? Garrison's "evolutionary readiness" motif had the merit of allowing for new apprehensions of truth, and it contributed to an irenic spirit in relation to those who might disagree with him, but it does not hold up under questioning. It entails that the Old Testament is at best like other kinds of evolutionary records: fossils trapped in the sediment of purely "geological" interest. By definition it can have little or nothing to say now.

Garrison's evolutionary motif allowed him to maintain that there could be a "continual and never ending progress in the knowledge of the truth," since "the wine of Christianity is always new, and that bottle which is to contain it must be capable of continuous and indefinite expansion."[30] Nevertheless the *principle* of truth for Garrison was fixed: "Christ himself, in his glorious personality, and Messianic offices, is the object of saving faith."[31] Since "Jesus called attention to His own personality as the fundamental fact of religion," Christianity comes down to a simple yes-or-no question concerning the personality of Jesus (*HF*, p. 46). Apparently Garrison assumed that salvation is authentic self-understanding which, in turn, is an appropriation of Jesus' understanding of God.

Garrison's method here is familiar: he enumerates the "character traits" of Jesus and argues that they show us the nature of God. Five traits of Jesus stand out: (1) "we are struck at once by his intellectual superiority" (proven by his continual besting of his "Jewish" opponents); (2) he exhibited moral perfection and sinlessness: "Jesus never betrayed the slightest consciousness of His own sin or shortcoming"; (3) "he offered himself to man as one whose mission was to supply all their needs"; (4) "he wrought many mighty works, attesting to his divine power and mission"; and (5) he rose from the dead — "no student of the life of Jesus, today, seriously questions the fact of the resurrection" (*HF*, pp. 52-57). Moreover, his resurrection confounded "the Jews," who had put him to death out of a "narrow particularism" (*HF*, p. 93).

---

30. Garrison, "Lessons from Our Past Experience," pp. 431, 430.
31. Garrison, "Lessons from Our Past Experience," p. 444.

There are more than a few methodological and factual questions raised by this portrait. First, Garrison's quest for "an intelligent treatment of the Biblical literature" and antipathy to treating the Bible in a "level" manner did not apply here.[32] He took the Gospel accounts of Jesus at full face value (though more on this below) and did not question Jesus' claims of consciousness. He never addressed the epistemological issues involved in calling the resurrection a historical "fact" (not to mention the *ad hominem* view that no "thinking" person denies this). He said that those who raise such issues on "scientific" grounds are in fact exhibiting that they are "too puffed up with [their] own success."[33]

But for the purpose of understanding Garrison's place in what came to be called mainstream theology, the interesting questions involve such matters as what he meant when he talked of taking the Gospels at "face value" (*HF*, p. 51) and what criteria he used to designate Jesus as "the greatest man of all history" and "the only perfect personality" (*CW*, p. 22). It should come as no surprise, given Garrison's use of the evolutionary motif, that he considered Christ to be perfect in terms of the "highest" culture of Garrison's own day.

"We must test our religious beliefs, our practices, by the mind and character of Christ," wrote Garrison, and "we must test our industrial and social life in the same manner."[34] What does "the mind and character of Christ" sanction or enjoin? Garrison offers a list of things the personality of Christ either tests or is historically responsible for. Generally, "Jesus Christ is the only solution to our social problems" (*CW*, p. 41). Garrison rests this assessment on the historical work of Christ, concluding, for example, that "it is not difficult to trace the wonderful growth in democracy back to its source in the teaching and life of Jesus" (*HF*, p. 162). Where the church has failed to follow the mind of Christ, socialism instead of democracy has prevailed (*CW*, p. 39). Moreover, "to this same teaching . . . we are indebted for all those philanthropic and benevolent institutions" (*HF*, p. 162). The mind of Christ does not approve of "rapidly accumulating trusts, of those vast monopolies," but it does approve of appropriate relations between employer and employee, capital and labor. It impinges on questions of war, slavery, marriage, liquor, and corporations who "trample under their feet the rights of toiling men and women" (*CW*, p. 101). The "new revelation in Jesus" has been undermining "thrones and dynasties, breaking the chains of human slavery, rewriting constitutions and laws . . . , creating a vast empire of democracy" (*CW*, p. 35). Each of these issues can be adjudicated by being "submitted to the extreme test of Christ's wish and will" (*CW*, p. 101).

While there are worse ways to theologize than to begin with the question of what would God have us do in some social situation, the problem with

32. Garrison, "Lessons from Our Past Experience," p. 455; and see Garrison, *Memoirs and Experiences* (St. Louis: Christian Publishing, 1926), pp. 199ff.
33. Garrison, "Lessons from Our Past Experience," pp. 441-42.
34. Garrison, *Memoirs and Experiences,* p. 234.

Garrison's approach is that the line between American (especially North American) cultural triumphalism and the demands of the gospel is blurred. An upshot of the "evolutionary" motif is that Garrison's own cultural locus became the implicit norm for our "highest and worthiest conceptions of Godhood" (*HF,* p. 61).

Such an approach to theology comes with two prices. First, Garrison exhibited either an incredible naivete or willful disingenuousness about the nature of the world. Amazingly, he wrote in 1926, against the background of the desolation of World War I, that "men are seeing in [Christ] as never before the Way out of all our religious, social, and industrial difficulties and the Way to the City of God — the goal of perfected humanity and redeemed society" (*CW,* p. 5). And he asserted with great confidence that "men who are enemies out of Christ, on coming into His kingdom, become friends" (*CW,* p. 56). Moreover, he dismissed those who thought otherwise, who were skeptical about the ever-improving state of things (*HF,* p. 233). Reflecting on the Civil War, Garrison complained of "how unnecessary it was, had reason controlled the two sections." It would have been a simple matter, he said, to have held a conference to "adjust" the question of slavery "to preserve the Union without war."[35]

The more serious problem with Garrison's way of theologizing is that it leaves little opportunity to criticize the culture one is a part of (if, by evolutionary definition, the culture is the highest expression of moral values). At best such theologizing can lead to a banal conflating of gospel and culture: "I had been advocating and fighting for the view of the States under one flag and one constitution. Why not stand for the union of Christians under one Leader and one Bible as our common rule of faith and practice?"[36] At worst, Garrison's procedure produced the kind of responses he gave to the Spanish-American War and World War I, in which one has "difficulty distinguishing between his religion and his patriotism."[37] For example, he described Admiral Dewey's victory at Manila as "thrilling," and said that it reminded him of "the great spiritual conflict, and of the ships of Zion, panoplied with the armorplate of righteousness, moving through the world's moral darkness on her sublime mission"; the war, he said, was "the Lord's way of pointing us to our national duty and destiny."[38] The Spanish-American War provided important tactical lessons for evangelists: enthusiasm, strategy, organization, and cooperation "are some of the elements of success in spiritual warfare."[39] Garrison's method

35. Garrison, *Memoirs and Experiences,* p. 34.

36. Garrison, *Memoirs and Experiences,* p. 48.

37. Charles Blaisdell, "The Attitude of *The Christian-Evangelist* towards the Spanish-American War," *Encounter* 50 (1989): 3.

38. Garrison, quoted by Blaisdell, in "The Attitude of *The Christian-Evangelist* towards the Spanish-American War," pp. 238-39.

39. Garrison, quoted by Blaisdell, in "The Attitude of *The Christian-Evangelist* towards the Spanish-American War," p. 240.

of theologizing from "the mind of Christ" allowed him no way to correlate *critically* the gospel and culture, and so the gospel message became the uncritical correlate and justification for cultural triumphalism. The definition of *Christian* was identified with the highest values of the culture. Only in the light of these values could he criticize warfare.

Garrison's methodological focus for doing theology was the personality of Christ, but there were other elements to his theology. He argued on natural theological grounds that humans are "conscious of a desire to worship," that "in human nature as we find it" there is a "higher capacity than that of mere reasoning," and hence that "the facts of human nature . . . find their only explanation in a Creator who possesses in an infinite degree those qualities and faculties which we find germinal in man" (*HF*, pp. 20, 19, 23). And he dismissed any who might question this conclusion: those who offer a materialist explanation of humanity are simply "not to be reasoned with" (*HF*, p. 23).

These "qualities and faculties germinal in man" find their fullest expression in Christ. From the natural-moral argument and the personality of Christ we can deduce certain things about God (although a great deal is obviously implicit). The overriding principle is that God is love: "love is the supreme motive of God in all his dealings with man" (*HF*, pp. 75-76). Again and again, Garrison came back to this point: compare with McGarvey's view that of Garrison's that "God will meet any of his penitent children, at any time, in any world, with pardon"; "if God in His infinite goodness shall choose to give further opportunity beyond death for any soul to repent . . . that would be cause for thanksgiving," and we should never "put limits to the mercy of God" (*HF*, pp. 185, 186).

How shall we evaluate Garrison's contribution to Disciples theology? It can safely be said that his influence was enormous. In a career roughly paralleling McGarvey's, Garrison reached through his journals thousands of church persons on a weekly basis. While one may fault various aspects of his theology, his irenic and open temperament was preferable to McGarvey's closed-off stance. Garrison was widely (although perhaps not deeply) read — he cited the ideas of Kant, Harnack, and Wellhausen among others — and universalistic in his outlook (with the sad and notable exception of his virulent anti-Catholicism, an attitude that was of a piece with his evolutionary cultural triumphalism). The Disciples historic willingness to be a part of the larger mainstream was molded and nurtured by Garrison's insistence that "a Christian having the spirit of his Master will bid Godspeed to whatever and whoever is building up the Kingdom of God."[40] His failure lay in formulating an understanding of the nature of God as the love that "is the motive power that lies behind creation" on the basis of a portrait of Christ uncritically painted in the hues of Garrison's own socioeconomic and cultural circumstances (*CW*, p. 19).

---

40. Garrison, "Lessons from Our Past Experience," p. 429.

Nevertheless, Garrison asked questions that allowed the Disciples to engage the world rather than spending all their energies on intramural debates. One can find worse beliefs than the insistence that "nothing is . . . so fundamental . . . as the questions concerning God. What kind of being is he, and what is his attitude toward mankind?" (*CW*, p. 17). The willingness to put the question this way and to continue to engage it, even when it is not answered with as much clarity as might be desirable, is a trait that continues to animate the Disciples of Christ in particular and mainstream theology as a whole.

EDWARD SCRIBNER AMES

Thus far we have distinguished between two ideal types of theologians, conservative and liberal. Between 1900 and 1940, liberal Protestant theologians split into two rather different groups: "evangelical liberals" and "modernistic liberals." The evangelical liberals were serious Christians searching for a theology that intelligent moderns could accept.[41] They sought to preserve what they took to be "essential" to Christianity in terms that would be intelligible to the modern world. The modernistic liberals, on the other hand, were "intelligent moderns" who nonetheless saw themselves as "serious Christians." Their thinking was basically oriented to a self-consciously modern outlook that provided the standard for measuring the abiding values of Christianity. "Jesus was important — and even unique — because he illustrated truths and values which are universally relevant. However, these truths and values can be validated and even discovered apart from Jesus."[42] The leading figures in the "Chicago school" of theology — Gerald Birney Smith (1868-1929), Shailer Mathews (1863-1941), and Edward Scribner Ames (1870-1958) — were all clearly modernistic liberals, as was the chief theologian whom they influenced, Douglas Clyde Macintosh (1877-1948). Of these, we are here concerned with Ames and Macintosh, the former a Disciple who deeply influenced Disciples, and the latter a longtime Yale professor who made considerable impact on the many Disciples who studied there.

Ames begins *The Divinity of Christ* by asserting that Christianity is "founded upon Jesus Christ. It sprang from his personality, derived its vital conception from his words and its inspiration from his vision and example."[43] Jesus was the "founder" of Christianity, important for his personality, teachings, and example. Jesus himself "preferred to be acknowledged by deeds rather than by words" (*DC*, p. 5), thereby emphasizing the importance of his

41. See Kenneth Cauthen, *The Impact of American Religious Liberalism* (New York: Harper & Row, 1962), pp. 27-28.

42. Cauthen, *The Impact of American Religious Liberalism,* p. 29.

43. Ames, *The Divinity of Christ* (Chicago: Bethany Press, 1911), p. 3; subsequent references to this volume will be made parenthetically in the text, using the abbreviation *DC*.

own example, which takes precedence over the "theoretical correctness of a man's ideas about Christ" (*DC*, p. 7). Christ's personality was characterized by an "enveloping love" for God and people. What proved Christ divine was his "voluntary choice to do his Father's will" (*DC*, p. 16). He accomplished an inner self-surrender "in order to give himself wholly to the purposes of the divine will," thus establishing his "oneness with God" (*DC*, p. 16). Rather than beginning with God and proceeding to try to understand the divinity of Christ, it is better to begin with the life of Christ and proceed to try to discover "what kind of a being God is" (*DC*, p. 9).

Our knowledge of Christ comes by way of an empirical inquiry into Jesus that deals critically with the biblical records and worldview (*DC*, p. 23). Abandoning the traditional two-substances-in-one-person christology of Chalcedon in favor of a modern understanding of personality, Ames concluded that Jesus differs from us in degree, not in kind (*DC*, p. 28). Jesus really was "like us," born in the normal fashion, steeped in the tradition of his people, responsive to the prophetic and wisdom traditions and capable of translating them into the idioms of beatitude and parable, able to practice genuine friendship with Zaccheus, the Samaritan woman, and Judas, and able to forgive those who crucified him (*DC*, p. 30).

However, when Ames turned to the issue of the relation of Christ to God, he confessed that he had "lost interest in ontological questions" (*DC*, p. 31) and limited himself to saying that somehow "the personality of Jesus reveals the heart of the world" (*DC*, pp. 30-31). The point of christology is not Jesus' relationship to God but his example for us. The "supreme empirical test of Christ" is whether his wisdom and spirit can "be actualized in the world, in a society of men, in a heavenly kingdom of love and peace" (*DC*, p. 35). The question is not so much "What think ye of Christ?" as "What will you do about Christ's example and ideal of life?" (*DC*, p. 36).

In spite of his claim that Jesus is to be understood historically as one steeped in the tradition of his people, Ames nonetheless declared that Jesus' newness constituted a "far higher state than religion had ever before consciously attained. The law came by Moses, but grace and truth came by Jesus Christ" (*DC*, p. 69). "So new, so unique" was Jesus' "gospel of friendship between God and man" that it left the religion of Israel behind and at a lower stage of evolutionary development. Thus, like Garrison, Ames used an evolutionary model to reinstate the old ideology that the Christians had superseded the Jews.

Ames confessed that William James had "opened new doors to the understanding of the human mind"[44] and that John Locke had become his hermeneutical key for reading Alexander Campbell. His Lockean interpretation of Campbell stressed the reasonableness of Christianity, the *one* article of faith

---

44. Ames, *Beyond Theology: The Autobiography of Edward Scribner Ames,* ed. Van Meter Ames (Chicago: University of Chicago Press, 1959), p. 37; subsequent references to this volume will be made parenthetically in the text, using the abbreviation *BT.*

in Jesus as the Messiah, and "a practical faith in his attitude and way of life" (*BT,* p. 43). He rejected "speculative theological metaphysics" and the teachings of "innate human depravity, and of emotionalism as essential in conversion" (*BT,* p. 43). John Dewey's instrumentalism, however, played a larger role in Ames's outlook than did James's radical empiricism.[45] Nor apparently did it ever occur to Ames that there is a vicious circularity to understanding faith as acting upon certain hypotheses and thereby producing certain results. How are the hypotheses to be tested if the worth of the results is to be decided by reference to the value judgments that are hypothesized in the first place? The "assured results" of empiricism seem shaky.

All of this is reflected in Ames's statement that "religion is a practical concern in the sense that it projects ends and ideals and works for their realization."[46] The human mind is "but an aspect of endeavor to control and direct activity to fruitful and significant ends" (*BT,* p. 45). Consequently, Ames's course on Campbell consistently took a "practical, common-sense, non-theological approach" to the discussion of all topics, producing a nontheological reading of Campbell (*BT,* p. 46).

The content of these "ends and ideals" that Christianity projects is at the heart of Ames's faith. "In the higher religions the sacred things are the human values to which the good life is devoted, such as love, intelligence, and practical techniques" (*BT,* p. 89). These, in turn, are unpacked by the concerns of the Social Gospel: "politics, child labor, intemperance, tuberculosis, woman's suffrage, better housing, sanitary shops, public education, white slavery, the race problem, prison reform, immigration, public playgrounds, labor legislation, and the conservation in every way of the sources and functions of life" (*BT,* p. 114).

In a 1913 sermon, with which he still agreed in 1959, Ames declared that each age of church history had its distinctive ideal of the Christian life, from the martyr to the ascetic to the crusader knight to the mystic to the theologian. Yet "now . . . the Christian ideal is undergoing another transformation. The theological saint is losing prestige. His creeds are discredited by greater knowledge and broader vision. As the image of the theologian dissolves and fades from view, there is emerging the ideal of the social worker" (*BT,* p. 115). Ames remained convinced that "our age demands a non-theological, practical faith which is earnestly loyal to the spirit of Jesus Christ, a faith which labors for the welfare of all mankind with the very love and ardor of Christ, a faith which is scientifically intelligent and experimentally adventurous in dealing with social problems" (*BT,* p. 118).

Compatible with this outlook was Ames's definition of faith as "a psychological attitude" of confidence or assurance that "a person, a principle, a

---

45. According to Charles Arnold, "he never really went 'beyond' Dewey" (*Near the Edge of Battle,* p. 55).

46. Ames, *Religion* (Chicago: Henry Holt, 1929), p. 70.

project will not disappoint us in action or in eventuation" (*BT,* p. 215). Faith is a thrust into the future, a "great venture . . . on behalf of the possibility of a better society" undertaken in the absence of any certainty as to its success (*BT,* p. 215). Likewise, Ames's doctrine of God was an empirical-pragmatic view. Early in his career, Ames initiated his remarks about God by commenting that "it is not an accident that we think of great social entities as great personalities." Just as we personify institutions, so it is "just as natural to sum up the meaning of the whole of life in the person and image of God."[47] Doing so is the "most natural and simplest way to represent to our minds and wills the moral values and the spiritual realities of life." In this sense, he called God "the great *Ideal* Companion."[48] He argued that as the search for an objectively real soul within persons has been dropped, so has the search for God as an objective reality transcending the world: "A more fruitful course is to inquire whether God may not be more truly and more fully understood as the reality of the world in certain aspects and functions — in what is here characterized as reality idealized." Yet he insisted that "idealized" did not mean "fabricated or imagined" but rather selected. "God is the world or life taken . . . in those aspects which are consonant with order, beauty, and expansion." Such "empirical facts" as the real presence of love constitute the "ground for the religious interpretations of reality as God."[49]

Yet in a chapter entitled "How God Is Used," Ames reopens the question of the actuality of God. As the "reality of Alma Mater is not to be found in any particular noble woman," so "the word god is not properly taken to mean a particular person, or single factual existence, but the order of nature including man and all the processes of an aspiring social life."[50] God is the "working hypothesis of religion and corresponds exactly to the working hypothesis in natural science."[51] "The idea of God, when seriously employed, serves to generalize and idealize all the values one holds."[52] However much Ames may have wanted to move beyond understanding God as an idealization or projection, his controlling motif was that religion's primary motivation is not the thirst for knowledge; its central concern is using the idea of God for effecting human behavior.[53] Hence, Charles Arnold asserts that Ames was ontologically a humanist who regarded the universe as friendly.[54]

Throughout his life, Ames "was seeking a religious ideology for myself and for any who would think with me. I did not want a theology. I disliked

47. Ames, *The New Orthodoxy* (Chicago: University of Chicago Press, 1918), p. 50.
48. Ames, *The New Orthodoxy,* p. 51; italics ours.
49. Ames, *Religion,* pp. 151, 154, 155.
50. Ames, *Religion,* p. 176.
51. Arnold, *Near the Edge of Battle,* p. 56.
52. Ames, *The Psychology of Religious Experience* (Boston: Houghton Mifflin, 1910), p. 318.
53. See Ames, *Religion,* p. 173; and Larry E. Axel, "God or Man at Chicago: The 'Chicago School' of Theology" (Ph.D. diss., Temple University, 1976), p. 185.
54. Arnold, *Near the Edge of Battle,* p. 57.

the word, and my religious training had taught me that theology was not necessary and might be dangerous, because it suggested dogmas that churches required people to believe whether the dogmas made sense or not" (*BT,* p. 75). For Ames, the term *theology* meant conservative theology, and conservative theology meant authoritarianism. If the equation holds, one must do what Ames did — reject theology. But the price was high. Having taken this route, Ames could not, by definition, engage in a critical and constructive theological reappropriation of the Christian tradition or the Disciples tradition. He opted instead for a philosophical and psychological reading of religion "as a natural growth in human life," to be studied with all the appropriate empirical tools (*BT,* p. 81). He made of religion "a natural, social, cultural process."[55]

One implication, which Ames recognized, is that the norms by which Christianity is to be assessed are drawn from the culture: "In our culture the highest religion is Christianity. It stands for the best in our civilization."[56] This apparent lack of a norm of appropriateness intrinsic to Christianity, even if any such norm is understood to be context-dependent for its meaning, is a key to understanding how modernistic liberalism's impact on Disciples increasingly resulted in a loss of identity. For if the identity of higher religions is drawn from the surrounding cultural values, then Christianity will inevitably resemble all other higher religions.

But the strengths of Ames's theology, in its time, were several, and they deserve to be appreciated. For many intelligent Christians, the problem with Christianity was precisely its authoritarianism, its requirement that they accept ideas on the authority of the Bible or the church with no critical appeal to reason or experience. Ames liberated many students from fundamentalism and, however much they might later have come to disagree with him, they remained in his debt. Second, Ames sought ways to make his religious or theological ideas both theoretically and practically intelligible. He sought to accomplish both goals with his pragmatic version of an empirical theology, in which the meaning of a religious idea *is* the difference it makes to human behavior and its ability to address the major social problems and goals of the times. (These problems and goals, some of which have been listed earlier, are strikingly similar to many of the problems central to the agenda of the various current liberation theologies.) Third, Ames worked to liberate the Disciples from the clutches of biblical literalism, which, had it not been successfully challenged, would have left them largely indistinguishable from the Churches of Christ. Among Disciples the major alternative to Ames, particularly early in his career, was McGarvey, and it behooves us to remember this.

Nonetheless, Ames's theology had its weaknesses, which in retrospect stand out clearly. He apparently could not locate within the Christian tradi-

---

55. Ames, *Religion,* p. v.
56. Ames, *The New Orthodoxy,* p. 12.

tion any articulable norm of appropriateness, even in a new and revised form, that would serve to govern or criticize proposed theories and practices. He does appeal to Jesus Christ, but the Jesus to whom he appeals is the Jesus of liberal theology generally, the one whom liberals thought they saw at the bottom of the well of history when it was really their own reflection staring back at them. This lack of a norm of appropriateness results in silence concerning the grace of God as that which warrants acts of love and justice. Hence, his pragmatic gospel is task-oriented and, lacking a doctrine of grace, works-righteous.

Another result of the lack of a norm of appropriateness is that Ames never engaged in a mutually critical conversation with the culture. His Christ was the Christ *of* culture, not the Christ in a dialectical relation to the culture. His Christ was identical with the highest cultural values, values shared by all the other "high" religions. Ames was not uncritical of the culture, but, as with Garrison, he criticized it in terms of its own highest values, not in terms of what might loosely be called a Christian perspective on the culture. Hence Ames simply did not know what to make of neo-orthodox theology when it arose, except to talk of it as a supernaturalism and to analyze it as a product of "war psychology." Asked if he were planning to attend a lecture by Emil Brunner, Ames answered: "I wouldn't go across the street; I wouldn't waste my time with him."[57] He went on to say, "Next, they'll be inviting Karl Barth!"

Third, Ames's confidence that civilization and culture were imbued with the same message the church was also to bear meant that he did not help the church to pay sufficient attention to its distinctive witness. The possibilities that the culture might become pluralistic and fragmented in its values, that many of its values would be established by quantitative, secularist, and economic concerns for the "bottom line," or that groups other than liberal Protestants might actually be in charge of the culture never seem to have occurred to Ames. In retrospect it seems fair to assess his assumptions about the culture as Constantinian. In our day, when the culture clearly cannot be counted on to bear the Christian witness (was it ever appropriate so to depend on it?), the church still suffers from the kind of nontheological self-understanding that Ames urged upon it. For all his radical innovation in religious thought, Ames shared with his denomination (and with his polar opposite McGarvey) an antitheological bias. In an age in which mainstream churches, to be revived from their lassitude, need to learn again to ask and answer the question of what they have to say that no one else can say, such an antitheological bias can no longer be afforded. Important as Ames's concerns for theoretical and moral intelligibility remain, we need an approach to theology that engages in a mutually critical correlation with our situation.

57. Axel, "God or Man at Chicago," p. 192.

DOUGLAS CLYDE MACINTOSH

While Douglas Clyde Macintosh was not a Disciple, he was deeply influenced by Ames's kind of theology and, in turn, had a significant impact both on other theologians and on two generations of theological students at Yale, among whom were many Disciples. A Canadian, Macintosh did his graduate work in theology at Chicago, where he was exposed to the concerns of empirical theology. A modernistic liberal, he sought rigorously to carry out the project of an empirical-pragmatic theology. His central concern was the problem of religious knowledge.

Macintosh was equally disturbed by two problems left over from nineteenth-century theology. He rejected both conservative theology, with its rationalism unrelated to empirical data, and the retreat of faith in the face of scientific progress. He held that scientific method itself could discover religious knowledge as it could every other kind of knowledge. The example of William James inspired him to think that theology could be based on the study of the varieties of religious experience wherein the empirical method could be used to defend the Christian faith itself.

Macintosh began with epistemology. He rejected *dualism,* the view that phenomena are totally different from things in themselves, as entailing an extreme agnosticism with regard to whether there is anything to be experienced.[58] Dualism overlooks the continuity to existence. Macintosh also rejected idealistic *monism,* which posits a complete identity between objects as given in experience and objects in their independent reality. Such a view, contended Macintosh, is so clearly at odds with common sense that arguments for it are inadequate to establish its truth.[59]

Macintosh instead argued that an adequate theory of knowledge must be a *critical realism* that acknowledges a partial identity and a partial dissimilarity between reality, in any of its guises, and its appearances in human experience. There is enough continuity in existence to permit us to say that independently real objects are "directly known, even though not all the qualities of the independent reality have been directly presented, and even though not all of the qualities of the object as presented need be thought of as belonging to it in its independent existence."[60]

Based on these epistemological arguments, Macintosh sought to develop theology as an empirical science. He concluded that his rejection of dualism enabled him to set aside the work of such neo-orthodox theologians as Barth, Tillich, and Brunner. In them, dualism comes to voice as an uncritical dogmatism whose claims cannot be tested by the realities of religious experience.[61]

---

58. See chaps. 2-3 of Macintosh, *The Problem of Knowledge* (New York: Macmillan, 1915).
59. See Macintosh, *The Reasonableness of Christianity* (New York: Scribner's, 1925), pp. 193ff.
60. Macintosh, *The Reasonableness of Christianity,* p. 198.
61. See chaps. 13-19 of Macintosh, *The Problem of Religious Knowledge* (New York: Harper, 1940).

By the same token, however, the idealists in religion who reduce God to some form of idea (e.g., Feuerbach and Freud) can be rejected on the same grounds on which idealism per se can be rejected. Since our relation to God is at the heart of the Christian faith, the idealist view of God as a mere projection would deal a lethal blow to it.[62]

Hence, Macintosh turned to the method of science to ground theology. As with all sciences, scientific theology assumes the laws of thought, the methods and principles of scientific inquiry, and the results of other sciences. Additionally, theology assumes the existence of God. Macintosh justified this assumption by noting that every science provisionally presupposes the existence of its object and that apart from this assumption there can be no such science. Such assumptions are based on practical experience of the object. In assuming the existence of its special object, theology simply does what any science does.[63] Macintosh allowed for the possible falsification of this assumption and contended that its verification was to be carried out by a consideration of the empirical data of theology.[64] Further, as all empirical sciences posit the dependability of nature, so Macintosh posited the dependability of God. Without such dependability, generalizations from specific data to conclusions about how God will act in the future would be impossible.[65]

Macintosh's next move was to stipulate which of various kinds of experience should be singled out as religious. Arguing that religion unites our awareness of absolute dependence and awe with our sense of absolute and universally valid values, he contended that the distinctive interest of religion is in the relation between ultimate reality and values.[66] The hallmark of deity is the unity of value and power. For a ground to establish these absolute and universal values, Macintosh turned to ethical intuitionism.

This understanding of religious experience yields a definition of God as "the value-producing factor and behavior in the universe, driving toward right adjustment on man's part."[67] The expression "in the universe" is important: we are aware of God as immanent within nature and human beings as the power "within experience" that "makes for a certain type of result in response to the right religious adjustment."[68] God's action toward us depends on our having adjusted rightly to God. Such an adjustment is composed of (1) concentration on the right values and on God as their source; (2) absolute self-surrender to God; (3) responsiveness to God's guidance; and (4) persistence in these attitudes. If we meet these conditions, we will experience the working of God in our lives.[69]

62. See chaps. 4-10 of Macintosh, *The Problem of Religious Knowledge.*
63. Macintosh, *Theology as an Empirical Science* (New York: Macmillan, 1919), p. 28.
64. Macintosh, *The Problem of Religious Knowledge,* p. 193.
65. See Macintosh, *Theology as an Empirical Science,* p. 35.
66. Macintosh, "Experimental Realism in Religion," in *Religious Realism,* ed. D. C. Macintosh (New York: Macmillan, 1931), p. 312.
67. Macintosh, "Experimental Realism in Religion," p. 395.
68. Macintosh, *Theology as an Empirical Science,* pp. 31-32.
69. Macintosh, *Theology as an Empirical Science,* p. 144.

Theology must express itself in laws if it is to be truly scientific. Macintosh first formulated his law in this way: "On condition of the right religious adjustment with reference to desired truly moral states of the will . . . God the Holy Spirit produces the specific moral results desired."[70] Later he restated it so as to presume less about God's person: "A divinely functioning reality, on condition of the right religious adjustment for a specific volitional effect (the promotion of the good will) tends to produce a desirable change in that direction in the will and character of the individual concerned, and this may be regarded as the basic, dependable 'answer to prayer.' "[71]

Beyond scientific theology, however, lies what Macintosh called "normative theology." Its basis lies in what he called the religious or "imaginal" intuition, and its content consists of those convictions, mostly subjective, that we entertain as characterizing ultimate reality. We do not know these beliefs to be true empirically, but Macintosh considered them reasonable if they met the test of a pragmatic criterion: "We have the right to believe that those theological doctrines are true which are necessary for the maintenance of the morality which is necessary for the maintenance of the highest well-being of humanity."[72] Or, "We have the moral right to believe as we must, if we are to live as we ought."[73]

Among the things we may believe in this fashion (the content of normative theology) are (1) that God is the kind of God necessary for the satisfactory pursuit of the religious life, purposeful, conscious, and personal; (2) that immortality is the ultimate conservation of all spiritual values, including that of individual moral personality; (3) that God can overcome, in this sense, every ultimate threat; (4) that God will respond appropriately to the right religious adjustment; and (5) that humans are free to make this adjustment.

The christology of normative theology finds warrant for the claims of normative and scientific theology in the person of Jesus as reconstructed by historical-critical method. Typical of the formulators of modern revisionist christologies, Macintosh finds Jesus to have been the chief exemplification within history of the right religious adjustment to God. His faith was perfect: "To employ this idea of the Christ-like as a norm for the criticism of all intuitive faith in God is to make use of what is known as the Christocentric principle."[74] Jesus functions as both the true religious and moral example through his commitment to the divine in all that he did.

Criticisms of Macintosh are worth noting here. First, his procedure has long been noted to be speciously circular. He is naive in prescribing the absolute and universal values for deciding what is a right religious adjustment. That they are his values and those of early twentieth-century North American

70. Macintosh, *Theology as an Empirical Science*, p. 148.
71. Macintosh, *The Problem of Religious Knowledge*, p. 203.
72. Macintosh, *Theology as an Empirical Science*, p. 22.
73. Macintosh, *The Problem of Religious Knowledge*, p. 382.
74. Macintosh, *The Problem of Religious Knowledge*, p. 367.

liberals is apparent; that they are absolute and universal is not. Macintosh seems to have thought that he and others like him had made "sufficient progress in religious discrimination to be able to distinguish the distinctly divine element in religious experience." Second, his pragmatic test of the contents of normative theology fares no better on the issue of specious circularity. Do his findings mean more than that, having chosen "on faith" to act upon certain value hypotheses, one can expect certain results to follow? "Are the hypotheses themselves thereby proved valid or invalid, since the worth of the results is itself to be decided in terms of value-judgments?"[75]

Third, Macintosh never breathes a word about the grace of God. But if some formulation about the priority of grace is normative in the sense of appropriateness for the Christian faith, this is a serious failure. Macintosh's theology is at heart a works righteousness: on the condition of our making the right religious adjustment, God will react appropriately. While we are yet sinners, God is helpless to act.

Fourth, Macintosh's christology, like all liberal christologies, reduces Jesus from the one *in* whom we believe to the one *with* whom we believe, the first and best to make the right religious adjustment. He is the Christ because he did the right work, but we are not saved by his work. We must emulate his example. This is an inappropriate christology if our norm of appropriateness is the promise of the love of God freely offered to each and all and if it is this freely offered love that empowers us to respond appropriately in love for God and neighbor. If we achieve "right religious adjustment," it is in this way. Macintosh got it backwards.

Were Disciples to have been deeply affected by Macintosh, in what would that have resulted among them? An assumption that our values, shared with liberal culture generally, are absolute and universal and the standards by which to assess religion and the Christian faith? An outlook that prizes acting on pragmatic value hypotheses? A silence about the gospel and the grace of God? A christology according to which Jesus Christ is the highest example of our values? How deeply Macintosh influenced Disciples is a matter of conjecture, but it is clear that there is nothing in his thought that would divert them from the general direction established by Garrison and Ames.

CHARLES CLAYTON MORRISON

We next turn our attention to Charles Clayton Morrison (1874-1966), who was first a pastor and then an editor. In 1888 a Disciple paper, *The Christian Oracle*, which appealed to Disciples liberals, moved from Des Moines to Chicago; in

---

75. James Alfred Martin, Jr., quoted by James C. Livingston, in *Modern Christian Thought: From the Enlightenment to Vatican II* (New York: Macmillan, 1971), p. 428.

1900 it was renamed *The Christian Century.* A financially struggling operation, the paper was offered for sale in 1908, and Morrison purchased it for $1,500.[76] Under his leadership *The Christian Century* in 1918 became "an undenominational journal of religion" reflecting Morrison's lifelong commitment to an ecumenical vision encompassing Protestant liberalism.

Along with such other Chicago Disciples as Edward Scribner Ames, Herbert L. Willett, and Winfred E. Garrison, Morrison was among the intellectual leaders of the Disciples for many years. From his editorial chair he exercised considerable influence on the leaders of all of the more liberal or mainstream Protestant churches. Over his long career he also reflected the changing theological moods that swept across the first half of the twentieth century, although he did not change in his fundamental conviction, as will be seen below.

Morrison's first book, *The Meaning of Baptism,* opposes the rigid "immersionist dogma" of Disciples. He frankly announced that the problem was Alexander Campbell and his views.[77] He wrote from what he called "the functional view," a socially alert pragmatism, and sought to understand baptism primarily as a social act, arguing that it could not be reduced to the physical act of immersion. Disciples legalism isolated baptism from the life of the church, he maintained, whereas the social view notes that "its whole meaning is derived from the church" (*MB,* p. 74). In baptism the church defines and constitutes itself, and baptism "is a means of social control" whereby the "ideals of the Christian community are defined in the soul of the initiate as obligations" (*MB,* p. 84). Along the way, Morrison used historical-critical scholarship to undermine legalism and argue for his own position.

Morrison did assert that baptism is "an act of grace" (*MB,* p. 157), but while he spelled out what it means to call baptism a social act, he did not indicate what it means to say that it is an act of grace. Because the social-functional view predominates in this book, his contention that baptism is an initiation rite is much more evident. While he did probably not want to say that baptism is merely an initiation rite, his view cuts in that direction.

In his Rauschenbusch lectures at Colgate-Rochester Divinity School, Morrison's approach almost mirrored that taken by Rauschenbusch's *Theology for the Social Gospel.* Rauschenbusch begins this book by claiming that "we have a social gospel." What we need, he goes on to say, is "a systematic theology large enough to match it and vital enough to back it."[78] Giving practice total precedence over theory, Rauschenbusch consistently asked of every theological idea whether it would support the Social Gospel, never

76. William E. Tucker and Lester G. McAllister, *Journey in Faith: A History of the Christian Church (Disciples of Christ)* (St. Louis: Bethany Press, 1975), p. 328.

77. Morrison, *The Meaning of Baptism* (Chicago: Disciples Publication Society, 1914), pp. 7ff.; subsequent references to this volume will be made parenthetically in the text, using the abbreviation *MB.*

78. Rauschenbusch, *A Theology for the Social Gospel* (New York: Macmillan, 1917), p. 1.

whether it was appropriate to the Christian faith or whether it was credible. He assumed that the function of theology was to justify what he already knew ought to be done. And this is how Morrison proceeds in *The Social Gospel and the Christian Cultus*. Christianity, he declares, has a "new gospel and an old cultus."[79] The Social Gospel has been arrested by an "inflexible and static" cultus that is well on the way to becoming sterile (*SG*, p. 31). Accordingly, Morrison's thesis was that "if catastrophe is to be averted, the Christian cultus must be radically and thoroughly reconstructed so that the social gospel may be made to feel at home within it" (*SG*, p. 33). The liturgy had to be recreated "so that the social imperative may be explicitly related to the will of God" (*SG*, p. 45). "Nothing short of a revolution in the whole Christian cultus will meet the demands of the new day" (*SG*, p. 54).

Theology, too, was disintegrating and required adaptation to the Social Gospel for its own survival (*SG*, p. 81). It had to learn an idiom capable of "convey[ing] the social aspiration of our time" (*SG*, p. 90). Further, the church as a social organization had to be retooled to be an adequate carrier of the Social Gospel; the churches had to become genuinely ecumenical: "It is the coming of the social gospel, which is the gospel of the kingdom, that is causing the churches to draw together in the hope of realizing organic unity" (*SG*, p. 137). Sectarianism bars effective actualization of the Social Gospel: "The social gospel waits upon the creation of a church competent to practice it" (*SG*, p. 140).

Christianity's ethics had to expand to encompass the Social Gospel. The church "must either assume its unique ethical responsibility or be regarded as a cumberer of the ground, an opiate of the people" (*SG*, p. 150). Protestantism had to cut its alliance with the capitalist system to which it has capitulated (*SG*, p. 155). It could recapture its ethical autonomy only by rediscovering "the mind of Christ" (*SG*, pp. 172, 97) — that is, of the historical Jesus. Writing in the depths of the Great Depression, Morrison contended that in the earliest church the Social Gospel took priority over alternative understandings of religion: "The early Christian movement was as passionately social — in its way — as is the communist enterprise in Russia" (*SG*, p. 186). "The Christian gospel in its first proclamation," Morrison avowed, "was a social gospel" (*SG*, p. 191).

Throughout, Morrison contended that the Christian cultus had to recover its autonomy. The church had to release itself from its own capitulation to the state (its Constantinian tendency) and to business (its dependence on capitalism). The church's readiness to support war, to provide chaplains to the military, to warrant nationalism, and to give comfort to capitalists while ignoring the plight of workers all testified to Protestantism's status "as the private chaplain of both the state and the economic system," a situation that did much to account for Protestantism's decadence (*SG*, p. 245).

---

79. Morrison, *The Social Gospel and the Christian Cultus* (New York: Harper, 1948), p. 3; subsequent references to this volume will be made parenthetically in the text, using the abbreviation *SG*.

Reinhold Niebuhr was no less a critic of the church on these points than was Morrison. In light of the churches' shameful support, on all sides, of World War I and their lack of response to the Depression, Morrison's book can be read as genuinely prophetic. The problem is that he never specified what the "autonomy" of Christian faith consists in except for the Social Gospel. Obviously, this was his norm of moral plausibility, but he did not test it in this book by bringing it into conversation with distinct norms of appropriateness to the Christian faith and credibility.

Therefore we turn to his 1940 book, *What Is Christianity?* with some expectation. In this volume Morrison sought to define Christianity "as a phenomenon."[80] Consideration of its generic characteristics led him to the conclusion that Christianity "is the revelation of God in *history*" (*WIC*, p. 21). In its sectarian phase, Protestantism abandoned the revelation of God in history in exchange for ideology, and liberalism in turn abandoned ideology in exchange for psychology (*WIC*, p. 28). Morrison understood history as primarily a "living historical continuum" in which events and movements occur and from which they cannot be isolated (*WIC*, p. 44). It "is the continuum of human community, which exhibits itself to us as multiple orders or strands of particular continuing communities" (*WIC*, p. 54). On revelation, Morrison wrote, "I do not know that I can define it without raising questions which do not lie within the scope of our present inquiry" (*WIC*, p. 54). He denied, however, that revelation is primarily a disclosure of cognitive truth to the intellect, preferring to talk of it as "an activity of God manifesting itself in events in history through the medium of a historical community whose corporate life is oriented toward him" (*WIC*, p. 58).

We move closer to a definition with the observation that Christianity is "the historical community which conceives itself as the divine revelation" but which is not "a racial, or national, or class community, but a universalistic community whose character is determined on the one hand by its potential inclusiveness of all men because they are children of God, and on the other hand by the person of Jesus Christ, whose place as the head of the Christian community determines the internal character of the community's life and defines its saving work in the total life of mankind" (*WIC*, p. 64). Cults of nation, of blood and soil, such as Shinto, fascism, and nazism, "do have, in form at least, certain elements of kinship with Christianity at the time of its emergence in history, that is, with primitive Judaism. No doubt Judaism, which is the mother of Christianity, began essentially as a religion of blood and soil. The tragedy which has overtaken it in history consists of the fact that, even to this day, Jewry has not been able to separate its religion from its particular racial consciousness" (*WIC*, p. 65). This quotation is cited here not only because it indicates how Morrison's mind was working two years after *Kristallnacht* but also for the light it sheds on his understanding of Christianity.

---

80. Morrison, *What Is Christianity?* (Chicago: Willett, Clark, 1940), p. 10; subsequent references to this volume will be made parenthetically in the text, using the abbreviation *WIC*.

Morrison's anti-Judaism becomes clear when we note how he worked out his understanding of the church as the revelation of God in history. Because he understood history as a continuum and refused to take historical events out of context, Morrison began his discussion in the context of the history of Israel. Jesus of Nazareth "appeared in a history, in a specific historical continuum which was itself the revelation of God" (*WIC*, p. 88). He did not come into history from beyond it, nor could he have appeared in any other historical continuum. "He would have gone unrecognized had he appeared in Rome or in Greece. He could not have found twelve disciples in the whole Hellenic world outside of Jewry — nor three, nor one" (*WIC*, p. 88). We are required to affirm the "unqualified solidarity of Jesus with the community that bore him" (*WIC*, p. 89).

This looks like a promising beginning for understanding Christianity in relation to Judaism, but observe his development of the subject. Christianity should not reject Judaism, Morrison insisted, because "it is the true Israel . . . the Israel which rejected Christianity was untrue to itself and to the divine purpose which had called it out from the nations to be the revealer of God to all mankind" (*WIC*, p. 89). The religion of Israel, unfortunately, was founded "upon their inalienable corporate self-consciousness as a racial and national community which had emerged in history for the accomplishment of the divine purpose" (*WIC*, p. 95). Therefore, although "there would have been no Christianity had there been no Judaism" (*WIC*, p. 96), and although all the great Christian ideas were borrowed from Judaism (*WIC*, p. 98), nonetheless the significance of Jesus is "that he saved Judaism . . . by separating it from Jewry" (*WIC*, p. 108). He "plucked the heart of Israel's faith from the breast of racial Israel" and handed over to the whole world the revelation of God in Israel (*WIC*, p. 109). In this way he saved God's revelation in history for history, "though the house of Israel was left desolate" (*WIC*, p. 109). Jesus did this by preaching "the abandonment of the religion of blood and soil in obedience to the ethical and universal will of God. This preaching Israel would not heed" (*WIC*, pp. 109-10). Its "vast illusion . . . of its racial superiority" could not be overcome (*WIC*, p. 110). Over against this Israel, Jesus "set another Israel. He called it the Kingdom of God. It was the *true* Israel" (*WIC*, p. 112). His only concern with historical Israel was to destroy it; the eschatological catastrophe that he anticipated "was not the violent crushing of Israel's oppressors, but the crushing of Israel itself" (*WIC*, p. 113).

His 1942 book, *The Christian and the War,* repeats these themes. In Jesus Christ God did not break into history; "it would be closer to the Christian truth to say that in Christ God 'broke out of' or 'broke through' history."[81] Here, too, he showed his awareness of the Nazi claim to a religion of "blood and soil," which he had already attributed to Jewry. Morrison's theme of Jesus' opposition to Israel's hope of liberation from oppression explained, in his view,

---

81. Morrison, *The Christian and the War* (Chicago: Willett, Clark, 1942), p. 33.

the antipathy to which Jesus' preaching gave rise: "The proposal of Jesus encountered opposition from every partisan group in Israel — the militant Zealots, the super-pious Pharisees, the opportunistic Sadducees — and it made them all his enemies" (*WIC*, p. 117). He waged a lonely, frontal attack "upon Israel's fanaticism and vanity" (*WIC*, p. 117). What traditional theology called the "work of Christ," which was to save us from sin and death, was assigned a new meaning by Morrison. What Jesus did "was to create a church — the Church of the Remnant" (*WIC*, p. 126). This new, organic community, with himself as its head, is the true Israel, "a community not bound by racial and national pride but, with Christ as its center and head, destined to embody the inner meaning of Israel's orientation toward God" (*WIC*, p. 135). The work which Jesus started was brought to completion by Paul, who emancipated "the Christian community from racial Judaism" and transformed "the concept of an absentee Messiah into the concept of the incarnation" (*WIC*, p. 149). He cut through Jewish particularism and made straight the way to the Gentile mind (*WIC*, p. 150).

Throughout *What Is Christianity?* Morrison is in conversation with theologians of major importance at the time, notably Barth, Bultmann, and Troeltsch. He rejects Barth's understanding of the relation of God to history, Bultmann's understanding of history, and Troeltsch's relativism in favor of his own view of historical revelation. A more rigorous conversation with these thinkers might have helped Morrison temper his anti-Judaism and led him to see the inappropriateness of defining the Christian community as *itself* the revelation of God in history (*WIC*, p. 64), a theological mistake which Barth, Bultmann, and Troeltsch would not make. Morrison's alternative, defining Christianity as other than Jewish, anti-Jewish, and better than Jewish, fails to improve on traditional Christian anti-Judaism.

In his last two books, Morrison returns to his favorite theme, ecumenism. In 1948 he published *Can Protestantism Win America?* and in 1953 *The Unfinished Reformation.* In the former he argues that Protestantism has two serious rivals for the soul of America — Roman Catholicism and secularism — each of which is incompatible with the other two.[82] Protestantism itself, Morrison argued, was in a weakened condition in relation to Roman Catholicism and secularism. Quantitatively, it was in decline; qualitatively, its interior life was waning in spiritual depth, in an intelligent grasp of its faith, and in the bonds that make for its solidarity (*CP*, p. 6). No longer ascendant in American culture, Protestantism faced a more complex situation than obtained in the era of Puritanism (*CP*, p. 13). Also, in secularism and Roman Catholicism it faced two "magnitudes which have risen over against it," whose strength could not be doubted (*CP*, p. 15).

Protestantism had lost the public school to secularism (*CP*, pp. 17-32), and

---

82. Morrison, *Can Protestantism Win America?* (New York: Harper, 1949), p. 1; subsequent references to this volume will be made parenthetically in the text, using the abbreviation *CP*.

Morrison advocated instituting "departments in the pedagogy of Religion" (*CP*, p. 27) to correct the religious illiteracy of young people. Each community or parish should institute a parochial school, because "if Protestantism is to win America it must take up the religious education of its children with the same seriousness which characterized its churches before the public school came into existence" (*CP*, p. 31). Also, Protestantism had to "win science" if it was to win America. The point was not to win America from science but to win science from secularism and from the value-neutral attitude toward its accomplishments (such as the atom bomb). Protestantism was the only religion that could win science, because only it could create the world community necessary to the proper harnessing of science and only it could live together with science intellectually (*CP*, p. 40).

With Roman Catholicism, Protestantism struggled with a "magnitude" that had a clear psychological advantage over it. "It offers to fill the vacuum with only the barest minimum of responsible reflection and decision on the part of the individual" (*CP*, p. 61). Roman Catholicism was "a system of irresponsible and authoritarian power — a kind of power which no human institution should presume to possess and exercise, a power which is radically incompatible with both Christianity and democracy, and which carries within itself the seeds of its own destruction" (*CP*, p. 64). It was "a monarchical and feudal institution," and "the perfect embodiment of the principle of fascism" (*CP*, p. 64). It dominated national and state politics and made great inroads into "organized labor and the Negroes" (*CP*, p. 72).

Clearly, Protestantism, in Morrison's eyes, had its work cut out for it. It had to learn to "live in the modern world" (*CP*, p. 81) and overcome its sectarianized, localized, and individualized mindset. It had to gather to itself both the organization and technique necessary to gain the respect of the collectivities that dominated the landscape of America (*CP*, p. 83). Its task was to *"confront the contemporary scene as if the Christianization of America depended, under God, upon it alone"* (*CP*, p. 86; italics Morrison's). It had no hope of doing this if it remained liberal in its theological outlook. America was secularized and liberalism "played into the hands of secularism by offering it a Christianity which was itself secularized" (*CP*, p. 89).

Moreover, Protestantism was not ready. It held a false tolerance for other religions, failed in its divisions to express the power of the Christian faith, and had never developed a conscience with respect to its unity in Christ (*CP*, pp. 91-101). Localism and denominationalism wasted its power. Its economic power was swallowed up by congregational and denominational expenses that supported the staffs of some 230 headquarters.

If Protestantism was to win America, said Morrison, it had to ecumenize! Sectarianized Protestantism was neither big nor efficient enough for the job. While cooperation in councils of churches and some denominational mergers were steps in the right direction, what was demanded was *"an ecumenical church now"* (*CP*, p. 165). Asserting that the only authority under which such a church could operate was that of Christ himself, Morrison urged that all differences over belief and practice be defined as part of the "fellowship" of the church and not its "constitution," thereby muting the theological dimension of ecumenism (*CP,* pp. 181ff.). And he insisted that ecumenism did not extend to Catholicism: "Protestantism can never have ecclesiastical fellowship with a church which maintains itself as a system of irresponsible power derived from the abject submission of its members" (*CP,* p. 211).

Morrison's conception of ecumenism was thoroughgoingly utilitarian. The issue was whether the culture of America would be Protestant, Roman Catholic, or secular (*CP,* p. 216). If the outcome was to be favorable, Protestantism would have to overcome its weakness and actualize its potential strength by reawakening to its ecumenical commitment "as a moral imperative" (*CP,* p. 216). In this book, Morrison's whole concern with ecumenism was that it was instrumental in doing the job of winning America.

Morrison further developed his understanding of ecumenism in *The Unfinished Reformation.* Here he no longer gave a merely instrumental justification for ecumenism but contended instead that it was the "will of God" that "the Church of Christ should be one church."[83] His argument was based on the Reformation. First, he reasoned that the Reformation was an ecumenical movement but that its commitment to church unity was thwarted by a continuing acceptance of the interdependence of church and state and by attempts to achieve unity through theological agreement (*UR,* p. 17). The magisterial Reformers did not seek to split the church but to liberate it "from its bondage to a sacerdotal authoritarian hierarchy" (*UR,* p. 23). Ecumenism in our time, he argued, is the church's awakening to the fact that it has inherited "an unfinished reformation," that "under the divine judgment . . . [it] is perennially in need of reformation (*UR,* p. 27).

Morrison then criticized denominationalism, and in his critique we find the reason for his refusal to give a "merely" instrumental justification for ecumenism. In his dissection of denominationalism he basically repeats what he said in *Can Protestantism Win America?* Denominationalism (1) wastes resources, (2) is embarrassing on the mission field, (3) frustrates the Social Gospel, (4) weakens Protestantism in its competition with Roman Catholicism, (5) provincializes the Protestant mentality, (6) creates moral insincerity among Protestants, (7) localizes congregations, (8) hampers ministers, and (9) denies the freedom that is in Christ by confusing it with denominational freedom (*UR,* pp. 28-29). A united church would release us from denominational uniformity into ecumenical diversity (*UR,* p. 81), from bondage to denominational class systems into the inspiring fellowship of a classless church (*UR,* p. 83). Congregations would become manifestations of the ecumenical church in a particular locality (*UR,* p. 89), and all Christians would be free to be ourselves and to appropriate the spiritual heritage of the whole church (*UR,* p. 96).

---

83. Morrison, *The Unfinished Reformation* (New York: Harper, 1953), pp. 1, 7; subsequent references to this volume will be made parenthetically in the text, using the abbreviation *UR.*

Such unity was still staunchly Protestant, in all respects unlike Roman Catholic unity. What he wanted was the "realization of the ecumenical intention of the Reformation itself" (*UR*, p. 100). Such Protestant unity would assure the "personal fulfillment" of individual Christians, not their "depersonalization" (*UR*, p. 105). It would be a unity of diversity, not uniformity (*UR*, p. 110), and its morality would be one of "personal depth and dignity," not one that is "superficial" (*UR*, p. 113).

Morrison caps off his book with a discussion of loyalty and freedom in a united church, a criticism of restorationism, and an analysis of three major obstacles to church unity (the historic episcopate, immersion baptism, and polities of congregational autonomy). His proposals in these regards are sage and worthy of consideration.

While *The Unfinished Reformation* may be said to begin better than it ends, in that Morrison here comes closer than elsewhere to articulating a critical principle or norm of appropriateness in the light of which he offers criticisms and proposals for church life, nonetheless the instrumentalist approach to Protestant unity and the anti-Catholicism of his earlier work persevere in this one. The anti-Catholicism may be somewhat relativized by remembering that he was talking about pre–Vatican II Catholicism, which was indeed different from the Roman Catholic Church today. Yet it is anomalous that Morrison could espouse such a narrow ecumenical vision and fail so thoroughly to see the promise and possibility that ecumenical discussion with Roman Catholics might hold. Visionary as he was with regard to Protestantism, Morrison could not envision a different future for and with Roman Catholicism.

CONCLUSION

What we have seen in this study of Disciples theology is a problem that plagues all theology. Properly understood, theology seeks to criticize and revise the Christian tradition in the light of a set of distinct but related norms. That is, theology works with norms of appropriateness to the Christian faith, credibility, and moral plausibility. Every adequate theology must defend some interpretation of all three norms as well as some interpretation of the situation to which it would have the Christian tradition, so criticized and revised, speak.

The difficulty is that while these norms are distinct but not separable, in practice they often fall apart. In theory it is quite clear that if a position is clearly immoral, it must also fail to be appropriate to the Christian faith. Likewise, it is clear that unintelligible utterances are also inappropriate (since we cannot make sense of them, they cannot even be argued). In the heat of theological conflict, however, it is common for this set of three interrelated norms to fail to hold together. Hence, when liberalism threatens to lose sight altogether of the gospel of Jesus Christ, meanwhile claiming to make sense and to be morally plausible, there can occur a neo-Reformation reaction that throws credibility and moral plausibility to the winds and claims that the only task of theology is to criticize the witness of the church in the light of some norm of appropriateness. Likewise, when some form of fundamentalist or classicist theology claims to be the only appropriate bearer of the tradition, thinkers concerned to make intellectual and moral sense may, in effect, abandon concerns for appropriateness in favor of intelligibility or moral plausibility.

Exactly this seems to have happened in the period of Disciples theology here under review. Thinkers like McGarvey laid claim to the Disciples tradition and held that they were interpreting it appropriately. The content of their norms of appropriateness were narrow and provided a clear sense of identity, but they prevented real conversation with thinkers concerned with intelligibility and moral plausibility. In reaction, other Disciples thinkers concerned themselves almost exclusively with matters of intelligibility and morality, paying scarcely any heed to questions of appropriateness. We cannot quibble with their concerns in these regards, although we are not compelled today to agree with them as to what constitutes intelligibility and moral plausibility. What we cannot fail to note, however, is that Disciples today, sharing similar concerns, particularly with moral plausibility, have little capacity to think critically about matters of appropriateness or identity and remain vulnerable to fundamentalist backlashes on that score. What is needed is a genuine revival of critical and constructive theological reflection that seeks to work with criteria of relative adequacy with regard to all three issues — those of appropriateness to the gospel, breadth of intelligibility, and moral plausibility.

Disciples Theologizing amid Currents of Mainstream Protestant Thought, 1940 to 1980: Sketchbook Observations

James O. Duke, with Joseph D. Driskill

We attempt here to sketch the efforts made by a number of Disciples scholars between 1940 and 1980 to address the principal concerns of the field of systematic theology. It must be readily admitted that at this late date, 1989, the "principal concerns of systematic theology" are whether there is any such field and, if so, what its principal concerns are. But not so very long ago systematics was commonly known for its critical and constructive dealings with such perennial theological problems as foundations and methodology and the question of authority; God; christology; the Spirit; theological anthropology; ecclesiology; and creation, redemption, and "last things." Disciples scholars with something to say about these matters are our chief interest.

To cover what all of them had to say would take more than a sketch. We have had to be selective. It is an open secret that since the word *theology* was long taboo among Disciples, the history of Disciples theology has to be reconstructed from a mass of literature falsely called "nontheological." The lifting of the taboo during the last half of the twentieth century gave us our theme, "scholars confess to be theologians." Highlighting "the theologians" with a public(ation) record, our sketch brings into view the placement and character of their work in the context of mainstream Protestant thought.

Ours is then a modest handling of this topic. Scholarship is by no means the only form or index of theological reflection in the church, and the concerns of systematic theology are by no means the whole of theology, but these are nonetheless matters that deserve some attention. Although it is hard to speak with any assurance of what "the church" (not to mention "the unchurched") expects from its theologians, they have been permanent fixtures within mainstream Protestantism. Since Disciples came to accept them on much the same

139

terms as other mainstream Protestants did, their work has a place in the story of this church.[1]

THE POSTWAR LIBERAL DILEMMA

Shortly after the end of World War II, the United States experienced a phenomenal upsurge of interest in religion. To mainline Protestants the post-war boom brought, along with much else, a "theological renaissance." This episode in the history of Christian thought featured a mixed assortment of theological alternatives to liberalism and fundamentalism, the most prominent of which may be called for simplicity's sake "realistic" and "neo-orthodox" theologies.[2]

The Disciples emerged from the war as a mainstream Protestant denomination within American Christianity's denominational system, though neither the term *denomination* nor *system* was altogether to their liking. For roughly two decades they were to gain their fair share of the rewards — growth, prosperity, esprit de corps — that came with the postwar boom. To do so, they had to respond to a long list of challenges from building starts and beatniks to world mission(s) and war and peace. It was more a sense of urgency than complacency that for a time kept "the brotherhood" intact despite its serious internal discord. The code words of dissension — "Unity or Restoration," "Cooperative or Independent," and "Liberal or Conservative" — were known to all. As some Disciples promoted bold new programmatic initiatives, others warned that such changes jeopardized the historic "plea" to restore primitive Christianity.

Among the initiatives were efforts to expand, upgrade, and mainstream education for those who sought ordination. To provide a theological education justly called second to none, Disciples needed educators, teacher-scholars, on a par with those in the graduate seminaries that served the other mainstream Protestant churches. This need was met, following a well-established pattern, by faculty appointments of Disciples (and sometimes others) with advanced work at the Ph.D.-granting institutions of mainstream Protestantism. In due course "Cooperatives" claimed five fully accredited denomi-

---

1. See George G. Beazley, Jr., "Who Are the Disciples?" and Ronald W. Osborn, "Theology among the Disciples," both in *Christian Church (Disciples of Christ): An Interpretative Examination in the Cultural Context,* ed. George G. Beazley, Jr. (St. Louis: Bethany Press, 1973), pp. 5-80 and 81-115; and James O. Duke, "Scholarship in the Disciples Tradition," *Disciples Theological Digest* 1 (1986): 5-40.

2. These variegated trends went by many other names: dialectical theology, Word-of-God theology, Christian realism, neo-Reformation theology, existential theology, crisis theology, biblical theology, and ecumenical theology. Neo-empirical and neonaturalistic theologies were often classified among the new forms of "theological realism."

national seminaries as well as four "houses" affiliated with well-known Protestant schools.[3]

Disciples faculty members on a par with their professional peers were obliged to undertake critical inquiry, engage in ecumenical dialogue, and adjudicate the claims of Christianity and modern culture. For all but a few, signing up for such duties meant making common cause with the liberal-leaning rather than the restorationist wing of their church. Upon entering the world of postwar theological scholarship, these Disciples confronted a dilemma of the first order. To be a Disciples liberal was to disavow theology in favor of free scholarly inquiry, but to engage in free scholarly inquiry was to contend with theological critiques of liberalism at nearly every turn.

Consider, for example, what Edward Scribner Ames — the most eminent of the Disciples liberal scholars — had to say in his 1945 article "The Disciples Are Modernists."[4] To Ames, neo-orthodoxy was simply "revived Protestant Fundamentalism," and the fame of Barth, Brunner, and, "with some qualifications," Reinhold Niebuhr merely confirmed that "the old creedal theology" lies in the background of the great Protestant denominations. Disciples, he observed approvingly, cared little for neo-orthodoxy: they were, after all, modernists by birthright and by choice.

As Ames read history, they had been modernists since their founding, long before the word had been coined, and loyalists were still true to their origins.

> They vigorously rejected Catholicism and the scholastic theology. With equal vigor they discarded protestant theology, all creeds and ecclesiasticisms, and accepted the Bible as viewed in the early stages of higher criticism, and modern science as the method of useful and fruitful knowledge. They sought and taught the *"reasonableness* of Christianity" and gained amazing success in its advocacy for a hundred years. They are still motivated by the hope of cultivating Christian union upon a non-dogmatic basis.

Theirs was a "movement" created not by the Reformation, but the Renaissance, the Enlightenment, and frontier America, where pioneers "matched the political democracy of their day with a free, democratic, religious faith." As such, it had no need or desire for any dealings with neo-orthodoxies. Here, of course, Ames was offering less a studied commentary on the past than a manifesto for the future, a preemptive strike on the second half of what liberals envisioned to be "the(ir) Christian Century." Though not even many of his best friends

---

3. Butler School of Religion, now Christian Theological Seminary; College of the Bible, now Lexington Theological Seminary; Drake, Phillips, and Brite Divinity School of Texas Christian University. The houses were at Chicago, Claremont, Vanderbilt, and Yale.

4. Ames, "The Disciples Are Modernists," *The Scroll* 42 (1945): 289-98; see especially pp. 293-94, 298. Illuminating comments on the responses of Disciples liberals to the new theological climate are found in Samuel C. Pearson, Jr., "The Campbell Institute: Herald of the Transformation of an American Religious Tradition," *The Scroll* 62 (1978): 1-63; see especially pp. 34-42.

shared his fondness for the term *modernism,* he had not become the patron saint of liberal Disciples without cause. In essentials, his views of the heritage and commitments of the Disciples were only liberal commonplaces. Staking out an advanced position against restorationism, Ames had time and again helped make his church safe for cooperatives, for liberals, and for scholars.

But not for "theological" scholars. And this is why his article — though brief, popularized, and tendentious — is of more than passing interest. It is one thing to reject Catholicism, "the scholastic theology," and "all creeds and ecclesiasticisms." It is quite another to dispense with Protestant theology per se. At the very moment mainstream Protestants were gearing up for a "theological renaissance," Disciples were setting out to build theological faculties second to none, and neo-orthodoxies were on the way to prominence, Ames warned that to bother with Protestant theology was to act in a manner unbecoming Disciples.

There is perhaps some comfort in recalling that Ames, like Campbell and Stone, was opposed to creedalism, dogmatism, and speculation, not serious thinking about religion. In retrospect, however, this point — true as it is — is small comfort indeed. No church can wage a hundred years' war against theology and come through the ordeal unscathed. Disciples had tapped into American anti-intellectualism, a reservoir whose waters never run dry. Liberals, before and after Ames, would be quick to note the anti-intellectual impulse at work in restorationism. But who then was left to detect its workings within liberalism, with its advocacy of an utterly simple gospel, a thoroughly practical Christianity, and an altogether nondogmatic unity?

The Amesian either/or — to be a Disciples scholar or a Protestant theologian — was to have some long-lasting effects. Of the fair number of Disciples who went on to become theological scholars, few became "theologians" by trade, and few of them systematicians. So long as liberals and restorationists agreed that Disciples history contained no "Protestant theology" at all, those who took an interest in the issues of systematic theology were left to fend for themselves, orphaned by their own tradition. And they would have liberal associates no less than restorationists to keep them ever mindful that their studies must never be so systematic, so theological, or so scholarly as to be impractical.

The liberal dilemma might have completely blocked any aspiring Disciples educator from coming to grips with the new trends in theology were it not for guidance from veteran scholars other than Ames. Two — Charles Clayton Morrison and William Robinson — were especially important in this regard.

Morrison's contribution was an alternate reading of neo-orthodoxy. His 1950 article in the *Christian Century,* "The Liberalism of Neo-Orthodoxy," amounted to a public censure of Ames's view: "To identify the new theological movement as a revival of the orthodoxy of the traditional creeds represents a failure to discern its most inward characteristics." These, Morrison said, were at base the further workings of the spirit of critical inquiry that was the hallmark of genuine liberalism. The target of neo-orthodox attack was not this but an "arrested liberalism" with a fixation on certain time-bound notions that it then held to be immune to critical re-examination.[5]

Right or wrong, Morrison's interpretation of neo-orthodoxy gave Disciples the green light to adapt to the newer currents of thought. How to do so, and why, were lessons taught not by Morrison but by another senior scholar, William Robinson. Robinson had realized, long before Morrison, that the "new theology" was neither uncritical nor anticritical. He also recognized that it was to be taken seriously for reasons other than this. Robinson saw in it a renewed awareness of the sovereignty of God and with it a sense of grateful appreciation for the means that God had provided for the salvation of sinful humanity. Its chief motifs — biblical theology, an existential emphasis, and an eschatological note — were in his view the essentials of a critical orthodoxy deeper than that of any scholasticism. It was along these lines, and at this level, that Robinson worked out his own theological proposals.

In so doing he was functioning as a Protestant theologian who was at the same time fully and truly a Disciple. He was able to do so because he looked at Disciples history with a revisionist eye. He was convinced that the emphases essential to orthodoxy at its deeper level and prominent in ecumenical discussion were manifest in the works of such nineteenth-century thinkers as Coleridge, Maurice, and Alexander Campbell. To his credit, Robinson never claimed that Campbell was a theological superstar; he merely noted — as no one else had — that he took Protestant theology very seriously, that his own thinking was now and again theologically insightful, and that his "new reformation" was a high-church movement in which the church's doctrine, structure, and means of grace were valued.[6]

How a Disciples theological educator surely more "typical" of the class than Ames, Morrison, or Robinson coped with the postwar dilemma can be seen in two related publications by T. Hassell Bowen. The first, "A Disciple Looks at Theology," appeared in 1948. Echoes of Ames are clear. Insisting that Disciples had always held that "Christianity is essentially a way of life, not a way of theology," Bowen advised that neo-orthodoxy is a threat to "the plea" so dire that "Disciples cannot be true to themselves if they make peace with it."

Yet Bowen parted company with Ames. He urged Disciples to counter this threat by rededicating themselves to theological inquiry. Only by means of systematic thinking could Disciples identify, defend, and commend the set of beliefs inherent in the way of life and the "plea" to which they were committed. The necessity of such thinking was acknowledged by the founders of the Disciples, who as members of "the Arminian branch of protestant theology" engaged in theology under a different name. Bowen also took a

5. Morrison, "The Liberalism of Neo-Orthodoxy," *Christian Century,* 7, 14, and 21 June 1950, p. 697.

6. See, e.g., chap. 1 of Robinson's *Whither Theology? Some Essential Biblical Patterns* (London: Lutterworth Press, 1947); and "Three Recent Movements in the Field of Theology," *Shane Quarterly* 13 (1952): 5-30.

slightly more nuanced, Morrisonian view of neo-orthodoxy. His critique of neo-orthodoxy was tempered by the view that it represented a corrective to certain "excesses" of liberalism that was in some respects an ally in the attempt on the part of Disciples to promote biblically based Christianity.[7]

Where Bowen situated his own theology — and where he hoped others might position themselves — became clear exactly one decade later in "Contemporary Theology and the Modern Minister." His aim was to orient ministers to the three currently leading types of theology: humanism, neo-orthodoxy, and realistic thought. The second of the three parts of this essay repeats the text of a 1948 lecture almost in toto, though revisions show that Bowen was now well aware that Bultmann and Tillich were hardly neo-orthodox purists. Of main interest is his description of the three varieties of realistic thought: atheistic realism, naturalistic or theistic realism (e.g., Whitehead and Wieman), and Christian realism (the Niebuhr brothers, Walter Horton, John C. Bennett, et al.). Bowen cast his lot with the theistic and Christian realists and suggested that by starting out from this base camp, Disciples could move on toward a genuinely biblical realism.[8]

Bowen's "biblical realism" never matured into a theological program. His lectures, however, were signs of the times. A number of Disciples went on to become theological scholars. In the seminaries, what had been the lone faculty post in Christian doctrine or the philosophy of religion was renamed "theology," and in most cases one or more additional slots were opened up. By the end of the decade an "Association of Disciples for Theological Discussion" had formed, and the church had mandated an ad hoc "Panel of Scholars" to diagnose its theological health. The issues, motifs, and above all the telltale vocabulary of the theological renaissance gained relatively widespread currency.

These changes did not represent a neo-orthodox takeover that swept liberalism from the field. They were the results of the mainstreaming of theological education, which brought increased numbers of teacher-scholars determined to hold their own among their peers. Classical liberalism lived on. Yet the weight of scholarly opinion had tilted.

Even before the war, the Anglo-American tradition of philosophy and theology took a neo-empirical and, with Henry Nelson Wieman, a theocentric turn. In the fifties came blendings of this "radical empiricism" and Whiteheadian process thought (e.g., Wieman, Bernard Loomer, Bernard Meland, and Daniel Day Williams), some in their own way as "realistic" in their estimates of the relationship between God and humanity as the neo-orthodoxies.

Moreover, as time passed the realization grew that "neo-orthodoxy" was no more than a handy catch-all category for a wide range of theological

---

7. See Bowen, "As a Disciple Looks at Theology," *College of the Bible Quarterly* 25 (1948): 3-18; see especially pp. 3, 7.

8. See Bowen, "Contemporary Theology and the Modern Minister: Three Lectures," *College of the Bible Quarterly* 35 (1958): 1-96.

programs. The careers of Rudolf Bultmann, Reinhold Niebuhr, and Paul Tillich, for example, had led them to positions far removed from any easy association with Barth, Brunner, or even one another. Since each of them kept up a critical dialogue with "modernity," they seemed to confirm Morrison's view that theirs was a deepening and broadening of the liberal tradition.

These mediating forms of liberalism on the one hand and neo-orthodoxy on the other were the theological options to which Disciples scholars, especially those who came of age in the fifties, tended to gravitate. Even so, the point remains that what came into favor was less one or another of these contemporary schools of thought than it was "the issues, themes, and telltale vocabulary" of the theological renaissance.

By the mid-fifties, "theology" had become a somewhat broader church-wide concern. Illustrative of this development were two sets of reports by study committees of the World Convention of Churches of Christ (Disciples). Under the title *Doctrines of the Christian Faith,* each set dealt with six topics — the first (1955) with the nature of the church, the place of theology in the church, baptism, the Lord's Supper, ministry, and hope; the second (1961) with evangelism, Christian unity, authority and revelation, christology, the congregation and the body of Christ, and Christian ethics.[9]

The reports indicated how "the church" itself was moving to overcome its postwar dilemma. The study on the role of theology stressed that this was an issue Disciples could not escape and then went on to contest the Amesian reading of church history:

> It is sometimes held that we have no theology and that we are opposed to the theological enterprise. This was clearly not true of our early leaders, many of whom were competent theologians. . . . They did not question whether theological formulation had a legitimate place. They did maintain that theology should be kept within its limits and usefulness; namely, as a clear affirmation of one's faith and a stimulus to a mutual sharing of understanding of a common revelation.

The report concluded that their heritage did not forbid but rather encouraged Disciples to engage in theology, insofar as the field was defined as "conversation and recital in biblical terms" and had as its focus the facts of revelation, creation, and redemption with the person of Jesus Christ at their center.[10]

Contemporary critiques of liberalism were dealt with by recasting historic Disciples views, once routinely phrased in restorationist or liberal idiom, in the language of current ecumenical discussion. The Campbell-Stone stress on the

---

9. *Doctrines of the Christian Faith: Six Reports by Study Committees of the World Convention of Churches of Christ (Disciples), 1955* (St. Louis: Christian Board of Publication, 1955); *Doctrines of the Christian Faith (Edinburgh Study Pamphlets): Six Reports by the Study Committee of the World Convention of Churches of Christ (Disciples), 1961* (St. Louis: Christian Board of Publication, 1961).

10. "The Place of Theology in the Church," in *Doctrines of the Christian Faith* (1955), p. 6.

oneness of the church is explained in terms of its paradoxical reality — its divine and human elements, its universality and locality, the continuity of its mission and the variability of its structure. In like fashion, what was once called the "simple gospel" was now called "the kerygma," and "no creed but Christ" was said to express an existential relation between Christ and the believer.

Historic Disciples practices such as believer's baptism by immersion and weekly communion were upheld by appealing to their theological meaning rather than legalistic or pragmatic considerations. Though "sacramentalism" was (again) repudiated, it was now noted that the two "ordinances" indeed have a certain sacramental status inasmuch as their "symbolic" meaning involves an awareness of the gracious action of God.

Eager to permit — and wherever possible to reconcile — a wide range of theological opinion, none of the study groups managed to achieve a systematically coherent formulation of church doctrine. In most cases what resulted was an alloy of varied and even discordant elements. The report on the person and work of Christ, for example, argues that the kerygma ("the Christ-event") necessitates a doctrine of incarnation, but readers are then asked to ponder the meaning of the two-natures doctrine. At length a patently liberal suggestion emerges: the presence of God in the person of Jesus Christ is the "attainment of a climax in a spiritual process," in that the spirit of God "imminnent [*sic*] in men" came to dwell in him without measure as "the perfect receptacle for the Spirit."[11]

In short, the reports bear the telltale marks of theology by committee, but they were a bold venture in corporate theologizing nonetheless. Disciples were ready to try their hand at formulating church doctrine and to admit that this was what they were doing.

The centerpiece of the theological renaissance within the church was the work of the Panel of Scholars (1958-62), printed in a three-volume set of reports entitled *The Renewal of the Church*. W. B. Blakemore, Jr., the Panel's chair, did his best to ease the fears of an audience unaccustomed to theology. First came reassurances that Disciples considered the Scriptures a "sufficient guide" in matters of belief; then came word that the times called for new ways to think together about the fundamental convictions of their faith. The Panel had no mandate or wish to develop an "official" theology for the church. It sought only "to search out and clarify the theological, biblical, sociological, and historical issues involved in our practical life."[12] Why the times required theological reflection was made all too clear in Ronald Osborn's lead article, "Crisis and Reformation." Though the article focuses on a crisis and a reformation peculiar to "the corporate career of Disciples of Christ," its title resonates with overtones of neo-orthodoxy, also known as "crisis" or "neo-

11. "Who Is Jesus Christ?" in *Doctrines of the Christian Faith (1961)*, pp. 12-13.
12. *The Renewal of the Church: The Panel of Scholars Reports,* 3 vols., gen. ed. William Barnett Blakemore, Jr. (St. Louis: Bethany Press, 1963), 1: 12. This document will subsequently be referred to as Panel Reports.

Reformation" theology. Osborn's words give pause to those tempted to view the era with nostalgia:

> Theology as a discipline and the particular theological emphases of the "ecumenical line" proved foreign to Disciple idiom, whether traditional or reformulated in terms of liberalism. With a strange sense of discomfiture Disciples found themselves neither taking the country nor moving in the center of the ecumenical stream. Suddenly the familiar formulations of our position — traditional or amended — seemed no longer very pertinent to our own situation as a denomination or to the preoccupations of the Christian world at large.

The thrust of the article is that the key planks in the unity platform of the Disciples had buckled. The New Testament provided neither a pattern of church order to be restored nor a statement of the gospel so simple that theological judgments were superfluous. The success of the ecumenical movement was due not to the withering away of ecclesiasticism but to the persistence on the part of denominational bodies to negotiate issues of faith and order, life and work, and merger. Anticlericalism had backfired: practical necessity had led to a professionalized ministry that differed from others mainly by the absence of a cogent theological rationale for ordination. The insistence on believer's baptism by immersion was now "an ecumenical stumbling block" that neither pastors nor scholars could justify.[13]

In sum, Osborn let it be known that too little theology had turned out to be as harmful as too much. And what has here been referred to as the postwar dilemma is shown to have been by no means a tempest in an academic teapot. Its effects were deep, touching on the church's sense of theological identity or lack thereof, and broad, pervading every aspect of church practice — governance, preaching and worship, education, evangelism, social involvement, mission(s), and above all ecumenical relations.

Assessing the work of the Panel is no easy task. How widely the reports circulated and whether they reflected or altered grass-roots opinion within the churches remain open questions. Those inclined to think that as scholars the panelists surely spoke to their own kind (if no one else) must reckon with the fact that the reports were too popularized and the positions too predictable to induce scholarly peers to modify their own views.

The Panel covered a wide range of topics, but its chief preoccupations were three: (1) the task and place of theology in the the church, past and present; (2) christology or, as things developed, christocentrism or christomorphism (it was not so much the doctrine of the person and the work of Christ as the figure or image of Christ that counted in these volumes); and (3) issues of ecclesiology.

The Panel fulfilled its mandate to search out and clarify issues involved in church life, and the strengths of the reports are exposition, analysis, and

13. Osborn, "Crisis and Reformation," *Panel Reports* 1: 23, 25-26.

evaluation. Theological originality, insight, and argument can be found embedded in the articles. But there are few full-fledged constructive proposals.

Gene Peters made one such proposal regarding the relationship of Christ and culture, however. He was troubled by what he saw to be a false choice between "old-fashioned liberalism," which lent divine authority to human achievement, and neo-orthodoxy, which denied ultimate worth or value to any human endeavor or cultural attainment. The proper view, he argued, was the one that Daniel Day Williams spoke of as assuring a "real redemption" — that is, a genuine transformation of life in history under Jesus Christ.[14]

Two essays by Frank Gardner were devoted to the doctrine of revelation. Alarmed by continental theology's "assault against reason," Gardner sought to demonstrate the intelligibility of the doctrine of revelation by appeals to linguistic analysis, neo-naturalistic and process thought, and a reasonable reading of the Bible. One essay, focusing on the revealer, surveys the messianic titles ascribed to Jesus, which are traced back to his capacity to elicit in others a loyalty to his person that was at the same time a loyalty to God. The variety of the titles implies not that the words are empty ciphers for the God who is and remains "wholly other" (as Gardner reads Barth) but that they are, as Wieman would say, "operational ideas open to amendment." Thus Gardner concludes that the historic Disciples affirmation of "no creed but Christ" is more adequate than the use of any specific christological formulas as tests of fellowship.[15]

The second essay, focusing on the God who is revealed, takes as its starting point "the religion of Jesus," at the core of which is the affirmation that God is Love, immanent in humanity and the world. Revelation may then be understood as the experience of a transforming and creative good that reorients the human personality toward an increase of love for God and neighbor. Gardner insists that while this transformation is by no means a natural or a human work, it is conditional upon the willing acceptance of Jesus Christ.[16]

Since both of these proposals are strictly aligned to the view that God and Christ are known only through their benefits, the ambiguity in Gardner's accounts of the interplay of nature and grace in redemptive experience is most unfortunate. His essay on "Man and Salvation" leads one to surmise that this ambiguity is not altogether accidental: "There is no such thing which could be characterized as 'Disciples anthropology' or 'Disciples soteriology,' for from its very beginnings there has been considerable diversity of thought in these areas." Gardner is untroubled by such doctrinal fuzziness; he contends that differences of theological interpretation produce "plasticity and freedom" conducive to "growth and creative development."[17]

14. Peters, "Authority: Human and Divine," Panel Reports 2: 227-38; see especially pp. 236-37.

15. Gardner, "The Revelation of God in Jesus Christ, with Reference to the Phrase 'No Creed but Christ,'" Panel Reports 1: 98-110; see especially pp. 103, 107-8, 110.

16. Gardner, "The God Who Revealed Himself in Jesus Christ," Panel Reports 2: 135-48.

17. Gardner, "Man and Salvation: Characteristic Ideas among Disciples of Christ," Panel Reports 1: 135-57; see especially p. 157.

Warnings against pressing theological points too far and appeals for the toleration of diversity appear often in the reports. Good theological and political reasons can be cited for this, but the cumulative effect of the Panel's work is a mixed message about the church's need for theology — a message memorialized when Blakemore characterizes "the mind of the Disciples of Christ" as "reasonable, empirical, and pragmatic."[18]

This is not to imply that the reports were theologically insignificant. On the contrary, the very fact that they were commissioned and published amounted to the public legitimation of theology of, by, and for the church. In terms of their own content, the case on behalf of theological inquiry was in substance the same as that made in the World Convention reports, but now extended, clarified, and sharpened. The advances were two.

One was the discovery that Disciples have a tradition, and "that tradition is Jesus Christ."[19] The new and fateful aspect of this discovery was the realization that the slogan "no creed but Christ" was not antitheological but was in fact itself a theological assertion. As such, it could suddenly be put to uses never before dreamed of by restorationists or old-line liberals. It enabled cooperatives to condemn restorationism on theological rather than purely pragmatic grounds. It made it possible to (re)connect the Disciples heritage to the apostolic kerygma, to the clause on ecclesiology in the Nicene Creed, to Protestant theology, and above all to contemporary Christian thought.

The second line of advance was the realization that the church's theological tradition gave it freedom to "disavow certain formulations of the fathers and work out new doctrinal expressions in keeping with our present understanding of the Lord's will."[20] Thus familiar Disciples emphases were (again) transposed into categories appropriate for contemporary theological dialogue, and a variety of theological concepts were called upon to indicate what it meant for this church to confess "no creed but Christ" at mid-century.

No wonder some critics were quick to complain that these panelists were like-minded "liberals" unable and unwilling to represent the diversity of opinion within the church. George Beazley vigorously protested that this criticism was unjust, for the scholars were not of one mind.[21] In a way he and the critics were both right. Diversity there was. Panelists such as Clague, Gardner, and Peters were oriented toward a liberalized Anglo-American "empirical theology," and the little they had to say about neo-orthodoxy was unflattering. Others, such as Baird, Routt, Wilburn, and even England, inclined in the direction of current biblical, ecumenical, and neo-orthodox theologies.

18. Blakemore, "Reasonable, Empirical, Pragmatic: The Mind of Disciples of Christ," Panel Reports 1: 161-83.

19. Blakemore, "Where Thought and Action Meet," Panel Reports 3: 16.

20. Osborn, "Crisis and Reformation," Panel Reports 1: 29.

21. Beazley, "Accusation, Debate and Dialogue and the Future of the Christian Churches (Disciples of Christ)," *Mid-Stream* 3 (1964): 1-18. A theologically substantive critique of the Panel's work can be found in Walter S. Sikes, "A Denomination Looks at Itself: Comments on 'The Panel of Scholars Reports,'" *Encounter* 25 (1964): 482-93.

Yet it is also true that viewed en masse the papers occupy bands on the theological spectrum set aside for Christian "realism," be it that of chastened liberalism or mild neo-orthodoxy. And since all the panelists were open to critical inquiry, points of dispute that loomed large in their own minds might well seem to others (e.g., restorationists) distinctions without differences.

The continuities, and within that framework some of the changes, that mark Disciples theology from the early fifties to the late sixties are graphically displayed in the career of Ralph Wilburn. There were other well-published and important figures — Beazley, Blakemore, Osborn, and Walter Sikes among the most notable — but of the "theologians," Wilburn can serve as well as if not better than any other to illustrate the efforts made during this era to address not only a variety of theological issues but an assortment of audiences (academic, ecumenical, and intramural).

The constant throughout Wilburn's entire career was an abiding concern to clarify the relationship between faith and the relativities of history. This was a concern shared by the many theologians of the day who recoiled from the tendency — whether conservative or liberal — to equate anything finite with the call, the claim, the Word of God. The recoil "let God be God" set in motion a familiar train of thought.

To "let God be God" is to acknowledge that God, alone the ultimate, is "other" than all else. Yet the "wholly other" God in whom faith trusts is known to be the One who is God because of a self-revelation in saving acts of history culminating in "the Christ event." This self-revelation in history, to which the Bible is the normative witness from faith to faith, brings Good News to all the earth: the assurance of God's mercy, care, and saving power. Those who confess the Lordship of Jesus Christ are formed by the power of the Spirit into a new people, the church. This community, living within the relativities of history, is called to make manifest the gospel by its every word and deed.

Given such a view, clarity about the relationship between faith and history is essential to the church. Without it the church may mistake its true calling. And the greatest mistake of all is to absolutize the church itself, to forget that it too — its Scriptures and traditions, its structures of polity, rites, programs, and all the rest — shares in the relativities of history. The awareness that the gospel is a treasure that is not to be confused with any earthen vessels, even those that carry it, is due to a self-critical impulse within faith itself. Wilburn called it "the prophetic spirit."

He devoted his first major work to this topic. *The Prophetic Voice in Protestant Christianity* (1956) was a methodical attempt — the first by a Disciple — to work through the basic issues that led from and hence separated Protestant orthodoxy, classical liberalism, and neo-orthodoxy.[22] It also introduced three subtopics to which Wilburn would often return.

---

22. Wilburn, *The Prophetic Voice in Protestant Christianity* (St. Louis: Bethany Press, 1956).

The first of these is the historical-theological placement of the Disciples tradition within Protestantism. Wilburn saw Campbell, like Schleiermacher, as the originator of a post-Enlightenment attempt to frame an adequate doctrine of revelation for modern Christians. The attempt, however, is said to have been marred by a failure to break lose from doctrinaire biblicism. With this, Wilburn began a case against restorationism that was brought to its completion in the Panel of Scholars. Also in the Panel reports he developed more fully, and with more sophistication and insight, his view of where the Disciples fit within the "polarities" of the Protestant theological tradition.[23]

Dialectically related polarities are also the means he used to discuss Christian unity, his second major concern. *The Prophetic Voice* ends with a look at ecumenical issues, and it there becomes clear that Wilburn's historical-theological analyses of the doctrine of revelation are meant to serve the cause of church union. From first to last Wilburn pressed for the "real organic unity" of Christians, a goal that was in his judgment true to the biblical witness and to the Disciples heritage alike. He viewed the oneness of the church in Christ as an eschatological reality, already given but not yet fully and visibly realized. As such, Wilburn called it a sacramental reality — that is, a sign and seal of God's gracious presence.[24]

Wilburn's third chief concern had to do with the basics of theology — revelation, authority, and theological method. He returned again and again to the contest between Schleiermacher, the champion of neo-Protestantism, and Barth, defender of neo-orthodoxy. Throughout the fifties his verdict on the debate went in Barth's favor. Schleiermacher's anthropological starting point seemed subjectivistic to him, and he considered Schleiermacher's cultural apologetic insensitive to the otherness, the over-againstness, the judgment of God.

Yet, like Bultmann and Tillich, Wilburn remained ill at ease with Barth's undialectical No to Schleiermacher's program. He read Schleiermacher with uncommon sensitivity and took seriously the mandate to be at once modern and Christian. Nor was he uncritical of Barth's biblical positivism. Although Wilburn found Barth's critique of *Kulturprotestantismus* to be based on sound instinct, he was nonetheless interested in a more critical and self-critical solution to the issue of faith and history than Barth provided.

23. See Wilburn, "A Critique of the Restoration Principle: Its Place in Contemporary Life and Thought," Panel Reports 1: 215-53; and "Disciple Thought in Protestant Perspective: An Interpretation," Panel Reports 2: 305-36.

24. See Wilburn, "Reflections on the Nature of the Unity We Seek," *The Scroll* 56 (1959): 3-13; "The Unity We Deplore and the Unity We Seek," *Encounter* 22 (1961): 175-96 (reprinted as "The Unity We Seek," in Panel Reports 3: 335-62); "A Theology of the Sacraments: The Nature of the Church and Our Salvation," *Encounter* 24 (1963): 280-302; and "The One Baptism and the Many Baptisms," *Theology Today* 22 (1965): 59-83.

His key works on ecclesiology also include "The Relevance of Existential Philosophy to the Task of Preaching," *The Scroll* 51 (1960), and the following in Panel Reports: "The Lordship of Jesus Christ over the Church," 2: 170-90; "The Place of Theology in the Church," 2: 17-44; and "The Role of Tradition in the Church's Experience of Jesus as Christ," 2: 106-32.

By the time Wilburn wrote "Widening Horizons in Theological Education" in 1962, many others had obviously joined him in this quest. Neo-orthodoxy, a prophetic protest against every human attempt to confine God within the limits of human thought and action, was itself coming under attack for precisely this reason. Without at all sanctioning a return to classical liberalism, Wilburn was led to conclude that "the blast of the Barthian trumpet has done its best, and theology demands entering into the cultural situation." It must respond directly to such contemporary issues as desegregation, Jewish-Christian relations, pluralism, and cold-war confrontation.[25]

Three years later Wilburn declared that Barthianism had been an "over-correction" to the flaws of liberalism.

> It is *kerygmatic* to the exclusion of any *apologetic*. Unless, however, theology correlates the biblical emphasis with an apologetic concern, it always heads for serious difficulty. Only an apologetic concern can *relate* faith meaningfully to the on-going present, in its total depth and breadth. . . . The "biblical way of thought" and "other modes of thought" seem to be separated by an unbridgeable chasm, for Barth. Any *other* mode of thought is essentially "unfit" for understanding the gospel. Barth is fundamentally wrong at this point.[26]

Wilburn did not thereafter repeat Barth's mistake. His writings took a more apologetic, Schleiermacherian vein.

In *The Historical Shape of Faith* (1966) he examined the issues posed for traditional faith by the modern idea of history, and with it historical consciousness and historical relativity. His constructive responses are, as ever, dialectical. But the dialectic is now not that of Barthian but of mediating theology, fully in line with the post-Bultmannian "new quest of the historical Jesus."[27]

Equally mediatorial are the views of science and religion set forth in his articles of the late sixties. Warnings against absolutizing any knowledge claims, scientific or theological, reappear, but emphasis now falls on the complementarity, the cross-fertilization, of scientific and theological inquiry. As science challenges theology to adjust its claims to the reality of the world, so theology challenges science to acknowledge that the givenness of the world of experience is a "gift" and that the needs and aspirations of human beings transcend the nexus of cause and effect.[28]

---

25. See Wilburn, "Widening Horizons in Theological Education," *College of the Bible Quarterly* 38 (1961): 1-10.

From *Prophetic Voice*, Wilburn's course leads to "Barth and Bultmann: An Essay in Comparison," *Encounter* 18 (1957): 387-99; "The Theology of Karl Barth: Its Genesis, Motif, and Method," *Encounter* 20 (1959): 53-71; "The Role of the Theological Seminary in Modern Culture," *College of the Bible Quarterly* 39 (1962): 30-37; "The Role of Tradition in Schleiermacher's Theology: The Nature and Value of Tradition," *Encounter* 23 (1962): 300-315; and "A Reappraisal of the Theology of Karl Barth," *Encounter* 25 (1964): 228-43.

26. Wilburn, "A Reappraisal of the Theology of Karl Barth," p. 240.

27. Wilburn, *The Historical Shape of Faith* (Philadelphia: Westminster Press, 1966).

28. See Wilburn, "What Science Contributes to Theology," *Lexington Theological Quar-*

In his move toward apologetics, theology of culture, and direct responses to current sociopolitical issues, Wilburn reflected a shift in orientation that had been under way in mainstream Protestantism, and among Disciples, for some time. Yet there had been an ever-so-slight delay factor in the tracking system of the Disciples. At first reluctant to make peace with neo-orthodoxy, they linked up with the theological renaissance just as it began to wane. So, too, the lengthy process of church restructure came to fruition a split second after public enthusiasm for "big government" of any sort had peaked. The 1967 adoption of a "Provisional Design" was an event to celebrate, well worth — many would say — the risk of schism. But anti-institutionalism and discontent with "the establishment" were on the rise among the cooperatives themselves, and this would prove to be of more consequence to the church than the loss of some opponents of restructure.

The watchword of the day was "relevance," a call for the church to take its stand on current social issues. That the church should do so had long been a popular refrain in mainline Protestantism. Liberalism wished to promote "the best" of Christianity and American culture at home and abroad, to hold realistic and neo-orthodox theologies together in dialectical tension. The invariable result was an ethics of meliorism. But as the fifties gave way to the sixties, national problems — race relations, poverty, the war in Southeast Asia, the generation gap, and the counterculture — grew into national crises. Meliorism came to be seen first as inadequate, then as immoral. And once consensus broke down with regard to what, if anything, was "the best" of American culture, mainstream Protestantism imploded.

In a 1970 retrospective on the sixties, Yale church historian Sidney Ahlstrom spoke of a watershed, a "radical turn," in theology and ethics. Secular theologies, the "God is dead" movement, situation ethics, the "new morality," and activist, often confrontational social ethics were cited among the signs of the changing times.[29] That "the Christian tradition," even in its untraditional mainstream Protestant forms, was "relevant" to the needs and aspirations of people in the contemporary world could simply not be taken for granted.

IN QUEST OF A NEOLIBERAL AGENDA

The "radical turn" took its toll on the newly restructured Christian Church (Disciples of Christ). The 1973 findings of "an interpretative examination in the cultural context" were doleful. George Beazley lamented that the church,

---

terly 2 (1967): 13-24; "What Theology Contributes to Science," *Lexington Theological Quarterly* 2 (1967): 47-58; "Christian Secularity," *The Scroll* 64 (1967): 3-7; and "The Problem of Verification in Faith-Knowledge," *Lexington Theological Quarterly* 4 (1969): 33-45.

29. Ahlstrom, "The Radical Turn in Theology and Ethics: Why It Occurred in the 1960's," *Annals of the American Academy of Political and Social Science* (1970): 1-13.

like the nation, was polarized to an extent unknown since the pre–Civil War era and that the future was at best uncertain. Secularism, "religionless Christianity," and theologies of revolution were in his view outright attacks not only on the status quo but on liberal and humane culture itself. His hope was for a renewed commitment to that culture, and with it fresh emphasis on freedom, the authority of the New Testament, and respect for institutions.[30]

In his survey of Disciples theology, Osborn reported that " 'The short career of neo-orthodoxy' has spent itself. Radical theology has taken the center of attention, and if something more nearly approaching traditional Christianity does triumph in this decade, it appears likely to be a form of neo-liberalism."[31] He agreed with Beazley that theology and church would (if they ever could) recover their health only by reconnecting — that is, "re-relating" — their message to "the world." As Beazley put it, the task was to reformulate the "most lasting insights" of the heritage in terms of a current school of theology that might deal "realistically with the contemporary crisis of faith and with the present tendency of theology to involve itself in questions of power and liberation."[32]

During the seventies neoliberalism was indeed the preferential option of many mainstream Protestant theologians, Disciples included. It did not offer, however, what in 1952 William Robinson claimed to be a great benefit of the newly formed "biblical theology" movement: "a common language and a common insight enabling scholars of long-separated Churches to speak to one another with a new degree of mutual understanding."[33] On the contrary, the breakdown of neo-orthodox and realistic syntheses issued in an era of unprecedented theological ferment.

The neoliberal impulse had as its aim the forging of new links between theology and the modern — or postmodern? — world. It was therefore destined to assume many and varied forms, depending on where in the world the link might be made. Since nothing was to be "taken for granted," questions of theological method again came to the fore. These were, for some, career-consuming preoccupations; for others, only springboards to one or another of the myriad thematic or programmatic theologies to appear from the late sixties to 1980 and beyond.

Even a partial listing of the new options is lengthy: theology of hope; theology of the future; theology of revolution; narrative and story theology; process theology; political theology; and theologies of liberation, among them those of blacks, feminists, and Third World Christians. And though mainstream Protestants might not favor them, at the one extreme resurgent evangelicalism

30. See Beazley, "Who Are the Disciples?" p. 11, and "A Look at the Future of the Christian Church (Disciples of Christ)," in *Christian Church (Disciples of Christ): An Interpretative Examination in the Cultural Context,* pp. 369-70.

31. Osborn, "Theology among Disciples," in *Christian Church (Disciples of Christ): An Interpretative Examination in the Cultural Context,* p. 113.

32. Osborn, "Theology among Disciples," p. 402. He speaks appreciatively of process theology in this regard.

33. Robinson, "Three Recent Movements in the Field of Theology," p. 118.

was forging its own new links between Christianity and culture, while at the other extreme God-is-dead theology was coupling with postmodernity to create deconstructive atheology.

All told, changes in the social order, the cultural ethos, patterns of religious affiliation, and the academic study of religion were reshaping mainstream Protestant theology during the sixties and the seventies. For Disciples, the critical era seems to have been 1963 to 1973, from "The Renewal of Church" to its "Interpretative Examination in the Cultural Context." During this season the plantings of the previous decade came to harvest (or went to seed) and those of the decade to come took root.

When the critical era began, Disciples had by most measures been successful in providing theological education justly called second to none and in locating teacher-scholars on a par with those in other graduate seminaries. No longer would it be unusual to find Disciples scholars who held their own among peers in the various theological disciplines. The Amesian either/or had lost its terror. The church expected its seminarians to study a bit of theology, and its seminaries to hire at least one Disciples theologian to teach the subject.

As time passed, a new generation of Disciples theologians took their posts in the denomination's schools, either as replacements or additions to the faculties, and in other mainstream Protestant institutions. For the first time in history, Disciples had in place a cadre of credentialed theologians, junior, senior, and emeriti.

That Disciples theological scholars generally were "responsive" to the changes in mainstream Protestant theology goes almost without saying. Their profession demanded no less. To the cadre of theologians in particular fell the awesome tasks of mastering an ever-expanding field, rethinking issues once thought settled and tackling issues never before seen, and as ever proposing adequate accounts of the faith of the Christian Church, ecumenical and denominational. Their first step was to decide where to situate themselves within their field; their second step was to construct an agenda of their own.

By 1980 several of them had compiled records of scholarly publication of sufficient length to give some indication of the trajectory, and the character, of their thought. Snapshots of the work of five such scholars — William Barr, H. Jackson (Jack) Forstman, David Griffin, Eugene (Gene) Peters, and Clark Williamson — may serve as helpful resources for understanding the state of Disciples theology from 1960 to 1980.

But be warned: help here is limited. Except for Gene Peters, whose career was cut short by his untimely death in 1983, these theologians are still active and very much "on the way." Their thinking has moved on, in some cases elsewhere, since the 1980 endpoint of this study. Thus this 1980-bound view is not merely brief but partial and skewed: what comes later may well afford a revisionist perspective on all the materials.

The work of William Barr of Lexington Theological Seminary has been in a sense a barometer of mainstream Protestant theology. In his inaugural lecture of 1965 Barr spoke of the tasks that faced systematic theology in his time. Noting that the field in the postneo-orthodox, postliberal, or neoliberal era is fluid and variegated, he argued that theological reflection dare not avoid addressing the issues of (1) the essential ground and norm of theology, (2) hermeneutics, or (3) the reopening of a dialogue with culture. His work on this agenda over time led him to consider varied currents of thought in the church and the academy: the legacy of Barth, secular and radical theologies, the new hermeneutic, theologies of hope and the future, political theologies including the theology of revolution, and theologies of liberation.[34]

Barr's point of departure was the conviction that theology is to be very much a church theology oriented to "the event when God and man are together, viz. Jesus Christ."[35] Here he followed his mentor Hans Frei of Yale in extending Barth's later insights in the direction of a narrative christology. In Barr's case, the extension led to two major shifts in his own thinking — the first toward a theology of hope and the second toward a theology of liberation.

These shifts reflect a deep underlying continuity of his thought, however. They result from an expanding self-critical understanding of what it means to orient theology to "the event when God and humanity are together, viz. Jesus Christ." This event must not be located exclusively in one moment of the past, for to speak of God's activity in Jesus Christ is to refer not only to a moment in history but also to a promise for the future. And this future already breaks into the present as the experience of God at work today in the struggle for a more humane social and political order, for renewing the world in terms of freedom, justice, shared power relations, peace, and ecological care.

Whereas it has been typical of Barr to assimilate recent trends of theology into his thinking, Jack Forstman of Vanderbilt Divinity School has routinely sought to cast light on the meaning of Christian faith for today by probing changing understandings of the claim of the gospel at crucial junctures in the tradition. This "probing" involves pressing beyond mere historical description to identify how key questions of theological foundations, method, and hermeneutics come into view and are played out in the course of "faith seeking understanding."

34. The works of William Barr consulted here are "The Task of Theology Today," *College of the Bible Quarterly* 42 (1965): 1-11; "New Radical Theology: A Review and Initial Assessment," *Lexington Theological Quarterly* 1 (1966): 119-32; "Man on the Way to His Future," *Lexington Theological Quarterly* 3 (1968): 97-106; "Word of God and Word of Man in Word-Event," *Lexington Theological Quarterly* 4 (1969): 122-35; "The Meaning of 'God' in Secular Experience," *Lexington Theological Quarterly* 5 (1970): 111-16; "Shape of White Liberation Theology," *Lexington Theological Quarterly* 9 (1974): 113-38; "The Struggle for Freedom in America: A Theological Critique," *Encounter* 37 (1976): 229-44; "Political Power and the Power of the Cross," *Lexington Theological Quarterly* 11 (1976): 3-8; "The Struggle for Freedom in America: A Theological Critique," *Encounter* 37 (1976): 229-44; "Theology as Hermeneutic," *Lexington Theological Quarterly* 12 (1977): 1-14; and "People and Books That Have Influenced Me Most," *Lexington Theological Quarterly* 31 (1978): 33-38.

35. Barr, "People and Books That Have Influenced Me Most," p. 35.

This might aptly be called an issues-oriented approach to historical theology. Forstman first used it in his dissertation on Calvin's doctrine of biblical authority. Here an analytical study of Calvin's views of Scripture served to bring to light a crucial distinction between biblical and biblicistic theology. History is put to similar use in *Christian Faith and the Church,* where biblical and Reformation sources are used to clarify how faith and church belong together, and in other writings, whether they deal with the early church, the Reformers, or key figures in modern theology.[36]

Varied as it is, Forstman's work is not scattered. It recircles, now from one angle and now from another, two fundamental themes: the dynamics of faith and the possibility and limits of human knowledge of God. Since faith — Christian faith — is life *coram deo,* Christians cannot do other than to understand themselves to be free to live for God and neighbor. Refusing to absolutize the relative, they make no unqualified claims for themselves, their aims, or their achievements.

Christian language about God — in Scripture, church doctrine, worship, and ethics — arises from the response of the community of faith to God's gospel in Jesus Christ. As a response to the *gospel,* what Christians have to say of God, the world, and humanity is to be a confident and joyful testimony

36. Works by H. Jackson Forstman consulted here are "The Nonchalance of Faith," *The Pulpit* (1960); "What Does It Mean to 'Preach from the Bible'?" *Encounter* (1960): 218-31; "The Subject-Object Relation and Its Relevance to the Problem of Authority," *Encounter* 22 (1961): 248-64; "Have the Disciples Become Irrelevant to Today's World?" *The Christian* 99 (1961); "Theology in the American University: To Teach and to Learn," *Encounter* 22 (1961): 435-44; *Word and Spirit: Calvin's Doctrine of Biblical Authority* (Palo Alto: Stanford University Press, 1962); "Bultmann's Conception and Use of Scripture," *Interpretation* 17 (1963): 476-81; "The Relevance of the Church in Its Theology," *The Christian* 102 (1964); "Theology and Other Disciplines," *Encounter* 25 (1964): 145-61; *Christian Faith and the Church* (St. Louis: Bethany Press, 1965); "Samuel Taylor Coleridge's Notes toward the Understanding of Doctrine," *Journal of Religion* 44 (1964); "Paul Tillich and His Critics," *Encounter* 25 (1964): 476-81; "Barth, Schleiermacher, and 'The Christian Faith,' " *Union Seminary Quarterly Review* 21 (1966): 305-19; "Luther's Understanding of Christian Liberty and Its Implications for Human Creativity," in *One Faith,* ed. Robert L. Simpson (Enid, OK: Phillips University Press, 1966), pp. 91-102; "What Does It Mean 'To Preach from the Bible,' " *Encounter* 27 (1966): 28-38; " 'Leben Schleiermachers,' vol. 2: A Review Article," *Journal of Religion* 47 (1967): 347-55; "The Understanding of Language by Friedrich Schlegel and Schleiermacher," *Soundings* 51 (1968): 146-65; "Language and God: Gerhard Ebeling's Analysis of Theology," *Interpretation* 32 (1968): 187-200; "Theology as Transcendental Jest? Friedrich Schlegel's Concept of Irony and the Theology of Schleiermacher," *Journal for Theology and the Church* 7 (1969): 115-24; "On the History of Christian Doctrine: A Demurral to Jaroslav Pelikan," *Journal of Religion* (1975): 95-109; "Thomas Mann's Seance and the Argument from Triviality," *The Disciple* (October 1975); "Expressing our Common Faith," *Study Encounter* 11 (1975): 20-22; "A Beggar's Faith," *Interpretation* 30 (1976): 262-70; "Giving an Account for the Hope That Is in Us," in *Giving an Account of the Hope Today,* Faith and Order Paper No. 81 (Geneva: World Council of Churches, 1977); "Find the Center. Make It Known," *Christian Century* 93 (17 November 1976): 1007-10; "The Nicene Mind in Historical Perspective," *Encounter* 38 (1977); translation (with J. Duke) of Friedrich Schleiermacher's *Hermeneutics* (Missoula, MT: Scholars Press, 1977); *A Romantic Triangle: Schleiermacher and Early German Romanticism* (Missoula, MT: Scholars Press, 1977); and "Is Christian Faith a 'Systematic Negation of Religion'?" *Religion and Life* 48 (1979): 217-26.

to the reality of utter grace. As a *response* to the gospel, their testimony is altogether human — finite, limited, flawed, subject to error, and always in need of reform. Thus for Forstman the "general" issue of how to be at once Christian and modern is also the existential issue of the dynamics of faith itself — how to be, as a Christian, at once committed and self-critical.

A distinguishing feature of Forstman's thought is a refusal to link Christian theology to any given philosophical framework. Although he clearly stands within the continental (post-Kantian) line reaching from Schleiermacher to Troeltsch to Bultmann and Tillich and on to Ebeling, he persistently resists the inclination to consider theology to be dependent on grounding or translating the language of faith into a philosophical idiom. In order to avoid authoritarianism, heteronomy, and parochialism, theology sets out to express the "one word" of faith clearly in words and deeds — ordinary words and deeds of life! — that are at once appropriate to the gospel and to present-day life.

Forstman's view that philosophy is one of the relativities of history that Christian theology need not court was by no means universally shared. Among the most prominent of the neoliberal initiatives in mainstream Protestant scholarship have been those associated with radical empiricism, neonaturalism, and process thought. This Anglo-American tradition, long cultivated at the University of Chicago, has appealed to many Disciples.

One was Gene Peters. His scholarly career got under way in the late fifties and early sixties with a set of evaluative comparisons between the basic choices facing young philosophical theologians. He found neonaturalism demonstrably preferable to Kantian-existential philosophy, the metaphysics of Whitehead preferable to the ontology of Tillich, the theocentric empiricism of Wieman preferable to neo-orthodoxies.[37] The die was cast; Peters did not thereafter return to these choices or even bother with the comparisons.

What he did instead was to develop the most purist process theology perspective of any Disciple to date. This begins with *The Creative Advance* of 1966, a primer on process theology of use to the church public and with an afterword by Hartshorne himself to specialists as well. It continues throughout the rest of his work, which includes major analytical interpretations that are sympathetic but not uncritical of Hartshorne's thought and constructive essays on arguments for the existence of God, on neoclassical theism, and on the problem of evil.[38]

37. Included here are "The Isolated Ego in Modern Theology: Philosophical Sources of the Concept," *Encounter* 20 (1959): 26-32; "Form, Power, and the Unity of the Individual in Whitehead and Tillich" (Ph.D. diss., University of Chicago, 1960); "Sebastian Franck's Theory of Religious Knowledge," *Mennonite Quarterly Review* 35 (1961): 267-81; "Authority," Panel Reports; and "Tillich's Doctrine of Essence, Existence, and the Christ," *Journal of Religion* (1963): 295-302.

38. Other works by Peters consulted here are "A Framework for Christian Thought," *Journal of Religion* 46 (1966): 374-85; *The Creative Advance: An Introduction to Process Philosophy as a Context for Christian Faith* (St. Louis: Bethany Press, 1966); "A Theological Typology," *Lexington Theological Quarterly* 3 (1968): 20-28; *Hartshorne and Neoclassical Metaphysics: An Interpretation* (Lincoln, Neb.: University of Lincoln Press, 1970); "Hartshorne on Actuality,"

In 1962 Peters moved from a seminary (Phillips) to a college (Hiram) context. After *The Creative Advance,* the primary audience for his advanced and often highly technical work was that of academic peers in philosophy and theology. This is not to say that his agenda was by any means intellectually or personally remote from the challenges facing church theology or the Christian life. On the contrary, Peters was chiefly, ultimately, concerned from beginning to end to demonstrate in the face of any claims to the contrary, whether those of neo-orthodoxy, secularism, or the death-of-God, the viability of a truly humane Christianity.

In his view, theism alone was capable of grounding and sustaining "the affirmation of the worth of things human." In developing his process theism in dialogue with Whitehead and Hartshorne, he was attempting to show that this affirmation was fully justified by Christianity and philosophy alike, so long as classical theism was revised to assure that "man and all his problems are included in the reality of God."[39]

Like Peters, David Griffin found in process thought the resources for reconstructing theology in the postneo-orthodox setting. His training during the late sixties made him sensitive not only to the process critique of classical (monopolar and as it were "monarchical") theism but to the attempts of John Cobb, Gilkey, and Ogden to move through and beyond the (now) unstable conceptual frameworks of Bultmann, Tillich, and the biblical theology movement. Based at the School of Theology at Claremont, Griffin quickly emerged during the 1970s as one of the most able of the younger process theologians.

This reputation was due to his analytical and constructive skills in dealing with a wide range of themes from revelation and christology to ecology and liberative praxis, as well as with major thinkers not only within but outside of the tradition of process thought, among them Bultmann and his school, H. Richard Niebuhr, Gordon Kaufman, Kai Nielson, and the liberation theologians. His first two books, *A Process Christology* (1973) and *God, Power, and Evil* (1976), are cases in point.

In the first he attempted to bring together into a coherent whole the scattered and often discordant insights of the new quest of the historical Jesus, the neo-orthodox stress on God's self-revelation in history, and a process theism based on Whitehead and Hartshorne. The result is a christology in which "the vision of reality" in the message of Jesus can be said to be in objective terms the "supreme expression of God's eternal character and purpose" and in subjective terms the "decisive factor" in the lives of his followers.[40]

Process Studies 7 (1977): 200-204; "Philosophical Insights of Charles Hartshorne," *Southwestern Journal of Philosophy* 8 (1977): 157-70; and "Divine Foreknowledge," *Encounter* 40 (1979): 31-34. A full bibliography of Peters's works is available in *Faith and Creativity: Essays in Honor of Eugene H. Peters,* ed. George Nordgulen and George W. Shields (St. Louis: CBP Press, 1987).

39. Peters, "A Theological Typology," p. 28.

40. See Griffin, *A Process Christology* (Philadelphia: Westminster Press, 1973), especially pp. 218, 220.

In the second he attempted a full-scale reconsideration of the problem of theodicy in light of process theology. He disengages the central biblical witness to the power of God from the notion of absolute control over nature and history. The power in God's preservation and providential ordering of the world may be understood to be persuasive rather than coercive, he argues. In that case, the created world exhibits finite necessity and finite freedom, and as the "recipient of the totality of Good and Evil that is actualized," God can be said to be the One who is the Good that "promotes nothing without a willingness to suffer its consequences."[41]

Griffin's works, even and perhaps especially his high-level philosophico-theological analyses, are expressive of a commitment to clarify and justify the meaning of Christian faith in an age of theological uncertainty. The passions of this faith are, and in his view surely must be, linked to a vision of the relationship of God, world, and humanity that rightly identifies how matters really are. A clear, coherent, and cogent account of the reality claims of Christian faith strengthens the ministry of the church.[42]

Disclosing the fundamental reality claims of the Christian faith and exploring their implications for the Christian life in the world may also be said to be tasks determinative of the work of Clark Williamson. His formative training at Chicago made it possible for him to draw heavily on process thought, but his thinking has been shaped as well by the ongoing Chicago tradition of radical empiricism represented by Wieman and Meland and elements of the later Tillich's theology of culture.[43]

The question of faith's reality claims that Williamson describes in his early work has both theoretical and practical dimensions. The views of historical relativity, secularity, and at length "the death of God" typical of modern culture indicate that the Christian tradition has eroded to such an extent that even its bedrock affirmation of the transcendent has come under suspicion and

---

41. See Griffin, *God, Power and Evil: A Process Theodicy* (Philadelphia: Westminster Press, 1976), especially p. 310.

42. See, e.g., Griffin, "Philosophical Theology and the Pastoral Ministry," *Encounter* 33 (1972): 230-44. Other works by Griffin consulted here are "Is Revelation Coherent?" *Theology Today* 28 (1971): 278-94; "The Essential Elements of a Contemporary Christology," *Encounter* 33 (1972): 170-84; "Gordon Kaufman's Theology: Some Questions," *Journal of the American Academy of Religion* 41 (1973): 554-72; "Whitehead and Niebuhr on God, Man, and the World," *Journal of Religion* 53 (1973): 149-75; "A New Vision of Nature," *Encounter* 35 (1974): 95-107; "Relativism, Divine Causation, and Biblical Theology," *Encounter* 36 (1975): 342-60; "North Atlantic and Latin American Liberation Theologians," *Encounter* 40 (1979): 17-30; and "Values, Evil, and Liberation Theology," *Encounter* 40 (1979): 1-15.

43. Works by Williamson include "The Death of God: A Survey," *Encounter* 27 (1966): 283-98; "Did Ritschl's Critics Read Ritschl?" *Evangelical Quarterly* 44 (1972): 159-68; "Tillich's Two Types of Philosophy of Religion: A Reconsideration," *Journal of Religion* 52 (1972): 205-22; "Response to Jay J. Kim on Bernard Meland," *Journal of Religion* 53 (1973): 216-27; "Secular Ecumenism: A Different Ballgame," *Encounter* 34 (1973): 343-50; "The Ideal Is More Real Than the Real (Fichte)," *Encounter* 35 (1974): 132-52; "Notes on a Theology of Work," *Encounter* 37 (1976): 294-307; "Preaching the Easter Faith," *Encounter* 37 (1976): 41-52; and "The Adversus Judaeus Tradition in Christian Theology," *Encounter* 39 (1978): 273-98.

attack. At the same time, he asserts that American youth are struggling against a *"secularized* world devoid of feeling, meaning, religion and value; they detect that problem-solving secular man, so celebrated by some of the radical theologians, is less than fully human."[44]

The occasion requires, in Williamson's judgment, a neoliberal reordering of the theological enterprise.[45] This begins with a rededication to the apologetic task, reviewing liberalism for lessons of use in a fresh attempt to show why, where, and how radical trust in the transcendent retains a place in human life. Like the question of faith's reality claims, the answer of apologetics has both a theoretical and a practical dimension.

The constructive thrust of Williamson's dealings with the theoretical dimension is to show that modernity's challenges to religion themselves presuppose, depend upon, and point to religious sensibilities in what, citing Eliade, may be called "the deepest being" of human selfhood. Williamson agrees with Gilkey that, taken with full seriousness, "secular experience contradicts secular self-understanding in the precise sense that the anxieties, the joys, and the tone of ordinary life reflect the context or framework of ultimacy."[46]

By the same token, Williamson argues that if historical relativity is taken with full seriousness, the experience of life in history is shown to be "a thick web of temporal relatedness involving a plurality of relata," and its meaning is caught and carried, at levels more fundamental than conceptual thinking, by myth and memory. Thus in the case of Christianity, the figure of Jesus Christ — one who accepts his own historical limitedness and relatedness — is revelatory of "a God for whom relations are real, i.e., to whom what happens in human history is not immaterial." To speak of accepting this revelation is "to act on faith, to suffer, and to forgive; otherwise the love of the suffering Servant would not transform the hearts of men. In this manner, history is overcome through historical action which has the courage to embrace history."[47]

Such comments here and elsewhere make it plain that for Williamson the Christian response to the question of faith's reality claims necessarily entails practical involvement in and with the world. During the seventies the mandate led him to reflect, for example, on the task of "secular ecumenism," the goal of which was reconciling not merely a divided church but a divided humanity, a divided world. His own commitment in this regard can also be seen in his treatment of social issues, Christian-Marxist dialogue, a praxis-oriented "theology of work," and Jewish-Christian relations.

44. Clark Williamson, "The Divine Obituary Was Premature: A Review Article," *Encounter* 31 (1970): 398.

45. See, e.g., Clark Williamson, "Rediscovering Our Grandfathers: Trends in Theology — A Review Article," *Encounter* 28 (1967): 161-67.

46. Williamson, "The Divine Obituary Was Premature," p. 397, citing Langdon Gilkey's *Naming the Worldwind* (Indianapolis: Bobbs-Merrill, 1969), p. 362.

47. Williamson, "God and the Relativities of History: An Installation Address," *Encounter* 28 (1967): 199-218; see especially pp. 215, 218.

It was fitting, then, that Williamson's first book, a primer on church theology for a "popular" audience, would have as its title *God Is Never Absent* (1977) and as its theme the "primacy of action" in Christianity. "Faith is a verb," Williamson says, and then goes on to explain the life of faith and the doctrines of the church in terms of action — being, becoming, and doing. The Alpha and Omega of faith's action is, in keeping with faith's reality claim, the divine purpose. And God's intention is to fulfill, to realize, the potential for good in, for, and among all creatures. It is "to bring into being a community in which reconciliation and the power of a holy life should become a reality. Reconciliation means the overcoming of all the disharmonies, conflicts, and divisions in our life — between us and God, between each another, and within ourselves. A holy life means a life of justice, peace, safety, liberty, and equality for all peoples." This community is "the church," but that word must be taken as inclusively as possible. God's will is not done on earth until "all peoples" lead a holy life of "justice, peace, safety, liberty, and equality for all."[48]

Williamson had developed this view in the course of sorting through the issues and options of mainstream Protestant theology, but it proved to be in perfect harmony with what, in 1980, he came to suggest was the very essence of Disciples theology:

> Disciple theology is a quintessentially American theology of sanctification, the goal of which is to baptize or transform the worldly into the spiritual. It shares the theocratic vision of Puritanism, seeking not to build the Kingdom of God in this world but to prepare this world for the coming of that Kingdom. . . . The goal of this theology is not another world; it is this world, other.[49]

This reading of the Disciples tradition of theology is not beyond dispute. Williamson himself calls it only a "suggestion," and perhaps since 1980 he has come to think differently. But it does capture a unifying theme in the works of the theologians, with the exception of Forstman, whose careers from 1960 to 1980 have been here briefly reviewed.

It is also fuel for a few concluding thoughts about where this account of Disciples theology from 1940 to 1980 has led. Consider the phrase "the Disciples tradition of theology." E. S. Ames condoned the first word alone: Disciples there were, modernists unencumbered by tradition and theology. In taking this view, Ames and like-minded liberals of the first half of the century had the best of intentions: to make their church a place for diversity of opinion and a force for good in the world.

It was not a view that went over or held up well in the new, postwar context. Its chief failing, given the climate of opinion in mainstream Protestantism and the ecumenical movement, was that it no longer served the high

---

48. Williamson, *God Is Never Absent* (St. Louis: Bethany Press, 1977), p. 139.
49. Williamson, "Theology and Forms of Confession in the Disciples of Christ," *Encounter* 41 (1980): 65-66.

ideal(s) for which it had been conceived. Instead of making the church a place for diversity of opinion and a force for good in the world, it now impeded the church's programmatic responses to the intellectual, ecclesiastical, ecumenical, and social issues of the times.

To this liberalism, and to restorationism as well, mainstream Protestantism's theological renaissance offered tempting alternatives, neo-empirical, realistic, and neo-orthodox. Of greatest appeal to Disciples were those most compatible with prior liberal emphases on the simplicity of the biblical message, faith experience, critical reasoning, moral accountability, and social concern. But even renaissance themes with an antiliberal edge — "let God be God," "confessing the Lordship of Christ," "Christ and culture in paradox," "the eschatological oneness of the church," and others — proved valuable in opposing restorationism, commending denominational restructure, and promoting Christian action in ecumenical, national, and world affairs.

Instrumental in bringing this new line of Protestant products to the church were the benefactors and beneficiaries of the process of mainstreaming Disciples theological education. Perhaps the toughest job they faced was to persuade Disciples, themselves included, that their heritage did not forbid any and all dealings with the Protestant theological tradition. Thanks to cues from Morrison and Robinson, and after many fits and starts, this case was finally made — by the Panel of Scholars.

Contra Ames, the Panel spoke not only of Disciples but of tradition, the Disciples tradition. Its core was Jesus Christ; in confessing "no creed but Christ," Disciples were granted the freedom and responsibility to express their faith in words (theological terminology), deeds (church programs), and structures (a new polity) suitable for effective ministry in the contemporary world. The "discovery" of this tradition enabled the panel, a loose coalition of rather conservative neo-empiricists and rather liberal neo-orthodox, to reassure Disciples that their church could be at once diverse and relevant.

What the discovery failed to provide was full assurance that the Disciples tradition was in any sense a source or guide for (re)formulating church doctrine. Indeed, a great deal of the theological scholarship in the Panel Reports seemed to imply that theological scholarship was actually not very important, so long as the church remained a place for diversity of opinion and a force for good in the world.

For a season Disciples flourished along with mainstream Protestantism generally on the basis of coalition theology and coalition politics — centrist, mediating, and melioristic. The "radical turn" in theology and ethics and the "sixties revolution" in American culture combined to change all that. As the center collapsed, mediation failed, and meliorism was indicted for gross immorality, mainstream Protestantism and the Christian Church (Disciples of Christ) as well entered a time of uncertainty and testing.

In this era, until 1980 at least, Disciples theologians set out on mainstream Protestantism's neoliberal quest for new linkages between Christianity and the modern, or postmodern, world. This quest would lead many — perhaps most, but not all! — of them to single out some one or another thing, person, group, or cause in this world as the "good" to which the church too should lend its full force.

It also led at least one Disciples theologian to press beyond received opinion in search of the *theology* within the Disciples tradition. This step was the culmination of a process, under way for almost forty years, toward the full acknowledgment that Disciples were — and are — a mainstream Protestant church with a tradition of theology. Thus by 1980 inquiry entered a new stage, with efforts to discern the theological identity of the Christian Church (Disciples of Christ) within the context of "Protestant theology," past and present. These efforts, still in progress, fall into the story of the 1980s and perhaps beyond.

Working Group Response: Bible and Theology

Karen D. Binford, Recorder

In addition to early drafts of the chapters by Boring, Perdue, and Williamson and Blaisdell, the working group on Bible and Theology of the 15-18 April 1989 conference also heard a presentation entitled "Changing Patterns of Disciples Worship," by Judith Jones.

GENERAL OBSERVATIONS

1. Disciples were definitely influenced by what was going on in their world. Examination of their biblical scholarship showed intense and thorough inter- actions with the controversies of the time, particularly the issues raised by empiricism and its effects on the development of higher criticism. Disciples fell on both the conservative and liberal sides of the spectrum. Patterns of worship fell pretty much in line with liturgical developments going on throughout mainstream Protestantism.

Also apparent was the influence that being a Disciple had on the direction and approaches used by these scholars and in the format and content of the worship services. This was particularly apparent in the theology study. The historic Disciples aversion to creeds, which grew during the period under study, and toward anything having to do with doctrine was strongly reflected in the works of those examined, in their reluctance to deal systematically with theo- logical issues or for that matter even to consider themselves theologians, even though they were continuously engaged in doing theology.

Our reflection revealed several areas of concern. Primary was the strong evidence of the loss of a consistent and coherent Christian witness, which had been present in the writings of Campbell and Stone and the Reformed tradition that birthed them. Because of their attitude toward creeds, the Disciples have generally failed to retain, from the era of Campbell and Stone, clear, systematic essentials of what it means to be Christian. As a result the

Disciples church is presently seen as having nothing to offer that is different from the rest of the culture.

2. There was a perceived dichotomy between academia and the local congregation. Historically Disciples pastors have served as theologians and teachers of the Christian faith. The laity has engaged in theological debate of issues raised in widely read publications to which the pastors contributed frequently and on a regular basis. More recently, however, theology and ministry have become separated. Today there is little or no theology being done on any systematic or widespread basis in the congregation. Pastors have become counselors, administrators, and program directors, and the teaching of the Christian faith generally has been relegated to the seminaries.

3. There has been a development of what was termed generic biblical scholarship which has lost not only denominational flavor but also the flavor of church in general. There is a perceived attitude on the part of the laity that biblical scholarship is not an appropriate part of the devotional and spiritual life of the average churchgoer. Systematic study of the Bible using the tools of higher criticism is generally relegated to the academics, while the laity at best tends to use the Bible in sporadic and undirected spiritual exercises. Knowledge of the Bible on the congregational level is generally lacking, in spite of recognition by laity that it is the definitive book of the faith.

RECOMMENDATIONS

This group felt that the basic need was for development of strong, clear statements of what it means to be Christian. Of particular concern here was a failure to focus on the nature of God evidenced both in the works of the examined authors and by the laity. The group believed that development of a strong doctrine of God, with clear connections to soteriology, would affect both biblical studies and the content and structure of worship in positive and effective ways.

The group also felt a need to return, at least somewhat, to the concept of pastor as teacher of the Christian faith. The main concern here was for a reintroduction of theology and serious Bible study into the local congregation. The group felt very strongly that the voice of professional theologians needs to be heard in the congregations and that the focus should shift toward writing more theology that can be understood and struggled with by the laity. Connected with this was the feeling that biblical studies using higher criticism can strengthen the congregation; it is presently being used in some congregations with excellent results. It was also felt there should be an emphasis on integration of biblical scholarship and use of the Bible for devotions. These two presently are seen as totally separate, an unfortunate view that limits the strength that can be drawn from the Bible.

In the area of worship, the group noticed a change in the role of the congregant from participant to spectator. The responsibility for both the design and implementation of worship has shifted from the laity to the pastor, and the laity has become more and more separated not only from the content of the worship but also from its meaning. This group saw a need to reintegrate the laity into the worship process, to increase their involvement in what is going on and determining what it means. Crucial to this is developing an understanding of what we do in worship, who participates, and why.

In its recommendations for further study, the group saw three areas of need. First was a need to examine those congregations that are dynamic faith communities regardless of whether they exhibit numerical growth. There are those that exhibit the characteristics of a reconciling, redemptive, prophetic church. Examination of their worship, leadership, and study and teaching patterns may provide some clues concerning the causes of decline in other congregations.

Second was a need for a broader study of worship practices, particularly in small congregations. Information on such things as which hymnals are used and how, what is said and done at the table and by whom, and the content of the liturgy, prayers, and so on could be illuminating and helpful in developing stronger and more inspirational worship services. Coupled with this was mention of the possible relationship between the liturgical expertise of the pastor and the content, structure, and effectiveness of the worship.

Third was a need for passionate discussion of important issues within the church. The group noted a lack of any incisive, constructive conflict. The only thing to come along that even comes close to this has been the controversy over the doctrine of salvation through Jesus Christ alone. Noting the positive effects of past controversies and discussions conducted in a public setting, the group felt the structure that necessitates immediate voting on issues at general and regional assemblies thwarts the possibilities for real, genuine, and fruitful discussions of crucial issues on a denominational level. The wish was expressed that there could be some format for such discussions that would not be subject to the voting rules of the assemblies, at least not immediately.

III. MISSION AND IMAGE

Disciples Leaders' Changing Posture regarding the United States and "Denominationalism," 1880-1980

Anthony L. Dunnavant

In 1880 Disciples of Christ leaders generally affirmed the United States and considered denominationalism to be illegitimate. The United States was seen as blessed with a special millennial vocation: it was more than just a nation. Denominations were seen as mired in their human traditions and therefore obscuring the fullness of the New Testament faith: they were less than the church. These were positions the Disciples had inherited from their early nineteenth-century forebears. By the 1980s Disciples leadership was often critical of the United States but generally affirmative of the denominations. When did these changes in viewpoint occur? What were the contexts for these changes? How might these changes have affected the recent history of the Christian Church (Disciples of Christ)? These are the questions this essay addresses.

In order to document the process of change that has occurred in Disciples leaders' views of the United States and denominationalism, this essay focuses primarily on what the Disciples popular press published on these two themes. "Leaders" are operationally defined as those writing for publication, principally in *The Christian-Evangelist* and its successors, *The Christian* and *The Disciple*. Some material such as letters to the editors of these publications is used to support or offer counterpoint to leaders' views. Writings from *The Christian Standard* are used only through the second decade of the twentieth century, beyond which the *Standard* cannot be unambiguously viewed as relating to the same constituency as these other publications. Special attention was given to material that relates directly to theological interpretation of the United States and to the idea of denominationalism. However, in the course of the research it became clear that the treatment of Catholicism (and later communism) often elicited statements on these two issues. Attention was also given to the presence and tone of reporting on interdenominational work.

A survey of the sources described above shows that the posture of

Disciples leadership regarding the United States remained largely the same from 1880 to the middle 1930s, after which it underwent a significant change. In the case of their viewpoint concerning denominations, however, one can trace an evolutionary change in perspective from 1880 to the 1930s.

From the 1880s to the 1930s the Disciples popular press gave persistent expression to the view that God had chosen the United States to establish democracy and spread pure Christianity at home and abroad. In September of 1880 *The Christian Standard* asserted that "no nation of history . . . ever was so favored of God," who "means to work out through [the United States] the problem of Christian civilization for the world."[1] Within this framework of interpretation, the Spanish-American War of 1898 was seen at least "indirectly" as "a religious war."[2] The expectation was that "evangelical missions will flourish under the Stars and Stripes."[3] The kind of "Christian patriotism" that underlay such an expectation was seen, at the turn of the century, as "the greatest factor in the onward progress of the world."[4] Although there were significant "internationalist" and pacifist expressions in the first decade of the twentieth century,[5] the entry of the United States into World War I brought with it a resurgence of patriotism. "Ever since the Pilgrim Fathers landed at Plymouth Rock with Bibles under their arms and prayers in their hearts, our country has been God's country," said a *Christian-Evangelist* writer in 1917. "Israel failed to serve God as they ought and were scattered to the four winds. . . . God then made a new nation in America to serve Him and represent Him in bearing the torchlight of truth."[6] Even in the midst of postwar disillusionment in the 1920s, there was an effort to sustain the notion that there is a "patriotism that can save," that is "unselfish," the "soul" of which is "re-

1. O. F. Lane, "The Pulpit: Relation of Christianity and Civil Government and the Duty of the Citizen," *The Christian Standard,* 25 September 1880, p. 305. This language is reminiscent of Thomas Campbell's view that the United States was a "highly favored country" that would be the context for "reformation in all things . . . according to [God's] word" (*Declaration and Address, by Thomas Campbell: Last Will and Testament of the Springfield Presbytery, by Barton W. Stone and Others* [St. Louis: Bethany Press, 1960], pp. 30-31).

2. "The Past History of Our Present War," *The Christian Standard,* 4 June 1898, pp. 729-30. See also Jerry Coleman Smith, "The Disciples of Christ and the Expansionist Movement, 1898-1899" (D.Div. thesis, Vanderbilt University, 1970), pp. 28-82. The *Christian-Evangelist's* support for the Spanish-American War is documented and analyzed by Charles R. Blaisdell in "The Attitude of *The Christian-Evangelist* towards the Spanish-American War," *Encounter* 50 (Summer 1989): 233-45.

3. "The Nation's Responsibility," *The Christian Standard,* 16 July 1898, pp. 928-29. See also Smith, "The Disciples of Christ and the Expansionist Movement," pp. 82-93.

4. William Drummet, "Christian Patriotism," *The Christian Standard,* 10 August 1901, p. 1012.

5. Andrew Carnegie had facilitated the creation of the Church Peace Union in 1914. As late as 1916 *The Christian-Evangelist* editorialized hopefully about "the new internationalism," which, it said, "looks beyond any mere geographical boundaries to the world-wide kingdom of Christ" (*The Christian-Evangelist,* 11 May 1916, pp. 578-79).

6. Claire L. White, "Most Vital Patriotism," *The Christian-Evangelist,* 12 July 1917, p. 786. See also Gen. Z. T. Sweeney, "The Duty the United States Owes to Civilization," *The Christian Standard,* 30 June 1917, p. 1137.

ligion."[7] The United States wished unselfishly for "the gifts of God to extend to all people as well as to ourselves."[8] When the Depression appeared to be interrupting this extending of God's gifts *The Christian-Evangelist* nonetheless affirmed that every time "the nation has seemed to be turning back toward the jungle and the cave, God always raises up a patriot, a preacher, a statesman, a president, a prophet who turns it right about face again." Therefore, remembering God and knowing that God had remembered America, it was possible to have "assurances" of "our deliverance and our perpetual progress."[9]

In the 1880s the Disciples press put forth the idea that "Christ and his apostles laid the fundamental principles of democratic government."[10] "Patriotism, intelligent and rational," was identified as "a virtue in the sight of God. Fathers should inspire their children with it, and no man has a right to the pulpit or professor's chair, who does not teach it."[11] In 1895 a writer in *The Christian-Evangelist* suggested the converse: "No man known to be an unbeliever can now be elected to the office of the President of the United States." Furthermore, "no man has ever been a Justice in the United States Supreme Court who has not been a believer in God, in Jesus, and in the Bible."[12] The desire for patriotic pulpiteers and believing politicians reflected a perception that "the flag of our country" and "the cross of Christ" should "always stand aloft side by side as the emblems of the best there is in this life and in eternity."[13] A generation later *The Christian-Evangelist* anticipated Independence Day 1930 with a call for a limitless patriotism in which "every hour is dedicated to God and country." The familiar theme of patriotism's roots in Christianity was recapitulated: "Jesus Christ was the greatest patriot who ever lived," and "the church is the greatest of all patriotic societies." However, by this time there were admonitions that patriotism be "free from jingoism" and "above boastfulness."[14] As the decade of the 1930s unfolded, these warnings became much more prominent.

Throughout the period from the 1880s to the 1930s the Disciples leadership wrote of threats that they thought might undermine the success of the United States as the "redeemer nation."[15] The undermining influence of that

7. "The Patriotism That Can Save," *The Christian-Evangelist,* 17 February 1921, p. 180.

8. "Elements of American Patriotism," *The Christian-Evangelist,* 29 June 1922, p. 798.

9. "Going on to Perfection: The Fourth of July, 1932," *The Christian-Evangelist,* 30 June 1932, pp. 835-36.

10. "Religion and Politics," *The Christian-Evangelist,* 5 February 1885, p. 88.

11. R. W. Gentry, "A Sermon: On the Relations of Christians to Human Government; Suggested by the Attempted Assassination of the President," *The Christian,* 28 July 1881, p. 1.

12. B. B. T.[yler], "Religion in Our History," *The Christian-Evangelist,* 25 April 1895, p. 466.

13. John A. Lee, "Christianity and Our Country," *The Christian-Evangelist,* 19 June 1902, p. 428.

14. "The Patriotism for Today," *The Christian-Evangelist,* 26 June 1930, p. 835.

15. This phrase was used by Ernest Lee Tuverson to describe the idea that the United States was the "chosen race, chosen nation" fulfilling a "millennial-utopian destiny" for humankind (*Redeemer Nation: The Idea of America's Millennial Role* [Chicago: University of Chicago Press, 1968], p. vii).

which was "foreign" to the United States was an oft-sounded refrain. In 1888 *The Christian-Evangelist* observed that "the communists, anarchists, and saloon keepers of this country are nearly all foreigners" and suggested that recent immigrants had all too often come "with no idea of being absorbed into our Americanism." Rather, they came to "foreignize America."[16] The greatest dangers were seen as arising from "the Roman, Foreign, and Rum powers."[17]

In 1880 Disciples readers were warned that "the very genius of Romanism makes the [Catholic] church the natural foe of republican government."[18] During the next decade the "Romish church" was described as a "foreign, un-American, medieval power" opposed to public education and religious liberty. Catholicism's growth was presented as a "challenge . . . to Christian manhood, to Protestant zeal [and] to American patriotism."[19] The dangers of Catholicism were especially played up during wartime. The Spanish-American War (1898) was interpreted as "the Pope and the priests hav[ing] called down the wrath of destiny in the form of Protestant gunboats."[20] During World War I the Vatican was linked disapprovingly with the Kaiser. "Prussian methods and Papal tactics mean one and the same thing — force, correctly translated 'might is right.' "[21] In 1924 Disciples participants in the Federal Council of Churches' Fifth Quadrennial Meeting learned that Roman Catholics were "greatly persecuting and harassing the embattled Protestants" of Europe. This, of course, came as "no surprise."[22]

Though Catholicism was the greatest perceived threat, it was not alone. *The Christian-Evangelist* was not exempt from the red scare of the post–World War I era. A contributing editor made it clear that "we want no man among us who strives to tear down our government. We do not want the Reds." They were seen as "a real menace" who should be "hustled out of the country" in spite of "pious protests made in the name of free speech." "The unkempt Red,

16. "Immigration," *The Christian-Evangelist,* 14 June 1888, p. 366.

17. Justice, "Preachers in Politics," *The Christian-Evangelist,* 25 December 1884, p. 825. Sometimes the enemies of good American Protestant institutions were strange bedfellows. In defense of the pious observance of the Lord's Day, *The Christian-Evangelist* noted in 1885 that "Catholics, Seventh Day Adventists, German Free-thinkers and the whole crowd of such anarchists [were] cooperating to break it down" ("The Nation and the Lord's Day," *The Christian-Evangelist,* 19 February 1885, p. 115).

18. A. I. Hobbs, "Church and State: Number 3," *The Christian Standard,* 27 March 1880, p. 97.

19. "America for Christ," *The Christian-Evangelist,* 14 November 1895, p. 722.

20. "The Past History of Our Present War," pp. 729-30.

21. "Made in Germany," *The Christian Standard,* 20 October 1917, p. 64. Sometimes the linkage was slightly more subtle, such as in the following association of the Inquisition with a host of unsavory images: "Huns must receive the Inquisition, violate innocent women, crucify babies, [and] incite Mohammadans to holy war against innocent Christians" ("Don't Buy a Liberty Bond," *The Christian Standard,* 20 October 1917, pp. 64-65). See also Geo. P. Rutledge, "Roman Catholicism the Most Dangerous System of the Ages — II," *The Christian Standard,* 4 July 1914, p. 1148.

22. "The Fifth Quadrennial Meeting of the Federal Council of Churches in America," *The Christian-Evangelist,* 18 December 1924, p. 1627.

he of the fierce whiskers and the unlaundered shirt" was not "the greatest menace." No, it was "the manicured Red of the University" that represented the most peril. These "apostles of a pseudo internationalism" used the veil of "Academic freedom" to "sneer at everything in our Republic."[23]

Even during the year of the Spanish-American War, some criticism of the United States was accepted by Disciples, however, and not dismissed as "sneering." J. J. Haley took to heart the criticisms of American Christianity offered in a "humiliating rebuke" by the Hindu Vivekananda at the World's Parliament of Religions in Chicago in 1898. "A godless constitution, a godless education, and godless politics help to beget in the American people a secular and worldly temper," Haley concluded.[24] In a similar vein *The Christian-Evangelist* had in 1891 pondered whether "all in all, the influence of Christian nations upon the heathen has been bane or blessing in the last two or three centuries."[25] Even more basic was the question raised by a letter writer in 1927 as to whether the United States was a Christian nation. The writer alerted the editors of *The Christian-Evangelist* to less-than-altruistic elements in American wars, politics, economics, and crimes and concluded that "the best we can say and tell the truth, is that the United States is on the road that leads to Christianity. It is still some distance in the future."[26]

Even though dangers such as Catholicism, liquor, and communism were acknowledged and occasional criticisms were heard, for the most part Disciples leaders emphasized the good in American institutions and actions and the wholesome influence of the American context. It was observed in 1889 that even "Catholicism in the United States is somewhat different from the Catholicism of [Europe]. . . . The clergy cannot go the length with free American citizens that they go with the subjects of Spain and Belgium."[27] B. B. Tyler reported optimistically to *The Christian-Evangelist* in 1901 that "Roman Catholicism cannot flourish in such an atmosphere as that of the United States."[28] Part of the goodness of the "atmosphere of the United States" was its natural antipathy to "Old World despotism."[29] This theme was sounded clearly in interpreting World War I and its aftermath. American wars were "all

23. [G. H. Combs], "The Americanism We Need," *The Christian Evangelist*, 28 June 1923, p. 806.

24. J. J. H.[aley], "The American Man's Religion," *The Christian-Evangelist*, 3 February 1898, p. 66.

25. Even this moment of doubt, however, ended with the affirmation that "if the Anglo-Saxon race could once be brought to Christ, then it would carry the knowledge of Christ to the ends of the earth" ("Christian Nations among the Heathen," *The Christian-Evangelist*, 16 April 1891, p. 242).

26. H. J. Barnes, "The Evangelist Post Office: An Unchristian Nation," *The Christian-Evangelist*, 30 June 1927, p. 986. The opposing (and more prevalent) viewpoint appeared in "The United States a Christian Nation," *The Christian-Evangelist*, 30 June 1927, pp. 875-76.

27. "Ecclesiastical Development," *The Christian Standard*, 28 December 1889, p. 860.

28. "B. B. Tyler's Letter," *The Christian-Evangelist*, 21 February 1901, pp. 235-36.

29. "America and Rome," *The Christian Standard*, 1 February 1908, pp. 180-81.

altruistic in nature and purpose." President Wilson had "sought to establish peace after the great war by the principles of the Declaration of Independence." But this virtuous advocate of "self-determination" — "the very essence of Americanism" — was "thwarted by money-loving, power-loving, glory-loving, vengeance-seeking European statesmen."[30] The idea of a corrupted Europe in contrast to a virtuous United States is very much in evidence here. This contrast had special significance for Disciples who, from their early nineteenth-century beginnings, had seen the United States as the context for the restoration of the ancient faith and ancient order of Christianity. The goals of the Disciples' "restoration plea" were the unification and missionary triumph of Christianity. The nations of Europe were historically tied to the "apostasy" that had occurred between the ancient church and its restoration.

One of the clearest marks of the "apostasy" of the church was its division into denominations or sects. Disciples writers from the 1880s to the first decade of the twentieth century showed little ambivalence on the principle of denominationalism. They were against it. An 1882 writer described denominationalism as "a promoter of pride, hatred and selfishness" and "a waste of money." "There is enough of energy and money spent in keeping up sects and denominations to convert the world."[31] Later in the same decade denominationalism was compared to "the almost hopeless tyranny of caste in India."[32] The Disciples' perception was that "the plea for Christian unity on the Bible alone is utterly at war with the advocacy of denominationalism on party platforms."[33] After the turn of the century it was especially *The Christian Standard* that urged the view that "the different denominations are so many sins against God."[34] Condemning "the sin of schism,"[35] the *Standard* looked forward to denominationalism's falling before the advance of "Jesus Christ . . . and his religion, in its primitive purity, simplicity and saving power."[36] However, in 1906 it was *The Christian-Evangelist* that published the observation that denominations "caused division," "retarded missionary activity," were not biblical, and kept Christians from standing "fast in that liberty wherewith Christ had made them free."[37]

30. "Patriotism That Can Save," p. 180.

31. James L. Thornberry, "Suggestions to the Preachers of All Denominations," *The Christian Standard,* 7 October 1882, p. 318.

32. E. B. Wakefield, "The Caste of Denomination," *The Christian Standard,* 14 September 1889, p. 600.

33. "A Movement, versus a Denomination," *The Christian-Evangelist,* 10 July 1884, p. 434.

34. Chester Sprague, "The Disciples and Denominationalism," *The Christian Standard,* 6 July 1901, p. 845. The staunch antidenominationalism of *The Christian Standard* did not mean that it showed no interest in closer relationship with other Christian bodies. A 1904 article observed that "Baptists are not a denomination in the sense that Methodists, Presbyterians, Episcopalians, Lutherans, etc., are" ("Denominationalism and Liberty," *The Christian Standard,* 31 December 1904, pp. 1875-76).

35. S. T. Willis, "The Sin of Schism," *The Christian Standard,* 7 October 1916, p. 5.

36. "Back to Christ," *The Christian Standard,* 3 March 1917, p. 656.

37. J. K. Ballou, "Why I Am a Christian Only and Not a Denominationalist," *The Christian-Evangelist,* 13 September 1906, p. 1167. Like *The Christian Standard, The Christian-Evangelist*

Disciples not only condemned denominationalism but insisted that they were not a denomination themselves. These issues were linked because, argued *The Christian Standard,* "every brother who concedes that 'the Disciples are a denomination' is quite sure in the end to justify denominationalism in general." The terrible consequence of this would be to "give up everything which the Campbells and their coadjutors contended for half a century ago."[38] It was important, then, for the Disciples to see themselves as a "religious movement" that had sought to "advocate principles that would gradually pervade the various churches and conform their faith and usages to the New Testament pattern."[39] An 1895 correspondent to *The Christian-Evangelist* even took strong exception to the use of "Those Denominational Pronouns" in such phrases as "our Brotherhood" and "we as a people." The writer insisted that the use of such pronouns and of the term *the Disciples* in a particular sense was "sectarianism in thought."[40] The desire to distinguish between denominationalism and the Disciples' New Testament Christianity was shown in another way in *The Christian Standard* three years later: "If, by becoming a Christian, a person is brought into the one body — the church — of which we read in the New Testament," then "when he becomes a member of the denominational church, he gets to be a member of two churches."[41]

An 1884 *Christian-Evangelist* article attributed the existence of the Disciples as "a separate and distinct body" to "the hostility displayed towards those seeking to effect [the] needed reformation by the so called orthodox churches." This reformation called for "unity on the Bible alone."[42] A decade later the same periodical maintained that Disciples were "compelled at times, to distinguish ourselves from others in order to speak or write intelligently." But this was only because the "pleas for unity remain unfulfilled."[43] Into the twentieth century *The Christian-Evangelist* continued to publish the view that the founders of the Disciples "reformatory movement" had been "forced to occupy an independent position" by the insufficient "catholicity" and lack of "Christian forbearance" in the "different religious bodies."[44] In short, the

---

reported on conversations between Disciples and Baptists in the early years of the twentieth century. The coverage was not always optimistic, and the conversations ended inconsequentially. See "Is It a Case of Heresy?" *The Christian-Evangelist,* 7 November 1901, p. 1413; J. J. Haley, "Can Baptists and Disciples Unite?" *The Christian-Evangelist,* 17 May 1906, pp. 623, 627; Claris Yeuell, "Baptists — Disciples," *The Christian-Evangelist,* 19 September 1907, p. 1202; and R. Moffett, "The Report of the Committee on Union," *The Christian-Evangelist,* 1 November 1906, pp. 1402, 1408.

38. "A New Plea for Denominations," *The Christian Standard,* 7 May 1898, pp. 590-91.

39. "A Movement, versus a Denomination," p. 434.

40. "Those Denominational Pronouns," *The Christian-Evangelist,* 17 October 1895, pp. 658-59.

41. O. A. Carr, "Shall We Join Two Churches?" *The Christian Standard,* 15 January 1898, p. 68.

42. "A Movement, versus a Denomination," p. 434.

43. "Those Denominational Pronouns," pp. 658-59.

44. "The Attitude of the Disciples toward the Other Religious Bodies," *The Christian-Evangelist,* 18 April 1901, p. 485.

Disciples were antidenominational, and any appearance they themselves gave of being a denomination was yet another evil consequence of the denominationalism all around them.

Although Disciples remained, in some sense, opposed to denominationalism in principle, sharp differences of opinion arose early in the period from 1880 to the 1930s as to what this opposition meant in practice. An 1886 letter in *The Christian Standard* took B. B. Tyler to task for worshiping with a Presbyterian colleague and for "rejoicing" in the "success" of this colleague's ministry.[45] In response, Tyler observed that "you write as if you think that Disciples alone man the Ship of Zion," and asked, "Do you really mean to affirm this?"[46] A growing appreciation of the efforts of the denominations underlay an 1891 writer's celebration of the impending death of Catholicism, credalism, Mormonism, Quakerism, spiritualism, universalism, Unitarianism, and clericalism. "The whole brood of 'isms'" was giving way before the triumphant march of the Sunday Schools, the Y.M.C.A.s, Christian Endeavor, and interdenominational missionary alliances, conferences, and conventions.[47] The praise of Protestant denominational and interdenominational work was sung in *The Christian-Evangelist* in the opening years of the twentieth century within a pointedly anti-Catholic context.[48] The threat of Catholicism was invoked as an inducement for a "massing together in unity of Protestant forces."[49]

The movement toward Protestant interdenominationalism was not uniform throughout the Disciples. For example, a suggestion by *The Christian Century* in 1901 that the mission field be divided among the denominations provoked a strong protest from *The Christian Standard.* Such a policy, argued the *Standard,* "is based on the assumption that denominationalism is not essentially sinful." Disciples should not enter evangelistic fields as rivals of denominational churches nor in collusion with them but "as consistent opponents of denominationalism everywhere."[50] Such divergence and continuing debate led *The Christian-Evangelist,* in 1915, to confront head-on the question of "the proper attitude for a follower of the Restoration plea to assume toward co-operative denominational movements." The advice given is that "where no direct sacrifice of principle is involved, in the interest of Christian community it is the right thing to co-operate in any sort of work of the interdenominational type."[51]

Under the leadership of Peter Ainslie the Disciples' Council on Christian

45. G. W. Yancey, "An Open Letter to Bro. Tyler," *The Christian Standard,* 13 March 1886, p. 82.

46. B. B. Tyler, "Response," *The Christian Standard,* 13 March 1886, p. 82.

47. H. W. Everest, "Unrecognized Religious Revolutions," *The Christian-Evangelist,* 26 February 1891, p. 132.

48. "B. B. Tyler's Letter," pp. 235-36.

49. Cephas Shelburne, "Keep Your Eyes on Rome," *The Christian-Evangelist,* 30 July 1903, p. 139. Shelburne is less optimistic but otherwise in basic agreement with Tyler.

50. "An Old Plan in a New Place," *The Christian Standard,* 8 June 1901, pp. 719-21.

51. "The Disciples and Interdenominationalism," *The Christian-Evangelist,* 16 December 1915, pp. 1595-96.

Union came into being in 1910 and *The Christian-Evangelist* reported its activities appreciatively. The *Evangelist* also reported on Christian unity proposals by others, such as the Protestant Episcopal Church.[52] In 1915 the periodical compared four proposals for Christian unity: (1) the Roman Catholic Solution, (2) Federation, (3) the Anglican Solution (the Lambeth Quadrilateral), and (4) the Restoration Solution. Because "surrender to Rome is unthinkable to a Protestant," "federation is . . . no solution," and Protestantism would presumably prefer "democracy" to "monarchy" (Anglican episcopacy), the article concludes, "there never was a time that the Restoration plea . . . had the opportunity for acceptance which it has today."[53] This conception underlay the *Evangelist*'s presentation in 1916 of "The New Testament quadrilateral" in contrast to the Lambeth Quadrilateral. The difference between the two, said the article, was that "the one is at heart a Catholic position, the other is a universal — Protestant — one."[54] There is ambiguity here; *The Christian-Evangelist* was alert to the growing ecumenical movement beyond the "Restoration," but it still claimed priority for "the plea."

In 1918 what now seems to have been a significant departure from the thus-far familiar line on denominationalism appeared. George William Brown asserted in *The Christian-Evangelist* that "the unfortunate truth" was "that many Disciples [were] really denominationalists" because of their "spirit of narrowness and intolerance." Thomas Campbell's claim to being "free from denominational bias was justified . . . by his . . . sincerity," his "open-mindedness," and his "absence of dogmatism." Therefore, what was needed to fight denominationalist tendencies among Disciples was "love, brotherly love, humility, open-mindedness, [and] teachableness."[55] In a 1922 *Evangelist* article, W. E. Moore accused some Disciples of being "more loyal to a 'historic plea' and a 'reformation movement' than they are to the ideals of the Kingdom of God." The "denominationalism" of sticklers for the "plea" was seen as especially condemnable in the face of unifying efforts elsewhere in Protestantism. Moore then pointed to the fact that scholars of various denominations, including "an eminent Episcopalian," had criticized denominational division.[56]

The broader context for the development of the views of Brown and Moore was the increasing interdenominational involvement of the Disciples in the twentieth century. Reporting on Disciples' participation in the Federal Council of Churches and other interdenominational efforts was routine and sympathetic in *The Christian-Evangelist* of the 1910s and 1920s. During the

52. "Progress toward Unity," *The Christian-Evangelist,* 26 October 1913, p. 1403.

53. "Christian Unity Up-to-Date," *The Christian-Evangelist,* 30 December 1915, pp. 1659-60.

54. "The New Testament Quadrilateral," *The Christian-Evangelist,* 17 February 1916, p. 195.

55. Brown, "Denominationalism and Disciples," *The Christian-Evangelist,* 25 July 1918, p. 759.

56. Moore, "Loyalty to Denominationalism or to the Kingdom of God — Which?" *The Christian-Evangelist,* 21 September 1922, pp. 1197, 1202.

same period *The Christian Standard* sharply criticized such involvements. This criticism culminated in the efforts of the *Standard* in the late 1910s and 1920s to "rescue the Restoration movement." It was during the 1920s that the controversy over "open membership" (the policy of admitting nonimmersed persons to the church membership) in Disciples missions came to a head. It became clear that one segment of the Campbell-Stone movement would not support missions' being carried out in cooperation with other denominations. It became equally clear that missionaries related to the foreign department of the new United Christian Missionary Society could not adhere to the "restoration plea." It simply made no sense in the context of an overwhelmingly non-Christian missionary situation to make "summary disposal" of the "Christian standing" of nonrestorationist Christians.[57] Thus, by the end of the 1920s conservative Disciples had created essentially an alternative convention (the North American), and an alternative approach to the financing of foreign missions ("independent missions"). The group of Disciples that supported the International Convention and the United Christian Missionary Society was, consciously or unconsciously, supporting bodies that increasingly acted on an interdenominational basis. (For more on this, see the essay by Mark G. Toulouse on pp. 194-235 in this volume.)

During the next half-century, Disciples' interdenominational activities grew in new directions with their involvement in the National and World Councils of Churches, the Consultation on Church Union, and a number of bilateral conversations. It might be argued that, overall, the high hopes leaders had pinned on the United States shifted to the ecumenical movement. Certainly it was from that movement that some criticisms of the United States eventually arose. First, however, other factors eroded some of the earlier confidence in the nation.

Part of the new, more critical view of the nation was rooted in an interpretation of the causes of World War I that came to be accepted by a significant segment of the American public in the 1920s and 1930s. This interpretation was that America had been "drugged and driven into the world War" and that "Wall Street," "big business," and "the merchants of death" played especially crucial roles in the process.[58] Acceptance of this view of the war's origins fueled the peace movement of the era. Church leaders who accepted this perspective sought to further the goals of the larger movement within the churches. One such leader was Disciples minister Kirby Page, who "proved a most effective and vigorous leader in rallying the churches behind the cause of peace."[59] Page was not alone, for the 1930s also saw the creation

57. Stephen J. Corey, *Fifty Years of Attack and Controversy: The Consequences among Disciples of Christ* (St. Louis: Christian Board of Publication, 1953), pp. 60-96.

58. H. Stone Hull, Harold E. Fey, A. L. Porterfield, and Maurice W. Fogle, "A Symposium on 'Ministers and the Slacker Pledge,'" *The Christian-Evangelist,* 23 May 1935, pp. 677-79.

59. *A Documentary History of Religion in America,* 2 vols., ed. Edwin S. Gaustad (Grand Rapids: William B. Eerdmans, 1982, 1983), 2: 150.

of the Disciples Peace Fellowship, which grew to more than seven hundred members in its first year.[60] Meanwhile, *The Christian-Evangelist* celebrated "how greatly the passion of strife and fighting [had] died down in the world," the nations' "working for peace" (through the League of Nations, the World Court, the Briand-Kellogg Pact), and the "peace societies" that were "working day and night."[61] "We stand for peace," a 1934 editorial declared, and "we believe that the Christian church is apostate which does not stand for peace."[62]

Another factor behind the dramatic change in the posture of Disciples writers regarding the United States was the rise of Nazism in Germany. *The Christian-Evangelist* called "the surrender of the German people to Hitler's leadership and to a riot of vicious prejudices and false emotions" the result of "many decades of training in narrow nationalism." Furthermore, "the rise, under Hitler, of the so-called German Christians . . . [was] the result of patriotism corrupted into nationalism."[63] Later the paper noted the resistance both of "Karl Barth and the hundreds of German pastors . . . who joined in the New Reformation Movement."[64] The Manifesto of the German Evangelical Church was commended to *Evangelist* readers as "the position of the true-hearted Christian" because of its dissent from "the religion of the militarized nation-state."[65]

German Nazism raised the concern that rampant nationalism could happen in the United States, too.

> There are all too many evidences that patriotism is increasingly becoming *with us* a malignant nationalism. . . . The attacks of American Legionnaires on ministers who preach somewhat pointedly the universality of human brotherhood; . . . the "black-listing" by the D.A.R. of teachers, speakers, ministers, writers who preach good will and venture to criticize government activities which do not create it; the emphasis of the War Department on military training in tax-supported schools; the quarter-century-old propaganda of the yellow press against internationalism; the slogan of hundred–per cent Americanism; the slogan "Buy American"; the exclusiveness of our immigration laws; the rise and fall of the Ku Klux Klan; the glibness with which the myth of Nordic superiority is perpetuated as a reality. These are signs among many of a progressive spread of nationalistic feeling which, unless checked, will finally create *in us* just the kind of jingoistic spirit for which we now denounce Germany.[66]

60. Mark A. May, "Disciples Peace Fellowship: Historical Formation and the First Twenty Years — 1935-1955," *Discipliana* 40 (Summer 1980): 22-25.

61. "The Changed Torch of Flanders: An Armistice Day Vision of Christ Coming in the Clouds," *The Christian-Evangelist*, 3 November 1932, p. 1411.

62. "The Editorial Observatory: Armistice Day, 1934," *The Christian-Evangelist*, 8 November 1934, p. 1442.

63. "Patriotism and Nationalism: Independence Day Thoughts on Christianity and the State," *The Christian-Evangelist*, 29 June 1933, pp. 819-20.

64. "The Editorial Observatory: Assault on Christ," *The Christian-Evangelist*, 9 August 1934, p. 1026.

65. M. Searle Bates, "Caesar Challenges God," *The Christian-Evangelist*, 27 January 1938, pp. 130-32.

66. "Patriotism and Nationalism," pp. 819-20; italics mine.

This catalogue of concrete American expressions of nationalistic extremism indicates that, in the view of *The Christian-Evangelist,* the danger of "a malignant nationalism" growing in the United States was all too real.[67] Gone was the easy assurance that Old World vices could not flourish in the wholesome atmosphere of America. No, in the late 1930s, it was time to go "on record in regard to basic civil liberties which are the heart of Americanism."[68] "Americanism" meant "freedom of thought and expression not merely for the idea you like, but freedom for the idea you hate." Denouncing an attack on "a poor little communist 'college' " by a group of veterans, one writer called on the American Legion to "take a firm stand against this ugly red hysteria which is sweeping the country, carefully fostered by reactionaries, preparedness advocates, and similar 100 per cent patriots."[69]

The reality of Nazism in Europe and the specter of extremism in the United States were, of course, related to economic depression. The economic situation led to calls in the Disciples press for "far reaching measures" of reform.[70] In a 1934 article, C. E. Lemmon indicted the United States for its individualism and greed and confessed "that the Protestant doctrines of individualism fit into this picture all too well." The Jesus who had earlier been depicted as a great patriot was now set over and against American individualism and greed as "a prophet of a corporate and collective society . . . called the Kingdom."[71]

Despite the emergence of a new critical stance toward the nation and the consciousness that patriotism might have the capacity to become "malignant nationalism," echoes of the older affirming stance continued during the 1930s. An example is Edgar DeWitt Jones's "Thank God for America!" — a fervent patriotic speech delivered at the New York State Fair in 1937 and reprinted in *The Christian-Evangelist.*[72] These echoes continued and gained strength in the 1940s. There was little in *Evangelist* articles such as "Thank God I Am an American" (1940) and " 'In God We Trust': Christian Foundations of Our Government" (1946) to set them apart from articles in the same genre written in the 1890s.[73] Obviously, World War II was an important factor in the return to these emphases. Nevertheless, some of the pacifism and antimilitarism

---

67. For several examples of "the threat of fascism in the United States" as perceived in *The Christian-Evangelist,* see William O. Paulsell, "The Disciples of Christ and the Great Depression" (Ph.D. diss., Vanderbilt University, 1965), pp. 283-88.

68. "Plain Talk on Americanism," *The Christian-Evangelist,* 27 January 1938, pp. 127-28.

69. "Americanism," *The Christian-Evangelist,* 23 January 1936, pp. 112-13.

70. Joy Elmer Morgan, "The Church and Citizenship," *The Christian-Evangelist,* 5 July 1934, pp. 868-69.

71. Lemmon, "On Being a Christian in America," *The Christian-Evangelist,* 4 January 1934, pp. 8, 16.

72. Jones, "Thank God for America!" *The Christian-Evangelist,* 23 September 1937, pp. 1220-21.

73. Kenneth L. Potee, "Thank God I Am an American," *The Christian-Evangelist,* 23 May 1940, p. 556; Ida B. Wise Smith, " 'In God We Trust': Christian Foundations of Our Government," *The Christian-Evangelist,* 2 January 1946, pp. 12-13.

of the 1930s lingered in the early 1940s. One letter-writer posed the question "Why not try Christianity on Hitler?" He suggested that "the money planned to be used for killing" instead be simply given to the families of Germany.[74] A number of Disciples ministers also pledged not to "bless war."[75]

With the entry of the United States into the war, a kind of patriotism appeared that had little patience for the idea of "loving Hitler" and little concern about avoiding "jingoism." The following letter appeared in *The Christian-Evangelist:*

> In my opinion the thing most needed by a large group of our churches is some virile teaching on patriotism. We are overworking the word love, but love will not win a war against the kind of enemy we are being forced to fight. A machine gun or a tank in the hands of a well trained soldier will have a lot more audience with demonized aggressors than all the love we can shower upon them. . . .
>
> Loving the Japs and Germans is like giving "that which is holy unto dogs and casting pearls before swine." . . . I have attended 30 religious services within the past six months and have heard much loving and praying for Hitler and *one* prayer for the President of the United States.
>
> I am in sympathy with the trenchant saying of Stephan Decatur who said "My country, right or wrong." . . . If some people would put in as much time and effort in defending our God-given liberties as they do in loving Hitler and his Japs, it would be the means of Christianity commanding more respect and esteem from the general public.[76]

Sentiments this "virile" were not typical of *The Christian-Evangelist*'s editorial pages — this was, after all, a letter. But during the war years, fears that the United States would follow the paths of those "militarized nation-states" condemned in the previous decade were replaced on the editorial page by an impatience with "the tortured mind of the theologian" and a clear preference for "the practical attitude of the Christian soldier." Again, as in 1898 or 1917, the enemies of the United States were understood to be "foes of Christian civilization."[77]

During and after World War II, *The Christian-Evangelist* reflected and contributed to a resurgence of the view that the United States was, in some sense, the "redeemer nation." A 1942 cover featured an interpretation of the United States by its vice president: America would bring freedom, literacy, nutrition, and education "everywhere."[78] In 1950 a writer described America

74. Harry Trumbull Sutton, "An Open Forum for Readers: Why Not Try Christianity on Hitler?" *The Christian-Evangelist,* 19 June 1941, p. 736.

75. "News of the Brotherhood: Ministers Pledge Not to Bless War," *The Christian-Evangelist,* 19 June 1941, p. 737.

76. George F. Bradford, "An Open Forum for Readers: Patriot Believes in U.S., Right or Wrong," *The Christian-Evangelist,* 2 April 1942, p. 381.

77. "Theologian and Soldier," *The Christian-Evangelist,* 28 July 1943, p. 720.

78. Henry A. Wallace, "America, the Sun of Righteousness," *The Christian-Evangelist,* 3 September 1942, p. 965.

as "set for the saving of the world."[79] The United States was again, in 1951, called "God's chosen people of the twentieth century."[80] As in the late nineteenth and early twentieth centuries, these views were accompanied by a consciousness that the nation's redemptive vocation was threatened by hostile forces.

As in the case of the two earlier wars, World War II was an occasion for the Disciples press to warn of the peril of Roman Catholicism. *The Christian-Evangelist* of 1943 saw "the Catholic hierarchy [attempting] to make advantage for the Catholic church out of the war situation."[81] After the war, Charles Clayton Morrison pointed out "where the Roman Church violates the principle" of separation of church and state. He was especially critical of "the appointment by the late President Roosevelt of an ambassador to the pope."[82] A new "perilous situation" was the "Roman Catholic . . . demand that their parochial schools be supported with funds from the federal treasury." *The Christian-Evangelist* reminded its readers that "every nation which has knuckled down to the Roman hierarchy" had "lived to see [its] religious liberties . . . taken away."[83] A 1949 editorial maintained that "only a strong, united and militant Protestantism can hope to withstand . . . [the] aggressive and well-organized Catholic attack upon our American liberties."[84]

Taking special offense at the Catholic claim "that the Roman Church alone is the great bulwark against Communism,"[85] *The Christian-Evangelist* quoted the Methodist Bishop G. Bromley Oxnam: "Communism has made no headway in Protestant countries."[86] In 1950 a guest editorial in *The Christian-Evangelist* observed that "as systems of thought and practice, Roman Catholicism and communism are markedly similar." Erecting "iron curtains," preventing "free discussion," seeking to "control the minds" of people, practicing "excommunication, character assassination, and economic reprisals," both Catholicism and communism demanded "blind, unthinking loyalty from their followers." They represented two totalitarian threats to "American freedom and democracy."[87]

Despite the similarity of the traditional anti-Catholic and the newer anticommunist rhetoric and the linking of the two, it is clear that communism

79. Thomas Curtis Clark, "Christian Faith in Our American Heritage," *The Christian-Evangelist*, 9 August 1950, p. 775.

80. James L. Christensen, "Which Way America? — The Most Decisive Battlefield in the World," *The Christian-Evangelist*, 11 April 1951, pp. 346-47.

81. "Is This Church or State?" *The Christian-Evangelist*, 9 June 1943, p. 548.

82. Morrison, "Separation of Church and State: Where the Roman Church Violates the Principle," *The Christian-Evangelist*, 27 August 1947, pp. 839-41.

83. "A Perilous Situation: Act Now!" *The Christian-Evangelist*, 13 July 1949, p. 679.

84. "Is American Freedom Threatened?" *The Christian-Evangelist*, 26 October 1949, p. 1052.

85. "A Perilous Situation," p. 679.

86. "Protestants and Communism," *The Christian-Evangelist*, 12 October 1949, p. 1004.

87. William B. Lipphard, "The Roman Catholic System and the Communist System," *The Christian-Evangelist*, 25 January 1950, p. 76.

was increasingly viewed as the greater threat. During the Korean War, communism was described in *The Christian-Evangelist* as "diametrically opposed to the American way of life" and to "Christian democracy."[88] A decade later some of the impact of anticommunism on church life could be seen in the complaint of *Christian* editor Howard Short, who wrote of his receipt of a "stream of invectives, some in such strong language that they could not be printed, by Christians determined on calling other Christians Communists." Short was not so much bothered by the fact that some "fellow goes around saying that there are 7,000 Christian ministers who are Communist or 'Comsymps'" as he was by "the fact that some members of Christian churches believe this stranger and start on the prowl for the enemy!" Such tactics, Short pointed out, provided "an unexpected ally" for communism.[89]

Even though the traditional view of the United States as "chosen but threatened" reemerged powerfully in the World War II and cold war eras, the more self-critical and antimilitaristic position of Disciples leaders that had come dramatically to the fore in the 1930s was not entirely swept away. The *Evangelist* gave space in 1945 to James B. Miller's blunt statement that "God must find it extremely difficult to bless a land supposedly based on equality" but where the lynching of blacks, the exploitation of immigrant labor, and the throwing of "American citizens of Japanese descent into concentration camps" could occur.[90] Another writer in 1945 suggested that "the predominant spirit of America is idolatrous and materialistic."[91] And Disciple J. W. Fulbright's proposals for legislation promoting "international collaboration" were not "globaloney," according to the *Evangelist.*[92] There was opposition to universal military training.[93] James A. Crain of the United Christian Missionary Society (UCMS) even made the remarkable statement in 1951 that "the Western Christian church should prepare itself now for the possibility that circumstances may arise in which the church will have to break completely with the political powers."[94]

In contrast to the dramatic change in the posture of Disciples leadership toward the United States, the change in the posture of Disciples leadership regarding denominationalism continued along an evolutionary course in the 1930s. In speaking of "The Mission of the Disciples" to the International Convention of 1934, G. H. Combs stressed the need for the Disciples to recognize that the members of "various denominations are Christians, already

88. Christensen, "Which Way America?" pp. 346-47.

89. Short, "No Picnic," *The Christian,* 2 July 1961, p. 838.

90. Miller, "The Land I Love: A Call to Applied Americanism," *The Christian-Evangelist,* 31 January 1945, pp. 112-13.

91. Leonard Butts, "Is America a Christian Nation? — A Pertinent Question," *The Christian-Evangelist,* 6 June 1945, p. 550.

92. "This Is Not Globaloney!" *The Christian-Evangelist,* 13 October 1943, p. 984.

93. "Universal Military Training," *The Christian-Evangelist,* 13 February 1952, p. 148.

94. "United Society Executive Asserts That the Church May Have to Break With the Political Powers," *The Christian-Evangelist,* 25 April 1951, p. 417.

Christians." This, of course, was traditional Disciples thinking. But Combs also asked for the recognition that "the churches to which they belong are Christian churches." Combs believed that "Christian union [could] be arrived at only when on terms of perfect equality Christians, and Christians as representatives of churches, shall sit at a common table asking to be led by our Lord."[95] *The Christian-Evangelist* also supported Christian union on an interchurch basis.[96] Statements by Disciples leadership regarding denominationalism in the 1930s made explicit what their cooperative relations with other Christian communities had already implied. These Disciples had come to view the denominations as churches and no longer as obstacles to God's mission. But this affirmation did not necessarily mean that Disciples saw themselves as a denomination. In the decades surrounding World War II, the traditional Disciples "opposition to being styled a denomination" was still being voiced. In 1931 Frederick Kershner offered the suggestion that the Disciples were an "undenominational denomination."[97] Even in 1954 the more traditional aversion to "making a denomination out of Christ's church," to using expressions such as "the 'Disciples' church," or to "succumbing to the whole denominational idea" was shown in the letter of a "young minister" to *The Christian-Evangelist.*[98]

In the 1940s and 1950s Disciples continued to oppose denominationalism along the line of reasoning propounded by George William Brown (1918) and W. E. Moore (1922). A 1947 *Christian-Evangelist* editorial distinguished between the substance (exclusiveness) and the accidents (organizations) of denominationalism. Disciples were sufficiently alert to the dangers of organizations but not to those of exclusiveness. The editorial thus criticized the denominationalism of those who "insist upon immediate and complete restoration on their own terms."[99]

In spite of continuing ambiguity about denominationalism, interest in interdenominational unity work was sustained. In the 1940s one field of great promise seemed to be the discussions of the Commission on Baptist-Disciple Union.[100] In the 1950s Disciples' participation in the launching of the National

95. Combs, "The Mission of the Disciples," in *International Convention 1934* (St. Louis: Christian Board of Publication, 1935), p. 165.

96. "Presbyterians and Disciples," *The Christian-Evangelist,* 29 June 1939, pp. 657-76.

97. Frederick D. Kershner, "As I Think on These Things: Are We, or Are We Not a Denomination?" *The Christian-Evangelist,* 30 July 1931, p. 1009.

98. Norman Able, "Letters to the Editor: Denominationalizing the Church?" *The Christian-Evangelist,* 19 July 1954, p. 466.

99. "Denominationalism: Substance and Accidents," *The Christian-Evangelist,* 27 August 1947, pp. 835-36.

100. These conversations also met with some opposition that was expressed in a convention resolution in 1948. See *International Convention of Disciples of Christ: Program* (San Francisco, 1948), p. 182; see also pp. 181 and 185 for resolutions reflecting the continued commitment to interdenominational unity efforts. *The Centennial International Convention of Disciples of Christ: Souvenir Program* (Cincinnati, 1949) also contains several resolutions supporting this commitment; see, e.g., p. 185.

Council of Churches was fully and sympathetically treated in *The Christian-Evangelist*.[101] This was also true of Disciples' involvement in the World Council of Churches.[102]

The 1960s and 1970s brought mounting tensions between Disciples who stood in the tradition of affirming the United States and those who echoed the more critical view that had been strongest in the 1930s. Similarly divergent understandings of traditional Disciples antidenominationalism were evident between those who were committed to the ecumenical movement and those who feared or opposed it.

In contrast to the way that World War I had virtually silenced and World War II had dampened pacifism or criticism of the nation, the Vietnam War evoked a deeply divided response. In 1965 *The Christian* published a Fellowship of Reconciliation "Report on Vietnam" that called for cessation of the bombing of North Vietnam and the early initiation of broad negotiations. Two weeks later in the same periodical, Ben R. Hartley (editor of *Presbyterian Survey*) spoke of "the rightness and necessity of our nation's involvement in Vietnam."[103] Shortly thereafter *The Christian* published a series of letters responding to both viewpoints. One labeled Hartley's contribution "subtle government propaganda." Another letter expressed "shock" that *The Christian* "gave hospitality to this attack upon the Fellowship of Reconciliation's Report on Vietnam." A third writer affirmed "the right and responsibility" of citizens "to challenge those actions of our country with which we disagree." But there were those who called for the recognition that "those of us who support the present Vietnam policy are no less interested in long-range lasting peace" than other Christians. There were even those who bluntly affirmed that "Church leaders are out of line when they question a policy our government has adopted in a critical spot in our fight against communism."[104]

The dissenting voices that emerged relative to the Vietnam War were reminiscent of those that had been heard in the 1930s. At least one contributor to *The Christian* drew an explicit parallel between the situation that Dietrich Bonhoeffer faced under Hitler and "the situation that many Christians feel they

101. "A New Era in American Protestantism," *The Christian-Evangelist*, 20 December 1950, pp. 1250-51.

102. See, for example, Gene Irvine, "News: Movement Finding Itself . . . World Council Faces Perplexing Problems in Eight-Day Meeting in Toronto," *The Christian-Evangelist*, 9 August 1950, pp. 777-79; Jesse M. Bader, "World Council Meeting: Disciples at Conference," *The Christian-Evangelist*, 6 June 1956, p. 582. Convention resolutions in favor of Christian unity came steadily and were often, though not always, sponsored by the Council on Christian Unity. See, for example, *International Convention of Disciples of Christ: Program[s]* (Portland, 1953), p. 223; (Cleveland, 1957), pp. 234-36; (Denver, 1959), pp. 248-50.

103. "A Statement of The Clergymen's Emergency Committee for Vietnam — Fellowship of Reconciliation: Report on Vietnam," *The Christian*, 10 October 1965; Ben R. Hartley, "Fresh Insight into the War: First Impressions from Vietnam," *The Christian*, 24 October 1965, pp. 1350-51.

104. "Letters: Readers Report concerning Vietnam Articles," *The Christian*, 26 December 1965, p. 1658.

are facing in America today." The writer suggested that Bonhoeffer's experience provided "a useful model for considering our Christian response to American policy in Vietnam."[105]

In a 1973 *Christian* Raymond L. Ticknor wrote that "to be a Christian may require that we stand against our government, or, to be a 'patriot' could mean that we stand against God."[106] This is a fair summary of the perspective that increasingly underlay Disciples writings on the United States in the 1970s. A compelling series of texts in the Bicentennial Independence Day issue of *The Disciple* illustrates Disciples' ambiguity about the United States. On the one hand there was an article about the U.S. Central Intelligence Agency's use of missionaries. Dr. Itofo B. Bokeleale of Zaire was reported to have said that "issues like the CIA-missionary links will be resolved only when Christians are educated to the point where they can understand the difference between patriotic feelings and Christian commitment."[107] The same issue carried, on the other hand, "Symbol of the Patriot's Faith," which told of the use of a "pioneer preacher of the Disciples" as "the central figure of one of the most famous American patriotic paintings," Archibald M. Willard's "Spirit of '76." The article concluded that Disciples "can rightfully point with pride and no little emotion to the marching trio who were rallying the Continentals with strains of martial music, to return and meet the foe again to snatch victory out of defeat."[108] A few pages away James Merrell's editorial contained elements of both views. "Not many years ago, most Americans boasted (and believed) that they held the key to humanity's future," wrote Merrell, but "events of the past few decades had silenced such bold claims and . . . fostered a climate of dispirited isolationism." Merrell asserted that despite this, "America still has a global responsibility" and called upon his readers, "like the nation's Founders," to "see it as a divine call." Merrell was consciously advocating a "modified" form of the "messianic complex" that had "marked America's global relationship for two centuries." This "modification" was a deeply significant one — "we will need to learn what it means to accept others as equals and as partners in a common task."[109]

By the mid-1970s strongly worded criticisms of actions and policies of the United States government appeared in *The Disciple*. A 1975 writer took the role of Jeremiah and said, "America, your hundred-billion dollar defense budget is a scandal and a sure sign of your weakness." He condemned the

---

105. Harold L. Lunger, "Vietnam and Christian Responsibility," *The Christian,* 21 July 1968, p. 900. Lunger also makes a reference to Reinhold Niebuhr in this article (p. 901) that suggests that both the Christian resistance to Nazism and the related theology of neo-orthodoxy were factors in the growth of increasingly critical views of the state among Disciples.

106. Raymond L. Ticknor, "Citizens of Two Worlds," *The Christian,* 18 November 1973, p. 1446.

107. Robert L. Friedly, "Duty: Overseas Leaders Say CIA's Use of Missionaries Offers a Lesson," *The Disciple,* 4 July 1976, p. 12.

108. "Samuel R. Willard: Symbol of the Patriot's Faith," *The Disciple,* 4 July 1976, p. 2.

109. Merrell, "Viewpoint: Beyond the 'Shining Sea,'" *The Disciple,* 4 July 1976, p. 13.

nation for its "armed madness" and its "sin of extreme nationalism."[110] A similar frame of mind was expressed in a 1977 article that spoke of the United States' policy of "train[ing] the military and police of Latin American dictatorships in 'counter-insurrectionary techniques' and in methods of torture."[111] The older claims of the United States' "selflessness" were now contested.

Perhaps the clearest and most dramatic change in the posture of Disciples leadership regarding the United States and the denominations came in the 1960s and 1970s in relation to the understanding of Roman Catholicism. Rather than viewing Roman Catholicism as a threat to America, leaders called for the recognition of Rome as an ecumenical partner. The context was the "new ecumenical atmosphere" created by the Second Vatican Council.[112] By 1977 the Disciples of Christ–Roman Catholic International Commission for Dialogue had been formed and this commission's work soon revealed "a common yearning for catholicity" between Disciples and Roman Catholics.[113]

Disciples' involvement in seeking Christian unity interdenominationally continued to grow in the 1960s and 1970s. By this time many simply assumed that Disciples would be part of "the sweeping movement toward Christian unity that seem[ed] . . . to be a manifestation of the spirit of God."[114] The interdenominational initiative that most commanded the attention of American Protestants in the 1960s was "Blake's Church," which became the Consultation on Church Union (COCU). The editor of *The Christian* was "sorry to hear that it was said informally in San Francisco that there was no use to talk at this time with those who did not accept the form of baptism which is practiced by [The United Presbyterian Church, the Protestant Episcopal Church, the Methodist Church, and the United Church of Christ]."[115] However, the Disciples soon became a part of the Consultation on Church Union with a delegation empowered by the convention to participate in the Consultation's development of a plan of union and to keep the Disciples at large and the convention informed as to the Consultation's progress.[116]

110. Roger F. Davidson, "Broken Cisterns in America," *The Disciple*, 2 November 1975, p. 9. See also Gerald M. Ford, "The Nation's Problem," *The Disciple*, 7 December 1975, p. 8.
111. William D. Hall, "We Have Power to Build Peace!" *The Disciple*, 7 August 1977, p. 12.
112. This atmosphere was applauded in a 1966 convention resolution that urged Disciples to "seize every opportunity for creating a better understanding of the contemporary Roman Catholic Church." The next convention considered a congregationally sponsored resolution calling for the celebration of "Ecumenical Sunday" in place of "Reformation Sunday" (*International Convention of Christian Churches [Disciples of Christ]: Program[s]* [Dallas, 1966], p. 311; [St. Louis, 1967], p. 341).
113. Paul A. Crow, Jr., "Dialogue toward Communion," *Mid-Stream* 18 (October 1979): 341.
114. Clarence H. Schnars, "Vanishing Barriers," *The Christian*, 20 August 1967, p. 1060.
115. " 'Blake's Church,' " *The Christian*, 26 February 1961, p. 262.
116. Disciples ecumenist Paul A. Crow, Jr., became COCU's general secretary, and full and serious Disciples participation in COCU augmented Disciples support of church councils, local church unions, and celebrations of the Disciples historic emphasis on Christian unity (*Inter-*

Favorable coverage of the World and National Council of Churches continued in *The Christian*. A Disciple, J. Irwin Miller, was the first layman to serve as the president of the National Council of Churches (1960-1963). Miller praised the Council in a 1965 issue of *The Christian* that on the whole exhibited a defensive posture. It featured George G. Beazley's statement of "New Testament Reasons for Working in the NCC," a straightforward description of the council's work, "testimonials" by well-known Disciples on "Why We Believe in and Support It," and, most revealingly, an effort by Tulsa attorney John Rogers to "set the record straight" relative to "wild accusations" that had been leveled at the council — that it was "soft on Communism," advocated Red China's admission to the United Nations, had allowed "Comsymps" to work on the RSV, had sponsored an " 'invasion' of Mississippi by student volunteers in the summer of 1964," was " 'subversive' of parental authority," advocated "free love," recommended obscene literature, wanted to pressure churches into being politically monolithic, disagreed with the separation of church and state, was a lobby, and claimed to represent the churches.[117] That *The Christian* would give so much space to a defense of the council indicates the depth of its editorial commitment to the council's work. The content of the accusations reveals that, in a number of readers' minds, the council was linked to powers hostile to the nation.

Perhaps it was an unprecedented sense that Christian unity efforts in the 1960s might really bring significant change that drew forth opposition. Much of the opposition to Disciples Restructure in that decade was linked to fear of the kind of Christian union COCU was seen as representing — one in which Disciples identity would be lost. Such was the concern of a correspondent to *The Christian* who, early in the decade, declared that "if Blake's bunch ever approaches Disciple leaders on such a type of unity and our people seriously consider it I shall have to go off and start a cult of my own, dyed-in-the-wool Disciple that I am."[118] An occasional echo of the older antidenominational concept appeared even after Restructure. Sometimes these seemed quite nostalgic. "As a child," a reader wrote in 1976, "I was pleased that I didn't have another religious title tacked on me or above the door of the church to which I belonged. . . . I said I was a Christian . . . — a follower of Christ."[119]

---

national Convention of Christian Churches [Disciples of Christ]: Program[s] [Miami Beach, 1963], pp. 259, 257; [Los Angeles, 1962], p. 279; [Detroit, 1964], p. 292; [Kansas City, 1961], p. 259).

117. J. Irwin Miller, "Disciples Have a Stake in Its Success"; George G. Beazley, "New Testament Reasons for Working in the NCC"; Robert W. Burns et al., "Testimonials: Why We Believe in and Support It"; John Rogers, "Factual Answers to the Charges: A Well-Known Tulsa Attorney Defends the National Council of Churches," *The Christian,* 9 May 1965, pp. 580-85, 589-91, 592-94.

118. Mrs. Claude C. McDonald, "Letters: Dyed-in-the-Wool," *The Christian,* 11 June 1961, p. 30.

119. Mary Wren Reynolds, "Responses: Letters from Readers — Disciple vs. Christian," *The Disciple,* 21 November 1976, p. 32.

In the 1970s Disciples continued to participate in a wide range of inter-denominational Christian unity ventures including COCU, the National and World Councils, the dialogue with the Roman Catholics, Christian union conversations in Canada, and union conversations with the United Church of Christ. Disciples also formed their own Ecumenical Consultative Council. These activities were given leadership and advocacy by the Disciples' Council on Christian Unity.[120] *The Christian* and, after 1973, *The Disciple* gave appreciative coverage to these efforts.[121] Questioning of the fundamental appropriateness of participation in the ecumenical movement was largely limited to the "Letters" page.

CONCLUSION

1. The special significance of the United States in the evangelization of the world and the United States' Christian foundations and Christian character were prominent themes in the interpretation of the nation by the Disciples popular press. New World righteousness and United States altruism stood in contrast to Old World corruption and selfishness. Patriotism was, therefore, a Christian virtue and Christianity a requirement for full participation in the state. These perceptions were clearly predominant in the period from 1880 to the 1930s and resurgent in the 1940s and 1950s.

2. The most dramatic introductions of critical perspectives on the nation came in the 1930s and again in the 1960s and 1970s. The 1930s seems to have been an especially crucial decade. The appearance of Nazism and German Christianity simultaneously with visible right-wing activities in the United States made an indelible impression on the Disciples leadership. The resistance to Nazism of Karl Barth and the German Evangelical Church was also noted. Thus, the "New Reformation" (and its "prophetic realism") must be seen as part of the context for this major shift.[122] The shift in perspective also occurred in the wake of deep disillusionment about church endorsement of World War I

120. *Business Docket of the General Assembly: Christian Church (Disciples of Christ)* (St. Louis, 1979), pp. 104-8.

121. See, for example, Paul A. Crow, Jr., "If Not the Reunion of Christ's Church — Then What?" *The Christian,* 6 May 1973, pp. 548-52; and "News of the Church: UCC, Disciples Dialogue Could Bring Merger," *The Disciple,* 21 November 1976, p. 22.

122. This view holds that "a transcendent God stands over and above the nation rather than being directly identified with it" and remembers "the imperfect nature of political institutions and their leaderships" (Mark G. Toulouse, *The Transformation of John Foster Dulles: From Prophet of Realism to Priest of Nationalism* [Macon: Mercer University Press, 1985], p. xxiv). Christian Church (Disciples of Christ) General Assembly resolutions in the recent past have often reflected this perspective. See, for example, *Business Docket[s] of the General Assembly: Christian Church (Disciples of Christ)* (Cincinnati, 1973), pp. 112-14; (Kansas City, 1977), pp. 165-67, 176-78; (St. Louis, 1979), pp. 217, 234.

and in conjunction with a heyday for organized Disciples pacifism. The sobering experience of the Depression also contributed to the move away from an easy and optimistic association of the destiny of the nation with the mission of God. Therefore, even in the midst of the widespread patriotism during the World War II years and the widespread anticommunist sentiment in the postwar years, there were some voices of caution and even some of criticism.

In the 1960s and 1970s these voices became much more commonplace. Doubts about the Vietnam War, criticism of the CIA, and simply the clear statement that "we must not identify the people of God with any nation-state"[123] arose in these decades and signaled a resurgence of the kind of perspective that had appeared forcefully in the 1930s.

3. One of the most persistent themes in the period that relates to both the theological interpretation of the United States and to antidenominationalism is anti-Catholicism. Disciples' popular views were anti-Catholic, and remained so on largely the same bases from the 1880s through the 1950s. This fit into the idea that "our institutions" were threatened by some hostile, alien, and foreign-controlled power. The threat was typically cast in conspiratorial terms. The collusion of alleged "Roman, Foreign, and Rum powers" was contemplated in the 1880s with passions that resembled those directed toward allegedly "subversive" National Council of Churches members who were accused in the 1960s and 1970s of conspiring with communists. It almost seems as though anticommunism replaced anti-Catholicism.

4. Opposition to denominationalism, in principle, was persistent. However, interdenominational cooperation came into the picture very early. Those Disciples who became the Christian Church (Disciples of Christ) took up the task of reinterpreting traditional Disciples antidenominationalism to allow — even empower — interchurch ecumenical effort. One approach to reinterpretation was to define inappropriate denominationalism as the attitude that holds one's own community aloof from other denominations.[124] While these "cooperative" Disciples retained a version of antidenominationalism in principle, their practice was to be heavily involved in interdenominational

123. Truce V. Lewellyn, "The Spiritual Roots of America," *The Disciple*, 4 July 1976, p. 8.
124. It might be argued that the "definitive" repudiation of the Disciples' traditional (restorationist) approach to antidenominationalism came with Restructure and the groundwork for Restructure in the *Panel of Scholars Reports*. The traditional claims for the "restoration plea" were that it was a biblical, "timeless," and potentially effective way of bringing about the unity of the church and the evangelization of the world. These claims were pointedly contested in the following essays: Dwight E. Stevenson, "Concepts of the New Testament Church Which Contribute to Disciple Thought about the Church," in *The Renewal of Church: The Panel of Scholars Reports*, 3 vols., gen. ed. W. B. Blakemore (St. Louis: Bethany Press, 1963), 3: 49; Ralph G. Wilburn, "A Critique of the Restoration Principle: Its Place in Contemporary Life and Thought," in *The Renewal of Church*, 1: 215-16, 223, 226-33, 241; and Ronald E. Osborn, "Crisis and Reformation: A Preface to Volume I," in *Reformation of Tradition*, pp. 25-26. One way to think of Restructure, then, is in terms of Disciples leaders' coming to realize that the "pious subterfuge" of denying that Disciples were a denomination "could not be sustained" (Ronald E. Osborn, *The Faith We Affirm: Basic Beliefs of Disciples of Christ* [St. Louis: Bethany Press, 1979], p. 65).

Christian unity efforts. This reinterpretation and involvement has been greeted with some opposition, fear, regret, and nostalgia, but thus far these responses have not greatly affected Disciples leadership.

5. In recent times the Christian Church (Disciples of Christ) has witnessed both an overall numerical decline and evidence of some members' alienation from the denominational leadership.[125] In this context it may be pertinent to recall how profoundly Disciples traditions have been recast. Disciples leaders radically reinterpreted the traditional form of Disciples antidenominationalism. Furthermore, the earlier affirmation of the United States as the crucial context — and even the chosen instrument — of God's mission gave way to more ambiguous and even critical views. These shifts were linked because the criticism sometimes arose from ecumenical contexts, and hostility to the nation has been popularly associated with ecumenical commitment. In sum, the reinterpretation of antidenominationalism and re-evaluation of the United States constitute a long-term reversal on the part of Disciples leadership that may well have been disorienting to a significant number of Disciples.

125. For evidence of dissent on statements or actions of Disciples leadership, see J. L. Murray, "Letters: No Adverse Criticism," *The Christian*, 31 December 1961, p. 1690; Mrs. R. Thomason, "Letters: Communist or Ignorant," *The Christian*, 12 September 1965, p. 1182; C. E. Morgan, "Letters: Concerning UN," *The Christian*, 31 October 1965, p. 1406; and Mrs. Kimmie Hart, "Letters: Church and State," *The Christian*, 7 December 1969, p. 1566. Dissent has also been expressed in the form of congregationally sponsored resolutions calling for suspensions of financial support for the World Council of Churches, opposing the communist philosophy, and "calling attention to the violation of human rights in communist-dominated areas" (*Business Docket[s] of the General Assembly: Christian Church [Disciples of Christ]*, 1977, pp. 185-86; 1979, pp. 234, 238). The perception that underlay these resolutions was that Disciples leadership had become disproportionately critical of the West and "soft" on communism.

Practical Concern and Theological Neglect: The UCMS and the Open Membership Controversy

Mark G. Toulouse

INTRODUCTION

The United Christian Missionary Society possesses quite a distinguished history. No comprehensive description of its fifty-year existence has yet found its way into print. Over the years, Spencer Austin, Virgil Sly, and Joseph Edward Moseley all began the process of writing histories but were unable to see their work through to completion. Perhaps the Society's overwhelming accomplishments contribute to the elusive nature of its history. After all, whoever writes the history of the Society will also be addressing a half century of Disciples work in foreign missions, home missions, Christian education, social welfare, church development, and church evangelism. Of course, one should not forget that the histories of the Pension Fund, the Board of Church Extension, the National Benevolent Association, and the Division of Higher Education also have points of intersection with the life of the UCMS. If these aspects of the Society's history were not intimidating enough, the mounds of boxes in Nashville containing papers related to the UCMS would surely cause even the most ambitious of historians to have second thoughts before committing to such a project.

Having spent some six weeks rummaging through these boxes, I have come to a few general observations or conclusions about the nature and work of the UCMS. First, the Society's years of dedicated service at home and abroad represent accomplishments in which Disciples can, for the most part, take great pride. The fact that particular things could have and perhaps should have been done differently does not preclude one from offering the judgment that the achievements of the Society are nothing short of impressive. Many churches and social institutions all over the world owe their existence to the efforts of selfless individuals somehow related to the UCMS and to the Society's careful stewardship of limited resources.

194

Second, the Society's fifty-year existence arguably represents the most powerful and important factor in the development of Disciples church life in the entire history of the Christian Church (Disciples of Christ). When editorial influence waned around the turn of the century, the Society's leaders stepped in to fill the gap, maintaining that influence right up to the time of restructure. The UCMS served as a major propaganda resource for Disciples churches everywhere. It stood behind the preparation of Sunday School materials and offered the official interpretation of Disciples work whenever such an interpretation was needed. Its staff spoke endlessly in Disciples churches on about every topic imaginable.

In the pre-restructure polity of the movement, no real system of checks and balances operated to keep the UCMS from amassing too much power. Admirably, the UCMS usually utilized that power with a genuine sense of responsibility and without violating the trust of the churches supporting it. More importantly, under Virgil Sly's exceptional leadership, the Society readily surrendered its control to make way for the more responsible polity developed in the process of restructure.

One might even conclude that the work of the Society actually laid the necessary groundwork for restructure. If there had been no UCMS, something like it would have had to be developed before any official restructure could have found general acceptance among Disciples churches. Disciples came to recognize themselves as *Church* precisely because the UCMS operated as *Church* in the midst of those years when most Disciples churches acknowledged only a loose association with one another. Over time, the work of the Society clearly demonstrated the value of recognizing the denominational reality of Disciples existence. That contribution provided a key ingredient for accomplishing the relatively smooth transition into restructure.

These observations must, for now, remain hypotheses. My third and final observation, however, serves as the foundation for the focus of this essay. The history of the United Christian Missionary Society adds considerable weight to the judgment that twentieth-century Disciples of Christ have been a theologically impoverished people. This assertion cannot be entirely substantiated within these confines. However, Joseph M. Smith has already impressively demonstrated that Disciples of Christ did not even attempt to develop an adequate theology of mission until the 1950s.[1] Disciples took their first step toward an expressed theology of mission when leaders of the Society published a document entitled "The Strategy of World Missions" in 1955 (it was revised in 1959 and again in 1961).

As Smith has observed, even this document reveals "no fundamental,

---

1. See Smith, "A Strategy of World Mission: The Theory and Practice of Mission as Seen in the Present World Mission Enterprise of the Disciples of Christ" (Th.D. diss., Union Theological Seminary, 1961). This excellent work stands alone in its attempt to offer a critical appraisal of the missionary endeavors of the Society.

theological reconsideration of the nature and basis of the mission enterprise itself." Instead, it gathers excerpted material from more comprehensive theological statements prepared in ecumenical circles. Smith's analysis of these choices makes it clear that Disciples placed a heavy emphasis on pragmatic considerations and tended to overlook "the Biblical understanding of the cross and redemption as articulated in ecumenical missionary circles."[2] As William R. Baird, Jr., points out in his analysis of the document, "it is apparent that pragmatic and utilitarian concerns are foremost in the minds of the authors when in their 'Last Word' they insist that the real test of the proposed strategy is whether or not it will work."[3]

For most of its history, the Society simply left unexplored important theological questions related to world mission. There was no exploration of the nature of the "Word," for example. Most Disciples simply assumed that the Word was something one preached. They did not think about the possibility that the Word of God might be active apart from the Christian evangelistic preaching that "Jesus Christ is Lord" and in ways not readily understood by Christians in the West. Among Disciples, no one recognized that the incarnation itself expresses the theological truth that God's activities in history are always inextricably attached to cultural and historical forms. What implications might such a recognition have for world mission? These and other theological issues — the meaning of the gospel; the foundation, purpose, and hope of the church; the character of discipleship — remained unaddressed by the leaders of the UCMS until well into the 1950s.

Smith devotes the bulk of his dissertation (320 of 455 pages) to exploring the development of mission theory and practice after 1949. Though he addresses the question of why Disciples have only lately taken up the theological task with regard to missions,[4] he does not address the role the open membership controversy of the 1920s might have played in exhibiting and maintaining, or perhaps even substantially contributing to, the poverty of theological reflection among Disciples in the twentieth century. The open membership controversy represents an interesting example of the Disciples' inability to deal with theological issues. The controversy itself also represents a rather formative event for Disciples since it established precedents and directions in both missions and church life that later Disciples have had to struggle with for the remainder of the twentieth century.

---

2. Smith, "A Strategy of World Mission," p. 163. For Smith's analysis of the "Strategy" document, see pp. 155-233.

3. Baird, "The Strategy of World Mission: A Theological Study," *Ecumenical Studies Series* 4 (January 1960): 52.

4. Smith rehearses the Disciples preoccupation with the notion of a "simple" or "pure" gospel and gives considerable attention to the fact that Disciples, in their naive belief in the "perpetual virginity" of the church, have rejected historical considerations and assumed an all-too-simple dichotomy between religion and culture. This is a rather simplistic summary of an excellent section of the dissertation. See Smith, "A Strategy of World Mission," pp. 415-39.

The fact that the controversy coincided with the formation of the UCMS no doubt increased its significance. A stronger, more mature, more confident Society might have been able to respond somewhat differently. This factor, in combination with unreflective theological and cultural presuppositions held by Disciples, helped to generate a Society response to the open membership controversy that had unfortunate consequences both for mission work and for meaningful engagement in theological reflection. For these reasons, the Society's response to open membership deserves closer examination.

THE UCMS AND THE OPEN MEMBERSHIP CONTROVERSY

By the late 1890s, Archibald McLean had grown out of the strict restorationism that had captivated much of Disciples mission life in the nineteenth century. Strict restorationists refused to cooperate meaningfully with other Protestant groups, and some adherents refused even to recognize their legitimate status as Christians. McLean, through his world travels, moved joyfully into a fuller participation in the ecumenical movement.[5] He adopted what might be referred to as a "moderate" restorationism.

This moderate restorationism did not result from significant theological reflection; rather, Archibald McLean and others like him merely reached an understanding that the Methodists and the Presbyterians were well-meaning Christian people. No theological analysis had led to the conclusion that these people should be regarded as Christian or suggested what implications acceptance of them as Christians might hold for the practice of the church at home or on the mission field. Instead, Disciples encounters with these other denominational types simply led them to the conclusion that they could share with them in a common task: world evangelization. Donald McGavran put it rightly when he said in 1961 that "as missionaries proclaimed the Good News and served mankind in the blessed name of our Lord, we found ourselves doing the same things as Mennonites, Methodists, Baptists and Presbyterians. Where men are burning themselves out that Christ be obeyed, a deep unity comes naturally. One does not have to strain after it."[6]

Therefore, on pragmatic grounds, McLean and a few other Disciples

5. See Smith, "A Strategy of World Mission," pp. 74-78. It should be noted that Smith is overstating the case when he writes that there was a "clear abandonment of restorationism as defining either the goal or the method of Christian unity." The open membership controversy was resolved, ultimately, in favor of moderate restorationist understandings of baptism and church membership.

6. McGavran, "Disciples of Christ and the Christian World Mission: In Which We Consider How Our Concept of Mission Has Developed from 1810 to 1960," address delivered before the Commission on Theology of Mission, 3-4 April 1961, p. 7.

began to pursue an active participation in ecumenical gatherings. For example, Stephen Corey, a longtime assistant to McLean and soon to become a key figure in the history of the UCMS, served as the president of the 1921 Foreign Missions Conference of North America and, as one of its twelve representatives, attended the International Foreign Missionary Conference in the summer of 1920.[7] These many ecumenical connections enlivened Corey and provided him with a more energetic, more global, and more inclusive vision. He had matured considerably since his 1909 address in Pittsburgh, an address in which he not only talked in imperialistic terms of the "world conquest" of Christian missions but declared that Jesus Christ had given us a "manly gospel" and that the "very magnitude of this task marks it as a man's job."[8] No doubt his ecumenical involvements had something to do with his changing point of view in these areas.

Corey also attended the Oxford International Missionary Conference in the summer of 1922 as a representative of the UCMS.[9] While in Oxford, he made several notations in his travel diary affirming his belief that Disciples were "greatly helped by these exposures to international groups" and reminding himself "to bring before com. [the Executive Committee of the UCMS] the main points in this conference." His diary also indicated that the conference had given him a renewed sense of urgency with regard to missions: "A revelation," he wrote. "We must strike the note of the awfulness and helplessness of the dark illiterate pagan side of nonChristian world."

In reiterating the three great needs of missions discussed at Oxford, he described the third of these as "the need of bringing the constituency abreast of the processes now working — interpretation." This task would not be easy, and Corey recognized that the UCMS faced "putting over to our constituencies some of the greatest changes yet."[10] The irony of these words becomes clear only when one recognizes that they were written while the UCMS was in the midst of one of the most difficult struggles it would ever face and the need for crucial interpretation existed as never before or since.

Unfortunately, the leaders of the UCMS failed precisely where Corey had stressed the need to succeed: they failed to bring the "constituency abreast

7. See the articles written by Corey on this meeting, "International Missionary Conference," *World Call* 2 (August 1920): 27; and "International Foreign Missionary Conference, Geneva, Switzerland," *World Call* (October 1920): 28-30.

8. Corey, "The Challenge of World Conquest to Christian Men," address to the Brotherhood of Christian Men, Centennial Convention, Pittsburgh, October 1909 (UCMS papers).

9. Samuel Guy Inman tells the story of the founding of the International Missionary Council in "International Missionary Cooperation Restored," *World Call* 3 (December 1921): 36-39. Both Inman and Corey represented the Disciples of Christ as delegates at this third meeting of the International Missionary Council. Corey's attendance is noted in the *Third Annual Report,* p. 16 (UCMS papers).

10. Corey, Oxford travel notebook in a folder marked 1921-1922 of the Corey Papers, housed at Disciples Historical Society in Nashville. The other two needs were to demonstrate international and interdenominational cooperation and to bring up new missionary leaders.

of the processes now working" and to interpret new developments on the mission field. The open membership controversy presented moderate restorationists with an opportunity to undergo a second revision. The mission field context had led some of the UCMS missionaries to abandon one of the last vestiges of restorationism, the relationship between baptism and church membership. As a result, though even these missionaries remained convinced that immersion was the proper form, they advocated a new revision of the moderate restoration position occasioned by their experiences on the mission field.

By taking this position, these missionaries became part of a larger movement among Disciples that C. C. Morrison tagged as "the progressive movement." In his address before the 1919 Kuling Convention, G. B. Baird revealed his own position as he favorably quoted Morrison's description of this movement:

> The progressive movement among the Disciples . . . is characterized by sympathy with the work of modern scholarship and a willingness to accept the readjustments made necessary by the assured results of scholarly inquiry. The progressive movement clings to the ideal of an educated ministry as an essential condition of giving effective interpretation to the Disciples' Mission in the World. . . . [It] welcomes the leadership of scholars and prophets and sees no hope for a religious enterprise that despises or crucifies them. . . . [It] accepts the obligation to make of religion a thing of social service and social salvation, as well as of personal salvation [and] . . . pleads for the adoption of an attitude and practice in the relation of our Disciples' churches to other Christian people which shall be consistent with our historic ideal and our acknowledged duty to practice Christian Unity.[11]

Thus the open membership controversy introduced the possibility of a broad and fairly early acceptance of higher critical conclusions among the Disciples mission leadership. In missionary life, a new, and, as it turned out, short-lived group had joined forces with progressive Disciples at home and started competing with the moderate restorationists and the strict restorationists in the battle for the Disciple mind. The moderate restorationists in the vein of Archibald McLean, Stephen Corey, and Frederick Burnham, to name a few, could easily have accepted the newly revised and progressive views had it not been for several factors, some of them having to do with the uncritical acceptance of particular theological presuppositions.

Other factors, nontheological in nature, hindered theological reflection among Disciples missionary leaders and kept these moderates from being able either to accept the new revisionism of the mission field or interpret it for the "constituency" at home. These factors must be defined as cultural and practical, involving primarily a commitment to the democratic principle and a concern for the financial stability of the new missionary society. Missionary leaders,

11. Morrison, quoted by Baird, in "What Contributions Have the Disciples of Christ to Make to the Chinese Christian Church?" pp. 3-4 (UCMS papers).

in other words, ended up facing the open membership crisis during this crucial period more concerned with pragmatic questions than theological reflection. As a result, they frustrated the burgeoning hope of organic Christian union on the mission field, affected the mission churches in other seriously negative ways, and found themselves at least thirty years behind the rest of the ecumenical movement in developing a sound theology of mission.

THEOLOGICAL PRESUPPOSITIONS

AN EVANGELISTIC GOSPEL

The primary sources reveal little theological rationale standing behind the formation of the UCMS. Ever since the idea of a united missionary society emerged in 1906, articulate supporters usually emphasized the pragmatic advantages of such a society. As Frederick Burnham put it, "there was a growing conviction that, if the Societies could be unified the work could be prosecuted more effectively." The final report of the Unification Committee, presented at Pittsburgh in 1909, stated "that such unification of our home and foreign missionary work, if accomplished, will thrill our churches, bring new life to our missionaries, reduce the number of our problems at home and abroad, increase our receipts, and add to our efficiency."[12] As is often the case with structural questions, pragmatic concerns garnered more attention than discussion of theological commitments.

After looking through the papers of these leaders and articles in *World Call,* one comes to a clearer understanding that traditional notions of evangelism lay at the heart of the founding of the UCMS. But the theological commitments remained hazy. What are the biblical foundations for this gospel? What is the substance of the gospel message? How might the gospel's significance be communicated without violating the integrity of either its biblical foundations or its meaning?

Though the Society did not address any of these questions, its leaders had no doubt about its commitment to evangelism, not only generally, but also as a specific tool to recruit members for the Disciples of Christ. One of the first actions of the Society's executive committee was a recommendation "that immediate entrance be made into a five year worldwide program of New Testament Evangelism, seeking to have one million additions to the [Disciples] Church, at least five hundred thousand of whom shall be by baptism." In order to attain the goal, the committee stressed the need to "place a new emphasis upon individual witness bearing and personal soul winning on the part of all

---

12. Minutes of the Joint Convention called for organizing the UCMS, Cincinnati, 20 October 1919 (UCMS papers).

in the church." A recommendation also emerged from this 1920 meeting to hire Jesse M. Bader as the superintendent of evangelism for the UCMS.[13]

Archibald McLean, the guiding force behind foreign missions prior to the age of the United Christian Missionary Society, set the stage for later commitments to evangelism. In an article published a few years before his death, he insisted that "the Evangelization of the world is the one work the Lord gave the Church to do. . . . In his parting charge, [Christ] made no provision for suspending operations until the last man has heard the word of truth, the gospel of salvation." Like many others, McLean here simply assumed that the content of the gospel was self-evident. There is no theological analysis in this article. The emphasis falls on the fact that "the work must go on." Disciples have no choice. "If we would be loyal to our Lord we must go forward in obedience to his last command."[14]

William Hutchison points out in a recent essay that the rather naive commitment to the Great Commission "as a sufficient justification for missions" recalls the "pre-Edinburgh era." Early in the century, Robert E. Speer and other mainstream missionary leaders such as John R. Mott "had refused to ground the missionary rationale on the Great Commission, which they saw as an overused and simplistic form of biblical literalism that had, moreover, masked too much aggression or insensitivity in the past."[15]

McLean had exposure to these men, as did Stephen Corey and others. But a commitment to the Great Commission as the major rationale for missions continued to dominate the Disciples literature of the 1920s. The Society's widely circulated "Record of Policies" statement of 1922 made it clear: "The

13. Bader was employed for $4,000 per year and given $6,000 expense money and the right to hold two evangelistic meetings himself from which he could keep the proceeds (Minutes of the Executive Committee meeting, 23 November 1920). And see the "Proposed Advance of the United Christian Missionary Society" (UCMS papers). The Proposed Advance was a program of education put forth in recognition of three "outstanding needs of the work" — to initiate an "evangelistic effort toward the goal of winning a million new members in five years," to expand the work subsequently, and to raise the money to do so.

14. McLean, "The Work Must Go On," *World Call* 1 (January 1919): 13. In McLean's *History of the Foreign Christian Missionary Society* (New York: Fleming H. Revell, 1919), he offers the same kind of rationale for the founding of the FCMS. He lists five reasons for organizing. The first is "the desire to obey the will of God." His basic exposition of that point rests in demonstrating that the New Testament is "a missionary book." The Great Commission forms the heart of his argument. Reasons two through five are thoroughly pragmatic: "it might help the work at home"; the "American Society was not in a position to undertake any work in the foreign field"; the "Disciples might preserve their self-respect"; and "intelligent Christians wished to enjoy the culture that can come from the missionary propaganda and from no other source" (pp. 42-50). A picture published in the *World Call* (2 [December 1920]: 30) emotionally depicts the nature of some of that propaganda and suggests why such a work was necessary: it features a group of natives in native dress in the Congo and has as its caption, "For Whom the Gospel Came Too Late: In the Center Is Old Lonjataka, the Congo Chief Who Befriended the Missionaries but Died without Christ."

15. Hutchison, "Americans in World Mission: Revision and Realignment," in *Altered Landscapes: Christianity in America, 1935-1985*, ed. by David W. Lotz (Grand Rapids: William B. Eerdmans, 1989), p. 164.

measure of the faith and vitality of the Brotherhood is the measure of its devotion to the Commission of Jesus for the evangelization, education and elevation of the world. There can be no substitute for obedience to His last Command."[16] This use of the Great Commission kept the Disciples mission movement focused on "soul winning" throughout the 1920s. They maintained this position in spite of the fact that the ecumenical institutions, particularly the international student movement (viz., the Student Volunteer Movement, the YMCA, and the YWCA), worked hard during the same period to reduce "preoccupation with personal evangelism." The organizations representing that movement attempted "to heighten concern for social reform and world reconstruction."[17] Disciples heard this message but always understood it in terms of how it might contribute to personal evangelism.

Frederick W. Burnham, the first president of the UCMS, offers an example of this kind of commitment to evangelism. His most classic expression of evangelism as central to the UCMS appears in a 1926 article in *World Call*. Evangelism, he wrote, "is primary in the task of the church." It "is 'the tie that binds' all the work of the churches of the Disciples of Christ as carried on through the United Christian Missionary Society." Burnham defined evangelism as "any process by which disciples are made and baptized into union with Christ." Any "honorable, ethical method" that produced the "desired results" was, in his view, authorized by the New Testament. There were several "means of approach" that could be utilized in evangelism. "The doctor's medicine and the surgeon's scalpel," wrote Burnham, are also "the means of the entree to the individual soul."[18] Burnham usually expressed the same ideas whenever he commissioned new missionaries.[19]

The "Application for Appointment as a Missionary" had several questions indicating the importance of personal soul winning as the task of the missionary. One of the first substantive questions asked an applicant was "Have you had any experience in personal effort in bringing others to Christ? If yes, in what form of work, and with what success?" Later in the application, the form returned to the subject by asking several other questions: "Do you believe that personal effort to lead people to Christ is the paramount duty of every

---

16. "A Record of the Policies of the United Christian Missionary Society as Enunciated by the Board of Managers," p. 4 (UCMS papers).

17. Hutchison, "Americans in World Mission," p. 157.

18. Burnham, "The Thread That Ties the Work Together," *World Call* 8 (February 1926): 4-6.

19. For example, in 1929 Burnham challenged the new group with these words: "Nothing is more fundamental in this missionary service than the deep and abiding and ever fresh conviction that the highest service which we can render to our fellowmen is to bring them to the knowledge of Christ and to lead them to put their lives under His leadership. The churches in America which you go out to represent will ever count this the primary motive of their missionary support. Important as is educational or medical or agricultural or social service, it gets its supreme sanction as a means to this end" ("Charge to the Missionaries: Ordination Service," Indianapolis, 11 June 1929, pp. 2-3). A similar theme is sounded in a brief article by a woman missionary to Japan — Stella Lewis Young, "Evangelizing without Sermonizing," *World Call* 2 (August 1920): 13.

missionary? Do you propose to make such effort the chief feature of your missionary career, no matter what other duties may be assigned to you?"[20] These questions make it clear that the UCMS considered personal evangelism as the primary objective of the missionary task.[21]

The personal evangelism of Disciples missions during this time period also had a moderate restorationist twist to it.[22] Even though moderate restorationists took a much more generous view of other denominations, they nonetheless maintained some very real vestiges of the restoration viewpoint they had modified earlier. Elements of this moderate restorationism are evident in the 1922 "Record of Policies" statement. Though the Society recognized "the work of other Christian communions" and cooperated "with them as fully as possible without sacrifice of convictions," it also emphasized that Disciples needed to present the witness "for the reunion of the divided church by a restoration of the New Testament order in faith, practice and fruits." The Society could fulfill that work only as it undertook "the task which purified, united and impassioned the early disciples of Jesus."[23]

The restoration mindset, confident of its truth, is clearly represented in this statement. This attitude, accompanied by a clearly inadequate reflection about the theological content and theological implications of the gospel to be preached, separated Disciples from other missionary endeavors during the time period. Disciples had long since concluded that anything beyond the simple affirmation of Christ as Lord only led to dispute and division. Missionaries and missionary leaders were confident that they had the gospel, and Disciples were more interested in getting results than in questioning fundamental presuppositions about the content of that gospel.

20. "Application for Appointment as a Missionary," United Christian Missionary Society. The forms I looked at had been filled out by Nancy Adeline Fry in June 1920, Oswald Goulter in September 1921, and Grace Stevens Corpron in October 1922 (UCMS papers).

21. Alexander Paul, Executive Director of Oriental Missions, affirmed this personally in a letter to Margueritte Bro 17 February 1925. She was complaining that evangelism seemed to get lost on the mission field in the midst of good schools, first-class hospitals, and institutional churches. Paul wrote that "With you, I believe that no matter how well trained a man or woman may be, if they do not have the intense desire to reach the Chinese and link them up in a definite way with Jesus Christ and then be patient enough to train them to work for Him and His program, they are bound, in the long run to fall short of being ideal missionaries" (UCMS papers).

22. It should be pointed out, however, that there were two notions of restorationism operating. The conservatives wanted to teach the principles of the Restoration movement on the mission field. John T. Brown, for example, wanted all cooperation with other Protestant groups stopped. But Corey and the UCMS leadership were more interested in the basic principles of restorationism. As Corey put it in response to Brown, "No creed less Christ — No book but Bible — No name but Christian. . . . Why pagan never even heard of Calvin or Luther or the reason for Restoration movt. Do well enough if you get them to know Christ + God" (personal notes taken at the time of the passing of the Sweeney Resolution, Steubenville, Ohio [UCMS papers]). However, like the founders of the movement, the leadership found itself necessarily denying the possibility of church membership without immersion, even on the mission field.

23. "A Record of the Policies of the United Christian Missionary Society as Enunciated by the Board of Managers," adopted by the Board of Managers of the UCMS in St. Louis, 18-19 January 1922, p. 4.

As Joseph Smith has observed, the Society's administration "became more and more preoccupied with the practical and the procedural." Both the conservative and the innovator, on the mission field and off, tended toward "concluding that whatever gets results must be the gospel." Smith concludes that "the How of getting the job done precluded the possibility of asking seriously and fundamentally, *What,* after all, *is* the gospel."[24] The existence of such a vacuum in theological reflection no doubt led Virgil Sly, Chair of the UCMS Division of World Mission, to exclaim in 1959 that "The necessity of an adequate theology of missions must be faced. We need to know what we are trying to do, what we are trying to say, and what we are in mission for."[25]

B. SPIRITUAL AND PRAGMATIC UNION

One of the most significant factors in holding Disciples to their unreflective theological presuppositions was the strict restorationist group, composed of the *Christian Standard* and its supporters. A voice as passionate as theirs could hardly be ignored by the moderates as they contemplated the revisionist proposals being formulated on the mission field. These conservatives already believed that McLean and others had distorted the vision of the founders when they became involved in ecumenical conversations for the sake of evangelism. Battle lines had already been drawn. The new revisionism beginning to emerge in some circles at home and in missionary circles abroad only confirmed the greatest fear of these conservatives: in their view, the moderates were getting ready to abandon the restorationist ship altogether, hoping to take crew and provisions with them. The conservatives intended to stand in the way.

In 1919 two developing union movements in China caught the attention of the missionaries stationed there. A national movement under the direction of the Presbyterian, Congregational, and London missions looked very promising and indicated the need for some kind of formal statement from Disciples about mutual recognition of membership if they were to have any hope of being a part of it. Another proposed union movement was gaining steam in Nanking and was more local than national. The Disciples among the China Mission did not want to be left out. The Nanking movement wanted to unite all the evangelistic forces of the city into one "well organized movement,

---

24. Smith, "A Strategy of World Mission," p. 114.

25. Sly, "Mission and Change," 2 December 1959, p. 7 (UCMS papers). At the time those words were spoken, Disciples were about one year into their five-year reflection on the topic of a theology of mission. In August 1956 the Council on Christian Unity and the World Division of the United Christian Missionary Society sponsored the formation of a "Commission on Theology of Mission," composed of seminary professors and UCMS staff. Joseph Smith, professor at Christian Theological Seminary when the Commission began and executive secretary of the department of East Asia for the UCMS when the study ended, served as chair of the Commission and, no doubt, constituted the driving force behind the Commission.

including all the churches." The movement's goals related to "the free inter-change of membership, of Pastors, evangelists and other workers, subject to the direction of the union committee."[26]

Frank Garrett, secretary to the Central Christian China Mission, knew that the missionaries would need to deal with the question of open membership as a prerequisite to participation in the two union movements. He wrote a letter to George Baird, a Disciples missionary who served as pastor of the church at Luchowfu, asking him to deliver the keynote address before the annual convention of the mission in Kuling in 1919. He chose Baird because he knew Baird's position on the open membership question. Baird hesitated to accept the assignment because he still remembered his experience in 1909 after he had delivered a similar paper. F. M. Rains, secretary for the Foreign Christian Missionary Society, had been present, and, after Baird's paper, pushed for his recall. Garrett responded to Baird's hesitation by urging him to reconsider:

> This is a time when we must probe this question to the bottom. We cannot longer take a traditional view. We must re-examine our foundations. The crisis is upon us. . . . The question [of a potential break with the Society] seems to be a very vital one now in Nanking. It will come to all of us in a large way in the near future. . . . Do not let your former experience [with Rains] trouble you now. Give us the best you can.[27]

Baird reconsidered, accepted the offer, and delivered his paper. "I am firmly convinced," Baird preached, "that we should make this move and go on record as in favor of the free interchange of members with all evangelical churches. We dare not continue the position that would force us to continue as an isolated group in China in the midst of a great union movement."[28] The Central Christian China Mission unanimously affirmed Baird's call for "open membership" and then promptly elected him president of the next year's convention. Garrett immediately wrote a letter to R. A. Doan, an assistant to Archibald McLean, asking that the Society give the question its "consideration with the understanding that the step has the approval of the China Mission."[29]

Garrett and the rest of the China Mission underestimated the response at home. Because of suspicions resulting from the consolidation of the various missionary societies into one society, the United Christian Missionary Society's new leadership faced significant problems of its own in 1919.[30] When Garrett's letter arrived at the offices of the Foreign Christian Missionary Society, it only

---

26. Details of these union movements are found in a letter from G. B. Baird to Morrison dated 27 December 1919 (UCMS papers).

27. See copies of these letters in the correspondence carried on between Baird and C. C. Morrison, 19 October 1920 (UCMS papers).

28. Baird, "What Contributions Have the Disciples of Christ to Make to the Chinese Christian Church?" Kuling Convention Keynote, August 1919, pp. 8-9 (UCMS papers).

29. Frank Garrett to R. A. Doan, 11 August 1919 (UCMS papers).

30. See Stephen J. Corey, *Fifty Years of Attack and Controversy: The Consequences among Disciples of Christ* (St. Louis: Christian Board of Publication, 1953), pp. 60-61.

complicated the situation because it reopened the controversy over open membership precisely at the time that the *Christian Standard* was fighting the formation of the new United Christian Missionary Society.

When the executive committee of the Foreign Christian Missionary Society received Garrett's letter, Robert E. Elmore was the recording secretary. After the approval of the formation of the United Christian Missionary Society at the Cincinnati International Convention of 1919,[31] he resigned his position and began a long association with the *Christian Standard.* Elmore then started to attack the formation of the UCMS and, since he had knowledge of Garrett's letter, he used it as ammunition, writing editorials claiming that the China missionaries favored open membership.[32] These actions contributed to the new Society's decision to take a defensive posture.

The Society's response to Garrett did not result from any lack of sympathy for what the missionaries faced on the field. Most of the major players at home recognized the problems in China and in the Philippines, both areas where union movements were beginning in earnest. But UCMS leaders found themselves at a loss as to how to deal with conservative criticism of open membership. They had no reflective or compelling theological rationale to offer Disciples regarding the issue. When leaders in the UCMS and elsewhere among Disciples talked about union, they talked mostly in terms of a unity that was either practical (uniting together for a common task, such as evangelism) or spiritual (we are related as members of Christ's invisible church). Organic unity (visible merger of churches and institutions) occasionally received mention as an ultimate goal, but always with the additional emphasis that it needed to take place along New Testament lines, meaning, at the very least, that it had to develop in accord with restorationist understandings of baptism.[33]

Even Peter Ainslie, the well-known spokesperson for Christian union during these days, expressed these sentiments before the open membership

31. A constitution was adopted for the International Convention of the Disciples of Christ in 1917. Therefore, 1917 was the transition year, changing the annual conventions of the missionary societies into an autonomous International Convention.

32. See R. E. Elmore, "Does China Mission Endorse Open Membership?" *Christian Standard,* 7 August 1920, pp. 1107ff. There can be no question that this is exactly the proper interpretation of the Garrett letter. Though he later hedged, saying that the 1919 China Convention did not vote in favor of open membership but merely to raise the question with the home society (see Frank Garrett to A. McLean, October 11, 1920), the evidence is altogether one-sided that all the missionaries present at the 1919 China Mission Convention (with the possible exception of Elliot Osgood) favored open membership (see Pearl Taylor Sarvis to Steve Corey, 14 August 1922 [UCMS papers]). Joseph Smith evidently did not have access to all the mission field letters when he judged that "Garrett's letter was misinterpreted by some to mean that Garrett and other missionaries were advocating 'open membership'" ("A Strategy of World Mission," p. 83). It is clear from the correspondence and from the China Mission's resounding support of Baird's address that this is precisely what Garrett and the other missionaries were doing.

33. For further discussion about the differing Disciples notions of church union throughout the last century, see the essay by Douglas A. Foster on pp. 236-59 in this volume.

controversy surfaced. When he discussed the question of the "catholic administration of the ordinances" in an address before the Conference on Organic Church Union in Philadelphia in early 1919, he said that Disciples are "constrained to adopt the immersion of penitent believers as the one catholic baptism, recognized by all communions . . . and therefore the one baptism on which all Christians can agree and unite."[34]

Though Ainslie could hardly be considered a conservative, he still held to an essentially "spiritual" view of union in that he preferred placing emphasis on the equality of believers before Christ over seeking organizational strategies for unity. For some Disciples, however, this theology seemed too otherworldly; if believers are to be equal before Christ, then theology should also dictate that they should be, where possible, united in one church. George Baird, for example, stood in agreement with Charles Clayton Morrison that the church on earth needed visible unity, and the quicker the better. As a result, Baird felt that he could not ignore the content of Ainslie's address before the 1919 Conference on Organic Church Union: "Mr. Ainslie might be told that he recognizes as Christians millions of men and women whom he would not receive as members of his own congregation, unless they were willing to accept our interpretations of the Bible and our administration of the ordinances." Baird asked the other China missionaries whether they would "allow the union again to be broken on one of our so-called pillars of union, or will the union refuse to be broken and go on without us." Unwilling to accept either possibility, Baird then offered a rousing challenge to the missionaries to be true to the historic Disciples commitment to union in practice as well as in theory.[35] As he put the question to Archibald McLean in October of 1919, "Is any platform more important than the opportunity to enter into a union for which we have been praying as a people for one hundred years?"[36] "While desirous of promoting union in every way possible," McLean responded, in "seeking to unite, we must not divide."[37]

This great fear of divisive issues merged with a largely pragmatic and spiritual view of church union to produce a conservative reaction to the possibilities of achieving a truly organic church union on the mission fields. Baird's hope for unity, unanimously affirmed by the missionaries at the time he delivered the keynote address in 1919, lost the day. His open membership stance proved to be unacceptable to the leadership of the Society. He and his

---

34. Ainslie, "The Message of the Disciples of Christ," *World Call* 1 (March 1919): 24.

35. Baird, "What Contributions Have the Disciples of Christ to Make to the Chinese Christian Church?" pp. 3, 8-9 (UCMS papers). Baird gives a critical review of Ainslie's whole address in the opening pages of this address before the Kuling Christian China Mission Convention of 1919.

36. Baird to McLean, 5 October 1919. Frank Garrett, in a letter to R. A. Doan, described the Plan of Union as "a real, conscientious effort at church union of which we must take notice" (Garrett to Doan, 23 September 1919 [UCMS papers])

37. McLean to Baird, 24 November 1919 (UCMS papers).

wife were forced to resign after nearly sixteen years on the mission field.[38]
When they arrived stateside, his wife suffered a nervous breakdown and had
to be treated in a sanitarium while he took the pastorate of a very small
Congregational church. In retrospect, Baird's original hesitation about delivering the address appears to have been prophetic, while Frank Garrett's advice
that Baird ignore his former experience with Rains proved to be hopelessly
naive.

In 1920 the executive committee sent to the missionaries a clear message
that "organization and maintenance of the work on the mission field" had to
be conducted "in consonance with the teachings of the Disciples of Christ in
the United States." Only "those who have been baptized by immersion" could
be counted as candidates for church membership. Rebaptism was held to be
essential in cases involving those who had been baptized as infants.[39] Theological questioning of this practice had begun to emerge in some Disciples
circles, though it had not found any support among UCMS leadership.[40] The

38. The following letters document Corey's desire to recall Baird: Corey to Doan, 15
December 1921; Doan to Corey, 16 December 1921; Mrs. Eva Raw Baird to Corey, 25 February
1922.

39. The Corey Statement indicates that those Christians who are attending the church not
as members but as Christians "are taught the New Testament way as we understand it and, if they
desire immersion, are received formally into the churches" ("International Convention of Disciples
of Christ, the Coliseum, St. Louis, Mo., October 18-24, 1920: Minutes," *World Call* 2 [December
1920]: 29). One such case is recorded in "Report of the Commission to the Orient," *World Call*
8 (August 1926): 35. Even an advocate of open membership such as E. K. Higdon felt completely
comfortable with the concept of rebaptism. By 1922 he had rebaptized four or five such Christians
(see E. K. Higdon to John T. Brown, 16 March 1922). The UCMS publicized a letter from E. I.
Osgood, missionary in Chuchow, China, in which he mentions the rebaptism of Tsien Si-Lin, a
pastor among them: "So I had a few talks with him and he saw that to be loyal as a pastor amongst
us, he should be immersed. More than that he is a deep Bible student and had come to the conviction
that immersion is the Scriptural baptism. So he was immersed and we received him formally into
the membership." Osgood talks about the large number of rebaptisms that had gone on in Chuchow
of men who were sprinkled. "I feel that a 'sprinkled' man among us is not loyal to the people
who support him, nor to the religion he claims to be preaching as their representative" (Osgood,
quoted in a UCMS document entitled "Statement Concerning the St. Louis 'Medbury' Resolution
and Developments on the Mission Field," p. 6). The UCMS used evidence like this to confirm
the orthodoxy of those on the field. But Baird asserted that rebaptism on the mission field "certainly
has never been a general practice and no strong pressure has been exerted to get members of other
churches to accept re-baptism" (UCMS papers).

40. In the summer of 1920, C. C. Morrison referred to believer's baptism as a "passing
dogma." "Chief among these signs of a new state of mind," he wrote, "is the growing practice of
receiving unimmersed Christians from other communions without insisting upon their rebaptism.
This practice is becoming quite commonplace now, though the pioneers of the idea ten and fifteen
years ago endured the odium theologicum in its most drastic form" ("A Passing Dogma," *Christian
Century,* 26 August 1920, p. 7). This article caused the UCMS quite a bit of consternation because
Morrison also asserted in it that "Most if not all of the mission churches of Disciples in China
have been for some time receiving unimmersed Christians into their membership." The March
1936 issue of the *Scroll* lists twenty-two churches that responded to E. S. Ames's request for
churches practicing open membership to step forward. More are believed to have been practicing
it by that time, though they evidently preferred to remain anonymous. The University Christian
Church of Chicago practiced open membership and refused to rebaptize as early as the first decade

position taken by the UCMS could not help but carry with it an air of superiority. As Stephen Corey put it in early 1923,

> While care should be taken in the public recognition of these people and in the designating terms used, so that they will not be confused with the regular membership of the churches, they should be accorded a real part in the congregational life of the churches while separated from their own congregations where they hold membership, and *while they are being instructed in the way of the Lord more perfectly.*[41]

Ainslie's view of unity prevailed. This meant that the most one could do on the mission field was talk in lofty principles about either spiritual or practical union. Stephen J. Corey described this practical unity as "the division of territory or acceptance of responsibility in the great heathen fields of the world."[42] Such a description finds various modes of expression in the UCMS literature,[43] as in the almost motto-like phrase, "the promotion of Christian unity for the evangelization of the world."[44]

---

of the twentieth century. In 1942 Clarence E. Lemmon, who happened to be pastor of an open membership church, was elected as the first president of the International Convention. But the UCMS remained committed to a policy of not advocating open membership for the mission fields through the mid-1950s.

41. Corey, "Statement concerning the Report of the China Mission," p. 3 (UCMS papers); italics mine.

42. Corey, in an unpublished "Open Letter to John T. Brown," p. 17 (UCMS papers).

43. See also Corey's statement in the minutes of the St. Louis Convention, *World Call* 2 (December 1920): 29. In this context, Corey defined practical union on the mission field in terms of "matters of cooperation in education, in medical work and in the problem of such a division of the vast populations to be evangelized so that the fields could be most quickly covered with the teachings of Christ, always endeavoring to eliminate all possible friction and trying to assume worthy responsibilities in the great fields." Peter Ainslie and others signed a statement put forth by the Committee on Fraternal Relations of the International Convention in St. Louis which read, "The Disciples are co-operating on the mission field with other Christian bodies and thereby are bearing practical witness to the necessity of co-operative work among Christians. We are likewise cooperating in the work of the Federal Council of the Churches of Christ in America and thereby are testifying again to the necessity of co-operative work among Protestants. We have likewise joined hands in the internationalizing of the Federal Council of the Church of Christ for Life and Work" (p. 30). W. F. Rothenburger affirmed this vision of practical unity in much the same way: "On the average, 98 per cent. of the Orient still bows down to pagan gods. Can we not see how the two per cent. will gravitate together that they may carry the cross of Jesus Christ? It is no sin to court the fellowship of all people who desire that Jesus Christ and His cross shall prevail in the Orient" ("Report of Commission to Orient," *Christian Standard*, 4 December 1926, p. 13).

44. See "Report of the Commission to the Orient," *World Call* 8 (August 1926): 42. The official "Record of the Policies of the UCMS" put it this way: "The first duty and responsibility of the United Christian Missionary Society is the establishment everywhere of churches of Christ. While doing this it recognizes the work of other Christian communions and cooperates with them as fully as possible without the sacrifice of convictions in order that the open Bible and a knowledge of Christ may be made accessible to the whole world at the earliest possible moment" ("A Record of the Policies of the United Christian Missionary Society as Enunciated by the Board of Managers," adopted by the Board of Managers of the UCMS, St. Louis, 18-19 January 1922, p. 2). Corey also indicates his commitment to this understanding in his "Open Letter to John T. Brown" when he emphasizes that practical unity "has never been accepted with any infringement on our

In Corey's 1921 Oxford travel diary, he noted that he came back from the conference "more than ever believing in a spiritual and practical unity with a common confession of faith, but more doubtful as to unity in forms of worship and ordinance." For him, the "great question" had become "whether we will come at union from standpoint of formula or life." By "formula" he meant uniting around a creed; by "life" he meant uniting in spirit. Disciples historically preferred "life" over "formula." The ironic point here is that it was the Disciples' "formula" (one might even say "creed") regarding believer's immersion, and the unlikelihood that other traditions would accept it, that led Corey and other Disciples through time to choose spiritual unity rather than organic unity. Following a long Disciples heritage, Corey lifted up spiritual and practical unity for the mission fields over the possibility of organic unity. The arguments put forth for spiritual and practical unity were essentially pragmatic, most of them pertaining to cooperative evangelism on the mission field. The rationale for organic unity would have had to come from solid theological reflection. It appears that only a few missionaries on the field, perhaps largely due to the circumstances they found themselves in, were attempting to do much of that.[45]

Guy Sarvis approached the theological heart of the matter when he wrote Corey expressing his belief that "the real underlying question [pertains to] what relations of fellowship or opposition or separation should exist among people who are honestly trying to be disciples of Christ." He concluded by saying that "those who were responsible for the statements of the Society either didn't see [this question] or didn't care to face it."[46] In response to a policy statement passed by the Executive Committee in September 1921, Frank Garrett, more conservative than Sarvis or George Baird, addressed the same point when he told Corey that the UCMS leadership had tried

> to make the scripture say what it does *not* say and teach what it does *not* teach. . . .
> It seems to me your statement condemns the present and blocks the future, and

convictions or practice whatever" (p. 17). At one point, Leslie Wolfe, a conservative missionary in the Philippines, led a challenge to the comity agreements that had been worked out with the Methodists and also questioned the working relationship that Disciples had in particular cooperative enterprises such as schools and hospitals. The UCMS was forced to demonstrate that the comity agreement in question, originally made in Manila in 1923 and approved in Oklahoma City in 1925, did not involve any "sacrifice of principle nor surrender of our people to other religious bodies." The "Report of the Commission to the Orient" (*World Call* 8 [August 1926]: 34-43) verified this (p. 35) and exonerated the UCMS and the Philippine missionaries. Mr. and Mrs. Leslie Wolfe were recalled because of their participation in the "alienation of native workers," his "inefficiency . . . as an evangelistic leader," and "incompatibility or unfortunate incapacity for doing team work." See *United Society News* 1 (July 23, 1926): 1 for a summary of the longer report found on pp. 34-35 of the "Report of the Commission" in *World Call* (UCMS papers).

45. Material related to this issue can be found in Baird's addresses to the 1919 and 1920 China Mission Conventions and in various letters from Guy Sarvis to Steve Corey. In a letter dated 31 August 1922 Sarvis wrote, "I will not serve in a mission or under a Board which in any way limits the completeness of the fellowship in service in a local congregation of all those who are mutually recognized in that congregation as disciples of Jesus Christ" (UCMS papers).

46. Sarvis to Corey, 1 January 1921 (UCMS papers).

that without any scriptural warrant. . . . The question is what relation did the New Testament church sustain to those whom they recognized as in Christ, in the Kingdom, in vital relationship with God — having found peace in Him — but though they had enjoyed this relationship for years were yet unimmersed? What is the New Testament teaching and practice on this relationship? If you are not speaking to the last point you are evading the issue and causing greater trouble for the future. If you are speaking to the last point you are dead wrong and neither the missionaries nor the churches will stand by you.[47]

Garrett's restorationism found a more logical expression than that of the leaders at home. Though he believed immersion to be the "more perfect" way, he consistently urged that it should not be made "a test of fellowship for those who are recognized Christians." "Was [Christ's] promise to the baptized to hinge on the form [utilized by the baptizer]?" asked Garrett. He maintained that in the absence of a "thus saith the Lord," the spirit of Christ and of the early church demanded that Disciples receive into membership "recognized Christians" who had not come to a full or proper understanding of baptism, without ever requiring them to become immersed believers.[48]

The moderate restorationism of the Society's leaders at home was not as generous. Their presuppositions about Disciples distinctives in relation to a restored church and their affirmation of a spiritual over organic view of church unity militated against their ability to affirm *in practice* the theological concept of the catholicity of the church.[49] As Joseph Smith pointed out in his analysis of Disciples missions, "in rejecting Christendom [Disciples] also renounced their heritage in the universal Christian community and became, in point of fact, not a primitive New Testament church, but an indigenous, American religious community."[50]

The Society's inability to recognize that "the church always and everywhere *is,* in its very existence, a catholic community"[51] blocked missionary efforts working toward organic union. The promising union movements in China temporarily died out, largely because of the controversy among Disciples. In 1925, the Union Seminary in China threatened to break up when the Society asked the Disciples to urge a change of constitution to suit Disciples needs.[52] In the Philippines, when the Society struck down a policy of "affiliated membership," Frank Stipp, a leading missionary there, wrote

47. Garrett to Corey, 26 December 1921 (UCMS papers).
48. Garrett to Robert Doan, 10 January 1921 (UCMS papers).
49. In these beliefs, these leaders were really fairly close to Alexander Campbell's position. He recognized as Christians those who had not been immersed, but, due to his commitment to the establishment of a restored church, and believing that such a restored church must include only those who were properly baptized, he found himself unable to admit any Christians into the membership of the church who had not been immersed as believers. For a further explanation of this point, see my brief essay, "An Open Question," in *The Disciple* 15 (May 1988): 25-27.
50. Smith, "A Strategy of World Mission," p. 428.
51. Smith, "A Strategy of World Mission," p. 454.
52. Garrett to Corey, 22 October 1925 (UCMS papers).

Corey expressing the certainty that "it is useless for us to sit longer with the committee planning for the United Church . . . and in fact our presence would be embarrassing in taking up in a frank way the question of interchange of members."[53]

When, by 1928, both a United Church of Christ in China and a United Church of Christ in the Philippines had been launched successfully, the Disciples stood on the sidelines. Alexander Paul, Oriental Secretary of the UCMS, offered a weak explanation in the pages of *World Call*.[54] Virgil Sly's assessment, offered when he was an officer of the UCMS in 1954, described the Society's posture toward these unions more accurately as "a tragic mistake."[55]

---

53. Stipp to Corey, 27 November 1925 (UCMS papers). Stipp wrote this letter in response to the Society's rejection of the Philippine missionaries' proposal for participation in the Filipino union movement. Stipp had at one time offered new members an option of church membership involving the following statement: "Retaining membership in the Evangelical church of which I am now a member and coming as a guest to enjoy the fellowship of this church and to participate in its congregational life" (see letter from W. H. Hanna to the *Christian Standard,* 11 July 1925). At the twenty-fourth annual convention of the Philippines Mission 4 April 1925, the Disciples met to consider the plan for a United Church in the Philippines and passed the following resolution in order to bring permanence to the makeshift way Stipp handled the question in his church: "Whereas members of churches of other communions are often located in communities where we have the only church, and Whereas we wish to give them the fullest possible recognition in our churches, Be it resolved, that it is the sense of the Christian Mission that evangelical Christians who have not conformed to our requirements for regularly entering the church should be listed as affiliated members while still retaining their memberships in their home churches." Corey prevented the use of the term "affiliated members" but basically supported the concept. In a letter to Burnham he commented that "There is no 'open membership' in the Philippine Islands, but simply a friendly plan on the part of our people to nourish and affiliate isolated Christians who come to our towns. They may have been a little unfortunate in the use of the term 'affiliated membership', but what they are trying to do is certainly just what we would want them to do" (Corey to Burnham, 30 September 1925). In its official response, however, the Society "wrote the mission agreeing with their desire to make other Christians feel at home in the churches, but calling in question the advisability of using the term 'affiliated members' in connection with the recognition and welcoming of Christians of other communions into the churches, because of misunderstanding and criticism which might arise. The mission has replied that they wish to conform in every way to the wishes of the Society, that the resolution was only a statement of opinion for our approval, and has never been put into effect and that the matter has been dropped. They also state that they had recommended the recognizing of other Christians, or 'affiliated members' in order that our churches might be a part of the Union Filipino Church if it should come in the Islands" ("A Statement with Regard to the Issue of 'Open Membership' as Raised in Connection with our Missionary Work" [UCMS papers]). The UCMS stopped Disciples participation in the union movement through this action. By the time the Orient Commission (an official investigative group representing the Executive Committee of the UCMS) visited the Philippines in early 1926, all practices of "associated membership" had ceased. Unimmersed worshipers at Stipp's Taft Avenue Church were only said to have a "spiritual home" and were "not identified with the congregation in any form of church membership." Here is more evidence of spiritual unity as opposed to organic unity. See "The Report of the Commission to the Orient," *World Call* 8 (August 1926): 35.

54. Paul, "Why Are the Disciples of Christ out of the United Church in China: Analyzing Its Constitution," *World Call* 10 (March 1928): 9-10. Though the article seems slanted toward China, it does treat the Philippine situation as well.

55. Sly, "Christian Unity and World Missions," Speech at Disciples Pre-Evanston Consultation, Chicago, 8 August 1954 (UCMS papers).

Largely due to the Society's handling of the open membership question, organic union did not emerge on the mission field at all for Disciples until it became a coerced necessity brought on by the Axis powers during World War II. In this respect, actions during this first period set back by decades the cause of Disciples missions in comparison to other mainstream traditions.[56]

CULTURAL PRESUPPOSITIONS AND PRAGMATIC CONCERNS PROHIBITING THEOLOGICAL REFLECTION

In addition to unchallenged theological presuppositions, cultural assumptions and pragmatic concerns also stood between the Society and the development of a more enlightened posture from which to deal with the whole question of open membership. For example, the Society's leaders understood the UCMS as an organization of the church carrying out the will of the constituency that supported it. Frederick Burnham, president of the UCMS from 1919 to 1929, illustrated how this served as a guiding principle when he indicated in a letter to E. L. Thornberry of Kentucky that "the United Christian Missionary Society does not attempt to deal in theological matters. It is a missionary society and carries on the enterprises which the brotherhood commits to its charge."[57] As Burnham's comments illustrate, the UCMS did not understand its task to be a theological one, leading the churches to more serious theological reflection about the nature of world mission; rather, the Society defined itself as an agency responsible to the will of the majority. This democratic principle received uncritical affirmation throughout the open membership controversy. Only a few clear-thinking missionaries questioned the wisdom of operating in this way.

The practical question of financial support made it difficult to question this democratic principle. Any possibility of open membership on the mission fields, the leaders quickly learned, considerably threatened the UCMS coffers.

56. It is interesting to note that Donald McGavran points out the disastrous effects of the open membership controversy from a different perspective. In 1961, he wrote, "The open membership war — it was an American war remember — wrecked our Church in the Philippines and stopped its growth for twenty five years. It prevented the salvation of at least forty thousand souls and condemned us to a minor position among the churches in those islands" ("Disciples of Christ and the Christian World Mission," pp. 8-9 [UCMS papers]).

57. Burnham to Thornberry, 9 April 1928 (UCMS papers). In two crucial addresses before the Board of Managers intended to defend the inherent right of private opinion, Burnham stressed his belief that the UCMS could "retain its democracy and yet be efficient . . . in effectively promoting and administering the work of the Kingdom of God on earth" ("Address to the Board of Managers of the United Christian Missionary Society," St. Louis, 18-19 January 1922). This was the meeting that passed the Sweeney Resolution; see also "Address to the Board of Managers of the United Christian Missionary Society," St. Louis, 2-3 December 1925, occasioned by the passing of the Oklahoma City resolutions (UCMS papers).

Since the UCMS had only just begun its work when the open membership controversy flared up, the financial implications were hard to ignore. Without money, the evangelistic task could not be accomplished. Anything that threatened the support of the Society struck at the very heart of what it hoped to accomplish.

Both of these factors — the democratic principle and the great concern for financial support — led to another rather unfortunate development that assumed a bit more permanence due to the open membership controversy. Since the UCMS took its marching orders from the democratic majority who paid the bills, the mission churches also had to take their directions from those who paid the bills. The extension of the democratic principle in this way eventuated in a paternalistic attitude toward mission churches that took decades to overcome.[58] Such a perspective only served to reinforce an attitude of cultural superiority that greatly affected the work of mission churches through mid-century.

A. THE ASSERTION OF THE DEMOCRATIC PRINCIPLE

When the open membership issue surfaced in the fall of 1919, the new UCMS leadership responded that "the whole question is of too much importance to be determined by any small group."[59] As McLean put it, to decide the issue as the China Mission had suggested would mean "a departure from what has been believed and practiced by our people."[60] The Executive Committee therefore communicated its belief that "in the final analysis the decision does not rest with our board but with the entire brotherhood."[61] In other words, even before the UCMS had approval to act as a legally constituted unit of the International Convention, it asserted its commitment to the democratic principle of operation.

Stephen J. Corey had more influence over Disciples missionary endeavors during this time period than any other person. When thinking through what posture one might assume in order to get along with those who disagreed, he jotted down the following sentence in his travel diary: "Somewhere between

58. This paternalistic stance toward the new churches held sway until at least 1949. A principle asserting the autonomy of mission churches was not finally written into policy until the adoption of the "Strategy of World Missions" in 1955 (see Sly, "Christian Unity and World Missions," p. 24; see also "Strategy of World Missions" [Indianapolis: Foreign Division of the United Christian Missionary Society, 1955], pp. 11-12: "The Society acknowledges that the church on the mission field has the right of decision. By this we mean the principle of the autonomy of the local church is applicable to the church in mission lands as well as to the church at home. However, it must be pointed out that the right of decision also assumes the willingness of the group who makes it to accept the results such decision may entail" [UCMS papers]).

59. Doan to Garrett, 19 November 1919 (UCMS papers).

60. McLean to Garrett, 24 November 1919 (UCMS papers).

61. Doan to Garrett, 19 November 1919 (UCMS papers).

the modern mind and the fundamentalist is safe ground."[62] Throughout his long ministry with the UCMS, and later as president at Lexington's College of the Bible, he worked hard to maintain that ground.

Corey had great confidence in the democratic process.[63] He evidently never thought much about how establishing and executing a missionary policy on the basis of democracy might frustrate theological responsibility. Instead, he emphasized that the democratic approach protected against the more autocratic tendencies represented in the conservative wings of the church. In his handwritten notes to himself, one of his favorite ways of thinking things through, Corey wrote, "When our good people, who do this work and are interested in it want to change me they can do it. This is a spiritual + democratic agency subject to our people." That was much preferable, in his view, to the direction of the "work by a publishing house [*Christian Standard*] which is autocratic + subject to the whim + predjudice [*sic*] of one man + which is impregnable to opinion + cannot be changed."[64]

These notes were written just after the passage of the so-called Sweeney Resolution by the Board of Managers. That resolution, passed in January of 1922, stipulated that only "immersed, penitent believers" were to be received into membership. Further, it stipulated that only missionaries "in sincere accord with this policy" should be appointed or continue in service. The context of Corey's notes makes it clear that he hoped to find a way to affirm the future in the light of these resolutions. He expressed his conclusion in a general letter mailed to all missionaries in the field in March of 1922: "At the time I felt it unwise to express the matter just as it was expressed, but now that it has been done, I feel like going on just as in the past, with the thought that we are a democracy and that things will work out all right as we proceed."[65] Corey's confidence in the democratic process paid off. Later in the year, the Board of Managers relieved the problem considerably by offering an interpretation of the resolution Corey considered acceptable.[66] However, the fancy footwork

62. Corey, Oxford travel diary (1921-22 folder, Corey papers). About the time of the Memphis Convention in 1926, Corey wrote, "I have been attacked by extremists on both sides. The *Christian Century* has assailed me for going too slow and the *Christian Standard* for going too fast. I consider both as compliments" (UCMS papers).

63. In 1942 Corey delivered an address to the International Convention entitled "Educating toward a Christian Democracy" in which he stated, "Christianity and the ideals of true democracy are intimately related." He then called for Christians to "restore faith in the ideals of democracy itself." Evidence of this kind of affirmation exists throughout the work of the United Society. The 28-29 July 1947 Trustees Minutes contain a "Resolution on Christian Democracy" urging the International Convention to reaffirm "its faith in the high ideas of a Christian democracy . . . that we call upon our people to help supplant inferior ideas by making the superior ideals of Christian democracy a reality in national and international affairs" (UCMS papers).

64. From Corey's notes written at the time of the passing of the Sweeney Resolution, Steubenville, Ohio, 1922 (UCMS papers).

65. Corey, in a letter sent to all missionaries addressed to "Dear Fellow Worker," 30 March 1922 (UCMS papers).

66. The Board passed an interpretation of this resolution as follows: "Our interpretation

involved in "interpreting" resolutions only intensified the frustration of missionaries on the field and conservatives at home.

The democratic process ultimately resulted in more frustration when, in the darkest days of the open membership controversy, the 1925 Oklahoma City International Convention passed a resolution calling for the firing of any missionary who had "committed himself or herself to belief in, or practice of, the reception of unimmersed persons into the membership of churches of Christ."[67] In response, Corey pulled out his pencil and jotted down his innermost thoughts in incomplete sentences on scraps of paper.

> *I do not believe in open membership — divisive — but . . . I believe in open membership in Kingdom of God by fruits know them. . . .* I am far beyond the point where I have any hesitancy whatever in recognizing a man who is unimmersed as a full Christian if he loves and serves Christ. While I have never done it in *practice* I will not put myself in the place of not being able to *think* that David Livingstone or Robert Speer might be acceptable for membership in a church of which I was pastor.[68]

In Corey's view, the Oklahoma City resolution represented "the most dangerous moment we have faced."[69] During the preceding five years, leaders of the Society had resolved the issue privately, among themselves, by defending the position that missionaries could personally *believe* in open membership but could not *practice* that belief on the mission field; publicly, therefore, they roundly condemned open membership. The Oklahoma City resolution asked for more. It dictated that the Society enter the realm of examining the private beliefs of its missionaries. As he reported in his own book dealing with the question, Corey came close to resigning over this issue.[70]

---

of the action of the Board of Managers with regard to church membership is that it has to do with the administrative policy to be pursued in carrying on the work, and does not concern personal opinions. We interpret the statement with regard to 'being in sincere accord' with the policy pronounced to mean that the missionary should be willing to earnestly carry on the work in the manner suggested." Both the resolution and this interpretation were passed at the Winona Lake International Convention in the fall of 1922 (UCMS papers).

67. This resolution, accompanied by another one that forbade employment of such people, was passed at the Oklahoma City Convention in 1925 as a result of the recommendation of the so-called "Peace Committee." The recommendations emerged from a series of statements made before the committee by John T. Brown, Z. T. Sweeny, W. R. Walker, P. H. Welsheimer, and S. S. Lappin (UCMS papers).

68. From notes written by Corey at the Oklahoma City Convention; italics mine. Note his distinction between practice and thought: to think about open membership is acceptable, but practice of it is not, because it is divisive. Note also his recognition of "spiritual" rather than "organic" union.

69. He wrote that the resolution curtailed "our liberty in Christ as greatly as our fathers enlarged it. As in N.T. times God adds to his ch. such as are being saved not us + we exalt a church roll into too high a place when we do not allow people to have opinions about it. . . . Not willing to do for mission field what I would not allow done to me in ministry . . . willing to put into effect working policy if not infringment of private opinion, but not this."

70. Corey, *Fifty Years of Attack and Controversy*, p. 104. Corey's struggles are recorded in his own hand on many other scraps of paper that illumine the inner turmoil of these years in a

His major difficulty with the Oklahoma City resolutions derived from his intense belief in the sanctity of individual opinion.[71] Those who had pushed the open membership controversy to this extreme had caused Disciples, in Corey's words, to "strain a gnat + swallow a Campbell."[72] "Are we going to give up that which our Fathers so heroically fought for, the right of individual interpretation, just when the religious world needs it so desperately?" he asked himself.[73] The Board of Managers stepped in to deal with this question when, perhaps in response to Corey's impassioned plea,[74] they interpreted the passage "committed to belief in" as "not intended to invade the right of private judgment, but only to apply to such an open agitation as would prove divisive."[75]

---

very graphic way. See also his letter to A. Cory of 26 October 1925, in which he expresses the sentiment "here's hoping there may be a way through." In response to the Oklahoma City Resolutions, on 8 December 1925 a Continuation Committee was organized. More than fifty Disciples of Christ from widely separated cities met at the Neil House in Columbus, Ohio. The purpose of the meeting was to express concern about the effect these resolutions had on the freedom of Disciples. The committee included E. M. Bowman of New York, E. S. Ames of Chicago, Peter Ainslie of Baltimore, Ida W. Harrison of Lexington, and R. A. Doan of Columbus. The committee also worked vigorously to develop a "delegate plan" for future conventions. R. A. Doan presented a major paper entitled "What Effect Will It [the Oklahoma City Resolution] Have on the Freedom of Missionary Work?" (UCMS papers) to this committee at its 8 December 1925 meeting.

71. This was also the case with Frederick Burnham, who on two occasions, at Board of Managers meetings held in St. Louis 18-19 January 1922 and 2-3 December 1925, delivered virtually the same sixteen-page address, rehearsing the traditional Disciples emphasis on the sanctity of personal opinion and prejudice against "faith in systems of theology." He also quoted Isaac Errett to the effect that "If I trust Jesus as my Savior, and obey His truth, I have a right to demand that the brightest angel in heaven shall not bring my soul into court" (1922 version, pp. 5, 19, UCMS papers).

72. Handwritten note dated 26 October [1926] (UCMS papers).

73. Handwritten question from fall of 1926 (UCMS papers).

74. Corey's handwritten ramblings, as was usually the case, eventually found rather eloquent expression in an address delivered either before the Committee on Findings or the Board of Managers meeting at St. Louis: "To surrender our liberty to think for ourselves to a convention resolution and to accept with docility a position instead of being rationally convinced of it, is to me, intellectual servility. The situation becomes even more intolerable when the missionaries, secretaries and members of the Board of Managers are placed under the penalty of disloyalty to the Brotherhood when they do not yield to this servility. It would seem that with perfectly good intention and desirous of expressing itself against open membership and in favor of immersion, our convention has succeeded in limiting the boundaries of liberty as zealously as our fathers enlarged them. I earnestly believe that this is the most dangerous moment we have faced in our history and that if this resolution is carried to its logical conclusion, one of the dearest principles we have cherished, as a people, that of Christian liberty, will be largely stultified" (untitled address, UCMS papers).

75. See "Statement of the Board of Managers of the United Christian Missionary Society," *World Call* 8 (January 1926): 38. This response is also found in the minutes of the Board of Managers meeting held in St. Louis 3 December 1925 — the meeting that initially voted to support this interpretation. It issued out of the "Committee on Findings," which had been established by the Board of Managers to report on the "Peace Committee Report" that had been presented to the Oklahoma City Convention. *The United Society News,* a new journal dedicated to publicizing the work of the UCMS among the churches, heralded the interpretation as presenting a "clear cut, sensible, scriptural policy for putting into practice the provisions of the famous 'Peace Resolution,' passed by the Oklahoma City Convention." See *United Society News,* 8 December 1925, p. 1 (UCMS papers).

This type of specious reasoning more than satisfied Corey. Though the inter-pretation obviously broke faith with the intent of the resolution, it did speak to his concern about private opinion and supported his concern about division.

Corey never expressed interest in defending the concept of open mem-bership. He opposed it, as he said, because it was divisive.[76] Since it proved divisive, it disrupted the work. Since the measure of the UCMS rested on the effectiveness of the work, and since open membership disrupted the work, the practice of open membership had to be opposed to the gospel. In a 1923 letter responding to Justin Brown, a missionary who resigned because of the Society's defensive posture, Corey wrote that "the main thing now is to have our organization function and hold together, without the sacrifice of prin-ciple."[77] The next year he echoed this concern when he told Guy Sarvis that the Society's position was "difficult because [it] cannot carry on [the] mission-ary work without a fair degree of unity in [the] brotherhood."[78] Once again practical and procedural matters took precedence over a theological under-standing of the question of church membership.

The intensity of the eight-year controversy over open membership took its toll on everyone. Most missionaries backed off the minute the UCMS communicated its disapproval of the practice. However, because several mis-sionaries had told John Brown during his independent fact-finding tour of the Orient and the Philippines that they practiced open membership, the issue did not die easily.[79] The missionaries involved merely meant to say that they recognized as Christians those who came to their communities from other Protestant traditions. Since Protestant churches, due to comity agreements, were miles apart, they usually welcomed these Christians into their churches as full participants, allowing them to vote and to hold church office. Most of these churches did not, however, list them on membership rolls. In fact, most churches on the mission field did not even maintain such rolls.

It did not help that John Brown, upon his return, resigned from the UCMS Executive Board and became a prolific writer for the *Christian Standard.*[80]

76. Corey wrote in October 1926 that "My friends everywhere know that I have never favored accepting into full membership in our churches at home or abroad, those Christians from other fellowships who have not been immersed, no matter how good their Christian lives are, because I believe it is divisive instead of unifying among our people and because I believe that we should stand for the New Testament forms and ideals. On the other hand, I have never felt that we should disfellowship those who hold differently on this point" (UCMS papers).

77. Corey to Justin E. Brown, 23 February 1922 (UCMS papers).

78. Corey to Sarvis, 26 May 1924 (UCMS papers).

79. See Margueritte Harmon Bro to John T. Brown, 12 February 1922; Lyrel G. Teagarden to Brown, 12 February 1922 (Ms. Teagarden died 9 December 1988 after a lifetime of distinguished service on the mission field); and E. K. Higdon to Brown, 16 March 1922, among others (UCMS papers).

80. See John T. Brown, *The U.C.M.S. Self-Impeached: A Review of Evidence of Public Record Which the Executive Committee of the U.C.M.S. Must Face* (Cincinnati: Standard Pub-lishing, 1924). This volume contains excerpts from all the missionary letters in question. Corey's personal feelings regarding John T. Brown are found in his "Open Letter to John T. Brown" in

Even though the UCMS quickly received written retractions from all the missionaries involved[81] and went to great lengths to explain the different conditions on the mission field resulting from the distance between Protestant churches,[82] the damage could not be repaired easily. Brown and other backers of the *Christian Standard* did not accept the subtle difference between recognizing the unimmersed as full participants in the church and recognizing them as full members of the church. Over the next several years, the democratic process forced the UCMS leaders to ask their missionaries to make finer distinctions between the unimmersed and the immersed in the life of the church on the mission field. These demands severely limited Disciples participation in union talks on the mission field.

The report of the "Peace Committee" delivered to the Oklahoma City Convention of 1925 further illustrates how the operation of the democratic principle worked to the detriment of theological reflection.[83] Instead of ex-

---

the UCMS papers. The letter was never sent; his coworkers talked him out of sending it or publicizing it in any way. But in a letter to Lela Taylor of 16 August 1922, Corey confesses that it was therapeutic to have written it: "it was burning inside of me and I had to get it out." Brown was not very highly regarded by the missionaries or the indigenous workers on the field either. Garrett reported in a letter to Corey dated 5 June 1922 that "the Chinese speak of him as the 'criminal judge' and of his interviews as 'hasty sittings of Criminal Court.' " The first official response of the UCMS to Brown was much more benign and unemotional and published in pamphlet form under the heading "Statement of the Executive Committee of the United Christian Missionary Society together with the Latest Report of the China Mission and All the Missionaries in China." Another thirty-two page pamphlet was issued by the UCMS and sent to the churches in early 1924 under the title "Facts about the Visit of John T. Brown to Some of the Mission Fields and Answers to His Statements in the *Christian Standard.*" This was a much more powerful and emotional statement, referring to his trip as "a ridiculous travesty of Christian ethics and mission principles." Anna Atwater referred to this pamphlet as "the facts about John Brown's 'body'" (Atwater to Cy M. Yocum, 25 February 1924, UCMS papers). Brown's *U.C.M.S. Self-Impeached* followed the publication of this pamphlet and first appeared in the pages of the *Christian Standard* of 31 May 1924. Corey details the chronology of events in *Fifty Years of Attack and Controversy,* pp. 85-94.

81. For an example of these retractions, see Corey to Margueritte Harmon Bro, 2 November 1922; Bro to Corey, 7 April 1923; Corey to Bro, 27 April 1926; Albin Bro to Corey, 13 July 1926; and Bro to Corey, 25 October 1926 (UCMS papers).

82. The minutes of the 1920 International Convention in St. Louis carry a detailed statement by Steve Corey describing the different conditions in China but assuring the convention that open membership was not practiced there. These minutes, including this statement, appear in *World Call* 2 (December 1920): 25-45; the statement appears on pp. 29-30.

83. The "Peace Committee" was constituted during the Cleveland International Convention of 1924 and charged with attempting to bring some resolution to the open membership controversy. The committee was made up of five people, two chosen by the agencies reporting to the convention, two chosen by "brethren dissatisfied with the management of some, or all, of these agencies," and one selected by the executive committee. The five members were Thomas C. Howe, Mrs. R. S. Latshaw, Will F. Shaw, M. M. Amunson, and Claude E. Hill. They met and heard arguments from five representatives of both sides of the issue. The representatives of the agencies presenting arguments were Steve Corey, Robert Hopkins, H. C. Armstrong, H. O. Pritchard, and Milo Smith. The dissatisfied group was represented by Z. T. Sweeney, S. S. Lappin, John T. Brown, W. R. Walker, and P. H. Welsheimer. See the minutes of the Board of Managers of the United Christian Missionary Society for 10 October 1925 (UCMS papers).

amining whether open membership had theological merit, the committee pointed out that "the majority of our people, and of our churches, do not consider it right and proper" and so concluded, "we esteem it to be our duty, a duty imposed upon us and made obligatory by the principles of democracy to which we have sought to adhere throughout our whole history, to act in harmony with the will of the majority of our brethren."

Most of the missionaries did not question the majority principle either, even those most drastically affected by it. E. K. Higdon put it plainly: "As long as the majority of the Disciples of Christ hold that only immersed Christians can be members . . . , I shall have to take the position that these other Protestants are not and cannot be members of the Taft Avenue Church." Frank Garrett weathered repeated calls for his recall by stating his belief that "loyalty to Christ is best shown by being loyal to the group, if there is no plain teaching of Christ to the contrary."[84]

G. B. Baird, Justin Brown, and a few others constituted exceptions on the mission field in their opposition to the democratic principle operating in the Society. Baird spoke for them all in his 1920 presidential address when he told the Central China Christian Mission that both missionaries and Society leaders, regardless of attitudes at home, "readily recognize" that the new development on the mission field surrounding the question of church membership "is a movement from God." Baird then posed the central question: "Should we obey men rather than God?"[85]

B. THE CONCERN FOR FINANCIAL SUPPORT

The leadership's commitment to democracy found pragmatic foundation in questions related to the financial security of the Society. The leaders realized that if the UCMS spent its time alienating the majority of the churches in the "brotherhood," the future of the Society itself could very well be jeopardized. They even explained some of their actions regarding the open membership controversy with references to this fact of life. As Corey put it, "We may make mistakes in these early days, but they can be rectified and the main thing is to continue to build up the missionary enterprise with the backing and support of our great people."[86] Such a posture was hardly conducive to developing a prophetic theology.

---

84. Garrett statement on open membership dated 3 July 1928; see also Garrett to McLean, 12 January 1920, where he declares his support for whatever the "rank and file of our Brotherhood" should decide (UCMS papers).

85. Baird, "Thirty Second Annual Convention of Central China Christian Mission, President's Address," April 1920, p. 7 (UCMS papers).

86. Corey to Justin E. Brown, 23 February 1922; see also Corey to Baird, 5 April 1923: "One who has not passed through the last five years here at home can hardly appreciate the deep anxiety all of us have had in trying to save the work from loss during these days of misunderstanding and criticism" (UCMS papers).

Archibald McLean, in a 1916 letter to C. C. Morrison, explained the problem rather clearly. Morrison had asked McLean to consider Edward Scribner Ames as a speaker for the Des Moines International Convention. "Dr. Ames is a prince among men; he is a gentleman and a Christian, . . . a man that I would like to honor," wrote McLean. "But we must look at the interests of the kingdom." He then proceeded to tell Morrison that the refusal to recall a missionary back in 1911 had cost "us a hundred thousand dollars at least. . . . It would be within bounds to say that it cost us twice that amount." If Ames were invited to speak, it would only "alienate good men and churches and cut off our receipts." To use any of the "Chicago men . . . could be suicidal." Even though they were "men of clean lives and men of marked ability . . . who would do credit to any convention . . . they have alienated themselves from the rank and file of the brotherhood and because they have they are not available for convention purposes. I wish it were otherwise. But the facts are as they are."[87]

The leaders of the UCMS recognized rather quickly that open membership had "made inroads . . . upon the receipts," or at least they thought this was the case.[88] Even G. B. Baird, the missionary who raised the open membership issue so prominently, realized immediately that the "work in China depends on money raised in America." In attempting to get a feel for how the Society might respond to the issue, he asked C. C. Morrison for his opinion on the question of "what influence" advocating open membership might "have on the missionary contributions."[89]

Baird knew that the Society would express concern about the probable effect any change in policy might have on the bottom line. Several missionaries expressed rather severe criticism of the Society's handling of the whole issue precisely because the UCMS reacted as Baird expected. Because of their worries about financial stability, the leaders of the Society ended up ignoring opportunities to educate the churches about the mission field and missionary

87. McLean to Morrison, 21 August 1916 (UCMS papers). Morrison responded that he had "tried to satisfy my soul with the hope that a continuation of our policy of silent forbearance was right but I am growing more doubtful of it all the time" (Morrison to McLean, 27 December 1917 [UCMS papers]).

88. Alexander Paul to Oswald J. Goulter, 15 July 1924 (UCMS papers). The actual statistics are interesting here. From 1920 to 1929, there was a growth in income overall every year. Designated giving to the foreign field grew every year between 1921 and 1926 (to a total growth of 48.7%), except for a seven percent decline in 1927 and a nine percent decline in 1928 (see "Expenditure of the Foreign and Home Departments," a sheet in the budget papers showing receipts and expenditures from 1921 to 1936 [UCMS papers]). It is true that the number of churches contributing to the Society peaked in 1923 at 3,388 and reached its low mark in 1935 (the year for the low mark in just about every category) at 1,839. But the Depression certainly had an effect here. Missionary giving (including home missions) peaked in 1928. Total giving to the United Society peaked in 1926, the year after the very restrictive Oklahoma City resolutions. Offerings from individuals peaked in 1927. It appears either that their preoccupation with finances was overblown or that their strategy was successful. (Statistics from minutes of the Cabinet Conference, Mitchell, Indiana, 31 October–4 November 1939, p. 37 [UCMS papers].)

89. Baird to Morrison, 26 August 1919 (UCMS papers).

understandings of what needed to transpire there. They also failed to express a theology of stewardship that could stand over against the tendency to identify giving money to God's work with a right to control mission activities.

In his presidential address to the April 1920 Central China Christian Mission, Baird did not mince words, even though R. A. Doan, an officer of the UCMS, sat in the audience. He pointed out that Archibald McLean and Mr. Doan had both argued that the open membership question constituted an issue that should be decided by the "rank and file of the brotherhood." But Baird argued that "there is a concerted effort to prevent the rank and file and most of the leaders of the brotherhood from knowing that any such question even exists." He went on to say that the leaders believed "we must wait until we have the 'assurance that we know the mind of the brotherhood and have the support of the brotherhood.' " But, Baird asked, "how are we to know, when all the discussion of the question on Christian Union in China is tabooed?"[90]

Justin Brown, an early missionary to China (1906) and among the most respected, expressed strong disagreement with the conservative posture of the Society. He contended that the UCMS had demonstrated its "desire to have as little said as possible" and for "that little to be a partial statement of the truth" in order to "appeal" to the "home constituency."

> I think I understand the point of view of those responsible for shaping the policies + raising the funds to carry on the work. I know how disturbing it is to you to have any question come up that threatens to cause contention or to reduce the receipts. Yet I am convinced this attitude is a mistake + is certain to defeat the ends it is meant to accomplish, is in fact defeating them.

Brown believed the mission fields suffered because of this style of administration. "Conditions on the mission fields" had to be altered, Brown told Corey, in order to "adjust to the attitude of mind of the home constituency." To rectify the problem, the UCMS needed to develop "a policy of constructive education + . . . courageous leadership" that would adjust "the attitude of mind of the home constituency . . . to the conditions on the mission fields."[91] Brown resigned from the field early in 1922 to begin that work, or as he put it, to "bring a message to the pagan element in the church here in America."[92]

---

90. Baird, "Thirty Second Annual Convention of Central China Christian Mission, President's Address," April 1920, p. 7 (UCMS papers).

91. Brown to Corey, 5 November 1922 (UCMS papers). Guy Sarvis, another missionary in the field, agreed that "a wide statement of the real facts might be one of the best answers to the critics." As he put it in a letter to Doan dated 1 January 1921, the Society's actions with regard to open membership seemed "essentially an effort to hide the truth in the fear that the people will not understand the whole truth if presented to them. . . . Is it not possible to appeal to intelligent people on the basis of the facts in the case, fully and frankly stated?"

92. Brown to Corey, 5 February 1922; see also Corey to Brown, 23 February 1922. Brown also wrote that although the Sweeney Resolution was "not . . . the chief consideration" in his resignation, "it proved the deciding one" (UCMS papers). Ray E. Hunt, pastor of Park Avenue Church in East Orange, New Jersey, echoed these sentiments from the field. He told an officer of

A few months later, the Society's leadership asked the China Mission to sign a statement claiming open membership had never occurred in China. Some of the missionaries believed the statement less than honest. Pearl Taylor Sarvis refused to sign it, stating that the document was "designed to accomplish a certain purpose at home" and was "so constructed with lights and shadows and design so placed to accomplish that purpose rather than reveal the situation here in all clarity. . . . How petty, time-serving and spineless our action looks in the face of the challenges, the demands, the opportunities presented by the Chinese leaders of the China Christian Conference in Shanghai."[93] Though her husband, Guy Sarvis, signed the statement in question, he expressed his utter frustration with this "whole equivocating business." He told Corey that it would only "cause the leaders of the young church in China to look upon us with contempt . . . [and] alienate our young people."[94]

Nearly a dozen years later, the problem still bothered missionaries on the field. Harold E. Fey, while serving in the Philippines, wrote and circulated throughout the home churches a letter that caused some problems for the Society because it noted that during its first twenty-five years in the Philippines, the Disciples church had split into "fourteen sectarian groups." Alexander Paul wrote Fey and gently cautioned him about "how easy it is for friends here at home to misunderstand statements."[95] Fey stood his ground. "Missionary interest will come alive again in our churches when they are taken into the full confidence of our leaders," he wrote. The Society had too often "fed [churches] . . . selected facts portraying only one side of the picture" rather than "the whole truth about the missionary enterprise." The "modern" missionary's "biggest problem" was dealing "with that set of ideas and emphases . . . of the preaching of the older days . . . and its fruits of discord and schism." "How is it possible," he asked Paul, "that the supporters of missions have any adequate idea of the problems of a modern missionary . . . unless they are . . . given the facts?"[96]

No doubt Fey still remembered that as he was preparing to leave for the Philippines, Paul Hutchinson, editor of the *Christian Century,* had offered him a job as the Philippine correspondent for the weekly. When the Society officials found out about it, they "solemnly warned" him to turn it down, fearing that a "young and inexperienced writer would cause trouble." Fey had nearly resigned over the incident, but Alexander Paul had talked him into going on to the Philippines, where he could "carry on" as if he "had never received the

---

the Society that the UCMS had "allowed itself to be dominated by the reactionary group of churches and preachers who were willing to make the threat of the withholding of missionary funds." By so doing, "it has failed to understand that some of us who have always been loyal to our organized interests may have a conscience on this matter" (Hunt to Bert Wilson, 7 February 1922 [UCMS papers]).

93. Pearl Sarvis to Corey, 14 August 1922 (UCMS papers).
94. Sarvis to Corey, 9 April 1924 (UCMS papers).
95. Paul to Fey, 24 July 1930 (UCMS papers).
96. Fey to Paul, 17 March 1931 (UCMS papers).

warning." He followed Paul's advice and, as he put it in his autobiography, learned how "to hold in proper and courteous disrespect the 'Nervous Nellies' of the church bureaucracy."[97] He also spent the latter part of his career in the freer air surrounding the editor's chair at the *Christian Century*.

At their Cabinet Conference in the fall of 1939, the Society's leaders talked some about implementing a better program of missionary education. "Traditional interpretation of missions stressed too largely the financial support of missionary program as the goal of missionary education, rather than the development of Christ-like persons for whom the missionary spirit is an integral part of the Christian experience."[98] Years later these same concerns continued to surface. During Virgil Sly's presidency, just prior to restructure, the UCMS commissioned Loren Lair as a "consultant on matters of organization and administration" and sent him to India and the Philippines on a fact-finding tour. Disciples missionaries expressed frustration that "free expression was not possible because of the danger of misunderstanding by church constituencies here in America."[99] These missionaries were not necessarily blaming the UCMS for this problem (at least not to the extent that the earlier missionaries had), but they strongly felt the need for better education in this regard. For whatever reason — and the worries about upsetting the delicacy of church support no doubt played a role — the Society had not done its job properly. Missionaries in 1968 still felt the problem of miscommunication rather acutely.

C. PATERNALISM ON THE MISSION FIELD

The twin concerns of democracy and the bottom line did not affect the posture taken by the UCMS only in America; there were obviously implications abroad as well. The fact that the UCMS formulated policies for the mission field based on the democratic principle and the need for financial support constituted only half of the equation; those policies then had to be enforced on the mission field if they were to have any meaning.

The enforcement of those policies led to a rather unfortunate paternalistic attitude that proved very hard to conquer in the years of the Society's history. The Society felt the need to protect the churches at home from what they would construe as a misuse of their funds. At the same time, this attitude produced the end result of a Society acting to protect the doctrinal purity of the churches on the field. And, of course, those who supplied the money decided what constituted doctrinal purity.

97. Fey, *How I Read the Riddle: An Autobiography* (St. Louis: Bethany Press, 1982), pp. 59-60.

98. "Missionary Education Report," from the Cabinet Conference held in Mitchell, Indiana, 31 October–4 November 1939 (UCMS papers).

99. "A Preliminary Report to the Board of Trustees of UCMS," minutes of the 18-19 June 1968 Board Meeting (UCMS papers).

In a statement signed by the Executive Committee and published in the *Christian Century*, the Society indicated that since "friends in America" still supported the churches in China, "no native church" in the China Mission could "exercise its own prerogative" on open membership "even if it were inclined to do so."[100] In response to the statement, George Baird told C. C. Morrison that "well informed people" consider such a policy "a pernicious doctrine whether in politics, industry, religion or social life." "I repudiate," Baird wrote Morrison, "the doctrine that the contribution of money gives an ecclesiastical control over churches benefited by it."[101]

Baird had long believed that the mission churches ought to be free from foreign control, to "have a right to do" what "any congregation in America has a right to do" in deciding policy matters related to its life and work. In his 1919 address before the Kuling convention of the Christian Chinese Churches, he told missionaries and others gathered there that "one curse of the churches in America has been and is the policy that large contributions carry an insidious power of control." To communicate such a message to the Chinese Church was to break faith with other principles the missionaries hoped to convey, particularly the "fundamental principle of the Disciples" that each Christian stands before God as a member of the "common priesthood of all believers." Therefore, issues of "authority and independence of action," Baird emphasized, should never be based on practical questions related to who supplies the "financial support" but should rather rest on "evidence of consecration to the ideals of the church and ability and willingness to assume responsibility and really face problems and solve them."[102]

A little less than a year later, in his address as president of the Thirty-Second Annual Convention of the Central China Mission, Baird picked up the matter again. R. A. Doan, vice president of the Foreign Christian Missionary Society under the UCMS umbrella, sat in the audience. Baird argued forcefully that the issue of open membership should be one that is resolved by "the Central China mission and the Disciple Churches in China." In his view, "to leave matters" with the "Brotherhood" was "to postpone indefinitely any

100. "A Communication," *Christian Century*, 16 September 1920, pp. 14-15. This statement was written by Stephen Corey (see Corey to Morrison, 29 September 1920) and signed by the members of the Executive Committee of the Foreign Christian Missionary Society (the foreign division of the new UCMS). The statement was a response to Morrison's editorial in the 26 August 1920 *Century* which enthusiastically claimed that, on the China mission field, belief in the exclusivity of believer's baptism was becoming "a passing dogma" (pp. 6-7).

101. Baird to Morrision, 19 October 1920. See also Baird to Morrison, 27 December 1919. Unfortunately, at the same time Baird was asserting the need for autonomy, Frank Garrett wrote McLean stating that "the China missionaries desire to be in perfect harmony with the brotherhood at home . . . to do just what our supporters expect us to do" (Garrett to McLean, 11 October 1920 [UCMS papers]).

102. Baird to Morrision, 19 October 1920, and "What Contributions Do the Disciples of Christ Have to Make to the Chinese Christian Church," p. 5 (UCMS papers).

prospect of our mission taking any leading or constructive part in this movement to form a united church."[103]

Immediately after Baird's address, Doan stopped him and told him that the mission "could not think of acting independently in deciding questions such as this." He told Baird that his notion of autonomy was "entirely eroneous [*sic*]" and informed him "that they who contributed support had the right to dictate what action [the mission] should take."[104] Guy Sarvis stood up for Baird's position when he wrote Doan a few months later and told him he considered the Society's attitude "an insult to the Chinese churches and to the missionaries." The "only hope for [the] future" of the Chinese churches, Sarvis insisted, "does not come from the Society at all." Rather, hope comes from the fact that the churches "are made up of *people*." "Money," he told Doan, made up "the least essential part" of the life of the Chinese churches. Sarvis also wrote Corey a month later encouraging him to recognize that the "chinese church" has a "right to be free from the dogmas and bonds that have so hindered the church at home."[105]

The Society, however, stuck to its policy of paternalism. In May 1921, Frank Garrett, acting on behalf of the China Mission, wrote the UCMS indicating that the Chinese churches "accept the evident fact that they are not free to manage their own affairs, but must submit to the control of the Brotherhood responsible for their establishment and support." He added, however, the mission hope that "the time will come when the lives of the missionaries, and more important, the sacrifice of and labor of the Chinese membership, will be more largely recognized as entitling them [to] the leadership of the Word and practice of the Chinese Church."[106]

The UCMS turned a deaf ear to the expressed desires of their missionaries to place more trust and confidence in Chinese leadership at the very time when, as William R. Hutchison has demonstrated, some leaders in the ecumenical movement strongly supported increased indigenous leadership on the mission field. As early as 1910, Robert Speer advocated that the missionary movement, in order to free itself of the impossible "burden" of designing theological statements that would be meaningful in other cultures, had to "build up native churches which will themselves carry this burden, which will deal with their own apologetic problems, work out their own institutions, support

103. Baird, "Thirty Second Annual Convention of Central China Christian Mission, President's Address," April 1920, p. 8 (UCMS papers).

104. Doan to Garrett, 7 November 1920; and Baird to Morrison, 19 October 1920 (UCMS papers).

105. Sarvis to Doan, 1 January 1921, and Sarvis to Corey, 1 February 1921 (UCMS papers). Ray Hunt, pastor of Park Avenue Church in East Orange, New Jersey, wrote that the UCMS policy deprived "the missionary of his freedom of interpretation" and kept "the native church on the foreign field [from] finding its own expression of faith and life" (Hunt to Bert Wilson, 7 February 1922 [UCMS papers]).

106. "A Reply to the St. Louis Convention Resolution, May 26, 1921," signed by Frank Garrett, secretary to the China Mission, Nanking (UCMS papers).

their own activities, and evangelize their own lands."[107] In 1925, Daniel Johnson Fleming of Union Seminary in New York argued for the imposition of a new "test for the fitness of missionary recruits." Hutchison summarizes Fleming's argument as one that would restrict all mission boards from certifying "any candidate for foreign service who could not accept a status of equality or subordination in the overseas post." Missionaries, said Fleming, should maintain a job description characterized by the words "temporary, secondary, and advisory."[108] But Hutchison, in his analysis of American foreign missions, concludes that these two men were well ahead of their times.

Even though those gathered at the meeting at Edinburgh in 1910, including Archibald McLean, heard quite a number of voices, especially those from Germany, advocating indigenous self-sufficiency, none of the delegates rushed home to put such a policy into practice. In 1922 Stephen Corey heard speakers at Oxford stress the necessity for "native leadership and control of mission churches,"[109] but it appears to have made no difference in his approach to the administration of the Society. None of the major denominational mission boards took steps during the 1920s to ensure changes in policy to reflect the wisdom found in these voices. Whatever the reasons behind the general hesitancy found in other mission boards, it is clear that among Disciples one of the primary factors had to do with practical financial concerns. In this instance, therefore, monetary considerations forced the Disciples at home to take a rather uncomfortable position that stood at odds not only with developing understandings of indigenous leadership but also with their own long-held belief in the autonomy of the local congregation, itself a doctrine influenced more by culture than supported by theology.

Because of its lack of theological reflection, the particular brand of paternalism practiced by Disciples in this early period of the UCMS naturally supported the ever-present sense of cultural superiority. Obviously, this notion of superiority did not find its roots in the paternalism of the UCMS. At least half a century of liberal ideologies, including American adaptations of Herbert Spencer's Social Darwinism and Hegel's theories of civilization as progress, affirmed America's unique institutions as the hope of the world. And these adaptations were merely building on understandings that could be traced all the way back to Jonathan Edwards and John Winthrop.

Disciples in the early twentieth century, supported by a sense of their duty as caretakers of developments abroad, carried on this tradition. Its marks included stereotypical characterizations of "heathen" and "pagan" peoples, little appreciation for non-Christian religions, strong anti-Catholicism, confusion of Christian-

107. Speer, quoted by William R. Hutchison in *Errand to the World: American Protestant Thought and Foreign Missions* (Chicago: University of Chicago Press, 1987), p. 122. The quotation is taken from Speer's *Christianity and the Nations* (New York: Fleming H. Revell, 1910), p. 73.

108. Hutchison, *Errand to the World,* pp. 150-55. See also Fleming, *Whither Bound in Missions?* (New York: Association Press, 1925), pp. 143, 171-72, 187.

109. *Third Annual Report (July 1, 1922–June 30, 1923),* p. 16 (UCMS papers).

izing with "civilizing," and identification of Christianity with American diplomatic goals. Remnants of these characteristics, stronger in some areas than others, remained in Disciples missionary endeavors well into the 1950s.[110]

110. "Pagan" and "heathen" remained in the vocabulary throughout the 1950s. Examples are everywhere in the literature. For examples of stereotyping, see the *First Annual Report of the United Christian Missionary Society, October 1, 1920–June 30, 1921* ("Submitted to the International Convention of the Discipels of Christ, Winona Lake, Ind., August 30, 1921"), p. 22, which describes the tribes of Wema in stereotypical ways: "The Baseketulu, a Mmongo tribe, are capable workmen but very headstrong"; "The Bakutu tribe . . . are the more tractable as workmen, but very suspicious and fickle." See also "Trustees Minutes," 19 April 1938, where Cy Yocum describes his travels to Africa and mentions that "the Congo native is . . . always a born trader, . . . [with] an insatiable desire for more possessions." The minutes from 10-11 May 1955 reveal that there remained "a paternalistic attitude on the part of the mission toward the [Congolese] Christians in its employ." For attitudes toward non-Christian religions, see Eliot T. Osgood, "Victory — Celebration in China," *World Call* 1 (March 1919): 9; and J. B. Hunter, "Making Contacts in Japan," *World Call* 8 (January 1926): 44. During the fifties and early sixties, attitudes toward non-Christian religions generally reflected more appreciation for the insights contained in them, but this appreciation was still overshadowed by an insistence that Christ provides the fullest revelation of any truth within them. The most liberal presentation I found still affirmed that Christ was the "one way," while affirming that Christians could learn something from other faiths (Harry B. Partin, "The Gospel and the Non-Christian Religions," presented for the Commission on Theology, 7 February 1961).

Anti-Catholicism remained strong throughout the life of the Society and later; competition between Protestants and Catholics was often the theme. See, for example, UCMS Trustees minutes dated 15-16 May 1951, p. 44, and 19-20 June 1951, p. 113. But there were also reports that demonstrated a stronger anti-Catholicism in the 1950s; see, for example, the minutes from 17-18 January 1950, in which the Catholic Church is accused of playing "on the fears and superstitions of the people [in Paraguay] because they are ignorant and fanatical." Or, again, from a report of a "Commission to Japan," dated 5 September–8 October 1954 and chaired by Riley B. Montgomery, president of the College of the Bible at Lexington, with Virgil Sly as consultant: "The Catholic Church, with the evils which adhered to Catholicism four centuries ago, is the most obvious and dominating institution in the Philippines society. . . . For the most part, the Catholic leaders are content to have the church live upon the people instead of for the people. . . . Protestant missionaries and evangelists must win their converts from an ancient Catholic society." A paper written by Paul Stone for Dr. T. Hassell Bowen at the College of Missions in 1952 demonstrates the general attitude toward Catholicism in the 1950s. Entitled "The Other Catholic Church," it begins, "The Roman Catholic Church is dominant in Latin America. But the form of Romanism existent in that continent is so radically different from that practiced in Europe and North America that it is scarcely recognizable."

Christianizing and "civilizing" were generally connected to the idea of a "Christian Democracy." Regarding identification of Christianity with diplomatic goals, see Oswald J. Goulter, "How the Missionaries Left Luchowfu," *World Call* 9 (July 1927): 24. See also Alexander Paul, "Radio Talk," 1939, upon his return from Japan and China: "Is the whole world returning to Paganism or will the influence of our own country together with that of the democratic Scandinavian democracies be able to turn the tide and call the nations at war back to sanity and build up a comity of Nations based on righteousness and peace?" For a later example, see H. B. McCormick's interview with General Douglas MacArthur, 5 April 1950, at which Virgil Sly was also present (UCMS papers). McCormick, president of the Society at the time he conducted the interview, concluded that MacArthur was "a real Christian gentleman who is making a most sincere effort to transform a nation into a democracy from feudalism and that he was most sincerely attempting to teach the worth of the individual, but based that conception on the teachings of Christ. In short, he is laying a sure foundation for the future of Japan and deserves the support of everyone who is backing the Christian movement." In earlier days, it was not all that unusual for

CONCLUSION

The open membership controversy finally settled down in the fall of 1926. A year earlier, the UCMS commissioned a team of three men — Cleveland Kleihauer, John R. Golden, and Robert N. Simpson — to visit the Orient and conduct a full investigation of the fields in Japan, China, and the Philippines in order to report on all the matters currently troubling the churches at home. After a fifteen-week tour of the Orient during the winter and spring, the Commission offered its report to the Memphis International Convention in November 1926.[111] Among other things, the commission reported that no open membership existed on any of the mission fields visited and that no missionaries advocated its practice.[112]

When the Commission brought the report before the Convention, the moderate leadership of the Society expected a big fight from the strict restorationists. Representative restorationist leaders did raise questions from the floor designed to challenge the integrity of the Commission and its report, but they were unsuccessful in their efforts. As W. R. Warren put it in his diary, "the opposition failed dismally in their effort to discredit the report." Frederick Burnham wrote in his diary, "Big attack fails. 3-1 vote approval on Report of Com'n to Orient." Edwin R. Errett of the *Christian Standard* offered an interesting interpretation of the reasons for the affirmative vote: "The really remarkable thing is that, though this conservative group never really made an effort to vote down the commission's report, and most of the leaders of the group did not vote upon it, there was a strong bass note in the negative (though not a majority) against the largely feminine vote in favor of the report's adoption."[113]

Errett's complaints were not, however, directed only toward the women. He reported that two weeks before the International Convention, John Golden, a member of the Commission, had contacted P. H. Welsheimer, well known as a member of the "loyal brethren" (strict restorationists called themselves by this name), and told him that "he had many damaging facts to reveal; that, moreover, he was being persecuted by members of the foreign department because of his fight to have those facts revealed and acted upon."[114] Therefore, Welsheimer, Mark Collis, S. S. Lappin, and W. E. Sweeney prepared questions to be put to Golden at the time of the report's presentation designed to enable

---

Disciples missionaries to be in constant contact with American consulates. This was particularly true for missionaries in Tibet and their constant contact with consulate officials in Chungking, China, and the military attache in Peking. See the William M. Hardy and the R. A. Peterson papers in the Disciples Historical Society.

111. For background on the Commission to the Orient, see "Report of Commission to Orient," *United Society News,* 23 July 1926, p. 1 (UCMS papers); and "Executive Committee's Charge to the Commission to the Orient," *World Call* 8 (March 1926): 28-29.

112. "Report of the Commission to the Orient," *World Call* 8 (August 1926): 35. The report appears on pp. 34-43.

113. Errett, "Convention of Bad Faith," *Christian Standard,* 27 November 1926, p. 4.

114. Errett, "Convention of Bad Faith," p. 1.

him to reveal these hidden facts. But the answers the "loyal" group expected Golden to provide did not surface.[115]

Convinced that the report constituted a cover-up of the fact that the heresy of open membership still existed on the field, and knowing full well that missionaries who had advocated it were still on the field, Errett concluded in the *Christian Standard* that "the UCMS and the International Convention . . . are hostile to the very purpose of the Restoration movement."[116] Those in attendance at the Convention, Errett concluded, were "predominantly loyal to the idea of the United Society, and . . . apparently as well trained for a demonstration in their favor as are Al Smith's adherents."[117] Conservatives such as Welsheimer and Collis, due to "political trickery,"[118] had "been led into a blind alley," and "were soon left in the unlovely attitude of being a bunch of hecklers."[119]

Errett's report about Golden's actions have the ring of truth to them. Warren wrote in his diary that at the 6 October 1926 Executive Committee meeting of the UCMS, John Golden presented a resolution moving that "Mr. and Mrs. A. C. Bro [of China] and Mr. and Mrs. Frank V. Stipp [of the Philippines] be not continued in the foreign missionary service." Golden based his argument on the fact that these missionaries, at that time on furlough, had violated the policy of the Society by having "shown themselves to be in favor of open membership." Cleveland Kleihauer, another member of the Commission, agreed with the resolution. The Executive Committee referred the resolution to their next meeting, scheduled for 25 October, in order that the Bros and the Stipps might meet with them on that date.

At that next meeting, the Bros and the Stipps presented written and oral statements to the Executive Committee. Alexander Paul's diary records that "it was a tense day for all concerned." Stephen Corey scribbled on the back of a half sheet of paper his comment that the recalling of the Bros and Stipps "will satisfy no one — If you do this it will but whet the appetite for others. Higdon, Sarvis, Garrett, Teagarten, + all." When the vote was taken, both sets of missionaries were exonerated. Warren noted in his diary that the vote was unanimous for the Bros and "for the Stipps there seemed to be two adverse votes." Just two days before the Commission presented its report to the International Convention, the Board of Managers unanimously affirmed the Executive Board's decision to return both missionary couples to the field, but decided "to keep [the Stipps] home another year."[120]

115. The whole transcript of the question-and-answer session is found in "Report of the Commission to Orient," *Christian Standard,* 4 December 1926, pp. 12-18.

116. Errett, "The Memphis Convention," *Christian Standard,* 27 November 1926, p. 10.

117. Errett, "Convention of Bad Faith," p. 4.

118. Errett, "The Memphis Convention," p. 10.

119. Errett, "Convention of Bad Faith," p. 4.

120. Entry in Alexander Paul's diary for 10 November 1926. See also W. R. Warren's diary entries for 6 and 25 October and 11 November 1926; and Alexander Paul's diary entry for 25 October 1926. See also Corey to Margueritte Bro, 27 April 1926, and Bro to Corey, 25 October

None of this was discussed publicly at the Convention. The Society's Board of Managers and Executive Committee considered the matter concluded. Golden had evidently indicated to Welsheimer just before the second Executive Committee meeting that details were withheld from the report and would be forthcoming. By the time of the Convention, these details were settled in ways that Golden had not expected.

The strict restorationists viewed Memphis as a major defeat for the Restoration movement. The next year, they formed the North American Christian Convention and from that time forward moved more and more into a separate existence as a group of independent churches. The Convention, Errett wrote shortly after the Memphis meeting, was a "nuisance . . . to be given over wholly . . . to be a spouting place for the officialdom of agencies which have forfeited . . . respect."[121] "In short," he stated as he wrapped up his major article analyzing the Convention, "if we had to believe that this gathering at Memphis represents the disciples of Christ in the Restoration movement, then we must conclude that we don't belong."[122]

Joseph Smith has described the Memphis Convention as a "decisive turning point." He argues that the Commission's report called for new "freedom for missionaries" and for the "emerging church" on the mission field.

> In facing the threat of disintegration of their organized mission effort in the struggle over "open membership," Disciples achieved a hitherto unknown degree of common commitment to an innovationist policy in the conduct of their foreign missions program. Basic to this policy were the principles of individual liberty of opinion for missionaries and Christian nationals, and a recognition of the right of the church on the mission field to some freedom of interpretation as it witnessed to the gospel.[123]

My own analysis of the open membership controversy is the opposite of Smith's. The Society's response to the open membership controversy repre-

---

1926 — letters demonstrating the anxiety experienced by the Bros. Direct quotes were taken from the diaries of Spencer Austin, which are available in his papers at the Disciples Historical Society.

121. Errett, "The Memphis Convention," p. 10.

122. Errett, "Convention of Bad Faith," p. 4.

123. Smith, "A Strategy of World Mission," pp. 97-99. Don Pittman and Paul Williams accept and repeat Joseph Smith's interpretation of Memphis in their essay "Mission and Evangelism: Continuing Debates and Contemporary Interpretations," in *Interpreting Disciples,* ed. Larry Bouchard and Dale Richesin (Fort Worth: Texas Christian University Press, 1987), pp. 217-19. The strength of the Pittman-Williams essay comes from their recognition of two different conceptions of the mission task operative in Disciples life. They define these two as the "homiletical" and the "relational." Though their essay does not describe the historical context leading to the development of the second view (generally the changes occasioned by the Jerusalem Conference in 1928 along with an increasing commitment to a christocentric liberalism that begins to stress "building the Kingdom" through social reconstruction), Pittman and Williams are, I think, right in their assessment that some tension still exists between those who assert the primary purpose of missions as the "salvation of individual souls" and those who assert that missionary activity is rather distinguished by "compassionate service to others and the establishment of human community."

sented, if anything, a decisive commitment to the status quo. The Commission's report did affirm that "the Church of Christ in the Orient can not accomplish its task unless it is an Oriental Church of Christ," but at the same time it stated that "many of the nationals are more willing to oversee than to undergird the task . . . more willing to accept responsibility for providing the staff than the stipend." Following a series of rhetorical questions clearly indicating the inability of the indigenous church to deal with its own affairs without outside guidance, the report concludes that, among both missionaries and nationals who urge autonomy for the mission churches, "expectancy outweighs experience in their judgments."[124] The Society's own newsletter summarized the report as stating that "few churches are ready for self-support and self-direction."[125]

This commitment to the status quo in the 1920s had its effect on mission work after that time. The problems revealed in this study of the open membership controversy — pragmatic rather than theological justifications, paternalism and control of churches in "foreign" fields, cultural and Protestant and Christian superiority, support of a divided church, inability to utilize developments in missions abroad as opportunities for education at home — still, to some degree, plagued Disciples through the 1950s. Speaking to Disciples at a meeting in Chicago in August 1954, Virgil Sly indicated that the autonomy issue had only recently been resolved in favor of the indigenous churches. He pointed out that the Society did not resolve "the point of local autonomy" until 1950. Even then, it resulted from events beyond the Society's control and no theological justification supported it.[126]

Perhaps this is why Disciples continued well into the 1960s to talk as if the issue really was the autonomy of the local church instead of the responsibility to learn from the theological reflections of churches located in other cultures. Leaders among the Disciples, thankfully, have learned that autonomy is tough to defend theologically. Unfortunately, the vast majority of people in the pew still defend autonomy and are unfamiliar with the theological affirmations standing behind the covenantal relationship described in *The Design for the Christian Church (Disciples of Christ)*.

Not only were Disciples tardy in coming to terms with indigenous leadership, but they also failed to change their stance on open membership until the early 1960s.[127] In its "Strategy of Ecumenical Concerns," approved in 1961, the

124. "Report of the Commission to the Orient," *World Call* 8 (August 1926): 41-42.

125. "Report of Commission to Orient," *United Society News,* 23 July 1926, p. 1 (UCMS papers).

126. The churches in the Philippines and in Japan had been forced into union by Axis powers. After the war, they chose to remain in union, causing a "crisis" for the UCMS. What would the Society's relationship be to these churches? Were historical Disciples positions threatened by these unions? See "Christian Unity and World Missions," 8 August 1954, pp. 19-20 (UCMS papers).

127. After the autonomy issue was settled in 1950, the Society began to respond to inquiries about open membership by stating something similar to what Dale Fiers told P. H. Welsheimer in a letter in 1955: "while the Society follows its historic practice of not advocating open membership

Division of World Mission, while recognizing that the mission churches would practice baptism only by immersion, recommended that all mission churches "participate in a plan of ecumenical membership." Such a plan placed members who were not baptized on a separate "ecumenical roll" and allowed for "full fellowship with the church." The Society concluded that such a policy was "not open membership" and "not closed membership." One might conclude that it was not full membership either. As the final position put forth in the document might indicate, the theological justification for the change remained weak. Pragmatic justification remained strong, as it did for those dealing with the open membership question at home. Since the 1940s, churches increasingly implemented open membership more on the merits of its practicality than as an inherent part of systematic theological reflection on the nature of the church.

Significant theologizing about mission among Disciples began in 1958 when the Society and the Council on Christian Unity cosponsored a Commission on the Theology of Mission. The Commission did its work for four and a half years. Composed primarily of theologians, missionary administrators, and missionaries, it met several times a year to hear and discuss papers prepared by members. The Commission's stated purpose "was to seek a clearer grasp of the essential nature of the Christian mission" and "to help stimulate the Brotherhood to deep levels of theological understanding of our knowledge of God and our urgent privilege to proclaim His love to the whole world." It clearly fulfilled the first portion of the charge[128] and clearly failed to fulfill the second.

Many of the papers presented over those years offer first-rate theological assessments of questions related to missions. Papers dealt with such topics as non-Christian religions, ecumenical membership, the gospel's relationship to Western culture, the nature of the church, and theologies of evangelism, mission, and history. The summary of the Commission's work, written by William Barr and published in an issue of *Midstream,* suffered some from Barr's desire to be true to the divergence of opinion represented by the members of the Commission.[129] In a letter to Joseph Smith accompanying delivery of the final report, Barr describes it as "much too sophomoric in tone and . . . filled with far too many statements which make only the broadest and vaguest generalities."[130] Even though this statement is mostly on the mark, the report still

---

it would not necessarily break fellowship with a church if in the exercise of its own rights as a New Testament church under Christ it should decide to receive the unimmersed into its fellowship" (Fiers to Welsheimer, 24 February 1955 [UCMS papers]).

128. The 1961 "Strategy of Ecumenical Concerns" owes its origin and development to this Commission.

129. Members of the Commission were Joseph Smith (chair), William Baird, William Barr, George Earle Owen, Oliver Read Whitley, Donald McGavran, Mae Ward, Donald West, Margaret Owen, Virgil Sly, Robert Tobias, Carl Belcher, Robert Heckard, Wayne Bell, Walter Bingham, James Clague, Searle Bates, Donald Salmon, Warner Muir, Glenn Routt, Jessie Trout, Irvin Lunger, Leonard Brummett, William Hall, Ralph Palmer, W. B. Blakemore, and Robert Nelson.

130. Barr to Smith, 26 June 1964. Joseph Smith agreed with this assessment; see Smith to George Beazley, Jr., 17 July 1964 (UCMS papers).

represents the best Disciples statement in print up to that time on the topic of a theology of mission.

The work of the members of the Commission as recently as twenty years ago, however, perhaps reveals that the earlier problems of interpretation remain for Disciples. The most theologically reflective of their working papers collect dust along with the others in the archives of the Historical Society or on the shelves of libraries in the midst of mostly unread journal pages. How do these things get communicated to the laypeople of the churches? The Commission's work never did succeed in that regard.

More recently, the Division of Overseas Ministries developed a statement of "General Principles and Policies" which the 1981 Anaheim General Assembly overwhelmingly endorsed. As a recent essay by Don Pittman and Paul Williams points out, the DOM statement "represents a consensus" never reached before. It confidently asserts that "God has never, in any time or place, been without witness."[131] Interestingly enough, a missionary applicant, some thirty-four years earlier, beat the board to the punch in using these words from Acts 14:17 to say that God speaks to other cultures in God's own ways, even if the people in those cultures know nothing of Jesus Christ. In response to a question asking about "attitude to other religions," Glyn Adsit wrote in 1947, "God has at no time left his people without a witness."[132] Robert Thomas, former president of the DOM, has pointed out that this use of Acts 14:17 in the "General Principles and Policies" statement has raised some controversy.[133]

This affirmation ultimately stands behind the concerns of those who brought Resolution 28, the so-called "Jesus Resolution," to the 1987 Louisville General Assembly. As Disciples struggle with the theological nature of issues surrounding whether or not Jesus is the *only* source of salvation, may they also discover how to encourage meaningful theological dialogue at grass-roots levels. As Clark Williamson has recently said so well, "When the church quits thinking theologically, . . . it tends to lose its ecclesial existence and to proceed aimlessly toward becoming a privatistic, alienated association of people providing such services as the relief of psychic distress and institutional maintenance."[134] Perhaps too much of twentieth-century Disciples history serves to confirm that observation.

---

131. "General Principles and Policies," Division of Overseas Ministries, p. 16.

132. From Adsit's missionary application, 1947 (UCMS papers). I believe the point of convergence here is probably in Paul Tillich, though I was unable to find the location of the precise reference.

133. See Pittman and Williams, "Mission and Evangelism," p. 235.

134. Williamson, "Theological Reflection and Disciples Renewal," in *Disciples of Christ in the Twenty-First Century* (St. Louis: Christian Board of Publication Press, 1988), p. 101. Williamson defines the function of theology as follows: "Christian theology is the effort to understand and interpret the Christian faith in a way that is (1) appropriate to the gospel of Jesus Christ and that is (2) intelligible in the dual sense of enabling us both to think (intellectually) and to act (morally) as the ecclesial community." For an excellent exposition on this definition, see pp. 86-101.

A pragmatic approach to problems is typically American; no doubt the Disciples, as an indigenous religious movement, came by it naturally. But the overarching effect of this kind of mindset has seriously retarded theological development of the Disciples in the twentieth century. Though the leadership of the UCMS, by the late fifties and early sixties, had begun to break out of this mindset, the people in the pews have not really been enabled to join them. Disciples leaders, like those in many other mainstream traditions, have long suspected that the average churchgoer is incapable of serious theological reflection. This suspicion has only encouraged an elite mentality, complete with "us" and "them" language.

This situation constitutes a potentially debilitating dichotomy. The task ahead for Disciples leadership as it heads into the twenty-first century would seem to demand an absolute commitment to its own continued theological development and to the theological education of the lay members of its churches. The complexities facing Disciples in the next century will demand of them the development of a relevant theology of mission. It is not enough to be marginally committed to theological competence among leadership alone; unless an educated commitment to the importance of the theological perspective emerges among the church people in general, the Disciples of Christ will be unable to contribute much to the work of God's church in the days ahead.

The Disciples' Struggle for Unity Compared to the Struggle among Presbyterians, 1880-1980

Douglas A. Foster

INTRODUCTION

From their beginning Disciples devoted themselves to Christian unity, a goal understood by the group's founders as essential for the conversion of the world and the coming of the millennium.[1] Yet their original program for achieving unity was antagonistic toward cooperation with other bodies. It involved "rectifying" Protestants and converting the world to the Disciples understanding of the scriptural terms of pardon, church membership, and the ancient order.[2] When Disciples began their quest for unity in the early nineteenth century, religious division embodied in the ecclesiology of "denominationalism" was generally defended as positive — a remedy to enforced uniformity and religious tyranny. When in the late 1800s other groups became increasingly concerned with pursuing Christian unity, Disciples faced the choice of either continuing to insist that all true Christians come to them or becoming part of the growing call for cooperation, federation, and union. This essay will attempt to chart the Disciples' struggle to define and carry out a concept of Christian unity that harmonized with a changing religious world and their own evolving self-concept. The similarities and contrasts in the same struggle among the

1. See, for example, Barton W. Stone, "Friendly Hints," *Christian Messenger* 13 (January 1844): 281-87; Thomas Campbell, *Declaration and Address of the Christian Association of Washington County, Washington, Pennsylvania* (1809; reprint ed., St. Louis: Mission Messenger, 1978), passim; Alexander Campbell, "The Foundation of Hope and of Christian Union," *Christian Baptist*, 5 April 1824, p. 177; Walter Scott, "On Union among Christians," *The Christian* 1 (August 1837): 154; and Douglas A. Foster, "The Struggle for Unity during the Period of Division of the Restoration Movement: 1875-1900" (Ph.D. diss., Vanderbilt University, 1987), pp. 1-46.
2. See Samuel Hill, "Campbell-Stone on the Frontier: The Only Ones Weren't the Only Ones," in *Lectures in Honor of the Alexander Campbell Bicentennial, 1788-1988* (Nashville: Disciples of Christ Historical Society, 1988), pp. 75-77; and Winfred E. Garrison, *Christian Unity and Disciples of Christ* (St. Louis: Bethany Press, 1955), p. 145.

northern and southern Presbyterian churches will serve to highlight and further illustrate changing Disciples ideas and actions regarding Christian unity.

DIFFERING CONCEPTS OF CHRISTIAN UNITY

Somewhat ironically, Disciples have often differed over the precise nature of the Christian unity they sought.[3] Even more ironic, in the late 1800s and again in the twentieth century Disciples suffered major divisions — schisms at least partially rooted in conflicting concepts of unity.[4] Most Disciples are unaware that variant ideas about unity have been the source of considerable friction in the movement. In recent years, however, Disciples Assemblies have given official recognition to this fact. Resolution 38, passed by the St. Louis Assembly in 1958, admitted that "our internal differences have largely stemmed from an inability to arrive at an agreement on the nature of unity," and it authorized the Disciples' Council on Christian Unity to organize discussions on "the nature of the unity we seek."[5] Between November 1958 and April 1959 eleven Disciples regional "Unity Consultations" were held in the U.S. and Canada. One of the chief questions the consultations were to address was, "What is the unity Disciples hope for (cooperation? 'spiritual'? organic?)?" When the March 1959 issue of the *Christian Unity Newsletter* reported the results of the first seven conferences, it noted "sharp diversity over the kind of unity Disciples seek — whether 'organic' or 'spiritual.'"[6] In 1972 Resolution 39 recognized continuing differences in opinions and concepts of "Brotherhood purpose and direction, especially in regard to Christian unity."[7]

3. See George G. Beazley, Jr., "The Present Place of the Disciples in the Ecumenical Movement," *Mid-Stream* 4 (Spring 1965): 78-79.

4. The most conservative group (known today as Churches of Christ), under the leadership of David Lipscomb of Nashville, insisted on strict adherence to what it saw as the clear truths of Scripture without addition or subtraction. A more progressive party, influenced by Isaac Errett of Cincinnati and, later, J. H. Garrison of St. Louis, emphasized a wide area of nonessentials in which diversity might exist without posing a threat to unity. The part of this group that retained conservative ideas of biblical interpretation eventually became the independent Christian Churches. J. H. Garrison came to advocate an organizational maturity for Disciples that would give them an official structure through which to participate in the ecumenical organizations. The part of the movement that became the Christian Church (Disciples of Christ) most closely reflects Garrison's ideas, yet diversity in concepts of unity within that part of the movement continued. See Foster, "The Struggle for Unity," chaps. 3-5.

5. *1958 Yearbook and Directory of the Christian Churches (Disciples of Christ)* (Indianapolis: Christian Churches [Disciples of Christ], 1958), pp. 37-38.

6. The report also pointed out striking ambivalence in two of the conferences. The plenary sessions approved statements embodying spiritual unity as the goal, but questionnaires filled out by individual participants showed the vast majority to favor organic union. "Unity Consultations Scheduled," *Christian Unity Newsletter* 4 (November 1958): 1; "Unity Consultations Report Findings," *Christian Unity Newsletter* 4 (March 1959): 1.

7. *1972 Yearbook of the Christian Church (Disciples of Christ)* (Indianapolis: Christian Church [Disciples of Christ], 1972), p. 173.

Two surveys taken in the past three decades confirm the conflict. In a 1959 study of Disciples churches in Southern California, Jerry P. Jones found considerable disagreement on statements such as "Denominationalism is a sin," "Open membership is a step toward unity," "Unity would be easier if theology were ignored," and "For unity to be achieved, some must be compelled."[8] In the 1984 Forrest F. Reed Lectures Lawrence C. Keene reported that Disciples ministers and elders in his surveys differed significantly concerning the desirability of closer fellowship with churches outside the Restoration tradition.[9]

As hinted, the chief difference in understanding Christian unity in the Christian world generally is whether it is essentially spiritual (invisible) or organic (visible). However, few if any early Disciples held the traditional Protestant "invisible church" idea of spiritual unity because of its inherent justification of denominationalism. Scattered statements allude to a spiritual unity of Christians, but most nineteenth-century Disciples understood this "unity" to have strict limits, referring to a faithful remnant scattered throughout "the sects" whom they called to come out and join them.[10]

A few in the Disciples mainstream have seemed to emphasize an existent underlying spiritual unity.[11] Recent statements include that of Harold Key, who, in speaking of internal problems facing Disciples during the move toward restructure, insisted that the Spirit of God through Christ had already produced unity. The problem for Disciples has been how to maintain the unity of the Spirit in the bond of peace.[12] Paul A. Crow, Jr., contended in 1983 that "the unity of the church is a spiritual reality which already exists and is founded upon the nature of God."[13] Even these statements in context embody more than traditional Protestant ideas of spiritual unity.

Early Disciples leaders such as Barton W. Stone and Thomas Campbell put almost total emphasis on individual responsibility for effecting Christian unity. Each person must first be united to Christ; all those thus united to Christ

8. Jones, "The Historical and Contemporary Positions of the Christian Churches (Disciples of Christ) Concerning Christian Unity" (M.Th. thesis, Southern California School of Theology, 1959), p. 56.

9. Keene, "A Family Portrait: A Focus on Attitudes and Beliefs," in "Heirs of Stone and Campbell on the Pacific Slope: A Sociological Approach," *Impact* 12 (1984): 70.

10. Thomas Campbell in the *Declaration and Address* firmly established this notion for Disciples with his statement that "The Church of Christ upon earth . . . consist[s] of all those in every place that profess their faith in Christ and obedience to him in all things according to the scriptures." See also L., "A Plea for Union," *Millennial Harbinger* 41 (September 1870): 524; Isaac Errett, *Our Position* (Cincinnati: Standard Publishing, 1873), p. 7; "Spiritual and Organic Union," *Christian Standard,* 19 March 1898, p. 362.

11. See, for example, J. V. Coombs, "Organic Union Not Sufficient," *Christian Standard,* 14 June 1919, p. 898; "Is Christian Unity a Fact?" *Christian Standard,* 2 June 1951, p. 346; Joseph Fort Newton, "The Underlying Unity of Spirit," *Christian-Evangelist* 37 (September 1900): 1129; "Spiritual Basis of Unity," *Christian-Evangelist* 92 (1955): 259.

12. See Key, "Practical Ways to Extend Fellowship and Reduce Tension," in *Fellowship Meeting, Rolla, Missouri, November, 1963,* ed. Martin M. Mitchum (N.p.: n.p., 1963), p. 16.

13. Crow, *The Anatomy of a Nineteenth-Century United Church* (Lexington: Lexington Theological Seminary, 1983), p. 43.

in a locality will be united with each other forming a church of Christ, inherently one with all other such groups.[14] In a similar vein, Peter Ainslie, the Disciples' "Apostle of Christian Unity," came to insist that Christian unity would result when all Christians possessed the spirit of Christ.[15] In 1929, in connection with activities of the Christian Unity League, Ainslie wrote what he called a "pact of reconciliation." In this document he urged Christians to "make the adventure of trusting other Christians as Christians" by receiving them into Christ's church and at his supper, and by accepting all Christian ministers as equals, regardless of differences in forms of ordination.[16] Ainslie saw this unity as coming through a process of spiritual, not organizational maturity. He believed that an underlying spiritual unity was already in place but that an acknowledgment of that unity in full mutual acceptance was essential for bringing it to completion. Ainslie's position can be understood as a modification and integration of both the spiritual and organic unity ideas — a middle position much like the individualistic stance of the founders of the movement.[17] Conservative James DeForest Murch also held a form of this middle position but maintained further that to work together Christians must hold similar beliefs. Like Ainslie, he saw a progression toward realization of the underlying spiritual unity, but he altered Ainslie's idea by insisting that true cooperation could exist only between those with conservative convictions, especially about the divinity of Christ and the inspiration of Scripture.[18]

Charles Clayton Morrison, editor of *The Christian Century* from 1908 to 1947, objected strongly to any form of the idea that unity was essentially spiritual. Morrison contended that the concept was false and a great hindrance

14. See Barton W. Stone, "Christian Union," *Christian Messenger* 3 (December 1828): 37-38; and "Remarks," *Christian Messenger* 9 (August 1835): 180; Don Herbert Yoder, "Christian Unity in Nineteenth-Century America," in *A History of the Ecumenical Movement, 1517-1948*, ed. Ruth Rouse and Stephen Charles Neill (Philadelphia: Westminster Press, 1968), p. 239.

15. Ainslie, "Will Christian Union Come by Absorption or Compromise?" *Christian Union Quarterly* 5 (January 1915): 197; and Ainslie, *The Scandal of Christianity* (Chicago: Willett, Clark & Colby, 1929), pp. 26-27. See also Wilbur S. Hogevoll, "The Meaning of Christian Unity in the Theology of Peter Ainslie" (M.A. thesis, University of Chicago Divinity School, 1936), pp. 20-22.

16. Ainslie, Intro. in *The Equality of All Christians before God* (New York: Macmillan, 1930), pp. 8-10.

17. Ainslie earlier upheld the traditional Disciples idea of immersion as the "one Catholic baptism," but the inconsistency of recognizing many as Christians who were excluded from membership in Disciples churches moved him to an open membership position (on which, see Mark Toulouse's essay on pp. 194-235 in this volume). See his sermons "Highway through Protestant Christendom," 24 June 1924, Baltimore, Maryland, and "Have the Disciples a Place in the Christian World?" 20 March 1927, Baltimore, Maryland, in Peter Ainslie Papers, Disciples of Christ Historical Society, Nashville. For a description of Ainslie's move toward open membership, see Hilary Thomas Bowen, "Dr. Peter Ainslie and Open Membership," manuscript in Disciples of Christ Historical Society.

18. See, e.g., Murch, "United Evangelical Action," *Christian Standard* 78 (1943): 482; and George Hugh Wilson, "Unity and Restoration in the Ecumenical Thought of the Disciples of Christ: With Special Reference to the Disciples' Part in the Evolution of the World Council of Churches" (Ph.D. diss., Hartford Seminary Foundation, 1962), pp. 240-49.

to the movement toward true Christian unity. The claim that unity already exists in the "invisible church" lulled Christians into complacency and even defense of division, he insisted. Morrison contended that the church is historical, that it exists only in history, visible and verifiable.[19]

At least three ideas about unity can be seen from this material: (1) it already exists spiritually in the invisible church — we merely need to acknowledge what is already there, (2) it is essentially spiritual but will not truly exist until each professed Christian truly has the spirit of Christ (including for some a set of conservative doctrines) and is united with all other such Christians; it is, therefore, in the process of becoming, and (3) the only true unity is visible organic unity. Interestingly, each of the stances conceives of unity in terms of an evolution. As early as 1895, J. H. Garrison described his idea of the process as advancing from unity within Protestant families to a federation of all the churches for cooperation in benevolence and missions, finally ending with the dropping of sectarian names and creeds so that all would be united in one church.[20] Ainslie believed that the Disciples had to follow the ecumenical movement wherever it went, because in it God was leading the church to union.[21] W. E. Garrison insisted in 1955 that those who opposed what were admittedly imperfect fulfillments of the ideal, such as federation, would actually become enemies of Christian unity "if devotion to an ideal were made the excuse for refusing to take any intermediate steps in the direction of its realization."[22] Inevitably participation in such efforts required structures that could be in some sense representative of Disciples as a whole.

A common theme among the most progressive Disciples was that the basis for unity cannot be doctrinal uniformity. Morrison argued that if theological agreement is necessary to unity, it can be reached only on Rome's terms — that is, in "submission to one supreme earthly authority conceded to have a divine commission to define the truth and to enforce its acceptance by ecclesiastical and spiritual penalties."[23] W. E. Garrison expressed concern that

19. Morrison, *What Is Christianity?* (Chicago: Willett, Clark, 1940), p. 277; *The Meaning of Baptism* (Chicago: Disciples Publishing Society, 1914), p. 212; and "The Quest for Unity," *Christian Century* 54 (1937): 1065. Morrison shared this idea with some earlier Disciples such as J. H. Garrison. See "Christian Unity — What Is It?" *The Christian-Evangelist*, 3 January 1887, p. 66. See also Crow's interview with Lillian Moir, 6 January 1970, Office of Interpretation, Christian Church (Disciples of Christ), in the Paul A. Crow, Jr., biographical file, Disciples of Christ Historical Society, Nashville, p. 9.

20. Garrison, "Three Steps to Christian Unity," *The Christian-Evangelist*, 21 November 1895, p. 738; see also "The Union Problem," *The Christian-Evangelist*, 29 May 1890, p. 338.

21. See George G. Beazley, "The Present Place of the Disciples in the Ecumenical Movement," *Mid-Stream* 4 (Spring 1965): 80; Ainslie, "The Breaking Down of Barriers," *Christian Union Library* 2 (July 1912): 4; and "The Shame of Division," *Christian Union Library* 2 (October 1912): 3-4.

22. Garrison, *Christian Unity and Disciples of Christ* (St. Louis: Bethany Press, 1955), p. 244.

23. Morrison, "Faith and Order or Life and Work," *Christian Century*, 25 September 1935, p. 1199; "All Christians Equal before God," *Christian Century*, 23 October 1929, pp. 1306-8.

the principle of freedom for diversity within the church was being neglected in the ecumenical movement itself. He accused the Faith and Order movement, for example, of being overly occupied with trying to secure agreements in areas of doctrinal divergence.[24]

Conservatives predictably mounted strong resistance to relaxing traditional Disciples standards.[25] Influential editor Isaac Errett argued in 1888 that to achieve union *in Christ,* Disciples had to seek the beliefs and practices generally acknowledged by those who accepted the authority of the New Testament. The safe way would be to adhere "to that which is clearly the universal voice of the faithful of all ages," along with "our own best knowledge of the divine word."[26] James DeForest Murch insisted in the forties and fifties that no essential Christian belief could be compromised for unity or cooperation.[27] Nevertheless, for an increasing number of Disciples leaders, unity in diversity was the only possible unity.[28]

Early in the Disciples movement the pursuit of unity at an organizational level — from the top — was usually opposed.[29] However, as leaders became convinced of the need for structures to participate in the ecumenical movement, the individualistic appeal of the founders was heard less and less in Disciples literature. Those who continued to emphasize the individual and local nature of unity insisted that unity could only be achieved from the bottom up.[30] Nevertheless, as will be seen, with few exceptions twentieth-century Disciples have focused their unity efforts increasingly on the corporate merger model — organizational union from the top.

In contrast to Disciples, early sentiment among Presbyterians maintained

24. Garrison, *A Response to Amsterdam* (Indianapolis: Association for the Promotion of Christian Unity, 1950), pp. 14-15.

25. See, however, Charles Clayton Morrison, "The Southern Presbyterians Withdraw," *Christian Century* 48 (1931): 764; Winfred Ernest Garrison, *The Quest and Character of a United Church* (New York: Abingdon Press, 1957), p. 217.

26. Errett was referring here to the Disciples' insistence on immersion ("Reply to Zetesis," *Christian Standard,* 23 July 1881, p. 236).

27. Murch, "Spiritual Unity," *United Evangelical Appeal* 15 (1956): 280; "The Unity We Desire," *Christian Standard* 75 (1940): 149; and "A Liberal Eclipse at Evanston," *United Evangelical Appeal* 13 (1954-55): 142.

28. See Winfred Ernest Garrison, *The Quest and Character of a United Church* (New York: Abingdon Press, 1957), pp. 12-13. Jerry Jones's survey of California Disciples churches in the late 1950s indicated strong disagreement with statements such as "All must accept Disciples' New Testament theology," and "Union is impossible without universal immersion," and strong agreement with statements such as "Unity is possible without conformity," and "The bond of union is love" (Jones, "Positions of the Christian Churches," p. 56).

29. See Barton W. Stone and John T. Johnson, "Editors' Address," *Christian Messenger* 7 (January 1833): 1.

30. "How 'Union at the Top' Works," *Christian Standard,* 6 July 1907, p. 1114. The author argues that "there is no higher divinely approved religious organization on earth than that of the local congregation of Christian believers." This approach has become the focus of much ecumenical effort in recent years. See, for example, F. D. Bonvillain, "The Thread of Unity: A Report on the Merger of Christ Church Uniting Disciples and Presbyterians in Kailua, Hawaii" (D.Min. project, Claremont School of Theology, 1976).

the legitimacy of "denominationalism." The development of European confessionalism provided welcome relief from persecution of dissenters like themselves.[31] A prodenominationalism continued among Presbyterians throughout
the nineteenth and twentieth centuries. In 1880 Princeton theologian Charles
Hodge listed five duties of denominational churches for preserving "the unity
of the entire church": (1) mutual recognition, (2) intercommunion, (3) recognition of each other's sacraments and orders, (4) noninterference, and
(5) cooperation in extending the kingdom of Christ.[32] Hodge joined most
Presbyterians in assuming the normative nature and perpetual existence of
denominational Christianity. Francis Miller epitomized this attitude in a 1948
article titled "The Church in Everytown." The nature of humans and the world,
he asserted, will never allow for one Christian organization, but there is room
for infinite expressions. Denominations should continue as long as they represent living, dynamic traditions, existing as brotherhoods within the church.[33]
As recently as 1963 in an official statement by the Commission on Ecumenical
Mission and Relations of the United Presbyterian Church in the USA, Church
official Harold Nebelsick explained that "many of the new confessions and
denominations which resulted in the fragmentation of the body of Christ were
caused by a movement of the Spirit" to preserve truths in danger of being
neglected by the church as a whole.[34] The following year the Southern General
Assembly adopted a statement echoing the Northern Church's sentiments: "We
do not subscribe to the view . . . that *all* divisions in the organized church are
sinful. It can be forcibly argued that a pattern whereby differently organized
churches recognize one another is a more appropriate visible expression of our
underlying unity in Christ than would be a progressive obliteration of denominational distinctions through unions."[35]

The underlying philosophy embodied in these statements is that the
nature of Christian unity is spiritual and invisible. Southerner Russell Cecil
declared in 1918 that Presbyterians were in agreement on the spiritual nature
of Christian unity and insisted that the necessity of visible organic unity could
not be defended from Scripture.[36]

Henry Sloane Coffin expressed the opposite end of the spectrum for

31. See Lefferts A. Loetscher, *The Problem of Christian Unity in Early Nineteenth-Century
America* (Philadelphia: Fortress Press, 1969), p. 4; Donald Herbert Yoder, "Christian Unity in
Nineteenth-Century America," in *A History of the Ecumenical Movement: 1517-1948,* ed. Ruth
Rouse and Stephen Charles Neill (Philadelphia: Westminster Press, 1954), pp. 221-26.

32. Hodge, "Church Unity," *Presbyterian,* 17 January 1880, p. 10; "Unity of the Church,"
Presbyterian, 30 May 1885, p. 10.

33. Miller, "The Church in Everytown," *Presbyterian Life,* 17 January 1948, p. 5.

34. Nebelsick, "United Presbyterian Basis for Ecumenical Relations," Significant Papers,
no. 7 (New York: United Presbyterian Church in the USA, 1963), p. 7.

35. *A Digest of the Acts and Proceedings of the General Assembly of the Presbyterian
Church in the United States: 1861-1965* (Atlanta: Office of the General Assembly, 1966), p. 59.

36. Cecil, "Union of Presbyterian Churches," *The Union Seminary Review* 29 (January
1918): 102-3.

Presbyterians in a scathing sermon in 1950. After arguing that the Presbyterian Church was not the sole guardian of any essential truths and that denominationalism is a sin, Coffin said, "The world would not easily detect an invisible unity in spirit. The unity Jesus willed was to be manifest, impressive, cogent. To me the continued maintenance of our denominations in their separatedness is a sin against Christ, a denial of our obedience to him."[37]

As with conservative Disciples, conservative Presbyterians believed that the organic approach to unity characterized by Coffin's speech tended to deemphasize the importance of doctrine. A Presbyterian heritage of emphasis on doctrinal rightness caused much opposition to ecumenical initiatives based on their perceived tendency to minimize correct doctrine. In 1961 the Southern General Assembly issued a statement declaring that "Unity on theological terms and under the constraints of theological conviction is the only unity to which the Church . . . should address itself."[38]

The earliest Disciples unity impulse, then, was a modification — a hybrid perhaps — of the spiritual and organic unity ideas. The idea was not that unity was already perfect in some intangible spiritual plane but rather that all true spiritual Christians should and must leave the sectarian/denominational organizations and come together to be visibly/organically united in congregations of Christians. The unity was envisioned not as organic in the sense of mergers of corporate structures but rather in terms of individual Christians uniting with other individual Christians in congregations without any features that would denominate them from other such Christians. These disciples would recognize as Christians all who professed to believe in Christ and demonstrated that belief in their conduct. At first the proponents of this vision believed that most Christians in "denominational churches" would see the rightness of their plea and join them. When other ecumenical opportunities became available in the latter years of the nineteenth century, however, this position was gradually supplanted in the minds of many by the idea of organic union in the sense of organizational merger.

In other words, among Disciples, who have always emphasized Christian unity, some moved from a "middle" position that condemned denominational structures to an organic-union position that required a legal corporate organization with which to pursue unity. Peter Ainslie was one who continued to emphasize the spiritual basis for any eventual visible union. Presbyterians, in contrast, began with a strong classical notion of spiritual unity that legitimized

37. Coffin, "Are Denominations Justified?" *Presbyterian Life,* 21 January 1950, p. 19.

38. *PCUS Digest,* p. 56. In the twentieth century the southern journal *Concerned Presbyterians* and the northern *Presbyterian Layman* were especially vocal in their accusations of internal theological liberalism and doctrinal laxity destructive of their understanding of truth. In recent decades resistance has focused on ecumenical outreach, particularly the Consultation on Church Union (COCU). See Arthur Carl Piepkorn, *Profiles in Belief: The Religious Bodies of the United States and Canada,* vol. 2: *Protestant Denominations* (San Francisco: Harper & Row, 1973), pp. 306-10.

the perpetuation of denominational divisions but moved rather rapidly in the middle of the century to an emphasis on organic union. In the last decade of the period under study, both groups were deeply influenced by developments in the Consultation on Church Union process which, it will be shown, produced another major thought shift. During the whole period under study, Disciples and Presbyterians have continued to demonstrate, within their communions, diverse ideas of unity. The clash of these views has itself contributed to defections and divisions.

EFFORTS TOWARD INTERNAL UNITY

As previously noted, Disciples have suffered two major divisions since their beginning. The U.S. religious census of 1906 recognized the first by listing Churches of Christ separately from Christian Churches (Disciples). The official restructure of the Christian Churches into the Christian Church (Disciples of Christ) in 1968 served to complete the second. In both cases, the dates indicate the end of a long process of alienation and division. Peter Ainslie believed that the first task in reaching Christian unity was to reconcile the divisions within each communion, and the Disciples were his first concern.[39]

Despite the feelings of Ainslie and many others, only two major efforts at internal reconciliation have been made. The first began in 1936 between members of Churches of Christ and the still officially undivided Christian Churches (Disciples). Claude F. Witty, minister for the West Side Central Church of Christ in Detroit and James DeForest Murch, then literary editor for the *Christian Standard,* brought ministers from the two groups together to discuss divisive issues and the possibilities of unity. A *Christian Unity Quarterly* was begun as a forum for the efforts. Murch and Witty encouraged the organization of local meetings and conducted two national conferences in Detroit (1938) and Indianapolis (1939).[40] Opposition to the meetings from the most conservative segment of the Churches of Christ, represented by the *Gospel Advocate,* led to a cooling of enthusiasm, and the efforts ended in the early 1940s.[41]

The other attempt at internal unity took place in the 1960s between

39. Ainslie, "First Things First," *Christian Union Quarterly* 4 (July 1914): 138.

40. These meetings were actually more closely akin to recent informal discussions taking place between members of Churches of Christ and independent Christian Churches. See *Restoration Forum V* (Joplin, Mo.: College Press, 1987), and *Restoration Forum VI* (Joplin, Mo.: College Press, 1988). Murch proved to be a staunch opponent of the liberal Disciples, opposing participation in the ecumenical movement and restructure.

41. See Murch, *Christians Only* (Cincinnati: Standard Publishing, 1962), pp. 274-76; Earl Irving West, *The Search for the Ancient Order,* vol. 4 (Indianapolis: Religious Book Service, 1988), pp. 231-33; James DeForest Murch and Claude F. Witty, "A Plea for Unity among Churches of Christ" (N.p.: n.p., 1937).

leaders of an already well-defined group of dissident independent Christian Churches and what would soon become the Christian Church (Disciples of Christ). Between 1959 and 1963, immediately following the regional "Unity Consultations" mentioned previously, Disciples ministers and leaders met for a series of four Consultations on Internal Unity of the Christian Churches. The tensions between evangelical/fundamentalist elements and those who favored restructure of the movement into a full-fledged denomination had almost reached the final breaking point. Some in the Consultations attempted to hold the movement together by arguing for broad diversity and tolerance — which they insisted had always been the Disciples' position. Differences in understandings of the nature of unity were apparent. Some insisted that the unity was primarily spiritual (invisible), involving a common core of faith with neither unity of action nor theological interpretation essential. Even those who advanced this idea differed in their understandings of the common core, however, with ideas ranging from simple acceptance of Jesus as Lord to insistence on a long list of essentials.[42] Woodrow Phillips expressed conservative fears: "If we cannot defeat a liberalism that negates Scriptural authority we can never have unity, for one issue will rise upon another to divide us."[43] Some Disciples liberals insisted that true unity could never be made contingent on rigid doctrinal uniformity. They called for cooperation in spite of significant differences even in matters of faith. Without cooperative action between churches, they maintained, there was no unity.[44] Others who had been supporters of Restructure eventually came to fear that the more rigidly defined structure would no longer permit nominal unity with the independents, a feature many liberals cherished as evidence to the religious world that unity in diversity was possible. The Atlanta Declaration Committee was especially insistent on the spiritual nature of unity as opposed to the creation of organizational boundaries.[45]

Needless to say, the Consultations were not successful in maintaining the internal unity of Disciples. The independent Christian Churches exist

42. See George Earl Owen, "Unity and Diversity among Cooperatives," in *The Second Consultation on Internal Unity of the Christian Churches* (Oklahoma City: Consultation on Internal Unity, 1960), p. 54; John Greenlee, "Summation," in *Consultation on Internal Unity of Christian Churches* (N.p.: Council on Christian Unity, 1959), pp. 77-78; Cecil K. Thomas, "The New Testament Church," in *The Second Consultation on Internal Unity of the Christian Churches*, pp. 14-15; James B. Carr, "Can We Have One Brotherhood?" in *The Third Consultation on Internal Unity of the Christian Churches* (N.p: n.p., 1962), p. 26.

43. Phillips, "The Basic Issues, Past, Present and Future," in *The Third Consultation on Internal Unity of the Christian Churches*, p. 38.

44. See Cecil K. Thomas, "The Holy Spirit and the Unity of Christians," in *Consultation on Internal Unity of the Christian Churches (Fourth Series)*, ed. Charles R. Gresham (Manhattan, Kans.: n.p., 1963), p. 47.

45. See discussion of the Atlanta Declaration Committee in Anthony LeRoy Dunnavant, "Restructure: Four Historical Ideals in the Campbell-Stone Movement and the Development of the Polity of the Christian Church (Disciples of Christ)" (Ph.D. diss., Vanderbilt University, 1984), pp. 509-20.

separately from the Christian Church (Disciples of Christ) with 1,063,469 members compared with Disciples' 1,106,692.[46]

In contrast to Disciples, Presbyterians have experienced considerable success at healing internal divisions. One of the most significant Presbyterian mergers took place in 1906 between the PCUSA and the Cumberland Presbyterian Church, prompted by the PCUSA General Assembly's 1903 approval of a "Declaratory Statement" modifying some of its interpretations of the Westminster Confession.[47]

By far the most important move toward unity among Presbyterians was the continuing effort to unite the northern and southern churches. The relationship between the groups from the 1882 reciprocal withdrawal of all past offensive measures to the 1983 merger forming the new PCUSA was increasingly cordial, though filled with ups and downs. The PCUS, undoubtedly influenced by the "southern civil religion" ideas of the doctrinal purity of the southern churches, was as a whole less anxious to talk about organic union.[48] Southern objections to union included accusations of northern doctrinal laxness, the assertion in early talks that the PCUSA did not understand the "negro question," and numerous matters of polity and organization.[49] On the other hand, arguments for the reunion from both sides included the contention that the "late unpleasantness" had been forgotten in every major field of social activity except the religious, and it was time to move beyond differences in that field too.[50]

Both General Assemblies approved union talks in 1929 and 1943, the latter eventually including the United Presbyterian Church of North America. Despite a concerted effort by influential ministers from all three groups to answer objections, when the vote came in 1955 the PCUS rejected merger. The other two continued talks until the merger of 1958, which produced the United Presbyterian Church.[51]

46. Constant H. Jacquet, Jr., ed., *Yearbook of American and Canadian Churches* (Nashville: Abingdon Press, 1988), pp. 39, 41.

47. A large minority of Cumberland Churches rejected the union and continued to exist as a separate denomination. John T. Ames, "Cumberland Liberals and the Union of 1906," *Journal of Presbyterian History* 52 (Spring 1974): 8-9, 15; William H. Roberts, "The Reunion of the Cumberland Presbyterian Church and the Presbyterian Church in the U.S.A.," *Journal of the Presbyterian Historical Society* 3 (September 1906): 301-5.

48. See Charles Reagan Wilson, *Baptized in Blood: The Religion of the Lost Cause, 1865-1920* (Athens, Ga.: University of Georgia Press, 1980). Initiatives for talks toward union always came from PCUSA presbyteries and were usually rejected by the PCUS General Assembly. See, for example, *Minutes of the General Assembly of the Presbyterian Church in the United States of America* (Philadelphia: Office of the General Assembly, 1918), pp. 121-22, 212.

49. See W. R. Minter, "Organic Union or Federation," *The Union Seminary Review* 29 (January 1918): 127-31; James H. Taylor, "Organic Union or Federal Union?" *The Union Seminary Review* 29 (January 1918): 95-97.

50. Ernest Thompson, "Organic Union of the Presbyterian Churches," *The Union Seminary Review* 29 (April 1918): 113; "Presbyterian Union," *Christian Evangelist,* 8 February 1917, p. 164.

51. W. Stanley Rycroft, *The Ecumenical Witness of the United Presbyterian Church in the U.S.A.* (N.p.: Board of Christian Education of the United Presbyterian Church in the USA, 1968), p. 143.

In 1969 the General Assemblies of the PCUS and the UPCUSA agreed to "seek a plan for the reunion of the two churches" and authorized the appointment of a Joint Committee on Presbyterian Union. Between 1970 and 1982 the Committee and its task forces joined in hundreds of meetings with churches, presbyteries, and synods to determine the thinking of the churches about union. Drafts of Plans for Reunion were submitted to the churches in 1971, 1974, and 1978 for discussion and comment. Opposition continued, particularly among southern dissidents, who increasingly opted to leave the PCUS. In 1973 several presbyteries met in Birmingham, Alabama, to form the National Presbyterian Church, later renamed the Presbyterian Church in America.[52] The 1982 meetings of the General Assemblies approved the final revision of the Plan of Reunion and sent it for approval to the presbyteries. The groups met in Atlanta in 1983 and there merged to form the Presbyterian Church (USA).

Disciples, who began the nineteenth century as a unity movement, have been rather surprised by the divisions that invaded their ranks. Internal unity attempts have centered on maintaining the unity they believed they had; little effort has been expended on seeking reunion after the divisions were realized. Perhaps a chief reason for Disciples failures at reversing internal schism is the nearness of the divisions. Time tends to heal wounds inflicted in painful separations; perhaps healing will come in the future.

More important for understanding Disciples failures at internal unity, however, is recognizing that the Disciples divisions are enmeshed in the bitter controversies of modernism/liberalism vs. fundamentalism/conservatism, a congeries of issues that has pulled American Christianity increasingly apart in this century. The wrenching fights of fundamentalism vs. modernism began building even before the first Disciples division was finalized and were a major factor in the second.[53] Successful Presbyterian unity actions took place between groups that were moving in the same directions ideologically and doctrinally. The groups produced in the Disciples divisions were inherently moving in different (though not necessarily opposite) directions. They have more in common with Presbyterian rifts like the defection of the Presbyterian Church in America, which has no prospect of future reunion with mainstream Presbyterianism.

---

52. *The Encyclopedia of American Religions,* 2d ed., ed. J. Gordon Melton (Detroit: Gale Research, 1987), pp. 254-55; Frank Joseph Smith, *The History of the Presbyterian Church in America: The Continuing Church Movement* (Mannassas, Va.: Reformation Education Foundation, 1985).

53. See James Brownlee North, "The Fundamentalist Controversy among the Disciples of Christ, 1890-1930" (Ph.D. diss., University of Illinois at Urbana-Champaign, 1973).

COOPERATIVE/FEDERATIVE EFFORTS

Disciples have been party to no unions since the "merger" of the Stone and Campbell movements in 1832. Mainstream Disciples, however, became increasingly open to cooperative efforts in the century under consideration.[54] Disciples established their first permanent organization to pursue contacts with other Christian bodies in 1910 through the efforts of that year's International Convention president, Peter Ainslie. In his address to the convention at Topeka, Kansas, Ainslie told Disciples that the task of seeking unity with their brethren in other communions was part of God's program and therefore should be part of theirs. He optimistically called for a Disciples unity council that would be endowed as well as any of their colleges and that would be given equal footing with the missionary societies. Late that year Ainslie and others incorporated the Council (or Commission) on Christian Union as an agency to bring the Disciples' plea to the Christian world, arrange conferences on Christian union, and work with the commissions of other religious bodies to arrange a world conference on Christian union.[55] In 1911 Ainslie began publication of the *Christian Union Library* (it became the *Christian Union Quarterly* in 1913), which carried articles on Christian unity by members of various communions. Ainslie and the Council on Christian Union were in the forefront of a movement sparked by the Edinburgh World Missionary Conference of 1910. That meeting and a unity conference held in London immediately afterward resulted in the creation of cooperating commissions in many denominations. In his history of the Faith and Order Movement, Tissington Tatlow places Ainslie's efforts in the vanguard of this surge of unity committees.[56]

In 1917 the Council was reorganized and renamed the Association for the Promotion of Christian Unity, becoming a department of the Disciples General Convention, the first American denominational unity committee to be elevated to such a status.[57] In 1954 the charter of the Association was changed to unite the ecumenical interests of the United Christian Missionary Society, the International Convention, the Board of Higher Education, and the Com-

---

54. See Charles Richard Dawson, "Elder Isaac Errett: Christian Standard Bearer" (B.D. thesis, College of the Bible, 1948), pp. 109-10; J. H. Garrison, "The Union Problem," *The Christian-Evangelist*, 29 May 1890, p. 338; "Our Relation to Other Religious Bodies," *The Christian-Evangelist*, 21 March 1895, p. 178; Howard Elmo Short, *Christian Unity Is Our Business: Disciples of Christ Within the Ecumenical Fellowship* (N.p.: Bethany Press, 1953), pp. 41-44; Winfred E. Garrison, *Christian Unity and Disciples of Christ* (St. Louis: Bethany Press, 1955), p. 141.

55. *The American Home Missionary Containing the Yearbook of Disciples of Christ 1913* (Cincinnati: American Christian Missionary Society, 1913), p. 50.

56. Tatlow, "The World Conference on Faith and Order," in *A History of the Ecumenical Movement*, pp. 407-8. See also Winfred E. Garrison, *Christian Unity and Disciples of Christ*, pp. 159-64.

57. *The American Home Missionary 1917, Containing the Yearbook of Churches of Christ (Disciples)* (Cincinnati: American Christian Missionary Society, 1917), p. 48.

mittee on Relief Appeals. It was then renamed the Council on Christian Unity, which name it still retains.[58] When Disciples restructured themselves into the Christian Church (Disciples of Christ), the Council became a "unit" of the denomination. This organization in its various forms took the lead in twentieth-century Disciples unity overtures.[59]

The General Assemblies of the northern and southern Presbyterian churches created committees to pursue unity even earlier than the Disciples. These early committees were, however, only temporary, created to handle talks in one specific circumstance. The PCUS confined its efforts exclusively to talks with other Presbyterian bodies, and that remained the chief thrust of the PCUSA as well. The Disciples Council was quite different from the Presbyterian committees. It was wide-ranging and adventuresome in its contacts with other religious groups.

Both northern and southern Presbyterian churches and the Disciples became members of the Federal Council of Churches at its beginning in 1908. Disciples endorsement of federation had come six years earlier when Garrison asked Elias B. Sanford, secretary of the Federal Council's predecessor National Federation of Churches, to speak to the Disciples convention in Omaha. A resolution in favor of the principle of federation was questioned by the editor of the *Christian Standard,* who suggested that its adoption would imply "recognition of the denominations." Garrison responded that it would recognize the existence of denominationalism and anticipate its elimination by promoting the spirit of cooperation. Garrison argued that association with other bodies in the Federal Council could be a vehicle for promotion of the Disciples' unique plea for unity.[60]

With the Presbyterians' spiritual understanding of unity, it is understandable why those who favored church cooperation welcomed the idea of federation. Many in fact contended that federation was the ultimate goal — the best that could be hoped for.[61] Despite sporadic efforts to force a with-

58. See Peter Ainslie, "Our Fellowship and the Task," *Christian Union Library* 1 (April 1912): 18-21; "The Temper of the Times and the Opportunity," *Christian Union Library* 2 (April 1913): 3; and "Work of the Commission of the Disciples of Christ," *Christian Union Library* 1 (October 1911): 3-5. See also "Association Becomes Council on Christian Unity," *Christian Unity Newsletter* 1 (January 1955): 1.

59. Statements appear in several yearbooks, beginning with the 1968 volume, which stressed that the unity commissions of the Council were authorized only to prepare plans of union for presentation to the Assembly and that no coercive power whatsoever could be exercised by the Council or the Assembly on any congregation. See *1968 Yearbook and Directory of the Christian Church (Disciples of Christ)* (Indianapolis: Christian Church [Disciples of Christ], 1968), pp. 44-45.

60. J. H. Garrison, "Church Federation: What Is It and What Should Be Our Attitude toward It?" *The Christian-Evangelist,* 28 May 1903, p. 449. For a more recent expression of this attitude, see Paul A. Crow's interview with Lillian Moir.

61. See Thornton Whaling, "Unity and Union," *The Union Seminary Review* 32 (January 1921): 146; see also Thomas Thornton Whaling, "The Federation of American Presbyterianism," *The Union Seminary Review* 27 (October 1915): 53.

drawal, particularly in 1931, the PCUSA consistently reaffirmed its support of the Federal Council.[62]

In the PCUS, however, dissidents introduced protests concerning the church's relation to the Council into almost every General Assembly. The chief objections were that liberals and communists dominated the Council leadership and that the Council involved itself in moral and social activities violating the southern body's idea of the spirituality of the church.[63] The church withdrew from 1911 to 1912 and again from 1931 until 1941.[64] Although the southern church reentered the FCC in 1941 and endorsed the formation of the National Council in 1949, a vocal minority continued its objections.[65]

Although Disciples never withdrew from the Federal Council, their relation to it parallels closely that of southern Presbyterians. Participation in the Council was marred by increasingly harsh attacks from the Cincinnati-based *Christian Standard,* which became the organ of the conservative independent Christian Churches. The attacks were prompted largely by the conservatives' refusal to see their movement as a denomination among denominations and the fear of being manipulated by a powerful centralized structure led by liberals or communists.[66]

The initiative for the first major attempt to move beyond federation to a multilateral union of denominations came from the 1918 General Assembly of the PCUSA. It called for a convention of the "National Bodies of the Evangelical Communions of America" for the purpose of formulating a "Plan of Organic Union."[67] Nineteen communions participated in the initial meeting. The Association for the Promotion of Christian Unity responded for Disciples.[68] Consistent with its policy of participating in unity talks only with Presbyterian bodies,

---

62. See *The Presbyterian Constitution and Digest,* ed. William P. Thompson (Philadelphia: General Assembly of the United Presbyterian Church in the U.S.A., 1970), pp. 1582-1617.

63. See Charles S. Macfarland, *Christian Unity in the Making: The First Twenty-Five Years of the Federal Council of the Churches of Christ in America* (New York: Federal Council of the Churches of Christ in America, 1948), pp. 83-84, 100, 118-20. The PCUS doggedly maintained the principle of absolute separation of church and state and the totally spiritual and "nonsecular" nature of the church. The position was rooted in the controversy attending the formation of the body and was embodied in the church's Confession of Faith (chap. 33, par. 4). In 1939 the church even rejected an overture to petition the president of the United States "to guard against any diplomatic act that would violate the principle of the separation of Church and State" since such a petition would itself violate the church's own policy of absolute separation (*A Digest of the Acts and Proceedings of the General Assembly of the Presbyterian Church in the United States* [Atlanta: Office of the General Assembly, 1966], pp. 25-42).

64. "The Three Presbyterian Assemblies," *Christian-Evangelist,* 29 May 1913, p. 737; Ernest Trice Thompson, "The Relation of Our Church to Other Church Bodies," *Union Seminary Review* 51 (April 1940): 286-89.

65. *Digest, PCUS,* pp. 466-72.

66. See Stephen J. Corey, *Fifty Years of Attack and Controversy* (St. Louis: Committee on Publication of the Corey Manuscript, 1953), pp. 143, 145, 212, 224.

67. *Minutes of the General Assembly of the Presbyterian Church in the United States of America* (Philadelphia: Office of the General Assembly, 1918), p. 154.

68. H. C. Armstrong, "The Union of Protestants," *World Call* 1 (February 1919): 27-28.

the PCUS declined to appoint delegates. Delegates at the second meeting in Philadelphia devised a plan for "The United Churches of Christ in America," and the American Council on Organic Union was established to promote it. Unlike the Federal Council, the stated goal of the Philadelphia Plan was eventual organic union with a progressive surrender of denominational matters to the Council. The denominations involved, however, came to believe that the plan would create confusion, appearing to be a rival of the Federal Council. Conservative Disciples urged nonparticipation while others such as Peter Ainslie saw the Philadelphia Plan as an imperfect but positive step.[69] Within two years the Plan simply faded away.[70] No church body ever approved it, and the northern Presbyterians who had initiated the action were the first to end it.[71]

The Disciples and Congregational Christian Churches (now part of the UCC) initiated the second major attempt to move beyond federation to a multilateral union of denominations with the Conference on Church Union, which met at Greenwich, Connecticut, in December 1949. Eight bodies were represented, including the northern Presbyterians. This time the PCUS participated but made it absolutely clear that its delegates were "authorized to make no commitments of General Assembly to any proposed plan of union."[72] An American Conference on Church Union was organized which developed a plan of union. Disciple Charles C. Morrison presented the initial draft of the plan.[73] The Greenwich plan provided that local churches would be free to determine their own modes of worship, baptism, and communion. Administrators exercising the function of bishops would be located at the presbytery level, with regional synods and a national council. Although the denominations could maintain their identities for a while, they would be expected to fade away. The plan was revised in 1953 and 1958 but never reached a form delegates considered satisfactory to present to their denominational assemblies and constituencies. Attention to the World Council of Churches and the incipient National Council left the "Greenwich Plan" to fade away as had the "Philadelphia Plan" almost forty years before.

Both Disciples and Presbyterians claim significant roles in the creation of the World Council of Churches.[74] Carl Taylor articulated the feeling of most

---

69. Russell Errett, "Philadelphia Plan for Union," *Christian Standard,* 23 October 1920, pp. 1403-7; Peter Ainslie, "The Union of Evangelical Protestantism," *Christian Union Quarterly* 9 (April 1920): 9-10.

70. Samuel McCrea Cavert, *American Churches in the Ecumenical Movement, 1900-1968* (New York: Association Press, 1968), pp. 112-13.

71. Paul A. Crow, Jr., "The Christian Church (Disciples of Christ) in the Ecumenical Movement," in *The Christian Church (Disciples of Christ): An Interpretative Examination in the Cultural Context,* ed. George G. Beazley (N.p.: Bethany Press, 1973), pp. 275-76; H. C. Armstrong, "The Union of Protestants," *World Call* 1 (February 1919): 27-28.

72. *Digest, PCUS,* p. 372.

73. Garrison, *Christian Unity and Disciples of Christ,* pp. 168-69.

74. See Samuel Macrea Cavert, *Church Cooperation and Unity in America: A Historical Review, 1900-1970* (New York: Association Press, 1970), pp. 34-38; Rachel Henderlite, "Presbyterian Ecumenicity: A Heritage and an Opportunity," *Journal of Presbyterian History* 57 (Summer

pro–World Council Disciples when he stated that they sought "organization on a high level which will enable us to unite in great causes but will allow us to retain our uniqueness and individuality as separate denominations," which is precisely what the World Council of Churches offered.[75]

Disciples viewed the National Council of Churches in the same light and gave both World and National Councils significant economic support. Conservative opposition continued, however, and Disciples membership in the councils was a factor in the continuing separation of the independents.[76] Both northern and southern Presbyterian churches entered the National Council of Churches in 1950, but the PCUS continued its pattern of objecting to social and political pronouncements by the Council and its agencies. It insisted on the right to disassociate itself from any action of the Council it disapproved of and cautioned against the centralization of power in the Executive Committee. In 1965 overtures from the Presbyteries of Nashville and Birmingham strongly denounced the Council's Commission on Religion and Race in its call for ministers to demonstrate in Selma. As with Disciples, continued PCUS membership in the National Council contributed to a modernist-liberal vs. fundamentalist-conservative division — the formation in 1973 of the Presbyterian Church in America.[77]

The most hopeful and long-lasting of the group efforts for unity in which the three bodies have participated is the Consultation on Church Union. This movement began with the now-famous 1960 sermon of United Presbyterian Stated Clerk Eugene Carson Blake calling for the United Church of Christ, United Presbyterian, Episcopal, and Methodist Churches to enter serious union discussions. Within two years the governing bodies of these churches had approved the formation of the Consultation. Because of their previous union negotiations with the UCC (discussed below), the Disciples were invited to become the first addition to the original four bodies in 1963, with the PCUS entering in 1966.

The Consultation (COCU) has met annually since its inception for serious theological study. Unlike the sketchy outlines of the Philadelphia and

---

1979): 162; "Contemplating Christian Union," *Christian-Evangelist*, 16 June 1938, p. 668. The PCUS also endorsed the concept of a World Council but at its 1938 Assembly expressed concern that the Council maintain strict autonomy of constituent churches (*PCUS Digest*, pp. 473-75).

75. Taylor, "The Contributions of the Disciples of Christ and Their Periodical Literature to the Cause of Christian Union" (Thesis, College of the Bible, 1954), pp. 210-11. See also Wilson, "Unity and Restoration in the Ecumenical Thought of the Disciples of Christ," p. 137.

76. Disciples contributions to the Councils are recorded in the *Yearbooks* beginning with 1941, when $4,053 was given to the Federal Council and $490 (between 1938 and 1942) to the World Council by Disciples congregations. By 1950 the figures had increased to $17,481 and $15,237 respectively. The Association for the Promotion of Christian Unity constantly spurred congregations to support the Councils, but while support increased, quotas were often missed. See Wilson, "Unity and Restoration in the Ecumenical Thought of the Disciples of Christ," pp. 166-68.

77. Frank Joseph Smith, *The History of the Presbyterian Church in America: The Continuing Church Movement* (Manassas, Va.: Reformation Education Foundation, 1985); *The Encyclopedia of American Religions*, pp. 254-55.

Greenwich Plans, COCU seeks to examine completely what a church should be in faith, mission, structure, worship, witness, and service. The immediate goal has come to be a "Church of Christ Uniting" — that is, a process that will eventually encompass all Christian churches in America. A preliminary Plan of Union was drafted in 1970 and sent to the churches for study. January 1972 was the deadline for the first round of evaluations and responses.[78] A tremendous psychological blow was dealt COCU in 1972 when the General Assembly of the United Presbyterian Church voted to withdraw in reaction to the plan. Although the Presbyterians reentered the following year, COCU's approach shifted in emphasis. The Consultation moved from an attempt at corporate merger — to impose union from the top down — to a focus on local parish activities like Eucharistic Fellowships and "Generating Communities." In 1980 a document entitled "In Quest of a Church of Christ Uniting" was issued to be studied by the participating churches. This and other descriptive documents detail a "covenanting" process designed to create increasingly closer relations over an indefinite period and allowing each participating body to carry into the relationship what is dear to it.[79]

Disciples have participated in COCU wholeheartedly, struggling with it to envision the kind of unity they wanted to effect. They hosted the 1965 meeting in Lexington, Kentucky, and provided Paul Crow, who served as COCU General Secretary from 1968 until 1974. In 1974 the General Assembly of the restructured Christian Church (Disciples of Christ) adopted a procedure for "Making a Decision on Church Union with Other Bodies" partly to be ready for any possible COCU union but also to define the rights of regions and congregations that might oppose such unions.[80]

Even more importantly, COCU's move toward a "covenanting" model of unity has become integral in the Disciples concept. A recent pamphlet describing the work of the Council on Christian Unity states, "The unity we seek is not a merger of existing organizations, but looks to the emergence of new forms of church life centered in worship, witness and mission." This echoes the sentiments in the COCU pamphlet "Covenanting: What Does It Mean?" Perhaps the most tangible illustration is the 1989 "Ecumenical Partnership" between Disciples and the United Church of Christ.[81]

---

78. Cavert, *American Churches in the Ecumenical Movement,* pp. 254-56; Paul A. Crow, Jr., "COCU — The Potential of a Decade" (N.p.: n.p., 1970), pp. [1-8].

79. "The Ecumenical Stance of the United Presbyterian Church in the U.S.A." (New York: Office for Ecumenical and Interchurch Relations, 1981), pp. 11-12; J. Rodman Williams, "The Plan of Union: Impressions — Theological and Otherwise," *Austin Seminary Bulletin Faculty Edition* 86 (December 1970): 25; *The COCU Consensus: In Quest of a Church of Christ Uniting,* ed. Gerald F. Moede (Baltimore: Consultation on Church Union, 1985), pp. v-3.

80. *1974 Yearbook and Directory of the Christian Church (Disciples of Christ)* (Indianapolis: Christian Church [Disciples of Christ], 1974), pp. 190-93.

81. "Ecumenical Partnership With UCC," and Resolution 8915, *1989 Business Docket and Program of the General Assembly of the Christian Church (Disciples of Christ)* (Indianapolis: Christian Church [Disciples of Christ], 1989), pp. 216, 308.

EFFORTS WITH INDIVIDUAL BODIES

The earliest effort by Disciples toward unity with a single group was the response of the General Christian Missionary Convention of 1887 to the Protestant Episcopal Church's Chicago-Lambeth Quadrilateral. The Quadrilateral was based on the ideas of William Reed Huntington, who attempted in 1870 to reduce Episcopalianism to four essentials upon which he believed all Christians could unite. Approved earlier by the Lambeth Conference and then by the 1886 Episcopal General Convention in Chicago, its four essentials were: the Holy Scriptures as the Word of God, affirmation of the Apostles' and Nicene Creeds, recognition of two sacraments — baptism and the Lord's Supper, and acceptance of the historic episcopate. The Disciples Convention that year responded cordially to the Episcopal overture and appointed a committee to study the proposal. But Disciples ultimately concluded, as did most other churches, that the Quadrilateral was an invitation for everyone to become Episcopalians.[82]

Disciples engaged in long-running and seemingly promising talks with American Baptists. Serious union discussions began in the 1890s, and a lively effort flowered in the first decade of the twentieth century. The groups conducted local conferences, speaker exchanges, and editorial discussions, with official congresses meeting biannually after 1911. In 1928 the groups created a joint commission which submitted a report calling for union at each group's 1929 assembly. The Disciples adopted the report unanimously, but the Baptist Convention referred it to a special committee for study. In 1930 the Baptists rejected the recommendations of the Joint Committee, citing the Disciples teaching of baptismal regeneration as the barrier to unity. Underlying reasons included fear of jeopardizing relations with the Southern Baptists and pushing congregations into the Southern Baptist fold. The Association for the Promotion of Christian Unity then began a series of informal meetings to maintain contacts. In the early 1940s the two groups cooperated in preparation of joint Sunday School literature, a hymnal, and devotional and family magazines. In 1944 joint committees were again appointed to promote cooperation between the ministers of both churches.

The most promising period of negotiations occurred between 1947 and 1952. In 1947 both committees received official status from their respective assemblies and were authorized to pursue serious union talks. The Joint Commission on Baptist-Disciple Relations began meeting in December 1947 and actively promoted unity discussion in publications and meetings. In 1949 the Commission prepared a timetable for moving toward union, including joint conventions in 1952, the preparation and presentation of a "Basis for Union" in 1954, and a vote in 1955. In 1952 the two groups held joint conventions in

---

82. Winfred E. Garrison, *Christian Unity and Disciples of Christ* (St. Louis: Bethany Press, 1955), pp. 47-49.

Chicago, meeting separately during the day and together at night. A joint communion service scheduled for the third evening was almost a disaster when the Baptists insisted that communion was a function of a local congregation, not a convention. The matter was finally solved by holding the communion service under the sponsorship of the Evanston First Baptist Church, with the Disciples delegates considered "guests" of the congregation.

Following the 1952 conventions, the Baptist section of the Joint Commission recommended that it be dissolved and that future talks with Disciples be carried on through the Convention's standing Committee on Relations with Other Religious Bodies. When the Disciples part of the Joint Commission heard of the dissolution of the Baptist section, they recommended the same for theirs, assigning any further talks to the Association for the Promotion of Christian Unity. This time the fear of losing dissident congregations to the Southern Baptist Convention was the most overtly expressed reason for breaking off talks, although the matter of baptism was mentioned. Baptists and Disciples have conducted no serious union talks since 1952.[83]

Talks began with the Congregational-Christian and the Evangelical and Reformed Churches in 1946. These two groups were themselves then engaged in merger talks that resulted in the formation of the United Church of Christ in 1958. Both the UCC and Disciples assemblies gave the talks official status in 1961, and yearly meetings from 1962 to 1966 made progress toward a united church. Both groups were, however, involved in the continuing COCU discussions and in 1968 mutually agreed to suspend the individual meetings to devote full attention to COCU. They believed COCU would produce a united church within five to seven years. When in the early seventies it became apparent that a united church was much farther away than thought, representatives of both groups made overtures toward renewing negotiations. In 1978 commissions of both churches began meeting with the object of producing a "union, i.e., a new Christian community with diversity, not merger" within ten years, while still maintaining commitment to the COCU process.[84] This articulation of their unity goal was clearly based on the developing COCU "covenanting" process.

Disciples began talks with representatives of the Roman Catholic Church in the United States in 1967 "to discuss similarities and differences." In 1977 international conversations were begun sponsored by the Council on Christian

---

83. Franklin E. Rector, "Baptist-Disciple Conversations toward Unity," in *Institutionalism and Church Unity,* ed. Nils Ehrenstrom and Walter G. Muelder (New York: Association Press, 1963), pp. 253-74; Garrison, *Christian Unity and Disciples of Christ,* pp. 166-68; A. T. DeGroot, "Three Fourths of a Loaf: A Historical Study of the Movements Looking toward the Union of Baptists and Disciples of Christ," *The Chronicle: A Baptist Historical Quarterly* (April 1948): 6-7.

84. *1977 Yearbook and Directory of the Christian Church (Disciples of Christ)* (Indianapolis: Christian Church [Disciples of Christ], 1977), p. 149; *1978 Yearbook and Directory of the Christian Church (Disciples of Christ)* (Indianapolis: Christian Church [Disciples of Christ], 1978), p. 261. This process was culminated in the summer of 1989 with passage of a resolution for full communion between the churches.

Unity and the Vatican Secretariat for Promoting Christian Unity. The talks are not intended to lead to union (at least in the foreseeable future) but are for the development of communion between the churches, the sole channel presently for relations between the two churches.[85]

As already indicated, most serious unity talks conducted by Presbyterians were with other Presbyterian and Reformed groups. In fact, until relatively recently, the southern church believed that its constitution prohibited it from entering negotiations toward organic union with any non-Presbyterian body.[86] The PCUSA, on the other hand, engaged in two union negotiations with non-Reformed bodies during the century under consideration. From 1928 to 1937 the PCUSA's Department of Church Cooperation and Union engaged in serious talks with the Methodist Episcopal Church. The Methodists, however, were then moving rapidly toward their own internal reunion, and the talks were ended unsuccessfully.[87]

The most significant attempt at union was with the Protestant Episcopal Church. The first overtures were made in 1887 in response to the Chicago-Lambeth Quadrilateral. The snag in the talks resulted from the refusal of the Episcopal Church to recognize the legitimacy of Presbyterian ordination. Negotiations ended after the Episcopalians rejected a suggestion for a pulpit exchange in 1893.[88] In 1937 the Protestant Episcopal Church again made overtures to the PCUSA, whose Department of Church Cooperation and Union endorsed cooperation "in the study and formation of such plans as may make possible the union contemplated." In 1939 the Churches distributed a primer on church unity designed to promote interaction and discussion at the grass-roots level. At the end of the primer a proposed Concordat for uniting the groups was printed. The plan addressed the ordination problem by requiring ministers from either group to submit to an "extension of ordination" before assuming the position of minister for a congregation of the other: an Episcopal bishop or the moderator of a Presbytery would lay hands on the minister and say a short formula. In 1946 Anglo-Catholics in the Episcopal Church began a vociferous campaign against the plan. The argument used in the 1890s was used again here: Presbyterian ordination was invalid, and Presbyterians entering the Episcopal ministry would have to submit to "reordination." The threat of schism among Episcopalians coupled with Presbyterian irritation led to the abandonment of the plan.[89]

85. *1977 Yearbook and Directory of the Christian Church (Disciples of Christ)*, p. 149; Ann Updegraff, "The Church Must Make Unity Real," in *This We Believe*, ed. James C. Suggs (St. Louis: Bethany Press, 1977), p. 96.

86. *Digest PCUS*, pp. 134-35.

87. Thompson, *The Presbyterian Constitution and Digest*, pp. 1536-37.

88. John T. McNeill and James Hastings Nichols, *Ecumenical Testimony: The Concern for Christian Unity within the Reformed and Presbyterian Churches* (Philadelphia: Westminster Press, 1974), pp. 217-19; F. D. Power, "Washington Letter," *Christian Standard*, 3 June 1893, p. 445.

89. National Council, Protestant Episcopal Church and Board of Christian Education, Presbyterian Church in the USA, *A Primer on Christian Unity* (New York: n.p., [1939]); McNeill and Nichols, *Ecumenical Testimony*, pp. 228-29.

Disciples participation in efforts toward unity with other bodies was promoted and executed primarily by the Council on Christian Union and its successors. This body received increasing support from the denomination throughout the twentieth century. Opposition came from conservatives who believed that denominationalism was wrong and that participation in these efforts endorsed and legitimized this divisive evil. These conservatives increasingly pulled away from the Disciples to form independent Christian Churches, the matter of unity and ecumenical action being a chief factor in the split. The same sort of thing went on among the Presbyterians, as evidenced in the 1973 defection of the Presbyterian Church in America from the PCUS.

Participation in efforts that operated on the model of corporate merger of church organizations, particularly the long-running COCU meetings, have tempered Disciples enthusiasm for that approach to unity. Disciples have moved with COCU toward a more "spiritual" model that emphasizes activities such as joint communion services primarily at the local level. This seems to be a return to a form of earlier Disciples ideas articulated by the movement's founders and more recently by Peter Ainslie.

Disciples and northern Presbyterians have experienced similar frustrations in their pursuit of unity with individual bodies. Interference from other unity efforts stalled or aborted early Disciples-UCC (and its predecessors) and PCUSA-Methodist talks. Long-term promising dialogue between Disciples and American Baptist Churches and the PCUSA and Protestant Episcopal Church ended in Baptist and Episcopal departure, each regarding its ecumenical partner as defective in some crucial point of doctrine (baptism and episcopacy).

CONCLUSIONS: DISCIPLES STRUGGLE FOR UNITY

Early Disciples agreed that there were true Christians in all denominations but that they should not remain in the divisive structures, that they should instead come out and be simply Christians, disciples of Christ, on the Disciples New Testament platform. When the Disciples plea did not work, many in the mainstream moved away from this notion of individualistic unity to a organic model of corporate merger. This movement in turn led to a defense of denominationalism — a radical shift from the movement's early attribution of religious division itself to "man-made" denominational divisions. In this context, denominational structure came to be seen as essential for carrying out their program for Christian unity. What they initially rejected because of its inherent defense of religious division they embraced as a means to unity, with some paradoxical results. Even as they have accepted denominational status, their zeal for ecumenical progress has led Disciples generally to view strong doctrinal positions as barriers to unity, and this has affected the character of their theological effort.[90] As Disciples moved toward an organic union–corporate merger model of unity, variant doctrinal positions held by groups with which the Disciples were talking, as well as their own peculiar tenets concerning baptism, communion, and the like, posed threats to union. The abortive attempts at unity with American Baptists illustrated the problem. If the promotion of Christian unity was conceived of as their raison d'être, Disciples had to find ways to overcome or minimize the doctrinal barriers by which denominations are, in part, identified. Even more ironic, the formal design created by the 1968 Restructure (and anticipated by earlier structures) tends toward an institutional conservatism that will inevitably resist its own demise.[91]

In contrast, early Presbyterians began with the idea of the legitimacy of denominational Christianity, viewing unity as primarily spiritual in a traditional Protestant sense. Yet, like Disciples, Presbyterians have become increasingly open to the idea of organic unity with non-Presbyterian and Reformed bodies, as evidenced in their participation in the Philadelphia and Greenwich Plans and the COCU process. Yet during the 1970s, Disciples, Presbyterians, and others who are part of the COCU struggle began to embrace a spiritually based "covenanting" model of unity that recognizes the persistence of denominational Christianity.

The following conclusions concerning Disciples unity ideas and actions seem warranted from the evidence in this study. (1) Disciples have been divided over what Christian unity really is. Shifts in concepts among denominational leaders and constituencies during the past century have produced tension and confusion in the denomination. (2) Liberal denominational leaders have moved away from doctrinal positions that were once strongly held, at least partially for the sake of unity. (3) Some denominational officials have taken the lead in talks and actions for unity, often leaving their "grass-roots" constituencies to imagine all sorts of evildoings by the hierarchy. The result has been defections by those who support a conservative doctrinal basis for unity. (4) Disciples have faced problems with independence. Their congregational polity imposes no sanctions on congregations that dissolve their ties with the denomination. No congregation is bound by rulings of Assemblies. In fact, the Assemblies actually serve as forums for the opinions of dissidents. Yet defection has occurred, and ecumenical matters have been a major factor in division. (5) Disciples have been party to no unions with bodies outside their own tradition. Initial movement toward creating representative structures for the sake of participating in an organic merger model of unity has been tempered by the repeated failures, culminating in COCU's shift away from the corporate model to a spiritual "covenanting" model. In the words of a recent

90. See Williamson and Blaisdell's discussion of C. C. Morrison's theological efforts on pp. 107-38 in this volume.

91. See Updegraff, "The Church Must Make Unity Real," p. 97; Ehrenstrom and Muelder, *Institutionalism and Church Unity,* pp. 59-76, 145-78.

Disciples Council on Christian Unity brochure, the quest has been altered to "the emergence of new forms of church life centered in worship, witness and mission." The full reciprocal recognition of each other as Christians with the continuation of denominational expressions deemed worthwhile by each group is now the goal.

Disciples have moved increasingly in the same directions as other mainstream American denominations through shifts of concepts of unity and participation in the joint efforts mentioned in this study. They appear to be headed for similar successes and problems in the future.

Faith on the Frontier: Historical Interpretations of the Disciples of Christ

W. Clark Gilpin

The magnetic draw of a continent, abundant and unexplored, pulling a diverse people into its interior to generate there the institutions and ideals of a new society — this image of the frontier has shaped American self-understanding in profound and complex ways for more than two centuries. In the hands of novelists, poets, and historians it has been the most evocative theme in our civic mythology. Like the nation as a whole, the Protestant churches of America have incorporated the symbolism of westward expansion into their histories, and, since the Christian Church (Disciples of Christ) actually originated on the frontier at the beginning of the nineteenth century, its self-perception, more than that of most churches, has felt the influence of the frontier as symbol and myth. This essay is an inquiry into that influence.

The inquiry is prompted by recognition that more than fifty years have passed since a persuasive effort was made to argue a comprehensive thesis about the general historical development of the Disciples of Christ. This comprehensive interpretation was proposed by Winfred Ernest Garrison (1874-1969) in three books that established him as the dean of Disciples historians: *Religion Follows the Frontier* (1931), *An American Religious Movement* (1945), and, with A. T. DeGroot, *The Disciples of Christ: A History* (1948; rev. ed. 1958). Garrison's writings represented a revision of the "frontier thesis" of historian Frederick Jackson Turner (1861-1932), who had argued that expansion into the "free land" of the West created the conditions for the emergence of distinctively American character and institutions.

Turner's ideas gave Garrison and other American church historians a basis for explaining the changes in doctrine and organization that Christianity had undergone in the United States, and the frontier thesis thus had a general influence on American religious history in the years from approximately 1920 to 1950. This adaptation of the frontier thesis to the purposes of American religious history is, for two reasons, particularly important to understanding historical interpretations of the Disciples of Christ. First, in general histories of religion in America, the most common occasion for an extended discussion of the Disciples is as an exemplar of the "Americanization" of Christian belief and practice within the frontier environment, from roughly 1800 to 1890. Second, for the Disciples of Christ themselves, the frontier thesis, as mediated through Garrison, has been the predominant historical self-interpretation of their tradition, ordering the principal textbooks of the twentieth century and supplying a host of popular images expressive of denominational identity. For these reasons, appraising the role of the frontier thesis in the writings of W. E. Garrison has significance not only for a historical understanding of the Disciples but also for the Disciples' own contemporary self-interpretation. What the social historian Richard Hofstadter has said of history in general may, in this respect, be said of the role of history in the life of a church: "Memory is the thread of personal identity, history of public identity. Men who have achieved any civic existence at all must, to sustain it, have some kind of history, though it may be history that is partly mythological or simply untrue."[1]

THE NINETEENTH-CENTURY HISTORIANS

The writing of Disciples history began not with the professional historians of the twentieth century but with scholarly ministers and editors of the later nineteenth century such as Robert Richardson (1806-1876), William Thomas Moore (1832-1926), and James Harvey Garrison (1842-1931). Richardson, friend and biographer of Alexander Campbell, composed his two-volume *Memoirs of Alexander Campbell* at the request of the Campbell family, and the work has exerted significant influence on twentieth-century interpretations of Campbell and the British backgrounds to his religious views. W. T. Moore was the first author to attempt the task he announced in the title of his best-known book: *A Comprehensive History of the Disciples of Christ*, a massive volume of 830 pages issued in conjunction with the denominational centennial in 1909. Garrison, in the course of his work as editor of the *Christian-Evangelist*, pondered the meaning and direction of Disciples history at the turn of the century and collected a set of essays setting forth the message and progress of *The Reformation of the Nineteenth Century* (1901). These authors approached historical subjects with explicit religious and theological purposes, and three assumptions that organized their narratives are significant for understanding later historiography.

First, each situated the movement that became the Disciples of Christ within the larger designs of providence. The centuries of the Christian era,

1. Hofstadter, *The Progressive Historians: Turner, Beard, Parrington* (New York: Knopf, 1969), p. 3.

wrote W. T. Moore, told the doleful tale of a great lapse, in which the church had lost "its primitive simplicity, beauty, and unity" and had thereby thwarted its own destiny of global evangelization. The restoration of Christianity to its primitive power was the task of the Disciples of Christ, who have "undoubtedly . . . been called by Divine Providence to meet this emergency in the onward course of Christianity around the world."[2]

Second, they believed that America itself played a role in this providential westward movement of the gospel: "the new world offered itself to a new experiment."[3] The religious liberty of the new nation gave opportunity for throwing off the traditions of state interference and clerical authority that had prevented European Christianity from achieving a full reformation. The very land nourished liberty, and, through the struggle to subdue it, bred a simple, vigorous, self-reliant American character. Robert Richardson epitomized these convictions in his arcadian portrait of Alexander Campbell's arrival in America:

> He . . . plunged into the depths of the American forest. In the exaltation of his youthful feelings he seemed to have reached a land of enchantment. The moon, already high in heaven and nearly at the full, seemed to mingle its silvery beams with the sun's golden radiance reflected from the western sky . . . while, beneath, he trod upon the soil of a new world — the land of liberty and of Washington, whose liberal institutions had long been the object of his admiration. All nature around him seemed to sympathize with his emotions. The balmy air, fresh from the wild mountain slopes, the new varieties of birds, which from almost every tree seemed, to his fancy, to chant their evening song in praise of the freedom of their native woods, the approaching shades of evening, veiling the distant landscape in a gentle haze, — all seemed to speak of liberty, security, and peace.[4]

The pattern of providence and the American land, so these writers believed, had come into conjunction at the beginning of the nineteenth century and, in so doing, marked the destiny of the Disciples of Christ. No writer expressed these sentiments with greater millennial fervor than W. T. Moore:

> Christ visited this earth at exactly the time it was ready for him. Luther began his reformation at precisely the supreme moment. The age was waiting for him. Likewise, we see the Restoration Movement of the Disciples of Christ was the answer of a providential call for a new religious day to begin with the ushering in of the Nineteenth Century. America was the country where the new day had to dawn, and where the Sun of Righteousness had to rise with healing in his beams. America is on the road to the conquest of the nations; it is the continent

---

2. Moore, *A Comprehensive History of the Disciples of Christ* (New York: Fleming H. Revell, 1909), p. 35. See also *The New Living Pulpit of the Christian Church*, ed. William Thomas Moore (St. Louis: Christian Board of Publication, 1918), p. 20.

3. Moore, *A Comprehensive History of the Disciples*, p. 35.

4. Richardson, *Memoirs of Alexander Campbell*, 2 vols. (Philadelphia: Lippincott, 1868-70), 1: 206-7.

where the Christian forces must be organised for the great and final forward movement to evangelise the countries lying Westward on the other side of the Pacific Ocean. But America, at the beginning of the Nineteenth Century, was a religious wilderness, and much rough work had to be done before the people could be made ready for the day of "sweetness and light," a day which finally did come at exactly the time when it was most needed and when it could be most effective in conquering the world for Christ.[5]

Third, in this onward march of providence, the church, too, must step forward at a lively pace, proclaiming what James H. Garrison liked to call "the present truth," by which he meant "the adaptation of the ever-living truth to the current needs of the time." The necessary first step of this advance, editor Garrison believed, was "a return to the simple, original constitution of the church," in which the essential truth was "the Messiahship and divinity of Jesus of Nazareth" and the rule of life was "the will of Christ." From that unshaken foundation could then proceed "a progressive reformation, which, by virtue of its underlying principles, will be held in loyalty to Christ, while it is capable of adjusting itself to the new phases of thought and of life as they arise, and of accepting all duly accredited truth, however new it may be."[6]

This early group of Disciples historians, by placing America and the Disciples of Christ within the panorama of divinely directed destiny, was not so distant as one might suppose from the assumptions that guided the writing of American history generally in the nineteenth century. In the background of their work stood such figures as the great romantic historian of America George Bancroft, for whom the grand lesson of history was the providential guidance of human affairs toward the goal of liberty. As late as the 1880s, this providential assumption persisted, somewhat disguised, in the "scientific history" pursued by Herbert Baxter Adams at Johns Hopkins University, even though, as Richard Hofstadter has remarked, the Adams school refurbished the old providential theory "with biological metaphors and evolutionary language."[7] Thus, at the end of the nineteenth century, as professional historians entered the fields once occupied by scholarly amateurs, the traditional providential view of America remained a powerful influence. In this regard, historian Dorothy Ross has observed that the new generation of professional scholars, trained in scientific norms, "explicitly avoided reference to Providential power or America's millennial destiny, but the prehistoricist cast of mind that accompanied that national vision was still present."[8] The "frontier thesis," both as it

5. Moore, *A Comprehensive History of the Disciples,* pp. ix-x.

6. *The Reformation of the Nineteenth Century,* ed. James Harvey Garrison (St. Louis: Christian Publishing, 1901), pp. 495-97; and "The World's Need of Our Plea," in *Historical Documents Advocating Christian Union,* ed. Charles A. Young (Chicago: Christian Century, 1904), pp. 343-44, 359.

7. Hofstadter, *The Progressive Historians,* p. 39.

8. Ross, "Historical Consciousness in Nineteenth-Century America," *American Historical Review* 89 (1984): 921.

was applied to American history and to American *religious* history, developed in this era of transition from narratives grounded in a theology of history to those based on the more explicitly historicist assumption that "all events in historical time can be explained by prior events in historical time."[9]

THE FRONTIER AND AMERICAN RELIGIOUS HISTORY

First in a famous address to the American Historical Association in 1893 and subsequently in a collection of essays, Frederick Jackson Turner creatively recast the nineteenth-century rhetoric of the West, the future, and democracy into a historical explanation for the development and distinctive form of American democratic society. Turner found the key to this development in the process of national westward expansion into "free land," and he argued that, as settled civilization receded on the eastern horizon of the advancing pioneers, society was continually "beginning over again on the frontier." This perennial social rebirth furnished "the forces dominating American character."[10]

The frontier, Turner declared, forced a return to more primitive economic and political conditions, and, as frontier society gradually developed toward greater complexity, the result was not a duplication of European society but something distinctively American, a society created out of the elemental interaction of the pioneers with a new environment. In the Mississippi Valley there had evolved, "not by revolutionary theory, but by growth among free opportunities, the conception of a vast democracy made up of mobile ascending individuals, conscious of their power and their responsibilities." Indeed, he concluded, "the advance of the frontier has meant a steady movement away from the influence of Europe, a steady growth of independence on American lines." To study the institutions and traits of character that emerged from this interaction of "an expanding people" with the wilderness was, therefore, "to study the really American part of our history."[11]

One facet of Turner's interpretation was a form of primitivism which, although different from that of nineteenth-century Disciples, rivaled their vision of escape from the bondage of history. In his 1893 address, Turner declared that

> For a moment, at the frontier, the bonds of custom are broken and unrestraint is triumphant. There is not *tabula rasa*. The stubborn American environment is there with its imperious summons to accept its conditions; the inherited ways of doing things are also there; and yet, in spite of environment, and in spite of custom, each frontier did furnish a new field of opportunity, a gate of escape

9. Ross, "Historical Consciousness in Nineteenth-Century America," pp. 910-11.
10. Turner, *The Frontier in American History* (New York: Henry Holt, 1920), pp. 1-4.
11. Turner, *The Frontier in American History,* pp. 1-2, 4, 203.

from the bondage of the past; and freshness, and confidence, and scorn of older society, impatience of its restraints and ideas, and indifference to its lessons, have accompanied the frontier.[12]

As this quotation suggests, "the West" for Turner was not so much a geographic area as it was a social "moment" when, under the transforming influence of free land, "the cake of custom is broken." When older institutions and ideas enter this new environment, "new activities, new lines of growth, new institutions and new ideals, are brought into existence." As the line of the frontier passes onward, a new society has emerged in the now settled area that "bears within it enduring and distinguishing survivals of its frontier experience."[13]

But Turner's interpretation had another, more somber side. If the democratic ideals and institutions of American society arose on the frontier, what did the future hold, given the closing of the frontier in 1890? Without the renewing environment of the frontier, was the American character that had emerged there in danger of becoming self-destructive? As society developed in the West, a troubled Turner found that the history of the frontier carried unexpected consequences. On the one hand, the frontier "ideals of individualism and democracy" had begun, with the industrialization of the nation, to conflict with one another. Americans, who built the Western states while believing both in competitive individualism and equality, had learned by the 1890s "that between the ideal of individualism, unrestrained by society, and the ideal of democracy, was an innate conflict; that their very ambitions and forcefulness had endangered their democracy."[14] On the other hand, this same process of industrial consolidation was threatening to distort the American ideals, and Turner therefore called upon the Middle West to conserve the values to which it had given birth: "It is in the vast and level spaces of the Mississippi Valley, if anywhere, that the forces of social transformation and the modification of its democratic ideals may be arrested."[15]

Stimulated by the publication in 1920 of Frederick Jackson Turner's collected essays, two church historians at the University of Chicago, Peter G. Mode and William Warren Sweet, used Turner's thesis to explain the origins and evolution of the principal features of American church life. Indeed, if an academic discipline involves the application of a method of inquiry to a constitutive question, one may say that in using the Turner thesis to interpret the institutions and practices of religion in America, Sweet, Mode, and their contemporaries "created" the discipline of American religious history. As Peter Mode explained in 1923, Christianity had "manifested a keen sensitiveness to its environment" throughout its history, and in America the dominating feature

12. Turner, *The Frontier in American History,* pp. 37-38.
13. Turner, *The Frontier in American History,* p. 205.
14. Turner, *The Frontier in American History,* p. 203.
15. Turner, *The Frontier in American History,* p. 203.

of the environment was the frontier. To recognize the fact that entrance into
"the unappropriated domain of the interior" was "the one unifying feature in
all the vicissitudes of our national development," therefore, made possible "a
much clearer insight into what constitutes the Americanizing of Christianity."[16]

William Warren Sweet, in his application of the frontier thesis, sought
to answer a question about the relative growth and influence of the various
American denominations. Why was it, Sweet asked, that the Baptists,
Methodists, and Disciples of Christ had grown so rapidly in the period from
1790 to the Civil War and that the style of religious life they represented had
shaped so substantially the culture of nineteenth-century America? To put the
question another way, how had these denominations overtaken in numbers and
equaled in social impact the churches of the colonial establishment, Presbyterians, Congregationalists, and Episcopalians? His answer was that the ethos
of the frontier, with its fluid social order and its celebration of democracy,
equality, and self-reliant individualism, was an environment that epitomized
the basic conditions of religious life in America and molded churches that
could flourish in such a setting. Hence, the churches of the frontier expansion
became the largest and "most typically American churches in the nation."[17]

Within Sweet's scheme, the Disciples of Christ were the quintessential
frontier religious group, revolting against "aristocratic" Calvinist theology in
the name of a simple scriptural message that was available to all regardless of
education and revolting against hierarchical church government in the name
of a simplified and lay-oriented polity that recognized the democratic self-
reliance of the pioneer. Arising in "the most democratic and classless society
in the world, that of the middle-western frontier," the religious movements that
coalesced around Barton Stone and Alexander Campbell "may be characterized
as attempts to simplify religion both organizationally and doctrinally in order
better to meet the religious needs of the frontier."[18]

Later historians of religion in America have not necessarily followed
Sweet's appeal to the frontier as a sweeping interpretive category, but they
have almost universally agreed with him that the frontier phase of the Disciples tradition captures the denomination's distinctive contribution to American religious history. For this reason, the principal contemporary histories
of religion in America give extended descriptions of the Disciples at only
one point, the era of what Sydney Ahlstrom termed "the great revival in the
West and the growth of the popular denominations," approximately 1790 to
1840. Historians as different in overall approach to American religious history

16. Mode, *The Frontier Spirit of American Christianity* (New York: Macmillan, 1923), pp.
1-14.

17. Sweet, *The Story of Religion in America* (New York: Harper, 1939), pp. 1-7; and
Religion in the Development of America Culture, 1765-1840 (New York: Scribner's, 1952), pp.
96-99, 134-37, 146-53. See also James L. Ash, *Protestantism and the American University: An
Intellectual Biography of William Warren Sweet* (Dallas: SMU Press, 1982).

18. Sweet, *Religion in the Development of American Culture*, pp. 190-233.

as Catherine L. Albanese and Winthrop S. Hudson, for example, nevertheless offer quite similar descriptions of the Disciples of Christ: they are a product of the era of revivalism and frontier camp meetings, and they succeed on the expanding perimeter of the American nation by virtue of their simplification of Christian doctrine, the leadership role they give to the laity, and their evangelistic appeal for Christian unity on the basis of Scripture.[19] Along with Methodists and Baptists, the Disciples are what Martin Marty has termed "the frontier 'big three,' " that wing of modern mainstream Protestantism that expanded as the nation expanded over the course of the nineteenth century. The portrait of the Disciples common to all of these histories is the one drawn most crisply by Sydney Ahlstrom: "What Presbyterians, Baptists, and Methodists apparently faced during these decades of Disciple expansion was a remarkable projection into the American frontier scene of a popular, down-to-earth form of eighteenth-century Christian rationalism, a movement all the more striking because it was successfully propagated in the ethos of revivalism and by an adaptation of its methods."[20]

W. E. GARRISON AND THE FRONTIER THESIS

Against this backdrop of the Turner thesis, its application to American religious history, and the common identification of the Disciples of Christ with the frontier phase of Protestantism's development within American culture, I now wish to place the historical writing of Winfred Ernest Garrison in the foreground of our attention. As a colleague of Peter Mode and William Warren Sweet at the University of Chicago, Garrison shared their interest in the frontier thesis, reading not only Frederick Jackson Turner but Turner's critics as well.[21] However, in writing the history of the Disciples of Christ, Garrison shifted the emphasis of the frontier thesis in several important ways, modifying the thesis more fundamentally, perhaps, than he himself recognized. These shifts of emphasis enabled him to account for the religious situation to which history had brought the Disciples of Christ in his own time and, usually implicitly, to suggest a line to march into the future. In so doing, Garrison disclosed his general assumptions about the relation between history and theological reflection, with which he had replaced the providential history of the preceding generation.

19. Albanese, *American Religions and Religion* (Belmont, Ca.: Wadsworth, 1981), p. 100; Winthrop S. Hudson, *Religion in America,* 4th ed. (New York: Macmillan, 1987), pp. 118-22, 131-34, 142.

20. Ahlstrom, *A Religious History of the American People* (New Haven: Yale University Press, 1972), pp. 451-52.

21. Garrison made use, for example, of a collection of essays reassessing the Turner thesis edited by Dixon Ryan Fox, *Sources of Culture in the Middle West: Backgrounds versus Frontier* (New York: Appleton-Century, 1934).

Garrison's account of the beginnings of the Disciples of Christ presented them as "a typical case of a group originating on the frontier, embodying in its first period the intellectual characteristics of the frontier."[22] Like Frederick Jackson Turner and William Warren Sweet, Garrison described how the immediate, concrete exigencies of pioneer life modified inherited ways and thereby encouraged habits of mind that inclined strongly toward individual freedom and a self-reliant pragmatism. From such an intellectual vantage point, the pioneer was fully prepared "to believe that even the most fundamental institutions — such as state and church — could be made over if they did not serve his need."[23] In a general way, Garrison thus agreed with William Warren Sweet about those social and intellectual characteristics that set the broad pattern followed by frontier religion. The early successes of the Disciples of Christ hinged upon the compatibility between these characteristics and their reforming message, which announced a reunited church arising from the freedom of individuals to read and replicate an authoritative Bible, unencumbered by the complex theological "opinions" of historic creeds and clergy.

But Garrison took his analysis a step further by observing that, although these individualist and utilitarian qualities served admirably to meet the basic economic and political issues of the frontier, they did not prepare the pioneer "for dealing either with the more complex social situations or with intellectual problems."[24] The pioneer view of the world lacked a philosophical basis, and so, when arguing for change in existing institutions, the frontier political and religious leaders had a tendency to buttress pragmatic changes with abrupt appeals to authority.

> If he did not like the government, he reverted to the Constitution, whose stability and assumed perfection afforded him a fixed point of reference in the otherwise obviously variable and often chaotic political order. If the church seemed to need reconstruction, his appeal was from the proximate and provisional authority of the clergy to the basic authority of infallible Scripture. He was an individualist — up to a certain point — and then he became a thorough authoritarian. He had complete confidence in his ability to handle the concrete and factual details of life, but none at all in his or any man's competence in the realm of the spirit. Even the wholly new religions which sprang up, like Mormonism, must ground themselves upon new revelations.[25]

By suggesting that frontier society rested on a unstable synthesis of pragmatism and authoritarianism, Garrison was adding a dimension to the portrait of religion in the Middle West that would have particular pertinence for his interpretation of the Disciples of Christ. And this interpretation fit within

22. Garrison, *Religion Follows the Frontier: A History of the Disciples of Christ* (New York: Harper and Brothers, 1931), p. xi.
23. Garrison, *Religion Follows the Frontier,* pp. 55-58.
24. Garrison, *Religion Follows the Frontier,* pp. 55-58.
25. Garrison, *Religion Follows the Frontier,* p. 56.

a larger historical project. Like Turner, who saw the social modifications of the frontier in relation to the broader issue of the tension between individualism and equality in American democracy, Garrison sought to place the frontier origins of the Disciples of Christ in relation to the central social and intellectual issues of the modern epoch. Both in *Alexander Campbell's Theology* (1900) and in *Religion Follows the Frontier* (1931), Garrison identified the tension between personal liberty and the unity of social groups as the fundamental religious problem that the nineteenth century had inherited from the age of the Reformation. During the era in which the Disciples of Christ emerged, the churches of Europe and America faced a major question: "How is it possible to reconcile the individual's liberty of conscience and intellect with that degree of unity of the church in spirit and organization which is demanded by the will of Christ and by the practical requirement for efficiency in his service?"[26]

The tension between personal liberty and the common aims of social life was especially pronounced within the United States, and there especially on the frontier. In America the guarantee of religious liberty and the separation of church and state underscored the voluntary character of religion and stimulated the creation of new religious groups, not only further dividing the churches but also making any Christian union a purely religious problem to be solved only by voluntary action of Christians rather than the state. The beginnings of the Disciples of Christ, with their hallmark allegiances to Christian liberty, Christian union, and the restoration of the New Testament church constituted one of the most notable religious responses to this social challenge of the frontier. In introducing Alexander Campbell's theology, Garrison asserted that "the need of the hour was for the discovery of a principle of synthesis by which, without restricting the liberty of any man, a practical and effective union of religious forces might be obtained."[27] Garrison argued that Campbell had achieved such a synthesis by interpreting the Christian life as willing citizenship within the kingdom of God, a kingdom whose forms and duties had been authoritatively set forth in the New Testament.

But however appropriate Campbell's synthesis may have been for frontier religion, could it serve equally well in other, later periods of history? It was this question that gave Garrison's appropriation of the frontier thesis its distinctive twist. As noted above, Frederick Jackson Turner in several key passages left the impression that the ideals of the Middle West somehow arose from the frontier soil itself and needed to be preserved from undue "modification" by subsequent industrialization. Garrison, on the other hand, was especially interested in the way ideals evolved over time, receiving particular reformulations in particular settings. He was concerned to show what concepts and presuppositions the pioneers brought with them to the frontier and what

---

26. Garrison, *Alexander Campbell's Theology: Its Sources and Historical Setting* (St. Louis: Christian Publishing Co., 1900), p. 25.

27. Garrison, *Alexander Campbell's Theology*, p. 68.

happened to those ideas in the new setting. "What we have to consider," wrote Garrison in 1931, "is not merely the story of a religious body preserving and propagating its faith, but a study in social evolution — the natural history of a group under the changing circumstances which have constituted the real history of the United States, and especially of the Mississippi Valley, from the beginning of the nineteenth century to the present time."[28]

As this suggests, Garrison's real focus of attention was not on the frontier per se but rather upon the social process of the revision and adaptation of tradition, of which the American West provided a particularly clear instance. From this perspective, the frontier was neither a stationary, permanent condition of society nor an escape from the complexities of society represented by Europe or the American East. Instead, religious groups like the Disciples that originally developed in a frontier setting found that both they and their social environment were "maturing" and becoming more sophisticated. Features of religious life that had been appropriately adapted to the frontier now faced a new social environment, and the history of the churches could not, therefore, be written wholly in terms of the character and movement of the frontier.[29] In the years between the Civil War and approximately 1925, the cultural life of the Middle West was transformed by education, technology, and the greater sophistication of town life. In *The March of Faith: The Story of Religion in America since 1865* (1933), Garrison describes the general impact of this transformation on the American churches, while in *Religion Follows the Frontier* he pays specific attention to the story of his own denomination. The Disciples of Christ were an integral part of this total population "whose ideals were moving from simplicity toward elegance," which included the development of a desire for "architectural respectability," the use of musical instruments in worship, and a demand for ministers "with some training in the arts of speech and some professional skill in the management of church affairs."[30] For Garrison this meant that the Disciples of Christ in his own time were passing through a critical phase of their life, as, following the close of the frontier, they faced the new environment of the socially developed Middle West.

Different responses to this social process created tensions within the religious group. Some held on to the older frontier ways, an authoritarian appeal to Scripture and forms of worship characterized by stark simplicity. Others adapted to the advancing social life of the Middle West, appropriating new views of biblical interpretation and preferring worship that included organ music and preachers with graduate degrees. These different responses to the modernization

---

28. Garrison, *Religion Follows the Frontier,* pp. ix-xii.

29. Garrison, *An American Religious Movement: A Brief History of the Disciples of Christ* (St. Louis: Christian Board of Publication, 1945), p. 5; Garrison and Alfred T. DeGroot, *The Disciples of Christ: A History,* rev. ed. (St. Louis: Christian Board of Publication, 1958), pp. 16-17, 59.

30. Garrison, *Religion Follows the Frontier,* pp. 225-27.

of the frontier went far to explain the divisions and controversies that beset the Disciples in the opening decades of the twentieth century. "The deeper meanings of all the controversies which have disturbed the harmony of the Disciples during the past thirty years must be sought in the diversity of attitudes toward what may, to use a somewhat vague term, be called 'liberalism'; and this, in turn, rests upon a diversity of reactions to those social, cultural, and intellectual changes which have accompanied the passing of the frontier."[31]

In what ways was Garrison's portrait of the Disciples comparable either to that of the nineteenth-century Disciples historians or to Turner's interpretation of the significance of the frontier in American history? Both Turner and, in a quite different way, the nineteenth-century Disciples historians could be characterized by David W. Noble's phrase as "historians against history."[32] Turner looked to the generative power of the American frontier to redeem American history from the social complexities of Europe and to provide the sources of American democratic life. The earlier Disciples historians had also looked beyond history — not to the primitive frontier environment but rather to the primitive gospel — as the source of escape from history. To return to apostolic Christianity was to overleap the intervening centuries of "human opinion" by which historical Christian life had encrusted and distorted the original simplicity of the Christian life and message.

Garrison, however, focused his attention upon neither the environment nor the message but rather precisely upon the social process of interaction between inherited beliefs and changing environments by which communities are changed over time and in time. He sought, in other words, to situate the Disciples of Christ *in* history rather than against it.

This effort to contextualize the Disciples of Christ led, of course, to a crucial question: What is the context? It was a question Garrison never directly resolved. Obviously, one of his answers was that the growth of American democratic society provided the context for Disciples history. This view appeared not only in his writings about the denomination but also in such works as *Catholicism and the American Mind* (1928), a fair but far from uncritical book in which he inquired whether Roman Catholic understandings of religious authority were compatible with the American polity. But another answer appeared with equal vigor in Garrison's work. In this case, the context was the historical development of Christianity. He emphasized the church's continuing but never fully successful effort to embody its ideals in particular settings. From this perspective, the Disciples of Christ as a reform movement were necessarily connected by continuity and by distinction to the entirety of the Christian tradition, and he regularly sought to place their development in relation to more comprehensive issues in the history of Christianity.

---

31. Garrison, *Religion Follows the Frontier,* pp. 301-2.

32. Noble, *Historians against History: The Frontier Thesis and the National Covenant in American Historical Writing since 1830* (Minneapolis: University of Minnesota Press, 1965).

As this suggests, decisions about context are decisions that reflect the interests or aims of the historian; some of these aims are explicit, but others are tacit or unacknowledged. It is, perhaps, all too obvious to us today that the frontier thesis, whether in the hands of Turner, Sweet, or Garrison, can contribute to notions of American exceptionalism, encouraging Americans "to play down the deficiencies of their culture or to think of themselves not as a part of Western civilization or of the world community but as a unique and self-contained society perpetually marked off by the frontier tradition from the common fate of modern societies."[33] To no small degree, Garrison's commitment to the context of the history of Christianity checked the potential excesses of his commitment to the context of American democracy. But, as African American and feminist historians have reminded us, interpretations of Christian history are themselves by no means immune to distortion by unacknowledged norms.

At times Garrison was quite alert to such problems, and he demonstrated his alertness in his historical study of 1934, *Intolerance,* which traces that phenomenon in Western cultural history from the beginning of the Christian era to his own time. But in the case of the historical relations between the Disciples and the Civil War, Garrison was not successful. His assumptions about the progress of the American democratic experiment and about the progress of the Disciples commitment to Christian union led him to minimize the roles of race and sectionalism in Disciples history, including the division between the Disciples of Christ and the Churches of Christ. The research of David E. Harrell, which demonstrates the centrality of race, sectional differences, and the Civil War in the division of the Disciples of Christ, indirectly exposes the limitations of Garrison's contextualization of Disciples history and is thus one of the most important pieces of Disciples historiography of the past twenty-five years.[34] But Garrison's failure on this important interpretive question should not be taken as evidence that he was unaware that the implicit norms of the historian shape what is historically "known." For him this was finally a theological question, the problem of the relation of historical context to transcendence of that context, a topic with which I will conclude this essay.

HISTORY AND THE SACRED

What larger motives prompted W. E. Garrison's attraction to the frontier thesis and his revisions of it? As we have seen, Garrison found that this thesis explained how the Disciples of Christ had "succeeded" on the American scene by adapting

---

33. Hofstadter, *The Progressive Historians,* p. 148.
34. Harrell, *Quest for a Christian America: The Disciples of Christ and American Society to 1866* (Nashville: Disciples of Christ Historical Society, 1966).

— indeed, by "efficiently" adapting — the Protestant tradition to the ethos and material conditions of the frontier. As the reader proceeds through Garrison's historical narratives, it becomes clear that the actual center of his interest was precisely this process of the revision and adaptation of tradition rather than an interest in the frontier itself. The frontier was one instance of a general process of social adaptation — an important instance for the Disciples, to be sure, but no more important in Garrison's view than the process of social adaptation through which the Disciples of Christ were proceeding in his own time.

Simply stated, Garrison's historical project was compatible with and supportive of his liberal theological convictions, and these theological convictions affected his historical project in at least three ways.

First, the theological liberals within the mainstream Protestant denominations conceived the task of theological scholarship in relation to the canons of free, critical inquiry that characterized university scholarship. They argued that theology should be thought of as proceeding by a method of empirical investigation, for which no presuppositions are, in principle, reserved from criticism. For this reason, when some Disciples of Christ suggested that the denomination should "build a university for ourselves," Garrison's response was vigorously negative.

> No religious body can dominate a genuine university. As an institution becomes great, it either ceases to be dominated or it never becomes a university in any true sense. The highest and holiest cause in the world cannot use a university as the agency of its propaganda. A university is not a place where boys and girls are taught to think as their teachers think. It is a place where every particular truth, or supposed truth, must take its chances in the search for *truth*.[35]

The University of Chicago philosopher of religion George Burman Foster clearly enunciated the liberal commitment to the unrestricted pursuit of truth when he asserted that religious authority "rooted in God's dictation and donation of truth" was "no longer tenable." Theological scholarship had to be revised, he insisted; "the study of a deposit of truth must give way to the search for reality," and "theology must come to terms with the scientific and philosophical theories which are current."[36] From this perspective, W. E. Garrison would argue in 1928 that in religion and theology there was a contention between "two types of mind," one that rested on authority and the other that tried to base its conclusions on an open review of the evidence. "The hope of the future," he declared, "lies in a type of religion, of theology, and of Christian ethics which is perfectly open-minded toward facts — the facts of history and nature and of the moral and spiritual experiences of men — and is willing to

35. Garrison, "A University for Ourselves," *Christian-Evangelist,* 16 February 1922, p. 208.

36. Foster, "The Contribution of Critical Scholarship to Ministerial Efficiency," *American Journal of Theology* 20 (1916): 161-78.

weigh and accept new evidence." Indeed, he concluded that "the concept of authority is foreign to religion."[37]

Second, Garrison and the liberal theologians, because of their general emphasis upon the immanence of God in history, were attentive to the underlying structure, direction, and meaning in the process of social evolution; divine providence, for them, manifested itself in an interactive social process. In their various efforts to apply scientific scholarship to the "needs" of the church or to correlate traditional Christian doctrines with the "needs" of modern humanity, the watchword came to be *efficiency*. To construe this word merely in technical or instrumental terms would, however, obscure the explicitly religious dimension of liberal theological inquiry. The "adjustment" or "adaptation" they sought was an adjustment to the largest features of experience, the personality-evolving and -sustaining structures of reality that made possible and supported the valued and valuing human enterprise. Garrison's social and historical inquiry into the religious adjustment of each age to its environment was an inquiry into the encounter of human life with the divine forces immanent within nature and history. The rhetoric of needs, efficient adaptations, and environments represented for him and for other liberals an articulation of the experience of the sacred within the process of history.

Following from these two points is a third. When Garrison read the history of the Disciples of Christ as necessarily including a continuing process of change to meet new conditions, he was in effect raising a theological objection against conservative Disciples of his own era. Their efforts to retain the biblicism of the frontier age mislocated the sacred by displacing the sacred from contemporary experience and mistakenly locating it in the irretrievable apostolic past of restorationism. He called instead for an affirmative, open encounter with experience, the accumulated corporate experience of the church and humanity, the aesthetic experience of the ideal contained in the "mystical" dimensions of art and poetry. He agreed with his Disciples of Christ colleague at the University of Chicago, the religious educator William Clayton Bower, who argued that the sacred was encountered in "the stream of current experience."

> Christianity is for [Christians] a quality of life, real and present, and growing directly out of their immediate interaction with their objective physical and social world. In the going experience of this community beliefs are not remote and abstract theological structures; they are instruments for interpreting the present experience of living human beings and for rendering it manageable. Its rituals, ceremonials, sacraments, and symbols are not detached and self-consistent entities; they are techniques for expressing and reproducing appreciations that well up out of cherished values and for establishing effective relations with the spiritual forces that are resident in and beyond the group.[38]

37. Garrison, *Affirmative Religion* (New York: Harper, 1928), pp. 19, 23, 27, 183-84.
38. *The Church at Work in the Modern World,* ed. William Clayton Bower (Chicago: University of Chicago Press, 1935), p. 2.

Such an encounter, Garrison concluded, finally exceeded either frontier faith in authority or modern faith in empirical evidence, because it led toward a future that was unknown, and it had to do "with ultimate values which lie beyond the reach of demonstration and with enterprises which call for the spirit of divine adventure."[39]

There are a number of things to be commended in Garrison's theological position, but I am concluding with them not to commend them. Garrison, in fact, would have insisted upon caution in commendation, since you and I live in a new situation and must seek our own "theologically efficient adjustments." I conclude with them, instead, as a reminder that a long time has passed since the Disciples of Christ attempted a comprehensive reappraisal of their history. When that historical task is once again taken up, it will, like Garrison's work, inevitably be shaped by the tacit aims and norms of class or ethnicity, nation or denomination. Both the facts selected for inclusion and the context within which they are placed will be embedded in a broader, even if unseen, pattern of moral and religious assumptions, and in this way the denomination's historical "image" will truly reflect its deepest character. The challenge will be to join Garrison in the effort, always partial and limited, to disclose and appraise those human interests by means of a theological judgment about the wholeness of all that is.

39. Garrison, *Affirmative Religion*, pp. 188-89.

Working Group Response:
The Disciples' Mission and Self-Image

Martha Grace Reese, Recorder

The Disciples are a denomination that was born on the American frontier, with a passionate vision of a united world won to Jesus as Lord, with themselves as servants of that vision, and with America as its vehicle.

That vision guided Disciples into the future, but it has experienced many hardships and problems along the way. The context in which we live today is global, and this fact challenges nineteenth-century American ethnocentrism (or parochialism). Renewal of our mission today depends on our cognizance of and participation in the mission of God already at work in the midst of this new global context.

Disciples are also faced with a crisis of self-understanding. Our own history is fraught with an enormous sense of our struggle to be faithful. This struggle for faithfulness has always taken place within an ambiguous relationship to our historical and cultural context. Our self-image in the midst of our history has been characterized by our commitment to church unity. Even though Disciples have greatly contributed to the worldwide ecumenical movement, the challenge to our self-understanding lies in the recognition that we are a people who have divided twice and who have not experienced organic union since 1832. We confess the failings of our past, accept God's forgiveness, and in the midst of our confession and forgiveness seek a renewed understanding of ourselves as the people of God.

The focus of our search for identity cannot be self-preservation, however; it must be centered on faithfulness to the Gospel. Our more recent written histories have emphasized the development of our organizational and institutional life. In order to form a renewed self-image, it is crucial that we formulate a theological understanding of where we have been as a people. It is essential that a critical theological history of the Disciples of Christ be commissioned by the Church. The history should be placed within the context of the whole history of Christianity and address Disciples reflection on the content of the gospel, the meaning of faith, the character and work of the church, and the nature of God's mission in the world.

This conference teaches us that we must face both our past and our present with candor, something that we have not always done. Historically, our pragmatism and commitment to individualism have kept us from appropriating our best theological reflection. Disciples, like other mainstream traditions, have long assumed that the average churchgoer is incapable of theological reflection. This suspicion has only encouraged an elite mentality, replete with "us and them" language. As a community of faith, we cannot abide this kind of division.

The task ahead for Disciples leadership demands a commitment to the theological education of the whole church. Unless a commitment to the importance of the theological perspective emerges among all the people of the church, Disciples will be incapable of contributing meaningfully to the work of God's church in the days ahead.

IV. EDUCATION

Disciples Theological Formation: From a College of the Bible to a Theological Seminary

Richard L. Harrison, Jr.

In 1880 the Disciples had but one theological seminary, the College of the Bible in Lexington, Kentucky. Over the next hundred years, that institution educated more Disciples ministers than any other Disciples seminary. By 1980, however, the College of the Bible had long since evolved into Lexington Theological Seminary. The change of name symbolized a significant shift in institutional self-understanding and in the theological education of ministers for the Disciples. This essay will look at the College of the Bible/Lexington Theological Seminary during this period, from 1880 to 1980, in order to analyze the changes in theological outlook of the institution and how those views have been reflected in the education of several generations of ministers.

The College of the Bible was initially founded in 1865 as the ministerial training program of Kentucky University, now Transylvania University.[1] The University had its roots in both the old Transylvania Seminary of 1780 (which evolved into Transylvania College, supported in its early years by Kentucky Presbyterians) and Bacon College, established by Disciples in 1836.[2] Education of clergy as well as the laity was central to the initial concerns of each of these institutions.

When the College of the Bible was created in 1865, it had the form of an undergraduate curriculum for students preparing for ministry, although there was an advanced program available for those with a baccalaureate degree. An important part of what would happen to the institution over the next sixty years

1. The best treatments of this history are found in three places: Dwight E. Stevenson, *Lexington Theological Seminary, 1865-1965: The College of the Bible Century* (St. Louis: Bethany Press, 1964); John D. Wright, Jr., *Transylvania: Tutor to the West* (Lexington, Ky.: Transylvania University, 1975); and Richard M. Pope, *The College of the Bible: A Brief Narrative* (Lexington, Ky.: College of the Bible, 1961).

2. See Dwight E. Stevenson, *The Bacon College Story, 1836-1865* (Lexington, Ky.: College of the Bible, 1962).

was the development of the College of the Bible from a mixed, largely under-graduate school to a graduate theological seminary.

Within a few years of the founding of the College of the Bible there was a sharp conflict within the University over the relationship of the church to the University. The result of this conflict was the creation of the College of the Bible as a fully independent institution.

In the period from 1878 to 1950, Transylvania and the College of the Bible shared a common campus, some classroom space, dormitories, library space, faculty, student bodies, administrative staff, and even, at times, a president. Nevertheless, from 1878 forward, the College of the Bible was an educational institution legally separate from Transylvania.

The early faculty of the College of the Bible was dominated by four persons: Robert Milligan (1814-1875), Robert Graham (1822-1901), John W. McGarvey (1829-1911), and Isaiah Boone Grubbs (1833-1912). All four were committed to the cause of the Campbell-Stone movement as understood in the post–Civil War era. They represented a second generation of leadership, a conserving force in the movement, and they even had some affinity for those who would soon form the Churches of Christ, a very conservative group of Disciples who separated themselves from the main body of the Disciples over a number of issues.

All four had studied under Alexander Campbell at Bethany College. None had studied elsewhere on the collegiate or graduate level. In the spirit of Campbell, they approached education and ministry as matters of reason, reasonableness, and practicality. The College of the Bible was thus shaped by Campbell's own emphasis on a reasonable Bible and an educational experience in which theological formation was understood as an engagement with the text and what was believed to be the clear meaning of the Scriptures.[3]

By 1880 and the time of the separation of the College of the Bible from the control of Transylvania University, the faculty and the curriculum of the College of the Bible was well established and solidly grounded in a sense of purpose and a philosophy of education.[4]

The catalogue of the College of the Bible for 1879-1880 describes the curriculum as centering in a study of Scripture (in English and in the original languages) along with a study of English literature and philosophy. While the purpose of the institution was "to prepare young men for usefulness in the

---

3. See Alexander Campbell, "Principles of Interpretation," in *A Connected View of the Principles and Rules by Which the Living Oracles May Be Intelligibly and Certainly Interpreted . . .* (Bethany, Va.: M'Vay & Ewing, 1835), pp. 15-100. (Note: this material is not found in subsequent editions of this work published under the title *The Chrisitan System*). See also Cecil K. Thomas, *Alexander Campbell and His New Version* (St. Louis: Bethany Press, 1958), and M. Eugene Boring, "The Formation of a Tradition: Alexander Campbell and the New Testament," *Disciples Theological Digest* 2 (1987): 5-62.

4. There were no tuition fees for students in the College of the Bible. Room, board, and related fees came to as little as $105 per academic year (*Annual Catalogue of the College of the Bible*, 1879-80, p. 12).

Church," it was not to be seen as "a *professional* school, its classes being open to all religious young men who wish to extend their knowledge of the Scriptures."[5] (It was another twenty years before women were permitted to study in the College of the Bible.)

More was at stake here than announcing that the courses of the College of the Bible were open to those with no professional ministerial goals. The denial of "professional school" status was a way of affirming a "low" view of clergy, of emphasizing an understanding of the priesthood of all believers in such a way as to avoid as far as possible any sense of clergy as a superior caste.[6]

The curriculum was divided into an English program and a classical program. The English course of study was for those students who had as yet little or no collegiate experience. It was a four-year program with no elective courses.

Most of the courses in Bible were listed under the heading of "Sacred History," and had two concerns: (1) to acquaint students with the "historical facts of the Bible" as a basis for all further study of the Bible, and (2) to explore the Bible in order to give the student "a large amount of material suitable for discourses and illustrations." Thus the study of the Bible and the use of the Bible for the work of the preacher were held closely together. There was to be expected yet a third result. The catalogue states: "Incidentally, the faith of the student is greatly strengthened by his acquaintance with the actual contents of the Bible." Knowledge of theory, resources for praxis, and enrichment of *piety,* then, were the goals of the biblical studies program in 1880.[7]

The teaching of Scripture focused on the historical books of the Hebrew and Greek testaments "together with all the historical information to be gleaned from the other sacred books, and the subsidiary information found in secular history." The Scriptures were to be presented as a unified whole, with "all obscure passages . . . made clear, and apparent discrepancies . . . reconciled."[8]

McGarvey, the primary teacher in Bible, placed great emphasis on the geography and topography of the biblical lands. His book *Lands of the Bible* was an essential textbook for his courses, and one of few works other than the Bible that was assigned.[9]

To complete the English diploma, a student studied the Bible with McGarvey five days a week for four years. McGarvey lectured, assigned substantial amounts of the biblical text to be memorized, and provided questions to be answered in precise ways. He made broad use of lower (i.e., textual) criticism. While he read many of the scholars who practiced higher criticism

5. *Annual Catalogue of the College of the Bible,* 1879-80, p. 5.

6. See D. Newell Williams, *Ministry among Disciples: Past, Present, and Future* (St. Louis: Council on Christian Unity, 1985).

7. *Annual Catalogue of the College of the Bible,* 1879-80, p. 6.

8. *Annual Catalogue of the College of the Bible,* 1879-80, p. 6.

9. John W. McGarvey, *Lands of the Bible* (Philadelphia: J. B. Lippincott, 1881).

(i.e., dealing with issues of authorship, setting, theological intent, etc.), he generally, often very caustically, disagreed with most of the more modern authors. Nevertheless McGarvey did employ some of the methods of higher criticism in his own interpretation and teaching.[10]

The goal of the four years of memorization and carefully structured instruction was to provide the student with "a thorough knowledge of the historical parts of the Bible, and the best methods of defending it against the objections of the ignorant and the attacks of unbelievers."[11]

Students in the department of sacred literature studied hermeneutics and theology — the latter referred to as "Christian doctrine." It was here that students in the classical course, the program for students who already had a Bachelor of Arts degree, would study Hebrew and Greek as a major part of their two-year curriculum.[12]

The study of theology was related entirely to the "exposition and defense of the scheme of redemption as taught in the Holy Scriptures," along with a very brief survey of church history. Sacred literature included courses in homiletics that all students had to take.[13]

The courses offered in philosophy were spread out over three years in the English course and sought to teach epistemology and "furnish . . . the weapons to be used in defending the Faith and assailing the strongholds of error; and to lay open the secret springs of the heart and Will, and how to lead both to the obedience of the gospel." The content and discipline of the philosophy courses were said to be "in utility to the preacher second only to . . . knowledge of the word of God."[14] Again, the integration of theory and praxis provided for a clarity of purpose in the life of the institution.

By 1900 some development had occurred in the curriculum, though little change can be noted in purposes and procedures. The classical course had become a three-year program, with courses added in both academic and practical areas. Church History and Christian Doctrine and Polity were now required as separate courses, along with a course entitled "Biblical Criticism." This was taught by a new member of the faculty, Benjamin Cassell Deweese.[15] Deweese was one of a new breed of teacher at the College of the Bible, having studied at institutions other than Bethany College, including the University of Missouri and Harvard.

---

10. Stevenson, *Lexington Theological Seminary,* p. 86.

11. *Annual Catalogue of the College of the Bible,* 1879-80, p. 7.

12. *Annual Catalogue of the College of the Bible,* 1879-80, pp. 10-11. Hermeneutics, or principles of interpretation, was described as "first, the exegetical analysis of the Scriptures into sectinos [*sic*], paragraphs, elements of thought, sub-elements, etc.; and, second, exegetical discussion at the end of paragraphs containing words or expressions which demand additional explanation." The authors cited as models in hermeneutics were all older, conservative, traditional interpreters of Scripture (*Annual Catalogue of the College of the Bible,* 1879-80, p. 7).

13. *Annual Catalogue of the College of the Bible,* 1879-80, pp. 7, 10.

14. *Annual Catalogue of the College of the Bible,* 1879-80, p. 8.

15. *Catalogue of Kentucky University,* 1899-1900, pp. 42, 43.

Biblical criticism was described as a study of "the history and present condition of the New Testament text," including questions of authorship, "and the evidence of the credibility and the inspiration of these books." The Hebrew Scriptures were similarly treated. "Throughout the course, the position and arguments of the modern destructive critics are set forth and their merits discussed."[16] Although the tone of the course was clearly antagonistic towards higher criticism, it nevertheless gave the students some insight into the methods and concerns of the discipline.

A class in church history was taught by Isaiah Boone Grubbs and provided a very brief overview.[17] The Christian Doctrine and Church Polity course, also taught by Grubbs, was described as "more nearly [approaching] the subject usually styled Systematic Theology than any other course in this college, but it differs from that branch in adhering strictly to Scripture teaching, and discarding all philosophical speculation." The text for the course was Robert Milligan's *Scheme of Redemption.*[18]

There are several interesting aspects to this entry in the catalogue. The first is that the Disciples prejudice against the term *theology,* and in particular, systematic theology, is evident here. At the same time, the mere reference to systematics is an indication of some change. In the 1880 catalogue the course was listed simply as "Christian Doctrine." Here the subject is broadened and specifically linked to the more traditional language of theological study. Second, there is implied here a "correct" over against an "incorrect" way of doing theology. The proper way is strictly to follow Scripture rather than to engage in "philosophical speculation." Third, the reference to Milligan's work, in many ways little more than a second-generation summation of Alexander Campbell's theology, indicates that the theological perspective of the institution in 1900 was still that of its founders. It is likely that Professor Grubbs, surely with the support of McGarvey, would not trust his charges to any other mentor in the faith than the one who had systematized the founding father — namely, Milligan's recapitulation of Campbell.

The classical course also included two classes that were clearly practical in orientation: Elocution and Homiletics. The latter was taught by Samuel Jefferson, who had received his B.A. from Bethany and his M.A. from Columbia. Jefferson was a more cosmopolitan figure than his predecessors, having made at least two voyages to Europe, and he was very demanding of his students. A former student recalled him saying, "I like to see people at home in foreign languages, but I don't like to see them appear as foreigners in their own language."[19]

16. *Catalogue of Kentucky University,* 1899-1900, p. 43.
17. "It being impossible within the limits of a college course to impart a thorough knowledge of this vast and ever growing subject, only those historical facts are set forth, and those phases of teaching, that every preacher should be acquainted with in the beginning of ministry. The rest are left as studies of a lifetime" (*Catalogue of Kentucky University,* 1899-1900, p. 40).
18. *Catalogue of Kentucky University,* 1899-1900, p. 40.
19. Stevenson, *Lexington Theological Seminary,* p. 121.

The homiletics course was a year-long class with opportunities for students to practice writing and delivering sermons. The second semester included a study of worship. It is interesting that one of the textbooks used was Washington Gladden's *The Christian Pastor and the Working Church.*[20]

Gladden was one of the founders of the Social Gospel movement in America, and the book throughout reflects the basic social concerns and optimism characteristic of the movement. Gladden argues that "the Christianization of society, in all its parts and organs, is the high calling of the church." For this reason, the minister should devote significant time and interest to the study of society, to sociology as understood at the turn of the century. According to Gladden, salvation is a matter of social concern, for "the distinctive quality of the saved is their power of saving the society in which they live."[21]

At the same time that College of the Bible president John W. McGarvey was writing a weekly column for the *Christian Standard* attacking higher criticism and any, including Gladden, who would cast doubt on the veracity of the entire text of the Bible, Professor Jefferson was using a book by Gladden that offered a liberal interpretation of the Bible:

> The Bible, intelligently studied will throw just as much light on questions of conduct, on the laws of the spiritual life, under the new hypothesis as it has ever given us under the old hypothesis — perhaps a little more. Some moral confusion may be avoided by recognizing as altogether human certain elements which were formerly supposed to be divine. It is a great gain to be discharged from the task of defending the historicity of certain narratives, and to be able to give our whole attention to their moral and spiritual values.[22]

Gladden specifically cites as examples some of those parts of the Bible most debated by the modernists and conservatives of the day. He says, for instance, "The question whether Jonah was swallowed by a fish or not can have no possible relation to the life of any living" person, "but the moral and spiritual questions which the story so vividly brings before us are well worthy of our attention."[23] Even if Jefferson provided his students with critical editorial comment on Gladden, his use of such a book, with such a blatantly liberal perspective, did give students an opportunity to read for themselves ideas quite different from those generally taught in McGarvey's College of the Bible. It certainly seems likely that if Gladden had been included as an example of what not to teach and believe, the book would have been so noted in the catalogue listing.

During this period, one other member of the College of the Bible faculty continued to make an impact on the institution and the church. Charles Louis

---

20. *Catalogue of Kentucky University,* 1899-1900, p. 41.

21. Gladden, *The Christian Pastor and the Working Church* (New York: Scribner's, 1898), pp. 102-3.

22. Gladden, *The Christian Pastor and the Working Church,* p. 99.

23. Gladden, *The Christian Pastor and the Working Church,* p. 99.

Loos (1823-1912), a native of Woerth-sur-Sauer in the Alsace, had a distinguished career in Disciples education. He served as president of Kentucky University from 1880 to 1897 and continued to teach in the College of the Bible after his retirement from the presidency. He taught Greek in a two-year course, during which students read both the New Testament and the Septuagint in Greek.[24]

Those students who added a year's study of Hebrew to the three-year classical course received a solid grounding in the content of Scripture and the basic tools with which to become more critical scholars. Although the curriculum was highly traditional and carefully conservative — even combative — with regard to the rising tide of modernism, the move from McGarvey to a much more liberal interpretation was not nearly as great a jump as would have been the case had the curriculum been less rigorous. The key to this is the study of Scripture in the original languages and the active engagement with modernism. Students were exposed to other ways of thinking even if this exposure was usually very tightly controlled.

Up to 1900, the faculty of the College of the Bible was composed largely of individuals whose own formal education had centered on Bethany College and the legacy of Alexander Campbell. Robert Graham, Isaiah Grubbs, James C. Keith (taught homiletics 1898-1900, diploma from the College of the Bible), John W. McGarvey, Robert Milligan, and William T. Moore had been educated primarily through Bethany College and/or the College of the Bible. Only the newcomers, Benjamin Deweese and Samuel Jefferson, had attended other institutions. But neither these nor any of the others had earned a doctoral degree.

Over the next dozen years much changed for the College of the Bible and for the Disciples. New faculty members were added. Most of the founding saints passed on to their reward. Even the most conservative of the new faculty represented a broader educational background, and some came from a decidedly more liberal perspective. The changes were reflected in the subjects taught, the character of the curriculum, and the ways in which teaching was done.

A watershed period approached for the Disciples and for the College of the Bible. Just as other denominations in America and Europe were struggling through what came to be known as the modernist-fundamentalist controversy, so the Disciples confronted the issues raised — and each other. The results were painful. Schism and new directions characterized the age. The numerically rapid growth of the Disciples slowed, though often perhaps for reasons beyond ideological stance. At the College of the Bible the hour of confrontation of modernism with narrow dogmatism came in the wake of the death of President McGarvey.

24. Stevenson, *Lexington Theological Seminary,* pp. 124-25; Wright, *Transylvania,* pp. 247-48; *Catalogue of Kentucky University,* 1899-1900, p. 42.

McGarvey died in October 1911. The dean of the school, W. C. Morro, had left that summer for another position. The faculty consisted of Deweese, Jefferson, W. F. Smith, and Hall L. Calhoun. Morro had come to the College only five years earlier, in 1906. He was liberally educated, having studied at Missouri, Transylvania, and the College of the Bible and having received a Ph.D. from Harvard. He was also the first of a line of faculty members who were natives of Australia.

Morro later emerged as one of the leading liberal Disciples educators. While at Lexington, he called for expanding courses in church history and developing a department of Christian Sociology, clearly under the influence of the Social Gospel movement. "I believe," Morro wrote the trustees, "that we are on the eve of a great social change; with other things the church also will be changed. . . . It will have for its task not merely the saving of the individual, but the transforming and christianizing of the social fabric."[25]

While Morro's vision took a while to develop, the College of the Bible did make one additional major contribution to the education of ministers under McGarvey's leadership. With the support of the Kentucky Christian Bible School Association (one of the predecessor organizations that would later form what has become the Christian Church [Disciples of Christ] in Kentucky), the College of the Bible established in 1909 the first department of Religious Education and the first endowed professorship in Religious Education in the country. William Francis Smith, a graduate of the College of the Bible, was brought to the faculty to fill the new position. He served until 1912.[26]

The addition of Hall Laurie Calhoun (1863-1935) to the faculty of the College of the Bible signified two things: the institution had its first teacher with a Ph.D. and it had its first home-grown instructor. Calhoun had graduated from Lexington in 1892. Nine years later McGarvey led the Board of Trustees to make it possible for him to attend Yale, where he earned the Bachelor of Divinity degree, and then Harvard, where in 1904 he received a Ph.D. in textual criticism of the Bible. That same year he began a fateful term of service on the faculty of the College of the Bible.[27]

By 1914 Jefferson had joined McGarvey in death, and Deweese was chronically ill. W. F. Smith, unhappy with how he was being treated by students and other faculty, apparently because of his lack of graduate degrees, left in 1912. Within three short years after McGarvey's death, only Calhoun remained of those who had taught with and under McGarvey.

Calhoun was made dean when Morro left in the summer of 1911. When McGarvey died, he was also made acting president. Calhoun clearly believed that it was McGarvey's wish that he would be the successor to the venerable

25. Morrow, quoted by Stevenson, in *Lexington Theological Seminary,* p. 135.

26. Stevenson, *Lexington Theological Seminary,* pp. 128-29.

27. See Adron Doran and J. E. Choate, *The Christian Scholar: A Biography of Hall Laurie Calhoun* (Nashville: Gospel Advocate, 1985), p. 86.

one. The Trustees had other ideas. Richard Henry Crossfield, president of Transylvania since 1908, was made president of the College of the Bible as well in January 1912. Crossfield had urged a joint presidency soon after McGarvey's death and had tried to resign from the presidency of Transylvania so as to allow the trustees of both institutions to act freely. The trustees of both institutions liked his thinking and gave him the opportunity to lead the two schools into new avenues of relationship and service.[28]

Crossfield moved quickly to fill vacancies on the faculty. Alonzo Willard Fortune had graduated from Colgate-Rochester Divinity School (where prominent Social Gospel leader Walter Rauschenbusch taught) and received a Ph.D. in New Testament from the University of Chicago just before beginning his duties at Lexington. William Clayton Bower replaced Smith in the chair of Bible School Pedagogy. He had studied at Columbia and Union and received a Ph.D. from Columbia in 1916. Like Fortune, Bower had already earned a reputation as an excellent parish minister before joining the faculty of the College of the Bible.[29]

Jefferson's position was filled by E. E. Snoddy. He taught philosophy in Transylvania and practical theology in the seminary. He had an M.A. from Yale. Bower's brother-in-law, George W. Hemry, also came to the faculty in 1914. He initially taught religious education, missions, and comparative religion. Hemry had an M.A. from Butler and had completed much of the work for a Ph.D. at Chicago.[30]

A new faculty eagerly responded to changes in the institution. In 1914 the College of the Bible decided to offer a degree as well as diplomas. The Bachelor of Divinity degree was to be a post-baccalaureate degree and generally required three years of graduate work and a thesis. Within five years the classical diploma was no longer offered.[31]

Elective courses were first made available to students in 1915-1916.[32] In addition to such possibilities as choosing majors, electives meant that students were able to exercise their own judgment about part of the curriculum. This was an enormous change from the days of McGarvey, when students had all of their courses determined for them, and, at least in McGarvey's classes, had answers as well as questions given to them for rote memorization. Electives contributed to a process of educational change in which diversity and a certain kind of freedom of thought was encouraged by the very structure of the curriculum.

Perhaps of equal importance to electives was the move by the younger faculty to require a wide range of reading by the students.[33] McGarvey's method had been to limit reading to the Bible and his own books for all students except those in the most advanced courses. Other faculty members followed

28. Stevenson, *Lexington Theological Seminary,* pp. 138-39.
29. Stevenson, *Lexington Theological Seminary,* pp. 138-39.
30. Stevenson, *Lexington Theological Seminary,* pp. 150-51.
31. Stevenson, *Lexington Theological Seminary,* pp. 162-63.
32. Stevenson, *Lexington Theological Seminary,* pp. 163-64.
33. Stevenson, *Lexington Theological Seminary,* p. 164.

similar patterns, with the possible exception of Jefferson. Only after 1912 did the library begin to replace a few textbooks as the primary resource for students. Again, encouraging students to go to the library and choose from a number of books had the effect of stimulating a level of intellectual freedom and curiosity that had not been the case earlier. It should be noted, however, that in the first years of the College of the Bible, most of the students came to Lexington ill-prepared for collegiate, not to mention graduate, study. McGarvey's curriculum was intended to educate persons deemed too intellectually immature to have much say in the character of their education.[34]

With so much change coming so rapidly, it is not surprising that conflict erupted. The story of the "heresy trial" at the College of the Bible in 1917 has been told often and well, and it does not need repeating here except in briefest summary. Dean Hall Calhoun, increasingly at odds with his colleagues on the faculty, became involved with a group of students who opposed the more liberal directions of the younger faculty. The conservative students called for a return to the methods and perspectives of McGarvey — methods and perspectives followed faithfully by Calhoun.

Under the leadership of student Ben Battenfield, the conflict became a matter of public discussion. Battenfield worked closely with the Standard Publishing Company and its weekly magazine, the *Christian Standard,* widely read among Disciples. The *Standard* used front-page headlines to call for an investigation of the situation in Lexington. The involvement of the *Standard* arose not only out of concern over this particular issue but over a whole series of conflicts with Disciples leaders during the preceding ten years, including some involving Transylvania/College of the Bible President R. H. Crossfield.

The trustees of the College of the Bible met in emergency session in May of 1917 with the intent of investigating the faculty and the curriculum. When the faculty, led by W. C. Bower, said that they would not participate in a heresy trial, the trustees agreed that such was not the "Disciples way" of doing things. They subsequently proceeded in a more informal manner and concluded with a full exoneration of the faculty.

This controversy pushed the Disciples far down the path of a schism that would not fully conclude until about 1970, with the implementation of a plan of reorganization for the Disciples called *Restructure.* A new church, variously known as the Independent Christian Churches or Christian Churches and Churches of Christ, emerged from this period.[35]

34. Stevenson, *Lexington Theological Seminary,* pp. 88-91.
35. See Alfred Thomas DeGroot, *New Possibilities for Disciples and Independents* (St. Louis: Bethany Press, 1963), a revised and expanded version of *Church of Christ Number Two* (Birmingham, England: A. T. DeGroot, 1956). See also Stephen J. Corey's apologetic Disciples work *Fifty Years of Attack and Controversy: The Consequences among Disciples of Christ* (St. Louis: Committee on Publication of the Corey Manuscript, 1953), and James DeForest Murch's Independent interpretation of the period in *Christians Only: A History of the Restoration Movement* (Cincinnati: Standard Press, 1962).

The two major players on the conservative side soon left the College of the Bible. Ben Battenfield eventually helped run a religious commune in the Ozarks.[36] Hall Calhoun left for Bethany College, where he taught until 1925. At that time, Bethany was supportive of the conservative Disciples. Calhoun then moved to Tennessee as a member of the very conservative noninstrumental Churches of Christ. He served their cause for ten years, during which time he was a preacher, college administrator, and teacher.

The conflict over modernism in the College of the Bible resulted in fundamental and lasting change in the institution. The conservative tradition of John W. McGarvey carried on by Hall L. Calhoun was gone. In its place was a theologically moderate to liberal institution that continued to serve the Disciples. The most vociferous opponents of these changes gradually separated themselves from the Disciples, leaving the College of the Bible and sister institutions in place to educate ministers of the Disciples.

The first signs of change were found in new faculty appointments. George William Brown replaced Calhoun as professor of Old Testament. Brown was a former missionary with a Ph.D. from Johns Hopkins. Charles Lynn Pyatt came in 1920 to teach Bible. Pyatt had a classical diploma from the College of the Bible, an M.A. from Transylvania, a B.D. from Yale, and a Th.D. from Harvard.

The deanship was filled by A. W. Fortune, who served until 1921, when he accepted a position as pastor of Central Christian Church in Lexington, one of the most prominent Disciples churches in Kentucky. In that position, Fortune continued to support and work with the College of the Bible, continuing to serve for many years as a part-time professor.

Rodney L. McQuary, with a B.D. from Yale and some work there toward a Ph.D., came initially to teach Old Testament but then moved into New Testament and church history after Fortune's resignation. Vernon Stauffer also came in 1922 to teach church history. He held a Ph.D. from Columbia. Neither McQuary nor Stauffer remained on the faculty long. Stauffer died in 1925, and McQuary returned to parish ministry in 1927.[37]

The curriculum in the years after the "heresy trial" reflected the more liberal views of the remaining faculty. The easing of the structure of the curriculum which had begun just prior to the conflict evolved into a program in which students could specialize in areas of their choice, with thirty-eight of the ninety-two hours required for the Bachelor of Divinity degree available as electives.

No longer eschewing the language of "theology," the college described the B.D. degree "as a recognition of distinct scholarship in the field of theology." Some of the old rhetoric remained, however: there continued to be a

36. Doris Thompson, "History of an Ozark Utopia." *Arkansas Historical Quarterly* (Winter 1955): 1-15.
37. Stevenson, *Lexington Theological Seminary,* pp. 211-13, 221-22.

department of Doctrine rather than of Theology, but on the other hand, the first required course in the field was described as a study of "theology; its importance, its relation to religion; the sources and qualifications for theological study; the special task of the modern theologian." Two theology courses were required of all B.D. students — one on the doctrine of God, the other on the doctrine of sin and salvation. A course on the history of Christian thought included "special emphasis . . . on the changing thought of the modern world, and a study is made of the conditions which make this change inevitable."[38] This was certainly a far more positive appropriation of "theology" than had been the case in 1900.

The courses in Bible clearly reflected the changes in the few years since the death of McGarvey. The catalogue refers to "written reports and outside reading" as required, over against the carefully controlled content and memorization McGarvey and colleagues had enforced. A more advanced Old Testament course is described as dealing with "questions of textual and historical criticism. . . . The principles of criticism, both textual and historical, pertaining to the books are set forth, and a practical application of these principles to problems of criticism in the Old Testament is made." Even questions of canon were discussed, with the overall aim of giving "the student an intelligent acquaintance with the subject of Old Testament Criticism." This was a clear acceptance of the modernist approach to biblical studies.[39]

There is more. A course entitled "Institutions of the Hebrews" included a study of the Jewish law and "a comparison . . . between these laws and other ancient codes, such as that of Hammurabi." Another course studied wisdom literature of the Hebrew Bible, with Job described as "a dramatic poem." The Wisdom of Sirach and the Wisdom of Solomon were also listed as materials of the course without denoting them as apocryphal or somehow less than fully biblical and authoritative.[40]

Courses in the New Testament reflected the same level of significant change in approach and interpretation. The basic required course on "The Life of Christ" was described as "a study of the sources of the life of Christ, with emphasis on the purpose of the various Gospels, their relation to each other, and the manner in which the writers used the materials at their command."[41]

Instead of emphasizing the "historical facts of the Bible" and the purpose of providing a defense of the Bible "against the objections of the ignorant and the attacks of unbelievers," as stated in 1880,[42] the 1920 curriculum made use of historical, literary, and source criticism for the purpose of enabling "the student so to relate Jesus to the life and thought of his own age that he can

38. *The College of the Bible Quarterly Bulletin* 10 (May 1920): 17, 31, 42-43.
39. *The College of the Bible Quarterly Bulletin* 10 (May 1920): 35-36.
40. *The College of the Bible Quarterly Bulletin* 10 (May 1920): 36-37.
41. *The College of the Bible Quarterly Bulletin* 10 (May 1920): 38.
42. *Annual Catalogue of the College of the Bible*, 1879-80, pp. 6-7.

interpret his wonderful life and message."[43] The curriculum sought to use modern interpretation of the Bible not to destroy piety but to undergird it, much as foreseen in the work of Gladden long in use at the College of the Bible.

In a series of articles published in the *College of the Bible Quarterly* for 1920, various members of the faculty defended the use of modernism in interpreting Scripture and supporting the faith of the church. Fortune argued that while some of the nineteenth-century critics went too far — generally because they followed their own "philosophical theories which determined their conclusions" — they did provide a helpful direction for serious critics of the twentieth century: they maintained that "the Bible must be studied as other literature." Further, Fortune suggested that the work of Darwin, far from undermining faith, provided a way of understanding "God's method of working." He was taken with the progressive understanding of knowledge, the idea that each age develops, progresses, and receives assistance from the scientist as well as the biblical critic.[44]

Other courses in the curriculum give evidence of how broad and deep the changes in educational philosophy and theological outlook actually were. In a course on the history of the Disciples — one of six courses in the field of church history, as opposed to one under McGarvey — the description avoids using the language of "Restorationism." Instead, the emphasis is on context, leading figures, ideas, documents, theology, and the "plea for union."[45]

Courses in the area of "Practical Theology" — religious education and missions — reflect as much change as occurred in other areas in the curriculum. Throughout there is a strong flavor of the Social Gospel, first encountered in 1900 with Prof. Jefferson's choice of the Gladden textbook and reinforced by Morro's concerns in 1909. By 1920 the Social Gospel was in full force. The description of the first course in preaching speaks of the "adjustment of the preacher's message to current intellectual and social ideals." An elective course entitled "The Working Church" used Gladden's text *The Christian Pastor.* The course dealt with "the relation of the local church to other organizations of the community, and also to the more widely organized movements for missions and moral reforms, and the work of pastoral leadership in the church and in the community."[46]

43. *The College of the Bible Quarterly Bulletin* 10 (May 1920): 38.

44. Alonzo Willard Fortune, "The Search for a Basis of Faith," *The College of the Bible Quarterly* 10 (December 1920): 10-11.

45. *The College of the Bible Quarterly Bulletin* 10 (May 1920): 42.

46. *The College of the Bible Quarterly Bulletin* 10 (May 1920): pp. 45-46. Several courses listed under the category of missions also evidenced this concern with the Social Gospel and a generally liberal view of human society and history. This can be seen in the courses on anthropology, ethnology and ethnography, sociology, and especially the course entitled "Modern Social Problems," which was described as dealing "with the origin, development, and present instability of the family, the problem of population, immigration, the negro problem, the modern city, poverty and pauperism, crime, socialism, and education as a means of social control." Students were to

Professor George Brown, writing in the *College of the Bible Quarterly,* argued that "modern Christianity dwells little on statements and forms; it demands a life based on Christ's life, and lived like his, with the welfare of man constantly in view." For the twentieth-century Christian, the "ideal is Christ's ideal; all men united in one great fellowship here and now; all men brothers; the one God father of all mankind; eternal fellowship continuing into the life beyond."[47] Here was classic liberalism and the classic Social Gospel proclaimed together just three years after the departure of McGarvey's protégé Hall L. Calhoun.

W. C. Bower's courses in religious education reflected advances of psychology related to human religious development. By 1920 he was already teaching courses entitled "The Psychology of Religion" and "The Organization of Play," the latter based on a psychological analysis of play as a part of education and social development.[48]

In the mid-twenties the curriculum was described in terms that revealed the influence of Bower, calling for a "combination of theory and practice" wherever possible. One aspect of Bower's concern is evident in the change of attitude toward student preaching. Prior to 1902 student preaching was largely discouraged. For the next several years it was very carefully monitored and limited by the faculty. After 1915, however, a much more positive approach was taken, and student service in churches was understood to be of positive educational benefit. The college also provided financial support for chronically poor students. By 1920 the catalogue stated that small churches in the area presented "a particularly favorable opportunity for self-support to students preparing for the ministry, especially if they have had some experience in preaching and the care of churches."[49]

In 1927 George V. Moore came to the faculty with a charge to develop a strong field education program. For most of his thirty-five years on the faculty he had responsibility for overseeing student field work and education. Moore was a graduate of the College of the Bible (B.D.), with an M.A. from Kentucky and a Ph.D. from Chicago.[50]

It is not a little surprising that an emphasis on student service in churches came after the turn of the century. On this point we should note (1) that the students in the period prior to 1900 were largely unprepared for student preaching assignments and (2) that Bower's educational philosophy encouraged prac-

---

use Lexington and surrounding towns as sources for doing case studies, and theories of sociology were to be applied that were very much in line with values and concerns of the Social Gospel (*The College of the Bible Quarterly Bulletin* 10 [May 1920]: 50-51).

47. Brown, "The Social Challenge to Modern Christianity," *The College of the Bible Quarterly* 10 (December 1920): 22.

48. *The College of the Bible Quarterly Bulletin* 10 (May 1920): pp. 47-49.

49. Stevenson, *Lexington Theological Seminary,* pp. 108-9, 210-11; *The College of the Bible Quarterly Bulletin* 10 (May 1920): pp. 28-29.

50. Stevenson, *Lexington Theological Seminary,* p. 223.

tical experience as a way of integrating and truly learning more abstract principles. As the curriculum became more intentionally academic and theoretically rigorous, it also placed more stress on "learning by doing" while learning about doing. And increasing student opportunities for church work represent another way in which the curriculum allowed students to make their own decisions about what it was they needed and wanted to know.[51]

The shape of the curriculum and the theological assumptions underlying the basic educational concerns of the College of the Bible in the early 1920s reflected a radical change from the era of McGarvey. Indeed, the change from 1917 to the 1920s was a profound departure from the past. The degree of change from 1911 to 1925 was far greater than from 1925 to 1980. The reason is clear. In the struggles of 1917, the modernist perspective of the moderate liberals won. The conservative, certainly the fundamentalist perspective (which, technically, never did have a voice in the College of the Bible), lost.

Henceforward, changes were incremental. They reflected a refining of the more liberal perspective but never a repudiation of that view. By the 1940s courses in the Bible were even more specialized than in years past, with a number of courses on specific books of the Bible. But there was little indication of a fundamental change in perspective from that of 1920. Literary, source, and canon criticism came to be more prominent, but this only took further the basic perspective already in control. Changes in approach to the study of Bible and theology reflected changes in the mainstream of liberalism, not a departure from liberalism. For example, in 1943 a course in "The Canon of the New Testament" dealt with "the stages by which the early church reached the consciousness of possessing a new collection of sacred writings, equalling, if not surpassing, the authority of the Old Testament."[52]

One of the most telling changes in the approach to biblical studies between the forties and the sixties (and later) is the omission of all pietistic language from the catalogue descriptions. No longer is John described as "a bold recast," nor are the prophets cited as a source of "timely teachings" useful "for present day living."[53] Rather, by the sixties courses are described

51. *The College of the Bible Quarterly Bulletin*, 1923-24, p. 37. In a statement about the general philosophy of the curriculum found in the 1923-1924 issue of the catalogue, the ideas of Bower are clearly stated: "Wherever possible the student is given opportunity to work out his theoretical training in actual practice. In pastoral theology he prepares and delivers sermons under criticism. The students who preach have stated periods for conference where the concrete problems arising in the administration of their churches are discussed under faculty supervision. Students in religious education are given experience in the actual conduct of religious education."

52. *The College of the Bible Quarterly: Catalogue Issue, 1942-1943* 20 (January 1943): 40-41. That the liberal view of scriptural interpretation was still well entrenched in 1943 is evident in a description of a course on the Gospel of John which reads, "this gospel must be studied apart from the other three because its contribution is not in the realm of fact but of truth; not in the realm of history but of devotion." John is offered as "a bold recast of the synoptic story of Jesus in the light of universal Christian truth" (p. 42).

53. *The College of the Bible Quarterly: Catalogue Issue, 1942-1943* 20 (January 1943): 39, 42.

dryly as "a study," "a survey," "an investigation," with no hint of doxological perspective.[54]

In the early forties theology was still categorized in the "Doctrinal Field," though the rich currents of Christian theology of that time were given significant treatment in an array of courses focusing on problems or particular doctrines (man, God, sin, salvation, christology, etc.) as well as on such topics as fundamentalism and modernism, humanism and supernaturalism, and empirical theology. The works of Wieman and Barth and other leading interpreters of the Christian faith at that time received serious attention in the curriculum of the College of the Bible.[55]

Practical theology continued to develop. Worship particularly was becoming increasingly prominent in the courses listed. It was even possible by this time to have a course entitled the "Priestly Functions of the Minister," which included study not only of baptism and the Lord's Supper but also funerals, weddings, and ordinations. The growing dominance of psychology as a way of interpreting all of life is evident in a description of a course said to link the new social science with ancient human practice and to address the matter of "psychological experiences which worship should satisfy." The pastoral functions of the minister as well as church administration were also receiving greater attention. It would again appear that as the classic academic fields expanded in scope and in specialization, much the same occurred in the more "practical" fields as well.[56]

As the College of the Bible entered the fifties, an expansive, optimistic time for the churches of America, the school began to see itself in new ways. In 1950 it severed all ties with Transylvania and moved to a site opposite the University of Kentucky.

These were heady times. Enrollments were increasing annually. New buildings were being built. Calls for a new name reflecting the true character of the institution were finally enacted in 1965, when the College of the Bible became Lexington Theological Seminary. This was not a change merely of the sixties, however; it was a response to changes that had taken place in the second and third decades of the twentieth century. It took the College of the Bible almost forty years to realize the significance of what had happened in those tense days of 1917.

Curricular changes in the fifties and sixties were modest by comparison to what happened between 1917 and 1920. Faculty changes looked much the same in 1970 as they did in 1925, but in comparison to those of 1900 they were revolutionary. The changes to be seen in curricular offerings between 1930 and 1980 reflect the dominant streams of thought to be found in theological circles from decade to decade.

54. *The College of the Bible Quarterly: Catalogue Issue, 1961-1962* 38 (1961): 39-44. Curiously, this particular catalogue lists courses in Old Testament after the New Testament.
55. See *The College of the Bible Quarterly: Catalogue, 1942-1943* 20 (January 1943): 45-47.
56. *The College of the Bible Quarterly: Catalogue, 1942-1943* 20 (January 1943): 47-49.

Perhaps one of the greatest institutional changes is to be seen in the gradual move to accept the language of "theology" as opposed to "doctrine." This development was already evident in the twenties, and it continued through the decades. In the early sixties, theology was still subsumed under the heading "Doctrinal Field," but subdivisions used the word *theology* — as, for example, "systematic theology." By 1965, the year of the change in the name of the institution to Lexington *Theological* Seminary, the heading "Doctrinal Field" had been dropped, replaced by "Area of Theological Studies."[57] Except for specialized studies of recently developed schools of thought, the basic approach to theology seems to have changed only modestly since the 1920s. That is to say, the positive, liberal, ecumenical perspective that can be seen in 1925 continued in place over the next several decades.

Also of interest are the already noted changes with respect to the "doing" of ministry in the curriculum. There is a clear parallel between the increasing attention in the curriculum given over to issues of praxis on the one hand and the more narrow specialization of the traditional classical courses on the other. By the 1960s, just as the number of courses in Bible and theology had expanded significantly, so had the numbers of courses in practical ministry studies. In 1942, outside of Religious Education, there were thirteen courses listed under "Pastoral Theology." By 1965 there were forty-nine. During the same period, the number of courses offered in theology doubled, rising from fifteen to thirty.[58] It would seem that the educational philosophy encouraged by W. C. Bower as early as the teens continued to have a significant role at Lexington.

The College of the Bible/Lexington Theological Seminary has played a major role in the education of ministers for the Christian Church (Disciples of Christ). Although one cannot correlate the views of the faculty and the curriculum with those of the graduates of the institution, it is reasonable to assume that some of the views disseminated in courses, structures, and relationships have found their way into the ministry of those educated there.

The story of Lexington Theological Seminary and the Christian Church (Disciples of Christ) is one common to most mainstream American churches: a move from nineteenth-century conservative evangelicalism to an increasingly liberal stance. This change is seen in curriculum — both what is taught and how — and faculty, particularly where those faculty received their highest degrees.

For Lexington the change in curriculum is clear. So is the change in faculty. Every one of the early members of the faculty was a student of Alexander Campbell and Bethany College. Only in the waning years of the nineteenth century do we see a broader educational background. Since 1900

57. *The College of the Bible Quarterly: Catalogue Issue, 1960-1961* 37 (1960): 51; *The College of the Bible Quarterly: Catalogue Issue, 1964-1965* 41 (Summer 1964): 29.
58. *The College of the Bible Quarterly: Catalogue, 1942-1943* 20 (January 1943): 44-50; *The College of the Bible Quarterly: Catalog Issue, 1965-1966* 42 (Summer 1965): 27-32, 34-46.

the dominant sources of graduate education for full-time faculty at the College of the Bible have been those major interdenominational schools that have been the leaders in liberal theological education in America.[59]

The evolution of the College of the Bible into Lexington Theological Seminary reflects the experience of the Disciples over the past hundred years. No longer a frontier religious movement, the Disciples have become a church. No longer Bible colleges, their ministerial education schools have become theological seminaries.

59. The following table is a listing of schools attended at the graduate level by individuals who have had full-time faculty positions at the College of the Bible or Lexington Theological Seminary from 1865 to 1987. The Bethany listing comprises individuals who did not do any postgraduate work. Only institutions appearing five times or more are listed. The numbers reflect work done regardless of whether it led to a degree, and no distinction is made among graduate degrees that were awarded.

Institution	Number attending
College of the Bible	20
Yale	11
Chicago	10
Union/Columbia	7
Vanderbilt	6
Bethany	5
Harvard	5
Kentucky	5

Disciples Higher Education in the Age of the University

Virginia Lieson Brereton

Over the past hundred years the Disciples of Christ colleges have closely followed a script we might call "the fate of the denominational college in the twentieth century." The plot runs something like this: over the decades the colleges, originally creations of zealous religious leaders, distance themselves from the denomination. They choose trustees and presidents who are less likely to be ministers or even laypeople from the denomination, and they attract a progressively smaller proportion of students from the communion. Sometimes the break with the denomination becomes official, as the college pulls away from its associated denominational agency.

Other aspects of the plot include an attention to upgrading academic standards as determined by the accrediting agencies: the school builds up an endowment if it is able, collects a respectable library, selects a more specialized faculty that holds graduate degrees, especially Ph.D.'s, and that has done its graduate training outside the denominational educational orbit. Specialization affects the administration as well; the college amasses a bureaucracy — registrars, librarians, admissions officers, fund raisers, publicity experts, deans, and alumni directors. Along with loosening the denominational ties, the school secularizes: chapel becomes less frequent and less likely to be required; organized intramural athletics and Greek letter societies absorb an increasing amount of energy and attention; the religious organizations such as the Y's and the missionary bands lose their vitality and perhaps are discontinued. The twentieth-century proliferation of knowledge is reflected in replacement of the classical curriculum, in which Greek and Latin held so prominent a place, by a multiplication of subject offerings. Vocational and career courses become more prominent than in the past. The religious teaching content not only assumes a smaller place in the total curriculum, but often a part of it is removed into a separate graduate theological seminary.[1]

---

1. William C. Ringenberg lays out this "plotline" in *The Christian College: A History of Protestant Higher Education in America* (Grand Rapids: William B. Eerdmans, 1984); see also

Butler University illustrates some of these developments. In 1855 it opened as Northwestern Christian University in Indianapolis. Staffed by a handful of professors, it offered the typical old-time college curriculum: mathematics, the natural sciences, and above all heavy doses of the "ancient languages" — Greek and Latin. It also provided some vocational subjects: civil engineering and teacher training. As at the vast majority of other colleges, the students below the college level — that is, the preparatory students — far outnumbered the regular college students. Classes consisted largely of text recitations; as at other schools students found part of their intellectual stimulation not in the regular curriculum but rather in student-run literary societies, under whose auspices they debated, read current literature, and composed essays and plays.

One of the Northwestern's prime movers, Ovid Butler, hoped the new school would one day become a great Midwestern university. Early on, in 1877, the institution left behind its overt "Christian" identity by changing its name to Butler University. In the late seventies it acquired two medical schools. In 1891 Scot Butler, son of Ovid, became the first nonpastor president. In 1898 the university announced a three-year graduate seminary, Butler Bible College, the first such school among the Disciples. Between 1904 and 1906 Butler University raised $250,000 in endowment, $25,000 of it in non-Disciples money, a gift from Andrew Carnegie; by 1913 the endowment had climbed to $400,000. The presidents of the early twentieth century had Harvard and Chicago Ph.D.'s. Realizing that competitive athletics was one way to advertise the school, not least among the graduates, Butler went enthusiastically into organized sports. In fact, matters got out of control and in the early 1930s Butler was briefly dropped from North Central, its accrediting association, for athletics violations.

Butler, aided by its location in a growing city, followed the secularizing, upgrading script quite rapidly. This is not to say, however, that the plot did not have its twists and turns. In the late 1870s the Indiana State Christian Convention, alarmed lest it lose control of the institution, resolved that all future employees must be Disciples. But as a result of the ensuing outcry over this move, from Disciples and non-Disciples alike, the convention moderated its position to mandate enlarging the board of trustees to include more Disciples. In the 1890s the appointment of a European-trained higher critic, Hugh C. Garvin, to the Bible department came under such heavy attack from the *Indiana Christian*, among other sources, that the Bible School had to be closed in 1896 and Garvin "retired," despite support for him from the board and local university community.[2]

D. Duane Cummins, *The Disciples Colleges: A History* (St. Louis: CBP, 1987). Many of these developments are clear in the nondenominational liberal arts colleges; see George Peterson, *The New England College in the Age of the University* (Amherst, Mass.: Amherst College Press, 1964).

2. For a sketch of Butler history, see Henry K. Shaw, *Hoosier Disciples: A Comprehensive History of the Christian Churches (Disciples of Christ) in Indiana* (Bethany Press for the Association of the Christian Churches in Indiana, 1966).

Among the Disciples the story of secularizing forces and rising academic standards, though apparently an irreversible one, was not always a simple linear development. In almost pendulum style Hiram College in Ohio came under a succession of presidents who alternated emphases; one would stress the school's Disciples identity and its role in preparing ministers and dedicated laypersons; the next would concentrate on Hiram's standing in the larger academic universe. Occasionally Hiram attracted a leader who managed more or less to balance both focuses. Thus, in the Civil War and immediate post–Civil War period the school went from the helm of James Garfield and B. A. Hinsdale — men with their eyes on the broader educational world — to the presidency of E. V. Zollars (1888-1901), who devoted his energies to the training of preachers for the denomination. There followed Miner Lee Bates, who appears to have tried to balance the two poles, then Kenneth Brown (1930-1940), whose main inspiration came from experimentation being fostered elsewhere in collegiate education.

At some Disciples colleges the question of required chapel was not simply a matter of moving from more required to less required. They started with chapel that was voluntary though doubtless strongly recommended, then moved to compulsory chapel (was this a sign that students were starting to resist?), and eventually to voluntary chapel or no chapel at all. Nor did the campuses suffer a steady declension from pious beginnings: sometimes at a school's founding piety was more assumed than actively cultivated; at many schools the late nineteenth and early twentieth century — the high point of the YMCA and YWCA, the student missionary organizations, and the interest in popular Bible study — was in fact the most self-consciously religious period.

Phillips, founded in 1908 in Enid, Oklahoma, remained close to the Disciples churches in the Southwest well into the twentieth century. The first two presidents, Zollars and I. N. McCash, emphasized the training of pastors. The separation of undergraduate and graduate Bible courses did not occur until 1959, and the seminary remained legally a part of the university until very recently. Joe Jones, who became president in 1979, worked to bolster the school's distinctive Christian identity. Economic crisis intervened to produce one of those ironies common in the history of church schools. Faced with the possibility of the school's closing, Jones negotiated a sale–lease back agreement with the city of Enid. Phillips sold its campus to Enid for $14 million, then Enid rented the campus back to Phillips for a dollar a year. But in order for this arrangement to be permissible in the eyes of the courts, Phillips was required to allow its graduate seminary separate incorporation and, through a change in its covenant, to loosen its ties with the denomination. Thus, whatever Jones's original intentions, the secularization process at Phillips was accelerated by his measures.[3]

3. Conversation with Mark Toulouse, September 6, 1989. Mark Toulouse to Virginia Brereton, 1 May 1989. Mark Toulouse, "A Neglected Tide: A History of Dean England's Push toward Incorporation, 1953-59" (Paper delivered to the Seminary Council of Phillips Graduate Seminary, Enid, Okla., 22 October 1985).

As the rather late secularization timetable at Phillips may suggest, the Disciples schools did not proceed in lockstep with each other. Southern and western schools like Phillips, usually the later foundations, looked like old-time colleges longer than their counterparts in the Midwest. In the early twentieth century the North Central Association of Colleges and Secondary Schools had the reputation for being the most powerful and the most exacting among the accrediting agencies, and accordingly those midwestern Disciples schools that had the requisite resources fell into step earliest. The southern and western universities did not feel as much pressure from accrediting agencies until later.[4] The midwestern Disciples schools early realized that competition with the great state universities then in the process of formation was futile and settled for small college status. In Texas, where most of the public universities remained weak and underfunded, the support of larger Disciples universities such as Texas Christian University was feasible.

Various elements in the Disciples heritage simultaneously slowed and hastened the movement of denominational colleges on the route to modernity outlined above. First, among the retarding factors was the Disciples' traditional preference for training their ministers in colleges rather than in theological seminaries. Alexander Campbell had always argued against the preparation of pastors in separate educational institutions; he was convinced that this practice encouraged them to regard themselves as a class set apart, an inclination he wished to discourage. Thus, though in retrospect the move toward the establishment of graduate theological seminaries seems to have been unstoppable, Disciples were slower than members of other communions to join the seminary bandwagon. Even the College of the Bible, which as early as 1877 was a separate institution concentrating on the training of ministers — the closest thing to a seminary the Disciples had at the time — eschewed the granting of graduate degrees until 1915. One consequence of this relative reluctance to establish separate graduate divinity schools was that religion and the training of preachers remained an integral part of the Disciples college curriculums longer than at the colleges of other denominations. The result, as one would expect, was to delay the process of secularization.

Another factor retarding the march of Disciples colleges into modernity was lack of money. Modernization required generous funding. Disciples educators were not alone in crying poverty; no doubt most denominational college leaders lamented the reluctance of their denomination to support their schools as generously as they would have liked. But with Disciples the lament seems

4. To be sure, Phillips was in North Central territory and was accredited as early as 1919. It came under pressure in the twenties to increase its endowment, and in 1942 to raise low teacher salaries and increase funding for its library (Frank H. Marshall, *Phillips University's First Fifty Years,* 3 vols. [Enid, Okla.: Phillips University, 1957, 1960, 1967], 1: 84-85, 3: 49.

particularly prolonged and bitter. Ironically the most strenuous complaints came in the twenties when in fact Disciples support for their colleges seems under the prodding of the denomination's Board of Education to have become more generous. A survey done by the Council of Church Boards of Education at the request of the Disciples Board of Education in the early twenties complained about the "pauperization" of the colleges by the denomination.[5] A chart comparing "Investments in Education by Leading Communions" showed the Disciples trailing behind most of the major denominations.[6]

Whether or not Disciples really fell behind other established denominations in funding their colleges, they may well have had special reasons for feeling less attached to them. First, most of the early schools were the creations of Disciples individuals, not denominational organizations. Denominational loyalty to them was not automatically built in, except perhaps in the case of Bethany. Second, Disciples would have been uncomfortable with rhetoric about supporting their colleges in order to preserve their denominational identity; the call for denominational particularity clashed with their traditional "plea" that the church of Christ be unified.

On the other hand, the forces that propelled the Disciples colleges into the twentieth century were legion and in the end probably far outweighed the retarding ones. Traditionally Disciples had looked favorably on science and scientific method. The first college — Bacon — took its name from Francis Bacon. Bethany College from its beginnings had emphasized the natural sciences as well as the classical languages. In the 1860s James Garfield, as teacher and principal at Hiram, engaged in reconciling science and religion and introduced geology — that most troublesome of sciences — into the curriculum. The understandings of Campbell, Garfield, and others of science and scientific method differed from those of the twentieth century; nevertheless the basic tradition of sympathy for scientific pursuits predisposed the successors of these men to look favorably on new developments in science and to embrace the scientific spirit that permeated the new universities.[7]

The Disciples also claimed a tradition of free inquiry that accorded well with university ideals. From the time of Campbell, Disciples prided themselves on their championing of the freedom to think and teach and their tolerance toward the views of others. Campbell was frequently quoted in support of this ideal:

> it is safer and happier for society that the mind should be permitted to rest with full assurance only upon its own investigations, and that perfect freedom of

5. Board of Education Seventh Annual Report, 1922, p. 20. The author of the survey was Lura Beam.

6. Board of Education Fifth Annual Report, 1920, p. 24. This chart is somewhat suspect, since no apparent allowance was made for varying membership sizes of the various denominations.

7. For a discussion of Protestant ideas about science, see David Dwight Bozeman, *Protestants in an Age of Science* (Chapel Hill: University of North Carolina Press, 1977).

inquiry should be guaranteed to every man to reason, to examine and judge for himself on all subjects in the least involving his own present or future destiny, or that of society.[8]

President Cramblet of Bethany, invoking Campbell, wrote in 1936, "The effective Christian college for today and for the future must have this same fearless attitude toward truth, toward the spirit of free inquiry after truth."[9] In fact, faculty in Disciples colleges appear to have largely avoided conflicts over the teaching of evolution that disturbed other church colleges. The only times the prevailing ideology about free inquiry faltered was over a central issue for Disciples: how to approach the Bible. Between 1899 and the teens the Drake administration dismissed four higher biblical critics who had studied at Chicago or in Europe, including a head of the Bible College. One of the dismissed professors, Ambrose Dudley Veatch, complained to the Carnegie Foundation of his treatment and was reinstated. The other three were not so fortunate.[10] Nevertheless, even if Disciples sometimes violated their own ideal, it was there to be appealed to by teachers who felt their freedom to think and teach being abridged. It also was there to be reinforced by the doctrine of "academic freedom" imported by American university leaders as a result of their contact with German universities.

Since traditionally Disciples have maintained an antisectarian stance, their colleges have been loosely tied to the denomination. Occasional attempts by the church to control them more closely have usually failed. At times college leaders have worked hard to serve the needs of the denomination, most notably in preparing ministers but also in turning out loyal laypersons, but they have done so voluntarily rather than under obligation. The relatively light denominational yoke has meant that school administrators have been freer than most to take their schools in the directions urged by accrediting agencies and prevailing educational norms.

Then too, Disciples have long prided themselves on their pioneer origins; they are conscious of the fact that they were the first sizable religious group bred on the American frontier rather than in Europe. No doubt the frontier ideology has become partly nostalgic myth, but all the same it has remained very powerful. One of its components has been a boast by Disciples about their pioneer inventiveness, their readiness to use new methods to accomplish what needs to be done, their openness to novel ideas. Would-be educational reformers and innovators among the Disciples have been able to appeal to this "pioneer" spirit. Since at the turn of the century the standards of the university and the increasingly secular society represented the new and the daring in

8. Campbell, quoted by W. H. Cramblet, in "The Second Century: A Challenge," in *Educational Beginnings and Present Problems* (Indianapolis: College Association of Disciples of Christ and Department of Higher Education of the United Christian Missionary Society, 1936), p. 25.

9. Cramblet, "The Second Century," p. 25.

10. Charles J. Ritchey, *Drake University through Seventy-Five Years, 1881-1956* (Des Moines: Drake University, 1956), pp. 136-44.

higher education, many Disciples were disposed by their heritage to fall into step behind them.

SURVIVING IN THE AGE OF THE UNIVERSITY

So far I have told an unexceptional story about the Disciples colleges: held back by some factors, propelled forward by others, they behaved pretty much as did other denominational colleges in the age of the university: as nearly as possible they came up to the standards of the university. Though many Disciples colleges had their triumphs — winning accreditation, attracting substantial Carnegie or Rockefeller money — they all had to adjust in some way to the inescapable reality of life in the twentieth century: very few denominational schools would ever be able to catch up with the public colleges and universities in the areas of enrollment, wealth, and physical equipment.

Accommodation to the new facts of life came hard. True, church colleges founded in the nineteenth century had traditionally been small and struggling, but to be tiny and penurious was not so painful when most of one's counterparts were likewise struggling. Also, when a school offered the only opportunity for advanced education in its area, its leaders did not have to worry overmuch about their reason for being. Clearly they served the community, supplying a higher education that people would otherwise have lacked. Their chief worry was not purpose but rather survival.

The growth and expansion of the universities, especially the state universities, in the late nineteenth century completely altered this situation. The universities introduced different criteria for excellence, usually criteria having little to do with the presence of religion in the curriculum. In fact, some state universities, because they equated religion and sectarianism, avoided the teaching of religion at all. They drew away the young people of all the denominations, including of course Disciples young people. By the nineties most of the state universities were still weak and rudimentary, but religious-education leaders could easily see the shape of the future. While enrollments at many denominational colleges were stagnating or even declining, the numbers at public universities were mounting. By 1920 the Board of Education reported that 6.87 percent of students in fifteen large state universities were Disciples.[11] And in 1929 a survey found that "During recent years the enrolments of state-supported institutions have been increasing much more rapidly than the enrolments of institutions supported by religious bodies."[12] Denominational

11. Board of Education Fifth Annual Report, 1920, p. 34.
12. Floyd W. Reeves and John Dale Russell, *College Organization and Administration: A Report Based upon a Series of Surveys of Church Colleges* (Indianapolis: Board of Education, Disciples of Christ, 1929), p. 25.

colleges could strive to raise their standards and achieve accreditation, but they could hardly hope to compete with the public universities as long as the latter defined the criteria of excellence.

Perhaps because they appreciated the virtues of the universities, Disciples seem to have been unusually inventive in discovering ways to live within an educational world dominated by these institutions. First, they came up with educational programs located near the university and designed to supplement university work — the Bible chair, intended mostly for undergraduates; the divinity house at a graduate level; and the school of religion that combined the functions of the first two. These supplemental institutions probably represent the Disciples' most original contribution to American higher education in the twentieth century. Second, in conjunction with other denominational educators, they redefined the role of the small religious college, so that it was seen as providing an education distinctly different from what the universities and larger colleges were capable of offering.

THE BIBLE CHAIRS

As Disciples educators watched a substantial proportion of their college-age young people go off to what many of them thought of as the "godless" state universities, they worried about losing them forever. One remedy they came up with was to follow Disciples students onto the campuses through the vehicle of the Bible chair. The term usually described one or two Disciples instructors, often housed in a special building of their own on or adjacent to the university campus. They offered classes in subjects such as Bible study, methods of Christian work, and New Testament Greek at low cost to all interested undergraduates. In some cases these classes eventually qualified for university credit and their instructors received faculty status.

The idea of the Bible chair was not a new one. Thomas Jefferson had envisioned some arrangement of this sort on the University of Virginia campus early in the nineteenth century; each sect would be able to instruct its own adherents at the university. Leonard Bacon at Yale suggested a similar institution in the 1880s. But the Disciples were the first actually to try out the idea. The early chairs were financed by the Christian Women's Board of Missions, which regarded them as mission projects in the pagan land of the state university. In 1893 they set up a first chair at the University of Michigan in Ann Arbor. It seems strange that the CWBM chose Michigan, since the state contained relatively few Disciples. Apparently the Ann Arbor pastor was the first to make the plea for such a chair. More important, in the early nineties Michigan was regarded as the foremost state university in the country: why not try the experiment there? The first occupants of the chair were Herbert Willett and Clinton Lockhart, who taught "scientific and practical" courses in

Old and New Testament (especially popular were courses in the life of Christ and methods of Christian work). They stayed for only a year (Willett went on to become dean of the Disciples Divinity House at Chicago) and were followed by G. P. Coler (1896-1913) and Thomas Iden, who stayed until the chair was terminated in 1932. Other chairs were set up at the University of Missouri (1896), University of Virginia (1899), University of Kansas (1900), University of Texas (1905), and the University of Indiana (1910).[13]

The Bible chairs achieved qualified success. Undoubtedly they benefited from the turn-of-the-century swell of interest in English Bible study.[14] At times they attracted impressive enrollments. In 1911 the Kansas Bible Chair enrolled 400. The Michigan instructor carried on a correspondence course from 1899 to 1909 that attracted such a large number of subscribers — three thousand in September 1902 — that he had to abandon the effort. Some chairs, such as the one at the University of Virginia, were partly endowed. Eventually other denominations set up their own Bible chairs, including the Churches of Christ after their break with the Disciples.

In a sense the very popularity of the Bible chairs led to their decline. While the efforts of other denominations to set up their own chairs was flattering, they also drew students away from the original chair. Though the achievement of university credit and faculty status for the Bible chair offered obvious advantages, it also had its nether side. G. P. Coler, the longtime occupant of the Michigan chair, never made any effort to gain credit for his courses, nor did his successor. In a letter to Frank L. Jewett of the Texas Bible Chair, Coler explained the dangers of too cozy a relationship with the university. If the instructor joined the faculty, he wrote, he "may become a mere part of the university machinery and not be disposed to become a positive moral and spiritual force in the community." The "Bible chair effort," he added, should be "characterized by intelligent, but rugged moral and spiritual initiative. . . . We cannot afford to make entangling alliances."[15]

Of course, the reverse side of an "entangling" relationship with the university was a hostile one, and Coler seems to have encountered this too. He wrote of two "enemies" on the faculty, one of whom "represent[s] our work as lacking in scholarship." President Angell, he claimed, had not paid more than lip service to the Bible chair effort: "He has never commended our work to the students and never will," Coler lamented, and compared the Michigan president's lukewarm attitude with the enthusiasm of Chancellor Strong at the University of Kansas. Even B. A. Hinsdale, a former president of Hiram and now a University of Michigan professor, refused to help: "He never used his

13. Ronald B. Flowers, "The Bible Chair Movement in the Disciples of Christ Tradition: Attempts to Teach Religion in State Universities" (Ph.D. diss., University of Iowa, 1957).

14. The Y.M.C.A. enjoyed a peak enrollment of 50,000 in its Bible classes in 1908 (Frederick Nile Harper, "The Thought and Work of Harrison S. Elliott" [Ed.D. diss., Columbia University, 1964], p. 45).

15. Coler to Frank L. Jewett, 19 January 1907 (Disciples of Christ Historical Society).

influence in behalf of our work, and his casual remarks about it were against us." The most sympathetic professors on the Michigan faculty were in fact not Disciples.[16]

Even the religious organizations on campus were hostile. Coler complained that "Ever since the fall of 1902, officers and committees of the S.C.A [Student Christian Association], the Y.M.C.A. and the Y.W.C.A. have met me with coolness. I am sure that I have given no just excuse for this change in their attitude toward our work; and I am equally sure that outside influences are operative."[17] Other problems presented themselves. When the Bible Chair consisted of only one instructor, as was often the case, his character and teaching ability were crucial. Apparently Coler had his weaknesses. A report characterized him and his work: "Mr. Coler's courses are not practical. . . . Sweet-spirit, everybody loves him. Not offering kind of course to attract anybody."[18] Coler himself complained that when he arrived in Ann Arbor he was neither prepared in Bible study nor had he been a pastor. Yet he was expected to teach Bible and pastor the Ann Arbor church, a crushing burden. He added that he was not a "very good public speaker" either.[19]

Probably the greatest difficulty of all came when the university created its own department of religion. This happened at Michigan in 1925, and surely contributed to the Bible chair's demise in 1932 (the Depression delivered the final blow). An optimist might say that the establishment of a religion department represented a final triumph for the Disciples: the Bible chair had successfully filled a vacuum in religious instruction until university leaders realized its value and made it part of the regular curriculum; its obsolescence in fact constituted the ultimate seal of its success. The more skeptical might point out that the teaching in an academic religion department was a far cry from the more pious, practical approach of the typical Bible chair occupants. Even when the Bible chairs provided the seeds for a later university religion department, the progeny often looked very different from the parents.

DEFENDING THE SMALL RELIGIOUS COLLEGE

The creation and funding of the Bible chairs caused some Disciples educators to protest that scarce resources were being drained away from the colleges, which could ill afford it.[20] Certainly they felt embattled as they saw the public

16. Coler to "Sr. Atkinson," 31 January 1905 (Disciples of Christ Historical Society).

17. Coler to "Bro. Jennings," 29 January 1912 (Disciples of Christ Historical Society).

18. Author and date unknown, report on the Disciples' work at Michigan (Disciples of Christ Historical Society).

19. Coler to "Sr. Atkinson," 31 January 1905.

20. A supporter of the Bible chairs observed that "Many of our colleges felt that if the Christian Women's Board of Missions had money to put into professors for teaching the Bible,

and private universities steal away some of the best of their students and faculty. "Is there really any place today in our educational system for the small church college?" asked Miner Lee Bates, president of Hiram, in 1913.[21] Over the next few decades his query, with minor variations, became a key question for Disciples educators.

Of course, the public answer to Bates's question was always a resounding Yes, except perhaps when Disciples educators were referring to the very weakest of their colleges. And indeed, these educators developed a rationale for the continued existence of their colleges and an argument for why Disciples should continue and even increase their support for them. At the core of their arguments was the discovery of virtue in the very fact of smallness. And in fact, by the twenties and thirties, the rest of the educational world was inclined to agree with them. By this time, the original glamour and excitement of the new universities had worn thin; their drawbacks were beginning to be apparent — a large anonymous student body in which individuals could get lost, an elective curriculum with no apparent integrating principles, a faculty more devoted to research than to teaching students. Some educators were beginning to feel nostalgia for the best elements of the old-time classical college of the nineteenth century. By 1927, Frederick Rudolph notes, "a mythology had developed around the vanished small colleges of the nineteenth century."[22] The philanthropic organizations that had been instrumental in the spread of the university standards began to fear that their efforts had resulted in curricular dead-ends and started financing educational innovations designed to counter the worst effects of the educational innovations they had so lately fostered.[23]

The leaders of small religious colleges were quick to pick up on the criticism of the universities and the nostalgia for the old colleges. Since few small colleges had graduate departments, they argued, teachers were free to focus most of their attention on undergraduates. While the small college teachers were well-trained scholars, they did not make the discovery of new knowledge their top priority. Rather, they focused on teaching. Furthermore, students in small colleges could count on ample individual attention from their teachers. This extra attention would not only aid their academic performance but would also strengthen them as they struggled toward emotional, religious, and moral maturity. The small college faculty was selected not only for its academic training; teachers were also chosen for their characters. In 1913

---

they should put it into our own colleges. They missed entirely our viewpoint. We were doing real missionary work, we felt, when we gave to the State Universities the opportunity of Bible teaching from an entirely non-sectarian standpoint" ("ARA" to the Committee on Proposed Bible College, Lawrence, Kansas, 6 March 1916 [Disciples of Christ Historical Society]).

21. Bates, "The Function and Future of Our Colleges," *Bulletin of Hiram College* 6 (December 1913): 6.

22. Rudolph, *Curriculum: A History of the American Undergraduate Course of Study* (San Francisco: Jossey-Bass, 1977), p. 277.

23. Rudolph, *Curriculum*, p. 226.

Miner Lee Bates praised the small church college faculty for offering "intimate companionship, counsel and oversight of men in whom broad scholarship, Christian faith and consecrated life form a consistent whole." Through its faculty, the small religious college offered "conditions favorable to the growth of the moral and religious sentiments and to the culture of definite Christian convictions and purposes." The small college, he continued, provided "intimate association of the students and all members of the faculty."[24] President Hieronymus of Eureka wrote, "education is defective which does not inspire right living, which does not make for private and public morality. . . . We aim at high scholarship, but do not neglect the weightier matter of high character."[25] In 1938 President Eugene Stephen Briggs of Phillips University declared that

> Phillips believes that Christian teachers are indispensable to the Republic. No amount of intellectual achievement unaccompanied by character and moral balance can guarantee the safety and welfare of a people. We believe that teachers with a sane view of life and activated by Christian principles are the greatest (single) factor in the proper guidance of youth, with the one possible exception of right-thinking parents.[26]

Even as late as 1950, Hiram College's historian, Mary Treudley, insisted that "character has always been valued at Hiram more highly than brilliant intellectual ability or outstanding worldly success."[27] At its best, then, the small church college furnished a moral and religious environment in a higher educational world largely devoid of such concerns; it shouldered the old-time college's task of concentrating on the moral and religious dimensions of student development.

Such a college, the argument continued, could also provide the curricular unity that was so clearly missing at the large universities. But this contention had to be muted. Since the small colleges had embraced many of the same subjects and departmental divisions as the universities, they found themselves grappling with many of the same problems of coherence. Nevertheless, President Riley B. Montgomery of Lynchburg College made bold to claim in 1947 that the Christian college "guides the students through the confusing maze of knowledge to some constructive principles and Christian conclusions. The

24. Bates, "The Function and Future of Our Colleges," pp. 5 and 7. Riley B. Montgomery, president of Lynchburg College in Virginia, echoed Bates's drift when he wrote that the faculty of Christian colleges ought to have "wholesome personalities," and "must be persons of positive Christian faith who of their own volition are active and useful members of the working church. Their lives should always give strong testimony to the things of religion for which the college stands" ("Educating toward a Christian World," address delivered at the Buffalo International Convention of Disciples of Christ, 31 July 1947, p. 11).

25. Hieronymus, quoted by Harold Adams, in *History of Eureka College* (Eureka, Ill.: Board of Trustees of Eureka College, 1982), p. 127.

26. Briggs, quoted by Marshall, in *Phillips University's First Fifty Years,* 3: 27.

27. Treudley, *Prelude to the Future: The First Hundred Years of Hiram College* (New York: Association Press, 1950), p. 39.

Christian college has a philosophy of life that is based upon Christian teaching and it is obligated to reveal in positive fashion the relation of all knowledge and all problems to this Christian philosophy." The faculty member should make sure this happens; he "should in his teaching field relate effectively the subject he teaches to vital Christian truth and religious life."[28] Presumably Arthur Braden, president of Transylvania University, was attempting to do this when in 1930 he offered a course entitled "The Bible and Civilization," "in which an effort was made to interpret civilization and progress from the Christian viewpoint."[29]

In the twenties the leaders of small colleges began to articulate another rationale for their existence. Because of the smallness of their institutions, they claimed they were ideally placed to try out educational innovations.[30] The twenties and thirties turned out to be a fruitful period for educational experiment, at the small college as well as at the university level. Many of the ideas spawned by the small colleges were aimed at enhancing the virtues they already claimed for themselves — fostering even more contact between faculty and students and channeling more faculty attention to individual students. Leaders of Disciples colleges did not originate most of these educational experiments, but, given their frontier image of themselves, they tended to be receptive to new ideas and kept their antennae out for promising departures.

One such promising area was freshman orientation. In 1911 Reed College initiated a class on how to function in college for its incoming freshmen. Other schools followed Reed's lead, some providing their freshmen with orientation classes in Western civilization or contemporary problems. By 1920 colleges were offering over a hundred general orientation courses for freshmen. One of those who introduced this innovation to Disciples education was J. C. Miller, dean and later president of Christian College in Columbia, Missouri. Miller was the logical Disciples educator for such a role, for he had written his 1930 doctoral dissertation on "The Induction and Adaptation of College Freshmen."[31] Cloyd Goodnight, president of Bethany 1919-1932, set up a week of orientation for freshmen prior to the opening of school and also assigned first-year students to faculty advisers.[32] In 1926 Transylvania came up with a "General Culture Unit" for freshmen and sophomores.[33]

Another widely celebrated small college innovation was the honors program which had been tried out originally at Swarthmore College. Swarth-

28. Montgomery, "Educating toward a Christian World," p. 7.

29. See John D. Wright, *Transylvania: Tutor to the West* (Lexington: University Press of Kentucky, 1980), p. 370.

30. *Time* magazine said, "Small colleges, like small countries, are often more fertile of ideas than big ones" (28 December 1936, p. 23).

31. Reeves and Russell, *College Organization and Administration,* p. 117.

32. W. K. Woolery, *Bethany Years* (Cincinnati: Standard Publishing, 1941).

33. Reeves and Russell, *College Organization and Administration,* p. 117; and Wright, *Transylvania,* p. 369.

more's experiment was funded by the General Education Board. Beginning in 1922, it offered its most able students a special program made up of seminars, tutorials, and exemption from the usual tests and exams; it required of them a written thesis and comprehensive written and oral examinations. The Swarthmore experiment inspired imitation. By 1930, ninety-three colleges had adopted honors programs. Advocates saw the honors program, among other things, as a way to give promising students more individual attention. Bethany College under President Perry Gresham tried out the idea of honors seminars, though not until 1961.[34]

One aspect of the Swarthmore honors program — the comprehensive examinations — was itself an innovation. In the nineteenth century, senior examinations had been oral and were designed mostly for public consumption (the exam was a public affair). In 1916 Harvard introduced written comprehensive examinations for its seniors. Hiram initiated comprehensive exams for seniors during the thirties. In the same decade Bethany introduced exams at the end of the sophomore year to test for mastery of general knowledge and another set of exams during the senior year to check for competency in the major field.

Another innovation of the early twentieth century was the two-year junior college. In 1900 there were only six such colleges; between 1909 and 1923, 173 were established, according to one count.[35] Between the early teens and late twenties Transylvania maintained Hamilton College, a two-year school for women, the first two-year college in Kentucky.[36] The junior college form was an ideal solution for Disciples colleges with very small or nonexistent junior and senior classes. They simply narrowed the scope of their efforts and declared themselves junior colleges. Christian College took this route, for instance, as did William Woods College.

Of the Disciples colleges, Hiram and Bethany seem to have tried out new educational ideas original with them, or at least not clearly borrowed from an already existing curricular bandwagon. Most likely these two old, relatively stable institutions were best able to assume the risks of new educational ventures.

Hiram's best-known experiment, the "Hiram Study Plan," had its beginnings in 1930, with the appointment of Kenneth I. Brown as president. Born in Brooklyn, Brown received a B.A. from Rochester and a Ph.D. in English from Harvard. Immediately before coming to Hiram he had been teaching English at Stephens College, which was then well known for its experiments in the education of women.[37] Brown received a mandate to change Hiram's curriculum; he recalled that the trustees told him just prior to his arrival,

34. James W. Carty, Jr., and David Lynn C. Hobe, *The Gresham Years* (Bethany, W.Va.: Bethany College, 1970), p. 18.

35. Reeves and Russell, *College Organization and Administration,* p. 254.

36. Wright, *Transylvania,* p. 276.

37. See Treudley, *Prelude to the Future,* p. 215.

We make no apology for Hiram's past. But we do aspire to a stronger future. We hope that Hiram will continue to remain a small college, but it is our dream that in some small way she may find a means of doing her educational task or a portion of that task with an extra measure of success, so that at least in some area she may enjoy uniqueness. . . . We do not ask you to seek new ways for their own sake. We should be happy, however, if the faculty and administration of our small college were able to blaze new trails which others might count worthy of following.[38]

Some of the faculty had been restless for curricular changes as well but had found their peers unwilling. The would-be reformers explained to Brown that the previous president (Miner Bates) had "tried hard enough to get them to agree to do something that would make Hiram different, and he never succeeded."[39] The Hiram Study Plan developed out of summer school courses designed by a group within the faculty and offered in the summers 1931-33. Instead of taking two or more courses, students enrolled for only one "intensive" course that met every day during the summer term. Though the summer school, introduced in the Depression years, failed after three years, the majority of the Hiram faculty was converted to the idea of intensive courses and voted to introduce them into the regular curriculum.

The intensive study plan remedied several problems faculty and students had complained of in the standard curriculum. First, when students had to take four or five courses concurrently, their time and attention seemed to be fragmented; they had a hard time studying anything in depth, and their teachers ended up competing with each other for their time and energy. Furthermore, students had no time in their schedules for such special events as field trips, special conferences, or speakers. Their days were strictly regimented by the ringing of the bell.

What Brown and his colleagues did was arrange the school year into four terms of nine weeks each. Each term students chose a course that met every day between nine-thirty and four-thirty. The exact use of class time was up to the professor and students. There could be a lecture or discussion in the morning, with student conferences in the afternoon, or perhaps a field trip, a movie, or a laboratory. In addition, a "running" or continuing course met for an hour at eight a.m. three days a week; the rationale was that subjects such as the study of languages did not lend themselves very well to the intensive format.

Intensive study offered several advantages. The faculty had the opportunity to try out new and varied teaching approaches. They got to know their students better, since they had only one class that met daily. With fewer students at any given time to care for, they could give individuals more help and

38. Kenneth I. Brown, *A Campus Decade: The Hiram Study Plan of Intensive Courses, 1930-1940* (Chicago: University of Chicago Press, 1940), p. 8.
39. Brown, *A Campus Decade,* p. 31.

attention. The Hiram Study Plan also had public relations value: it stirred up considerable excitement in the educational world in the late thirties and also seemed to attract students who otherwise might not have chosen Hiram.[40] Two other Disciples colleges followed Hiram's lead: Eureka and Chapman. In 1941 Transylvania adopted a four-quarter calendar, with two to three courses per term and each class meeting for seventy-five minutes per day six days a week.[41]

Whatever its successes, the plan also had its weaknesses. Most prominently, it was difficult to fit in physical education and sports. Theoretically the late afternoon was reserved for this part of the students' program, but the physical education staff had difficulty handling the whole student body in such a concentrated time slot. Scheduling student employment was also a problem. Further, the "running" courses proved vexatious: teachers of these courses complained that students neglected them, and students complained about the early hour at which they met — especially the Saturday morning classes. Not all faculty took advantage of the opportunity to try out new pedagogies, and uninspired teaching was especially glaring in the intensive setting. More muted were worries about whether students could absorb so much material in nine weeks and whether they would remain interested in one subject for so long. Under this program juniors and seniors often went for as long as a term or two without contact with professors in their major fields.[42]

Some of the opportunities offered by the Hiram Study Plan simply went begging because of lack of money to implement them. Hiram chronically suffered from shortage of funds, but especially so during the Depression of the thirties. In 1938, however, the Carnegie Corporation gave the school $7,500 "toward support" of Hiram's "reorganization program." Hiram used these funds for several projects, among them budgets for movies and supplemental library purchases. The most successful project made possible by the Carnegie funding was one called the "English conference." Under it the college provided extra help and attention for promising students who were handicapped by poor reading and writing skills. Constance McCullough came to Hiram from the University of Minnesota to direct the program. The students, whose need for the program was determined by a standardized test, took three classes a week (during the running course hour) and also met for a half-hour conference every week. Hiram leaders

40. For some of the publicity, see Kenneth I. Brown, "A One-Course Study Plan," *Journal of Higher Education* 5 (June 1934): 323-26; "Shall Education Be Served Whole or Hashed?" *Graphic Survey* (July 1934); and "The Hiram Study Plan," *School and Society,* 30 October 1937, pp. 1-3. See also "Midnight Oil and Black Coffee Passé at Hiram Now," *Cleveland Plain Dealer,* 19 December 1936; "Hiram Plan," *Time,* 28 December 1936, p. 23; Alvin Silverman, "Hiram's Democracy Marks Her Campus," *Cleveland Plain Dealer,* 4 October 1937; "Study Plan for Relieving College Pressure," *Christian Science Monitor,* 2 November 1937.

41. Wright, *Transylvania,* p. 372.

42. On the Hiram Study Plan, see Brown, *A Campus Decade;* a series of reports in *From Hiram* 4 (January-April 1937); Harold E. Davis, "The Single Course Plan of Instruction," *Bulletin of Hiram College* 33 (December 1941): 196-207; Arthur H. Benedict, "The Hiram Study Plan: A Quarter Century of Experimentation," *Bulletin of Hiram College* 49 (August 1957): 1-7.

regarded this program as so successful — test scores went up dramatically — that they continued to budget for it after the Carnegie money had run out. This attention to the "remedial" reading and writing needs of students, though it would become a standard feature of later college programs, was unusually enlightened at the time. To be sure, "bonehead" English — for athletes and slow students — had been around for a long time, but was regarded as a necessary evil. A genuine interest in creative methods of dealing with student deficiencies, a remedial class that was treated as a worthwhile pursuit in and of itself, was an unusual development in the undergraduate curriculum of the time.[43]

Bethany also tried new directions, though its era of greatest experimentation came under the administration of Perry Gresham, who arrived only in 1952. A graduate of Texas Christian University and Brite Divinity School, Gresham had taught philosophy at TCU and filled several prominent pastorates. Summers he had attended the Disciples Divinity House at Chicago and also Columbia and Union Theological Seminary in New York. One emphasis introduced by Gresham, "Education for Responsible Citizenship," was meant to give training to a few select liberal arts and preprofessional students in "the nature and art of politics at local, state and federal levels in preparation for responsible citizenship. . . ."[44] The citizenship program involved internships in government, mostly at the state and local level, field trips, workshops, seminars, and visiting speakers. Some of the conferences and seminars involved the participation of businessmen, citizens, and politicians, as well as the students.

In 1968 Bethany under Gresham adopted the 4-1-4 or January term plan. This academic schedule had first been tried at Florida Presbyterian College in the early sixties and by 1972 had been incorporated into the academic calendars of five hundred colleges.[45] Like many other plans, the Bethany January term provided opportunities for students to take a single concentrated course at Bethany, do independent study, engage in work-study, or spend the term at another campus. Among the Bethany courses in 1972 were a course in "Tropical Ecology" that took students to Puerto Rico, the Virgin Islands, and the Florida Everglades; an offering in photography "as applied to biological sciences"; a course in "Hebraic Sources of Western Civilization" that involved travel in Greece and Palestine; and a course in the "Stock Market."

One thing might surprise observers of Disciples colleges. Alexander Campbell's inclusion of Bible teaching as part of the curriculum at Bethany was an innovation, and instructors at other Disciples colleges followed Campbell's

43. See Brown, *A Campus Decade,* pp. 94-95.
44. Bethany College *Bulletin,* 1962-63, pp. 78-79.
45. James R. Davis, "The Changing College Calendar," *Journal of Higher Education* 43 (February 1972): 145. Davis notes, "Oddly enough, a calendar of successive seven-week courses had been in existence at Hiram College for thiry years, long before the 4-1-4 had become popular" (p. 146).

example in giving Bible instruction a prominent place in the curriculum. Given this beginning, one might expect a tradition of innovation and creativity in the teaching of Scripture to undergraduates. Outside the Disciples fold there was a great deal of ferment, especially at the turn of the century, surrounding the subject of how to teach the Bible, particularly to a popular audience. At the fundamentalist Bible schools considerable attention was paid to *methods* of teaching the Bible; New York Theological Seminary was built on a single man's notion of how the Bible could most effectively be taught; and the first generation of higher biblical critics (W. R. Harper preeminently) expended a great deal of effort on the task of explaining their insights to a general audience. But one looks in vain for a similar preoccupation among Disciples Bible teachers of undergraduates. An observer can look at the Bible lectures of E. V. Zollars (president of Hiram, TCU, and founder of Phillips) and read the outlines of G. P. Coler (occupant of the Michigan Bible chair) and Arthur Braden (occupant of the Kansas Bible Chair and president of Chapman College and Transylvania University) without finding anything much that is new in approaches to teaching the Bible. There is a suggestion that Kenneth I. Brown, president of Hiram from 1930 to 1940, had unusual success in teaching the Bible to undergraduates before he came to Hiram, but he does not mention it in either of his books.[46] A 1928 report contains a tantalizing allusion to a Conference of Bible Teachers in connection with the Board of Education meeting at which the teachers discussed such questions as "What shall be the content of Bible courses? How shall Bible courses be related to courses in other departments of the college?" But we have no indication of how they answered these questions, or whether the answers actually affected Disciples college Bible classes.[47] Probably much of the creative energy went into higher critical scholarship. Coler at Michigan hinted that Herbert Willett, who occupied the Bible chair for only a year, had been widely admired as a teacher. But his tenure in that position was brief, and it is difficult to know much about his teaching approach or technique with the Michigan undergraduates.[48]

In the end one is inclined to ask in what ways the Disciples' approach to higher education was uniquely theirs. Hiram's Study Plan was a new departure, and the Bible chair represented a true innovation, an attempt to accommodate the

46. Treudley, *Prelude to the Future,* p. 215.
47. Board of Education Thirteenth Annual Report, 1928, p. 13.
48. Certainly Willett achieved a reputation for popularizing the higher critical teachings, but he accomplished this outside the confines of the undergraduate curriculum. He wrote *The Life and Teaching of Jesus* (1898) just before his year at Michigan. It seems reasonable to suppose that he used some of this material in his Bible Chair classes. The book mixes higher critical concerns about the dating of the Gospels and the historical context of Jesus' life with a thorough-going piety: "No students of the world's life or literature can evade his [Jesus'] personality" (p. 16); "To study the life of Christ is an act of worship" (p. 17).

new facts of life. Yet it is difficult to evade the fact that Disciples educators in the twentieth century have not differed greatly in their ideas or activities from their counterparts in other denominations. To be sure, the earliest schools of the denomination were distinctive, especially Bacon with its overwhelmingly practical emphases and Bethany with its Bible instruction at the center of its curriculum and its unusually heavy concentration on the natural sciences. Of course, in 1840 when Bethany was founded, Disciples were still proud of an identity as a "peculiar people." By the late nineteenth century, however, many of them had grown weary of peculiarity. And such was the impact of the university, the power of the philanthropic foundations with their thousands of dollars, and the clout of the regional accrediting associations with their insistence on uniform standards, that most church colleges with the wherewithal began to resemble each other and the secular liberal arts colleges. Phillips University educators used to joke about their slogan: "Fear God and obey the North Central."[49] Like most jokes it had a serious core, capturing the sense of conflict experienced by twentieth-century church educators. The glaring reality of the twentieth-century history has been the effectiveness of the secular society and culture in shaping the educational agenda of the mainline churches. That act of shaping has made for an ambiguous legacy.

49. Marshall, *Phillips University's First Fifty Years,* 2: 38.

Identity and Unity: Disciples Church Education

J. Cy Rowell and Jack L. Seymour

Christian religious education has been a theological battleground in the Disciples of Christ. In any noncredal church, education naturally reflects conflict because it is the place where denominational theology is taught to future generations.

The Disciples of Christ have been committed to and have given leadership to ecumenical Christian religious education. When the *Survey of Service* noted with pride in 1928 that the "Disciples of Christ, through the department of religious education are standing in the very van of the cooperative movement," the authors were speaking the truth.[1] The influence of Disciples on the field and profession of Christian religious education has been great.

Since the 1870s Disciples have provided leadership and scholarship for ecumenical religious education. The names of many leaders who were Disciples can be recognized: Francis M. Green, who wrote an early and widely praised Sunday school manual; Isaac Errett and J. H. Garrison, who provided model curricula; Robert Hopkins, who served as American secretary of the World's Sunday School Association; Cynthia Pearl Maus, who was an innovator in youth ministry; Hazel Lewis, who embodied ecumenical curriculum goals; Roy G. Ross, who served as executive secretary of the International Council of Religious Education and later executive for the National Council of Churches in the U.S.A. (NCC); Ray L. Henthorne, who chaired the Cooperative Curriculum Project for the NCC; and Robert F. Glover, who was an architect of Joint Educational Development.

In scholarship the contribution of the Disciples was significant as religious education became an academic discipline. Walter S. Athearn, a professor at both Drake and Boston Universities, helped set early standards for religious education. William Clayton Bower of the College of the Bible and the University of Chicago was one of the leading architects of progressive

---

1. *Survey of Service: Organizations Represented in the International Convention of Disciples of Christ* (St. Louis: Christian Board of Publication, 1928), p. 212.

religious education theory. Harry C. Munro was responsible for leadership training within the International Council.[2]

Through these efforts, the identity and boundaries of the Disciples of Christ were also shaped. Evangelical and spiritual depth were complemented with commitments to responsible citizenship; to scientific research on education, personality development, and society; and to reason in the religious life. Those who shared these commitments became the "mainstream."

At the same time, Disciples have addressed themselves to distinctively Disciples educational concerns. Our thesis is that developments in Christian religious education over the last hundred years evidence an enduring tension in the Disciples of Christ between unity and identity, or, in other words, between a commitment to ecumenical Christianity and a search for particular identity.[3] Recognition of the evidence of this continuing tension in the history of Disciples Christian religious education will help Disciples identify a challenge that needs to be addressed as they look to the future — the challenge to maintain an ecumenical witness while continuing to struggle with the issue of a particular identity.[4]

CONTRIBUTIONS TO RELIGIOUS EDUCATION

The history of Protestant Christian religious education is normally divided into four periods: (1) the Sunday school movement (1860-1910), from the acceptance of the Sunday school as an agency of the church to its challenge as an effective instructional agency; (2) progressive religious education (1903-1940), from the founding of the Religious Education Association to its challenge by neo-orthodox educators; (3) Christian education (1940-1965), from the beginnings of neo-orthodox Christian education to the completion of the Cooperative Curriculum Project of the NCC; and (4) church education (1965 to the present).[5]

When the history of Disciples Christian religious education is examined against this outline, it becomes apparent that Disciples have had significant

2. Unlike Athearn and Bower, whose careers were primarily academic, Munro was an editor, ecumenical executive, and professor. See Carol Ann Munro, "Progressive Theories for Christian Education: A Discussion of the Writings of Harry C. Munro," *Discipliana* 44 (Spring 1984): 8-10.

3. See W. E. Garrison and A. T. DeGroot, *The Disciples of Christ: A History* (St. Louis: Christian Board of Publication, 1948), p. 430. We agree with Garrison and DeGroot, who identify this tension as central for the life of the denomination.

4. We would like to thank David Otto (Peabody College, Vanderbilt University) and Allen Harris (Brite Divinity School, Texas Christian University), who assisted with research for this essay. We would also like to thank the executives of the department of Christian Education (Division of Homeland Ministries) and the Local Church Curriculum Division (Christian Board of Publication) and a host of retired educators who graciously shared their observations and insights with us. This essay describes and comments on the history of Disciples education as reflected in published reports by the church's leadership rather than focusing on congregational studies.

5. For a periodization of the field of Christian religious education, see chapter one of Jack L. Seymour, *From Sunday School to Church School: Continuities in Protestant Church Education in the United States, 1860-1927* (Washington: University Press of America, 1982).

influence in the larger history of Protestant Christian religious education and that as a consequence of the character of that influence the outline of their own story differs in one respect from the outline of the larger story. During the Sunday school period, because of their polity, Disciples contributed as individuals rather than as a denomination. A second period of Disciples education dates from the founding of the Christian Board of Publication in 1910 and the establishment of "official" Disciples religious education. In that period, Disciples were key leaders in the theory and practice of progressive religious education — so much so that the influence of the later neo-orthodox religious education period in Protestant Christian religious education was minor among Disciples. A third period dates from the late 1950s, during which Disciples continued as key leaders administering ecumenical church education.[6]

SUNDAY SCHOOL PERIOD (1874-1910)

Disciples initially rejected the Sunday school. Alexander and Thomas Campbell and Barton Stone opposed it as sectarian. Stone believed that associations such as the American Sunday School Union promoted division by advocating curricula that used Bible lesson books and catechisms instead of the Bible. These founders believed the Sunday school interfered with the rightful place of the family and the Bible in Christian instruction.[7]

Gradually, however, as they observed the Sunday school and heard Sunday school leaders call for Christian unity, Disciples accepted it. In 1847 Alexander Campbell explicitly affirmed the work of the Sunday school as an agency of evangelism and growth in biblical faith. Moreover, in 1849 the Sunday school was commended by the General Convention of the Disciples meeting in Cincinnati.[8] Disciples thus joined other evangelical Protestant communions in efforts to expand the Sunday school.

Evangelism was the foremost commitment during this period. The Sunday school was called the "nursery of the church" for good reason. Over seventy percent of new members came to the church through the Sunday school.[9] Moreover, the teaching of the Sunday school focused on the Bible. Biblical criticism entered the church only toward the end of the period, and

6. For the purpose of this study, we organize the periods of Disciples education as follows: (1) Sunday school movement (1874-1910), from the first International Sunday School lesson series printed by a Disciple to the founding of the Christian Board of Publication; (2) Religious education (1910-1954), from the founding of the Christian Board to Roy G. Ross's acceptance of leadership of the NCC; and (3) Church education (1954 to the present).

7. For the story of the early involvement of the Disciples founders in the Sunday school, see John Ralph Scudder, "A History of Disciple Theories of Religious Education," *The College of the Bible Quarterly* 40 (April 1963): 9-15; and *The Disciples and Religious Education,* ed. William Clayton Bower and Roy G. Ross (St. Louis: Christian Board of Publication, 1936), pp. 23-37.

8. Scudder, "A History of Disciple Theories of Religious Education," pp. 15-18.

9. Seymour, *From Sunday School to Church School,* pp. 25-78.

evangelical Protestants were still united in a common approach to teaching the Bible to promote morality. The rally, rather than the classroom, was the model of Sunday school instruction until the turn of the century. Enthusiasm and evangelism united Protestants (laity in greater numbers than clergy) across denominational boundaries.

By 1872, when the Interdenominational Sunday School Convention approved its uniform lesson plan as a strategy for Bible study throughout U.S. Protestantism, the Disciples ranked fifth in size of Sunday school participation. Almost immediately Disciples contributed to this plan. Because of their unique polity, Disciples did not establish official denominational curriculum agencies to prepare and market resources, as did Methodists and Baptists. However, series for Disciples were created by their leaders: Isaac Errett began in 1874 a series in *The Christian Standard,* and a year later J. H. Garrison followed with an alternative in *The Christian.*[10]

Errett himself was an interdenominational leader during the Sunday school period, participating in International Sunday School conventions. He served from 1884 to 1890 on the International Lesson Committee and was followed until 1908 by B. B. Tyler, who was later elected president for the Tenth International Sunday School Convention. Disciples also contributed through their writings to interdenominational education: Francis Green, who had joined Errett in 1876 to edit *The Teacher's Mentor,* wrote a manual for Sunday school work, *The Standard Manual for Sunday School Workers,* which was highly praised by the *Sunday School Times,* a leading interdenominational magazine.[11] Other teacher training manuals by W. W. Dowling, Herbert Moniger, and Marion Stevenson followed.

An analysis of these contributions, however, shows the tension between unity and identity in the Disciples. Unity was fueled by an evangelistic Sunday school theology that seemed for a time to unite all Protestants. Divisive theological insights remained outside the Sunday school. Denominational distinctiveness was also recognized and honored. Even though the International Lesson Committee divided the Bible into seven-year periods of study, each denomination had freedom to produce its own resources and teacher training helps for its own members. Sunday school conventions focused on educational strategies that extended Sunday school work rather than on theology.

A commitment to unity in the late nineteenth century meant evangelistic unity. Errett described the Sunday school as "the door through which the children may be led to the Bible schools of the family and the church where they shall be taught more, much more than the Sunday school, however good, can possibly afford."[12] As an evangelistic agency, the Sunday school brought people into congregations where they were provided with specific instruction.

10. Scudder, "A History of Disciple Theories of Religious Education," pp. 34, 37-38.
11. Scudder, "A History of Disciple Theories of Religious Education," pp. 38-41.
12. *The Christian Standard,* 13 January 1877, p. 12.

The concern with identity is clearly seen in Green's *Standard Manual*, which is markedly different from another well-respected manual, *The Modern Sunday School* by John H. Vincent, a leader in Methodist Sunday school work and chair of the International Lesson Committee until 1896.[13] While their pedagogical advice is almost identical, Green devotes much less space to it — only sixty pages; the other 130 pages are given over to an "apologetic" about biblical "doctrine" for Sunday school teachers.[14] Sunday school instruction for Green was about "the religion of the New Testament," by which he meant moral and dogmatic teachings, "ceremonial commands" about baptism and ordinances of worship, and historical facts about Jesus and the church.[15] Green's work expressed the need to declare a specific identity.

When issues of biblical criticism, the Social Gospel movement, experimentalism in education, and liberal Protestant theology began to "sneak" into interdenominational discussions about the Sunday school and "religious" education, those involved in education were themselves split. The Religious Education Association (REA), founded in Chicago in 1903, became the forum for new ideas. These "liberals" called for graded Sunday school lessons and the opening of the Sunday school to biblical criticism. By contrast, evangelicals supported the traditions of the International Sunday School Association.

Disciples were caught in these forces. Prior to 1900 all who called themselves Disciples were able to work within the International Sunday School Convention system as independent people and congregations in a loose association to assist themselves by expanding the influence of the Sunday school. But when the purpose of Sunday school began to shift from evangelism to instruction, hard questions about unity had to be faced. During the Sunday school period, the commitment to unity seemed easier. Denominations tended to cooperate at a surface level that did not challenge their special identity. However, as an agency of "liberal" instruction, the church school "meddled" with congregational theology and with denominational identity. Some within the Disciples went the way of the "progressives" to genuine ecumenical cooperation and openness about instructional content. This group laid the foundation on which present-day Disciples education was built.

RELIGIOUS EDUCATION (1910-1954)

Garrison and DeGroot in their denominational history accurately note that religious education "is one field, perhaps *the* one, in which Disciples have

---

13. Vincent, *The Modern Sunday School,* rev. ed. (New York: Eaton and Mains, 1900).
14. Green, *The Standard Manual for Sunday School Workers* (Cincinnati: Chase & Hall, 1878), pp. v-vi.
15. Green, *The Standard Manual for Sunday School Workers,* pp. 7-8.

contributed with distinction to the common store of scholarly and important religious literature."[16] Without question, after Disciples were officially organized in religious education, they became a leading force in the field. However, the tension between unity and identity was further strained.

From their beginning in 1910 the Christian Board of Publication and the Bible School Department of the American Christian Missionary Society were committed to ecumenical participation in progressive religious education. Disciples served in leadership positions in the ecumenical educational agencies, and the scholarship of Disciples led the field in its self-definition. In fact, *The Christian-Evangelist* was one of the earliest magazines to publish the new religious education scholarship.[17] Progressive educational theory, with the parallel "liberal" theology committed to democracy, openness, and public responsibility, became troublesome for the forces of identity, who began to operate competing structures.

The Disciples' contributions to ecumenical religious education are evident in three areas: their leadership in the International Council of Religious Education, their scholarly writing in progressive religious education theory, and their embodiment of progressive curriculum theory.

1. During the first fifteen years of the twentieth century, there was an uneasy relationship between leaders in church education. Attempts to improve the Sunday school by shifting its focus from evangelism and Bible content to instruction based on research in human development divided the forces in religious education. Progressive educators founded the Religious Education Association with the express intent of relating the church's educational work to research and scholarship in education and biblical criticism. Denominational leaders organized the Sunday School Council of Evangelical Denominations in 1910 to gain denominational control of the Sunday school so that it could be improved. However, International Sunday School Association members sought to hold onto the "evangelistic" gains they had made through the uniform lesson system.

Through this conflict Walter S. Athearn was a bridge. He chaired the committee that brought a plan for union for the three educational associations. Another Disciple, Robert Hopkins, the secretary of the Bible School Department (later called the Religious Education Department), also served on the committee. In 1922 these three competitive organizations were united into the International Council of Religious Education.[18] With this act, the forces of church education were united under the "progressive" banner.

2. Disciples led in the formation of the philosophy of progressive re-

16. Garrison and DeGroot, *The Disciples of Christ,* p. 546.
17. See George Albert Coe, "The New Era in Religious Education," *The Christian-Evangelist,* 5 February 1903, p. 109.
18. See Walter S. Athearn, *Report of the Committee on Education of the International Sunday School Council of Religious Education* (Kansas City: International Sunday School Council of Religious Education, 1922).

ligious education. They were in the forefront of establishing academic chairs and programs in religious education, beginning at the College of the Bible in 1909.[19]

Athearn chaired REA committees on teacher training and the correlation of the educational agencies of the local church.[20] The reports of these committees led to setting standards for the *church* (not Sunday) school — standards that were embodied by the Disciples in their "Front Rank" standard of efficiency. Moreover, Athearn popularized an innovation of weekday released-time education begun in a Disciples congregation in Gary, Indiana, which led to the cooperation of church and public schools in providing time during the week for religious instruction.

William Clayton Bower, however, was the pivotal force in the movement. Along with George Albert Coe, a Methodist who taught at Northwestern, Union Theological Seminary, and Teachers College (NY), Bower shaped the theory for religious education. His program at the University of Chicago trained many. Theoretically, he advocated focusing religious education on the "religious" nature of human beings and relating the experimental work in education and John Dewey's experiential method to church education. Moreover, he led the effort to coordinate agencies in the church which were involved in education, and to relate religious education to efforts in local communities for education for social responsibility and citizenship.[21] Bower chaired many committees for the REA and the International Council as well as for the Disciples. His ideas about the coordination of the educational agencies of the church were influential when the Disciples formed the United Christian Missionary Society (UCMS) and reorganized and unified Christian education work in 1935 and 1944.[22] These ideas also helped the Disciples focus educational efforts on social issues.[23]

19. A list of chairs and programs can be found in *Disciples of Christ Silver Anniversary of Religious Education* (St. Louis: Department of Religious Education, 1936), pp. 37-38.

20. See, for example, Walter S. Athearn, "Teacher Training Commission of the Religious Education Association," *Religious Education* 7 (April 1912): 81-87; and "The Church School: Report of the Committee on the 'Correlation of the Educational Agencies of the Local Church,'" *Religious Education* 8 (April 1913): 32-47.

21. For a discussion of Bower's contribution, see chap. 4 of Jack L. Seymour, Robert T. O'Gorman, and Charles R. Foster's *The Church in the Education of the Public: Refocusing the Task of Religious Education* (Nashville: Abingdon Press, 1984). Bower summarized his ideas in "Religious Education for Our Day," *Christian-Evangelist*, 6 December 1934, pp. 1, 4.

22. See *Report of the Commission on Educational Coordination* submitted to the International Convention of Disciples of Christ, 1934, and *Report of the Commission to Study Christian Education*, submitted to the Board of Higher Education, Christian Board of Publication, the United Christian Missionary Society, and the International Convention, 1945.

23. Regarding the need for social change, see *Disciples of Christ Silver Anniversary of Religious Education;* on issues of racism in education, see Mrs. John A. Towns, "Americans — Brown and White," in *International Convention of Disciples of Christ, Kansas City, Mo., October 12-18, 1936* (St. Louis: Christian Board of Publication, 1936), pp. 134-38. Also of interest in this regard is the interracial leadership represented in the early stages of the International Christian Youth Fellowship Commission.

3. The Disciples curriculum embodied the work of ecumenical progressive agencies of religious education. Throughout the 1920s the International Council of Religious Education worked to define the elements of a progressive curriculum. In particular, they worked to define how religion was made manifest in life and what life settings had to be addressed to transform a person's thinking and acting in faithful ways.[24] The economic collapse of 1929 seriously hampered extending the report into practice, however.

Nevertheless, for Disciples, Hazel Lewis, a leader of children's education who had worked on the background research for the International Council, continued to be involved in the development of curriculum materials.[25] Her contributions helped to ensure that the Disciples curriculum was directly influenced by progressive theory and research. While not as experiential as Bower would have liked, the Bethany Series still became the paradigm for progressive curricula. Its openness to scholarship and its basis in life experience was so great that Disciples continued to improve it into the 1950s when many other denominations turned to neo-orthodox curricula with a heavy focus on church history and doctrinal theology.[26]

Disciples thus embodied their commitment to unity (i.e., ecumenical cooperation). But at the same time, serious questions were being raised about identity. Some forces within the Disciples even feared that the church was losing its way and its commitment to being the "New Testament" church.[27]

Examples of the identity conflict are clearly evident in the *Christian Standard* in the period when it still claimed to be a Disciples journal.[28] Progressive developments in religious education were directly challenged by essays claiming, for instance, that "Our subject is not religious education, but Christian education. . . . Any system of education that dethrones Christ and enthrones the authority

24. See *The Development of a Curriculum of Religious Education,* ed. Paul H. Vieth (Chicago: International Council of Religious Education, 1930).

25. See Scudder, "A History of Disciple Theories of Religious Education," pp. 49-51, 71. See also Glenn McRae, "Fifty Years of Curriculum Production for Christian Churches," *Bethany Guide* 34 (May 1960): 4-5, 32; *The Experience-Centered Method,* Bethany Church School Guide Reprint, no. 7 (St. Louis: Christian Board of Publication, n.d.); and Hazel Lewis, *Bethany Primary Department Manual* (St. Louis: Christian Board of Publication, 1944).

26. The Methodist Episcopal Church joined the Disciples in declining to develop an explicitly neo-orthodox curriculum series. The paradigm for neo-orthodox education is the Presbyterian Christian Faith and Life Series. For a comprehensive treatment of this series, see William Bean Kennedy, "The Genesis and Development of the Christian Faith and Life Series" (Ph.D. diss., Yale University, 1950).

27. Although there was an identifiable "strict restorationist" group since at least 1927, when the North American Christian Convention met for the first time, a distinct public listing of the "Christian Churches and Churches of Christ" did not appear until 1971 in the *Yearbook of American Churches.* See Garrison and DeGroot, *The Disciples of Christ,* pp. 437, 526; and William E. Tucker and Lester G. McAllister, *Journey in Faith: A History of the Christian Church (Disciples of Christ)* (St. Louis: Bethany Press, 1975), pp. 33, 386. Through much of the 1920s and 1930s both "ecumenical" Disciples and strict restorationists called themselves Disciples.

28. See, for example, Isaac Errett, "What the Disciples Believe and Practice," *Christian Standard,* 16 August 1924, p. 5.

of inner consciousness is anti-Christian."[29] Experience-centered curricula were challenged as a fallacy unable to deal with the profound social changes of the 1930s. A contrasting style called "creative indoctrination" was advocated.[30]

In the early 1940s both the United Christian Missionary Society and Standard Publishing Company participated with forty other denominations and agencies in the United Christian Education Advance program of the International Council. A comparison of the themes of each evidences a concern for theological identity.[31] For UCMS the program focused on "reaching the unreached," Bible study, family life, peace, leadership education, world mission, stewardship, and curriculum production. The material emphasized the need for transformation in a warring world and the cooperation of Christians. At Standard Publishing Company the advance focused on church improvement, effective teaching, adequate equipment, evangelism, "scriptural indoctrination," "Christ-centered nurture," church loyalty, the Christian home, and moral influence in the community.

During the period of progressive religious education, the tensions between ecumenical unity and denominational identity came to the forefront. The identity that continues in present Disciples education was worked out with openness to the Protestant ecumenical movement. Disciples educators defined an identity committed to ecumenical cooperation.

CHURCH EDUCATION (1954-1988)

Christian religious education among the Disciples in the 1950s was shaped, in part, by continuing involvement in what then was called "interdenominational cooperation." During the 1950-51 church year, for example, Disciples participated in interdenominational conferences on adult education, the education of parents, and a summer workshop for local church directors of religious education where a third of those present were Disciples and the dean, for the third year, was Gentry Shelton, a Disciples director.[32] Several annual reports of the Division of Home Missions and Christian Education of UCMS in this decade noted that "the division gave substantial financial and leadership support" to many interdenom-

29. Mrs. Ira M. Boswell, "Christian Education," *Christian Standard,* 23 August 1924, p. 16. See also Frederick J. Gielow, Jr., "Religious Education versus Christian Education," *Christian Standard,* 20 April 1929, pp. 5-6.

30. See Clarence R. Athearn, "Experience-Centered Curriculum versus Creative Indoctrination," *Christian Standard,* 12 March 1932, pp. 3-4, 6.

31. Note the contrast between the Division of Christian Education's *Christian Education: The Church's Answer to the Savior's Concern for Today's World* (Indianapolis: United Christian Missionary Society, 1943) and *Christian Education Advance: Manual Simplified Program* (Cincinnati: Standard Publishing, n.d.). See also "It Is Time for Christian Education Advance!" *Christian Standard,* 6 September 1941, pp. 3-4; and Roy G. Ross, "Momentous Years," *Christian Standard,* 21 February 1942, pp. 7-8, 23.

32. *1951 Yearbook of the International Convention of Disciples of Christ* (Indianapolis: International Convention of Disciples of Christ, 1951), pp. 40-41.

inational agencies. "Through such participation" during the 1958-59 church year, it was reported, "the division strengthened the Disciples of Christ interest in the ecumenical movement and made available to the brotherhood the composite services of the major Protestant movements in this country."[33]

In this period the Bethany Graded Lessons were revised.[34] These were popular resources. Christian Board of Publication reported that in 1953 the sale of Bethany Graded Lessons, Uniform Lessons, and other courses were "the largest in the history of the Board. Statistics indicated that churches whose enrollment constitutes more than 68% of the church school enrollment of the Disciples of Christ use Bethany materials."[35] In the report for 1954 the percentage had increased to 76 percent. The growth of curriculum sales directly reflected the growth in church school enrollment in these years.

In 1945 Disciples church school enrollment in the United States and Canada was 1,013,679. The modern high was recorded in 1958 with 1,280,000, after which enrollment continued to drop, to 915,813 in 1963. After that the trend briefly reversed, recovering to 1,100,476 in 1966. Subsequent to that year, church school enrollment has declined almost every year — for example, to 383,141 in 1976, 328,325 in 1980, and 314,257 in 1985.[36] The post-1966 decline in church school enrollment is attributable, in part, to the 1968 decision to restructure the denomination, after which "approximately 3,200 congregations with an estimated membership of 650,000 took legal action to withdraw from the fellowship."[37]

Intentional efforts to help the Disciples deal with their particular identity as a North American denomination found expression in 1954 with the publication of *Choosing the Way,* a new resource for a "pastor's class" in church membership with a leader's guide and a pupil's book.[38] Historical identity was

33. *1959 Yearbook of Christian Churches* (Indianapolis: International Convention of Christian Churches [Disciples of Christ], 1959), p. 240.

34. While the Bethany Graded Lesson series was based on interdenominationally produced outlines, the series was essentially denominationally edited and produced. The primary and junior series of the 1960s was produced cooperatively with the American Baptists and Church of the Brethren, but it incorporated denominational specifics, such as separate missionary units.

35. *1954 Yearbook of the Christian Churches (Disciples of Christ)* (Indianapolis: International Convention of Disciples of Christ, 1954), p. 42.

36. All of the above statistics are from Christian Church *Yearbooks* except for the 1985 figures, which are from a CPB document. It is difficult to get accurate statistics for comparative purposes. The 1981 *Yearbook* (with 1980 figures) was the last modern *Yearbook* to report church school *enrollment.* Beginning with the 1982 *Yearbook* (1981 statistics) only average attendance in church school is reported. The average church school attendance in 1981 was 205,140 and has continued an overall decline to 180,484 in 1988.

37. Tucker and McAllister, *Journey in Faith,* p. 386.

38. This first "pastor's class" curriculum resource was followed in 1965 by *The Christian Way: Tracing the Covenant* in 1974, *Community of the Called* in 1981, and *Called to be Disciples* in 1988. Appropriately, all these resources pay specific attention to Disciples history, beliefs, and polity. In general the 1954, 1965, and 1974 courses place the Disciples in the context of the larger Christian community with little specific reference to the ecumenical movement or ecumenical cooperation. By contrast, the older youth/adult book in the 1981 series has a prominent ecumenical emphasis, as does the 1988 series, which makes extensive use of ecumenical references and sources.

also an intentional part of the Bethany Graded Lessons. A new youth series launched in the mid-1950s included a seventh-grade course, *My Church* (1955), on general church history with a Disciples emphasis. A twelfth-grade course, *Our Church's Story* (1961), was a study of church history for Disciples with an emphasis on the ecumenical movement.

By the end of the 1950s, ecumenical movements were under way that profoundly shaped Christian education among the Disciples.[39] The most far-reaching change took place in the way curriculum resources were conceived and developed. Beginning in the late 1950s, the National Council of Churches undertook a fresh exploration of issues in curriculum theory. Ultimately that effort led to a December 1960 meeting in St. Louis attended by representatives of twelve denominations. By March 1961 the Cooperative Curriculum Project (CCP) was a reality; it eventually included sixteen denominations. Its executive was a Disciple, Ray L. Henthorne, a CBP youth editor. On the eve of the creation of the CCP, Marvin E. Smith, director of the local church curriculum division of CBP, wrote of the significance of this new cooperative undertaking:

> It marks the first co-operative attempt of Christian educators to go beyond the planning of a curriculum for a particular age group or materials for a particular functional area of church work. Instead, a curriculum will be planned which will reflect the whole life, work, and faith of the church, as well as the whole lifetime needs of the individual. Second, it will be the first effort to involve all the functional groups and/or agencies that plan educational activities for the church.[40]

The CCP produced an overall curriculum design incorporating a single objective, five curriculum areas, and a "learning tasks" approach to teaching and learning — all set in the context of the church as a worshiping, witnessing, and nurturing community. The formal report of the CCP was published as *The Church's Educational Ministry: A Curriculum Plan* (1965). The forces of the Protestant educational mainstream were fortified through the CCP effort.

Following the completion of the CCP, each denomination used the findings as it saw fit. In 1964 the Disciples established the Disciples Cur-

---

39. As ecumenical movements impacted Disciples Christian education in this period, changes also occurred in traditional Disciples programs and structures of Christian education. For example, during the early 1950s the summer camp and conference program that had from its beginning been planned and administered as an integral part of the "national" program of Christian education was modified by state Disciples programs. A significant shift involved the transformation of the summer conference into a basic Christian education program open to all youth rather than a leadership education program for selected youth delegates. During this period the old Christian education age-level "field staff" model in which state directors of Christian education were considered the "field staff" of the Department of Religious Education of the UCMS and paid in part by national funds began to disappear under the initiative of state organizations. The first state Christian education staff who were not age-level specialists and not paid by UCMS funds were individuals employed in Missouri and Kentucky in 1957 and 1958.

40. Smith, "From the Editor: Historic Step in Protestant Curriculum Planning," *Bethany Guide* 35 (March 1961): 1.

riculum Project to develop a curriculum plan based on the CCP. The involvement of personnel from the total church (beyond editors and Department of
Christian Education staff) was aimed at producing a "churchwide" curriculum. The comprehensive focus of the ensuing Christian Life Curriculum
(CLC) was seen in the production of resources for church school, the home,
men and women's groups, youth fellowships, and retreat settings. The church
school materials constituted the interdenominational component of the Disciples project and were developed in cooperation with the American Baptists
and Church of the Brethren.[41] The CLC was launched in the fall of 1969 and
concluded in August 1978.

The CLC was a bold experiment in churchwide education. It was very
likely the most comprehensive, imaginative, and sophisticated set of resources
the Disciples have ever published. It was an expensive project both financially
and in staff time. Unfortunately the church school series was not popular for
various reasons. Reflecting on the history of the CLC, one editor observed that

> All of the CCP, the Disciple Curriculum Project and the development of the
> Christian Life Curriculum Project and the development of the Christian Life
> Curriculum took place in the turbulent decade of the sixties. The social revolution
> taking place outside the church had in time a profound impact on what was
> expected to happen inside.

And another editor said about the Christian Life Curriculum,

> This phase of curriculum development came along at about the same time that
> church school attendance began its downward slide. There are some who were
> willing to blame the curriculum resources for that decline but it parallels the
> decline that was taking place in most other "mainline" denominations. It may
> not be blameless but to make it carry the whole burden is scapegoating.[42]

One difficulty in producing curriculum resources is that decisions have
to be made far in advance of the anticipated termination of the existing
resources. Those decisions are also made in the context of what is occurring
in the life of the general church and society at that time. When the CLC was

41. In his study of the Christian Life Curriculum, Alan Mace raises the identity/ecumenical
question: "The Christian Church (Disciples of Christ) is an example of a church which has not
been significantly involved in independent curriculum development since the inception of CCP in
the early 1960s. Thus, for two decades it has not held actual control over the 'orthodoxy' of the
curricula used in Christian education by its member congregations. The question of theological
and educational consistency seems to be appropriate for the Christian Church (Disciples of
Christ). . . . For the future of the Christian Church (Disciples of Christ), it is important that its
curricular materials be consistent with its understood theological position." Mace's study gives
particular attention to the "consistency of the theological position of the Christian Church (Disciples of Christ)," and what he calls "the underlying curricular belief system of the Christian Life
Curriculum." He concludes that they were "substantially consistent" ("Curriculum Development
in Christian Education" [Ed.D. diss., George Peabody College for Teachers of Vanderbilt University, 1983], 7-8, 120-22).

42. Quotations from correspondence of retired CBP editors to J. Cy Rowell.

envisioned in the mid-1960s, there was genuine concern for the nature and mission of the church and concern for the wholeness of congregational life. By the mid-1970s, before the planned nine-year life span of CLC had been completed, new goals and problems were emerging that were to affect the planning of any future curriculum. One such factor was the optimism over the future of the ecumenical movement, especially as represented in the Consultation on Church Union (COCU). There was also concern that the mainline churches were in trouble and needed each other more than they had in the past.[43]

In the late 1960s, another new ecumenical partnership in Christian education emerged, initiated by the United Church of Christ, the Episcopal Church, and the United Presbyterian Church in the U.S.A. The result was Joint Educational Development (JED), an ecumenical structure that saw itself as a "process" by which partner denominations could work together on specific projects or task forces. In 1969 the Disciples became a JED partner, providing general staff persons who were to hold leadership positions in JED and the curriculum project.[44]

In time, the development of church school resources became the largest JED project. The new curriculum plan was Christian Education: Shared Approaches, offering four approaches to program and resources. By 1974 the Disciples decided to participate in the new CE:SA curriculum (launched in September 1978 and concluded in August 1988). In making this decision, the Christian education executives chose not to return (after the completion of CLC) to the Disciples' traditional pattern of a denominationally designed and produced curriculum, as was advocated by some.[45] In fact, CE:SA seemed to communicate that denominational differences were insignificant.

43. A *major* factor in moving the Disciples and other denominations toward the ecumenical production of curriculum resources is clearly financial, especially when curriculum sales are declining. Small and middle-size denominations simply cannot publish materials alone that will be as price-competitive as materials produced together. The competition is not so much with the two largest denominations — the Southern Baptist Convention (Disciples as a rule do not use SBC materials because of theological differences) and United Methodist Church (although UMC materials are popular in Disciples congregations) — as it is with the independent or commercial publishers.

44. Robert F. Glover, executive of the Department of Christian Education, chaired the JED Executive Committee 1977-81, after having served as secretary (1971-72), vice chair (1973-75), and acting chair (1974). Ray L. Henthorne, a CBP editor, was staff associate (half-time) for Christian Education: Shared Approaches, the new JED curriculum plan, from 1975 to 1977.

45. Shortly after the 1968 restructure action, a decision was made to terminate all existing denomination-wide general planning processes, including the Curriculum and Program Council that had been in place since 1953. However, there were some Christian education planning conferences jointly sponsored by the Department of Christian Education and CBP; the last one was held in 1982. It can be argued that the absence of "official" planning structures during the 1970s meant that curriculum decisions were being made by "unit" staff without direct input from a more representative body. The need for intentional planning was recognized in the late 1980s. Since 1987 there has been a series of conferences that will shape future Disciples planning: the March 1987 "reappraising" conference at Christian Theological Seminary, the 1-5 June 1988 Lexington Conference, the 28 February–2 March 1989 Christian education strategy session, and the 16-18 April 1989 CTS Conference.

One dream of CE:SA was that leadership education in congregations and regions might be done ecumenically, since the JED-related congregations would be using the same resources. The dream was realized to some extent in the early years of CE:SA. In general, however, CE:SA was not well received. Enrollments in church school, Vacation Church School, and summer conferences continued to decline. There was a dramatic loss in curriculum sales. The Disciples experience with CE:SA may have been best summed up by a Christian education professor who, reflecting on the Disciples history of being at the center of ecumenical development in education, commented that "Developments in JED and the CE:SA curriculum were the climax of that trend. The response of the churches to the shared approach has been, at least to some extent, a sort of ho-hum reaction."[46]

The modern period of Disciples Christian education was a time of significant change. Developments in curriculum design and production, although not the only events deserving attention here, graphically illustrate the quest of Disciples Christian religious education for the church's distinctive identity in the midst of a commitment to unity.

REFLECTIONS

THE SEARCH FOR IDENTITY

The history of the Disciples in Christian religious education has given evidence of tension in the church — the tension between commitments to unity and identity. Today the question for all mainstream churches is how to be committed to both unity and identity. As Disciples with a commitment to openness and unity, the task is to remain a public denomination, honoring the distinctiveness of the denomination within an ecumenical context. Martin Marty, in his contemporary classic *Public Church,* identifies public churches as both passionately open to others and passionately committed to their distinctiveness.[47] Disciples would do well to consider this identity.

The history of Disciples education points to the importance of examining the distinctive identifying marks that the Disciples contribute to the mainstream. The commitment to unity must remain while the denomination continues to define its identity with greater clarity. In other words, Disciples education will falter without a clear definition of its identity, including a commitment to ecumenical partnership. That is the challenge this educational history lays before the church.

---

46. From correspondence of a Disciples retired seminary Christian education professor to J. Cy Rowell.

47. Martin E. Marty, *Public Church: Mainline–Evangelical–Catholic* (New York: Crossroads, 1981), pp. 167-69.

MARKS OF IDENTITY

Some of the distinctive marks of Disciples identity are historical and theological; others have to do with worship practices and polity concerns. At the same time, the history of Disciples Christian religious education has contributed to the denomination's distinctiveness. Disciples "marks of identity" are more than theological doctrines; they include a style of education itself.

1. *Democracy.* The Disciples have demonstrated a commitment to what historically has been called "indigenous religious education."[48] This entails, in part, a recognition of the authority and responsibility that congregations (and regions) have in developing their own approach to Christian religious education. At the same time, they are dependent on others for appropriate resources, leadership education events, and cooperative programs that benefit congregations. The "democratization" of Christian religious education took a dramatic turn in the post-restructure period as the regions assumed more responsibility for planning programs and servicing the needs of congregations. In its best moments, the democratic approach to Christian religious education has produced innovative programs and resources; at other times, it has produced fragmentation and competition.

2. *Openness.* Disciples education historically has been open to new knowledge, has prized experimentation, and has emphasized reason over emotion. Disciples program planners and editors have welcomed new insights in personality and faith development, learning theory, and teaching methodologies. Disciples educators have also welcomed the culture's contribution to knowledge as a source of content in the curriculum. While there have been both liberal and conservative critiques of new knowledge and disputes over its appropriate use in Christian religious education, on balance the Disciples have been open to new insights from the sciences and the humanities.

3. *Unity.* Disciples have championed unity in two different senses. First, they have been significant leaders in the ecumenical planning and development of Christian education resources and programs. To this point, Disciples educators have seen their work as contributing to the unity of the church through cooperation. Second, Disciples education, especially with regard to the content of curriculum resources, has stressed the unity of the church and the need for Disciples to be open to the contributions and witness of the larger Christian community.

4. *Responsible Citizenship.* The Disciples understanding of the task of Christian education in relation to the life of the Christian has included an emphasis on Christians being responsible and intelligent citizens. Current events and social issues are topics frequently found in curriculum resources. Because of its attempts to avoid a sect-like dichotomy between citizenship and

---

48. See George Oliver Taylor, "Fifty Years of Christian Education Service," *Bethany Guide* 34 (May 1960): 6-7, 32-33.

faith, the Disciples emphasis on responsible citizenship has sometimes been perceived as equating the Christian faith with citizenship.

5. *Baptism and Communion.* The immersion of believers following their profession of faith and the weekly observance of the Lord's Supper are characteristic marks of the Disciples. How the educational program of the Disciples appropriately deals with these historic identifying marks in the midst of ecumenically produced resources is problematic. The curricular solution to this rather recent problem has been the development of pastor's class resources and elective study courses for adults. At the same time, Disciples have been open to ecumenical studies on the sacraments, especially in relation to those denominations, such as the United Church of Christ, with which it has been in conversation in recent years.

6. *Bible interpretation.* Historically Disciples have thought of themselves as "people of the Book." Educationally this has meant that the study of the Bible has a central place in Disciples education and is expected by congregations to be prominent in church school curriculum materials. The lay interest in Bible interpretation is primarily oriented toward gaining biblical information and guidance for daily living. Simultaneously, under the influence of biblical scholars and the academic community in the Disciples, the Bible has been approached by some writers with openness to the insights from biblical scholarship. The problem is that only occasionally has this scholarship appeared in resources for lay study.[49]

IMPLICATIONS FOR THE FUTURE

Implicit in the history of Disciples Christian religious education, especially in the "marks of identity," are unresolved tensions, ongoing problems, established patterns, and continuing challenges that need to be addressed as the Disciples look to the future. What follows are seven clusters of implications that require further exploration.

49. In an insightful discussion of Disciples theology, Larry D. Bouchard adds to the classic themes of restoration and unity what he calls the interpretation principle — "the imperative to interpret the meaning of Christ and the scriptures according to a free, reasonable, and responsible conscience in the context of community" ("The Interpretation Principle: A Foundational Theme of Disciples Theology," in *Interpreting Disciples: Practical Theology in the Disciples of Christ,* ed. L. Dale Richesin and Larry D. Bouchard [Fort Worth: Texas Christian University Press, 1987], p. 19). Although he applies the interpretation principle to Disciples doctrine and practice, Bouchard's treatment of this principle in relation to the Bible is particularly instructive. For example, he claims that "the import of the biblical norm is not that the Bible is the only source of truth Christians are to interpret, but that it is the only source of truth we *must* interpret. . . . The Bible is the objective, artifactual center of the community's experience of faith, and only in the interpretive encounter do its texts speak" (pp. 20-21). Bouchard's view of biblical interpretation, if made central and explicit in Christian education resources and congregational teaching strategies, would give new credence to the Disciples claim to be a biblical people. His discussion of restoration and ecumenicity is equally instructive for the educational task of the Disciples.

1. The relationship of *unity and identity*. Clarity is needed in defining the nature of the unity to which the Disciples are committed and the role of Christian religious education in undergirding that commitment. No doubt Disciples can benefit from and are called upon to share in some ecumenical planning for Christian education. However, the more difficult task is to know what understanding of unity is to be communicated in educational resources and strategies. Is more required than advocating openness to other Christians and describing ecumenical structures? And of equal if not primary importance is the need for Disciples education to articulate more forthrightly the denomination's historic marks of identity. Probably no other task presents a greater challenge than helping people better understand and become committed to the Disciples view of baptism and communion while simultaneously helping them to appreciate other views of baptism and communion.

2. Concern for the role of the *church in the educational ecology* of the United States. Too often Christian religious education is seen as only a function of the church school in the congregation. The reality is that in the history of Protestant education, local church education has been effective when it is related to and integrated with a larger public strategy of how the church is to educate or influence the culture. For example, in the nineteenth century, Sunday school education was related within an ecology of "public" religious education with church colleges, church publishing, philanthropic societies, the publication of Sunday school texts in major newspapers, the teaching of public schools, and denominational missionary societies. In the early twentieth century, progressive religious educators attempted to continue an ecology by coordinating church school education with denominational colleges, with efforts at community education, and with public schools in "released time" religious education.

The concern of the church with the public context of education has seemed to wane in recent years as Christian religious education has been restricted to church education.[50] The Disciples commitment to openness caused them to take the lead in the progressive era to search for strategies to influence the education of the public. It is imperative that Disciples again address public religious education.

3. The need for *new forms* of Christian education. The "democracy" mark of identity points to the need for a fresh covenant relationship among congregations and general Christian education units of the church, including regional structures. In an age of declining membership and shrinking denominational dollars and staff, the autonomous or marketplace approach to the planning of educational programs and resources on the part of congregations and regional/general structures should give way to a new sense of denominational partnership.

Several specific forms or dimensions of Christian education require atten-

---

50. Seymour, O'Gorman, and Foster, *The Church in the Education of the Public*, pp. 125-56.

tion. First, the educational needs of racial-ethnic congregations and their patterns of teaching and learning deserve serious exploration. Second, the difficulty of providing quality Christian education in small-membership churches is an ongoing problem. Third, a realistic assessment of the strengths and weaknesses of the church school as the dominant educational structure in the typical congregation, along with the development of optional models, should be undertaken. Fourth, the responsibility of the church to address and influence societal structures that educate (e.g., schools, the media, business) is of foremost importance.

4. The use of the *Bible and theology* in educational practice. The central issue is to clarify the appropriate use of academic, scholarly biblical and theological insights in Christian religious education. For all its emphasis on the Bible, the importance of people knowing what they believe, and the value of reason, Disciples education has tended not to make explicit the use of scholarly insights, especially biblical ones, in curriculum resources and congregational programs.[51] A related issue has to do with the need to define the "teachability" of resources in relation to how people become open to learning the Bible, theology, and doing critical reflection on ethical and social issues. The challenge here is to envision Christian education as a process of helping people to think critically and systematically.

5. The need to define Christian education's role in helping people distinguish between the *church and society* or between mature Christian faith and responsible citizenship. On the one hand, there is the need today to help people develop authentic, meaningful personal piety and spiritual disciplines. On the other hand, there is the need for Christian religious education to give greater attention to the difference between informed citizenship and the witness of Christians, as individuals and as a community, in the midst of a secular society. The emerging interest in the proper role of the academic study of religion in public education is an example of a church/society issue of historic concern to Disciples educators. Given the Disciples view of education and religion, this church is particularly well equipped to give direction and leadership to the discussion.

6. The need for a new *institutional history.* The Disciples have had a rich history in Christian religious education. The full story needs to be con-

---

51. Prior to the 1969 launching of the Christian Life Curriculum, teams of editors and general Christian education staff met with Disciples seminary faculties to discuss the new curriculum. Since then there has been no comparable involvement of the Disciples academic community in foundational planning for Christian education program and curriculum resources, although individual professors have contributed specific curriculum pieces. The call for academician and editor/general staff dialogue is coming from several sources. See, for example, Marvin E. Smith, "Crisis in the Christian Churches," *Disciples Divinity House Bulletin* 58 (Fall 1987): 1-3, 5-7. Smith, a retired director of the Local Church Curriculum Division of CBP, calls for "getting academic agreements about ourselves shared with and discussed by our total membership" as part of the reforming step to be taken "to clarify and justify our reason for being." He also makes a persuasive argument that Disciples should "devise some radical new ways of nurturing our congregations" and "restore and vitalize teaching and learning at the local church level."

served in a major volume.[52] Topics worthy of investigation include the story of education in Disciples racial-ethic congregations, the development of youth ministries (summer conferences, International CYF Commission, etc.), the difficulty of developing effective strategies for adult education and the various attempts to produce new resources for adult study, the contributions of the professional church educators organizations, and changes in regional and general Christian education organizations.

7. The need to *recruit and educate church educators.* Today the Disciples face an acute shortage of seminary-educated professional church educators for congregational positions. Although the Disciples have had congregational staff educators for many years (and a professional organization since 1947), it is now increasingly difficult to find people interested in these positions.[53] Systematic churchwide attention needs to be given to recruiting and equipping people for professional Christian education as a viable ministry career. As urgent, however, is the need to recover a sense of the "teaching pastor," given both the growing necessity for Disciples to deal more effectively with our identity and the fact that in the majority of Disciples congregations, the minister is the church's only professional teacher/educator. Attention should be given to helping seminary students and pastors catch a vision of the "teaching pastor" and develop appropriate insights and skills. The task of identifying and preparing people to teach Christian education in the seminaries also deserves fresh attention.[54]

The accomplishments and advances in Christian education that the Disciples experienced in the first half of this century were the result, in large measure, of the creative endeavors of its leaders. Today, Disciples are facing numerous issues in Christian education. The future of this historically mainline church in the upcoming century may well rest on its finding and equipping a new generation of professional church educators who can help it fulfill its distinctive mission as a particular people in the unity of the Body of Christ.

52. The first and only comprehensive institutional history of Christian education in the Disciples of Christ is *The Disciples and Religious Education,* ed. William Clayton Bower and Roy G. Ross.

53. The vacuum is being filled by part-time staff without seminary training. At a conference in February 1989 sponsored by the Department of Christian Education and Ministry and CBP, attention was given to this phenomenon and the "order of ministry" issues raised by the growing phenomenon of the lay educator.

54. The first Disciples seminary professor of religious education was William Francis Smith, who began teaching at the College of the Bible (now Lexington Theological Seminary) in 1909. He was succeeded in 1912 by William Clayton Bower. By 1925 all four of the present seminaries had a religious education professor and have continued, with only minor lapses, to have such a professor (or one responsible for religious education). Most of these professors have been Disciples. However, between 1979 and 1989 only one seminary has had a professor of religious education on a permanent basis who was a Disciple. Moreover, in recent years there has been only a very small number of Disciples with earned doctorates appropriate for teaching religious education. In 1989 three such individuals worked in non-Disciples seminaries.

Working Group Response: Education

Ann D. Beattie, Recorder

In addition to early drafts of the chapters by Brereton, Harrison, and Rowell and Seymour, the working group on Education heard a paper on "Yale and the Disciples" by Edwin L. Becker.

TOPICS FOR FURTHER DISCUSSION AND RESEARCH

1. A word that kept coming up was *passion*. We heard about the passion for the gospel of Alexander Campbell and the "Bethany Four" — their passion to declare God's gracious love for all sinners. Several wondered whether this same passion is still present, and various dates were suggested for its disappearance. We saw that this passion needs to come from having a well-defined "center," and we speculated about how that center might be defined now.

2. Surrounding this center is the suggested tension between our identity and our desire for ecumenical unity. Some contended that our ecumenicity can diminish our identity, as when we sometimes feel we have to say, "we can't do this or it will take away from our ecumenical witness." Others saw this ecumenicity as an essential part of our identity, and again we looked at Campbell's ability to hold these together. As some denominations seem to be moving into a time of wanting to hold to and declare their distinctive denominational characteristics more strongly, and as many of us who define ourselves as mainstream churches are feeling the hard times of declining numbers, we want to caution ourselves against having a redefinition of our identity result in the emergence of a sectarian spirit, as is happening in some denominations today. And yet, neither can we shrink from declaring our identity more clearly than we sometimes have in the past. These aspects of the task before us clearly require further exploration.

3. Connected with the issues of passion and identity was the subject of biblical authority. One participant noted the difficulties that emerge for one's

foundational faith and passionate proclamation when we move from viewing the Bible as witness to the viewing the Bible as religious study. An encouraging contribution to this discussion was the story of the history of the required Bible class at Bethany College: the instructor of this course regularly received Bethany's outstanding teacher award even though the class was required!

4. As we considered our center and our identity, what we declare and teach, we began to survey the state of religious education in our schools and churches. It is interesting that at this time there are only two Disciples Ph.D.'s in religion teaching this subject in seminaries. We noted that the Christian education position in most churches is a second-class position and that this is reflected in the individual's pay. We noted the diminishing pool of volunteers to teach Sunday School and midweek program offerings. And we noted the lack of teacher training. Pastors are often so busy with administrative duties and the like that they have little time to be either master teachers or trainers of the volunteers. We looked at the rising costs of producing curriculum materials, at the difficulty of planning materials in this fast-moving world (since materials have to be planned several years before they are produced), and at the content of our mainstream materials. We noted that many of our churches have lost a whole generation of baby boomers, asked how our Christian education fits into that, and wondered if we are going to be able to hold onto our youth, the next generation of leadership. What ways can we find to teach about our tradition in the future that will address our hunger and thirst for God?

5. As an outgrowth of the presentation on Yale, we began to ask questions about the place of field education in the training of pastors and looked at the connection between the seminaries and the churches. Is the seminary the place for broader exposure to prison ministries, for working with the homeless, and so on, or should seminarians be encouraged to pastor churches at the same time they are trying to adjust to seminary life and get the most out of this educational time in their lives? We heard both sides of this issue as we considered the difficulties of paying for a seminary education, especially for many second-career people with families. Given that an increasing number of seminarians have not been brought up in Disciples churches and that long-time Disciples students continue to need Disciples "community" while studying, we considered the difficult question of how they can continue to be "socialized," to grow as Disciples ministers, if they attend a seminary where there are few Disciples churches in the area. Can we do a better job of working together as churches, seminaries, and regions to pursue an action-reflection model of forming pastors?

Further, what should the church's role be with the colleges? Should we strengthen the relationship in the area of financial support? Should we place more qualified Disciples laypeople on the boards of trustees? Would more intentional cross-fertilization bring more growth for both sides? And might a stronger connection lessen the distance between the more liberally trained recent seminary graduate (often a woman) and the seemingly more conservative person in the pew?

We need to ask ourselves what our Disciples colleges have to offer that isn't available at secular institutions or at other denominational colleges. Again, we face the question of our unique identity: what do we have to offer that is not offered as well or better by others?

6. Finally, a significant area of discussion that kept re-emerging in different forms during our time together was that of the "privatization" of religion. "If we owned the colleges," it was asked, "would we ask them to change, to engage more forcefully in teaching the Christian faith? Or should we leave that to the churches?" It was suggested that to leave this to the churches would be to run the risk of giving up the connection of the faith to the public sphere, failing to accomplish the task of helping people see who they are in relation to the universe, and in the end making religion just one more option in the "good life." Where else will students hear that they are to be more than intellectual theorizers about religion or even good moral citizens — that they are to be Disciples in the broadest and deepest sense of the term?

V. STRUCTURE

The Changing Career Tracks
of Elite Disciples Professionals

Mark A. Chaves

It is now commonplace to observe that internal structural differentiation characterizes the twentieth-century organizational development of United States Protestant denominations. The expansion of administrative boards and specialist agencies and concomitant growth in managerial personnel reflect this increasingly differentiated organizational structure.[1] Whether one evaluates these developments as enhancing the efficiency of denominational management or disenfranchising local congregations, there is no denying the reality of increased organizational complexity and specialization.

Several consequences of this differentiation have been examined. Paul M. Harrison and Gibson Winter have discussed the problems that organizational differentiation pose for the legitimation of religious authority. Eric Woodrum has argued that social tensions and conflict within denominations arise from differentiated organizational structures: religious professionals who work in noncongregational settings believe and act differently than those in congregations. K. Peter Takayama has similarly placed organizational differentiation among the major sources of denominational strain. James A. Beck-

<hr>

1. See James A. Beckford, *Religious Organization* (The Hague: Mouton, 1975).

<hr>

The research reflected in this essay was supported by two separate grants from the Lilly Endowment, one through the Harvard Project on Historical Studies of Protestantism in American Culture and the other through Christian Theological Seminary. Several people provided helpful comments on earlier drafts of this paper: Elaine Backman, Julie Brines, Cy Goode, Bill Hutchison, Peter Marsden, Donald Nunnelly, Aage Sørensen, Newell Williams, the members of the New World Colloquium at Harvard University, and participants in the Christian Theological Seminary working group. I would also like to thank Pat Kelly for careful and diligent coding and May Reed for archival assistance. — MARK CHAVES

ford, following Karel Dobbelaere, Jaak Billiet, and Roger Creyf, has connected differentiation to internal secularization processes by pointing to "the increasingly autonomous operation within religious organizations of agencies that are governed by mainly secular considerations."[2]

In this essay I examine another consequence of the structural differentiation within denominations: segmentation of their professional labor market into congregational, educational, and agency career lines. It is important to examine labor market segmentation because it can be understood as an intervening mechanism between organizational differentiation and the consequences mentioned above. That is to say, one of the reasons organizational differentiation results in legitimation problems, intradenominational conflict, and internal secularization may stem from the fact that people are less likely to move among the various segments of the denomination. The social ties and lines of communication that might otherwise integrate the various organizational sites of a denomination are thereby weakened. As a result, the social distance between congregations, educational institutions, and agencies of a denomination increases, making conflict and crises of authority more likely.

I have investigated the labor market segmentation of the Christian Church (Disciples of Christ) by analyzing the careers of those occupying elite positions within this denomination at three points — 1909, 1942, and 1985. Before describing the data and methods used in this analysis, I will discuss the sociological perspective on careers employed here.

A SOCIOLOGICAL PERSPECTIVE ON RELIGIOUS CAREERS AND LABOR MARKETS

The careers of religious professionals, like the careers of many others, are not composed of a random sequence of jobs. Rather, they display certain regularities that are produced by the manner in which jobs are matched with people. Members of the clergy desiring a change of congregation are not free to move just anywhere. First of all, they are constrained by the number of available positions. Nor will all the positions that are formally open in fact be open to the job seeker. Some positions will be "beneath" what the applicants desire,

2. Harrison, *Authority and Power in the Free Church Tradition: A Social Case Study of the American Baptist Convention* (Princeton: Princeton University Press, 1959); Winter, "Religious Organizations," in *The Emergent American Society: Large-Scale Organizations,* ed. W. Lloyd Warner (New Haven: Yale University Press, 1967); Woodrum, "Towards a Theory of Tension in American Protestantism," *Sociological Analysis* 39 (1978): 219-27; Takayama, "Strains, Conflicts, and Schisms in Protestant Denominations," in *American Denominational Organization,* ed. Ross P. Scherer (Pasadena: William Carey Library, 1980); Dobbelaere, Billiet, and Creyf, "Secularization and Pillarization: A Social Problem Approach," *Annual Review of the Social Sciences of Religion* 2 (1978): 97-124; Beckford, "Religious Organization," in *The Sacred in a Secular Age,* ed. Phillip E. Hammond (Berkeley and Los Angeles: University of California Press, 1985), p. 129.

some will be "above" what they expect to attain, and others will be unattainable because of such things as gender discrimination. Hiring organizations will not give equal consideration to all formally qualified applicants. It is unlikely that the Country Club Christian Church of Kansas City (1985 membership = 3,050) would peruse the list of recent graduates of even prestigious divinity schools and seminaries to fill a vacant pulpit, for instance. Similarly, committees seeking a president for Eureka College or the Board of Church Extension will draw from a relatively narrow pool of labor. This serves to illustrate that the careers of religious professionals are worked out in a labor market that is patterned in certain identifiable ways.

With a little imagination, one can picture this religious labor market in a way that highlights its complexity. Imagine a map of the United States filled with dots representing specific religious organizations — congregations, agencies, seminaries, and the like. Each time a religious professional changes jobs, imagine a line connecting the old job to the new job. The map would have to be three-dimensional to represent job shifts within the same organization. Very soon, this map would be filled with criss-crossing lines, each of which represented the career of a single individual. The sociological problem would be to discern order in this picture. Regularities in these career tracks would represent the infrastructure of the denominational labor market. These patterned ways in which the matching of people to jobs occurs are one aspect of a religious organization; changes in these regularities represent organizational development.

Although a labor market can be understood most broadly as "a system of interconnected career lines" it is possible to distinguish various types of labor markets.[3] Several of these types, elaborated by Robert P. Althauser and Arne L. Kalleberg, will be useful here. They define an *internal* labor market as a cluster of jobs that have "(a) a job ladder, with (b) entry only at the bottom and (c) movement up this ladder, which is associated with a progressive development of knowledge or skill."[4] The cluster of jobs that constitute religious careers typically display these features, though as always it is possible to question whether movement up the ladder is associated with increasing knowledge and skill. For example, it is difficult to reconcile the relative absence of women from positions nearer the top of religious career ladders with the claim that movement up the ladder is determined by merit alone.

Althauser and Kalleberg further distinguish two types of internal labor markets: "*firm internal labor markets* (FILMs), established by and confined to a single employer (organization, corporation), though not necessarily embracing all jobs in a firm; and *occupational internal labor markets* (OILMs),

3. See Seymour Spilerman, "Careers, Labor Market Structure, and Socioeconomic Achievement," *American Journal of Sociology* 83 (1977): 551-93.

4. See Althauser and Kalleberg, "Firms, Occupations, and the Structure of Labor Markets," in *Sociological Perspectives on Labor Markets,* ed. Ivar Berg (New York: Academic Press, 1981), p. 130.

existing for incumbents of one occupation or of two or more associated occupations and not necessarily confined to a single employer."[5] The labor market in which religious careers develop is not easily classifiable as either an FILM or an OILM; it displays features of both. Most religious careers are characterized by job movement from one organization to another within the same occupation. From the point of view of the relatively small establishments that directly employ religious professionals (congregations, agencies, schools), the labor market of religious professionals looks more like an OILM.

There is, however, another level of organization: the denomination. Some have argued — pointing to high rates of denominational switching among churchgoers, great internal diversity, and increasing heterogamy — that denominational lines are no longer as sociologically salient as they once were.[6] Because the careers of religious professionals still track largely within a single denomination, however, the religious labor market may be where denominational boundaries persist. To illustrate with data presented below, approximately two-thirds of the jobs ever held by Disciples educational elites, three-quarters of the jobs ever held by Disciples agency elites, and more than 90 percent of the jobs ever held by Disciples congregational elites remained within denominational boundaries. Although these figures indicate that the denominational boundary is less permeable in the careers of eventual congregational elites than eventual educational or agency elites, the boundary continues to be a salient feature for all three categories of elite careers.

As a whole, then, the religious labor market is segmented into markets whose outlines largely correspond to denominational boundaries. Though movement in and out of these "firms" is not altogether absent in religious careers, most jobs are in organizations within a single denomination.[7] From this point of view, the labor market of a denomination looks more like an FILM, characterized by clusters of jobs internal to a particular firm — the denomination itself.

Fortunately, it is not necessary to pigeonhole a denominational labor market as either an OILM or an FILM. I introduced these concepts only because they help me to state my primary thesis concerning developments within the Disciples professional labor market. To anticipate, my main argument in this essay is that within the firm internal labor market represented by the Disciples denomination, segmentation has occurred along *occupational*

5. Althauser and Kalleberg, "Firms, Occupations, and the Structure of Labor Markets," p. 130.

6. See Robert Wuthnow, *The Restructuring of American Religion* (Princeton: Princeton University Press, 1988). But see also Wade C. Roof and William McKinney, *American Mainline Religion* (New Brunswick, N.J.: Rutgers University Press, 1987).

7. See Robert E. Mitchell, "Polity, Church Attractiveness, and Ministers' Careers: An Eight-Denomination Study of Inter-Church Mobility," *Journal for the Scientific Study of Religion* 5 (1966): 241-58; and James B. Wirth and Ross P. Scherer, "Lutheran Ministry: Portrait of a Strategic Elite within a Denominational Organization," in *Current Research on Occupations and Professions,* vol. 4, ed. Helena Z. Lopata (Greenwich, Conn.: JAI Press, 1987), pp. 109-39.

lines. The career lines leading to pastoring a very large congregation have become differentiated from career lines leading to the presidency of an educational institution, and both of these have become differentiated from career lines leading to an elite position in a national agency of the denomination.

This differentiation is complex. It is not the case that each of these three career lines has become differentiated from the other two at the same rate and during the same historical period. The labor markets separating careers leading to elite positions in educational institutions and congregations were already segmented to a high degree in 1909. Though there is some indication that they have become slightly more differentiated over this period, the primary development during this century has been the differentiation of a third religious career from these other two — a career in religious administration leading to an elite position in a national denominational agency. In other words, this period has seen the development of another OILM — the agency labor market — within the FILM bounded by denominational lines. Describing this development is my main goal in this essay.

Although the usual cautions about generalizing from a single case are in effect here, the broad organizational similarity among Protestant denominations permits some confidence that trends in Disciples organizational development are not atypical.[8]

This research has also been limited to a consideration of the careers of those who wind up in elite positions within Disciples organizations. A denominational labor market is certainly much more than the careers of those who wind up in elite positions, but the careers of elites — when viewed sociologically — offer one window onto the evolution of an extremely complicated organizational structure.

DATA

Data were collected on the careers of Disciples elites at three points in time — 1909, 1942, 1985. The most recent date is meant to represent the current situation. The earliest year was chosen because it represents a date more or less immediately prior to the beginning of serious movement toward centralizing the administrative apparatus of the denomination. (This movement culminated in the formation of the United Christian Missionary Society in 1919.) It therefore represents the situation of a denomination poised to enter a new organizational phase (this phase lasted until 1968, when some decentralizing

8. See Peter Berger, *The Sacred Canopy* (Garden City, N.Y.: Doubleday, 1967), p. 139; and Ross P. Scherer, "Organization Types and American Denominations," *Journal for the Scientific Study of Religion* 27 (1988): 475-98. But to appreciate the diversity of organizational form within Protestantism, see also Gary P. Burkart, "Patterns of Protestant Organization," in *American Denominational Organization*, pp. 36-83.

occurred). The 1942 date was chosen as a representative mid-century point because of available biographical source material produced in that year. Apart from these reasons, the choice of these particular dates rather than adjacent or nearly adjacent dates was arbitrary. It should be noted that since I examine the careers of people in elite positions at these dates, the period of study actually begins earlier than 1909. Similarly, the data from 1985 elites do not actually represent the labor market of 1985. That is to say, those now entering a career track are unlikely to face the same labor market encountered at entry by those who were near the end of their careers in 1985.

The "elite" group is defined positionally: the Disciples elite is composed of those individuals who occupy key positions in important organizations within the denomination. So the first step in identifying the elite is identifying the important organizations. Denominational annual reports indicate that four kinds of organizations compose the denomination: congregations, regional structures, general agencies, and educational institutions. These organizations are tied financially to each other, although the formality of those ties varies. They are also tied symbolically, in that they all report in some manner to the denominational convention and are listed in the annually published *Yearbook*. Most importantly for my purposes, these four kinds of organizations represent the primary options for career paths open to religious professionals within this denomination.

Choosing the elite positions within these organizations necessarily involves a degree of arbitrariness, because the hierarchical arrangement of positions is continuous. It is impossible to identify unambiguously those who have power and authority and those who do not; the distribution of these qualities is more diffuse than that. Nevertheless, there is a hierarchy, and I attempted to identify the positions at the very top of the pyramid in each kind of organization. There is no question that positions lower in the hierarchy are also part of the denomination's elite, but in trying to make the case as clear-cut as possible, I included only those in the topmost positions in the four categories.[9] Using this rationale, I included the following in the population of Disciples elite:

1. Top officers or staff members (e.g., presidents, vice presidents, executive secretaries) of periodicals and major units of the national structure
2. Presidents of the colleges and seminaries affiliated with the Christian Church (Disciples of Christ)
3. Pastors of the largest congregations
4. Regional ministers (or their functional equivalents) of the largest regions

9. It would, of course, have been possible to use an entirely different method of defining the elite population — reputational rather than positional, for example. But it would be extremely difficult to establish a reputational elite for the earlier periods. For further discussion of the consequences of defining an elite population by various methods, see George Moyser and Margaret Wagstaffe, *Research Methods for Elite Studies* (Boston: Allen & Unwin, 1987).

I call the first group the "agency elites," the second group the "educational elites," and the third and fourth groups together the "congregational elites."[10] The third and fourth groups are justifiably aggregated because regional ministers have constant contact with congregations, and inspection of their job histories reveals that in each period their careers have been characterized by a series of pastorates leading to the regional minister post. In both these senses they are congregational elites.[11] Lists of individuals occupying these positions in 1909, 1942, and 1985 were developed using Disciples *Yearbooks* from those years. The final lists contain 91 individuals in 1909; 116 individuals in 1942; and 128 individuals in 1985.

The next step in the research was to collect biographical information on as many of these elites as possible. For the 1985 group, several of the denominational offices cooperated by providing biographical information available in their personnel files. The "names file" kept at the Disciples Historical Society proved a valuable source for all three lists of elites. I also got biographical information from several editions of *Who's Who in America*, the 1976 and 1983 editions of *Who's Who in Religion*, the 1935-36 edition of *Who's Who in the Clergy*, and the 1941-42 edition of *Religious Leaders of America*. Using these sources, I was able to gather biographical information on 92.3 percent of the 1909 group (84 individuals); 91.4 percent of the 1942 group (106 individuals); and 83.6 percent of the 1985 group (107 individuals).[12]

Note that I used published biographical indexes only as *sources* of biographical information. This represents a shift from the usual practice in research on elites — *defining* the elite as those who are listed in these reference books — the shortcomings of which are well known.[13] I used these published indexes only as one among several sources of biographical data on an elite population defined independently of those sources.

10. Wirth and Scherer use a similar typology in their study of Missouri Synod Lutheran careers ("Lutheran Ministry"). They identify six types of ministerial positions: professors, executives, large pastorates, medium pastorates, small pastorates/assistants, and specialists. The similarities to my categories are clear; the differences are due to my focus on elites.

11. It would be interesting to examine the kinds of congregations from which regional ministers are drawn. I have reason to believe that they are drawn from midsize rather than large congregations: the move from pastoring a midsize congregation to serving as a regional minister represents upward mobility, whereas a move from one of the largest congregations to a regional minister position would represent downward mobility and not be undertaken voluntarily. I have not yet systematically examined this hypothesis. The results are not changed appreciably if regional ministers are excluded from the analysis.

12. These are the numbers of individuals on which I was able to collect *some* data, but in each group missing data prevented me from doing analyses on some of the individuals. The tables indicate the numbers of individuals on which I had enough information to perform analyses.

13. See E. Digby Baltzell, " 'Who's Who in America' and 'The Social Register': Elite and Upper Class Indexes in Metropolitan America," in *Class Status and Power*, ed. Reinhard Bendix and Seymour Martin Lipset (Glencoe, Ill.: Free Press, 1953), pp. 172-85; and Colin Bell, "Some Comments on the Use of Directories in Research on Elites, with Particular Reference to the Twentieth-Century Supplements of the Dictionary of National Biography," in *Elites in Western Democracy*, British Political Sociology Yearbook, vol. 1, ed. Ivor Crewe (New York: John Wiley, 1974), pp. 161-71.

I coded variables describing both background characteristics and characteristics of job histories. Background variables include the following:

- birth date and birth place
- gender
- educational attainment
- earned a postgraduate clerical degree or not
- earned a degree from a Disciples educational institution or not
- ordained or not

Variables describing aspects of elite job histories include the following:

- whether the first job in a career was in a congregation or not
- number of jobs held
- average number of years in each job
- proportion of jobs in Disciples organizations
- proportion of jobs that were in congregations
- proportion of jobs in educational institutions
- proportion of jobs in church administration

RESULTS

Table 1 presents summary results, broken down by type of elite and year. These results reveal interesting variation both over time and between the careers of the three elite groups. I will comment here on the results that bear most directly on my argument of this essay — that the period from 1909 to 1985 is characterized most markedly by the development of the agency segment within the Disciples labor market.

The trends apparent in the background variables may appear to contradict the claim that there has been increasing differentiation of career tracks leading to these three kinds of elite positions. These three groups of elites appear to have become more similar in various respects over this period. There are, for example, increasing proportions of educational and agency elites earning postgraduate clerical degrees and becoming ordained. By 1985, 79 percent of the educational elites had clerical degrees and 69 percent were ordained. For the agency elites, by 1985 67 percent had clerical degrees and 72 percent were ordained. While 100 percent of the congregational elites were ordained in all three periods, the proportion with postgraduate clerical degrees had dramatically increased over this period. It is interesting to note that in 1909 educational and agency elites were more likely than congregational elites to have earned a postgraduate divinity degree. The typical pattern for the 1909 congregational elite was to have earned a four-year degree from a college and no education beyond that.

Although the absolute difference in percentage points on educational

TABLE 1 Background and Career Characteristics of Disciples Elites

TYPE OF ELITE:	Congregational Elites			Educational Elites			Agency Elites		
YEAR:	1909	1942	1985	1909	1942	1985	1909	1942	1985
BACKGROUND VARIABLES									
Mean Age	48.0	51.6	54.8	52.0	52.3	54.7	50.6	59.9	53.3
s.d.	8.9	11.8	7.1	11.9	9.8	8.5	12.5	11.2	7.5
Number	27	32	25	24	21	9	24	33	29
Percent with earned postgraduate clerical degree									
Percent	5	33	97	21	45	79	15	19	67
Number	21	33	33	24	22	14	20	37	58
Percent with earned degree from a Disciples institution									
Percent	95	84	81	91	71	79	67	79	76
Number	21	32	32	23	21	14	18	34	55
Percent female	0	0	0	7	0	0	12	20	20
Number	28	42	46	28	23	16	34	51	66
Percent ordained	100	100	100	54	70	69	46	56	72
Number	28	37	35	24	23	13	28	45	58
CAREER VARIABLES									
Percent whose first job was with a congregation									
Percent	78	97	85	30	36	43	38	58	60
Number	27	37	34	23	22	14	26	38	58
Mean number of jobs	4.7	4.1	4.1	4.3	5.5	5.4	3.9	4.3	4.7
s.d.	2.3	1.9	1.4	2.5	2.1	1.9	2.6	1.8	1.9
Number	25	31	32	22	22	14	21	34	53
Mean number of years in each job									
Mean	3.9	5.7	6.0	4.9	4.8	4.4	9.9	7.4	6.0
s.d.	1.9	4.6	4.2	2.9	2.8	2.3	8.9	5.1	4.0
Number	23	27	25	22	22	12	20	32	51
Mean proportion of jobs with Disciples institutions									
Mean	.90	.98	.97	.67	.69	.55	.71	.79	.79
s.d.	.17	.06	.10	.32	.36	.40	.39	.36	.32
Number	25	31	32	22	22	14	21	34	53
Mean proportion of jobs with congregations									
Mean	.86	.86	.81	.34	.35	.21	.44	.50	.46
s.d.	.20	.23	.27	.40	.38	.31	.43	.39	.34
Number	25	31	32	22	22	14	21	34	53
Mean proportion of jobs in education									
Mean	.07	.06	.01	.60	.53	.70	.23	.11	.09
s.d.	.16	.13	.03	.43	.38	.37	.34	.23	.21
Number	25	31	32	22	22	14	21	34	53
Mean proportion of jobs in church administration									
Mean	.01	.08	.11	.00	.06	.06	.08	.17	.25
s.d.	.07	.21	.22	.00	.20	.13	.18	.25	.28
Number	25	31	32	22	22	14	21	34	53

attainment was larger among the 1985 elites than among the 1909 elites,[14] the 1909 difference was of greater substantive importance. This is because in 1909 the lack of a graduate clerical degree would almost completely differentiate the congregational from the other two kinds of elites. In 1985, despite the larger absolute difference, the overall prevalence of the degrees makes it less important in differentiating among the three elite groups. With respect to being ordained, even the absolute difference among these three groups decreases over this period.

These trends suggest that today there are more religious career paths open to those who enter the Disciples labor market with a postgraduate clerical degree and ordination than there were earlier in the century.[15] When *starting* a career, a young cleric has paths leading to three different places open to him.

The gender specificity is appropriate here: these results suggest that the young female cleric of today has only one path to an elite position open to her — the path leading to an elite agency position. The finding of William T. Bielby and James N. Baron that extensive gender segregation continues to operate in the workplace holds, at least at the elite level, for religious professionals within the Disciples of Christ.[16] Women elites are segregated into the agencies. Interestingly, early in the century two of the educational elite positions were occupied by women.[17]

One career variable — the percentage of elites whose first job was with a congregation — indicates a similar trend. Although more than 80 percent of the congregational elites in all three periods began their careers in a congregation, educational and agency elites were increasingly likely over this period to begin their careers in a congregation. By 1985 43 percent of educational elites and 60 percent of agency elites started their careers in a congregation.

On the surface, these results may seem to indicate a decreasing differentiation of the religious labor market, with those occupying these three kinds of elite positions looking more like each other in 1985 than they did in 1909. There is some truth to this, but the similarity is with respect to background and first job, not with respect to later career paths. The three kinds of elites become increasingly similar with respect to what they bring with them when they enter the labor market — education and credentials — and where they start. But this increasing similarity in background characteristics and first job makes the later differentiation of career tracks even more striking.

14. For example, in 1909 21 percent of educational elites had the graduate clerical degree while only 5 percent of congregational elites did. In 1985 79 percent of the educational elites had the degree while 97 percent of the congregational elites did. The first case is a difference of 16 points; the second a difference of 18 points.

15. As I indicated above, "today" actually means the labor market faced by those entering in about 1957 (the mean year of ordination for 1985 elites). It remains an issue for further research whether the labor market faced by those who entered in 1985 was substantially different.

16. Bielby and Baron, "Mean and Women at Work: Sex Segregation and Statistical Discrimination," *American Journal of Sociology* 91 (1980): 759-99.

17. Luella W. St. Clair was president of Hamilton College in Lexington, Kentucky, and Emma Frederick Moore was president of Christian College in Columbia, Missouri.

Variables measuring characteristics of career tracks present hints of segmentation.[18] The strongest hints are suggested by results regarding the proportion of congregational, educational, and administrative jobs held by the three different groups of elites. In all three periods, congregational elites have more jobs in congregations than other elites. The average congregational elite had more than 80 percent congregation jobs, the average agency elite about half, and the average educational elite about one-third in 1909 and 1942 and one-fifth in 1985. Although the decrease between 1942 and 1985 in the proportion of congregation jobs among educational elites might represent some increasing differentiation of the educational labor market, this market segment was already fairly well differentiated in 1909. The trends in the mean proportion of jobs in education tell a similar story. In all three periods, the educational elites have held a substantially higher proportion of jobs in education than the other elites, and the difference has increased over this period.

While all three elite groups have held an increasing proportion of administrative jobs, the steadiest increase is evident among the agency elites. In 1909 the mean proportion of jobs in church administration held prior to the elite agency position was only .08. This rises to .17 in 1942 and to .25 in 1985. While agency elites at the beginning of this century were apparently drawn from among those in congregational and educational labor markets, by 1985 they were drawn from among those whose careers were to a greater extent internal to this newer agency labor market.

These results, while suggestive, do not directly address the segmentation issue. In order to explore directly the increasing segmentation of the labor market over this period, I performed a discriminant analysis on these data.[19] I created a nominal variable representing for each individual the elite group to which he or she belonged — educational, agency, or congregational. This measure then served as the dependent variable in a discriminant function that included the background and career level measures as independent variables. The issue addressed by this kind of analysis was the degree to which it is possible to predict, using information about individuals' backgrounds and careers, the type of elite position they would occupy. Increasing power over time to discriminate, on the basis of these variables, between those who wind up educational, agency, or congregational elites can be interpreted as increasing segmentation of the labor market. Moreover, separating background variables from career variables enables some evaluation of whether differentiation into these separate paths rests on changing characteristics that individuals bring with them to the market or on organizational development that differentiates a labor market populated by people who possess, at least at entry, more or less similar degrees of human capital.

18. These variables measure characteristics of career tracks up to but not including the elite position itself.
19. For an introductory discussion of this technique, see William R. Klecka, *Discriminant Analysis,* Quantitative Applications in the Social Sciences Series, no. 9 (London: Sage Publications, 1980).

**TABLE 2   Classificatory Power of Discriminant Functions:
Background, Career, and Full Models**

Model	Number	% Congregational Elites Correctly Classified	% Educational Elites Correctly Classified	% Agency Elites Correctly Classified	tau
1909					
Background	54	47.1	59.1	33.3	.212
Career	68	84.0	68.2	19.0	.380
Full	41	76.9	89.5	44.4	.617
1942					
Background	75	53.6	10.0	63.0	.172
Career	87	89.9	50.0	35.3	.335
Full	64	50.0	73.7	59.3	.403
1985					
Background	60	87.0	0.0	53.6	.320
Career	99	65.6	64.3	64.2	.400
Full	49	77.8	66.7	90.0	.708

Note: Background Models use age, receipt of a postgraduate clerical degree, and receipt of a degree from a Disciples institution. Career Models use only proportion of jobs in congregations and proportion of jobs in church administration. The full models use both these groups of variables plus two additional career variables: number of jobs and average job length. These variables were excluded from the career models because it is inappropriate to include them without controlling for age.

I should make clear that despite the presence of "independent" and "dependent" variables, this analysis is meant to be descriptive rather than causal. Sets of coefficients that constitute the discriminant functions are interpreted as information about regularities in career patterns rather than as variables that "explain" why someone is an educational rather than a congregational elite. For example, although a variable measuring the proportion of jobs in congregations is increasingly powerful in differentiating among these three groups of elites over this period, having a career spent mostly in congregations does not "cause" one to be a congregational rather than an educational or agency elite. The causal direction might actually be the reverse — certain kinds of careers are pursued in order to arrive at certain elite positions. This analysis therefore should be understood as an attempt to describe three kinds of career tracks that become increasingly differentiated over this period, not as an attempt to explain which people are allocated to which careers.

Table 2 presents, for all three periods, the classificatory power of discriminant functions that include only background variables, only career variables, and both background and career variables.[20] *Table 3* presents the stan-

20. Not all variables from Table 1 are used in the discriminant analysis. Most exclusions are due to high collinearity. Being ordained, having a first job in a congregation, proportion of jobs in Disciples organizations, and proportion of jobs in education are all highly correlated with

dardized coefficients for the discriminant functions that include both background and career variables. The results in *Table 2* directly address the segmentation issue. Examining the *tau* measure of overall discriminating power, the 1985 model with both background and career variables discriminates better than the corresponding model in 1909. The full model discriminates least well in 1942.[21] In 1909, the full model predicts elite group membership 61.7 percent better than chance; in 1942, the full model predicts elite group membership only 40.3 percent better than chance; in 1985, this model predicts elite group membership 70.8 percent better than chance.

This alone would be rather weak support for a hypothesis of increasing segmentation over this period. But examination of how well the model is predicting membership in each particular group reveals in greater detail what is going on. The full model is about as successful in 1985 as in 1909 at classifying congregational elites correctly. It is noticeably less successful over time in classifying educational elites because attaining a postgraduate degree (one of the background variables) identifies an educational elite more reliably in the earlier periods.

The full model is substantially more successful over time, however, in correctly classifying agency elites. In 1909 44.4 percent of the agency elites are correctly classified; in 1942 59.3 percent are correctly classified; and in 1985 fully 90 percent are correctly classified. These results strongly support the main claim I make in this essay — that the primary development in this period is the differentiation of the agency labor market. The educational and congregational labor markets were already fairly differentiated segments in 1909.

Results from the career model tell a similar story. With respect to overall discriminatory power, the career model is about as successful in each period, accurately classifying cases between 33.5 and 40.3 percent better than chance. Like the full model, however, the career model is substantially more successful in classifying agency elites in the later periods. It correctly identifies only 19 percent of the agency elites in 1909, 35.3 percent in 1942, and 64.2 percent in 1985. The career model classifies educational elites at about the same rate in all three periods, but it classifies congregational elites less well in 1985 than in either 1909 or 1942.

Inspection of the misclassification pattern produced by the career model reveals that every one of the misclassified 1985 congregational elites was incorrectly classified as an agency elite.[22] This pattern is instructive, suggesting that differentiation of the agency and congregational labor markets is far from complete. This result also illuminates the otherwise puzzling decline over time

the proportion of jobs in congregations. (Pearson's r between these variables and the proportion of jobs in congregations ranges from an absolute value of .61 to an absolute value of .88.) Gender is excluded due to the very small number of females in the elite populations of all three periods.

21. The nonlinearity in the development of segmentation is discussed below.

22. These results are available from the author upon request.

TABLE 3 Standardized Coefficients from Full Discriminant Models

Year	1909		1942		1985	
Function	F1	F2	F1	F2	F1	F2
BACKGROUND VARIABLES						
Age	-.29	-.12	.23	.34	-.22	-.39
Clerical Degree	-.55	-.06	-.72	-.13	-.65	-.98
Disciples Degree	.08	-.34	.29	.06	-.56	-.06
CAREER VARIABLES						
Percent congregational jobs	.97	.31	.88	-.49	1.60	.46
Percent administrative jobs	.06	.83	.54	.34	.69	.75
Number of jobs	.27	.01	-.25	.13	-.32	.67
Mean length of job	.11	.78	.27	.48	-.04	.18
Number	41		64		49	
Percent of discriminating power in F1	56.99		70.60		81.87	

in the ability of this model to accurately identify the congregational elites. The congregational elites are in fact just as differentiated (perhaps more so) from the educational elites in 1985 as they were in 1909 and 1942. But the presence of the new agency labor market, which is not yet completely differentiated from the congregational segment, leads the career model to mistake congregational elites for agency elites and thereby reduces its ability to correctly identify the congregational elites. To put this another way, the increasing segmentation represented by differentiation of the agency labor market decreases the ability of the model to identify the congregational elites because the differentiation is not yet complete.

The standardized coefficients from the full models are presented in *Table 3*. Looking at the first function in all three periods, the proportion of jobs in congregations is the most powerful discriminating variable. Furthermore, in 1985 it contributes more than twice as much as the next important variable, whereas in 1942 it contributes only 22 percent more, and in 1909 only 75 percent more. In 1985 the second most powerful variable is the proportion of jobs in church administration. This is the least important variable in 1909 and the third most important in 1942 (though it is the most important on the second function in those years). The relative contribution of age declines from the third most important variable in 1909 to the least important in 1942 and the next to least important in 1985. Though these coefficients are not easily interpreted, the patterns of relative contribution complement the results of *Table 2*. Two of these labor market segments — the congregational and educational — were, by 1909, fairly differentiated in terms of the proportion of a career spent in congregational jobs. By 1985 another career variable — the proportion of church administration jobs — also carried discriminating power. Meanwhile, at least one background variable — age — contributed relatively less to the discriminant function over this period. Overall, the pattern is one of increasing importance of career variables and decreasing importance of background variables in discriminating among congregational, educational, and agency elites.

CONCLUSION

In this essay I have examined one aspect of a denomination's internal differentiation — the segmentation of its professional labor market. Exploring a complex religious organization from the perspective of its labor market results in a richer, more nuanced story of its development than is possible through examination of the mere growth in size of the educational institutions and agencies or through an analysis of formal polity. A segmented labor market is an example of a social structure that cannot be observed from organizational charts or denominational constitutions and yet is an important sociological reality with consequences both for individuals pursuing religious careers and for the denomination as a whole.

I have argued that segmentation has occurred and continues to occur within the Disciples professional labor market. The complexity of the segmentation suggested by the above findings can be summarized as follows. By 1909, the Disciples of Christ labor market was already differentiated into two segments — the congregational and the educational. The differentiation between these two segments remained in 1985, perhaps having become more severe. During this century a third segment — the agencies — has developed. But the set of careers leading to an elite position in a national agency is not yet completely differentiated from the set of careers leading to a position as a congregational or educational elite, though they may be on the road to complete differentiation.

These results point to several directions for future research. Attempting to locate more exactly the boundaries of the developing agency segment is one possibility for further exploration. I have suggested that this period is characterized by the development of another occupational internal labor market within the labor market bounded by denominational lines. While the evidence I have presented is consistent with this interpretation, it does not rule out other interpretations. An interesting alternative is that the agency labor market is actually internal to firms rather than to the occupation of church administrator. Perhaps each specific agency has developed its own internal labor market with very little movement between agencies. The continuing process of structural differentiation leads me to expect such a development. Further analysis of the characteristics of job shifts in the agency labor market (Are they within agency? between agencies but within denominations? between agencies and denominations?) is needed to settle this issue.

Another subject for future research is presented by the results for 1942 elites. The differentiation of the agency careers appears to follow a fairly linear development. Agency careers are more differentiated in 1942 than in 1909, and more in 1985 than in 1942. But the results do not support a similar linear story for the increasing differentiation of educational from congregational careers. Results in Tables 2 and 3 indicate that congregational and educational labor markets are more differentiated in 1985 than in 1909 but less differentiated in 1942 than in 1909. What explains this pattern? Two forces seem plausible. First, perhaps the post–World War I expansion in Disciples educational institutions drew individuals from the congregational labor market into the educational labor market. Increased demand for teachers and administrators in Disciples educational institutions would have the consequence of de-differentiating these two labor markets because there would not be enough people already in the educational labor market to fill all the available positions. Second, the 1942 elite careers spanned the Depression years. Lester G. McAllister and William E. Tucker have reported that during the 1930s "Some congregations discontinued a preaching ministry entirely or sought only weekend services of a minister. On every hand congregations were behind in salary payments to their ministers. Many ministers worked at reduced salaries. No statistics reveal the total number of ministers unemployed but it must have been considerable."[23] It is plausible that the career disruption caused by the Great Depression led some clergy to find jobs elsewhere if they could, perhaps in educational institutions. These two forces would lead us to expect that educational and congregational careers would become more intertwined in the period between 1909 and 1942.

Finally, the connections between a segmented religious labor market and other consequences of the internal structural differentiation of denominations should be examined. While this essay takes a necessary first step by documenting the segmentation within one denomination, more research is needed to increase our understanding of the ways in which labor market segmentation contributes to the intradenominational conflict, organizational strain, and crises of authority produced by differentiation.

23. McAllister and Tucker, *Journey in Faith: A History of the Christian Church (Disciples of Christ)* (St. Louis: Bethany Press, 1975), p. 388.

Working Group Response: Structure

Lawrence A. Burnley, Recorder

In addition to an early draft of the chapter by Chaves, the working group on Structure heard presentations entitled "American Baptists and Disciples, 1880-1980: A Search for a Denominational Integrity" by William Brackney and "Peculiar Restorationism of African-American Disciples and Baptists, 1880-1989" by James Washington.

GENERAL OBSERVATIONS

1. There's a need to look at how we live out our diversity within the church. The Disciples constituency reflects the diversity of God's creation. The problem is that we don't know how to live out this diversity in unity. There is a need to discover new ways to enhance unity in the church.

2. We recognize that we are all on a journey of faith. With the diverse membership of the Disciples there is an absence of a common vision.

3. A problem that the Disciples share with other mainstream denominations is a failure of nerve or what might be called a faith crisis. Our church structures must provide opportunities to come to consensus in community and to express our convictions with confidence.

4. Racism has always been and continues to be a pervasive problem within our denomination as well as in the larger society, yet there is no concerted effort within our denomination to fully utilize present structures to eradicate this problem.

5. There is a need to define what power is, who has it, and how it is being used.

6. Sexism is deeply ingrained in our society and in the church. We must continue to revise structures, leadership systems, and procedures in congregations and other manifestations of the church so that they are fully open to women.

359

7. A fundamental question that needs to be addressed is why we want growth in church membership. Until we answer this question we cannot execute effective evangelism.

8. Institutions tend to be self-serving and self-perpetuating. The church cannot begin at the point of self-interest and move into evangelism.

9. Career tracks that lead to being a pastor of a church, president of a Disciples college or seminary, or officer of a general unit of the denomination have become increasingly differentiated from each other during this century. Careers in congregations, education, and church administration are less likely to overlap now than earlier in the century, leading to a greater degree of structural segmentation.

RECOMMENDATIONS

1. Conduct a study of congregationalism. Are its structures helpful, inhibiting, or irrelevant?

2. Study more carefully the patterns of segmentation among the upper-level positions within the Disciples labor force. What are the implications of segmentation as they relate to church structures?

3. Give attention to the relationships between leadership styles and church structures.

4. Research needs to be done on the contributions of the African-American membership to the structures of the denomination, both in the past and today. Attention should also be given to the contributions of Hispanics and Asians within the Disciples.

5. Prepare a systematic and vigorous exposition of the strengths and characteristics of existing patterns of denominations with special attention to their impact on evangelization. Attention should be given to the following:

- African-American denominations
- Racially diversified denominations
- Cooperative relationships between racially separated and racially diversified denominations

6. Encourage existing Disciples structures to examine the re-emergence of overt racism in America as well as the institutionalized and covert racism that continues to pervade our society. As Christians we are challenged to do the hard work of confronting this problem.

7. Research existing models of dialogical decision making to enable the development of structures that will enable honest dialogue among the diverse membership of the Disciples, producing decisions that incorporate the gifts of that diversity.

VI. THEOLOGICAL, MORAL, AND SOCIAL PROFILE

Pastoral Politics in the 1988 Election: Disciples as Compared to Presbyterians and Southern Baptists

James L. Guth and Helen Lee Turner

INTRODUCTION

The social and political activities of Protestant ministers have long been a subject of interest to historians, social scientists, and church people. From the time of the Puritan clergy in Massachusetts Bay Colony, ministers have played an important if intermittent role in American politics, fighting for American independence in the 1770s, the abolition of slavery in the 1850s, and economic reforms in the Social Gospel era of the early twentieth century. During the 1960s and early 1970s, scholarly and popular interest focused on the highly visible actions of what Harvey Cox dubbed the "New Breed": young, theologically liberal ministers who often adopted unconventional tactics in the civil rights and antiwar movements. Pioneering studies of the New Breed by Jeffrey Hadden (1969) and Harold Quinley (1974) showed that theological modernism was highly correlated with political liberalism, that liberal ministers were both more approving of clerical activism and more active than conservatives, and that they faced considerable resistance from conservative laity.[1]

Even as Quinley wrote in the early 1970s, the tide of liberal activism was receding. Mainline churches were losing members and money (some said in response to the New Breed's political activism), liberal clergy were leaving the ministry in large numbers, and those remaining were more willing to accommodate the political and social sensibilities of their parishioners. Although Quinley argued for the continuing relevance of liberal activism,[2] countertrends seemed evident: reports abounded of growing mainline concern with

1. Hadden, *The Gathering Storm in the Churches* (Garden City, N.Y.: Doubleday, 1969); Quinley, *The Prophetic Clergy* (New York: Wiley, 1974).
2. Quinley, *The Prophetic Clergy,* p. 20.

traditional evangelism and spiritual priorities, the influx of conservative young people (and second-career clergy) into seminaries, and the increasingly conservative national mood on issues that the New Breed had championed. And when ministerial activism surfaced in the Nuclear Freeze and environmental movements of the early 1980s, scholars paid little attention, although conservative minorities in many Protestant churches continued to criticize the liberal "captivities of the mainline."[3]

The limelight had shifted to the new New Breed: the Christian Right. As the Moral Majority charged onto the national stage and the "Year of the Evangelical" threatened to turn into the "Decade of the Evangelicals," observers focused on analyzing the theological and political characteristics of this new movement. Perhaps because the Christian Right was viewed primarily as a popular phenomenon, clerical activists were somewhat neglected, at least in comparison with their liberal predecessors, but there were a few studies of conservative clergy.[4] Most suggested considerable revision in the findings of Hadden and Quinley: conservative pastors now seemed more comfortable with political involvement, considerably more active, and much more confident of parishioner approval. Still, excepting the recent work of Kathleen Beatty and Oliver Walter,[5] there have been few comparative studies of the liberal New Breed of the 1960s and the conservative New Breed of the 1980s. This comparison of Disciples ministers with Presbyterian and Southern Baptist pastors will fill part of that gap.

OVERVIEW

The purpose of this study is to examine the relationship between the theological perspectives and the social and political stance of Disciples ministers. For comparison, we also collected data on ministers of the Southern Baptist Convention (SBC), the nation's largest Protestant denomination, and the Presbyterian Church (U.S.A.) (PC[USA]), the newly united body of mainline northern

---

3. See Richard John Neuhaus, *The Naked Public Square* (Grand Rapids: Eerdmans, 1984).

4. See, for example, James Guth, "The Southern Baptist Clergy: Vanguard of the New Christian Right?" in *The New Christian Right,* ed. Robert Liebman and Robert Wuthnow (New York: Aldine, 1983), pp. 118-30; "Political Converts: Partisan Realignment among Southern Baptist Ministers," *Election Politics* 3 (1985-86): 2-6; and "A New Turn for the Christian Right? Robertson Support among Southern Baptist Clergy," paper presented at the annual meeting of the Midwest Political Science Association, Chicago, 1989; Mel Hailey, "The Political and Social Attitudes of Church of Christ Ministers," paper presented at the annual meeting of the American Political Science Association, Washington, D.C., 1988; Kathleen Harder, "Pastors and Political Mobilization: Preaching Politics," paper presented at the annual meeting of the American Political Science Association, Washington, D.C., 1988.

5. Beatty and Walter, "Fundamentalists, Evangelicals and Politics," *American Politics Quarterly* 16 (1988): 43-59; and "A Group Theory of Religion and Politics: The Clergy as Group Leaders," *Western Political Quarterly* 42 (1989): 129-46.

and southern Presbyterians. Ministers of these denominations were chosen for comparison for two reasons. First, the three denominations have much in common. The Disciples have historic connections with both Presbyterian and Baptist traditions, have enjoyed membership strength in many of the same areas, and to a considerable extent have competed with both for members. Second, the three denominations differ in important ways. The Southern Baptists are one of the most theologically conservative Protestant denominations, while both the Presbyterian and Disciples represent mainline or even liberal Protestant Christianity. The three denominations have different traditional orientations toward politics: the Baptists, with their emphasis on separation of church and state, reinforced by otherworldly theology, have at times verged on complete abstention from politics, except for occasional moral crusades such as prohibition. Presbyterians, with their Calvinist and moral reform heritage, and Disciples, with their twentieth-century social action traditions, have envisioned a much larger role for the church in public life.[6] So while they have much in common, these three denominations also embody much of the great range and diversity in American Protestantism. Consequently, the findings of this study not only relate to Disciples but provide ample material for a preliminary analysis of the broader American Protestant scene.

The survey began just after the November 1988 presidential election and was completed in August 1989. We sent survey forms to all 2,150 senior Disciples pastors and, for purposes of comparison, to random samples of 1,500 senior pastors produced by the Southern Baptist Sunday School Board Research Unit and by the National Office of the PC(USA). After three mailings we had received 1,305 responses from Disciples ministers (64% of the denominational subsample, after adjusting for deaths, retirements, etc.), 930 from PC(USA) clergy (64%), and 700 from Baptists (48%). The questionnaire was a 250-item form designed to elicit pastors' views on a wide range of theological, social, and political issues. We included theological and political items, assessing attitudes on most issues considered by the denominations' national meetings since 1975. We also asked several questions that surfaced during the 1988 presidential campaign. And we inquired about ministers' presidential choices in 1988 and their involvement, if any, in the campaign. In addition, the survey instrument for each denomination asked about internal controversies, factional and leadership preferences, and problems confronting the denomination. Many of these questions will be analyzed in future work; here we concentrate on political attitudes and activism.

The study is organized as follows: after a brief exploration of the theological alignments of the ministers, we address the following questions: (1) What is the attitude of these clergy toward political involvement? (2) What do ministers see as appropriate activities for "pastors in politics"? (3) What is

6. See *Ministry in America,* ed. David Schuller, Merton Strommen, and Milo Brekke (New York: Harper and Row, 1980).

the political agenda of these ministers in the late 1980s? (4) What ideological divisions appear among ministers? And (5) How active are ministers politically and who are the beneficiaries? In each case, we examine the impact of denominational tradition and theological orientation.

THEOLOGICAL ORIENTATIONS

Scholars have used several approaches to assess the theological worldview of ministers. The most traditional approach is simply to ask questions about a minister's adherence to traditional items of Christian orthodoxy or support for "liberal" or "modernist" interpretations of the faith.[7] More recently, analysts have considered self-identification items to be preferable, or at least more succinct, measures,[8] although the choice of items is problematic, given varying usage in different denominations. Whatever strategy is adopted, the importance of theological views for ministerial politics has been amply demonstrated: they influence political attitudes, views about the role of the minister, and the degree of commitment to social and political activism.[9] Thus they are part of a larger ministerial worldview, extending beyond theology proper. And we do have some basis for our expectations here: the Baptists should hold very orthodox views, the Presbyterians considerably more liberal beliefs, and the Disciples, by reputation at least, views somewhere between those of Southern Baptists and Presbyterians.[10] Table 1 reports responses to some of our questions.

Quite clearly these ministers live in different theological worlds. Southern Baptists are strongly orthodox or traditionalist and many adhere to the cardinal points of premillennial or dispensational doctrine, once an antipolitical, otherworldly perspective, but more recently linked to the New Christian Right.[11] Presbyterian clergy, as the controversies of recent years suggest, are quite divided in attachment to traditional formulations of Christian doctrine, but few adhere to premillennial or dispensational schemes. The Disciples clearly resemble Presbyterians more than Baptists, but, despite the common view of the denomination, they are slightly more liberal on some tenets, such as the exclusive role of Jesus in salvation (an important issue in both the 1987 and 1989 General Assemblies), the actual existence of a Devil, and the Virgin Birth.

7. E.g., Hadden, *The Gathering Storm in the Churches;* and Quinley, *The Prophetic Clergy.*
8. E.g., Guth, "The Southern Baptist Clergy"; Clyde Wilcox, "The New Christian Right and White Fundamentalists" (Ph.D. diss., Ohio State University, 1984); Beatty and Walter, "Fundamentalists, Evangelicals and Politics."
9. See Hadden, *The Gathering Storm in the Churches;* and Quinley, *The Prophetic Clergy.*
10. See Wade Clark Roof and William McKinney, *American Mainline Religion: Its Changing Shape and Future* (New Brunswick, N.J.: Rutgers University Press, 1987).
11. See Helen Lee Turner and James Guth, "The Politics of Armageddon: Dispensationalism among Southern Baptist Ministers," in *Religion and Political Behavior in the United States,* ed. Ted G. Jelen (New York: Praeger, 1989), pp. 187-208.

TABLE 1   Theological Orientations of Clergy

	Percent "Strongly Agree" or "Agree"		
	BAPTIST	PRESBYTERIAN	DISCIPLES
Jesus only way to salvation	97	65	46
Devil actually exists	96	49	37
Jesus will return to earth someday	96	56	38
Virgin birth a biological miracle	94	56	42
Hell is a real place	91	38	34
Adam and Eve real historical persons	86	21	20
Believe in "rapture" of the Church	79	19	19
Scriptures inerrant in all matters	78	14	14
Women's ordination against Scripture	71	7	13
Myth/symbol vital to understanding Bible	64	90	90
Israel special nation blessed by God	60	10	13
Bible teaches premillennialism	60	8	11
Jesus could understand all languages	55	18	22
Believe in "dispensationalist" theory	38	3	10
God directly influences elections	37	15	7
Bible only dependable ethical guide	—	41	25
Theological Self-Identification:			
Fundamentalist	14	0	1
Evangelical	—	26	15
Conservative	67	25	24
Moderate	16	—	—
Liberal	1	38	55
Theological Cluster			
"Conservative"	89	31	25
"Liberal"	11	69	75
Number	(700)	(930)	(1,305)

So both modernist and traditionalist clergy are well represented in these samples. The Baptist theological perspective is strongly supernaturalist and apocalyptic, expecting a cataclysmic end to history as a result of divine intervention and stressing a very high christology, biblical inerrancy, and soteriological exclusivism. The Disciples, on the other hand, exhibit more of a traditional eschatological perspective — seeing the activity of God in historical events and the work of the church. They have abandoned many orthodox views, preferring a more critical and symbolic interpretation of Christian doctrines, and they have abandoned Christian exclusivism in large numbers, believing that God has witnesses in every time and place and in other religious traditions.

The beliefs expressed on individual items are also reflected in pastors' self-identification. Although we offered ministers somewhat different options to accord with common usage within each denomination, and so the responses are not directly comparable, they confirm the results of the orthodoxy items: note the overwhelming choice of conservative labels ("fundamentalist," "conservative") among Baptists, the three-way Presbyterian split (among "evangelicals," "conservatives," and "liberals"), and the Disciples' striking preference for the "*L* word."

Although these results might suggest a theological continuum ranging from the most conservative to the most liberal, a recent work on American Protestantism has suggested that the division is really even simpler: there are but two "factions" or "clusters" constituting the new boundaries in American Protestantism: religious liberals and religious conservatives.[12] These factions, it is argued, are divided not only on theology but on the role of the church, social issues, economic priorities, and foreign policy. And although some denominations are dominated by one faction and some by the other, the bipolar struggle has displaced the old religious competition based on denominations, with their historic creeds and traditions.

To complement our analysis of differences among these three denominations, we used a procedure known as cluster analysis to divide the ministers into two distinct groups, based on responses to the theological items in Table 1. Although the details of the procedure do not concern us here,[13] various tests show that each cluster is indeed quite homogeneous: one is consistently orthodox or conservative in theology, the other modernist or liberal. As Table 1 shows, theological conservatives dominate the SBC, while liberals claim a solid majority of Presbyterians and a slightly larger majority among Disciples. For simplicity of presentation, we have not included data on each faction in the following tables, but we will make frequent reference to the political differences between theological liberals and conservatives.

PERSONAL ORIENTATIONS TOWARD POLITICAL LIFE

We should expect considerable disagreement about ministerial involvement in political life within our sample. First, the divergence in theological perspective should give rise to different responses: if Hadden and Quinley's earlier findings hold up, ministers with a traditionalist, orthodox, and "other-worldly" theology should be less interested in politics, have little desire to be involved, have lower estimates of pastoral efficacy, and perhaps see little to be accomplished by political activism. Modernist clergy, with their "this-worldly" orientation, should exhibit very different traits: intense interest, desire for personal involvement, high estimates of efficacy, and a feeling that the world is amenable to change. Thus we would expect Disciples and Presbyterians to outstrip Baptists in favorable orientations toward political life, and the predominant theological

12. See Robert Wuthnow, *The Restructuring of American Religion* (Princeton: Princeton University Press, 1988).

13. See Guth, "Pastoral Politics in the 1988 Election: The Political Mobilization of Protestant Clergy," paper presented at the annual meeting of the American Political Science Association, Atlanta, 1989.

liberalism in these denominations should be reinforced by historical traditions more favorable to social and political involvement than those found among Southern Baptists.[14]

On the other hand, if Wuthnow's analysis of the recent political mobilization of conservative Protestantism is correct,[15] we should find few of the differences that characterized liberal and conservative clergy in the 1960s — or perhaps even a conservative advantage. If this obtains, we would expect that Southern Baptists, with their overwhelmingly orthodox clergy, should have the most favorable attitudes toward involvement, joined perhaps by the smaller conservative factions among Presbyterians and Disciples.

We asked ministers several questions concerning political interest, desire for involvement, and personal efficacy (see Table 2). The results are provocative. First of all, the predominantly orthodox Southern Baptists report just as much interest in politics as Presbyterians and Disciples do. Nevertheless, within all three denominations liberals claim more political interest than their orthodox rivals. Still, even the *orthodox* Baptists match the most interested non-Baptist faction, the liberal Presbyterians. Obviously "other-worldly" clergy do not necessarily lack interest in the kingdom of this world. On a related issue, however, the tables are turned, with Presbyterians and Disciples expressing greater desire to be more involved personally in social and political action. Here again, liberal clergy have an advantage over their orthodox counterparts within each church. Still, liberal and orthodox Baptists alike express greater desire for involvement than their Presbyterian and Disciples counterparts; the Baptist disadvantage overall comes from the overwhelming predominance of the orthodox with their lower scores. When it comes to a desire for more denominational commitment to politics, Baptists look pretty much like the others, exceeding the Presbyterians and falling just short of the Disciples. Breaking each denomination into conservative and liberal clusters again, we find that Baptist liberals want much more corporate involvement, while Baptist conservatives, Presbyterian liberals, and Disciples liberals want the current level. Presbyterian and Disciples conservatives would prefer much less denominational activism: write-in comments and responses to other questions clearly indicate that these factions resent the liberal posture of national church leaders and bureaucracies.

Do ministers think their activities can make a difference? In some ways, yes. Ministers have a surprisingly strong sense of personal political efficacy — at least insofar as their congregations are concerned. When asked whether "ministers have great potential to influence the social and political beliefs of their congregations," most agreed, but Baptists (and other theological conservatives) expressed the strongest affirmation. This may reflect several factors:

14. See John Lee Eighmy, *Churches in Cultural Captivity: A History of the Social Attitudes of Southern Baptists* (Knoxville: University of Tennessee Press, 1972); and Robert Friedly and D. Duane Cummins, *The Search for Identity: Disciples of Christ — The Restructure Years* (St. Louis: CPB Press, 1987).

15. See chap. 9 of Wuthnow, *The Restructuring of American Religion.*

TABLE 2 Clergy in the Social and Political World

	Percent "Strongly Agree" or "Agree"		
	BAPTIST	PRESBYTERIAN	DISCIPLES
Ministers in Politics			
More than "mild" interest in politics	77	76	76
Like to be more involved	41	50	49
Denomination should be more active	39	35	42
Ministers can greatly influence congregation	77	55	62
Hard to know right channels for action	64	47	57
Clergy of varying faiths should cooperate	53	57	63
Faith and Society			
If more were converted, social ills vanish	67	28	33
Christianity emphasizes spiritual realm	44	9	14
More emphasis on "social" sanctification	14	33	36
Liberation theology has many valid ideas	—	57	59
World deteriorating, not much can be done	14	5	5
Religion in America			
U.S. founded as Christian nation	67	31	33
Religion losing influence in U.S.	67	56	52
Many groups threaten religious freedom	72	30	27
Hard to be Christian and political liberal	53	8	11
Only free enterprise can be Christian	47	7	11
Government must support religion to keep moral	38	16	16

the traditional conservative emphasis on the efficacy of the Word — that is, pastoral preaching, the firmer political agreement between ministers and congregations among conservatives, and (a cynic might argue) the absence of real efforts to influence.[16] Ironically, Baptists may not feel capable of directing a congregational consensus: both liberal and conservative Baptists tend to agree that "it is difficult for ministers to know the proper political channels to use in accomplishing some goal" — a feeling shared by a majority of Disciples but by only a minority among Presbyterians. A majority in all three denominations thinks ministers should cooperate more in politics even if they differ in theology. True to their ecumenical traditions, Disciples rate such cooperation highest among the three.

Thus far the picture is more complex than the classic studies might predict: on some indicators of political interest and competence liberals excel, but on others conservatives do. Of course, ministers' activism will be conditioned by their "social theology": their perception of the world around them, the role of the church (if any) in addressing public problems, and the proper vehicles for activism (Table 2). First note that ministers differ sharply about the nature of social ills and how to cure them. For Baptists, the basic problem remains individual conversions: two-thirds agree that if "more people were brought to

16. See Rodney Stark, Bruce Foster, Charles Glock, and Harold Quinley, "The Sounds of Silence," *Psychology Today,* November 1970, pp. 38-41.

Christ, social ills would take care of themselves." Only a third of the Disciples and even fewer Presbyterians concur with this easy equation of salvation with social betterment. Both Presbyterians and Disciples also reject the statement that "Christianity is clear about separating spiritual and secular realms and putting emphasis on spiritual values," whereas a plurality of Baptists agree (and many more are "not sure"). On the other hand, while neither Disciples nor Presbyterians are prepared to abandon individual salvation in favor of social reform, they are much more inclined than Baptists to think "the church should put less emphasis on individual sanctification and more on transforming the social order in conformity with Christ's teaching." (Indeed, close to a majority of the dominant liberal factions in each of these denominations accept this statement.) Even more striking is the strong Presbyterian and Disciples support for "liberation theology," often perceived as a radical political doctrine.

Although Disciples and Presbyterians would seem to have a theology that envisions a larger role for social and political action, the Baptists find reasons for activism as well. Although their theology has important elements of apocalyptic thinking, few are ready to believe that nothing can be done to improve the world. But their political motivation does seem to be based in a kind of historical pessimism. They see a past in which America was founded as a Christian nation, a present in which religion is losing influence (a view also held by many Presbyterians and Disciples), and a future in which religious freedom is threatened by groups opposing all religion (a perception not shared by Disciples or Presbyterians). For many Baptists, the enemy is clear: political liberalism, which they think incompatible with true Christian faith (they actually include free enterprise among the tenets of the faith!). Such beliefs are clearly the foundation of the contemporary Christian Right. Nevertheless, even the Baptists, with their separationist heritage, have doubts about whether government should actually support religion in order to uphold traditional morality. Overall, though, many Baptists (and theological conservatives in the other churches) have developed a sort of "civil theology" that may serve as the functional equivalent of the liberals' updated Social Gospel.

Given these perspectives, do liberals and conservatives differ on what the church should do? We asked pastors to rank from 1 ("Top Priority") to 10 ("Lowest Priority") possible corporate activities.[17] In Table 3 we report the percentage of ministers giving each purpose a "Top Priority." Baptists rank traditional evangelism as the most important duty of the church, and while Presbyterians and Disciples clearly see local evangelism as a vital task, they give much lower priorities to national and especially world missions. On the other hand, they put more emphasis than the Baptists on social reform, whether at the national, local, or personal levels. Indeed, a more complex statistical analysis, using all ratings, shows that Baptists are preoccupied with "soul

17. Cf. Dean Hoge, *Division in the Protestant House* (Philadelphia: Westminster Press, 1976).

TABLE 3   Priorities for the Denomination

	BAPTIST	Percent First Priority* PRESBYTERIAN	DISCIPLES
Evangelism in local area	56	34	38
Evangelism in the United States	31	17	19
Evangelism overseas	14	5	3
Work for Christian moral standards in U.S.	12	5	6
Charity to individuals in need	7	13	9
Guidance and counseling for individuals	5	16	10
Overcoming injustice and oppression	4	16	18
Community self-help programs	4	7	6
Solve social problems locally	3	5	10
Work on national social reform	2	4	4

*Columns total to more than 100% because some ministers gave a number 1 priority to more than one choice.

winning" to the exclusion of other purposes — except for "working for Christian moral standards in America." Presbyterians are distinguished by their emphasis on charity and counseling, while Disciples (especially liberals) rate social reform higher than either Baptists or Presbyterians do.

APPROVAL OF ACTIVISM AND GENERAL INVOLVEMENT

On balance the findings above suggest that the predominantly liberal Disciples and Presbyterian clergy should exhibit greater approval for ministerial involvement in public affairs and probably be somewhat more active. But we have also found, in several respects, attitudes that might inspire or at least undergird political activism among Baptists and other theological conservatives. What kinds of activities do ministers approve for themselves? In the 1960s and early 1970s, Quinley discovered a vast disagreement between theological traditionalists and modernists over what activities were appropriate for ministers, with the orthodox far less supportive of many tactics. We cannot be sure his findings would still obtain today. Indeed, critics have argued that Quinley overemphasized highly visible and nonconventional actions, characteristic of liberal civil rights and antiwar movements, and undermeasured more subtle political behavior common among the traditionalists.[18] Moreover, even using similar indicators, recent studies have hinted at a "closing of the gap" between the two types of ministers in approval of activism.[19]

18. N. Koller and J. Retzer, "The Sounds of Silence Revisited," *Sociological Analysis* 41 (1980): 155-61.
19. See James Guth, "The Politics of Preachers: Southern Baptist Ministers and Christian Right Activism," in *New Christian Politics,* ed. David Bromley and Anson Shupe (Macon: Mercer University Press, 1984), pp. 239-49; Beatty and Walter, "Fundamentalists, Evangelicals and Politics," and "A Group Theory of Religion and Politics"; and Harder, "Pastors and Political Mobilization."

TABLE 4 Approval of Ministerial Activism

Percent Approving Ministers Who:

	BAPTIST	PRESBYTERIAN	DISCIPLES
Urge congregation to vote	99	99	99
Take public stand on political issue	88	93	92
Deliver sermon on controversial issue	75	86	85
Contribute money to candidate, PAC, party	70	86	85
Take public stand on political candidate	69	64	67
Form public affairs study group in church	60	96	93
Take pulpit stand on a political issue	59	62	60
Join national political organizations	44	71	72
Run for office	42	57	67
Form action group to accomplish a goal	36	78	80
Participate in protest march	36	69	65
Participate in civil disobedience	27	54	50
Endorse a candidate from the pulpit	8	5	6

Our findings suggest both the closing of the gap and its resilience. Table 4 reports approval scores on several Quinley questions and on some added by Guth in recent studies of Southern Baptists. The table is ordered by the actions most generally approved by Baptists to those least often approved. Overall, Presbyterians and Disciples hold a more activist conception of the minister's role. Indeed, on items such as forming study and action groups within the congregation, joining political organizations, running for office, and participating in protests and civil disobedience, vast differences exist, with Presbyterians and Disciples exceeding the Baptists, reflecting both the effects of theological liberalism and, perhaps, longer traditions of political involvement. Disciples and Presbyterians are also more tolerant of nonconventional protests and civil disobedience. The overwhelming Baptist rejection of civil disobedience helps explain the SBC leadership's recent disapproval of Operation Rescue's antiabortion protests. Only pulpit endorsement of candidates still elicits more disapproval (from all three denominations) than committing civil disobedience.

Are these variations in attitudes toward clerical activism reflected in different levels of activity? We gave ministers a checklist of activities and asked them if they had participated in such activities "in 1988," "only in the past," or "never." Table 5 reports the responses for actions taken in 1988, ordered from the Baptists' most frequent to least frequent activity. The first point is important: ministers are remarkably active as compared to the general public or, for that matter, even college-educated Americans. To take just two examples: only 3 percent of Americans belong to a political organization, compared to 9 percent of the Baptist pastors and 22 percent of Presbyterian and Disciples pastors; 7 percent of Americans contribute money to any political candidate or organization, but 19 percent of the Baptist pastors and close to

TABLE 5   Ministerial Political Activism (1988)

Percent of Ministers Who:

	BAPTIST	PRESBYTERIAN	DISCIPLES
Touched on an issue during sermon	74	80	81
Took public stand on political issue	63	65	65
Signed or circulated a petition	58	53	55
Publicly supported a candidate	48	46	52
Wrote or contacted public official	37	49	50
Preached on entire sermon on issue	—	38	40
Gave money to candidate, PAC, party	19	38	37
Wrote a letter to the editor	13	18	21
Joined national political organization	9	22	22
Organized social action group	7	27	16
Organized public affairs study group	5	16	19
Participated in protest march	4	6	5
Endorsed candidate from pulpit	3	2	2
Ran for public office	0	2	1
Mean number of acts in 1988	2.91	3.15	3.25

40 percent of the Presbyterian and Disciples pastors do.[20] The second point worthy of note is the remaining participation gap between the Baptists and the other denominations. On some activities, there are few denominational differences: touching on political issues in sermons, signing or circulating petitions, taking public stands on both issues and candidates (outside the pulpit), but on others there is still a substantial difference. Southern Baptists are less likely to contact a public official, give money to political causes, write a letter to the editor, join a national political organization, or organize study and action groups. Note, however, that relatively few ministers in any denomination undertake such actions. Liberals are theologically more inclined to engage in most activities, although the orthodox are more likely to sign and circulate petitions. The activism of the Christian Right, though, is suggested by the strong showing of Baptist conservatives regarding petitions and taking public stands on issues and candidates — which are more central to the Right's strategy than study groups, an indirect ministerial tactic favored by liberals.

The mean activism rates for the three denominations confirm the overall pattern apparent in the table: the Disciples are the most active, followed by the Presbyterians, with the Baptists the least involved. (Interestingly, liberals are most active among Presbyterians and Disciples, but conservatives are slightly more active among Baptists.) Thus, on general political activism the mainline denominations' advantage still holds, but the large divergence characteristic of the 1960s no longer exists.

20. See Kenneth Wald, *Religion and Politics in the United States* (New York: St. Martin's Press, 1987), p. 9.

At this point, we should dispose of one alternative explanation for the continuing theological and denominational differences in activism. The SBC differs from the PC(USA) and the Disciples in having substantial numbers of clergy who do not have college and/or seminary degrees. Given the strong correlation in the mass public between political involvement and higher education, we might suspect that the findings here are spurious, the result of lower levels of education among Baptist and orthodox pastors. But when we applied controls for education, both the theological and denominational gaps remained relatively constant: at every educational level, Baptist and orthodox pastors are slightly less active than their Presbyterian and Disciples and liberal counterparts.

DIFFERENT POLITICAL AGENDAS

Knowing how active ministers are does not tell us much about their public impact. We also need to discover their political agenda: what issues do they care about? After our inventory of political acts, we asked ministers to report how often their activity, taken as a whole, addressed a series of issues. In this list we included major issues debated at national denominational meetings as well as items of political controversy in the 1988 presidential election. Table 6 reports the results, ordered by the issues most frequently taken up by Baptists.

A few issues do form a kind of common agenda for the three denominations, although their prescriptions for solving these problems may differ. Family issues, alcohol and drugs, and hunger and poverty elicit much attention from ministers generally. Education, the Middle East, and capital punishment attract about the same level of interest in all groups, albeit from only a minority of clergy. Southern Baptists, on the other hand, are far more likely to concern themselves with pornography, abortion, gambling, prayer in schools, and homosexuality. Note that although both the PC(USA) and the Christian Church (Disciples of Christ) have taken liberal (and very controversial) stands on several such issues, very few ministers report activity on these. As other data in our study show, these are the items on which clergy perceive the greatest gap between themselves and their congregations. Earlier surveys confirm these results from the other side: few Disciples recall their ministers mentioning these issues.[21]

Although Presbyterians and Disciples avoid the issues on the conservative agenda, they do report greater activity on civil rights, environmentalism, defense spending, economic issues, women's rights, apartheid, and Latin

---

21. See Friedly and Cummins, *The Search for Identity,* p. 136. See also Joseph E. Faulkner, "What Are They Saying? A Content Analysis of 206 Sermons Preached in the Christian Church (Disciples of Christ) during 1988," pp. 416-39 in this volume.

TABLE 6   Issues Addressed in Political Activity

	Percent "Very Often" or "Often"		
	BAPTIST	PRESBYTERIAN	DISCIPLES
Common Concerns			
Family problems	91	81	83
Alcohol and drugs	86	73	77
Hunger and poverty	69	87	91
Education in U.S.	47	39	38
Israel and Middle East issues	28	27	30
Capital punishment	36	21	31
Conservative Priority			
Pornography	73	29	33
Abortion	71	35	29
Gambling	56	14	19
Prayer in school	49	17	25
Gay rights, homosexuality	47	19	19
Liberal Priority			
Civil rights	35	63	69
Environmental issues	26	61	64
Defense issues	22	50	55
Economic issues in U.S.	27	54	55
Equal Rights Amendment	22	41	51
South Africa, apartheid	9	39	42
Deficits, federal budget	22	33	39
Relations with USSR	15	34	36
U.S. Latin American policy	7	29	26

American problems, although only a minority are active on some of these. The differences between the Baptists and the Presbyterians and Disciples are replicated in miniature within each denomination: conservatives are more likely to address social issues, especially abortion and pornography, and liberals are more likely to address other domestic and foreign policy questions.

Still, theological effects are usually dwarfed by the Baptists' distinctive preoccupations. If we reorder Table 6 by combining all three agenda areas and ranking each denomination's preoccupations, we produce a picture of distinct denominational priorities. Nine of the top ten issues identified by Southern Baptists as the subject of their involvement are social issues (though even such issues as "hunger and poverty" are probably addressed in very different terms in the different denominations). For Baptists, most domestic and foreign policy issues approach or fall into the mean response category of "seldom." Clearly Southern Baptists are still "morality specialists," despite efforts by Christian Right leaders to expand their political horizons into economic and foreign policy. Among Presbyterians and Disciples the issues identified by Baptists as the targets of most activity are usually at the bottom of the list: six of the ten least addressed issues for Presbyterians and Disciples are social issues (the rest are primarily foreign policy). The top Presbyterian and Disciples agenda items

TABLE 7 Political Preferences of the Clergy

| | Percent in Each Category | | |
	BAPTIST	PRESBYTERIAN	DISCIPLES
Ideology			
Extremely Conservative	12	0	1
Very Conservative	44	5	4
Somewhat Conservative	24	18	15
Moderate or middle-of-the road	14	27	24
Somewhat Liberal	6	33	35
Very Liberal	1	14	17
Extremely Liberal	0	2	3
Partisanship			
Strong Republican	25	9	7
Weak Republican	12	9	7
Independent-leaning Republican	31	15	16
Independent	10	9	10
Independent-leaning Democrat	8	20	20
Weak Democrat	8	15	14
Strong Democrat	7	24	26

include alcohol and drug abuse and family issues, but other topics dominate: hunger and poverty, civil rights, the environment, defense spending and arms control, the economy, and ERA. Certainly these denominational differences reflect not only the traditional preoccupations of each but the current priorities of denominational leadership.[22]

POLITICAL ATTITUDES AND ORIENTATIONS

Next we turn to the political attitudes and identifications of ministers. If past studies are any guide, we would expect a clear pattern: theological conservatives should be political conservatives, and theological liberals should be political liberals. We should find conservative politics dominating among Baptists and liberal identifications and attitudes among Presbyterians and Disciples. Party and ideological self-identifications provide a good entry point. Political scientists have used both measures as powerful, succinct indicators of political orientation. And both show unmistakable evidence of continuing partisan and ideological polarization among Protestant ministers (Table 7). Baptists strongly prefer the GOP, although the largest number fall into the Independent-leaning Republican category, while Presbyterian and Disciples clergy tip heavily toward the Democrats, in sharp contrast to the preferences of their parishioners. (As ex-

22. See Friedly and Cummins, *The Search for Identity;* and Anne Motley Hallum, "Presbyterians as Political Amateurs," in *Religion in American Politics,* ed. Charles W. Dunn (Washington: CQ Press, 1988), pp. 63-73.

TABLE 8　Issue Attitudes Among Clergy

		Percent "Liberal"	
	BAPTIST	PRESBYTERIAN	DISCIPLES
Social Issues			
Death penalty	13	58	58
Creationism in public schools	14	56	54
Abortion amendment	15	72	72
Gun control	19	80	73
ERA	19	60	63
Gay rights	29	80	79
Sex education	35	85	88
Affirmative action	35	77	74
Tuition tax credits	41	67	65
School prayer	44	72	71
Economic and Social Welfare			
Privatization of government programs	20	67	65
Federal encouragement of day care	—	76	80
National health insurance	46	78	79
Minimum wage increase	49	—	—
More Federal effort on social welfare	54	84	83
Environment top priority	68	90	89
Foreign and Defense Issues			
Strategic Defense Initiative	19	76	73
Aid to the Contras	24	79	77
Sanctions against South Africa	36	63	70
No increases in defense spending	37	90	89
Sanctuary for Latin American refugees	38	71	72
U.S. support of friendly dictators	41	68	69
Need concessions to Palestinians	48	89	85
Strategic arms talks top priority	60	90	89

pected, theological liberals in each denomination are political liberals and Democrats; the orthodox are political conservatives and Republicans.) A more elaborate statistical analysis shows that theology is the chief influence on party identification, with denomination adding only a modest effect, whereas both factors, but especially theology, influence ideological self-identification. That is to say, Baptists are somewhat more Republican, and Disciples and Presbyterians are slightly more Democratic, than theology alone would predict. And on ideology, Baptists are much more conservative and Presbyterians and Disciples considerably more liberal than theology alone would suggest. All in all, Martin Marty's "two-party system" in American Protestantism is literally that, not just a theological and social status divide.

Consistent ideological divisions stand out on the overwhelming majority of social, economic, and foreign policy issues. As Table 8 shows, Baptist pastors take lopsidedly conservative stances on most social issues, with two exceptions: they are deeply divided over school prayer and tuition tax credits for parents of parochial school children; here traditional Baptist separatism has not been entirely eclipsed by Christian Right campaigns for aid to Christian schools and a constitutional amendment allowing organized prayer. The Baptists are especially conservative on the death penalty, abortion, creationism, and gun control. On the other hand, without exception, the Presbyterians and Disciples hold distinctly liberal views on every social issue. (It should be noted that among both Presbyterian and Disciples ministers a veritable chasm exists between liberal and orthodox factions on these questions.) Further statistical analysis shows that theology is the more powerful predictor on most social issues, but denomination also contributes considerable explanatory power, especially on gun control, sex education, gay rights, abortion, and the death penalty, with Baptists more conservative, and Presbyterian and Disciples ministers more liberal than expected on the basis of theology alone.

The pattern shifts somewhat on domestic economic issues. Although Baptists strongly agree that the federal government is doing too many jobs that should be left to the private sector (a sentiment not shared by two-thirds of the Presbyterians and Disciples), on specific domestic policy questions the balance among clergy is distinctly on the "liberal" side: even a plurality of the Baptists favor a larger federal role on social welfare issues, a national health insurance program, an increase in the minimum wage (data not shown), and tough environmental policies. But on all these points Presbyterian and Disciples ministers are even more liberal, and within each denomination modernist clergy are more liberal than orthodox.

Finally, defense and foreign policy issues seem to lie in intermediate territory. First, the Baptists reveal only partial agreement with the Christian Right's foreign policy: they do support Star Wars and aid to the contras and oppose stronger sanctions against South Africa, but there is a substantial liberal minority that opposes increases in defense spending and American support of friendly dictators; a plurality favors Israeli concessions to the Palestinians, and a strong majority backs strategic arms talks with the Soviets. Second, the Presbyterians and Disciples take staunchly liberal positions on all these questions, very much in accord with their denominations' official positions. Once again, theology accounts for much of the difference between and within denominations, but denomination also plays its accustomed role, locating Baptists much further to the right than theology alone would predict, and Presbyterians and Disciples slightly to the left.

PASTORAL INVOLVEMENT
IN THE 1988 PRESIDENTIAL RACE

Are these contrasting preferences reflected in clerical activism during national presidential campaigns? If so, how? Here we have very little to go on. There have been very few previous studies of ministerial activism in electoral, as opposed to social and political movement, contexts. Indeed, with the exception of Hadden's documentation of the relationship between ministerial theology and presidential choice in 1964 and Benton Johnson's classic studies of Protestant pastors,[23] there has been little analysis of activism in "normal" electoral situations. In fact, the stress on generalized activism implicit in the customary inventory of activities, such as that used above, may be quite misleading if, for example, the crucial target is presidential elections.

We asked ministers about their political preferences and choices in the 1988 presidential race and also inquired about their role in primary or general election campaigns. The answers provide considerable insight into the ways that pastors' attitudes intrude into national politics. We first asked ministers for their initial preferences in both Republican and Democratic fields. Once again, there were stark denominational differences. In the GOP race, Southern Baptists clearly preferred George Bush, with Bob Dole and Jack Kemp far behind. Among Presbyterians and Disciples, Bush and Dole ran neck and neck, although Bush was distinctly more popular among theological conservatives, and Dole was more popular among liberals. Pat Robertson, the Christian Right candidate, had little backing in any denomination, not even breaking into double digits among his fellow Southern Baptists.[24]

On the Democratic side, the favorites were less clear. Almost a fifth of the Southern Baptists refused to choose *any* Democratic contender, but co-religionist Al Gore led the pack with 46 percent. The preferences of Presbyterians and Disciples were much more dispersed, with Jesse Jackson having the largest contingent (28% among Disciples, 23% among Presbyterians), followed by Al Gore (15% and 19%), Michael Dukakis (15% and 18%), and Paul Simon (16% and 16%). Among the dominant faction of theological liberals in each denomination, however, Jackson and Dukakis moved well out in front.

Participation in the primaries and caucuses was quite high among all three denominations, ranging from 64 percent among the Baptists to a whopping 73 percent of the Disciples, a turnout far above that of the general public (Table 9). As might be expected on the basis of party identification, 71 percent of the Baptists who voted did so in the GOP contest, while 74 percent of the Presbyterians and 73 percent of the Disciples chose the Democratic race. George Bush was the overwhelming choice of Baptists, while Jesse Jackson took a narrow advantage among Presbyterians and a clearer plurality among Disciples. Thus, Baptist ministers reflected fairly well the political choices of their laity, while the Presbyterian and Disciples ministers not only voted in the "wrong" party but backed a candidate with no constituency among their middle-class white parishioners.

---

23. Johnson, "Theology and Party Preference among Protestant Clergymen," *American Sociological Review* 31 (1966): 200-208.
24. See Guth, "A New Turn for the Christian Right?"

TABLE 9　1988 Presidential Choices and Activism

		BAPTIST	PRESBYTERIAN	DISCIPLES
PRIMARY TURNOUT:		64%	67%	73%
IF VOTED, CHOSE:	GOP PRIMARY	(71%)	(26%)	(27%)
	Bush	45	18	18
	Dole	9	6	5
	Kemp	9	1	1
	Robertson	8	1	3
	DEM PRIMARY	(29%)	(74%)	(73%)
	Gore	15	7	5
	Dukakis	6	28	25
	Jackson	4	29	30
	Gephardt	2	1	4
	Simon	2	7	8
	Babbitt	0	1	1
	Hart	0	1	0
		100%	100%	100%
ACTIVE IN PRIMARY:		17%	22%	26%
IF ACTIVE, WORKED FOR:	REPUBLICAN	(76%)	(17%)	(24%)
	Bush	55	14	18
	Robertson	11	2	3
	Other GOP	10	1	3
	DEMOCRAT	(24%)	(83%)	(76%)
	Gore	10	5	2
	Dukakis	8	37	34
	Jackson	2	33	29
	Other Democrat	4	8	13
		100%	100%	100%
PRESIDENTIAL VOTE	Bush	81%	36%	34%
	Dukakis	19	64	66
ACTIVE IN CAMPAIGN		38%	35%	42%
IF ACTIVE, WORKED FOR:	Bush	88%	29%	30%
	Dukakis	12	71	70

We also asked whether ministers worked for any candidate by "wearing campaign buttons, putting a sign in the yard, attending speeches and rallies, etc." during the primaries. Here the Disciples led the way, with 26 percent reporting active support beyond voting; among the Presbyterians it was 22 percent, and among the Baptists 17 percent. (By theological cluster, 26% of the liberals but only 17% of the orthodox were active. But among Southern Baptists 18% of the conservatives and only 12% of the liberals were involved.) Among Disciples activists, Dukakis had 34 percent, Jackson 29 percent, and George Bush 18 percent. Presbyterian activists were divided among Dukakis (37%), Jackson (33%), and Bush (14%). Finally, among

Baptist activists Bush was the overwhelming beneficiary, with 55 percent; of the other Republicans and Democrats, only Robertson and Gore had a significant proportion (10% each).

The partisan polarization suggested by the primary data is confirmed by figures for the general election. As Table 9 shows, there was an enormous denominational fissure: Baptists went for Bush by a four-to-one margin, while the Presbyterians and Disciples supported Dukakis two to one. Interestingly, the Baptist percentage is identical with that for Southern Baptist laity; the Presbyterian and Disciples ministers' preferences reverse those of their laity.[25] Again, theological orientations produced the expected results: modernists in all denominations voted for Dukakis, and orthodox pastors favored Bush, although Baptists in both theological camps were slightly more likely than their Presbyterian and Disciples counterparts to vote for Bush.

The slight advantage of Presbyterian and Disciples pastors (especially the liberals) in activism during the primaries disappeared in the fall. Both theological factions were quite active in the campaign, with liberals having a statistically insignificant greater showing (40-36%). Among the Baptists, 88 percent of all activists worked for Bush, while 71 percent of the Presbyterians and 70 percent of the Disciples activists worked for Dukakis. Looking at it another way, among the Baptists 40 percent of all Bush voters were active in some fashion, as were 40 percent of Presbyterian and 45 percent of Disciples Dukakis voters. The "minority" candidates did less well in each denomination: only 30 percent of the small group of Baptist Dukakis voters were active; among Presbyterians only 27 percent of Bush voters were involved, compared with 38 percent among the Disciples. Clearly, something in the denominational climate encourages greater activism among enthusiasts of the "favorite" candidate.

A final cautionary note: the apparent balance between liberal and conservative activism produced by our sample is somewhat misleading. Even with a slight disadvantage in the rate of participation, Southern Baptist clerical activists overwhelmed their Presbyterian and Disciples counterparts in numbers, size of congregations, and availability of organizational resources. To take the point on numbers, in 1988 there were over 37,000 Southern Baptist churches and over 63,000 ordained clergy, compared to 11,500 PC(USA) churches and 19,000 ministers, and 4,200 Disciples churches and 6,800 ministers. The imbalance is even greater when evangelists and other religious workers are considered. A major reason for the salience of conservative clerical activism in the 1980s is not so much a decline in liberal activism as the greater numbers of conservatives, resulting from a somewhat increased rate of activism among a much larger clerical corps.

---

25. Lyman Kellstedt, letter to author, 1989; cf. Paul Lopatto, *Religion and the Presidential Election* (New York: Praeger, 1985).

DISCUSSION

Although we have to examine comparative data from other denominations, the evidence presented here suggests that we may now be close to true "two party" mobilization in American Protestantism. Not only are modernist liberals of the Protestant mainline churches, such as the Disciples and the PC(USA), holding to their political commitments and activism, but they have been joined by their orthodox colleagues, who may still resist certain types of clerical involvement, especially in nonconventional modes, but have almost achieved parity in many kinds of participation, and perhaps even superiority in numbers — plus the advantage of picking the winning side, at least in presidential races.

These findings provide further impetus for reassessment of earlier research predicting the permanent superiority in activism of modernist, this-worldly clergy over their traditionalist, other-worldly counterparts. Although liberals are still more approving of activism and slightly more active, conservatives are seldom far behind, especially in conventional electoral politics, which, after all, may ultimately be the most effective kind. That this increase has come without fundamental changes in the basic social perspectives and organizational priorities of theological conservatism is even more striking. This suggests not only the malleability of theologies but also the possibility of a variety of religious avenues to clerical involvement. In fact, much analysis of clerical activism has focused too much on the ministers' political role as corporate leaders and not enough on their own definition of the proper political avenues for clergy. Write-in comments on our surveys, especially from conservatives, make it clear that other-worldly clergy can maintain traditional understandings of the role of the church but have very new and more activist definitions for the minister-as-citizen, outside the church. Hence the preference for petitions, for public (not pulpit) stands on candidates and issues, as opposed to study and action groups and political sermons within the church. We need in the future to focus less on *whether* ministers are politically involved, and more on *how*.

We have also seen the continuing impact of denominational traditions, preoccupations, and leadership. The evidence here does much to explain the distinctive traits of each denomination's politics in recent years: the positions adopted by national governing bodies are really quite representative of the attitudes of their *clergy*, though certainly not of the laity. The Disciples clergy exhibit a distinctive meld of theological and political liberalism, combined with an impressive degree of public activism; this combination is opposed only by a small and dispirited minority of pastors. The Presbyterians have many of the same traits, but experience a more vigorous internal debate over both theological and political liberalism and the proper role of the church in public affairs. Finally, the Southern Baptist Convention has moved even further rightward in recent years, in large part because of the new mobilization, inside and outside the church, of its conservative clerical constituency.

The origins of these distinctive theological and political orientations are quite complex. One important influence is region: ministers from the South (especially the Deep South) in all three denominations are much more conservative than their colleagues elsewhere. Thus, Baptist conservatism is at least partly "Southern," and the greater liberalism of Disciples and Presbyterians reflects their predominant location outside the South. (Here the recent Presbyterian merger has created the potential for greater conflict: ministers from the southern wing are substantially more conservative than their northern colleagues.) The ministers' own social class roots have some significance. Baptist ministers come from much lower socioeconomic status than Presbyterians, who are overwhelmingly middle-class. The Disciples fall somewhere in between. In all three denominations, ministers from farm and blue-collar origins tend to be more preoccupied with theological and social traditionalism. The nature of the ministers' childhood settings works the same way: those from rural areas are more theologically and politically conservative in all three denominations, but the SBC has the largest contingent of such ministers.

Although such background factors have some influence, they are almost overwhelmed by the impact of professional socialization and training. In all three denominations clergy become increasingly liberal in both theological and political orientation with each advance in secular and, especially, theological education. And ministers from the three denominations differ greatly in this regard. Fully 20 percent of Southern Baptists lack a college degree, and 40 percent do not have a seminary degree; only 21 percent have gone beyond the first seminary degree for further theological study. On the other hand, virtually all Presbyterian ministers have college and seminary degrees, and 44 percent have further training in theology or ministry. The Disciples are not far behind: 90 percent have college and seminary degrees, and 42 percent have done further theological work.

The substance and location of ministers' education are also vital. Here we gain some insight from from the study by Everett Carll Ladd, Jr., and S. Lipset of the political and religious leanings of American academics, which revealed that professors at the most selective and prestigious colleges and universities, those in the social sciences and humanities, and those most integrated into their disciplines were furthest to the left.[26] Applying this perspective to ministers produces analogous results, although the total educational pattern is distinct in each denomination. As undergraduates, most Southern Baptist ministers study either religion or an applied discipline, such as business, education, or computer science, almost invariably at small, nonselective denominational or state colleges. Presbyterians, on the other hand, major in the humanities, especially literature and history, or (increasingly) in the social sciences. They frequently attend selective private or "Public Ivy" institutions.

26. Ladd and Lipset, *The Divided Academy: Professors and Politics* (New York: W. W. Norton, 1975).

Not surprisingly, the dominant educational pattern among Baptists produces the most conservative ministers (among the college-educated), while the predominant Presbyterian route is followed by theological and political liberals. A similar pattern holds for seminary training: ministers from the most prestigious interdenominational seminaries, such as Yale, Vanderbilt, and the University of Chicago, are the most liberal in all three denominations; few Baptists attend such schools, but a significant minority of Presbyterians and Disciples do. On the other side, many of the most conservative Baptists attend independent fundamentalist seminaries, while Presbyterian conservatives often come from evangelical seminaries such as Gordon-Conwell or Fuller. In both of these denominations, graduates of the denomination's own seminaries exhibit some theological and political diversity but generally conform to the dominant pattern: conservative among Baptists, liberal among Presbyterians.

In many ways, the Disciples' clergy have the most uniform and distinctive recruitment and socialization pattern. The vast majority attend Disciples colleges and seminaries, all of which (with only slight variations) produce theological and political liberals in overwhelming numbers. They are joined by an even more liberal minority from schools such as Yale, Vanderbilt, and Chicago. The conservative remnant is composed largely of three different types: (1) ministers brought up in a more conservative denomination and/or trained in a conservative denomination's seminaries, (2) older ministers who have attended a Bible college and perhaps a year or two of seminary, and (3) the relatively few lay ministers among Disciples, those with little or no formal theological training.

These patterns have considerable significance for understanding our findings. First, the vast theological and political differences between the Baptists on the one hand and the Disciples and Presbyterians on the other are in part the product of very different denominational policies, traditions, and experiences in professional education for ministers. Second, the data help explain the very considerable political gap between the attitudes of Disciples and Presbyterian clergy and their laity, and the greater agreement between the political choices of Baptist clergy and laity. The ministers in the two mainline denominations have educational backgrounds quite unlike those of most of their parishioners, both in substance and extent, while the Baptists are less clearly differentiated by education from their congregations. Thus, given the persistence of established programs of professional education, it is likely that the political attitudes and choices described above will persist, ensuring continued conflict between opposing groups of Protestant ministers and between mainline clergy and laity.

Active and Inactive Disciples, Presbyterians, and Southern Baptists: A Comparative Socioeconomic, Religious, and Political Profile

Bruce A. Greer

INTRODUCTION

Who are the people who identify themselves as Disciples of Christ? What are their socioeconomic, religious, and political characteristics? How do they feel about the major social and moral issues of our time, such as race relations, civil liberties, crime, gender roles, abortion, and sexuality? How do they compare with other religious and denominational groups? In particular, how do Disciples compare with Presbyterians and Southern Baptists, those associated with the two traditions that have perhaps the closest historical ties to the Stone-Campbell tradition. These are the questions addressed in this essay.

The Method

To ensure breadth and balance in this study, the surveys of two national organizations have been utilized: the National Opinion Research Center (NORC) at the University of Chicago and the Gallup Organization. Eight NORC General Social Surveys from 1980 to 1988 provide the primary source of data for this study. Seventeen Gallup polls taken between 1985 and 1987

I wish to thank Wade Clark Roof of the University of California at Santa Barbara, Deborah Sellers of the University of Massachusetts at Amherst, Lois Timms-Ferrara of the Roper Center at the University of Connecticut, Tom W. Smith of the National Opinion Research Center, and D. Newell Williams of Christian Theological Seminary for their helpful assistance. — BRUCE A. GREER

provide a second, much more limited source of data. The total sample size for the eight NORC surveys is 12,704; the total sample size for the seventeen Gallup polls is 26,377.[1]

National surveys, as opposed to those conducted by denominations, are more useful for a comparative study such as this for three reasons. First of all, their consistency over time makes them well suited for meaningful analysis. This is the particular advantage of the comprehensive General Social Survey, which has been consistent in its content since 1972. Because the same questions are asked in any number of its annual surveys, the analysis of smaller subsamples is made possible by aggregating cases over a number of years. Though Gallup polls tend to focus on specific issues pertinent to a given time, they always include valuable sociodemographic information about the respondents. Using basic sociodemographic variables from Gallup polls (e.g., age, sex, marital status, education, income, political affiliation, religion, region, and community type), one can quickly aggregate an adequate number of cases in order to profile a subsample such as Disciples, Presbyterians, and Southern Baptists.

Second, for a variety of reasons, denominational surveys are difficult to use for comparative analysis. For example, the *Presbyterian Panel* provides an excellent profile of affiliates of the Presbyterian Church (USA); however, the content changes with each survey. Because denominational surveys are often in-house studies, they tend to focus on issues of interest to a particular denomination and often vary widely in the sampling technique and questions asked. Comparisons of such surveys are questionable, because one is inevitably comparing apples and oranges. Though such studies can be valuable and should not be overlooked, national surveys are the better choice for comparative analysis. Despite some of the nagging problems associated with denominational categorization in national surveys, their sampling techniques and consistency over time make them the better source of data.

Third, a truer and perhaps more useful profile of those who call themselves Disciples of Christ, Presbyterians, and Southern Baptists can be developed by comparing broadly across the three traditions in the general population. While denominational studies of the constituent members of these particular denominations must be given due consideration, national surveys have distinct advantages. Church members or not, there are national survey respondents who have at one time or another been a part of one of these traditions and shaped by them — at least to the degree that they have chosen to identify themselves as Disciples of Christ, Presbyterians, or Southern Baptists.

The broader profile to be obtained from national survey data seems more useful for all concerned. It is instructive, for example, to know about the

---

1. James Allan Davis and Tom W. Smith, *General Social Surveys, 1972-1988* (machine-readable data files; Storrs, Conn.: Roper Center for Public Opinion Research, 1988); *The Gallup Poll* (machine-readable data files for seventeen Gallup Poll surveys; Storrs, Conn.: Roper Center for Public Opinion Research, 1985-87).

characteristics and opinions of the "unchurched" among the three respective traditions. Only surveys of the general population can yield such valuable information. For obvious reasons, in-house, denominationally sponsored surveys of church members often tell us little if anything about those outside the flock who still claim some association with it.

To augment national survey data, surveys from the three denominations being compared were utilized: the 1986 *Disciple Churchwide Survey,* the 1987 *Presbyterian Panel* of the Presbyterian Church (USA), and the *1986 Survey of Southern Baptists.* While each denominational survey differed in its sampling technique — from self-selection among certain constituents, to random selection from within a constituency, to a sample of the general population — each amplifies the broader national surveys of NORC and Gallup.

These denominationally conducted surveys contained rather large samples. The 1986 *Disciple Churchwide Study* had the largest sample of all (12,165). The 1987 *Presbyterian Panel* obtained a sample of 1,128 church members and 998 elders, although only church members were used for comparison. The 1986 *Survey of Southern Baptists* obtained a sample of 1,072 people and was the only survey of the four using a sampling technique not involving constituent churches and their members. These data were used to enhance and expand upon the findings of the GSS and Gallup data.

The 1986 *Disciple Churchwide Study* could not be used as a primary source of data for this study for three reasons. First, the sampling technique was problematic. Because random sampling (or some variation of it) was apparently not used, these data cannot be considered to give "an accurate picture of the identity and views of Disciples."[2] Though the churches chosen to participate may have been selected randomly, the respondents within those churches seem to have been self-selected. This is problematic because there is no assurance that respondents were representative "active Disciple church members." How does one know, for example, what constitutes an "active" member? Was the method of questionnaire distribution the same in all places? Did they fall into the hands of individuals who rarely attend? Though there were 12,165 respondents — a sizable sample, to be sure — the sampling technique compromises the representativeness of the findings.

A second reason the *Disciple Churchwide Study* could not be used is that it tells nothing about Disciples *in general,* those on the outside and edges of the denomination as well as those involved within it. Only a survey of the general population can provide such information. In fairness to those who planned and conducted the study, it was not meant to describe Disciples in general nor was it designed to be used as a comparative tool. Its purpose was fundamentally different from that of this study.

As a study of "active" Disciples church members, the *Disciple Church-*

---

2. Ann Updegraff-Spleth and Charles Brackbill, *Report on Disciple Churchwide Survey* (Indianapolis: Christian Church [Disciples of Christ] Division of Homeland Ministries, 1986), p. 3.

wide Study may well provide, at best, an adequate description of church-affiliated Disciples. Its findings concerning demographic characteristics seem *intuitively* correct;[3] however, given the sampling technique, it cannot be said with confidence that its findings are "accurate," no matter how large the response rate in terms of the percentage of questionnaires returned or total respondents. Much smaller sample sizes (e.g., 1,500) can be far more accurate given good sampling technique. Unfortunately, the ostensibly "comprehensive" nature of the survey does not automatically guarantee accuracy or representativeness. Caution is therefore warranted when generalizing about Disciples from the *Disciple Churchwide Study*.

The Sample

Though a variety of data was used for this study, the primary data for the bulk of the analysis are taken from the eight annual General Social Surveys between 1980 to 1988. Out of a total sample size of 12,704 there were 983 Southern Baptists, 511 Presbyterians, and 206 Disciples. For reasons explained in the Appendix to this chapter, the Southern Baptist sample size was taken from the five General Social Surveys between 1984 and 1988 and therefore reduced to a total of 551. Out of the seventeen Gallup surveys with a total sample of 26,377, there were 1,973 Southern Baptists, 457 Presbyterians, and 565 Disciples.

Using General Social Survey data, the subsamples for each of the three denominations were divided into two groups, "frequent attenders" and "infrequent attenders." It is clearly useful to know how the three denominational constituencies differ from one another in general, but it is equally useful to know how frequent attenders and infrequent attenders compare both within and between the denominations. For the purpose of analysis, a "frequent attender" is defined as someone attending religious services twice a month or more, and an "infrequent attender" as someone who attends once a month or less. The breakdown of these six subsamples is shown in Table 1 (p. 390).

FINDINGS

1. SOCIOECONOMIC CHARACTERISTICS

Disciples, Presbyterians, and Southern Baptists will first be compared according to their general socioeconomic characteristics, comparing frequent and infrequent attenders within each denominational group. These characteristics include gender, age, race, ethnic origin, native birth, region, community type, mobility, education, occupation, occupational prestige, income, marital status, and family size.

3. Updegraff-Spleth and Brackbill, *Report on Disciple Churchwide Survey*, pp. 21-23.

TABLE 1   Denominational Samples by Church Attendance

	Disciples		Presbyterians		So. Baptists*	
Attendance	N	%	N	%	N	%
Frequent Attenders	100	(48.5)	202	(39.7)	270	(49.0)
Males	33	(33.0)	71	(35.1)	105	(38.9)
Females	67	(67.0)	131	(64.9)	165	(61.1)
Infrequent Attenders	106	(51.5)	307	(60.3)	281	(51.0)
Males	59	(55.7)	155	(50.5)	141	(50.2)
Females	47	(44.3)	152	(49.5)	140	(49.8)
Total:	206		509		551	
Males	92	(44.7)	226	(44.4)	246	(44.6)
Females	114	(55.3)	283	(55.6)	305	(55.4)

NOTE: Among all General Social Survey respondents about 45 percent attend religious services twice a month or more: 36.5 percent of males (N = 5,408) and 51.4 percent of females (N = 7,235) are "frequent attenders."

Gender Distribution

Both the Gallup Poll and General Social Survey show the gender distribution in each of the three denominations to be very similar, each having more women than men (see Table 1). The United States population on the whole tends to be more female than male, 52 percent female and 48 percent male.[4] All three denominations are not, therefore, very different from the general population. Survey samples, for various reasons, tend to have slightly higher ratios of women to men than the general population. This being the case, one might assume that the three denominational samples are biased in the direction of having a slightly higher proportion of women.

The gender distribution among frequent attenders, however, differs considerably from that of infrequent attenders. A consistent pattern is seen among the frequent attenders in all three denominations: women are much more likely to be regular church attenders than men. Among Presbyterians and Southern Baptists who attend infrequently, the male/female ratio is about even, whereas Disciples infrequent attenders are more likely to be male. The gender ratio among General Social Survey "frequent attenders" is strikingly similar to the gender ratio found in the *Disciple Churchwide Survey* and the *Presbyterian Panel* (64% women/36% men and 61% women/38% men, respectively). This similarity would seem to indicate two things about in-house surveys of constituents conducted by denominations: (1) they may have a greater proportion of women because church affiliates are more likely to be women and (2) their findings may be similar to those concerning frequent attenders in a general population survey.

---

4. *Statistical Abstract of the United States: 1989* (Washington: U.S. Department of Commerce Bureau of the Census, 1989), p. 16.

TABLE 2 Attendance by Age by Denomination

	DISCIPLES		PRESBYTERIANS		SOUTHERN BAPTISTS	
	N	%	N	%	N	%
Less than 30:						
Attenders	19	(39)	25	(29)	48	(44)
Nonattenders	30	(61)	60	(71)	60	(56)
Subtotals	49	(24)	85	(17)	108	(20)
30 to 49:						
Attenders	29	(41)	70	(39)	97	(44)
Nonattenders	41	(59)	109	(61)	124	(56)
Subtotals	70	(34)	179	(35)	221	(41)
50 and older:						
Attenders	52	(60)	107	(44)	125	(58)
Nonattenders	35	(40)	138	(56)	89	(42)
Subtotals	87	(42)	245	(48)	214	(39)
Totals:	206		509		543	

($p < .001$).

Note: Mean age for *attenders* among Disciples (50.3), Presbyterians (52.1), and Southern Baptists (48.3); for *nonattenders:* Disciples (42.5), Presbyterians (47.8), and Southern Baptists (44.0). Mean age for all respondents in each denomination: Disciples (46.3), Presbyterians (49.5), and Southern Baptists (46.1).

Age Distribution

Slight differences in age distribution seem to exist between Disciples of Christ, Presbyterians, and Southern Baptists. Southern Baptists and Disciples have a lower average age than Presbyterians by three to three and a half years. Southern Baptists and Disciples, on the other hand, are slightly older than the general population by about a year, and Presbyterians by more than four years, with the mean age for all General Social Survey respondents from 1980 to 1988 being 45.2. It is important to remember that the average age of respondents to national surveys will almost always be higher than the overall national average simply because survey respondents are usually 18 years of age or older. This eliminates all persons under the age of 18 from most samples, thus causing the average age to be higher.

Statistically significant differences occur within and between the three denominations when age distribution is cross-tabulated by frequency of attendance (see Table 2). As one might expect, infrequent attenders are younger than frequent attenders by four to eight years on average across the three denominations. The age difference is greatest among the Disciples and the least among Southern Baptists. Another striking feature of the age distribution is the rather high *average* age of frequent attenders, especially among Presbyterians and Disciples. In both cases more than half of their frequent attenders are over 50 years of age. Among Disciples and Southern Baptists there seems to be a linear relationship between age and attendance: the older people are, the more likely they are to be frequent attenders. This is not the case among Presbyterians, where infrequent attenders outnumber frequent attenders in all age categories.

Racial Composition and Ethnic Origin

Both the Gallup Poll and the General Social Surveys show the Disciples of Christ and Presbyterians to be in excess of 90 percent white, Presbyterians even more than Disciples. *The Disciple Churchwide Survey,* however, indicates a higher percentage of Disciples being white, a percentage comparable to Presbyterians.

It is difficult to know the racial composition of the Southern Baptist Convention. For some reason both the Gallup Poll and General Social Survey indicate that the Southern Baptist Convention is 22 percent black. Informal estimates of the racial composition of the Southern Baptist Convention obtained from knowledgeable sources within a national board of that body indicate the denomination to be about 95 percent white, although there is no way to verify this estimate. One thing certain in the experience of these knowledgeable sources is that the Southern Baptist Convention is not 22 percent black (see Appendix). Unfortunately, the *1986 Survey of Southern Baptists* did not ask its respondents their race.

Disciples, Presbyterians, and Southern Baptists have a common ethnic heritage. The vast majority have ancestry in the British Isles (England, Wales, Scotland, and Ireland) and Germany. Three out of four Presbyterians and Southern Baptists share this ethnic heritage as opposed to two out of three Disciples. Among the Southern Baptists, 12.5 percent claim some Native American ancestry. The next most common ethnic ancestry for all three denominations is "Western European" (not including Germany). In addition to ancestry from the British Isles, Germany, and other western European nations, Presbyterians also have a modest number of Scandinavians (6.1%). All three denominations are dominated by persons of western and northern European ancestry, as might be expected. In addition, the vast majority in all three denominations, 95 percent or more, are native born in the United States.

Region

The regional distribution of Disciples, Presbyterians, and Southern Baptists differs considerably, as would be expected. The numerical stronghold of the Disciples of Christ is found in the Midwest — the East North Central and West North Central census regions. Substantial numbers of Disciples are also located in the Pacific, East South Central, South Atlantic, and West South Central census regions. Approximately 90 percent of all Disciples live in these six regions, with very few living in the Mountain, Middle Atlantic, and New England census regions.

Presbyterians are more northern and eastern in their location. Six out of ten live in the Middle Atlantic, South Atlantic, and East North Central census regions, within a geographical triangle bounded by New York City, Chicago, and Florida. Another 22 percent live in the Pacific and West North Central census regions. The New England, East South Central, West South Central, and Mountain census regions each have somewhat sparse numbers of Presbyterians.

Southern Baptists still remain very much "Southern" despite the aggressive expansion of the Southern Baptist Convention into all parts of the United States since World War II. Eighty-two to 86 percent of all Southern Baptists live in the three southern census regions: South Atlantic, East South Central, and West South Central. Another 12 to 15 percent live in the East North Central, West North Central, and the Pacific regions. Small numbers will be found in New England, the Middle Atlantic, or Mountain states.

The greatest overlap among the three denominations is in the South Atlantic region. Disciples and Presbyterians have considerable overlap with each other in the Midwest. Disciples and Southern Baptists, on the other hand, overlap with each other in the East South Central and West South Central regions. Of the three denominations, the Disciples are perhaps the least concentrated geographically, and Southern Baptists the most concentrated. The Disciples of Christ, on the whole, tends to be a mid-American denomination, concentrated for the most part in the frontier lands of the late eighteenth and early nineteenth centuries. The Presbyterians, on the other hand, have greater concentration in those places once part of colonial America.

Disciples, Presbyterians, and Southern Baptists for the most part live in the same regions they lived in at the age of 16. It is interesting to note, however, that in all three denominations a greater percentage of infrequent attenders live in the West than is the case with frequent attenders. One out of every four Disciples who are infrequent attenders and one out of five infrequent-attender Presbyterians lives in the West. Three out of four Presbyterians, seven out of ten Southern Baptists, and nearly six out of ten Disciples living in the West are infrequent attenders, following the general pattern of church attendance in that area.

Residence

The general population in the United States is more urban and suburban in residence (72%) than any of the three denominations under consideration. Large percentages in each denomination live in cities of 50,000 or more, their suburbs, or the unincorporated areas next to them: 69 percent of Presbyterians, 61 percent of Southern Baptists, and 48 percent of Disciples, with minimal difference between frequent and infrequent attenders in all cases. Among the three denominations, however, the Disciples of Christ are the most likely to be rural. One out of three Disciples, versus one out of four Southern Baptists and one out of five Presbyterians, lives in small towns of less than 2,500, unincorporated areas of 1,000 to 2,500, or open country.

About half of all Presbyterians live in the top 100 Standard Metropolitan Statistical Areas (SMSAs) of the United States, versus about one-third of all Disciples and Southern Baptists. Nearly half of all Southern Baptists are found in smaller cities not in the top 100 SMSAs and towns over 10,000 in population, as opposed to about one third of Disciples and Presbyterians. About 37 percent of all Disciples live in counties without a town of 10,000 or more in population, nearly twice the percentage of Presbyterians and Southern Baptists. Presbyterians, therefore, are more likely to be found in the cities and suburbs of the top 100 SMSAs and Disciples more likely to be found in rural areas.

Of the three denominations, the Presbyterians are the most mobile, as might be expected due to their higher educational and occupational prestige levels. More than one-third of them live in different states from when they were 16 years of age. One-fourth of Disciples and one-fifth of Southern Baptists now live in a different state. Just under one-half of all Southern Baptists, on the other hand, still live in the same community they lived in at age 16, versus 44 percent of Disciples and 38 percent of Presbyterians.

Education

As expected, Presbyterians have the highest level of education among the three denominations, with an average of 13.4 years. Disciples average 12.1 years of education, versus 11.9 years for Southern Baptists. These statistics alone fail to reveal the rather significant difference in all three denominations between frequent and infrequent attenders. In every case, frequent attenders average one-half to nearly one year more education than infrequent attenders, a pattern that holds true for the general population as well. A curvilinear relationship exists between church attendance and education: people with less than high school education and those with postgraduate education tend not to go; on the other hand, high school graduates, those with some college education, and college graduates are more likely to attend.

There is a significant discrepancy between the educational levels found in the General Social Survey and Gallup samples and those reported in the *Disciple Churchwide Survey,* the *Presbyterian Panel,* and the *1986 Survey of Southern Baptists* (see Table 3). For the categories "some college" and "college or more," the Gallup Poll results are from 25 to 28 percent below those of the denominationally conducted surveys, and the General Social Survey results are from 21 to 23 percent below denominational surveys. Conversely, the percentage of Disciples, Presbyterian, and Southern Baptist respondents with less than a high school education is much higher in the Gallup and General Social Survey samples than in the denominational samples.

A partial explanation can be seen in the difference of educational levels by attendance in the three denominations. Among Disciples and Southern

TABLE 3   Distribution of Education

			Disciples			Presbyterians			Southern Baptists		All
	Glp	GSS	Den	Glp	GSS	Den	Glp	GSS	Den	GSS	
Education:											
(Ave. yrs.)			(12.1)			(13.4)			(11.9)	(12.5)	
Percent with:											
College or >	15	12	37	28	31	51	12	11	24	29	
Some college	16	25	21	21	24	26	16	19	29	33	
(Subtotal)	(31)	(37)	(58)	(49)	(55)	(77)	(28)	(30)	(53)	(62)	
HS grad.	45	32	31	36	27	20	41	38	35	20	
< HS	24	31	12	15	19	2	30	32	12	18	
(Subtotal)	(69)	(63)	(43)	(51)	(46)	(22)	(71)	(70)	(47)	(38)	
Ratio:											
Some college >	31	37	58	49	55	77	28	30	53	38	
High school or less (p < .0001).	69	63	43	51	46	22	71	70	47	62	

NOTE: *Glp* = Gallup Poll; *GSS* = General Social Survey; *Den* = Denominational surveys.

Baptists, respondents with less than a high school education are not as likely to attend church. Among all three denominations those with some college education or more are more likely to attend. Both the *Disciple Churchwide Survey* and the *Presbyterian Panel* may show higher educational levels because their samples are likely to contain active churchgoers. Thus one might conclude that the people in the pews of the churches in all three denominations may well have higher educational levels than those who are not in the pews.

Occupational Prestige and Income

The pattern among the three denominations for occupational prestige is similar to that of education. The average score on the Hodge-Siegel-Rossi prestige scale differs between frequent and infrequent attenders.[5] With prestige scores on the scale ranging from 9 to 82, Presbyterian frequent attenders have the highest average prestige score of 46.5. Disciples of Christ frequent attenders have an average prestige score of 43.6, and Southern Baptist frequent attenders have an average prestige score of 41.0. Presbyterians who are infrequent attenders have an average prestige score of 44.0, infrequent-attender Disciples 38.0, and infrequent-attender Southern Baptists 39.1.

Those in all three denominations who work in lower-prestige occupations are less likely to attend church. Only 37 percent of Presbyterians in this prestige

5. See James Allan Davis and Tom W. Smith, *General Social Surveys, 1972-1988: Cumulative Codebook* (Storrs, Conn.: Roper Center for Public Opinion Research, 1988), pp. 619-36.

category attend frequently, versus 40 percent of Disciples and 46 percent of Southern Baptists. Among Disciples of Christ and Southern Baptists, frequent attenders are in the slight majority among those in occupations of middle-range prestige; however, frequent-attender Presbyterians constitute only 39 percent of all Presbyterians in this prestige category. A very high percentage of Disciples and Southern Baptists in higher-prestige occupations (72% and 62%, respectively) are frequent attenders. Although only 48 percent of higher-prestige Presbyterians are frequent attenders, this is the highest percentage among the three Presbyterian prestige groups.

As would be expected, Presbyterians have the highest household income of the three denominations. One out of three Presbyterians has a high household income as opposed to about one out of five Disciples and Southern Baptists. Disciples and Southern Baptists, on the other hand, tend to be in the lower two income categories, 60 percent and 55 percent respectively. It is of interest to note, however, that there is only a modest difference between the household income of frequent attenders and that of infrequent attenders in all three denominations (see Table 4).

Marital and Family Status

About six out of every ten Disciples of Christ, Presbyterian, and Southern Baptist respondents to the General Social Survey claim to be married, with slightly more Gallup Poll respondents in the three denominations claiming to be married. Only modest differences exist between the percentage of frequent attenders and infrequent attenders who are married. More significant differences are found among the widowed, divorced, separated, and never married. Widowed persons are more likely to be frequent attenders in all three denominations, while the divorced, separated, and never married are more likely to be infrequent attenders. Divorced or separated Presbyterians are an exception, along with Southern Baptists who have never married, with nearly equal percentages among frequent and infrequent attenders. In all three denominations eight out of ten frequent attenders are either married or widowed. The *Disciple Churchwide Survey* and *Presbyterian Panel* both report even higher percentages of married and widowed people among their respondents.

Southern Baptists have had, on average, the most children among the three denominations, and the Presbyterians have had the least. Seven to eight out of ten respondents in all three denominations have had children, the vast majority with up to three children. Seven out of ten Disciples of Christ frequent attenders do not currently have children at home, as opposed to six out of ten infrequent-attender Disciples. The *Disciple Churchwide Survey* results indicate that 70 percent of Disciples "active church members" do not have children living at home — the same as frequent-attender Disciples in the General Social Survey. About two-thirds of all Presbyterians and frequent-attender Southern Baptists do not currently have children at home. On the other hand, 43 percent

TABLE 4   Income by Attendance

	Disciples		Presbyterians		Southern Baptists	
Income	N	%	N	%	N	%
Frequent Attenders						
High	16	(19%)	56	(36%)	60	(24%)
High Middle	17	(20)	36	(23)	55	(22)
Low Middle	27	(32)	27	(17)	53	(22)
Low	25	(29)	38	(24)	78	(32)
(Subtotal)	(85)		(157)		(246)	
Infrequent Attenders						
High	19	(20)	77	(32)	50	(19)
High Middle	19	(20)	49	(20)	66	(25)
Low Middle	22	(23)	51	(21)	63	(24)
Low	33	(37)	67	(27)	88	(33)
(Subtotal)	(95)		(244)		(267)	
No Answer	(26)		(108)		(38)	
Totals	206		509		551	

(p < .0001)

NOTE RE: Income categories.
   a. For Gallup data and GSS data 1986-88: "High" is $40,000 or more per year; "High middle," $25,000-39,999; "Low middle," $15,000-24,999; and "Low," less than $15,000 per year.
   b. For GSS data 1982-85: "High" is $35,000 and over; "High middle," $22,500-34,999; "Low middle," $12,500-22,499; and "Low," less than $12,500 per year.
   c. Income data from the GSS not used for 1980-81.
   d. Denominational survey data for income was adjusted according to the above categorization.

of infrequent-attender Southern Baptists have children living at home, the highest percentage among frequent and infrequent attenders in all three denominations. Only about one of every five respondents in each denomination expects to have more children.

2. RELIGIOUS CHARACTERISTICS

On matters of religious belief and practice, Disciples of Christ respondents to the General Social Survey fall for the most part in the middle between Presbyterians and Southern Baptists. At this point one could use labels such as "liberal" for Presbyterians or "conservative" for Southern Baptists; however, such descriptive labeling is often simplistic, inaccurate, and potentially pejorative. Acknowledging the inadequacy of these labels, the positioning of the three denominations will be done with appropriate care and qualification. Significant differences are likely to occur between the frequent and infrequent attenders within each denomination as well as between the denominations themselves.

Religious Practices and Attitudes

Disciples of Christ and Southern Baptists, on average, are more frequent church attenders than Presbyterians. One-third attend church every week or more as opposed to only one-fourth of Presbyterians. Conversely, more than half of all Presbyterians attend church rarely or not at all, whereas about 43 percent of Disciples and Southern Baptists rarely or never attend. Among frequent attenders, 78 percent of Disciples, 74 percent of Presbyterians, and 70 percent of Southern Baptists are members of church-affiliated groups. Very low percentages of infrequent attenders in all three denominations are members of church-affiliated groups: 18 percent of Disciples, 17 percent of Presbyterians, and 15 percent of Southern Baptists.

Taken together, the six groups within the three denominations do not express strong confidence in organized religion. With the exception of Presbyterian frequent attenders, the modal response among all groups was similar to that of the general population: respondents have, on the whole, "only some" confidence in organized religion. Predictably, frequent attenders are more likely to express "a great deal" of confidence in organized religion than are infrequent attenders. About half of Presbyterian frequent attenders and one-third of Southern Baptist frequent attenders claim to have a great deal of confidence in organized religion, compared to only three out of ten Disciples frequent attenders. While three out of four in all three denominations have some degree of confidence in organized religion, the confidence could be said to be lukewarm at best.

Frequent attenders in all three denominations are far more likely to call themselves strong adherents than infrequent attenders, as might be expected. Eight out of ten Disciple frequent attenders consider themselves strong adherents versus one out of four infrequent attenders. Among Presbyterians about six out of ten frequent attenders consider themselves to be strong adherents versus only one out of seven infrequent attenders. Two out of three Southern Baptist frequent attenders consider themselves strong adherents as opposed to one out of five infrequent attenders.

Frequent personal prayer (once a day or more) is somewhat more common among Disciples and Southern Baptist frequent attenders than Presbyterian frequent attenders: 85 and 79 percent respectively versus 71 percent. Nearly one half of Southern Baptist infrequent attenders (47%) pray once a day or more, versus 42 percent of Presbyterians and Disciples. Southern Baptist infrequent attenders are more likely than Presbyterians and Disciples to maintain personal religious practices, which could be a function of regional religious culture.

Religious Beliefs

Respondents in all three denominations maintain rather traditional images of God, Southern Baptists being the most traditional and Presbyterians being most

TABLE 5   Views on the Nature of the Bible

	Disciples	Presbyterians	Southern Baptists
Frequent Attenders	(N = 31)	(N = 78)	(N = 164)
Actual Word of God	48%	32%	70%
Inspired Word of God	39	59	29
Ancient book of fables	7	8	1
Other/Don't know/			
No answer	6	1	0
Infrequent Attenders	(N = 39)	(N = 97)	(N = 174)
Actual Word of God	36%	25%	51%
Inspired Word of God	54	55	43
Ancient book of fables	8	21	6
Other/Don't know/			
No answer	3	0	1
Totals	(N = 70)	(N = 175)	(N = 338)

(p < .0001).

like the general population. Some difference occurs between the three denominations as well as between frequent and infrequent attenders. About eight out of ten frequent-attender Southern Baptists and Disciples tend to view God as Father, compared with six out of ten frequent-attender Presbyterians. Among infrequent attenders in all three denominations, about two-thirds or slightly more tend to view God as Father. In spite of recent efforts to make religious language more inclusive, the male image of God remains strong in all three traditions.

A high percentage of frequent-attender Disciples (86%) and Southern Baptists (80%) prefer the image of God as Master over that of Spouse. A higher percentage of infrequent-attender Southern Baptists (71%) view God as Master than do all Presbyterians (about 65%). The greatest difference is between frequent- and infrequent-attender Disciples, with only 56 percent of the latter group viewing God as Master. Disciples frequent attenders (68%) and all Southern Baptists (63%) tend to be most traditional in viewing God as Judge rather than Lover. About one half of all Presbyterians view God as Judge, as is the case among infrequent-attender Disciples. Infrequent attenders in all three denominations are somewhat more likely than frequent attenders to view God as Friend rather than King.

On the important matter of biblical literalism, often used to measure fundamentalism or evangelicalism, Disciples fall in the middle between Presbyterians, who tend to be less literalist, and Southern Baptists, who tend to be more literalist (see Table 5). Seventy percent of frequent-attender Southern Baptists believe that "the Bible is the actual word of God and is to be taken literally, word for word." Fifty-one percent of infrequent-attender Southern Baptists have a literalist stance versus 48 percent of Disciples who are frequent attenders. Only 36 percent of infrequent-attender Disciples hold to a literalist view as compared to 32 percent of Presbyterians who are frequent attenders.

The majority of Presbyterians, frequent and infrequent attenders alike (59% and 55%), believe that "the Bible is the inspired word of God but not everything in it should be taken literally, word for word." Fifty-four percent of infrequent attenders among Disciples have this view as well, along with 43 percent of Southern Baptist infrequent attenders. The least literalist group of all is made up of Presbyterians who attend infrequently: 21 percent of them believe that "the Bible is an ancient book of fables, legends, history, and moral precepts recorded by men."[6]

Most Americans claim to believe in life after death. Seventy-one percent of all respondents to the General Social Survey from 1980 to 1988 claim such a belief. Seventy-one percent of all respondents to a 1988 Gallup Poll claimed to believe in life after death.[7] Disciples, Presbyterians, and Southern Baptists are no different. There is, however, a significant difference between frequent and infrequent attenders, the latter being more like the general population. Among frequent attenders, 95 percent of Disciples of Christ, 90 percent of Southern Baptists, and 88 percent of Presbyterians believe in life after death. This compares to 81 percent of "churched" respondents in the 1988 Gallup Poll used for the Princeton Religious Research Center study *The Unchurched American . . . Ten Years Later.* Among infrequent attenders, 82 percent of Southern Baptists, 72 percent of Disciples, and 66 percent of Presbyterians claim to believe in life after death. Fifty-eight percent of the "unchurched" in the Gallup-Princeton study believe in life after death.

Religious Background

Almost all Southern Baptists and Presbyterians, frequent and infrequent attenders alike, were Protestants at age 16 (91 percent or higher). Ironically, only 81 percent of frequent-attender Disciples grew up Protestant, versus 89 percent of infrequent-attender Disciples. Only 57 percent of Disciples and 58 percent of Presbyterians were in their respective denominations at age 16. On the other hand, eight out of ten Southern Baptists were Southern Baptist at age 16. One might speculate that in the three southern census regions, where most Southern Baptists live, Southern Baptists are never very far from a Southern Baptist church, and so it is easier for the denomination to maintain ties. Disciples and Presbyterians, on the other hand, are rarely the majority group in any part of the United States and therefore may be more vulnerable to the migration of its people into other denominations. On the other hand, Disciples and Presbyterians have also received people from other denominations: approximately 20 percent of their current adherents came out of Baptist and Methodist backgrounds.

---

6. All statements from Davis and Smith, *General Social Surveys, 1972-1988: Cumulative Codebook,* p. 159.

7. *The Unchurched American . . . Ten Years Later* (Princeton, N.J.: Princeton Religious Research Center, 1988), p. 28.

3. POLITICAL AND SOCIAL PROFILE

Politically, respondents in all three denominations tend to be more conservative than liberal. Although this is the case for the general population, it is somewhat more the case for the three denominations under consideration. Respondents to the General Social Survey were asked to position themselves on a scale ranging from "extremely liberal" to "extremely conservative." In general, these data clearly suggest that political liberals are in the minority among Disciples, Presbyterians, and Southern Baptists. A moderate to conservative pattern is consistently seen among all three denominations on any number of political questions.

Political Party, Viewpoint, and Voting

Among the three denominations, the group containing the highest percentage of respondents affiliated with the Democratic Party (47%) and the lowest percentage affiliated with the Republican Party (22%) is the Southern Baptist infrequent attenders. Very close to them are the Disciples of Christ infrequent attenders: 43 percent Democrat and 23 percent Republican. Southern Baptist frequent attenders have the same percentage of Democrats (43%) but more registered Republicans (32%). The most Republican group is the Presbyterian frequent attenders: 44 percent Republican and 31 percent Democrat. Disciples of Christ frequent attenders are a close second with 39 percent Republican and 29 percent Democrat. Presbyterian infrequent attenders are 38 percent Republican and 26 percent Democrat. Within denominational groups, the greatest difference is among Disciples of Christ, with infrequent attenders 43 percent Democrat and frequent attenders 39 percent Republican.

Only slight differences show up in the Gallup data. Southern Baptists overall are found to be somewhat less affiliated with the Democratic Party and Presbyterians somewhat more affiliated with the Republican Party. Disciples of Christ on the whole are found to be 39 percent Republican and 35 percent Democrat, just the opposite of the General Social Survey indication (36 percent Democrat and 30 percent Republican). One might conclude from this small discrepancy that Disciples are just about evenly divided in their political affiliation. It is interesting, however, that the Laurence Keene survey of Disciples of Christ ministers and elders found that elders were 50 percent Republican and 31 percent Democrat.[8] The *Presbyterian Panel* results show their respondents to be even more Republican (53%) and less Democratic (25%) than Presbyterian frequent attenders in the General Social Survey.

---

8. Laurence C. Keene, "Survey of Disciples of Christ Ministers and Elders," unpublished manuscript (Malibu: Pepperdine University, n.d.), p. 4.

With the exception of Disciples of Christ infrequent attenders, all others in the three denominational groups tend to consider their political viewpoint moderate to conservative. Although none of the Disciple infrequent attenders considered themselves "extremely liberal," 30 percent considered themselves slightly liberal to liberal versus 28 percent who considered themselves slightly conservative to conservative. The strongest conservative orientation is found among Southern Baptist frequent attenders (47%) and Disciples frequent attenders (45%). In spite of their Republican inclination, both frequent- and infrequent-attender Presbyterians are somewhat less conservative (37% and 38%, respectively) than Southern Baptist and Disciples frequent attenders. Except for Southern Baptist frequent attenders, the modal response for all denominational groups is a "moderate" political viewpoint, the most moderate-oriented group being Southern Baptist infrequent attenders (46%).

There are indeed some ironies in the political characteristics of the three denominations. Though Southern Baptist frequent attenders tend to be Democrats in their political affiliation, they are the most conservative group of all among the six groups in the three-denomination sample. This is not altogether surprising given the tendency of Democrats in the South to be politically conservative. On the other hand, Presbyterian frequent attenders are the most Republican group with regard to their political affiliation and yet they are the second most "moderate" group (41%) of the six groups within the total sample of the three denominations. The difference within the Disciples of Christ is rather striking: Disciples frequent attenders are more conservative (45%), and Disciples infrequent attenders more moderate to liberal. Some difference seems to exist between Southern Baptist frequent attenders, 47 percent of whom are conservative, and Southern Baptist infrequent attenders, 46 percent of whom are moderate. The greater political and ideological gulf seems to exist within the Disciples between frequent and infrequent attenders. The ideological distance between conservative Southern Baptist frequent attenders and moderate Southern Baptist infrequent attenders does not appear as great.

The voting record among all three denominations in presidential elections followed the conservative drift of the nation in the 1980s. In the 1980 presidential election, the majority of Disciples infrequent attenders and of all Southern Baptists in the sample voted for Jimmy Carter. A majority of Disciples frequent attenders and a strong majority of all Presbyterians voted for Ronald Reagan. In the 1984 presidential election, Reagan was the overwhelming choice in all three denominations. The strongest pro-Reagan vote in the sample was among Disciples frequent attenders (82%), with the Southern Baptist frequent attenders close behind (71%). The strongest Mondale vote was among Disciples infrequent attenders and Presbyterian frequent attenders (both with 33%). Disciples of Christ frequent and infrequent attenders show some political differences through their presidential voting patterns.

TABLE 6 Attitudes toward Federal Spending

	Disciples		Presbyterians		So. Baptists		GSS
	Frequent (N = 61)	Infrequent (N = 57)	Frequent (N = 122)	Infrequent (N = 208)	Frequent (N = 127)	Infrequent (N = 124)	All 8,219
Favor more spending on:							
Crime	61%	68%	62%	74%	67%	74%	68%
Drug problem	53	63	54	57	66	73	61
Education	59	63	57	54	59	67	59
Health care	46	56	49	51	58	61	59
Environment	44	60	46	54	51	64	55
Social Security*	53	66	40	42	48	62	54
Urban problem*	33	49	34	38	27	34	43
Defense	33	26	36	35	26	22	27
Welfare**	10	23	14	14	13	23	22

*$p < .0001$
**$p < .02$.

Attitudes toward Federal Spending

When asked about nine areas of federal government spending, statistically significant differences among the three denominations were found on only three issues: spending on Social Security, urban problems, and welfare (see Table 6). Considerable agreement is found among both frequent and infrequent attenders in all three denominations concerning the need for more federal spending on crime, the drug problem, and education, and somewhat less so on health care and the environment. Frequent and infrequent attenders in all three denominations are evenly divided on the matter of defense spending; however, Disciples of Christ frequent attenders and all Presbyterians are somewhat more in favor of defense spending than the general population.

The strongest proponents of increased spending for Social Security are the infrequent attenders among Disciples (66%) and Southern Baptists (62%). The fiscal conservatives on this issue, favoring less spending, are both frequent- and infrequent-attender Presbyterians (40% and 42%, respectively). Nearly half of Disciples infrequent attenders (49%) feel the need for more federal spending on urban problems, while all other groups are less supportive of such spending. The vast majority, three-fourths or more, of frequent and infrequent attenders among all three denominations felt that enough or too much federal money was spent on welfare. Frequent-attender Disciples and Presbyterians, along with Southern Baptist infrequent attenders, feel noticeably stronger than the general population that too much is spent on welfare.

Civil Liberties

A majority of Disciples, Presbyterians, and Southern Baptists agree with the general population on the issue of capital punishment. Seventy percent of all

TABLE 7   Civil Liberties

| | Disciples | | Presbyterians | | Southern Baptists | | GSS |
	Frequent (N = 80)	Infrequent (N = 76)	Frequent (N = 160)	Infrequent (N = 217)	Frequent (N = 195)	Infrequent (N = 213)	All 9131
Atheists:							
Let speak	58%	66%	70%	74%	53%	61%	66%
Let teach	30	47	40	49	26	37	45
Keep book	50	68	64	73	41	50	62
Racists:							
Let speak	53	70	58	67	46	57	58
Let teach	26	43	39	46	31	39	41
Keep book	54	66	63	68	44	58	61
Communists:							
Let speak	43	68	65	67	42	44	57
Let teach	25	53	39	50	26	30	44
Keep book	51	66	60	68	37	47	57
Militarists:							
Let speak	39	62	57	64	40	47	55
Let teach	19	43	38	48	21	30	39
Keep book	40	62	61	68	38	49	56
Homosexuals:							
Let speak	46	71	72	77	49	57	67
Let teach	34	62	56	62	34	46	56
Keep book	40	54	58	71	35	46	57

(Note: All items significant at $p < .025$ or below.)

respondents to the General Social Survey from 1980 to 1988 favor capital punishment. Of the six groups from the three denominations, only infrequent-attender Disciples are less likely than the general population to favor capital punishment, and that margin of difference is hardly significant. On the issue of gun control, only Presbyterians favor gun control to the same degree as the general population. Infrequent attenders among Disciples and Southern Baptists are the least likely to favor gun control among all groups in the three denominations. There is widespread agreement among all Disciples, Presbyterians, and Southern Baptists, along with the general population, that the courts are too lenient. Disciples, Presbyterians, and Southern Baptists in general seem to be looking for stricter controls on crime and criminals, favoring capital punishment, gun control, and tougher courts.

On the matter of civil liberties, Presbyterians seem most likely to be more tolerant of religious, political, and sexual diversity (see Table 7). Among the three denominational groups, Southern Baptists appear the least likely to be tolerant of such diversity. Respondents were asked whether they would be inclined to permit atheists, racists, communists, militarists, and homosexuals to speak publicly or to teach in a college or university or whether they would feel that any book written by such persons should be removed from the public library.[9]

Generally speaking, frequent and infrequent attenders among all three denominations are more likely to tolerate such persons speaking publicly and to object to the removal of any book written by such persons from a public library. They are, however, considerably less tolerant of permitting such persons to teach in a college or university.

Public Assistance versus Self-Reliance

On issues of public assistance versus self-reliance, modest statistically significant differences do occur among the three denominations, especially in comparison to the general population. On the issue of the federal government's "special obligation" to help improve the living standard of the poor, the modal response among all three denominations and the general population is that there should be a balance between public assistance and self-reliance. With the exception of Southern Baptist infrequent attenders, a slight tendency toward favoring self-reliance over government assistance is evident among all three denominational groups. A very similar pattern emerges on the question of whether the public or private sector has the primary responsibility for dealing with the nation's social problems. Once again, with the exception of the Southern Baptist infrequent attenders, both frequent and infrequent attenders in all three denominations feel more strongly than the general population that the burden of responsibility is with "individuals and private businesses."

The modal response among the general population regarding government assistance with medical expenses is that people should have help. Forty-six percent feel that the federal government should do more to assist people with medical expenses. With the exception of Disciples infrequent attenders, who concur with the general population, the modal response of all other frequent- and infrequent-attender groups within the three denominations is that there should be a balance between government assistance and self-help. About half of the respondents to the General Social Survey from 1980 to 1988 (48%) feel that the federal government has no special obligation to help improve the standard of living for blacks. Disciples frequent attenders and all Presbyterians responded similarly; however, two-thirds of Disciples infrequent attenders and two-thirds of all Southern Baptists feel that blacks should receive no special treatment.

Attitudes on Race Relations

On issues concerning black-white relations, some significant differences are observed. Two-thirds to three-fourths of all Disciples and Presbyterians oppose any laws that would prohibit the marriage of blacks and whites. Southern

---

9. Davis and Smith, *General Social Surveys, 1972-1988: Cumulative Codebook*, pp. 118-23.

Baptists, on the other hand, are evenly divided on the issue. The majority in all three denominations reject the notion that whites have the right to keep blacks out of their neighborhoods. Seven to eight out of ten Disciples and Presbyterian infrequent attenders reject such segregation, while Presbyterian frequent attenders and all Southern Baptists reject the notion somewhat less strongly. More significant differences are evident on the issue of whose rights are primary in the selling of a home. Forty-six percent of the general population believes that a homeowner can choose to sell to whomever he or she wishes, even if it means refusing to sell to prospective buyers because of their race or color. With the exception of Disciples infrequent attenders, all other groups within the three denominations favor the rights of the homeowner to a greater degree than the general population.

Because the majority of Southern Baptists (82% or more) are from the three southern census regions (South Atlantic and East and West South Central), their attitudes on racial issues must be seen in the context of their regional culture. It is important to compare Southern Baptist attitudes on racial issues with those of other southern white Protestants. The majority of southern white Protestants in six denominations — Disciples of Christ, Episcopalians, Lutherans, Presbyterians, Southern Baptists, and United Methodists — feels that the federal government has no obligation to improve the standard of living for blacks. A sizable minority of United Methodists in the South (45%) favor the legal prohibition of interracial marriage, compared with a slight majority of Southern Baptists in the South (53%). On average, six out of ten or more whites in the six denominations oppose the right to keep neighborhoods segregated; however, the majority in all six denominations in the South believe that homeowners have the right to sell to whomever they choose, even if it means refusing to sell to blacks.

Gender Roles

On the all important matter of gender roles, significant differences are observed among the three denominations (see Table 8). Comparing closely with the general population, seven or more out of ten frequent and infrequent attenders in all three denominations approve of married women working even if they have husbands capable of supporting them. Significant differences are seen on the notion that women belong in the private sphere (i.e., in the home), leaving leadership of the public sphere up to men. In general, Presbyterians were more strongly opposed to this than the general population, while Disciples and Southern Baptists were less opposed and therefore somewhat more traditional. Presbyterian frequent attenders disagree more strongly than the general population that men are better suited for politics than women. Frequent-attender Disciples, all Southern Baptists, and infrequent-attender Presbyterians, on the other hand, tend to feel more strongly than the general population that men are better suited for politics.

TABLE 8   Attitudes on Gender Roles

	Disciples		Presbyterians		Southern Baptists		GSS
	Frequent (N = 62)	Infrequent (N = 63)	Frequent (N = 93)	Infrequent (N = 180)	Frequent (N = 149)	Infrequent (N = 160)	All 7451
Percent who agree:							
Approve married women working	73%	71%	73%	80%	77%	77%	77%
Women belong in private sphere	40	30	18	19	32	28	24
Women not suited for politics	51	35	26	44	51	40	35

NOTE: The first item (women working) is not statistically significant. The second and third items are significant at p < .01.

Abortion

Eight out of ten Disciples, nine out of ten Southern Baptists, and nearly all Presbyterians agree that abortion should be legal in cases where the mother's health is endangered. All three denominations, to a slightly lesser degree, support legal abortion in the case of rape or a serious defect in the baby. Beyond these three reasons for abortion to be legal, much greater differences are seen. In the case of a family being too poor to afford more children, only a slight majority of Presbyterians feel that abortion should be legal. A slight majority of Presbyterians also feel that abortion should be legal for unmarried women who become pregnant, married women who do not want any more children, and women who wish to have an abortion for any reason at all. Disciples and Southern Baptists, on the other hand, tend not to favor legal abortion in any case except for the mother's health, rape, and serious birth defects. On the whole, Presbyterian infrequent attenders are the most pro-choice oriented, and Southern Baptist frequent attenders are the most pro-life oriented.

TABLE 9   Attitudes on Abortion

	Disciples		Presbyterians		Southern Baptists		GSS
	Frequent (N = 88)	Infrequent (N = 87)	Frequent (N = 179)	Infrequent (N = 262)	Frequent (N = 195)	Infrequent (N = 213)	All 10730
Legal abortion (agree):							
Mother's health endangered	81%	79%	97%	95%	85%	91%	86%
Rape	71	79	91	94	72	82	78
Serious defect	68	76	89	92	70	82	77
Family too poor	31	46	54	65	21	39	44
Single mother	32	40	52	62	22	38	41
No more children	23	46	50	62	22	37	41
For any reason	25	30	45	54	17	33	36

NOTE: All items significant at p < .0001.

TABLE 10   Attitudes on Sexual Morality Issues

| | Disciples | | Presbyterians | | So. Baptists | | GSS |
	Frequent (N = 62)	Infrequent (N = 63)	Frequent (N = 93)	Infrequent (N = 180)	Frequent (N = 149)	Infrequent (N = 160)	All 7451
Percentage who agree:							
Favor sex education in the schools	66%	83%	89%	86%	73%	86%	82%
Divorce should be more difficult	73	52	61	43	73	45	50
Premarital sex is always wrong	48	19	29	14	63	30	27
Extramarital sex is always wrong	85	80	79	62	94	80	72
Homosexual sex is always wrong	91	74	78	63	92	85	72
Pornography corrupts	83	53	72	53	86	63	60
Pornography should be outlawed	66	30	44	35	67	35	41

NOTE: All items significant at p < .0001.

Sexual Morality

Although all groups within the three denominations strongly favor sex education in the public schools, frequent-attender Disciples and Southern Baptists
are somewhat less enthusiastic about the idea (see Table 10). Across all three
denominations, frequent attenders tend to feel stronger than infrequent attenders that divorce should be harder to obtain in the United States. Infrequent
attenders in all three denominations tend to be much more tolerant of premarital
sex than frequent attenders; however, both frequent and infrequent attenders
alike feel strongly that extramarital sex and homosexual relations are always
or almost always wrong. Frequent attenders in all three denominations are
more likely to oppose pornography than infrequent attenders.

   Frequency of church attendance seems to be strongly related to more
conservative attitudes on issues of sexual morality among Disciples, Presbyterians, and Southern Baptists.

DISCUSSION

What is to be gained from reviewing such findings as these? What insights,
if any, can they provide about people who identify with the Christian Church
(Disciples of Christ), as well as the Presbyterian Church in the U.S.A. and
the Southern Baptist Convention? First of all, one might say that clearing
the fog about any constituency is an important and useful exercise. In light

of recent concerns about "Disciples identity" and the decline of mainstream Protestant denominations, this is indeed a good time to clear the fog about the Disciples of Christ constituency. Too often the temptation is to reach conclusions based on one's own observations, intuitive hunches, and common sense — and there is no guarantee that these will provide an accurate picture of the way things really are. National surveys, such as those utilized in this study, can at least provide some *general* ideas about a particular group or set of groups, and perhaps even more. Survey data can at least verify or call into question our hunches about many things, including denominational traditions.

Findings such as these can be even more useful when they are considered in conjunction with finding from other studies. For example, the results of this study should be linked with the findings of the other studies presented in this volume (pp. 363-65, 445-68, 491-508, 521-56). And in spite of my reservations about the sampling procedures and findings of the *Disciple Churchwide Survey,* I still believe it should be used for comparison, as should the Laurence Keene study. Indeed, all relevant surveys, be they national polls or surveys of denominations, can provide valuable complements to the material in this study. Though survey research techniques are by no means perfect, the probability of error can be minimized enough to ensure confidence in the findings. As we accumulate surveys, we should inspect the convergences and divergences. Convergences among surveys begin to tell us that something may, in fact, be the case about the subject at hand. Having read this study in conjunction with others, one may with more confidence arrive at particular conclusions about Disciples, Presbyterians, and Southern Baptists.

Seven Concerns from the Findings

1. *Disciples of Christ church leaders need to be concerned about the ratio of women to men among the frequent attenders in their churches.* It is a pervasive phenomenon in the United States that men are not as involved as women in religious institutions. While this study does not offer any answers to the question of why this is so, the findings clearly confirm what most frequent church attenders will already have observed. It is an important concern that warrants further investigation on the part of local, judicatory, and national church leaders.

2. *Disciples of Christ church leaders need to be concerned about the predominance of frequent attenders over the age of 50.* Where are the younger adults? Why do they choose not to participate? What does this say about both those who are not attending and about those who are attending? How are the younger folks who *do* attend different from those who do not attend? How does the numerical dominance of any generation affect modes of worship, service, fellowship, and leadership in local churches? In what ways might generational dominance discourage the participation of other generational

groups? Disciples of Christ church leaders have a responsibility to be "faithful to the faithful," the active frequent attenders, no matter what their age. On the other hand, the Disciples of Christ cannot proceed with an aging constituency for too long before problems show up on both the local church and denominational level.

3. *Disciples of Christ church leaders need to be concerned about the difference in the educational and occupational prestige levels of frequent attenders versus infrequent attenders.* Why is it that frequent church attenders, as a rule, tend to be better educated and of higher occupational prestige than infrequent attenders? Are Disciples congregations unwittingly excluding those of lower educational and occupational levels? Are Disciples congregations class-bound homogeneous units? Do new church development projects, for example, primarily target better educated, upwardly mobile groups? To what extent does ministerial training in the Disciples of Christ (i.e., college and seminary) distance clergy from people with lower educational and occupational prestige levels? Homogeneous units are quite natural to congregational life and can indeed enhance it when properly applied. On the other hand, for all of its obvious benefits for congregational vitality, homogeneity can turn congregations in on themselves and away from those on the outside who are different.

4. *Disciples of Christ church leaders need to be concerned about the fact that separated, divorced, and never married people are less likely to be involved in church life.* Are Disciples congregations so family oriented that they make singles of any variety, including single parents, feel awkward? In Disciples churches that offer couples classes and fellowships, are there also opportunities for single adult fellowship? Are Disciples congregations responsive to the needs of single parents? How many never-married, separated, and divorced people are there in the communities served by Disciples churches? What churches, if any, are attempting to be responsive to their needs? And how do Disciples congregations respond to those who are going through the agony of marital separation? Certainly this trend of single and single-again people drifting away from the church is not unique to the Disciples of Christ. Will Disciples congregations respond to this trend in their own communities, and in what way?

5. *Disciples of Christ church leaders need to be concerned about declining fertility rates and their long-term implications for church growth.* I am by no means implying that Disciples of Christ church leaders should embark on a denomination-wide fertility campaign, encouraging the fecund among the faithful to "be fruitful and multiply." Concern is warranted, however, regarding the apparently meager potential for biological growth within the denomination. There are fewer Disciples of Christ women of childbearing age, and those that are of childbearing age are having fewer children than the prior generation of Disciples mothers. The implications for evangelism are therefore rather obvious: Disciples of Christ congregations will increasingly need to recruit mem-

bers through means other than biological. Calling people on the fringes and outside of the church into Christian faith and fellowship has always been the imperative of the gospel; a weakening biological growth rate should bring that imperative into sharper focus.

6. *Disciples of Christ church leaders need to be concerned about the seemingly disparate ideological views of their denomination's constituency.* To what extent do Disciples clergy differ from Disciples laity on matters of theological, social, and political ideology? Should it be a concern that Disciples clergy seem to be more liberal than Disciples laity? Should it be a concern that Disciples laity seem to be more conservative than Disciples clergy? In what other ways and places do these ideological differences appear? What are the implications for a denomination in which the majority of clergy are Democrats and the majority of elders Republicans? How do Disciples clergy differ from Disciples laity on social and theological issues and the matter of biblical literalism? The question is not who is right and who is wrong; the question is how such differences should be acknowledged, discussed, and worked out in the life of Disciples congregations. What is it that holds them together and enables them to function? More sectarian denominations tend to have greater theological, social, and political homogeneity. Ideological distance between clergy and laity is usually minimal. Mainstream denominations such as the Disciples of Christ tend to be much more ideologically diverse, often acknowledging the diversity with the rhetoric of "unity amid diversity." But what is the cost of the relative lack of ideological consensus? How is the church's mission affected, and is it in any way, if not in many ways, compromised to the least common denominator?

7. *Disciples of Christ church leaders need to be concerned about the continued presence of racist and sexist attitudes among its constituency.* To what extent do racist attitudes exist among Disciples of Christ frequent attenders? How do such attitudes manifest themselves in the life of local churches and communities? In what ways are Disciples congregations and congregants alike leading or lagging behind on matters pertaining to racial harmony and equality? While almost all readers of this study will no doubt share a deep concern about the persistence of racist attitudes, not all will be so concerned about any alleged sexism within the Disciples of Christ. All ideological differences aside, one cannot avoid the issue of the changing role of women in our society. Great numbers of women are now in the labor force (i.e., working outside of the home), and increasing numbers of women are pursuing careers of their own and staying with them. The number of women clergy, for example, has doubled in the past ten years.[10] The implications for marriage and family life as well as the church are enormous. Can sexist attitudes be acceptable in Disciples churches, or any other churches, as women transform our society

10. Constant Jacquet, Jr., *Yearbook of American and Canadian Churches: 1989* (Nashville: Abingdon Press, 1989), p. 262.

into a more egalitarian social structure? The findings of this study do point to residual racism and sexism within the Disciples of Christ, and we dare not allow this to go unchallenged nor unchanged.

Concluding Comments

Disciples, Presbyterians, and Southern Baptists, spiritual cousins since the nineteenth century, seem to fall into three categories found in the common parlance. For the most part, Presbyterians are the most liberal of the three denominations. While their political views tend to be moderate to conservative, they score lowest on indicators of religious conservatism (e.g., biblical literalism) and higher on indicators of tolerance (e.g., civil liberties). Southern Baptists, on the other hand, are the most conservative of the three denominations. In spite of their traditional affiliation with the Democratic Party, their political views are by far the most conservative, as are their scores on matters of religious conservatism. Lower scores on the tolerance of diversity should not be interpreted pejoratively as simply evidence of ignorance or intolerance among Southern Baptists; they should be viewed to some extent at least as a reflection of the homogeneity of the culture in which Southern Baptists are most prominent. Disciples of Christ seem to fall in the middle between the liberal Presbyterians and the conservative Southern Baptists. Their moderate positions on political, religious, and social matters place them clearly in the middle.

This rather general, if not somewhat precarious, ideological placement of the three denominations is corroborated by the classification system used by the General Social Survey to classify denominations as liberal, moderate, or "fundamentalist." In the General Social Survey, all three denominations fall into the same scheme: Presbyterians are liberal, Disciples moderate, and Southern Baptists fundamentalist. These terms are meant to be descriptive of ideological tendencies rather than value-laden judgments. In *American Mainline Religion,* Wade Clark Roof and William McKinney place Presbyterians, Disciples, and Southern Baptists in the same liberal-moderate-conservative order. A review of the literature on the sociology of American denominations will produce a similar if not identical finding. This does not mean that there are no liberals to be found among Southern Baptists and no conservatives to be found among Presbyterians or Disciples. Nothing could be further from the truth. In the aggregate, however, the ideological/theological tendencies of the three denominations do fall rather consistently into the liberal-moderate-conservative scheme.

Though Presbyterians can be spoken of as liberals, Southern Baptists as conservatives, and Disciples as moderates, they must not be seen as mutually exclusive categories. There is in fact considerable overlap among the three denominations. These classifications really serve simply to point to degrees of difference. However much overlap there may be, differences between the three bodies are present and cannot be overlooked.

APPENDIX:
SOME CAVEATS CONCERNING NATIONAL SURVEY DATA

A particular problem with national samples is the small number of cases they yield in subsample categories. Most national polls sample about 1,500 people per survey, a sample size considered representative based on the probability that in 95 chances out of 100 the sample error will be minimal (plus or minus 3%). While such sample sizes are good for many analyses, when samples are divided into various groupings for comparative analysis, subsample size becomes a concern. Even a large denomination such as the Southern Baptist Convention, with 14 million members, produces only about 100 cases in a random sample of 1,500 taken from the U.S. population. The rule of thumb for statistical analysis is, quite obviously, the more cases the better. In the case of Southern Baptists, one could use perhaps three national samples to aggregate an adequate number of cases for analysis. In the case of smaller denominational groups such as the Disciples and Presbyterians, many more national samples have to be aggregated to produce an adequate number of cases for analysis.

Another challenge concerning the use of national surveys for a study such as this concerns defining the denominations to be studied when they are not otherwise specified by the survey organization. This is especially the case with the General Social Survey prior to 1984, when only generic denominational types were given. Two of the three denominations in this comparative study had to be "constructed" either partially or completely in order to use the General Social Survey. Of the three groups the least problematic was the Southern Baptist Convention and, unfortunately, the Disciples were the most problematic.

Defining Disciples of Christ

The Gallup Poll has a separate category in all of its surveys for "The Christian Church (Disciples of Christ)," but Disciples are not specified under the denominational rubrics given in the General Social Survey. The GSS rubrics are Baptist, Methodist, Lutheran, Presbyterian, Episcopal, and "other" — the Disciples belonging in the final category, along with a wide variety of other mainstream and sectarian bodies.[11] Disciples must therefore be constructed out of the numerous groups categorized in the "other" category, as Wade Clark Roof and William McKinney did in *American Mainline Religion*.[12] In my analysis I used the same method of construction as Roof and McKinney, working from four listings from the "other" category under Protestant denomination in the General Social Survey: "Christian, Central Christian," "Disciples

11. See Davis and Smith, *General Social Surveys, 1972-1988: Cumulative Codebook,* pp. 649-51.

12. See Roof and McKinney, *American Mainline Religion: Its Changing Shape and Future* (New Brunswick, N.J.: Rutgers University Press, 1987), pp. 253-56.

of Christ," "First Christian, Disciples of Christ," and "First Christian." While this combination does not ensure a pure sample of Disciples, exclusive of those in other Stone-Campbell traditions, it does constitute the best possible sample available for analysis. If there is any contamination in the sample, it is between Disciples and "Independents" and not with the Churches of Christ, which are specified elsewhere in the "other" category of the General Social Survey. To check for any significant differences among the subsamples used to create the Disciples sample, I compared them for racial composition, sex, age, marital status, education, income, political views and affiliation, region and type of community (urban, suburban, rural), and views on the Bible. While some differences were evident, I did not find them significant enough to challenge this sample definition.

Defining Presbyterians

Defining Presbyterians is somewhat less problematic in the General Social Survey. Presbyterians have been one of the five Protestant denominational rubrics used continuously by the General Social Survey since 1972. It will be difficult, however, to be precise about Presbyterians claiming affiliation with the newly formed Presbyterian Church (U.S.A.). The difficulty lies in the fact that many respondents are categorized as "Presbyterian, don't know which." While the category in the General Social Survey called "Other Presbyterian Churches" may well pick up most persons claiming affiliation with distinctly different Presbyterian bodies (e.g., the Cumberland Presbyterian Church, the conservative Presbyterian Church in America), it is safe to assume that some of these cases may be found in the "don't know which" Presbyterian category. On the other hand, it is also safe to assume that most of those in the "don't know which" Presbyterian category are associated in some way with the two bodies that formed the new Presbyterian Church (USA): the United Presbyterian Church and the Presbyterian Church in the U.S. In terms of the General Social Survey categories, I defined a Presbyterian as either United Presbyterian, Presbyterian Church in the U.S., or Presbyterian "don't know which." I included the latter group to ensure an adequate number of cases. The Gallup Organization's classification is a bit puzzling. "Presbyterian Church in the U.S." is the only category listed for Presbyterians.

Defining Southern Baptists

Even the Southern Baptist Convention is problematic. First of all, there is the problem of generic categories in the General Social Survey prior to 1984, when "Southern Baptists" would have to be defined as Baptists who live in the South. This raises the problem of "contaminating" the subsample with all sorts of southerners who are Baptists of every variety, from Independent to Primitive. There are evidently many Baptists who live in the South who think of themselves as "Southern Baptist" even though they are not affiliates of the Southern Baptist Convention. This is clearly evident in the racial composition one obtains for "Southern Baptists" from the General Social Survey as well as from the Gallup Organization. From 1984 to 1988 the General Social Survey contained 73 cases under the "Southern Baptist Convention" category with *22 percent* black. The 17 Gallup studies used contained 2,505 cases under the "Southern Baptist Convention" category, and *22 percent* of them are black. One must assume, albeit intuitively, that this does not correspond with the true racial composition of the Southern Baptist Convention, which would seem to be no more than about 5 percent nonwhite. Conversations with researchers familiar with the Southern Baptist Convention confirmed the fact that the denomination seems to be about 2 percent black and 3 percent ethnic, but there does not seem to be accurate data available on the matter.

Defining "Southern Baptists" was relatively uncomplicated because from 1984 to 1988 the General Social Survey does specify "Southern Baptist Convention." To avoid the racial composition problem, however, the 1984-88 General Social Survey data for Southern Baptists had to exclude blacks and other racial groups, thus making it impossible to obtain a more accurate estimate of racial composition. The seventeen Gallup studies I used suffered from the same racial composition problem, and therefore only whites claiming to be affiliates of the Southern Baptist Convention were used for comparative purposes. As a result, no racial composition data for the Southern Baptist Convention are given in this study, which is most unfortunate.

Sample Sizes

So defined, the General Social Survey yielded an adequate number of cases for the Disciples of Christ, and an ample number of Presbyterians and Southern Baptists.

"Christian Church (Disciples of Christ)":	N = 206	(1980-88)
"Presbyterians":	N = 502	(1980-88)
"Southern Baptists"		(1984-88)
All cases	N = 735	
All cases (excluding nonwhites)	N = 551	

The seventeen 1985-87 Gallup Organization surveys yielded a somewhat similar distribution, except for the Presbyterians.

"Christian Church (Disciples of Christ)":	N = 565
"Presbyterians":	N = 457
"Southern Baptist Convention" (whites only)	N = 1,973
All cases	(N = 2,505)

What Are They Saying? A Content Analysis of 206 Sermons Preached in the Christian Church (Disciples of Christ) during 1988

Joseph E. Faulkner

INTRODUCTION

"Jesus came preaching" (Mark 1:39), and the church has continued to view preaching as a primary means of fulfilling its mission. Church history is filled with distinguished (and some not so distinguished) names of men, and more recently women, of the pulpit. In colonial New England the pulpit and its message was the center of social and religious life. The sermon probably gave moral direction to the entire community in a way never since realized. This was the case in part because there were no alternative messages.[1] The pulpit did not have to compete with *Miami Vice*, Geraldo Rivera, Oprah Winfrey, or Johnny Carson. If you wanted to hear someone perform "on stage," you went to church. The preaching of the colonial minister was "for all intents and purposes, the only regular voice of authority."[2] This changed after the War of Independence. The church became democratized, and the pew came to share authority with the pulpit. As the country moved westward, the church, while not the dominant institution it had been under Jonathan Edwards in Northampton, nevertheless retained a place of importance in the frontier town.

1. See Harry S. Stout, *The New England Soul: Preaching and Religious Culture in Colonial New England* (New York: Oxford University Press, 1986).
2. Stout, *The New England Soul*, p. 4.

Many people contributed to this essay. I would like to thank Glenn Kreider, especially, for his computer consultation; Mike Pastor, Allen LeBlanc, Betsy Will, Jan Shoemaker, and Lois Seitz also provided valuable services. — JOSEPH E. FAULKNER

Back East the successors to Edwards and others were not without their prominent voices in community life. Henry Ward Beecher in Brooklyn and Phillips Brooks in Boston are generally referred to as "giants" of the pulpit in the late nineteenth century. They represented the establishment both politically and religiously. The twentieth century, sometimes viewed as the beginning of the decline of preaching in American life, does not offer totally confirming data. The preaching tradition has continued to be a seminal part of this society. Peter Marshall, Billy Graham, Norman Vincent Peale, and offspring of similar types following their tradition have been prominent spokesmen for the gospel in our day. The televangelists are household names, and their followers, while not as numerous as they themselves believe, are nevertheless numbered in the millions. While recent well-known scandals have rocked the televangelists and their prominence in American religious life, it would be premature to bury once and for all this aspect of preaching. The cast has already changed, but the play goes on.

What is evident from this thumbnail sketch of some two hundred years of preaching in America is that there has and continues to be an enormous variety of preachers in the pulpit. Preaching surely is no longer the "only regular voice of authority" for the church member. We have a surfeit of authorities now: Dear Abby for love affairs, Dr. Ruth for our sexual needs, Dan Rather and colleagues for political guidance, and hundreds of editorial writers in magazines and papers examining every conceivable topic. Contemporary men and women have no lack of guidance for any aspect of their lives. The survival of the pulpit at all in this climate may in fact be one of the great miraculous acts of God in our time.

PURPOSE AND METHOD

The purpose of this essay is to examine one aspect of the preaching tradition that continues to be an integral part of American religious life. Whatever voices point to the eventual demise of preaching — and there are many — it continues to be a regular part of church life. In no other single activity does the minister reach as large a portion of the congregation as when he or she stands up to preach. What is said? How is it said? What purposes lie behind the sermon? These concerns are important to the ongoing life of any church.

To answer these and related questions, a content analysis of 206 sermons preached in the Christian Church (Disciples of Christ) during 1988 provided information on types of sermons preached, doctrinal issues addressed, illustrations used, and similar homiletical issues. A 10 percent sample (N = 291) of churches with memberships of one hundred or more was randomly drawn from the 1987 *Yearbook and Directory of the Christian Church (Disciples of Christ)*. Each minister was asked to submit ten sermons preached consecutively at any time during 1988. Churches with associate ministers were asked to submit sermons in keeping with the proportion of preaching by the respective clergy. A total of 107 ministers responded, for a return rate of 37 percent. The 206 sermons chosen for analysis represent a 20 percent randomly drawn sample of all sermons received from the 107 participants. At least one sermon was randomly selected from each minister who participated in the study.

The analysis that follows is a document analysis using a computer program called Zyindex, which allows for searching through written documents to identify single words or a combination of words *in context*. It also allows for the precoding of themes, in this case theological and homiletical issues, and then searching for the occurrence or absence of these. For example, searching for the use of Old or New Testament books in the sermons was a simple matter of identifying the books by names. On the other hand, searching for a concept — evangelism, for example — involved searching for both the term itself and ideas previously coded. Two coders were used, except for the section on christology, where I had to assume full responsibility.

Content analysis is a valuable tool. It does not, however, take the place of insight into the nature of the material investigated apart from enumeration, and it does not eliminate the possibility of divergent interpretation by readers other than the coders. However, examples offered as representative illustrations of the content provide for some degree of external validity checks. The analysis here is sociological and not theological, since I can make no claim of expertise in the latter area. I do have a Bachelor of Divinity Degree (from Emory University) and two years' experience in writing more than two hundred sermons in a pastoral context. Thus I approach the interpretative task as one trained in sociology but with a modest background in homiletics and sermon construction. In addition I have used as a guide to what constitutes good preaching recent texts on homiletics written by current authorities in the field.

BIOGRAPHICAL DATA

In addition to the sermons forwarded, each minister was asked to fill out a one-page biographical data sheet. Table 1 (p. 419), assembled from this data, shows that the sample is composed primarily of married white male pastors serving churches located, for the most part, in the Midwest, Southwest, and California. The mean number of years spent in the ministry is seventeen, so these are veterans of the pulpit. Ninety-four percent of those responding were seminary graduates and two-thirds were graduates of Disciples of Christ seminaries. Nonwhite and female respondents are significantly underrepresented in the sample.

TABLE 1 Selected Biographical Characteristics of 100 Ministers*

	Percentage
Geographic Location	
Core States (CA, IL, IN, IA, KS, KY, NE, OH, OK, TX)	74
All Others	26
Time at Present Church	
Less than 4 Years	53
5 or More Years	47
Time in Ministry	
Less than 5 Years	15
6 to 15 Years	39
16 to 25 Years	24
26 or More Years	21
Highest Level of Education	
1 to 4 Years of College	1
College Graduate	11
B.D. or M.Div.	87
Other Degrees	
D.Min. or S.T.M.	24
M.A., M.Ed., Ph.D., Th.D.	12
Sex	
Male	93
Female	7
Age	
30 or Under	6
31 to 40	34
41 to 50	25
51 to 60	28
61 and over	7
Marital Status	
Married	97
Single	1
Divorced	1
Widowed	1
Race	
Nonwhite	1
White	99
Seminary Attended	
Brite Theological Seminary	16
Christian Theological Seminary	15
Lexington Theological Seminary	21
Phillips Theological Seminary	14
All Others	28
Missing Cases	6
Denominational Affiliation	
Disciples of Christ	73
Others	18
None	3
Missing Cases	6

*N = 100. A total of 107 ministers forwarded sermons, but seven did not forward biographical sheets.

AMERICAN CULTURE: THE SETTING OF EVERYDAY LIFE

James Earl Massey says that those who preach "will seek to know just what dominates the thought life of those who hear the sermons, and will want to understand the loyalties to which the energies and time of the people are being given."[3] What are the characteristic features of our way of life that impinge directly on us all and help to shape our thoughts and mold our loyalties? It is neither possible nor necessary in this context to do more than sketch a broad outline of some prominent features of American life in the last years of the twentieth century. Some will argue that this presentation omits some features more important than those included, and that may be the case. I am simply including features that I know to be significant, features that I know those who minister to congregations will encounter in some fashion in the lives of their people. I have gathered them into three basic categories.

The first category is the overwhelmingly individualistic value structure of American society. Values can be viewed as the "affective conceptions of the desirable,"[4] and in America individualism dominates our conception of what is desirable: "We insist, perhaps more than ever before, on finding our true selves . . . being responsible to that self alone, and making its fulfillment the very meaning of our lives."[5] This is expressed in part in arguments over the right to abortion, the right to use drugs recreationally or for athletic enhancement, the right to divorce and cohabit without legal marital status, the right to choose alternative sexual lifestyles, and other such pursuits designed to gratify individual needs and desires.

The second category is demographic changes that have changed the shape of our society. Those who preach every Sunday will have a sense of the changes that have taken place even if they don't possess specific census data. A quick glance at the profusion of white hair in the congregation is evidence of the "graying of America." The relative absence of large numbers of children indicates the trend toward increased numbers of singles and later marriage for both males and females. The presence of single parents with children points to the decline of the traditional family structure of mother, father, and 2.3 offspring. The consequences of these new demographic features for the church are tremendously important and can only grow in significance as the twenty-first century approaches.

The third category is the rise of technology as a guiding principle for much behavior in American society. Every day more and more decisions are being made on the basis of technology rather than ethics. It is becoming almost

---

3. Massey, *Designing the Sermon: Order and Movement in Preaching* (Nashville: Abingdon Press, 1981), p. 17.

4. Robin Williams, *American Society,* 3d ed. (New York: Alfred Knopf, 1970), p. 27.

5. Robert N. Bellah, Richard Madsen, William M. Sullivan, Ann Swidler, and Steven M. Tipton, *Habits of the Heart: Individualism and Commitment in American Life* (New York: Harper & Row, 1986), p. 150.

reflexive to look for a technological response when human problems arise. Can we solve it by applying even more sophisticated hardware? Indeed, many would be suspicious of any "unscientific" attempts to solve a problem. In the sphere of international relationships, for instance, we are more inclined to turn to Star Wars technology than to old-fashioned diplomacy. This is not to suggest that technology has absolute authority in our society or that whatever can be done will be done; rather, it is to recognize that our governing ethos is efficiency, and we view technology as the essence of efficiency. The German sociologist Max Weber recognized more than forty years ago that modern bureaucratic man bases his decisions on efficiency and rationality rather than conventional standards of morality. Alasdair MacIntyre, in one of the important recent philosophical analyses of Western society, argues quite simply that *emotivism* has become the central feature of Western culture: "what emotivism asserts is in central part that there are and can be *no* valid rational justification for any claim that objective and personal moral standards exist, and hence there are none."[6]

Describing where we are today, in the midst of secularity or a "post-Christian era," is not easy because of the considerable variety of lifestyles in our society. But those struggling with new technological innovations, new lifestyles, a changing demography, and the church's response to all of these agree that the old rules no longer apply universally. Many would agree with McIntyre that "what is abundantly clear is that in everyday life as in moral philosophy the replacement of Aristotelian or Christian teleology by a definition of the virtues in terms of the passions is not so much or at all the replacement of one set of criteria by another, but rather a movement towards and into a situation where there are no longer any clear criteria."[7]

It is into this environment that the members of the congregation go each day to pursue their careers. It is from this environment that they enter the church to hear the proclamation of the Word on Sundays. Fred B. Craddock argues that unless the minister recognizes this "new situation in which preaching" is occurring, "sermons will at best seem museum pieces."[8]

THE ANALYSIS OF THE SERMONS

My analysis of the sermons is fourfold. First, I look at the format, classifying the sermon as narrative, thematic, or expository. Second, to the extent possible I determine the overriding theme. Third, I describe the sources of authority for what is said. The two principal categories of sources are biblical and non-

6. MacIntyre, *After Virtue: A Study in Moral Theory* (Notre Dame, Ind.: University of Notre Dame Press, 1981), p. 18.

7. MacIntyre, *After Virtue,* p. 219.

8. Craddock, *As One without Authority,* 3d ed. (Nashville: Abingdon Press, 1986), p. 15.

biblical, but I further divide the latter category into personal illustrations, general illustrations, and special illustrations such as movies, television, sports, and related topical items. Finally, I examine the language of the sermons, noting particularly whether "religious language" is dominant in the sermon. Thielicke is only one of many who argue that there is an "odor of decay that clings to the old, worn-out language" when "it is simply passed on without being worked upon and digested."[9] Finally, I make an overall assessment of the sermons to determine if they are addressed to the life experiences of the congregation. Elizabeth Achtemeier argues that unless preachers are astute students of their age as it is reflected in the media, they may find themselves unable to make contact with the people in the pews.[10]

THE FORMAT AND THEME OF THE SERMONS

There are three major traditional sermon types: thematic or topical, expository, and narrative. A fourth type, referred to as experimental, may take several forms, including that of a dialogue between two ministers or between a minister and a layperson and that of a "first-person sermon," in which "usually the preacher assumes the role of a biblical character and speaks on behalf of that character."[11] (Among the sermons in the sample, there were two experimental sermons, one a dialogue between two ministers and the other a first-person sermon.) Although narrative sermons are widely praised and appreciated, only 4 percent of the sermons in the sample fell into this category. Of course, many sermons contain narrative sections, but few in the sample used narrative as the principal form. This was also the case for expository sermons, in which the "design . . . is determined basically by an extended passage of Scripture. In true exposition the thought and treatment are controlled by the textual passage."[12] Only about 4 percent of the sermons could be classified as expository. The remaining 91 percent were topical or thematic. This is not an unexpected finding, since this type has dominated much of the preaching in the history of the church. A majority of the topical sermons (and indeed of all the sermon types) were doctrinal in nature (focusing on faith, love, hope, evangelism, etc.). Table 2 presents a categorization of the themes of the 206 sermons.

Craddock contends that sermons should "treat subjects of importance and avoid trivia. . . . Theology urges upon the pulpit a much larger agenda: creation, evil, grace, . . . forgiveness, . . . care of the earth, . . . love, and the

9. Helmut Thielicke, *The Trouble with the Church: A Call for Renewal,* trans. John W. Doberstein (New York: Harper & Row, 1965), p. 50.

10. Achtemeier, *Creative Preaching: Finding the Words* (Nashville: Abingdon Press, 1980), p. 34.

11. Achtemeier, *Creative Preaching,* p. 81.

12. Massey, *Designing the Sermon,* p. 22.

TABLE 2   Percentage of Sermons Dealing with Various Themes

Theme	Percentage
Doctrinal	80
(a) Hope, Forgiveness, etc.	50
(b) Reconciliation with God	19
(c) The Church	11
Social Justice	5
Contemporary Issues	3
Evangelism and Mission	3
Biblical Study	2
Ministerial Authority	1
Miscellaneous	6
Total	100

reconciliation of the world to God."[13] I made a point of searching for these sorts of themes. As Table 2 reveals, 80 percent of all the sermons are doctrinal. Within the larger category of doctrine it is possible to single out more specific themes such as reconciliation of individuals to God. The church with its various concerns is treated in 11 percent of the sermons. What is striking, from one perspective, is that social justice is the theme in only 5 percent of the sermons. Contemporary issues such as marriage, divorce, and sexual attitudes and behavior account for another 3 percent. It is true that social justice and other contemporary themes can be dealt with in the context of a sermon on love, for example, but as my examination of sermon illustrations demonstrates, this is not often the case among the sermons in the sample. Contemporary issues are only a minor part of the preaching agenda for this sample of ministers.

I have chosen for a detailed analysis four of the major themes in Table 2: doctrinal issues (e.g., hope, foregiveness, reconciliation with God), the church, social justice, and contemporary issues.

Doctrinal Issues

Sermons dealing with doctrinal issues in the sample range from those that are well organized and use fresh and relevant illustrations to those that homiletic texts suggest be avoided at all costs — namely, the reciting of Scriptures without any application to the listeners' lives.[14] (This latter problem will be examined in the section on Language Use below.) One sermon dealing with forgiveness is based on the Old Testament story of Hosea and Gomer and the thirteenth chapter of 1 Corinthians. Referring to Gomer's adultery, the minister

13. Craddock, *As One without Authority,* p. 49.
14. I have purposely avoided using any sermon titles in this study to ensure the anonymity of the contributors. In some cases I have also changed geographical references and the names of individuals referred to in sermons. Quotations are direct and so include the grammatical errors and rhetorical problems of the original material.

uses a technique seldom employed in these sermons: he raises a question. "What would you do? What would I do — in such a case as unfaithfulness of a wife to her husband?" He then proceeds to bring the biblical message directly to the listener:

> This morning, like Hosea, you may have been tempted to give up on somebody because they have broken their covenant with you. You may have even given up on yourself! [But] this morning ask God to put into you the love of Christ that will not let you go and will allow you to reach out with a love to others that will not let them go from us.

In one of the more unusual sermons, one of the narrative sermons, the question of evil — God, the Devil, and you — is addressed. This theme of Satan and the Devil is not absent from the sample — it is addressed to some degree in 29 percent of the sermons — but this is the only sermon fully devoted to this topic. The sermon asks whether this idea of Satan is important in our day, whether people any longer believe in Satan, and related issues. The sermon also incorporates as illustrative material contemporary movies, and quotes with effectiveness contemporary theologians such as C. S. Lewis.

Having pointed to two effective sermons dealing with forgiveness and evil, I would also like to consider a sermon examining the Christian concept of love. The stated purpose is to move people to faith in the love of Jesus Christ and to reconcile the expectations of parents and children. It incorporates nine different illustrations, seven of which give every indication of having been taken from books of sermon illustrations. Example: an artist paints a picture of a man across the street filled with despair and defeat, but instead of portraying the despair, he paints "an inspired dreamer." When shown the picture, the man says,

> Who is that? Me! Well, if that's the way you see me, that's the way I want to be! [This illustrates] the love that Christ holds out to us even when we are incapable of any kind of response.

In another illustration, a father and daughter are standing on the shore watching the tide come in.

> The daughter said quite pensively, "Isn't it wonderful, how much the sea cares about the land?"

It is at least debatable how effective such illustrations are in revealing the love of Christ for us.

The Church

The church is a major concern in 11 percent of the sermons in the sample. Questions are raised concerning the nature of the church — what it is, what it should be. For example, some stress that it should be a house of prayer and not an ongoing business concern. The future of the church and the current decline in membership is recognized as a major source of concern. Expressions of hope are voiced in the belief that the church is of God, has been here before us, and will continue after we have gone.

One of the major concerns of the Disciples of Christ, and of all mainline Protestant bodies, is specifically addressed by one sermon:

> Mainline Protestant denominations almost without exception report a gradual but constant decline in membership. . . . How is it with us here and now? Advance or retreat, growth or decline, victory or defeat? Does God have some mission in his heart for us here? Has the work of this great congregation that has met for worship, study, and fellowship in this building for more than sixty years been completed?

The answer, not unexpectedly, is no. But there is a recognition that

> if we are to remain here and continue for the foreseeable future, certain things must happen. . . . We must seek all possible ways of attracting more persons to our church and when they come, have a worthwhile program of worship, study, fellowship, and genuine caring to offer them.

No other sermon in the sample is as candid in its assessment of the future prospects of the church as this one.

Social Justice

Five percent of the sermons deal primarily with social justice. This is not an unexpected finding. One study of ministers' sermons in California during the turbulent sixties produced an almost identical percentage: "we found that approximately 6% of the sermons . . . were mainly devoted to social and political topics."[15] The clergy are divided on the desirability of preaching on controversial social issues. I received two telephone calls while gathering these data that point to the ambiguity here. One midwestern minister said that if people could not find social relevance in a text, perhaps they had not understood it. A second minister, from Texas, said quite simply that the pulpit was not the place to discuss social issues. Two of the social justice sermons are among the better examples in the sample. The illustrations are pertinent and relevant, and the movement of the sermons from introduction to conclusion follows an orderly progression of idea development. One of the sermons has a universal focus. It deals with the question of whether or not liberty and justice do indeed exist for everyone. Presenting data on infant mortality rates around

---

15. Rodney Stark et al., "Ministers as Moral Guides: The Sounds of Silence," in *Religion in Sociological Perspective*, ed. C. Y. Glock (Belmont, Cal.: Wadsworth, 1973), p. 164.

the world, it raises the question of whether justice can be said to exist for mothers in underdeveloped countries with such high infant mortality rates. Are we as Christians concerned with such issues when their existence is so readily apparent?

Contemporary Concerns

Like sermons dealing with social justice, sermons addressing social issues such as marriage and divorce or sexual attitudes and behavior constitute a distinct minority in the sample. In some respects these sermons are unusual for the forthright and vigorous nature with which they address the topic. One sermon notes that throughout Scripture God blesses the institution of marriage, but the minister suggests that it has been debased in today's world. Then, after noting that "what I am about to say here will not be popular," he launches into a forthright assessment of sexual promiscuity in today's society:

> Fornication is a sin regardless of what the psychologists, sociologists, and sex therapists say.

Contemporary attitudes and behavior will bring forth the judgment of God, but

> the judgment spoken of here is not the fury of hellfire and brimstone. It's worse. This judgment is observed and felt in unwanted pregnancies, deliberate abortions, uncontrollable disease, disintegrated homes, and displaced children. . . . Let them say all they want to about "safe sex." . . . Let them install their condom machines and introduce their new curriculum.

Conclusion: it all leads to disaster and a breakdown in the moral structure. It is a safe bet that the congregation did not sleep through this sermon.

These are representative examples of the discussion of the various themes dealt with in the sermons. To aid further in understanding the discussion of these themes, I will turn next to the sources of authority cited in them.

SOURCES OF AUTHORITY

No matter what the format of the sermon or its topic, the minister must call upon some source of authority. In a very general sense the minister's authority is either biblical or nonbiblical. The Bible is used to offer validity for the claims or arguments advanced in the sermon. In addition to the Bible, the minister may use literature, newspapers, personal experiences, movies, television — an almost endless source of material from the world in which we all live. In these sermons the Bible is commonly cited simply to validate the propositions advanced — not the entire Bible, just the New Testament, and not the entire New Testament, just the Gospels. This is true even though more than half the ministers in the sample reported use of the lectionary in preaching. Overall in the sample, the New Testament is quoted more than three times as often as the Old Testament, and 62 percent of all the sermons draw the text from one of the four Gospels. John is the most frequently cited — (37%); followed by Mark (27%), Matthew (18%), and Luke (17%). The Pauline epistles are used in 30 percent of the sermons, and the remaining 8 percent use texts from the rest of the New Testament. Richard Lischer argues that "in both testaments God's comforting promise can be heard and his mighty salvation witnessed."[16] This may be theologically sound, but the sermons in the sample give little evidence that it is taken to heart. Old Testament references are offered as the textual base in 24 percent of the sermons. Of the thirty-nine books in the Old Testament, fifteen are cited at least once, but 52 percent of all the Old Testament citations are from three books: Isaiah, Jeremiah, and the Psalms. An additional 28 percent are from Genesis, Exodus, 1 and 2 Samuel, and 1 Kings. The biblical source of authority is primarily the New Testament and the Gospels. Christ is of course the central figure in the Gospels, and thus the question may be asked: What picture of Christ is presented in these sermons?

IMAGES OF CHRIST

In an effort to answer this question, I used Glen F. Chestnut's *Images of Christ* as a guide to analyze different images of Christ in the New Testament — "who he was and what he did: Christ as the sacrifice for our salvation, the Messiah, the Word of God, the revealer of God, the human being who was also divine, the head of a new humanity, and the conqueror of death."[17] I chose this book because it was written specifically for a lay readership — the same sort of people to whom the sermons were addressed. Table 3 (p. 428) shows the results of the analysis. I treated the eight images separately even though any given sermon could feature more than one (and many did).

One can readily agree with Chestnut when he discusses the meaning of Christ as the Word of God: "It hardly seems practicable . . . to instruct the laity in the metaphysical mysteries of the Stoic-Platonic Logos from the average pulpit."[18] It may well be that this advice applies to each of the images of Christ he discusses. Certainly there is little detailed and searching analysis of the pictures of Christ in these sermons. References do occur, but they are more often passing references than extended treatments of the meaning of the divinity of Christ, for example.

16. Lischer, *A Theology of Preaching: The Dynamics of the Gospel* (Nashville: Abingdon Press, 1981), p. 51.

17. Chestnut, *Images of Christ: An Introduction to Christology* (Minneapolis: Seabury Press, 1984), p. ix.

18. Chestnut, *Images of Christ*, p. 44.

TABLE 3   Percentage of Sermons Treating Various Images of Christ

Images of Christ	Percent
Christ as Sacrifice on the Cross	27
Christ as Messiah	10
Christ as Word of God	14
Christ as the Revelation of God	25
Christ as Human	10
Christ as Divine	5
Christ as Redeemer	39
Christ as Conqueror of Death	5

As Table 3 indicates, the image of Christ most frequently addressed is that of Christ as Redeemer. The least frequently considered images are Christ as divine and Christ as the conqueror of death. The relative lack of emphasis on Christ's victory over death is at least in part attributable to the fact that only four Easter sermons showed up in the final sample. Certainly it is a fair assumption that this is a primary theme preached every Easter. On the other hand, it is quite instructive to note that this major New Testament emphasis on Christ is restricted primarily to Easter sermons.

It is not possible to consider each of the eight images here, so I will restrict my analysis to the three images that appear most frequently: Christ as redeemer, sacrifice, and the revelation of God. How extensively these basic themes should be examined in preaching is subject to some debate. Lischer says that "the majority of Christians encounter theology only in this, its final form, preaching."[19] What the laity hear in these sermons is primarily a succession of snippets from the larger piece of cloth. In discussing Christ as Redeemer, Chestnut states that the "modern emphasis . . . is not on providing an explanation for why human beings as a race are so incredibly and universally sinful, but simply on pointing to the observable fact that this is so. Human beings are *sinful* and that is the problem Christ came to solve."[20] The theology expressed in these sermons readily conforms to this assessment, but most of the references sum it up by saying, for example, that

> Jesus . . . has the means for the cleansing or purification for sins and reigns with God at his right hand in heaven.

or

> the only eternal absolute that will always satisfy our deepest needs and our deepest desires is Jesus Christ, the Son of God, Lord, Saviour, and our Redeemer.

One sermon can serve as illustrative of the few cases in which an effort is made to expand on the meaning of redemption. The sermon pointed to a recent

19. Lischer, *A Theology of Preaching,* p. 28.
20. Chestnut, *Images of Christ,* p. 111.

tragedy that had occurred in the community and then posed the question of how such an event could be explained. Answer: it probably cannot be fully understood.

> But what is not beyond explanation is how the larger community may respond to such tragedies. It is here that our religious groups have an important contribution to make. The contribution is for those groups to do what they should do best: demonstrate redemptive love. . . . That redemptive love means a number of things — such as providing a sustaining presence, bearing one another's burdens, acknowledging that we are all bound together in the bundle of life, and offering compassion and patience and those difficult demands of "tough love" including forgiveness.

The sermon goes on to explore the meaning of redemption further and concludes with the statement that "love always does its work. It always has."

A majority of the references to Christ's sacrificial death are akin to the following brief statements:

> [We must] accept Jesus' act of salvation on the cross for our own living. We must do . . . this because, Only Jesus Saves!

The relationship with God in the Old Testament was predicated on the law, but

> we now have something else. That is the sacrifice of Jesus Christ. Nothing we can do will be good enough; so the only thing we can base our relationship with God on is the sacrifice of Christ. It is grace forevermore. It is as simple as the thief on the cross saying, "remember me."

Again, one example can serve as illustrative of the few efforts made to deal with the sacrifice of Christ in a detailed and more analytical fashion. One entire sermon examines the meaning of the power of the cross in our lives today. Contrasting political power, which may be used for good or evil, with the power of God to transform our lives and lead us into active caring (e.g., feeding the hungry and the dispossessed in the Third World), the sermon uses current illustrations and cites current theologians with pertinent statements.

USE OF ILLUSTRATIONS

Since most preaching is topical or thematic and "made up of affirmations and ideas and arguments," Achtemeier contends that "we need to intersperse the thought portions with picture portions."[21] Illustrations appear in 75 percent of the sermons in this study. The total number is 445, and the variety is so great that I settled on three major categories: general, particular, and personal.

21. Achtemeier, *Creative Preaching*, p. 104.

TABLE 4 Percentage of Various Categories of General Illustrations

Category	Percentage
Related to life experiences of congregation	45
Illustrations from printed matter that are relevant and meaningful	13
Illustrations from printed matter that are not relevant or meaningful	17
Miscellaneous and trivial	25
Total	100

General Illustrations

To help in the analysis, I subdivided this group into four types: illustrations related to the life experiences of the congregation, relevant and meaningful illustrations drawn from books, newspapers, magazines, and other printed material, illustrations drawn from printed material that were not relevant or meaningful, and a miscellaneous category. Distinguishing between relevant and irrelevant illustrations in the printed material category obviously involved a judgment call, but I think the examples I provide below will substantiate my choices in the matter. Table 4 shows the percentage distribution of the general illustrations by category.

Illustrations that are based on the life experiences of the congregation are often vivid and pertinent to the theme being discussed. For example, in describing Nicodemus's visit to Jesus and the difficulty of being born again, the preacher notes the pain and effort involved in any birth:

> You think being born is easy? You think a baby slides forth from the mother's womb like a ship being launched down a well-greased yard's ways? You know better than that from your experience as a mother, or even a father getting the story second hand!

I suspect every mother in that congregation perked up immediately and nodded vigorous assent.

A sermon using the book of Job as assurance that God is with us in hard times begins by asking first if it wouldn't be great if things always went well for us.

> Wouldn't it be great if there were no such things as *pimples, crooked teeth, hemorrhoids, age spots, baldness, or obesity?* Wouldn't it be nice if all of us men had builds like Arnold Schwartzneiger [*sic*] and you women were something like Vanna White, Bo Derek up into our 90's without having to work at it or diet and exercise?

A final and unusually powerful illustration dealing with the brokenness in our lives uses a poem written by a dying man expressing his wife's frustration at his coming death. She is angry when she knows she should be otherwise. But she resents the time he spent away from home when she had to keep the kids all alone. The poem concludes:

> I'll tell you one thing more:
> if a card comes drifting back,

> Postmarked from Hell or Lethe or Death's Other Kingdom
> I'll not read it to the children, 'nor prop it proudly on the mantle place
> I'll stuff it up your effigy.

"Don't you get tired of the brokenness in your life?" asks the minister.

Craddock says that "we are seeking to communicate with people whose experiences are concrete."[22] These illustrations refer to very concrete experiences.

On the other hand, many illustrations taken from printed matter bear little relationship to how people live their lives. In one example, the preacher is trying to stress that the church must reach out and not be consumed with self-serving.

> Do you remember the story of the man who toured the grease factory? "This is the world's largest grease factory," the tour guide said as they started through the gigantic plant. They walked through rows of machines with gears turning, wheels revolving. . . . Toward the end of the tour the fellow asked the guide, "What do you do with all the grease you make here? To whom do you sell it?" "Oh," said the guide, "We don't sell any of it. We have to use all that we produce to lubricate the machinery here at the factory."

Simplistic illustrations of this sort were not difficult to locate.

Particular Illustrations

Those who write on the art of preaching overwhelmingly agree that preachers must be "students of life," that they must be attuned to the lifestyles of those to whom they minister. They should go to the movies their congregations go to, listen to their music, and in short demonstrate that they live and breathe as others do. One indication of the extent to which they do this can be found in their use of illustrations drawn from contemporary life. Table 5 (p. 432) shows a partial listing of the topics most frequently used as illustrations in these sermons. Only a distinct minority of sermons contain illustrations from the movies or television, which are watched by millions of people each week. There is almost no use of classical or contemporary literature, drama, history, biography, or other similar sources. Of the television illustrations, only 40 percent actually seek to relate them to some particular theme in the sermon. One, however, is worth noting for its use of humor and relevance. The topic is evangelism. How would John have tried to attract both Jews and Gentiles to Jesus if he had had the use of television commercials?

> The Gentiles . . . come to Jesus saying, "He makes you feel great!" The Jews would be coming saying, "He gives less demanding rules than the law of Moses." At a lakeside picnic they'd argue, "Feels great!" "Less demanding!"

22. Craddock, *As One without Authority*, p. 60.

TABLE 5 Percentage of Selected Particular Illustrations Used in Sermons

Category	Percent
Literature	
Classical	10
Contemporary	10
Theologians or Preachers	
Classical Theologians	11
Contemporary Theologians	15
Contemporary Preachers	19
Music References	
Hymns	15
Current Issues	
Feminism	8
Drugs, Pornography, Crime, Violence	19
International Concerns	
War, Peace, Nuclear Arms Race	23
Movies and Television	
Movies	12
TV	21
Sports or Sports Figures	16
Science or Scientists	10
Business or Businesspersons	13

Another issue of more than passing interest in today's society is the feminist cause, the female liberation movement, consciousness raising, and similar terms used to describe the position of women. This issue receives attention in only 8 percent of the sermons. All but one of the references in the sample are supportive of women's efforts to achieve equal rights. In similar fashion, the use of drugs in an addictive sense is found in 13 percent of the sermons. In every case it is addressed as a serious national problem in need of attention.

Personal Illustrations

The reference to and use of the minister's own life and faith journey as sermonic material is controversial. Myron R. Chartier argues that "at some point in the sermon the preacher must be able to tell 'my story' as it relates to the Christian story."[23] William H. Willimon is less certain about how much of

23. Chartier, *Preaching as Communication: An Interpersonal Perspective* (Nashville: Abingdon Press, 1981), pp. 33-34.

a "personal 'presence' in preaching" there should be.[24] All agree, of course, that self-aggrandizement is wholly unacceptable.

Almost half of the sermons (48%) used one or more personal illustrations. Not surprisingly, they ranged from the utterly trivial to sincere efforts to relate the preacher's own faith journey to the gospel message. Approximately one-fourth were frivolous and dealt with the wife's lasagna, the inevitable travelogues, house pets, overweight problems, fishing, and the like.

Among the more serious material used to clarify and personalize the preaching of the Word, one illustration pointed up the dual standards by which we all operate, saying one thing but sending a different signal to those around us with our actions. The minister commented that "its like the elder in a church I once served who was a card carrying member of the K.K.K. and was always on my case because the church didn't teach enough Bible." Another minister notes that in making his own personal decisions for God, he has to first check out his "as-long-as" clauses: he will stick with God "as long as I can remain comfortable and don't have to be with people I don't know or don't like" or "as long as I can stay out of public controversy and everyone will still like me." One of the very best personal illustrations seeks to help us understand what the Bible means when it talks about the "orphans and widows" we are enjoined to help. The minister acknowledges that he really knows no orphans, and the widows he visits do not seem to fit the biblical image. He then describes a visit to his favorite widow, his mother, who lives with other widows in a community out West. When he goes to visit, they often get him into a card game where the conversation proceeds along these lines:

> One heart. Did I tell you dearie that I turned over some of my CD's last week and got 10.5 percent and I locked it in for 36 months? Two diamonds. Oh, no, I like municipal bonds. They are tax free. . . . Three hearts. . . . Preferred bonds — preferred stocks — that is what I like to be in. . . . Then it comes around to me and I look, and all I can say is, "Pass"!

While a majority of the personal illustrations are used effectively, it should be remembered that slightly more than half of those preaching do not use any reference to their own faith or lifestyle to "make God visible through the transparency of his or her own person."[25]

Finally it should be noted that although preachers use some sort of illustration to lead into the sermon in approximately 80 percent of the cases, the illustration is directly related to the theme that follows in only about 50 percent of the cases. It is clear that they feel it appropriate to use this device to open the sermon regardless of whether it enhances the theme.

---

24. See Willimon, *Integrative Preaching: The Pulpit at the Center* (Nashville: Abingdon Press, 1981).

25. Chartier, *Preaching as Communication*, p. 33.

LANGUAGE USE

While preaching is an oral form of communication, many ministers write their message in full manuscript form before presentation. Not all do, of course; six or seven ministers wrote me saying they would be happy to participate in the study but they did not write out their sermons — even in outline form. Among those who do write out the sermon, however, it is a fair assumption that the delivery follows as closely as possible the style and word usage that they have committed to paper. The choice of words to communicate receives extensive treatment in nearly all homiletical texts.

There is a consensus among homileticians that sermon language should be vivid, colorful, and convey a sense of the sounds, smells, tastes, and emotion of life. In the real world, however, as William D. Thompson points out, "sermonic language is frequently and justly criticized for being too abstract. . . . It is full of words like love, compassion, justice, right and wrong, happiness, evil, etc."[26] Craddock says that "it is difficult to conceive of a sermon that does not contain descriptions of persons, events, relationships, or places. . . . Description provides images. . . . When the appropriate word is spoken, an image stands out vivid and clear: nun, minister, German, communist, . . . car salesperson, lawyer."[27] These principles should also shape the presentation of theological concepts. Sin, grace, salvation, redemption, and similar concepts fill the pages of sermons, but are they connected to the life experiences of the congregation and described in terms which are vivid and colorful? They are derived from the Bible and the history of the church's teachings, but it remains a matter of debate how familiar a congregation is with the Scriptures and church history. Achtemeier, for one, argues that the "biblical record may be so strange to a congregation that it seems to be a message from another planet."[28] In a discussion of the use of religious language in a secular age, Langdon Gilkey asserts that "many are able to say that 'they believe' religious doctrines; what is so hard for them is to go on and say what these doctrines might *mean* and to *use* them in understanding their ordinary life."[29] It is the preacher's task to make clear the meaning and applicability of the theological terms widely used in sermons.

The focus of this section is on the use of theological language. Is it clear how such language is or can be used in everyday living? Or are the terms simply declaimed as if there were complete understanding of their meaning and import? To get at these questions, I analyzed two terms in detail: *sin* and *grace*. I chose these terms because the image of Christ most frequently touched upon in the sermons is Christ as Redeemer.

---

26. Thompson, *Preaching Biblically: Exegesis and Interpretation* (Nashville: Abingdon, 1981), p. 69.

27. Craddock, *As One without Authority*, pp. 200-210.

28. Achtemeier, *Creative Preaching*, p. 13.

29. Gilkey, *Naming the Whirlwind: The Renewal of God-Language* (Indianapolis: Bobbs-Merrill, 1969), p. 262.

The position of the Christian faith is, of course, that the grace of God overcomes human sin. But does that assertion have any meaning for a contemporary congregation? Does *grace* mean anything to them? Does *sin* connote anything more than gambling, drug usage, or sexual infidelity? In categorizing the use of these concepts in the sermons, I distinguished between abstract and specific usage. I considered the use abstract if the term appeared with no more than a sentence or two indicating what it meant. I considered the use specific if a greater effort was made to give flesh and meaning to an otherwise abstract theological concept.

Sin is examined in 40 percent of the sermons. In nearly every instance it is used in an abstract manner (83% of the time). There is little effort to present a conceptual treatment of sin embracing some given format such as legalistic, moralistic, or theistic piety — that is, sin as a failure to believe, or failure to perform right acts, or failure to love God with all one's heart, soul, and mind.[30] For example,

> The church must always be critical of sin and in conflict with those forces that would attempt to render her powerless, helpless, and voiceless.

Or

> When we talk about the things that are basic in existence, everybody understands us. Such as love and loyalty, need and failure, sin and salvation, hope and freedom — these are common to all people regardless of race or nationality.

The latter illustration links together a series of concepts with no specification whatsoever.

In those instances (17%) where an effort is made to move *sin* from the abstract to the specific, some language use is vivid and colorful and seeks to relate directly to experiences readily understood by the listener:

> Just like the alcoholic cannot control his drinking, we have lost control over our sinning. We don't care what God wants. And that's what sin is. It may express itself in different ways, by theft, or by gossip, or by murder. But, however we express it, it's all the same. It's saying to God, "I don't care."

Again:

> A few years ago, Karl Menninger's bestseller was titled and asked the question, *Whatever Became of Sin?* He chided those therapists and social scientists who sought to rationalize away all aberrant human behavior as the result of unfavorable social conditions. He also took to task the liberal theologians who, for decades, had been telling people, in effect, there is no such thing as sin. That ultimate authority by which all human behavior was once judged

30. This particular conceptual scheme was suggested to me in correspondence with Susan May, who graciously shared her insights concerning this discussion of the treatment of sin in the sermons.

(God) . . . blesses everything and damns nothing. "Hogwash," said Menninger. . . . There are in our world, infidelity, cruelty, racism, stealing, prejudice, lying, idolatry, and a host of other human behavior which can only be called sin.

Sin, when addressed in specific terms, is overwhelming personal sin. The quote from Menninger's book is one of only four which identifies sin as having any social nature at all.

One conception of sin examined in 10 percent of the sermons is that related to the "me" generation. The discussion of the "me" generation reflects the question that Thielicke raised more than twenty years ago and that is even more relevant in today's society: "Where is the average person today who, when he hears the word 'sin' really hears what the New Testament meant by that word? For whom today does this word still say that here man is being addressed at the point of his resistance and opposition to God, that this means man in his will to assert his autonomy, his insistence that everything centers in man."[31] While the term *sin* is not used directly in connection with discussion of the "me" generation, it is clear that self-actualization or self-realization is not looked upon with approval. It is interesting that these discussions are quite specific in nearly every case.

Several of you know that I'm — I [laughs self-consciously] am rather a stickler for grammar. People use the word *I* and *myself* too often incorrectly where the word *me* should be used. *I* is a subject pronoun and *me* is an object pronoun. And our incorrect overuse of the *I* tells the world who we want to be the subject of the conversation. . . . Using only half the vocabulary offered to us is to focus only on ourselves, and this shows our human weakness. We have . . . a self-infatuation. How crucial it is that we choose God above everything, including ourselves.

If sin is overcome by God's grace, is this made clear? Grace is treated in 25 percent of the sermons. In 85 percent of the cases the term is used as if full understanding is apparent and no further comment is necessary. In the 15 percent of examples where some effort is made to apply the meaning of grace to our lives, only two are detailed examinations. Examples of the abstract use can be seen in the following:

E. Stanley Jones once declared, "the early Christians did not say in dismay. Look what the world has come to," but in delight, "look what has come into the world." They saw that not only did sin abound, but that grace did much more abound. To which group do you belong?

In a discussion of Paul's debate in Ephesus over accepting Gentiles into the faith without ritual circumcision, Paul's conclusion is summed up as follows:

31. Thielicke, *The Trouble with the Church,* p. 36.

TABLE 6 The Purpose of Sermons

Comfort and inspiration	28
Exhortation	19
Challenge	18
Teaching and theological information	17
Affirmation of the faith	6
Purpose undefined	12
Total	100

> The fundamental nature of the gospel is grace. No adjustments or stipulations which suggest that the gospel might carry any conditions with it can be tolerated. The fundamental nature of the gospel is grace, alone.

It is clear that overall a preference for the abstract dominates language use in these sermons.

PURPOSE OF THE SERMONS

Even though their language is primarily abstract, ministers still have some specific purposes in their preaching. Charles L. Bartow has asserted that "preaching seeks the transformation of the life of [the] community. . . . It envisions new possibilities for the people."[32] A reading of these sermons suggests that "transformation," "new possibilities," "challenge," and related concerns are *not* dominant concerns here. Table 6 shows that the major purpose of the sermons is to offer comfort and inspiration to the congregation. This is followed by exhortation to live a better life, serve God, or witness. For example,

> We must join in the ranks of the faithful witnesses who are working to bring the good news to the whole world. God has left this vital task in our hands. We must not set it aside as of less than primary importance.

The sermons that seek to challenge the congregation do so primarily on a personal level. Parishioners are challenged to "release your song," to live up to the potential in their lives and work. The challenge to set new goals for the church and carry through with them is also a prominent theme. In the few sermons dealing with social justice, the congregation is urged to "bring about a more just social order" both nationally and internationally. Slightly more than one fifth (23%) of the sermons were designed to teach, convey theological information, or simply affirm the faith. More than one in ten (12%) had no readily discernible purpose.

32. Bartow, *The Preaching Moment: A Guide to Sermon Delivery* (Nashville: Abingdon Press, 1981), p. 19.

CONCLUSION

Preaching is a process, and as such cannot be wholly captured in written documents such as those analyzed in this study. But written sermons do provide valuable insights into the lives of those who prepare them. How they see the world and how they see the gospel answering the needs of that world are revealed in what they write and later say in their pulpits.

What needs are addressed in these sermons? Is there awareness of the complexity and moral ambiguity of the daily life struggles faced by the congregation? Is the preaching directed toward and related to our technological era and does it give awareness of this in the Scriptures chosen, the illustrations used, and the conception of the work of Christ in the late twentieth century? Or are the sermons largely devoted to the presentation of "eternal" truths that need to be put into a contemporary context to be rendered meaningful? On balance, the latter approach characterizes a majority of these sermons. The theme of the sermons is overwhelmingly doctrinal in nature. When these doctrines are examined in detail, there is more declamation than analytical explanation. The language used to describe the doctrines is almost completely abstract rather than specific. The assumption would appear to be that the congregation knows and understands the doctrine and thus needs simply to be reassured that God does indeed love us, will forgive us, and will save us. But it is clearly dangerous to assume much doctrinal sophistication or even biblical literacy on the part of a congregation.

The ministers themselves demonstrate an almost Marcionic approach to the bulk of the Bible — the Old Testament. They appear to have little use for the great narrative stories and even less for the indignation at social injustice expressed by the eighth-century prophets. This is reflected in the scant attention they pay to issues of social justice, racism, feminism, and other such contemporary concerns. They consistently exhibit a narrow focus on the Gospels as the primary source of authority for preaching and hence present a limited view of what data, biblical and nonbiblical, may be offered in support of what they proclaim as the "eternal truths."

There is an uneven quality in the sermons. Variation in preaching styles from more than 100 ministers around the country is not surprising, of course. But the uneven quality *within* sermons is surprising and is revealed in the use of all types of illustrations. Many of these, as noted, are quite pertinent, vivid, and related to life experiences. But within a single sermon it is not unusual to find a personal illustration used in a capable fashion being followed shortly by a hackneyed book-worn story. It would seem that illustrations are being used almost compulsively, perhaps to provide breaks in the continuous flow of information that characterizes most sermons.

Regular preaching is not an easy task. As one among many pressing ministerial responsibilities, sermon preparation can easily be shunted aside until the last possible moment. But the time to preach unavoidably arrives, once again, and so you speak. You dare to speak. You dare to lay your offering before them. And because you do, the word is let loose, the Spirit starts to rove among them, the bread is broken, and passed around, and, for better or worse, the gospel feast begins again. For the millionth time in our story, God's people hear the word, and they are fed.[33]

Let us pray that this is indeed the case.

---

33. Willimon, *Integrative Preaching,* p. 101.

Working Group Response: Social, Religious, and Moral Profile of Ministry and Laity

Kim Blakeley-Lombard, Recorder

In addition to early drafts of the chapters by Guth and Turner, Greer, and Faulkner, the working group on the Social, Religious, and Moral Profile of Ministry and Laity heard a presentation entitled "Family, Birth Control, and Sexuality in the Christian Church (Disciples of Christ): 1880-1980," by John P. Marcum.

We decided that our task was to take the data that had been gathered by the sociologists, draw our own conclusions from it, and provide a theological basis for making decisions.

Some members in our group suggested that we evaluate what we believe and how we live out our faith on the basis of the theological norm of God's love for all of creation. All that we say and do must be based on that norm. People know that the world is in bad shape and that the mainstream denominations are declining; what is exciting is that we continue to bear witness in the world today. It seems to suggest that in spite of all the claims for ultimacy in the advertising realm, people still have a need for the One who is truly ultimate. When they come to church, they deserve to have us deal with that which is truly ultimate, with the ways in which God is relevant to our lives, rather than finding another social club that conforms to the rest of society and hence lacks ultimate meaning.

The studies suggested openings for evangelism, openings for living out our faith in an all-inclusive God. One study pointed out that many single people are not involved in the life of the church despite the fact that they claim membership in Disciples congregations. Openings for evangelism were suggested for persons who are divorced, remarried, single parents, and those who choose not to marry. A group that tends to be ignored more than any other is homosexuals. One suggestions from our group is the need to redefine "family" in such a way that those who have been considered "nontraditional" will feel accepted in the church and can know that they are part of the everyone whom

God loves and accepts. If our theology understands God to be inclusive, our actions will tend to be more inclusive as well.

Sociological data suggest that the preponderance of Disciples are middle-class. The suggestion was made that we might do well to reach out to those in lower- and upper-income areas. Many people in upper-income areas have tried a little of everything in a search for ultimate meaning, and many have become disillusioned. Churches that take theology and meaning seriously may be able to meet some of the needs of those people in the unchurched popula-tions — the challengers and calculators, who are particularly selective and critical in choosing a church as they search for the Ultimate. We should be committed to such attempts not merely to get more members and keep our churches alive but to demonstrate a faithfulness to our mission to preach the good news of God's love for all of God's creation and of the meaning and fullness of life.

We surveyed data indicating a gap between the theological and political views of clergy and laity and also a considerable diversity of theological and political views among the laity. We did not draw any real conclusions con-cerning these matters, but we do consider them important areas for future study. Fulfilling our roles as teachers of the Christian faith and listening to the experiences of those to whom we seek to minister will facilitate dialogue between clergy and laity as we seek to be faithful to our belief in God's all-inclusive love.

Some in our group warned that as we work to reach out to other groups in our church, we must take care not to ignore the dominant group in our churches now: those who are fifty and over, many of whom are women. They are included in the all whom God loves and with whom God wants to be in relationship. They are part of our present, and it is with them that we look to our future and seek to live out our faith.

It was also suggested that we look at those congregations that are defying the mainline denominational trends and growing. What is the underlying the-ology being preached and lived out in these congregations? What programs are they providing?

The greatest implication for the issue of growth and decline that we discovered was the need to claim our history and to claim a theological basis on which to do theological reflection for teaching and action. The Disciples of Christ have a rich heritage, and yet one survey of our clergy indicates that the greatest problem facing the Disciples is our lack of identity. In looking to the future, we need to know and claim our past. Sermons and programs for education now being developed should emphasize our roots.

In looking to the future, it also seems vital that clergy engage in critical theological reflection. The sermons in Faulkner's survey tend to use theological terms that have little meaning for the congregation. There would seem to be a need for preachers to work to define these theological terms (i.e., sin, grace, salvation, redemption, righteousness) and explain how they have been understood by those who have gone before us (in our Scriptures, Luther, Stone, Campbell). Preachers also need to help their congregations understand such concepts through concrete and meaningful illustrations that are true to their experiences.

Since theology is very important, we suggest further study into the theological understandings of clergy and their congregations: How do they understand sin, grace, salvation, redemption? How do they communicate their theology? How is it lived out in the lives of their congregations? Members of our group were very concerned about how we live out our theology and that we not stop with theological reflection. The Disciples founder Barton W. Stone might suggest to us that once we see the beauty of God's love we cannot help but respond in acts of love toward God and neighbor.

Who are we? We are members of the Christian Church (Disciples of Christ), a part of the body of Christ, a part of the whole people of God. We have a rich heritage of critical theological reflection and an evangelistic passion that reaches out to all people to proclaim God's all-inclusive love. May it be that this heritage empowers our endeavors toward transformation and renewal.

VII. ECOLOGY OF GROWTH
AND DECLINE

Spatial Patterns of Growth and Decline among the Disciples of Christ, 1890-1980

Roger W. Stump

Since their origin early in the 1800s, the Disciples of Christ have developed a geographical distribution markedly different from those of other major religious bodies in the United States.[1] Emerging as settlement advanced through the Ohio Valley, the Disciples became one of the largest religious groups in the lower Midwest and remain more heavily concentrated there than any other major denomination. From this hearth area, the Disciples spread to many other parts of the country. They have achieved their greatest success in a large area reaching from Ohio to Texas, a "Disciples Belt" that has been the focus of their geographical distribution for over a century (Fig. 1, p. 446). Their widespread diffusion, however, has made them a group of national importance.

As the Disciples have spread across the United States, many factors have shaped their spatial patterns of growth and decline. The purpose of this essay is to determine how their geographical distribution has changed over the course of their history and to identify some of the key factors that have caused those changes. Specifically, the analysis examines the Disciples' distribution at five points in their history and assesses changes in their distribution during intervening years. Each of the five study years coincides with a major stage in Disciples history. The study begins with a survey of patterns in 1890, the year in which the settlement frontier closed in the United States and which thus marks the end of the Disciples' initial period of diffusion. Membership patterns in 1906 reveal the group's expansion around the turn of the century and the effects of the schism that produced the Churches of Christ, officially recognized as a separate body in that year. The Disciples' distribution in 1952 reflects the boom in church membership at mid-century. Recent trends are assessed at

1. See Edwin S. Gaustad, *Historical Atlas of Religion in America* (New York: Harper & Row, 1976), pp. 64-67; Bruce Bigelow, "The Disciples of Christ in Antebellum Indiana: Geographical Indicator of the Border South," *Journal of Cultural Geography* 7 (Fall-Winter, 1986): 49-58.

FIGURE 1   The Disciples Belt

two points in time: in 1971, shortly after a second schism produced the
independent Christian Churches; and in 1980, at the end of the decade in which
the Disciples underwent the first significant decline in their history.[2]

The discussion of changes in Disciples distribution from 1890 to 1980
focuses primarily on the effects of contextual factors, aspects of the social and
demographic contexts in which church growth and decline occur.[3] Such factors
include regional migration, population growth, and urbanization. Church
growth also depends on institutional factors associated with the denomination
and its congregations, such as the effectiveness of individual clergy, the quality
and scope of church programs, and the emphasis placed on new church development. While such factors can have a large impact on church growth, in most
cases the nature of their impact cannot be determined at a national scale using

2. Membership data for the five study years were taken from the following sources: U.S.
Census Office, *11th Census, 1890: Volume IX, Report on Statistics of Churches in the United States*
(Washington: U.S. Government Printing Office, 1894); U.S. Bureau of the Census, *Religious
Bodies, 1906* (Washington: U.S. Government Printing Office, 1910); Lauris B. Whitman and
Glen W. Trimble, *Churches and Church Membership in the United States, 1952* (New York:
National Council of the Churches of Christ, 1956); Douglas W. Johnson, Paul R. Picard, and Bernard
Quinn, *Churches and Church Membership in the United States, 1971* (Washington: Glenmary
Research Center, 1974); and Bernard Quinn et al., *Churches and Church Membership in the United
States, 1980* (Atlanta: Glenmary Research Center, 1982). Membership data from these sources
represent the full participating membership. Because the Disciples have had only a small presence
in Alaska and Hawaii, the analysis examines patterns only in the continental United States.

3. On the role of contextual and institutional factors in church growth, see David A. Roozen
and Jackson W. Carroll, "Recent Trends in Church Membership and Participation: An Introduction," in *Understanding Church Growth and Decline: 1950-1978*, ed. Dean R. Hoge and David A.
Roozen (New York: Pilgrim Press, 1979), pp. 38-40.

TABLE 1 Regional Distribution of the Disciples of Christ

Region	Percentage of all Disciples within a region				
	1890	1906	1952	1971	1980
New England	0.3	0.3	0.1	0.1	0.1
Mid Atlantic	2.6	3.6	3.3	2.5	2.8
East North Central	31.4	31.0	28.7	22.8	22.4
West North Central	25.6	28.5	20.6	21.3	21.0
South Atlantic	6.8	7.4	11.8	14.2	14.7
East South Central	20.9	15.7	10.5	9.5	9.8
West South Central	9.2	7.8	13.5	17.1	17.7
Mountain	0.6	1.6	2.8	3.3	3.7
Pacific	2.7	4.1	8.7	9.3	7.7
Total	100.0	100.0	100.0	100.0	100.0
Disciples Belt	73.3	74.9	65.6	62.7	63.2

New England: CT, MA, ME, NH, RI, VT
Mid Atlantic: NJ, NY, PA
East North Central: IL, IN, MI, OH, WI
West North Central: IA, KS, MN, MO, ND, NE, SD
South Atlantic: DC, DE, GA, FL, MD, NC, SC, VA, WV
East South Central: AL, KY, MS, TN
West South Central: AR, LA, OK, TX
Mountain: AZ, CO, ID, MT, NM, NV, UT, WY
Pacific: CA, OR, WA
Disciples Belt: IA, IL, IN, KS, KY, MO, OH, OK, TX

the data examined here. This study thus considers the effects of only one crucial institutional factor — denominational schism.

The goal of the following analysis, then, is to identify influential features of the larger context within which the Disciples' patterns of growth and decline have evolved. In elucidating the varied character of this context and its effects, this study also provides a foundation for examining how factors not considered here have influenced Disciples membership patterns, and serves as a framework for interpreting local case studies.

THE LATE NINETEENTH CENTURY

From the time of their beginnings in the early 1800s, the Disciples grew rapidly. They numbered 200,000 by 1860 and over 640,000 by 1890, making them the nation's eighth largest denomination in the latter year.[4] As they grew, the Disciples diffused into every region of the United States (see Table 1). By

4. See David Edwin Harrell, Jr., "Restorationism and the Stone-Campbell Tradition," in *Encyclopedia of the American Religious Experience,* vol. 2, ed. Charles H. Lippy and Peter W. Williams (New York: Charles Scribner's Sons, 1988), p. 851; and U.S. Census Office, *11th Census, 1890,* p. xvii.

1890 they had established churches in over half of the nation's counties, and New Hampshire and Nevada were the only states from which they were absent. In terms of their size and spatial distribution, the Disciples had become a denomination of national significance by the end of the century.

Despite their growing presence nationwide, the Disciples' distribution continued to reflect their Ohio Valley origins (Fig. 2). In 1890, a third of all Disciples lived in Kentucky, Indiana, or Ohio, the states that made up the early hearth of their movement. The largest concentration of members in this area stretched from Kentucky's Bluegrass region into southwestern Ohio. Other concentrations developed in southern and central Indiana and in eastern Ohio.

FIGURE 2   Distribution of the Disciples of Christ in 1890, by county.

From the Ohio Valley, the Disciples spread to a large area of the nation's interior. This diffusion proceeded mainly to the west, following the advance of settlement. Their concentrations in Kentucky and Indiana thus extended across Illinois into Iowa, Missouri, and Kansas. By 1890 over a third of all Disciples lived in the four latter states, and Missouri claimed the largest state membership, nearly 100,000. A second major path in their diffusion led south from the Ohio Valley. Tennessee developed a large membership by mid-century, and from there the Disciples spread south into Georgia, Alabama, and Mississippi and southwest into Arkansas and Texas. In 1890 the southern states together contained nearly a fifth of all Disciples.

The Disciples had less success on the Atlantic coast. Like other evangelical churches, the Disciples made their greatest gains during the 1800s on the frontier, where the scarcity of religious institutions created great opportunities for evangelism.[5] Still, by 1890 the Disciples had spread to most eastern states. Their main axis of membership here ran from southwestern Pennsylvania to eastern North Carolina. The latter contained an especially large cluster of Disciples, over 11,000 in 1890. The Disciples had also spread throughout the West by 1890, but their numbers there were still small. Altogether the western states contained slightly over 20,000 Disciples, most of them in California, Oregon, and Washington.

As they diffused across the country, the Disciples tended to remain in rural areas and small towns, a pattern that reflected their rural origins and the lack of extensive urbanization in the nation's interior, where most of them lived. A few urban centers of membership had appeared by 1890, but they did not contain many more members than nearby rural counties. The biggest urban concentrations developed in the Midwest and upper South, in Cleveland, Cincinnati, Louisville, Nashville, Kansas City, and Des Moines. Of these, Louisville claimed the largest membership, slightly over 4,000 in 1890. At the same time, however, over a hundred mainly rural counties contained at least 1,000 Disciples, including about twenty such counties with over 2,000.

By 1890, then, the Disciples had developed a distinctive geographical distribution focused on the Ohio, Mississippi, and Missouri Valleys. Their greatest concentration ran from Kentucky through Missouri, but growing numbers of Disciples could be found in other regions as well. Because they were concentrated in the nation's agricultural heartland, most Disciples still lived in farming districts or small towns.

THE EARLY TWENTIETH CENTURY

During the late nineteenth and early twentieth centuries, two major developments affected the Disciples' geographical distribution: rapid growth in membership and schism within the Disciples movement. From 1890 to 1906 the Disciples increased dramatically, to a membership of over 1.1 million. They were the fastest growing of the large Protestant denominations, increasing at a rate nearly twice that of all Protestants combined and over twice that of the total population.[6] As the Disciples grew, however, doctrinal disputes arose within the group, ultimately leading to the emergence of the Churches of Christ by 1906. Nonetheless, even after the Churches of Christ separated, the Disciples counted nearly a million adherents. Although these two developments are not unrelated, they are treated separately in the following discussion. The survey of growth up to 1906 thus focuses on the whole Disciples movement, including the combined membership of the Disciples and the Churches of Christ.

5. Gaustad, *Historical Atlas of Religion in America*, pp. 64, 66.
6. U.S. Bureau of the Census, *Religious Bodies, 1906*, vol. 1, pp. 25-26.

GEOGRAPHICAL DIMENSIONS OF GROWTH UP TO 1906

The Disciples grew rapidly between 1890 and 1906, nearly doubling their total membership, and this growth was widespread geographically. Membership increased in over 70 percent of all counties containing Disciples in 1890. Congregations were established in around 400 new counties as well, mostly located adjacent to counties having Disciples in 1890. At the state level, membership increased in all states except South Carolina, Delaware, and Utah.

The Disciples' growth at this time tended to follow a pattern of local contact diffusion. In such a pattern, a denomination's growth in a given area depends on its initial presence there; the larger its presence, the greater subsequent growth will be. Various factors may contribute to the development of this type of pattern. Individual members play a role by bringing children and friends into the church. Congregations contribute by attracting new adherents through their various programs or their prominence in the community. As membership grows, new churches are established, both in communities already having congregations and in new areas nearby. Through these processes of expansion, the group grows the most where it is already strongest, and its existing distribution is reinforced. This pattern is typical of Protestant denominations in the United States during the twentieth century and explains the persistence of regional variations in patterns of affiliation.[7]

Evidence that the Disciples followed this pattern appears in the strong correlation at the state level between membership in 1890 and increase in membership between 1890 and 1906.[8] The association between initial membership and subsequent growth indicates that the Disciples largely grew "in place," making their greatest gains where they were already most numerous. Most of their growth thus occurred within their traditional core region, extending from Ohio to Texas (see Fig. 1, p. 446). The nine states of this Disciples Belt accounted for an increase of 350,000 members, 70 percent of the Disciples' total growth.

Although growth was proportionate to initial membership in most areas, some states did not follow this pattern. In Oklahoma, the Disciples grew from 2,000 to 32,000 between 1890 and 1906, at a rate about 15 times their national average. This rapid growth reflected Oklahoma's Disciples Belt location and the sharp rise in its population after it was opened to white settlers in the late 1800s. The Disciples also grew rapidly in the West as its population expanded, but their absolute increase was small in most western states; the exception was California, which gained over 13,000 Disciples. Finally, in Tennessee the Disciples' growth was disproportionately small relative to their initial membership, increasing by only about one-third between 1890 and 1906. This slow

---

7. See Roger W. Stump, "Regional Divergence in Religious Affiliation in the United States," *Sociological Analysis* 45 (Winter 1984): 283-99.

8. The correlation coefficient between initial membership and absolute increase in membership at the state level was 0.94, which was significant at the 0.95 confidence level.

growth rate may reflect Tennessee's role as the center of the schism that produced the Churches of Christ. Tensions preceding the schism may have attenuated the Disciples' growth even before the division occurred.

The correlation between initial size and subsequent growth is weaker at the county level than at the state level.[9] The size of the Disciples' initial presence still affected growth at the county level, but factors other than simple contact diffusion were also important. Many such factors operated only locally, making their effects on patterns of change nationwide difficult to assess. At least one factor had a distinct effect across the country, however: urbanization. By 1906 a number of cities had emerged as important centers of growth for the Disciples, most of them in or near the Disciples Belt. Indianapolis, Chicago, Kansas City, and Pittsburgh claimed the largest increases between 1890 and 1906 and the largest total memberships in the latter year, each counting between 7,000 and 10,000 Disciples. Other major centers of growth in the Disciples Belt included St. Louis, Des Moines, Lexington, and Louisville. The leading center outside the Disciples Belt was Los Angeles, where membership increased by nearly 5,000 over this period.

Growth among the Disciples before the schism of 1906 thus involved two main trends. Most importantly, the Disciples were most successful in gaining new members in areas where they were already prominent. The presence of a substantial denominational infrastructure in those areas, and of large numbers of existing members, provided the many points of contact needed to attract new adherents. Second, urbanization had begun to produce large concentrations of Disciples in several major cities. The effect of urban growth on the Disciples' distribution was less pronounced at this time than later in the twentieth century, but its importance was becoming increasingly evident.

THE GEOGRAPHY OF SCHISM: THE CHURCHES OF CHRIST

As their numbers grew around the turn of the century, the Disciples became increasingly divided by doctrinal controversy. Dissension arose out of long-standing disagreements over several developments among the Disciples, including the creation of the American Christian Missionary Society and the use of instrumental music in worship services. In 1906 this dissension led to the official recognition of the separation from the Disciples of nearly 160,000 members, under the name of the Churches of Christ.[10]

Because the schism was largely regional in character, the withdrawal of

9. The correlation coefficient for initial membership and absolute increase in membership at the county level was 0.43, which was significant at the 0.95 confidence level. County-level membership data for the Disciples and the Churches of Christ are not provided for all states in the 1906 census of religious bodies. This correlation is thus based on data from 783 counties for which membership data for both groups were available.

10. Harrell, "Restorationism and the Stone-Campbell Tradition," p. 853.

the Churches of Christ strongly affected the Disciples' distribution (see Fig. 3). The Churches of Christ were heavily concentrated in the South; in 1906 about three-fourths of their membership lived in the three southern census regions, compared to less than a third of all Disciples. Their geographical center was Tennessee, which contained a fourth of their members. It also had the highest ratio of Churches of Christ to Disciples membership, the former outnumbering the latter by nearly three to one. The Churches of Christ also surpassed the Disciples in Arkansas and Alabama and had nearly as many members in Texas.

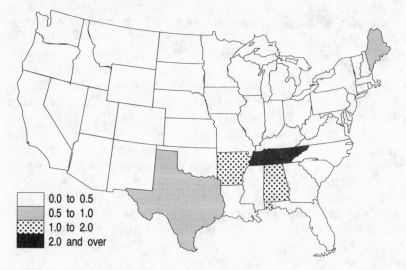

0.0 to 0.5
0.5 to 1.0
1.0 to 2.0
2.0 and over

FIGURE 3   Ratio of Churches of Christ to Disciples of Christ membership in 1906, by state.

The split between the Disciples and the Churches of Christ reflected broad cultural divisions between the North and South. According to David Harrell, "Southern church leaders frequently rallied sectional prejudice against the North to accompany their theological attacks on northern liberals" among the Disciples.[11] Socioeconomic contrasts also divided the two groups. Disciples were more urban, and the average value of their churches was over five times that of the Churches of Christ.[12] Sociologically, the Churches of Christ represented a southern, conservative reaction to the northern, liberal ideas and practices associated with the increasingly wealthy and urban Disciples.

After the schism, the Disciples' membership shifted to the north, as the proportion living in the East South Central and West South Central regions fell from 30 percent in 1890 to under 24 percent in 1906 (see Table 1, p. 447).

11. Harrell, "Restorationism and the Stone-Campbell Tradition," p. 853.
12. See Harrell, "Restorationism and the Stone-Campbell Tradition," pp. 853-54.

Outside the South, however, the schism had little effect on Disciples membership patterns. Nor did the Churches of Christ impede the Disciples growth in subsequent decades. Indeed, from 1906 to 1926 a fairly strong correlation existed between growth in the two groups.[13] The socioeconomic contrasts between the two groups suggest that they did not compete with each other for members, and thus growth in one did not detract from growth in the other.

THE MID-TWENTIETH CENTURY

The first half of the twentieth century was again a period of sustained growth for the Disciples. Between 1906 and 1952 their membership increased by over 80 percent, growing to a total of 1.8 million members in 1952. Their rate of growth was about equal to that of the American population, but somewhat lower than that of other large Protestant groups, including the Baptists, Lutherans, and Methodists.[14] The Disciples nonetheless retained their status as one of the nation's largest Protestant bodies. Their national significance was reinforced by a widely distributed pattern of growth. From 1906 to 1952, membership increased in all but six states: those of New England (except Maine) and North Dakota. Growth at the county level was more varied but still reflected widespread gains. Membership increased in two-thirds of the counties in which the Disciples were present in 1906, and they expanded into well over 200 new counties. In all, 1,805 counties contained Disciples in 1952 — close to 60 percent of all counties in the United States (see Fig. 4, p. 454).

As the Disciples grew, their spatial distribution changed significantly. These changes were generally brought about by two major demographic trends of the period: regional shifts in population and rapid urban growth. Contact diffusion also produced growth in place, but this process did not dominate the Disciples' expansion as it once had. Only a moderate correlation thus existed between membership in 1906 and changes in membership from 1906 to 1952.[15]

REGIONAL SHIFTS IN THE DISCIPLES' DISTRIBUTION

The most notable regional change in the Disciples' distribution during the first half of the century was a decline in their concentration within the Disciples

13. At the state level, the correlation between absolute growth in the Disciples and in the Churches of Christ from 1906 to 1926 was 0.43, which was significant at the 0.95 confidence level. Membership data for 1926 were taken from U.S. Bureau of the Census, *Religious Bodies, 1926* (Washington: U.S. Government Printing Office, 1929).

14. See Gaustad, *Historical Atlas of Religion in America*, p. 53.

15. Membership in 1906 and the change in membership from 1906 to 1952 had a correlation coefficient at the state level of 0.46, compared to a coefficient of 0.94 for the period from 1890 to 1906.

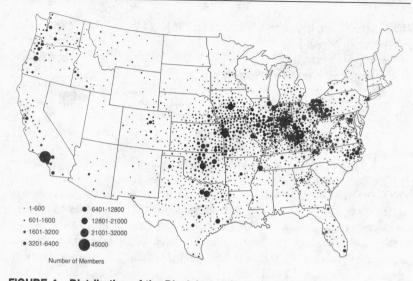

FIGURE 4   Distribution of the Disciples of Christ in 1952, by county.

Belt. This region still represented the core of their distribution, containing over 1.2 million Disciples in 1952. The four largest state gains also occurred there, in Indiana, Texas, Ohio, and Oklahoma. Nonetheless, the Disciples Belt ac-counted for little over half of the total membership growth from 1906 to 1952, and the proportion of all Disciples living in the region fell from three-fourths in 1906 to under two-thirds in 1952 (see Table 1, p. 447).

This shift resulted partly from slow membership growth in the Disciples Belt. Texas, Oklahoma, and Kansas were the only states in the region where the Disciples grew at rates above their national average; elsewhere in the region, the Disciples increased more slowly than they did nationwide. Their expansion here was limited by slow growth in the region's population. This slow growth in turn reflected the Disciples Belt's disadvantage in regional migration patterns, which led many people from the rural Midwest to industrial cities farther east or to the west coast.

Along with slow growth within the Disciples Belt, rapid growth else-where contributed to the regional shift in the Disciples' distribution. The group flourished in several areas adjacent to the Disciples Belt: West Virginia, south-western Pennsylvania, Tennessee, and southeastern Nebraska. Together these states added over 70,000 members. This growth developed partly through migration of members from the Disciples Belt, but growth in place also played a role, as Disciples had been present in these areas since the 1800s.

The South Atlantic region was a second focus of growth outside the Disciples Belt, with the five states from Virginia to Florida increasing by 110,000 members. Rapid population growth, based on both natural increase and migration to these states, was responsible for much of this increase. The association between population growth and gains among the Disciples was clearest in Florida, the fastest growing South Atlantic state in terms of both population and Disciples membership. The major exception to this pattern was North Carolina, an important center of membership since the 1800s. There, successful contact diffusion enabled the Disciples to grow much faster than the total population, especially in the eastern part of the state.

The largest focus of growth beyond the Disciples Belt arose in the West. In every state from the Rocky Mountains to the Pacific, the Disciples grew faster than in the nation as a whole, increasing by over 150,000 members in the western states combined. Most of the increase occurred in California, Oregon, and Washington, and nearly half of it in California alone. This growth chiefly reflected patterns of migration. The West, and especially California, experienced rapid population growth over this period, due mainly to migration from the eastern United States. The Disciples Belt contributed substantially to this migration, and thus the number of Disciples in the West rose sharply. Growth was most notable in Los Angeles, a major migrant destination. The Disciples grew by 40,000 in Los Angeles County from 1906 to 1952, the largest increase in any county and nearly five percent of their increase nationwide.

On a regional scale, then, important shifts developed within the spatial distribution of Disciples during this period. The Disciples Belt remained the group's geographical core, but substantial membership increases occurred outside the region, particularly in the South and West. These increases developed partly through the process of local contact diffusion, but migration played an important role as well, especially in the West.

THE EFFECTS OF URBANIZATION

As these regional shifts emerged, the Disciples' distribution underwent a second and perhaps more important transformation as it became increasingly clustered in the nation's expanding cities. From 1906 to 1952 the Disciples grew by 40,000 in Los Angeles, 25,000 in Dallas and Fort Worth, and 21,000 in Indianapolis. Kansas City, Oklahoma City, Tulsa, and Wichita each added over 10,000 members. The ten counties with the largest increases, each centered in a major city, added over 150,000 members — nearly a fifth of the Disciples' total gain over the period (see Table 2, p. 456). These counties also claimed the largest memberships in 1952, accounting for over ten percent of all Disciples. In contrast, the ten leading counties in 1906 had contained under five percent.

The urban shift in the Disciples' distribution accompanied the nation's rapid urban growth in the first half of the century. Cities expanded and rural areas declined as farm mechanization reduced the demand for agricultural labor

TABLE 2   Major Urban Centers of Disciples Membership, 1952

City	Number of Disciples in 1952[a]	Membership Growth, 1906-1952
Los Angeles, CA	45,373	40,012
Indianapolis, IN	30,205	21,694
Kansas City, MO	24,187	14,797
Dallas, TX	17,814	15,030
Oklahoma City, OK	15,012	13,341
Des Moines, IA	14,812	8,436
Tulsa, OK	12,684	12,299
Canton, OH	12,378	9,370
Wichita, KS	12,104	10,739
Fort Worth, TX	11,932	10,292
Total	196,501	156,010

a. Membership is reported only for the county containing the central city.

and as industrial growth increased the demand for urban labor. The Disciples made significant membership gains in the context of this urban migration, mainly in cities where their denominational infrastructure was already in place and could capitalize on the influx of migrants. Large gains were thus most common in the cities of the Disciples Belt, which contained the institutions needed to hold on to newly arrived Disciples and attract new members from the migrant population at large. Of the top ten urban centers of growth, all but Los Angeles were located inside the Disciples Belt.

Outside the Disciples Belt, urban growth contributed less often to large membership gains. The Disciples grew by only 1,500 members in New York City, they declined by 250 in Philadelphia, and Boston had no Disciples in 1952. In such cities, the scarcity of existing congregations limited growth. Migration to northeastern cities at this time also included a large number of Catholics, who were unlikely to change affiliation. Cities west of the Disciples Belt, on the other hand, attracted many Protestant migrants, including many from the Disciples Belt already affiliated with the Disciples. The group's membership in western cities thus expanded, especially where existing churches provided a foundation for growth. Again, Los Angeles saw the largest increase, and by 1952 contained considerably more Disciples than any other city in the nation.

A shift from rural areas and small towns to larger cities thus coincided with the regional expansion of the Disciples out of the Disciples Belt. This trend produced an increasingly nucleated distribution, dominated by a fairly small number of major cities. The development of these centers of membership was significant because it was through this process that the Disciples achieved much of their growth during this period. This trend was also important because it established the context within which the Disciples' membership patterns would evolve as the century progressed.

THE LATE TWENTIETH CENTURY

During the past several decades, two notable developments have shaped the Disciples' membership patterns: separation from the Disciples of a new body of independent Christian Churches (the Christian Churches and Churches of Christ) and a nationwide decline in the Disciples' membership. Some of the key causes and effects of these developments are in turn reflected in several significant trends in the Disciples' geographical distribution.

The Disciples' institutional evolution complicates the analysis of these trends. In 1968 the Disciples changed their structure from a confederation of churches, the International Convention of Christian Churches, to a distinct denomination with a strong national organization, the Christian Church (Disciples of Christ). Many members opposed this change, however, and in response formed the Christian Churches and Churches of Christ, which retained a looser organizational structure.[16] Given these changes, recent membership data are not fully comparable to those from before 1968.

To simplify the analysis of trends since 1952, I have divided the latter into three components. The first involves changes in the Disciples' membership approximately to the time of their reorganization in 1968. I assess these changes by comparing the combined membership of the Disciples and the independent Christian Churches in 1971 with that of the Disciples in 1952. The second component concerns the separation of the independents from the Disciples, which I examine by comparing the two groups in 1971. The third component involves declines in the Disciples' membership from 1971 to 1980.

CHANGES FROM 1952 TO 1971

The 1950s and 1960s saw little change in the Disciples' total membership. The Disciples and the independent Christians together claimed 70,000 fewer members in 1971 than the Disciples had in 1952, a decline of under four percent. This stability should be weighed, however, against a 35 percent increase in the American population over this period. Changes in Disciples membership also varied considerably throughout the country. The number of Disciples increased in half of the forty-eight contiguous states and in a third of the nation's counties. The apparent stability in the Disciples' membership thus disguises significant shifts in their distribution.

The contrast between growth within and outside the Disciples Belt, which had begun earlier in the century, became more pronounced after 1952 (see Table 1, p. 447). Seven of the region's nine states lost large numbers of members; indeed, each lost more members than any state outside the region. These losses were partly offset in Ohio and Indiana, which together added

16. See Harrell, "Restorationism and the Stone-Campbell Tradition," pp. 856-57.

nearly 30,000 Disciples, but the Disciples Belt as a whole still lost over 100,000 members. At the same time, growth occurred in over half of the states outside the Disciples Belt, for a net increase of nearly 30,000 members. Florida had the largest gain, of over 20,000 members, and California and Georgia added over 10,000 each. These patterns continued the group's shift toward the West and the Southeast, reflecting the influence of regional variations in population growth. Because most southeastern and western states had rapidly expanding populations during this period, their share of the Disciples' total membership rose.

Cities continued to serve as important centers of change, but they were no longer associated only with growth: many saw large declines in membership. Los Angeles, the leading center of membership in 1952, lost nearly 8,000 members. Large drops also occurred in Des Moines, Washington, Kansas City, and Denver; the four counties containing these cities lost 24,000 members from 1952 to 1971. These declines developed partly as a result of the rise of suburbanization. In most American cities of this era, large numbers of urbanites moved from the central cities into nearby suburbs. As Disciples followed this trend, their urban churches did not replace departed members with new adherents from the remaining urban population.

At the same time, the Disciples grew rapidly in the suburbs. While Los Angeles lost 8,000 members, membership rose by 13,000 in Orange, Riverside, San Bernardino, and Ventura Counties, into which the suburbs of Los Angeles extend. Johnson (Kansas) and Clay (Missouri) Counties, containing suburbs of Kansas City, grew by over 5,000 members. Denver's loss was partly made up by increases of nearly 2,000 members in Adams and Jefferson Counties. Around Washington the Disciples grew by over 2,000 in Montgomery (Maryland), Prince Georges (Maryland), and Fairfax (Virginia) Counties. Of course, suburban gains did not always offset urban losses. As city dwellers moved to the suburbs, many adopted new affiliations or did not establish an affiliation at all. Such patterns were uncommon during this period, however.

Although suburbanization produced losses among the Disciples in some cities, in others they continued to grow. Within the Disciples Belt, Columbus and Indianapolis had respective increases of 5,000 and 6,000 members, and membership rose by several thousand in Cincinnati, Lexington, Louisville, and Dallas. Urban growth also occurred outside the Disciples Belt, in the Southeast and West. Atlanta's two main counties, De Kalb and Fulton, saw a total increase of over 10,000 Disciples. The counties in Florida containing Orlando, St. Petersburg, and Ft. Lauderdale each grew by several thousand members. In the West, Disciples in Phoenix's Maricopa County grew by nearly 5,000, and California's San Diego and San Jose Counties each added 2,500.

Several trends thus characterized changes in the Disciples' distribution between 1952 and 1971. Growth outside the Disciples Belt brought expanding memberships to the Southeast and the West. This growth was offset, however, by a decline within the Disciples Belt, and the result was little change in the

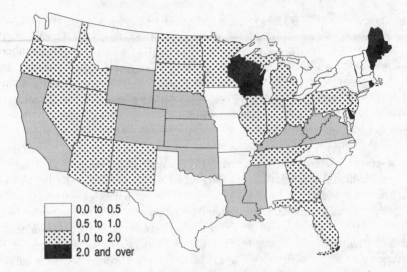

**FIGURE 5   Ratio of Independent Christian Churches
to Disciples of Christ membership in 1971, by state.**

total membership of the Disciples and independent Christian Churches. In addition, growth continued to be centered either in large cities or their suburbs.

GEOGRAPHICAL DIMENSIONS OF SCHISM:
THE INDEPENDENT CHRISTIAN CHURCHES

A second major influence on the Disciples distribution in the 1960s was the emergence of the independent Christian Churches. The loss of this group had a more widespread effect on the Disciples' distribution than the separation of the Churches of Christ. The latter began as a regional organization. In 1906 two-thirds of its members lived in Tennessee, Alabama, Arkansas, Texas, and Oklahoma, and they outnumbered the Disciples in just the first three of those states. The independents, on the other hand, emerged with a nationwide distribution, outnumbering the Disciples in half of the continental states (see Fig. 5). This fact reflects a second difference between the two schisms: in 1906 the Disciples outnumbered the Churches of Christ by more than 6 to 1, while in 1971 the former outnumbered the independents by less than 1.2 to 1.

The independent Christians were most successful in northern and eastern parts of the Midwest, much of the West, a few northeastern states, and the southeastern states of Georgia and Florida. In the Midwest, the Disciples' largest losses to the independents occurred in Ohio, Indiana, and Illinois. Around 60 percent of the combined membership of the two groups in these states belonged to an independent Christian Church. Thus, while these states

contained over 500,000 Disciples in 1952, they had around 200,000 members
of the Christian Church (Disciples of Christ) in 1971. Losses in the West and
Southeast were significant because both regions had previously seen rapid
membership growth. Independents did not outnumber Disciples everywhere,
however. Other than Ohio, Indiana, and Illinois, each state in the Disciples
Belt had more Disciples than independents in 1971. Disciples also outnumbered independents in California, many eastern states, and scattered states
across the South and West.

David Harrell has suggested that variations in the relative success of the
two groups reflected sociological contrasts between urban and rural areas, with
the more liberal Disciples having an advantage in the former and the more
conservative independents in the latter.[17] Membership data generally support
this hypothesis. Nationwide, the Disciples were most successful relative to the
independents in the cities. In urban counties, Disciples outnumbered independents by an average of nearly 600 members per county. At the same time, the
two groups did not differ significantly in size, on the average, in either rural
or suburban counties.[18] Parity in the two groups' suburban membership suggests the influence of factors other than the sociological contrasts cited by
Harrell. The fluidity of suburban church affiliation, for example, may have
benefited the independents in places which in other ways favored the Disciples.
Moreover, while sociological factors appear to have given the Disciples a
general advantage in urban settings, this trend had many local exceptions.
Independents in fact outnumbered Disciples in a third of all urban counties in
which either group was located in 1971. Nonetheless, the Disciples' total
membership in urban counties exceeded the independents' by 50 percent, while
the total number of Disciples living in rural or suburban counties roughly
equaled the number of independents (see Table 3). This pattern clearly supports
the hypothesis of an urban advantage for the Disciples.

In addition to the urban factor, the Churches of Christ appear to have
influenced patterns in the relative success of the Disciples and independents.
Specifically, the presence of a large Churches of Christ membership seems to
have limited the number of Disciples choosing to join an independent church.
By offering an alternative within the Restorationist tradition, the Churches of
Christ may have attracted adherents dissatisfied with trends among the Dis-
ciples, making new independent churches unnecessary. In areas with few
Churches of Christ, on the other hand, the independents could establish a

17. Harrell, "Restorationism and the Stone-Campbell Tradition," p. 857.
18. Urban counties are defined here as counties that were placed in a Standard Metropolitan
Statistical Area (SMSA) by the Census Bureau in 1971 and that also contained a large central
city. Suburban counties include those located in an SMSA but lacking a central city, and rural
counties are defined as those not included in an SMSA. The average difference between the number
of Disciples and independents was significant at the 0.95 confidence level in urban counties (with
a t-statistic of 3.63), but was not significant in rural or suburban counties (with t-statistics of 0.20
and -0.36 respectively).

TABLE 3 Urban, Suburban, and Rural Membership of Disciples and Independents, 1971

	Disciples		Independents	
Type of County	Membership	Percent	Membership	Percent
Urban[a]	417,192	43.9	280,704	34.5
Suburban[b]	90,821	9.6	95,850	11.8
Rural[c]	442,272	46.5	437,841	53.8
Total	950,285	100.0	814,395	100.0

a. Located within a Standard Metropolitan Statistical Area and containing a large central city.
b. Located within a Standard Metropolitan Statistical Area but lacking a large central city.
c. Not located within a Standard Metropolitan Statistical Area.

dissenting tradition with no competition. Thus, in Texas and adjacent states in the South, where the Churches of Christ outnumber the other two groups, few Disciples departed. In Ohio, Indiana, and Illinois, where the Churches of Christ are less common, most Disciples joined an independent church.

As a result of the separation of the independent Christian Churches, the distribution of the Christian Church (Disciples of Christ) in 1971 differed considerably from the International Convention's in 1952. About 90 percent of the counties with Disciples in 1952 had fewer adherents in 1971, counting only members of the Christian Church (Disciples of Christ), and the number of counties with Disciples fell from over 1,800 to under 1,500. The Disciples' membership decline was greatest in the Midwest and least pronounced in the South and West; in Florida, their membership actually rose. The independents' separation thus shifted the Disciples again to the south and west (see Table 1, p. 447).

CHANGES FROM 1971 TO 1980

In 1971 the combined membership of the Disciples and the independent Christians stood slightly below that of the International Convention in 1952. The decline was not great, however, and in part may have reflected differences in the ways these groups counted their members.[19] During the 1970s, membership decline among the Disciples was more definite. From 1971 to 1980, their membership fell from 950,000 to 820,000, a drop of 14 percent.[20]

19. Most importantly, the Christian Church (Disciples of Christ) reported only "participating membership" in the 1971 survey of church membership, rather than total membership (including nonparticipating members). The independents and the International Convention appear to have used a less restrictive definition of membership, including all adherents listed on the membership rolls of a church.

20. These membership figures again reflect the participating rather than the total membership. Total membership figures are somewhat higher, but were not reported by county in the 1971 survey of church membership and thus were not available for comparative analysis.

FIGURE 6   Gains in membership among the Disciples of Christ, 1971 to 1980, by county.

Changes in membership again varied spatially (see Figs. 6, 7, and 8). The largest drop occurred in California, where the Disciples lost 19,000 members, a third of their number in 1971. Ohio, Indiana, Illinois, Missouri, and Texas each lost over 10,000 members. At the same time, the Disciples grew in nine states located in the Northeast (Connecticut, Maine, New Jersey, and New York), the Southeast (Florida and South Carolina), and the West (Idaho, Nevada, and Utah). Nearly every state contained counties in which membership rose; in all, the Disciples increased in 29 percent of the counties in which they were located in 1971. They spread to few new counties, but also disappeared from few, for a net loss of only 60 counties among those with Disciples.

As in the two preceding decades, large cities were the main centers of decline. Los Angeles had the largest single loss, of nearly 10,000 members, or seven percent of the total drop in membership from 1971 to 1980. Dallas, Kansas City, Tulsa, and Chicago each lost several thousand members. The ten counties with the largest drops in membership, each containing a large city, together lost 32,000 members, a fourth of the total membership decline during the period. Of course, not all cities saw drops in membership. New York City and Ft. Lauderdale each added over 1,000 Disciples, for example, and these gains contributed significantly to statewide growth in New York and Florida.

Rather than a uniform decline, then, the Disciples experienced a complex pattern of growth and decline during the 1970s. The major question raised by this pattern is why they declined in some areas and grew in others. Many

FIGURE 7 Losses in membership among the Disciples of Christ, 1971 to 1980, by county.

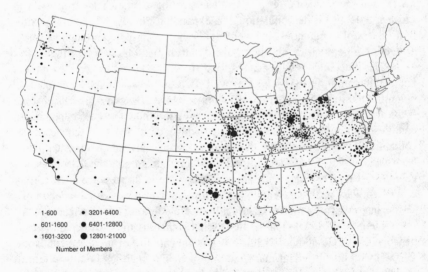

FIGURE 8 Distribution of the Disciples of Christ in 1980, by county.

factors influenced this pattern, involving features of the Disciples as a denomination, of individual congregations and clergy, and of the social settings within which they operated. A complete assessment of these influences is beyond the scope of this essay. The data examined here do, however, elucidate the effects of several major factors: suburbanization, variations in population growth rates, competition from independent Christian Churches, and patterns of membership change in other mainline churches.

Suburbanization had the least obvious effect. Suburban migration may have continued to contribute to declining urban memberships as it had in the 1950s and 1960s, but in the 1970s urban losses were not recovered in nearby suburbs. Membership fell by 10,000 in Los Angeles County between 1971 and 1980, for example, and in suburban Orange, Riverside, San Bernardino, and Ventura Counties it dropped by 3,000. Membership fell by 3,000 in Missouri's Jackson County, which encompasses central Kansas City, and by about half that many in the suburbs of adjacent Clay (Missouri) and Johnson (Kansas) Counties. Similar patterns occurred in many other cities as well. A simple shift in membership from cities to suburbs was thus no longer under way; other factors were instead producing both urban and suburban declines.

Variations in population growth had a greater effect. A comparison of slowly growing counties with rapidly growing counties clearly reveals that the Disciples were more successful in the latter. Of the counties that grew more slowly than the median for all counties in the 1970s, 25 percent saw growth in their Disciples' membership, compared to 34 percent of counties growing faster than the median.[21] The Disciples were thus somewhat more likely to grow in a county if its population was expanding rapidly. Under such conditions, the pool of potential new members is significantly larger than in a stable or declining population, enhancing the opportunities for church growth.

The independent Christians appear to have affected patterns of growth and decline among the Disciples as well. Because these groups have much in common, the independents may have impeded the Disciples' growth in some areas by competing with them for adherents. To test this hypothesis, I compared counties containing both Disciples and independents in 1971 with counties containing Disciples only. Of the counties lacking an independent Christian Church in 1971, 35 percent experienced growth among the Disciples. Of counties where Disciples and independents were both present in 1971, only 26 percent saw an increase among the former. The presence of independent Christians thus had a moderate effect on decline among the Disciples.[22]

Geographical variations in the Disciples' success are also related to membership trends among other mainline Protestant churches. During the 1960s and 1970s, membership fell in many such groups. The theories first proposed to explain this decline focused on institutional factors such as the demands a church places on its members and denominational commitments to new church devel-

21. The association between population growth and increasing Disciples membership produces a chi-squared statistic of 17.29, with one degree of freedom, which is significant at the 0.95 confidence level.
22. The association between the presence of independent Christians and increasing Disciples membership produces a chi-squared statistic of 14.00, with one degree of freedom, which is significant at the 0.95 confidence level.

opment.[23] Dean Hoge has shown that this trend depends on contextual factors as well, such as variations in birth rates and the shift away from traditional values.[24] The influence of such factors is likely to vary across the country, however, given the strong social and demographic contrasts among different parts of the United States. Some areas may thus prove more susceptible than others to decline among the mainline Protestants, including the Disciples.

The data examined here do not provide a means of directly measuring the aspects of an area's social and demographic character that might affect church growth, except for population growth. An indirect assessment of such influences can be developed, however, by examining variations in the success of other mainline churches. If the Disciples are affected by the same contextual factors, they should have grown where other mainline denominations grew and declined where those groups declined. To determine if such a trend exists, I compared patterns of growth and decline among the Disciples with those of two other mainline bodies with nationwide distributions, the United Methodist Church and the United Presbyterian Church. This comparison reveals that the Disciples grew in only 27 percent of the counties in which the combined membership of the other two groups fell, but in 36 percent of the counties in which the other groups expanded.[25] This finding suggests that contextual factors associated with membership change among other mainline denominations have also affected the Disciples.

Variations in the growth and decline of the Disciples are related, then, to patterns of population growth, competition from the independent Christians, and decline among other mainline churches. Moreover, the effects of these factors are statistically independent, and therefore cumulative.[26] The Disciples' membership was much more likely to fall when all three conditions conducive to decline were present than when none of them was. Of the 1,482 counties containing Disciples in 1971, 438 had a population growth rate below the national median, contained independent Christians, and saw decline among the United Methodists and United Presbyterians, and of these 438 counties, only 21 percent saw an increase in the number of Disciples. Of the 913 counties having one or two of the conditions tied to decline, 31 percent saw growth among the Disciples. In contrast, the Disciples grew in 45 percent of the 131 counties that had none of the conditions associated with decline.

23. The most prominent examination of such institutional factors appears in Dean M. Kelley, *Why Conservative Churches Are Growing* (New York: Harper & Row, 1972).

24. Dean R. Hoge, "A Test of Theories of Denominational Growth and Decline," in *Understanding Church Growth and Decline, 1950-1978*, ed. Dean R. Hoge and David A. Roozen (New York: Pilgrim Press, 1979), pp. 179-97.

25. The association between increases in the other two mainline churches and increasing Disciples membership produces a chi-squared statistic of 13.57, with one degree of freedom, which is significant at the 0.95 confidence level.

26. In a log-linear model with increase or decrease among the Disciples as the dependent variable, the main effects of each of the three factors was significant at the 0.95 confidence level. Each factor's effect was thus statistically significant while controlling for the other two factors.

The effects of all three negative factors were amplified, moreover, by the Disciples' concentration in counties where conditions were most conducive to decline. Nearly half of all Disciples in 1971 lived in counties having all three conditions related to decline, and three-fourths of all Disciples lived in counties having at least two of those conditions. Fewer than four percent of all Disciples, on the other hand, lived in counties having none of those three conditions. Most Disciples thus lived in places where conditions were particularly unfavorable for growth, and their numbers fell accordingly.

CONCLUSIONS

In addressing the issue of church growth and decline, David Roozen and Jackson Carroll conclude that patterns of membership change are not brought about by any single cause but are instead produced by "a complex pattern of multiple and often interacting factors."[27] The preceding analysis explores the effects of some of those factors on growth and decline among the Disciples up to 1980.

Of the various contextual factors considered, the related processes of urbanization and suburbanization had perhaps the greatest influence on the Disciples' distribution over the past century. Urbanization played a key role in their growth up to the 1950s, as they became increasingly concentrated in major urban centers. The religious revival at mid-century and the Disciples' own efforts to attract new members obviously contributed to this growth as well, but these gains would have been difficult to achieve if the Disciples had not had access to the large potential memberships that the nation's growing cities provided. To a considerable extent, the Disciples' growth during the first half of the century was driven by their large and prosperous urban congregations, which in turn were a product of urbanization itself.

The process of urbanization also had an impact on subsequent declines among the Disciples, in conjunction with the influence of suburbanization. After developing sizable memberships in many large cities, the Disciples, like other mainline denominations, were susceptible to sharp membership losses when migration to the suburbs began. Such losses could have been prevented by acquiring new members to replace those leaving for the suburbs, but this task has proven difficult for most mainline churches. The largest declines faced by the Disciples in recent decades thus appeared in those cities that had previously experienced the greatest increases. Moreover, migration to the suburbs did not guarantee membership increases there. The era of urban growth had seen the construction of an extensive urban infrastructure of churches and other denominational institutions. When Disciples began to move out of the

27. Roozen and Carroll, "Recent Trends in Church Membership and Participation," p. 39.

city, this infrastructure had difficulty keeping pace. Suburban membership did flourish in many places during the 1950s and 1960s, but by the 1970s cities and suburbs were both losing members.

A second set of contextual factors that significantly influenced growth and decline among the Disciples are population growth and regional migration. During much of their history, the Disciples benefited from rapid population growth in the Disciples Belt, their core region. Expansion of the region's population during the 1800s and early 1900s gave the Disciples access to a large number of potential members, fueling growth in place there. More recently, the states of the Disciples Belt have grown slowly or unevenly, as birth rates have fallen and migration to other regions has increased. Most Disciples congregations are thus located in regions lacking the population growth needed to sustain uninterrupted gains in membership. The Disciples continue to expand in regions whose populations have grown rapidly in recent decades, such as the Sunbelt states of the West and the Southeast, but these regions are not traditional areas of strength for the Disciples. The relative scarcity of Disciples institutions has thus limited their gains in such areas.

Larger trends in church membership have also affected patterns of growth and decline among the Disciples. Like other mainline churches, the Disciples grew rapidly during the first half of this century; in the 1950s and 1960s, when church membership rates were their highest, the Disciples' membership was at a peak. During the 1970s, when many mainline groups began to lose members, the Disciples also started to decline. Moreover, their losses have overlapped spatially to a degree with those of other denominations. This correspondence in patterns of denominational decline suggests that some areas are especially inhospitable to mainline church growth, presumably as a result of their social and demographic characteristics. If such is the case, the Disciples' recent declines may in part reflect a set of problems faced by all mainline churches, problems that are beyond the control of any single denomination.

The main institutional factor considered here, denominational schism, has affected Disciples distribution as well. When the Churches of Christ broke away in 1906, they greatly reduced the Disciples' membership in the South, but elsewhere had little influence. Social and economic differences between the Disciples and the Churches of Christ have subsequently prevented significant competition between the two groups. The separation of the independent Christian Churches in 1968 had a more widespread effect. Because the independents are similar to the Disciples in many aspects of worship and belief and are equally widespread across the country, the potential exists for continuing competition between the two groups for new and existing adherents. Such competition appears to have contributed to the Disciples' decline in the 1970s.

Of course these are not the only factors that influenced the Disciples' geographical distribution over the past century. Many other relevant institutional and contextual factors could not be addressed through the data analyzed.

But these factors nonetheless help to define the larger context within which patterns of growth and decline have evolved among the Disciples. Most importantly, the analysis identifies how various social, demographic, and religious factors external to the Disciples have affected their membership patterns and illustrates the geographical complexity of those patterns and the processes that have shaped them.

The resulting portrait of the Disciples' historical geography reveals that neither growth nor decline has been a uniform feature of the group at any time in its history. Trends in the Disciples' membership have varied considerably from one place to another, reflecting variations in the social, demographic, and religious characteristics of the places the Disciples have inhabited. These variations represent the context in which changes in the Disciples' membership patterns and contributions of other factors to those changes must be interpreted. In addition, an understanding of these diverse contexts of growth and decline provides a point of departure for assessing future trends in Disciples membership.

Disciples in a Mission Land:
The Christian Church in New York City

Mark S. Massa

*We raise the query, has not the importance and accessibility of
New York as a mission field been overlooked? The character of
New York Disciples warrants the expectation of greater things.
They are preeminently and almost universally a missionary people.*

Thus did the *Christian Standard* for 17 November 1894 call for a reconsideration of New York as mission territory for Disciples. In the strictest theological sense, of course, all climes and cultures were to constitute mission territory for zealous Disciples, but New York represented a special case, a case much closer to overseas cultures than to other parts of that land where Alexander Campbell had harbingered the millennium. Indeed, the *Standard*'s mission call for New York at the end of "Christianity's Greatest Century" (as the nineteenth was perhaps too effusively termed by America's most famous mission chronicler) has something of the eerily prophetic about it.[1]

The response to the *Standard*'s prophetic call for Disciples to reconsider New York as mission territory has been dramatically confirmed by demographic data at the end of our own less than triumphant century. For the contention of this essay is that the Disciples of Christ in New York City today do in fact represent a mission church. In this sense, the Disciples' traditional

---

1. "Christianity's Greatest Century" is the label given to the nineteenth century by Kenneth Scott Latourette in the fourth volume of his *History of the Expansion of Christianity* (New York: Harper, 1937-45).

I would like to thank Craig Pilant, a doctoral student at Fordham University, who helped to research this study during the summer of 1988, gathering the statistics reported in Tables 1 and 2. — MARK S. MASSA

historiographic identity as a church that flourished on the frontier holds true for their story in New York City as well.

There is, however, an ironic twist to the story. It has been the conservative restorationist impulses in the Disciples' heritage, as opposed to the ecumenical progressive impulses that define so much of their twentieth-century identity, that have proven to be most important to their growth in New York.[2] Indeed, the Disciples' growth pattern in New York City would seem to confirm Dean Kelley's theories as to why conservative churches grow — only in this case explaining the growth of congregations belonging to a resolutely progressive denomination.[3]

It is my contention that to the extent that Disciples have capitalized on their identity as missionaries of a restorationist gospel, over against the ecumenical gospel of New York's Protestant mainstream, their numbers have grown and their identity as a distinctive option on the evangelical spectrum has benefited; to the extent that they have identified with the ecumenical mainstream, becoming in the process a comfortable Protestant group indistinguishable from many others in the city, their numbers and presence in the city have undergone problematic decline. This thesis rests on both the fate of "mainstream," middle-class Disciples congregations in the city and the emergence of a new type of Disciples among New York minority groups, especially Hispanics and Haitians.

The style and ethnic identity of Disciples in New York City changed dramatically after World War II. Indeed, by 1980 the overwhelming majority of Disciples congregations were no longer predominantly white, middle-class, and formerly Midwestern as they had been earlier in the history in the city. Rather, the great majority of New York Disciples were working-class and lower middle-class black, Hispanic, or Haitian immigrants. The piety, worship, and ecclesiological self-understanding of these new congregations, moreover, re-sembles the sectarian identity outlined by Troeltsch and Weber much more closely than the denominational or mainstream identity that has characterized twentieth-century Disciples.[4]

2. This study takes as axiomatic the tension between the ecumenical ("progressive") and restorationist ("conservative") impulses within this "frontier" church. Disciples historiography has consistently stressed this point; see, e.g., David Harrell, *Quest for a Christian America*, vol. 1 of *A Social History of the Disciples of Christ* (Nashville: Disciples of Christ Historical Society, 1966), pp. 4ff.

3. Don H. Yoder, "Christian Unity in Nineteenth Century America," in *History of the Ecumenical Movement, 1517-1948*, ed. Ruth Rouse and Stephen Neill (Philadelphia: Westminster Press, 1967), pp. 249ff. John F. Woolverton, "Huntington's Quadrilateral — A Critical Study," *Church History* 39 (1970): 198-211. Dean M. Kelley, *Why Conservative Churches Are Growing: A Study in the Sociology of Religion* (New York: Harper & Row, 1972), pp. 2ff.

4. See Ernst Troeltsch, *The Social Teaching of the Christian Churches*, vol. 2, trans. Olive Wyon (New York: Macmillan, 1931), pp. 999-1000. On "denominational" identity, see H. Richard Niebuhr, *The Social Sources of Denominationalism* (New York: Henry Holt, 1929), pp. 17ff. The terms *sectarian* and *denominational* (or *mainstream*) seem to identify most precisely the fundamental differences between the two types of Disciples congregations discussed here. The groups considered by this study as "denominational" (occupying what William Hutchison has called a "Seven Sister Establishment Status" in American culture) are the northern Methodist, Congre-

The amazing growth of restorationist Disciples congregations among New York's Hispanics — centered in the La Hermosa congregation — is rivaled and even surpassed by the exponential growth of Haitian Disciples, centered in the Brooklyn congregation of the Reverend Philius Nicolas — the Evangelical Crusade/Fishers of Men. The dramatic appeal and success of the restorationist Disciples message among these latter groups — representing also a substantially different style of preaching, piety and Disciples identity from that associated with the traditionally middle-class, white, and theologically progressive denomination — raises interesting (and potentially fruitful) questions regarding mission ideology in some areas of the United States.

In the first part of this essay I focus on the history of two representative congregations in New York — Park Avenue and Bethlehem United — that offer some insights into the fate of mainstream, middle-class Christian congregations in the city. I also consider their histories in light of the demographic and sociological histories of the Baptist, Congregationalist, Episcopalian, and Presbyterian churches in New York during the same period. In the second part of the essay I examine the emergence of the new type of Disciples identity among New York Hispanics and Haitians since the 1960s. Finally, in the third part of the essay I draw some preliminary conclusions about Disciples identity in New York City, a city that I believe represents a mission territory.

I.

From the very beginning New York Disciples have been missionary: fully two decades before Alexander Campbell and Barton W. Stone merged their independent restorationist and ecumenical movements into a single stream, an independent "Christian" movement had been generated in New York City to missionize that ostensibly evangelized territory. On 10 October 1810, a group of Scots, largely influenced by Robert Sandeman's immersionist movement, withdrew from the Ebenezer Baptist Church in Manhattan to gather under the name of the "Disciples of Christ."[5]

---

gationalist (UCC), northern Presbyterian, northern Baptist, Episcopal, Lutheran, and Disciples churches (*Between The Times: The Travail of the Protestant Establishment in America, 1900-1960,* ed. William R. Hutchison (Cambridge: Cambridge University Press, 1989), pp. 3-6. The concept of this sevenfold evangelical establishment is useful if somewhat fluid; it serves general discussions well but should not to be pressed too literally. See Robert Handy, *A Christian America: Protestant Hopes and Historical Realities,* 3d ed. (Oxford: Oxford University Press, 1974), p. 52; Perry Miller, *The Life of the Mind in America,* 2d ed. (New York: Harcourt, Brace & World, 1965), pp. 36ff. My observations regarding the new "sectarian" Disciples congregations are based on interviews and visits to La Hermosa and Evangelical Crusade/Fishers of Men.

5. "Historical Note," *Forward: Newsletter of the Central Church of the Disciples of Christ,* 10 January 1935, p. 2. "Our Church," *Forward,* 24 May 1951, p. 1. "Our 150th Anniversary," *Forward,* 3 January 1960, back cover.

Taking the name "Primitive Christian Church of Disciples," this small group — like their city — grew both in numbers and in a northerly direction. In 1850, with 174 members, these Disciples incorporated and bought a building on West 17th Street for $10,500. Two moves later, in 1883, the cornerstone was laid for a much grander structure on West 56th Street. This northward, gentrifying trend culminated in 1944, two moves yet further down the road, when the congregation bought property in the exceedingly tony neighborhood at Park Avenue and 85th Street.[6]

For those familiar with the history of Manhattan topography, this peripatetic history of the Disciples' mother church in New York reflects the northward movement of the city's middle class from the Battery toward Harlem in search of cleaner air, quieter and safer streets, and more comfortable dwellings. But this topographical history reveals as well a perduring problem facing the Disciples' mission and identity in the city: to the extent that the Disciples identified with the climb of industrious laborers into the affluent middle class, they never developed an indigenous New York membership. While the congregational membership roll of First/Park Avenue Church continued to grow in both numbers and in giving power until 1960 — as it moved into ever more comfortable meeting houses — the overall growth involved negligible growth among native New Yorkers. In 1916, this fact of the congregation's life was troubling enough to draw its upbeat pastor, Finis Idleman, to observe that his flock, "although heroic and sacrificial in spirit, is unstable in its existence, one third of it changing every year." And forty years later Dr. Hampton Adams observed from that same pulpit that, while one thousand new members had been added to his congregation's rolls in the decade after 1945, the great majority of them had transferred from other Disciples churches, usually in the Midwest. In 1955 the official membership stood at 514, representing an overall gain of twelve members since 1925.[7]

The nature of the membership at New York's mother church indicated in Table 1 — namely, that the statistical increase in membership recorded in yearbooks actually represented transferred members from other Disciples churches and that the overall increase from such replacements was negligible — raises troubling questions about the success of the Disciples' ecumenical message in the city. Park Avenue Christian (under its various names) was famous in the city among both Disciples and among other Protestants for the number of its members actively engaged in ecumenical endeavors. From the first, the pastors of this affluent congregation had taken an active part in the

---

6. Rose M. Starratt, *A Sesquicentennial History of the Park Avenue Christian Church* (St. Louis: Bethany Press, 1963), pp. 15-16, 19, 21, 23-27, 60-63. "Pageant Reviews History of Church," *Forward*, 13 October 1960, pp. 2-5.

7. Starratt, *A Sesquicentennial History of the Park Avenue Christian Church*, pp. 46, 57; "Our Prospects in 1928," *Forward*, 13 May 1971; "Decade of Decision Special Meaning For Park Avenue Church," *Forward*, 5 January 1961; "Where Do the Members of Park Avenue Christian Live?" *Forward*, 28 September 1961, p. 1.

TABLE 1   Central/Park Avenue Christian Church*

Year	Number of Members	Additions by Baptism	Additions by Transfer	Total Amount Raised ($)
1913	425	NA	NA	NA
1915	336	NA	NA	7,514
1917	390	NA	NA	9,900
1919	450	NA	NA	11,631
1921	425	10	72	13,748
1923	430	17	50	14,561
1925	502	5	66	31,537
1927	424	13	77	25,250
1929	421	12	NA	20,620
1931	396	6	NA	21,178
1933	416	14	NA	16,500
1935	450	27	NA	16,540
1937	481	11	NA	14,800
1939	486	9	35	13,800
1941	425	8	26	12,700
1943	375	5	22	12,478
1945	436	10	100	48,225
1947	422	12	93	68,646
1949	458	18	90	72,453
1951	481	6	79	56,642
1953	510	18	47	65,323
1955	514	7	85	56,852
1957	529	7	73	75,611
1959	510	5	37	66,656
1961	512	6	50	138,751
1963	472	2	26	166,607
1969	374	4	19	113,012
1971	289	1	2	136,738
1972	280	6	10	120,650
1973	280	6	9	132,536
1974	271	1	19	401,827
1976	282	6	6	183,666
1977	279	3	6	151,133
1978	285	2	12	265,819
1979	278	0	16	269,575
1980	291	2	22	318,707

*Based on Yearbook information. Distinctions between those added by baptism or by transfer were not introduced until 1921.

various ecumenical programs and committees sponsored by the city's Protestant Council, as well as occupying official positions at the Federal (and later) National Council of Churches.[8]

8. Interview with the Rev. John Payne, Park Avenue Christian Church, New York City, 6 July 1988. "Our Battle Cry: Christian Union!" *Forward,* 30 June 1900, p. 1. "Why Not a Liturgical

Further, Disciples coming to New York from other areas to work in the various ecumenical offices headquartered there regularly established membership in the congregation because of its reputation for rich liturgy and music, progressive social outreach programs, and excellent preaching. Thus, at least part of the membership turnover at Park Avenue stemmed from its role as the official ecclesiastical residence for students at Union Seminary and bureaucrats at the National Council of Churches, who joined the congregation for a brief period before returning to other parts of the country.[9]

The history of the Flatbush (Third) Christian Church in Brooklyn replicates a number of features that define the story of the First/Park Avenue congregation, a replication that further defines one type of Disciples church in New York — that is, a group of middle-class Disciples moving into a new section of the city, transferring memberships from other Disciples congregations to form a new congregation. Flatbush — a stolidly middle-class, brownstone-lined section of Brooklyn built up at the turn of the century in the shadow of the patrician townhouses of Park Slope — saw an influx of Disciples in the early years of the twentieth century. On 29 November 1903, twenty-one people, many of them members of Brooklyn's Sterling Place Church, united to form the Third Church of Christ.[10]

The young congregation evinced the kind of evangelical fervor that quickly drew members: during the course of its first fall as an independent congregation, its "Evangelistic Meetings" netted 19 new members. As Table 2 indicates, at the end of 1906, the church reported sixty-five members. It grew steadily for the next two decades, and by 1922 its membership was estimated at 450. This dramatic growth of over four hundred new members in less than twenty years presents the historian with some intriguing questions. What made Flatbush Christian attractive to so many people moving into central Brooklyn?[11]

In light of the subsequent history of the congregation — itself a reflection of the history of the Flatbush neighborhood — this rapid growth might be explained more by demographics than by evangelism: the large influx of middle-

---

Calendar?" *Forward,* 27 March 1920, p. 2. "A Course in Comparative Religions," *Forward,* 25 November 1925, p. 2. "Prospects for the World Council of Churches," *Forward,* 6 January 1938, p. 1. "Formation of the Protestant Council of New York City," *Forward,* 1 February 1945, p. 1. "Fellowship of Churches and Synagogues," *Forward,* 5 October 1967.

9. Interview with John Payne, 6 July 1988. "Shall We Observe Lent?" *Forward,* 24 March 1917, p. 1. "Worship through Drama," *Forward,* 20 March 1931, back cover. "Central Church and Most Disciples," *Forward,* 24 October 1935, p. 2. "Where Do the Members of Park Avenue Christian Live?" *Forward,* 28 September 1961, p. 2. "Purpose, Program, Goals," *Forward,* 21 January 1971, pp. 1, 3, 5.

10. Interview with Alfred "Steele" Hughes, 12 July 1988, Flatbush YMCA, Brooklyn, New York. S. H. Stebbins, "Flatbush Christian Church," in *The Twenty-Fifth Anniversary, Flatbush Christian Church, 1903-1928* (Brooklyn, 1928), p. 1. Ralph Foster Weld, *Brooklyn Is America* (New York: Columbia University Press, 1950), pp. 48-85, 115-17.

11. Stebbins, "Flatbush Christian Church," p. 3. Weld, *Brooklyn Is America,* pp. 54ff. Harold X. Connolly, *A Ghetto Grows in Brooklyn* (New York: New York University Press, 1977), pp. 134-36. Interview with Alfred Steele Hughes, 12 July 1988.

TABLE 2   Flatbush (Third) Christian Church

Year	Number of Members	Additions by Baptism	Additions by Transfer	Total Amount Raised ($)
1913	150	NA	NA	NA
1916	275	NA	NA	3,500
1918	375	NA	NA	5,600
1922	e450	18	20	8,000
1924	338	16	62	10,695
1926	380	18	21	18,600
1928	310	11	0	16,500
1930	276	6	0	12,719
1933	250	12	0	8,080
1935	272	3	0	7,214
1937	261	5	0	6,121
1939	298	9	10	6,842
1941	274	7	12	7,401
1944	251	13	9	9,811
1948	245	5	11	11,347
1950	260	2	28	10,538
1952	209	3	6	10,596
1954	206	5	5	12,685
1955	181	1	3	11,287
1958	157	0	6	10,367
1960	129	2	2	9,997
1963	120	3	7	10,691
1969	63	2	0	5,108
1972	30	0	0	2,567
1974	20	0	0	3,159
1976*	123	2	3	27,200
1978*	125	3	5	32,914
1980*	132	0	0	38,850

*Designates Flatbush Disciples congregation merged with the Bethlehem United Church of Christ, affiliated with both the UCC and the Christian Church (Disciples).

class Protestants into Flatbush were looking for a congregational affiliation that reflected their own values, and Flatbush Christian provided a friendly and mildly evangelical atmosphere under the preaching of the Rev. Mr. Frederick M. Gordon. Gordon's preaching was evangelical enough to appeal to a wide range of Protestants beginning their climb into affluence, but its social life was genteel enough — with its Endeavor Society socials and a Parish Gymnasium that included bowling alleys — to radiate a distinctly churchly (as opposed to sectarian) identity for the respectable folk who swelled its rolls.[12]

12. Weld, *Brooklyn Is America,* pp. 126-34. "A Tribute to Brother Gordon, on the Occasion of His Leaving Us," an anonymous sermon delivered in December 1920 (files of the Northeastern Regional Office [hereafter NRO] of the Christian Church [Disciples of Christ], Buffalo, New York). Stebbins, "Flatbush Christian Church," p. 5.

Rev. Gordon resigned from the pastorate of Flatbush Christian in December 1920, well before the membership peak reported in 1922, but the style of preaching and congregational piety had been established firmly enough under him to survive the two-year search for a permanent pastor. Thus, when a unanimous call was extended to the Rev. Charles Bloom of North Tonawanda, New York, in the fall of 1923, the church was operating largely within the mildly evangelical, middle-of-the-road identity that Gordon had established, and the congregation was still growing at an impressive rate. But this constituted *both* the good news and the bad.[13]

The problem with this comfortable congregational identity that reflected the values of Anglo-Saxon, middle-class Flatbush was that Flatbush itself was changing, and the congregation's demographic/theological identity was not. Already in the early 1920s, Flatbush was attracting increasing numbers of Jewish and Irish immigrants. The membership statistics presented in Table 2 fail to show the dramatic numerical decrease during the twenties, in part because the official numbers remained fairly stable through memberships transferred from other "dissolved" Brooklyn congregations. Fifty of the sixty-two "Transferred Memberships" reported for 1924 came from members of Flatbush's mother church, Sterling Place, which was dissolved in 1923. This pattern of lateral growth would be repeated again in the future.[14]

By the end of the 1960s, the church drew so few members from its surrounding neighborhood — now largely Hispanic — that the congregation voted at a meeting in August 1969 to encourage the development of a Spanish Department in cooperation with Sinai Christian, a neighboring Hispanic congregation. By January 1970, however, this attempt at Hispanic outreach was judged to have been a failure, a core of twenty-five Hispanic families, the minimum required for financial viability, having failed to materialize, and the membership continued to decline, reaching a low of only twenty active members. The solution arrived at in 1971 was to merge the Flatbush congregation with the Bethlehem United Church of Christ — like Flatbush a white, middle-class, mainline congregation also suffering from declining membership. The resulting joint operation listed its denominational affiliation as both Christian Church (Disciples of Christ) and United Church of Christ. The resulting growth in membership listed in the Disciples Yearbook — the jump on Table 2 from twenty members in 1974 to 123 members in 1976 — really constituted, at best, a lateral growth that masked a dramatic membership decline between 1960 and 1970.[15]

---

13. Stebbins, "Flatbush Christian Church," p. 5. Yearbooks of the Disciples of Christ for 1920-1923 (Cincinnati: American Christian Missionary Society, 1920-23).

14. Interview with Alfred Steele Hughes, 12 July 1988. Elliot Willensky, *When Brooklyn Was the World, 1920-1957* (New York: n.p., 1986), pp. 70ff. Connolly, *Ghetto Grows,* pp. 135ff. Stebbins, "Flatbush Christian Church," p. 5.

15. M. L. Wilson (president of the New York City Council of Churches) to the Rev. Arthur Stanley, area secretary, 30 June 1969. M. A. Morales, "Agreements on the Meeting Held on the Flatbush Christian Church, August 26, 1969." "Minutes of the Merger Committees of the Bethlehem

TABLE 3 "Anglo" Disciples Churches in New York City

	1st/ Park Avenue	Lenox[a]	Sterling[b]	Ridgewood[c]	Boro Park[d]	Green Point[e]
1913	425	250	250	—	65	—
1915	336	—	320	12	89	86
1917	390	67	327	7	116	98
1919	450	(Disbanded)	240	525	70	80
1921	425		262	e175	107	e125
1923	430		e300	308	96	e125
1925	502		(Disbanded)	208	e96	90
1927	424			242	(Disbanded)	80
1929	421			245		50
1931	396			290		30
1933	416			325		e31
1935	450			350		110 (2d)
1937	481			400		e123
1939	486			419		75
1941	475			e375		104
1944	354			244		e75
1946	422			e262		e125
1948	471			e262		e125
1950	486			e262		65
1952	487			e262		e65
1954	485			130		(Disbanded)
1956	518			128		
1958	529			(Disbanded)		

a. Lenox Avenue, Manhattan; merged with Central/Park Avenue
b. 1st/Sterling Place; 478 Bergen; Hanson Pl. & S. Portland Ave., Brooklyn; merged with Flatbush Christian
c. Ridgewood Heights, Brooklyn. Forest Ave. & Linden. Formed from members of 2nd Church/Humboldt Place. Members joined Flatbush Christian.
d. Borough Park, Brooklyn. 12th Avenue & 45th Street; 49th St. & Ft. Hamilton Pkwy. Disbanded.
e. 199 Henry St., Brooklyn; formed from members of 2nd/Humboldt Place.

The histories of the First/Park Avenue and Flatbush/Bethlehem Christian churches, despite geographic and even demographic differences, give evidence of important features that define other mainline Disciples churches in New York City — such churches as Lenox Avenue in Manhattan, Second Church in the Bronx, Sterling Place and Humbold Street in Brooklyn (see Table 3). Among these features are a largely middle-class white constituency, mildly evangelical preaching and piety, and a wide range of parochial activities beyond the strictly evangelistic that characterized comfortable Protestant congregations between 1880 and 1930. It was precisely this identity that stood the

United Church of Christ and Flatbush Christian Church, April 9, 1973." Alfred S. Hughes, "To The Members of the Congregation of Flatbush Christian, December 2, 1970." Fred Benzenberg, "Trustees Report on the Fiscal Year 1971" (letter to the area secretary). "Memorandum from Lee Gartrell to Dan Kuhn, January 22, 1970." All of the above documents are found in a folder labeled "Flatbush/ Bethlehem United" in the files of the Regional Office, Buffalo, New York.

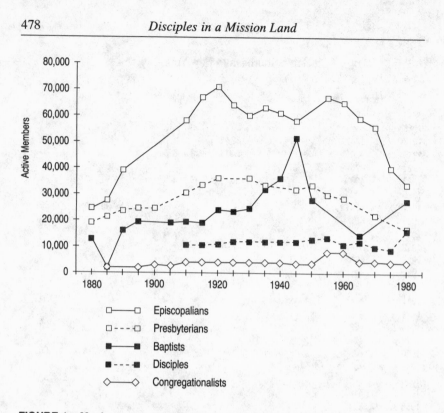

FIGURE 1 Manhattan and the Bronx: Active Members

New York Disciples in such bad stead over the long haul: mainstream Disciples seem to have had a much harder time holding onto their white, middle-class members than did the other Protestant bodies in the city.

As Figure 1 indicates, the Disciples' experience in New York City during the first five decades of the twentieth century most closely resembles that of the Congregationalists, another mainline regional group that experienced considerable difficulties in retaining an indigenous membership in the city, although for very different reasons.[16]

As can be seen in Figures 2 and 3, the Congregationalists had the most gradual and consistent pattern of growth, a pattern very similar to that of the Disciples. The denomination grew steadily in Brooklyn until 1921, after which admissions began to drop off (see Fig. 4, p. 480). The Congregationalist experience in Manhattan and the Bronx was much less dramatic, largely because the denomination's numbers were smaller outside of Brooklyn, and so it had fewer members to lose there. Except for a brief upsurge in the postwar era —

16. Among these "reasons" are the Plan of Union of 1801, which operated against Congregationalists outside New England. Likewise, the Congregational churches in the city were far more theologically liberal and far less restorationist than the Disciples.

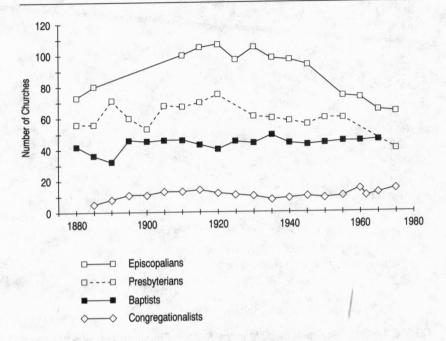

FIGURE 2 Manhattan and the Bronx: Numbers of Churches

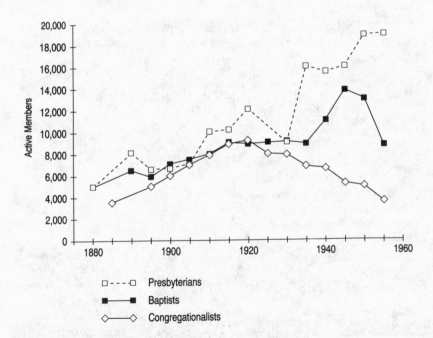

FIGURE 3 Brooklyn: Communicants and Active Members

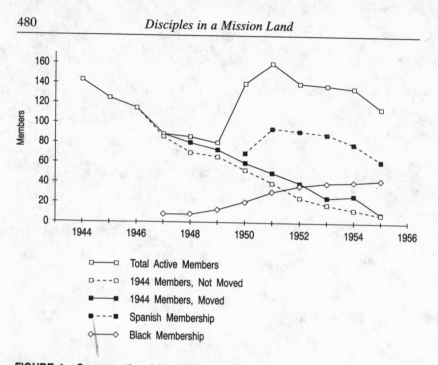

FIGURE 4   **Congregational Mobility in the Second Church of the Disciples of Christ**

a result of the Congregationalist affiliation with the influential and well-endowed Riverside Church in the early 1950s — Congregationalist churches remained relatively small and few in number. The postwar Congregationalist decline raises the question of whether the denomination might have an inherently limited regional-ethnographic appeal. The influx of large numbers of black and Hispanic immigrants into New York in the decades after the Second World War seems to have contributed in significant ways to the decline in the size and numbers of Congregational churches. It is precisely on this point that the Disciples' story takes a somewhat different turn.

II.

The new sectarian style that marked New York Christian congregations founded after 1945 — congregations such as La Hermosa, Evangelical Crusade/Fishers of Men, and Bronx's Second Church — witnessed to the dominance of a new type of Disciples identity in the city. This new type of Christian congregation emphasized the restorationist side of the Campbell-Stone heritage far more than the ecumenical side of the tradition that characterized such congregations as Park Avenue and Flatbush/Bethlehem United. And the new

Disciples that filled the membership rolls of these churches sought (and found) in their congregations a gospel and piety that emphasized a distinctive religious identity that shunned the permissive ethos of other mainstream churches — even other Disciples churches. These Disciples churches grew not on Park Avenue or in the middle-class enclaves of Brooklyn but in the barrios and the Haitian neighborhoods of Flatbush; their membership rolls swelled not because Disciples moved into the neighborhoods but because charismatic preachers, attracted by the Disciples' restorationist tradition, won converts in storefront churches and brought the reborn with them into official affiliation with the Christian Church (Disciples of Christ).

As Thomas O'Dea, Joseph Fitzpatrick, Renato Poblete, and other sociologists who have studied religious patterns among immigrant groups have already argued, the attraction of the sectarian religious identity to transplanted American blacks, Puerto Ricans, and Haitians can be explained, at least in part, by recourse to well-known sociological models: the flight from anomie and the cultural dislocation/isolation of immigration; the quest for meaningful and immediate personal communities in impersonal urban centers; the search for viable value systems in the face of the destruction of, or removal from, traditional systems; and the like. In this essay I am assuming the validity of these sociological insights as to why ethnic/racial minorities in America have consistently turned to sectarian religious organizations to locate themselves in a pluralistic culture.[17]

But this having been said, the question still remains: why the Disciples and not, say, the Baptists or the Assemblies of God? What does the Disciples tradition have to offer these new pilgrims — or, more specifically, the charismatic leaders of these new pilgrims — that other Protestant traditions, most obviously the various Pentecostal and holiness groups, do not? Once again, it is the restorationist side of the Campbell-Stone tradition that offers a decisive and unique appeal: what the Disciples of Christ seem to offer to the new immigrants that other comparably evangelical groups do not is the opportunity to wed their sectarian impulses with a tradition that is, at the same time, respectably mainstream.

It is *this* Disciples tradition — the progressive mainstream impulses wed, quite distinctively, with the restorationist concerns more visible among nineteenth-century Disciples — that exerts such great attraction to urban immigrants. Unlike other denominational affiliations, the Disciples promise the warm familiarity of evangelical worship and the prophetic satisfactions of "harbingering the millennium" through restorationist church order, while at the same time promising an established church identity in a denomination that, among other things, is quite distinctively American.

17. Thomas O'Dea and Renato Poblete, "Anomie and the 'Quest For Community': The Formation of Sects among the Puerto Ricans of New York," *American Sociological Review* 21 (1960): 18-36. Joseph P. Fitzpatrick, *One Church, Many Cultures: The Challenge of Diversity* (New York: Sheed & Ward, 1987), pp. 125ff. Joseph Fitzpatrick, *Puerto Rican Americans: The Meaning of Migration to the Mainland* (Englewood Cliffs, N.J.: Prentice-Hall, 1987).

The mission to Hispanics in New York City was undertaken by the Iglesia La Hermosa Discipulos de Cristo on 110th Street, along the northern border of Central Park. The history of La Hermosa's mission, in fact, represents something very close to a paradigm for subsequent Christian missions to the city's Hispanics — in several senses. La Hermosa not only offered a successful model of growing membership and community outreach for other Disciples churches; it also provided the founding members for several other Hispanic Christian congregations in the city. These offshoot congregations followed the example of their mother church in attracting members scattered throughout the city's five boroughs, a membership whose previous religious affiliation was overwhelmingly Roman Catholic.[18]

The increased rate of Puerto Rican immigration to New York City in the late 1930s led to the formation of La Hermosa ("the Beautiful") Christian Church in the tenement rooms of a young Puerto Rican seminary student in Spanish Harlem. The Christian designation given by this handful of worshipers to their congregation seems to have been a generic one, for the founding members of the congregation came from a number of Protestant backgrounds in Puerto Rico, although an ever-increasing proportion of the group was made up of disaffected Catholics. This latter demographic feature of La Hermosa's membership, in fact, adumbrated the shape of the future Hispanic membership of New York Christian churches; the consensus of Hispanic pastors in the late 1980s is that the percentage of former Catholics in their congregations hovers somewhere around 80 percent.[19]

In 1944 La Hermosa asked to be recognized as a congregation of the Disciples — an appealing denominational affiliation for the young congregation that would balance local independence with a broader identity — and was officially listed in the 1944 *Yearbook* as located on East 110th Street with eighty-eight members. The address listed in the *Yearbook* was a four-story tenement, about twenty feet wide, surrounded by crumbling rooming houses. La Hermosa flourished in this neighborhood: as Table 4 shows, the congregation grew steadily, reaching 429 members by 1969.[20]

By 1957 La Hermosa's fast-growing congregation could no longer fit twice each Sunday into its twenty-foot-wide sanctuary. With the financial

18. "Puerto Rican Work in New York: A Challenge," *Leaven* 9 (March 1957): 1-2; "A Worthy House of Worship," flyer for Capital for Kingdom Building Campaign, United Christian Missionary Society. "La Hermosa," in "Spanish Speaking Work," memo dated 21 November 1953 (New York Metropolitan Office files). "Northeastern Area Report," compiled by Arthur Stanley, 30 November 1978, pp. 9ff. (NRO files).

19. "The Christian Mission in the New York City Metropolitan Area: A Working Document, March, 1968," prepared by Leland Gartrell, Department of Planning and Research, Protestant Council of New York City, I-9, II-1-4, 36-37 (NRO files). Interview with Yolanda Marquez-Burgos, Metropolitan Office administrator, 29 July 1988, New York City.

20. Interview with Charles Lamb, Regional Minister of Northeastern Region, 19 July 1988, Buffalo, New York. "La Hermosa — The Beautiful," *Christian Evangelist*, 19 September 1965, pp. 5-6. "Missionary Opportunity in New York," *Christian Evangelist*, 6 February 1957, pp. 30-31.

TABLE 4 Iglesia La Hermosa Discipulos de Cristo

Year	Members[a]	Additions by Baptism	Additions by Transfer	Total Amount Raised ($)
1944	88	2	12	7,945
1946	107	13	17	7,999
1948	145	11	45	7,829
1950	180	17	12	11,000
1952	200[b]	—	—	—
1954	250	30	50	16,500
1958[c]	325	5	55	11,483
1960	375	35	2	24,172
1962	392	12	25	39,479
1965[c]	346	10	2	97,921
1969[c]	429	12	8	49,168
1971	435	27	3	54,836
1973	437	20	1	58,010
1976	438	20	1	58,061
1978	400[b]	—	—	90,304
1980	400[b]	—	—	96,396
1983	168	5	5	74,000
1986	211[b]	—	—	46,351[b]

a. Represents only *resident* members; nonresident membership varied from 5 to 120.
b. Estimated figure.
c. Represents a four-year increment from the previous statistics.

support of the United Christian Missionary Society, the congregation moved down the street from their old building to the corner of 110th and 5th Avenue. At that time, there were plans for the construction of a multipurpose Community Center for the congregation's outreach programs in Harlem and for housing "La Academia Cristiana," a private school offering bilingual education. This part of the building plan was never implemented, although Schomberg Plaza, a low-cost housing complex erected across Fifth Avenue from the church, represented a venture initiated by the Disciples and other neighborhood churches.[21]

But La Hermosa contributed in other, equally impressive ways to building up the Disciples' presence in New York: in 1956 the mission in Brooklyn, which the congregation had sponsored since 1951, became the First (Spanish) Christian Church of Brooklyn. In 1963 their Spanish ministry in the Bronx became the Iglesia Evangelica Cristianas Hispanas, while their outpost in the borough of Queens evolved into the Primera Iglesia Hispana de Queens. This process of creating daughter evangelical churches among New York's Hispanic population — an explicit goal of the congregation from early in its history —

21. Fred M. Michel, "A Task of Compassion," *Christian Evangelist,* 13 February 1957, pp. 11-12. "Proposed La Hermosa Project," memo of the "Committee of La Hermosa Project," undated (1957), showing a flow-chart of committee responsibilities (New York Metropolitan Office files).

went so well that by 1969 over one-third of the Disciples churches in New York City were Spanish-speaking.[22]

La Hermosa's lead in ministering to New York City's burgeoning Hispanic population after World War II was followed by Bronx's Second Church in May 1948. Second Church, a previously white, mainstream Disciples congregation, was in the midst of dramatic demographic changes, reflecting the changes taking place in the racial and ethnic makeup of the Bronx. In the early 1930s significant numbers of working-class blacks began moving into what had been the solidly middle-class neighborhood of Morrisania (the church's neighborhood), precipitating one of the earliest waves of "white flight" in the city. From 1950 to 1960, the Puerto Rican population of the neighborhood increased from 10 to 34 percent. These demographic changes are reflected in Second Church's membership statistics: while membership held its own for a while, the number of active members suffered a steady decline well into the 1960s.[23]

In February 1947 a survey committee that had been organized to discuss the future of the congregation declared that their geographic situation was actually a "mission field, peopled largely by Colored and Spanish-speaking." As can be seen from Figures 4 and 5, Second Church's response to this mission statement has largely defined its history in the past three decades. Figure 4 (p. 480) illustrates the undramatic but steady growth in black membership after 1947 as well as the far more dramatic growth in Hispanic membership.[24]

In response to the Survey Committee Report of 1947, Second Church initiated a missionary ministry to Puerto Ricans in the Bronx in May 1948. By November 1949 the English-speaking congregation voted to invite the faster-growing Hispanic congregation to join them as one congregation, holding services in both languages. This arrangement provided a short-term answer to Second Church's numerical problems, mixing the two Disciples emphases, mainline and sectarian. But as the number of whites continued to shrink, Second Church's two-tiered congregation entered a prolonged period of friction and debate in the 1960s, and a new type of Disciple began to dominate — largely nonwhite, non-English speaking, non-middle-class, seeking a more emotionally satisfying, less structured style of worship, more fervently evan-

22. Interview with Charles Lamb, 19 July 1988. "A Church That Grew . . . with the Odds against It: A Matchless Opportunity in Home Missions," flyer published by the United Christian Missionary Society, August 1959. Raymond E. Brown (Board of Church Extension) to Arthur J. Stanley, 29 January 1971 (NRO files). "Christian Mission in the New York City Metropolitan Area," II-37.

23. John Dolan, "Morrisania during the 1950s," *Journal of the Bronx County Historical Society,* Spring 1981, pp. 15-17. Lyle V. Newman, "Report of the Preliminary Study on the Puerto Rican Situation in the Bronx, April 11, 1948," pp. 3-4. Lloyd Ultan, *The Beautiful Bronx, 1920-1950* (New Rochelle: Arlington House, 1979), pp. 44ff.

24. Festus C. Carey, Jr., "A Summary Statement: Confidential Yet Serious" (New York Metropolitan Office files). Jesse M. Bader, "Report on a Consultation at the Second Christian Church, Bronx, March 17, 1962" (New York Metropolitan Office files).

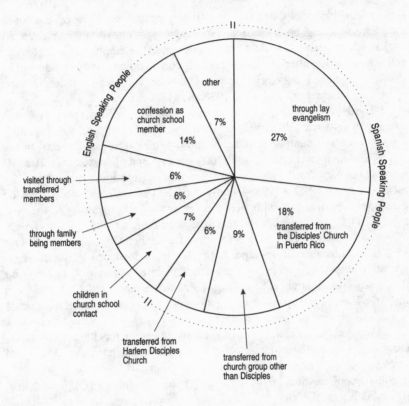

FIGURE 5 New Members of Second Church, the Bronx, in 1970

gelical preaching, and a more clearly drawn set of moral guidelines regarding smoking, alcohol, and social behavior generally.[25]

In 1949, Second Church reported 130 active members in the *Yearbook;* by 1970, the congregation — actually two congregations meeting separately under two different ministers in the same building — reported an "Anglo" congregation of 110 and a Spanish congregation of 191. Each congregation elected its own board, which met both jointly one month and separately the next. The two congregations shared the church's maintenance costs, but the Spanish-speaking congregation assumed two-thirds of the expenses. Because of the dynamic nature of the Hispanic ministry at Second Church, the congregation had impressive success in retaining members, despite the extraordinary social mobility of the

25. Leland Gartrell, "Report to Arthur Stanley on the Second Christian Church, Bronx, March 9, 1959," pp. 2-4 (NRO files). "Rules of Procedure for the Second Christian Church, Bronx, July 1, 1962" (NRO files). "Presentation Made to the Joint Board Meeting of the Second Christian Church, September 7, 1969," pp. 2-3 (New York Metropolitan Office files). Chester Sillars, "Field Staff Report on the Second Christian Church, 1964," pp. 1-2 (NRO files).

Bronx: from 1955 to 1960 there was a 40 percent turnover in the population of the Morrisania neighborhood; from 1960 to 1970 the rate of turnover increased to just under 50 percent. In light of such changes in the community, the retention and growth of membership in the Spanish congregation, while undramatic in absolute numbers, is nonetheless impressive; equally impressive is the doubling of annual giving reported between 1976 and 1980.[26]

The New York City Disciples, with their high percentage of Hispanic congregations (over 30 percent of their membership is Spanish-speaking), stands in marked contrast to other mainline Protestant denominations in the city. The American Baptists, with 200 churches and approximately 100,000 members in New York, reported 18 Hispanic congregations with a combined membership of 2,100 in 1988 — only 2 percent of their membership in the city. The Episcopalians, with 81 churches and 42,500 members in the city, reported 11 Hispanic parishes with a combined membership of 1,500 — only 3 percent of their membership in the city. The United Church of Christ, with 45 New York congregations reporting 8,263 members, listed 1 Hispanic congregation with 431 members — 5 percent of their membership in the city. And the Presbyterian Church, U.S.A., with 109 churches reporting 24,000 members in 1988, listed 17 Hispanic congregations with a combined membership of 1,500 — 7 percent of their membership in the city.[27]

And yet the amazing growth and membership retention of sectarian Disciples congregations among New York's Hispanics has been rivaled and surpassed by the exponential growth of Haitian Disciples, centered in the Brooklyn congregation of the Reverend Philius Nicolas — the Evangelical Crusade/Fishers of Men.

A Haitian immigrant to the United States, Philius Nicolas was ordained in the Church of God in Christ (Memphis, Tennessee). He organized a Church of God congregation among Haitian immigrants in the Flatbush section of Brooklyn in 1973. While continuing to pastor his fast-growing flock, Nicolas took additional courses at Union Theological Seminary, during which time he learned about the Disciples from Winthrop Hudson's *Religion in America*. He confesses today that while he was at Union he was looking for a "larger and more catholic group with which to affiliate," and he was immediately attracted by Hudson's description of Alexander Campbell's restorationist gospel. Nicolas's further

---

26. "Christian Mission in the New York City Metropolitan Area," I-9, II-16 (NRO files). Arthur Stanley, "New York Area Report: November 3, 1975" (NRO files). "A Provisional Design for Urban Ministries in Metropolitan New York, January 22, 1988" (New York Metropolitan Office files).

27. The information on American Baptist churches in New York was provided by the Rev. Jorge Aledo, associate executive minister for Hispanic Ministries in the Metropolitan Area (American Baptists), 24 July 1989; statistics for the Protestant Episcopal Church in the city were provided by the Rev. Michael S. Kendal, archdeacon of the Episcopal Diocese of New York, 20 July 1989; figures for the United Church of Christ were provided by Marge Royle, secretary for research and evaluation of the Metropolitan Office of the United Church of Christ, 21 July 1989; statistics for the Presbyterian Church, USA, were provided by the Rev. James Speer, executive presbyter for the Presbytery of New York, 20 July 1989.

investigations into Disciples tradition led him to the "Declaration and Address" and the "Last Will and Testament of the Springfield Presbytery," both of which called for the restoration of primitive Christianity and for an acquaintance with experimental religion — music to Nicolas's ears. More immediately, his investigations led him to discover the worship and preaching at La Hermosa and at Second (Bronx) Christian — liturgical styles very much to his taste and to that of his French-speaking, Pentecostal congregation, which observes three-hour Sunday morning worship services that include steel drums and an hour-long hymnfest before preaching and home-based prayer meetings.[28]

In 1976 Evangelical Crusade became officially affiliated with the Disciples of Christ. By 1986 it reported an active membership of 1,225, the largest Disciples church by far in greater New York. There remained, however, a problematic liturgical holdover from Nicolas's previous association with the Church of God in Christ: his church's monthly celebration of the eucharist, a practice that flew in the face of both mainstream Disciples practice and Disciples restorationist tradition.

Nicolas reports that most of his flock arrived in Brooklyn with Roman Catholic affiliations but joined the Crusade congregation because of the warmth and vibrancy of the worship and because of the distinctive identity that such affiliation offered. For immigrants struggling to establish a new life and identity in a strange new land, says Nicolas, his church offers an unambiguous model of what it means to be a Christian in pluralist, secular America: no drinking, no dancing, strictly chaperoned dating, clear stands against homosexuality, abortion, and the Equal Rights Amendment. To support and nurture this gospel identity, Nicolas's congregation offers a range of religious support groups — Bible Study, home visiting bands, prayer groups — as well as neighborhood outreach programs that include immigration processing, housing and rent-control committees, and youth groups.[29]

Nicolas's network of burgeoning Disciples congregations among Haitian immigrants stands in marked contrast to Haitian growth patterns among other mainstream Protestant groups in New York: the Presbyterians list one French-speaking congregation in the city (which serves for all French-speakers, not just Haitians), while the (American) Baptists list three full-fledged Haitian congregations among several dozen in the city.[30]

28. Interview with Philius Nicolas, 7 July 1988, Brooklyn, New York. "A Brief History of the Evangelical Crusade Fishers of Men, Inc." (Metropolitan Office files).

29. "Present Status of Evangelical Crusade, September 27, 1977." Raymond Brown (Church Extension), *Report to the Metropolitan Disciples Union* (New York Metropolitan Office files). Interview with Charles Lamb, 20 July 1988.

30. The French Presbyterian congregation is the French Evangelical Church in Manhattan; the three Haitian Baptist congregations are the Communite Fraternelle and the Haitian Baptist Church in Brooklyn and the Eglise Evangelicale Baptiste Haitienne in Queens. Another "associated" Haitian congregation, Redempteur Eglise Baptiste in Brooklyn, meets in a predominantly non-Haitian church (information from a phone conversation with David Meers, New York Office of the Presbyterian Church, USA).

Perhaps the closest analogue to the growth of Haitian Disciples churches is that of the growth of Korean congregations in the Presbyterian Church. In 1977 there were two congregations of Korean Presbyterians in New York (totaling 433 members), neither of which had its own church or church property; by 1987 there were eleven Korean Presbyterian USA congregations, totaling 2,491 active members; nine other congregations met in other Presbyterian churches or in Methodist or Baptist buildings. But these statistics actually underestimate the number of Korean Presbyterians in New York City because they do not include the burgeoning numbers belonging to the evangelically inclined Korean Presbyterian Church, a doctrinally conservative denomination that has grown dramatically among recent immigrants, largely at the expense of the Presbyterian Church USA. Like the Haitian Disciples, these sectarian Presbyterians are attracted to the Korean church — as opposed to the larger and more sedate Presbyterian mother church — because of its strong evangelical identity and moral code.[31]

By any standard of measurement, Nicolas and his support groups at the Evangelical Crusade have been immensely successful at attracting and retaining members: the congregation grew from 250 active members in 1976 to 1,225 members in 1986 — a year in which the total active membership for all Disciples churches in greater New York was 8,009. In 1983 the congregation claimed the eighth largest number of baptisms of any Disciples church in the country. Further, Nicolas's congregation supports six congregations in Haiti, the largest (in Gonaires) claiming 1,775 faithful, and the smallest (in Daran) claiming 358 active members — all, according to Nicolas, seeking Disciples fellowship. And, since affiliating with the Disciples in 1976, Nicolas has played a major role in bringing three other Haitian churches in Brooklyn to join the Disciples fellowship, leading Charles Lamb, regional minister of the Northeastern Region, to estimate that one-fourth of all active Disciples in New York are Haitians brought into the fellowship through Nicolas.[32]

III.

What is it, exactly, that this dramatic growth of sectarian Disciples congregations among Hispanic and Haitian groups in New York City in the past few decades tells us? Social scientists have always hedged their bets when it comes

---

31. Statistics on Korean Presbyterian church growth are from the Yearbooks of the Presbyterian Church, USA, 1977-1987, and from a phone conversation with David Meers, New York Office, Presbyterian Church, USA.

32. "Present Status of Evangelical Crusade, September 27, 1977." Raymond Brown (Church Extension), *Report of General Consultation, Evangelical Crusade, Brooklyn, New York* (New York Metropolitan Office files). Interview with Philius Nicolas, 7 July 1988. Philius Nicolas to Charles Lamb, 16 June 1982 (NRO files). "Field Report, Haiti, September 17-19, 1980" (NRO files). Interview with Charles Lamb, 20 July 1988. Yearbooks of the Disciples of Christ for 1978, 1980, 1983, and 1986.

to extrapolating from New York to the broader American experience — as well they might given the uniqueness of the city. There is scarcely any sense in which New York City could be said to constitute a cultural microcosm of the nation, and the religious experiences of so traditionally Middle American a group as the Disciples of Christ in faded and jaded Babylon cannot be read as normative in any sense for the great majority of American Disciples.

But it is precisely the unique quality of the Disciples' New York experience — what I have preferred to term a mission territory experience — that offers a broader perspective on both the past and the future of the Christian Church in other equally pluralistic urban areas that are designated (ironically or not) "homeland missions." The progressive identity that is generally characteristic of twentieth-century Disciples plays remarkably badly in these pluralistic urban areas.

The sad showing of the Disciples' unitive, ecumenical tradition in New York is especially surprising, given the city's important historical role in the American ecumenical movement, from the early efforts of the Evangelical Alliance headquartered in the city, to the broad-church unitive efforts of the New School Presbyterians centered at Union Theological Seminary, to the irenic ecumenical ministry of such New York Episcopalians as William Reed Huntington, himself the father of the Lambeth Quadrilateral and thus of much of what became the Faith and Order Movement in modern ecumenism. Such a long urban association with the American Protestant ecumenical impulse, perhaps culminating in the choice of New York as home for that Vatican of American unitive Protestantism, the National Council of Churches, should have made New York City a good bet for the ecumenically committed, broad-church Disciples of Christ, as it was for the Presbyterians. In point of fact, however, precisely those congregations most identified with this mainstream ecumenical identity — Park Avenue, Flatbush/Bethlehem United, and the like — evince the most difficulty in recruiting an indigenous New York membership and in maintaining a distinctive identity in the city.[33]

It is rather those Disciples congregations offering the restorationist side of the Disciples' heritage, churches such as La Hermosa, (Bronx) Second Christian, and Evangelical Crusade — congregations, in short, that offer a more sectarian as opposed to mainstream style of worship, doctrine, and identity — that evince far more success in attracting and retaining indigenous support, especially among immigrants of color (indigenous being a slippery identification in cosmopolitan New York). But does such a historical fact confirm the theories of Dean M. Kelley as to why conservative churches grow? I believe that it does, *in part.*

33. Don H. Yoder, "Christian Unity in Nineteenth Century America," in *History of the Ecumenical Movement, 1517-1948,* ed. Ruth Rouse and Stephen Neill (Philadelphia: Westminster Press, 1967), pp. 249ff. John F. Wolverton, "Huntington's Quadrilateral — A Critical Study," *Church History* 39 (1970): 198-211. Lefferts A. Loetscher, *The Broadening Church: A Study of Theological Issues in the Presbyterian Church since 1869* (Philadelphia: Westminster Press, 1949), chap. 1.

The membership of the Christian Church (Disciples of Christ) has held its own in New York City over the past two decades primarily because of the dramatic influx of Hispanic and Haitian members, under the lead of several charismatic ministers attracted to the restorationist side of the church's tradition. Clearly the ability of the national church to incorporate such nonmainstream congregations into its communion witnesses to the flexibility and broad-church principles that stand it in good stead in a pluralistic society, just as they did a century and a half ago on the middle border. The first preliminary lesson to be learned from this study may be that the most fruitful means for the church to recruit new members in eastern urban areas in the immediate future might involve a recovery of a side of the Disciples heritage generally slighted in the twentieth century.

A second lesson is closely related to the first: such a return *ad fontes* to the full Disciples heritage will involve more than an antiquarian appropriation of the past for the sake of, say, intellectual symmetry. Campbell and Stone were in touch with their missionary audience. The nature of contemporary American culture might very well need a reapplication of their missionary style, especially in eastern urban areas like New York City. The lively missionary fervor of nineteenth-century Disciples on the frontier of Ohio, Indiana, and Kentucky appealed to precisely those kinds of new arrivals — immigrants, if you will — that Philius Nicolas does: hard-working and quite serious-minded folks newly arrived in a liminal geographical area (and many newly arrived in the middle class) who seek a distinctive Christian identity that is soundly biblical, culturally relevant, and emotionally satisfying.

These lessons quite naturally raise the question of identity no less than of strategy. How much diversity is possible if a denominational body is to retain a meaningful identity? What is the appropriate relationship between identity and growth strategies? Is it, in fact, good theology to reappropriate an identity that many Disciples would now find problematic, however successful such an identity might be in attracting growth? History — alas, even church history — cannot answer these kinds of "ought" questions; it can, however, offer a larger perspective for considering them. And this brings us to the third lesson of the study.

Disciples of Christ — disciples with both a small and a large *d* in this case — ignore the past at their own peril. Increased pluralism with concomitant assaults on the unifying cultural faith, the exponential expansion of the urbanization process, and the complexities of addressing social justice problems in a mixed-market economy are facts of American history. They have been so since at least the decade following the Civil War, and they show no signs of going away. The experience of Disciples in New York City would seem to urge an increased study of our specifically *urban* history, a history that offers a somewhat different story line than the experience of Disciples in other parts of America. An examination of history on the urban frontier might very well point in the direction of a revitalized missionary ecclesiology not for Peru or the Malagasy Republic but for such exotic mission lands as New York City.

Denominational Switching, Social Mobility, and Membership Trends

C. Kirk Hadaway

Over the past two decades social research into denominational mobility has verified what conventional wisdom had always known — that a large proportion of Americans switch from one religious denomination to another during their lives. Just how many Americans have switched was unknown, however, until national surveys were able to show that at least 36 percent of Americans and 39 percent of Protestants indicate a religious preference different from the one they had while growing up.[1]

The fact that large numbers of Americans switch denominations is interesting, but it is far more useful for church leaders to understand *why* people switch denominations, the *patterns* of their switching, and the *impact* of these patterns on denominational membership trends. A number of efforts have been made in this direction, but their success has been mixed, because of the complexity of the problem. Much of what is assumed to be true concerning denominational switching in America may well be false.

One of the first "causes" or determinants of denominational switching to receive attention was its presumed relationship with upward social mobility. It was conjectured that as individuals rose in social status they would begin to feel an "incongruity" between their status and that of other members of the denomination to which they belonged and a "pull" toward denominations that were more consistent with their new status. This theory was championed by cynical social scientists who suggested that Americans were "playing musical church to a status-striving tune."[2] The Baptist who becomes a Methodist, then a Presbyterian, and finally an Episcopalian on his or her way up the corporate ladder is a familiar story, but to what extent is this social

---

1. James A. Davis and Tom W. Smith, *General Social Surveys, 1972-1988* (machine-readable data file; Chicago: National Opinion Research Center, 1988).

2. N. J. Demerath III, *Social Class in American Protestantism* (Chicago: Rand McNally, 1965), p. 71.

and denominational mobility typical? Hard research on this issue has been sparse.

In this essay I address the issue of whether increased social status does in fact tend to lead people to switch to higher-status denominations. I am particularly interested in whether such mobility (religious and social) has had any effect in recent years on the growth (or lack thereof) of the Disciples of Christ. For comparative purposes, I also pay special attention to two groups that have a clear historical link to the Disciples: Baptists, who have a lower average social status than Disciples, and Presbyterians, who tend to have a higher social status than Disciples.

PREVIOUS RESEARCH ON SOCIAL MOBILITY AND DENOMINATIONAL SWITCHING

Early research into social mobility and switching tends to provide some support for the notion that Americans switch toward status consistency. A national sampling conducted in the early 1960s showed a net status effect for individuals switching to higher-status denominations.[3] A sampling of a small number of natural scientists produced similar albeit more ambiguous results.[4]

One of the few studies to focus specifically on issue of social mobility and switching was conducted by Jerry Bode.[5] Unfortunately, Bode used a limited sample from Nebraska, and the results cannot be generalized to the larger population. Nevertheless, he found that people who have increased in social status are more likely to switch denominations and that upwardly mobile people who switch tend to join higher-status denominations. He found no evidence of a tendency for downwardly mobile persons to switch to lower-status denominations.

Jon Alston used data from a 1955 Gallup Survey to examine the relationship between switching and socioeconomic status.[6] Alston concluded that higher-status denominations were "more attractive" to switchers on the grounds that they tend to have higher proportions of switchers among their members. This interpretation is seriously flawed for two reasons, however. First, one of the categories ("other Protestant") that contains a very high number of "mobiles" (people who have switched in) can be shown to be *low*

---

3. James N. Morgan, Martin David, and Wilbur Cohen, *Income and Welfare in the United States* (New York: McGraw-Hill, 1962).

4. Ted R. Vaughn, Gideon Sjoberg, and Douglas H. Smith, "The Religious Orientations of American Social Scientists," *Social Forces* 44 (1966): 519-26.

5. Bode, "Upward Social Mobility and Change in Religious Affiliation" (Ann Arbor: University Microfilms, 1968).

6. Alston, "Religious Mobility and Socio-economic Status," *Sociological Analysis* 32 (1971): 140-48.

in social status. Second, Alston defined mobiles as people who have switched in, and yet the proportion of mobiles is actually affected by the number of those who *leave* as well as by the number who switch in. An unstable denomination could lose most of the people that had been reared as members, gain a few from the outside, and appear more attractive by Alston's criteria than a more stable denomination that gained about the same percentage from the outside.

Rodney Stark and Charles Y. Glock's analysis of denominational switching in *American Piety* is another example of how the complexities of the process can lead to misinterpretation.[7] They found that higher-status mainline denominations had net gains as a result of the switching process, whereas large conservative groups such as the Baptists experienced net losses. A net gain simply means that more people switched into a denomination than switched out. Stark and Glock explained the attraction of the Presbyterian Church, the Episcopal Church, and the Congregationalists as a matter of (1) upward social mobility and the tendency of upwardly mobile persons to switch from lower-status conservative denominations to higher-status liberal denominations, and (2) the appeal of "modernized theologies."

On the basis of their switching data, Stark and Glock dismissed reports of the rapid growth of conservative denominations as "a myth" and predicted that "the conservatives are likely to become an increasingly minor force in American religion." This short-sighted prediction seemed plausible at the time because most of the liberal denominations were still growing. Within a few years, however, these gains turned into very serious losses. Conservative denominations continued to grow, although at slower rates than in the past. (There has been no true conservative resurgence, at least in terms of membership growth.)

While it can be argued that Stark and Glock's analysis described "a bullish religious market" that is now past,[8] it is more likely that they simply misinterpreted their data. One major problem was their failure to acknowledge conservative sects when computing patterns of net gains and losses among liberal, moderate, and conservative denominational clusters. They turned up the small trend of higher-status liberal denominations gaining at the expense of the conservatives because they considered switching only within a restricted set of Protestant bodies. They did not take account of the impressive gains made by the sects through switching nor by the Baptists through switching from sects, other Protestants, and those claiming no religion. Nor did they consider the losses of the liberal groups to Catholics, other Protestants, and those claiming no religion.

7. Stark and Glock, *American Piety* (Berkeley and Los Angeles: University of California Press, 1968).

8. Wade Clark Roof and William McKinney, *American Mainline Religion* (New Brunswick, N.J.: Rutgers University Press, 1987), p. 163.

If we set aside the misleading treatment of switching data in *American Piety*, it becomes clear that the primary "winners" through the switching process are the high-status liberal denominations and the lower-status conservative sects. The "losers" are large moderate and conservative groups such as the Methodists, Lutherans, and Baptists. This was true in the 1965 National Opinion Research Center data used by Stark and Glock, and it remains true in National Opinion Research Center data collected in the 1980s. For this reason, it cannot be said that patterns of net gains support only an "upward movement" of switching from low-status to high-status denominations. This is not to say that such a trend does not actually exist; it is just that the data used by Stark and Glock do not support such a conclusion.

More recently, Wade Clark Roof and William McKinney took a closer look at the patterns of net gains through switching and the characteristics of those who switch. They found that "the net switching gains for liberal Protestants are wholly accounted for by *older* switchers."[9] They speculate that perhaps the stream of switching to liberal denominations was greater in the past than it is today or that switching to liberal denominations occurs primarily among *older* Americans (those beyond their child-bearing years). It is possible, in fact, that both are true.

With regard to "upward switching," Roof and McKinney conclude that "all evidence points to less upward switching, or conservative-to-liberal transfer of religious membership, now than in the past."[10] A small stream in this direction may still exist, but it is likely to be filled primarily with older people who have relatively low levels of religious commitment.

ARE THOSE WITH CHANGING SOCIAL STATUS MORE LIKELY TO SWITCH DENOMINATIONS?

It is a rather simple matter to address the question of whether changing social status tends to make a switch to another denomination more likely. National Opinion Research Center (NORC) data from the General Social Surveys contain questions dealing with education and occupational prestige for both the respondent and the parents of the respondent. For instance, by comparing the respondent's occupational prestige with that of his or her father, a measure of status change can be recorded. The series of NORC polls also includes questions that help classify respondents as denominational "switchers" or "stayers."

Table 1 shows four measures of socioeconomic change and the percentage of respondents who increase, decrease, or show no change in social status.

9. Roof and McKinney, *American Mainline Religion*, p. 171.
10. Roof and McKinney, *American Mainline Religion*, p. 175.

TABLE 1   Percent Increasing or Decreasing in Socioeconomic Status

	Educational Change (Mother-Resp.)	Educational Change (Father-Resp.)	Occupational Prestige Change[a] (Father-Resp.)	Occupational Prestige Change[b] (Father-Resp.)
Increased Status	66.7%	69.3%	45.7%	53.9%
No Change	19.9	16.5	8.1	4.9
Decreased Status	13.4	14.2	46.2	41.2
Number of Cases	19,215	16,699	18,394	17,992

a. Change in prestige score (Hodge-Seigel-Rossi classification)
b. Change in prestige score (Dictionary of Occupational Titles classification)

Educational change compares the respondent's years of education (ranging from no formal schooling to eight years of college) to the education of the respondent's mother or mother substitute. A similar variable compares the respondent's education to his or her father's education. As can be seen, the large majority of respondents have more years of schooling than did their parents. The two occupational prestige change variables compare the prestige of the respondent's occupation with the prestige of the respondent's father's occupation when the respondent was growing up. The first prestige variable uses the Hodge-Seigel-Rossi categorization of occupations based on perceived social standing. In the NORC sample, scores for respondents ranged from 12 (low) to 54 (high). The second prestige variable is much more detailed. It uses the Dictionary of Occupational Titles classification and accompanying prestige scores developed by Lloyd V. Temme.[11]

Table 1 shows that there has not been a major shift toward occupations with higher prestige. In the Hodge-Seigel-Rossi classification, the split is nearly even between respondents who had higher-rated occupations than their fathers and those who had lower-rated occupations. Only 8.1 percent had exactly the same occupational rating as their fathers. The more discrete DOT prestige classification yielded a slightly different pattern: only 4.9 percent had no change, and a slightly larger proportion increased in prestige (53.9%) than decreased when compared to their fathers' occupation.

Switching was measured by comparing responses to two questions: "What is your religious preference? Is it Protestant, Catholic, Jewish, some other religion, or no religion?" and "In what religion were you raised?" Protestant responses were probed with an additional question asking for a specific denomination. People who indicated a different religion or denomination from when they were growing up were considered switchers. Only respondents who said they were Protestant, Catholic, Jewish, none, or some other religion at the present time *and* when growing up were considered.

11. For more information on these categorizations, see Davis and Smith, *General Social Surveys, 1972-1988.*

TABLE 2 Percentage Switching by Change in Socioeconomic Status

	Educational Change (Father-Resp.)		Educational Change (Mother-Resp.)		Occupational Prestige Change[a] (Father-Resp.)		Occupational Prestige Change[b] (Father-Resp.)	
	Change	No Change	Change	No Change	Change	No Change	Change	No Change
Full Sample	31.8%	32.3%	31.6%	30.9%	32.7%	30.4%	32.4%	29.5%
Protestants	34.6%	35.6%	34.2%	32.8%	35.9%	32.8%	35.6%	32.3%
Young (under 25)	31.1%	30.7%	30.8%	29.8%	31.6%	30.7%	31.2%	30.7%
Older (over 44)	32.9%	35.1%	32.7%	33.0%	33.9%	30.1%	33.7%	28.3%
Young Protestants	31.7%	32.8%	31.0%	30.7%	32.7%	30.9%	32.2%	31.6%
Older Protestants	38.0%	39.6%	38.0%	36.1%	39.2%	34.6%	39.1%	32.7%

a. Change in prestige score (Hodge-Seigel-Rossi classification)
b. Change in prestige score (Dictionary of Occupational Titles classification)

For example, a respondent who switched from "no answer" or "don't know" to the Disciples of Christ was not considered a switcher and was dropped from the analysis.

Table 2 shows the relationship between change in socioeconomic status and denominational switching. The basic relationship is weak. Those who had experienced change in socioeconomic status (up or down) were slightly more likely to switch denominations on three out of the four measures of SES change in the full sample. Educational change produces the weakest relationships. Those who had the same educational level as their father were slightly *more* likely to switch than those with a different educational level. The reverse was true with regard to mother's educational level. In both cases, however, the relationships were so small that they do not approach acceptable levels of statistical significance.

Somewhat stronger relationships were found for the occupational prestige variables. As can be seen on the first line of Table 2, 32.7 percent of those who have changed occupational status have switched denominations, as compared to 30.4 percent of those with essentially the same occupational status as their father. A similar relationship is shown for the second measure of change in occupational prestige. In both cases the relationships are weak but statistically significant.

Additional analysis was performed to see if the relationship varied among Protestants, Catholics, younger respondents, and older respondents. Very little change was seen in the two measures of change in education. In all six categories the relationships for change in education were insignificant. For change in occupational prestige, however, the relationship with switching was stronger among Protestants and among respondents who were forty-five years old or older. The effects were additive, so that the strongest relationship between change in occupational prestige and switching was found for *older Protestants*. This association produced a gamma of -.14 and

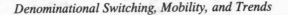

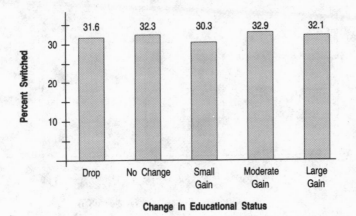

FIGURE 1 Percent Switching by Change in Educational Status (Father to Respondent)

a Pearson's correlation of -.04. The relationship increased in magnitude, but it remained quite weak.

IS INCREASED SOCIAL STATUS ASSOCIATED WITH DENOMINATIONAL SWITCHING?

Several studies have indicated that *rising* social status rather than a change in social status per se is related to denominational switching. In other words, social climbers may switch "upward," but there should be little reason for someone to switch "downward" because of declining social status.

Figures 1 and 2 illustrate the basic relationship between change in social status (both upward and downward) and denominational switching. In Figure 1 it can be seen that no relationship exists between upward or downward *educational* mobility and switching. However, for change in occupational prestige there is a small relationship. Those with no change in occupational prestige were least likely to switch denominations. A decline in occupational prestige was related to switching, as was an increase in occupational prestige. Further, the highest levels of switching were recorded for those with the greatest *increases* in occupational prestige.

In summary, those who experience change in occupational status are slightly more likely to switch denominations than those who remain at the same basic occupational level as their fathers. The relationship exists for both increasing and decreasing social status, but it is stronger for increasing social

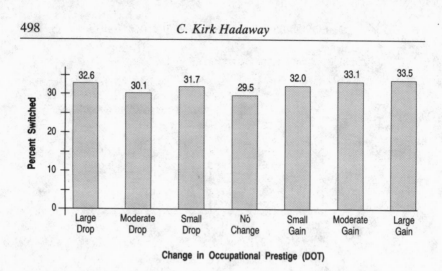

FIGURE 2   Percent Switching by Change in Occupational Prestige (Father to Respondent)

status. In all cases, however, the relationship between status change and switching is very weak.

DO SWITCHERS CHOOSE DENOMINATIONS CONSISTENT WITH THEIR SOCIAL STATUS?

Even if there is not a strong tendency for changing social status to "provoke" people to switch denominations, a status effect could exist if people who switch denominations tend to do so in the direction of status consistency. In other words, do people with gains in social status who switch denominations tend to affiliate with *higher*-status denominations, and do switchers who decline in social status tend to affiliate with *lower*-status denominations?

In order to examine this issue it was necessary to develop a ranking of denominations according to social status. Denominational groupings were obtained from *American Mainline Religion.*[12] Excluding the "miscellaneous" and "no religious preference" categories, I was left with a total of twenty-five religious groupings. I then ranked each denominational grouping according to the mean levels of education, General Educational Development needed for the respondents' occupations, and occupational prestige (two variables) of its adherents. To develop a composite status ranking of the denominations, I added the individual SES rankings, entering the educational ranking twice. Denom-

12. Roof and McKinney, *American Mainline Religion,* pp. 254-56.

TABLE 3 Socioeconomic Ranking of Religious Bodies

	Cases	Mean Education	Mean Occupational Prestige[a]	Mean Occupational Prestige[b]	Mean GED Score[c]
1. Unitarian	52	15.9	51.9	536.4	449.1
2. Jewish	515	14.1	48.0	498.6	426.6
3. Episcopalian	586	13.8	45.3	462.7	404.4
4. *Presbyterian*	1,036	13.2	44.4	449.3	398.0
5. Christian Science	60	13.4	41.7	433.2	392.6
6. United Church of Christ	332	12.9	42.9	437.7	387.3
7. Mormon	307	12.9	40.2	408.6	371.9
8. White Methodist	2,291	12.3	41.4	418.7	377.5
9. Evangelical/ Fundamentalist	159	12.2	39.0	401.0	367.6
10. Lutheran	1,699	12.0	40.0	399.8	367.4
11. Catholic	5,815	12.0	39.4	399.8	363.5
12. *Christian Church (Disciples)*	365	11.7	39.1	394.9	365.5
13. Reformed	99	11.4	38.5	384.8	354.9
14. Northern White Baptist	986	11.5	37.1	371.3	345.5
15. Church of Christ	301	11.3	37.8	374.9	349.3
16. Adventists	95	11.4	35.9	361.4	347.2
17. *White Southern Baptists*	2,192	11.0	37.8	377.2	351.2
18. Nazarenes	120	11.2	35.6	358.6	340.7
19. Black Methodist	370	11.1	34.4	347.3	336.8
20. Assemblies of God	150	10.6	36.1	365.7	344.4
21. Black Northern Baptist	864	11.1	32.9	331.7	322.0
22. Jehovah's Witnesses	141	10.9	32.9	333.2	325.3
23. Pentecostal/Holiness	535	10.3	33.0	327.8	325.1
24. Church of God	159	9.8	33.3	325.7	318.2
25. Black Southern Baptist	1,023	10.0	29.7	288.9	306.4

a. Change in prestige score (Hodge-Seigel-Rossi classification)
b. Change in prestige score (Dictionary of Occupational Titles classification)
c. General Occupational Development needed for the respondent's occupation

inations could score in a range from 5 (highest status) to 125 (lowest status). The results of this composite ranking are shown in Table 3, along with the mean values used to create the rankings.

Unitarians, Jews, and Episcopalians were the top three religious groups in terms of the social status of their adherents. The bottom three were black Baptists living in the south, the Church of God, and Pentecostal/Holiness denominations. The Disciples/Christian Church cluster falls in the middle of this ranking. There are relatively few surprises in the rankings, especially at the top and bottom. The only true oddity was the high ranking of the Evangelical/Fundamentalist cluster.

Once the denominational status ranking was developed, it was possible to measure the extent to which respondents were switching from lower-status denominations to higher-status denominations and vice versa. For instance,

TABLE 4   Association of SES Change with Change in Denominational Status

	Educational Change (Mother-Resp.)	Educational Change (Father-Resp.)	Occupational Prestige Change[a] (Father-Resp.)	Occupational Prestige Change[b] (Father-Resp.)
Full Sample	.08	.06	.06	.08
Females	.07	.05	.06	.08
Males	.09	.08	.07	.07
Female Protestants	.07	.04	.05	.07
Male Protestants	.10	.06	.08	.09
Young Female Protestants	.02	.05	.04	.06
Older Female Protestants	.06	.01	.07	.07
Young Male Protestants	.06	.01	.03	.05
Older Male Protestants	.13	.10	.13	.12

a. Change in prestige score (Hodge-Seigel-Rossi classification)
b. Change in prestige score (Dictionary of Occupational Titles classification)

someone who switched from the Church of God to the Episcopal Church would score +21, and someone who switched from the United Church of Christ to the Assemblies of God would score -14. People who did not switch denominations were not considered.

The next step was to see if change in socioeconomic status was related to change in denominational social status among switchers. Table 4 (p. 500) shows the Pearson's r coefficients between changing denominational status and four measures of socioeconomic change. Positive coefficients indicate switching toward status congruency, whereas negative coefficients suggest that people switch *away* from status congruency. As can be seen, there is a tendency for people who switch denominations to do so in the direction of status congruency. The relationship is stronger among older male Protestants than among any other group, but in all cases it remains rather weak.

Figure 3 shows the relationship between increase in denominational status with change in years of education (from mother to respondent) among older male Protestants. As can be seen, switchers with a drop in educational status are least likely to move to higher-status denominations. In addition, the difference between those with a drop in educational status and those with a small gain in educational status is very small. Apparently the impact of educational status change on switching is seen primarily among those with moderate to large gains in socioeconomic status.

So we see that change in socioeconomic status is related to switching. People who gain or lose status are slightly more likely to switch than those who retain the status of their parents. In addition, people who increase in social status are slightly more likely to switch than persons who decline in social status. However, switchers who drop in social status do not tend to switch to lower-status denominations. About half switch "up" and half switch "down." Switchers with small gains in socioeconomic status are also nearly evenly split

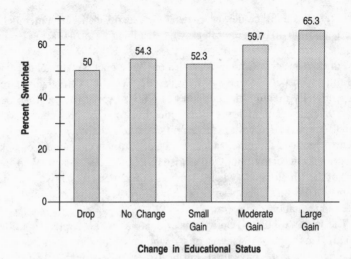

Change in Educational Status

FIGURE 3 **Percentage with Increase in Denominational Status (among Switchers) by Change in Education (Mother to Respondent)**

in the direction of their switching. A trend toward "upward switching" on the part of switchers rising in social status does exist, but it is weak and it operates most clearly among older Protestants who have seen substantial increases in social status.

SWITCHING AMONG PRESBYTERIANS, DISCIPLES, AND BAPTISTS

It is particularly interesting to look at switching among Presbyterians, Disciples, and Southern Baptists, because, as noted earlier, they represent high-status, middle-status, and lower-status denominations and they share a common thread of history — in that the Christian Church/Disciples of Christ/Church of Christ denominational family emerged as a movement primarily among Presbyterian and Baptist churches.

It should be noted at this point that the merged General Social Survey does not identify individuals by their specific denomination unless there is absolutely no possibility of misclassification, as would be the case with the Episcopal Church, Jehovah's Witnesses, and the Church of the Nazarene. However, the three denominations of interest here — the Christian Church (Disciples of Christ), the Presbyterian Church (USA), and the Southern Baptist Convention — cannot be so easily separated from their respective denominational families. Further, the survey deals with identification, not membership, and perhaps 30 to 40 percent of those we call adherents are not actually church members.

For the Christian Church/Disciples of Christ denominational cluster, we are dealing with people who say they identify with the Christian Church or who specifically mention the Disciples of Christ. About half of these people will be Disciples (although not all are members of Disciples churches). The other half are affiliated with *independent Christian churches*. Because of this problem, I reduced the independent Christian Church component of this de-nominational cluster by removing Christian Church respondents who live in regions of the United States where members of Independent Christian churches outnumber Disciples. The results of this effort are preliminary and are not reported in the tables that follow.

The white Southern Baptist cluster contains white Baptists who live in the South. This excludes black Baptists, who constitute less than 2 percent of the Southern Baptist Convention, but it also excludes roughly 15 percent of true SBC members who live outside the South. On the other hand, it *includes* members of independent Baptist churches in the South, such as members of Jerry Falwell's church in Lynchburg, Virginia.

The Presbyterian data are somewhat purer, especially since the merger of the northern and southern branches of the church. Still, this denominational cluster includes members of several small but growing conservative Presby-terian groups that have split off from the main Presbyterian Church.

Although data such as these may not be the ideal, they are the best national samples available, and merging several similar national polls provides the only way to investigate switching patterns for a small denominational group like the Christian Church. The information gained may not be all that is needed to understand the impact of switching on any of the three specific denomina-tions, but it should give insight into the patterns of shifting and sorting among these three denominational families.

Having said all this, I turn now to the consideration of patterns of switching among the denominational clusters. I do so in two ways: first, I look at just these three groups, as if they were a closed system; second, I consider switching to and from "other denominations" and the category of no denom-inational affiliation.

As can be seen in Table 5, there does not appear to be a great deal of switching among Presbyterians, Disciples, and white Southern Baptists. Of the three groups, the Baptists keep the largest share of their adherents (96.7%), and Disciples keep the smallest share (89.3%). Those leaving the Baptists tend to become Presbyterians, and vice versa. This is probably a function of size more than anything else. Disciples who switch, on the other hand, are evenly split in their destinations.

The pattern of net gains through switching indicates that Presbyterians are faring the best in the interplay among these three denominational clusters.

TABLE 5   Switching among Presbyterians, Disciples, and Baptists

Present Denomination	Religion When Growing Up				
	Presbyterian	Christian Ch. (Disciples)	White So. Baptists	(N)	Net Gain or Loss
Presbyterian	92.8%	5.1%	2.7%		+2.8%
(N)	(570)	(11)	(47)	(628)	(+14)
Christian Church	1.5%	89.3%	0.6%		-1.4%
(N)	(9)	(191)	(11)	(211)	(-3)
So. Baptists	5.7%	5.6%	96.7%		-0.5%
(N)	(35)	(12)	(1,707)	(1,754)	(-9)
(Total N)	(614)	(214)	(1,765)	(2,593)	

They gain 14 persons (2.8%). The Baptists and the Disciples both lose. Baptists drop 0.5 percent in the switching process, while Disciples drop 1.4 percent. Since Presbyterians are higher-status on average than Disciples and Baptists, Table 5 seems to provide modest support for a conclusion that a higher-status denomination will gain adherents at the expense of lower-status denominations. As we have seen, however, to suggest that this small trend is due to the impact of rising social status at the individual level is probably not warranted, given the weak relationships.

A much more meaningful way to look at switching among these three denominational clusters is to consider the patterns within the the larger context of switching in America. In Table 6 other religious bodies and the no-affiliation category are added to the switching data. This changes the situation dramatically.

Several points can be made from this table. First, Presbyterians and Disciples are much less stable than white Southern Baptists. A full 76.2 percent of those raised Southern Baptist remain in this denominational category as

TABLE 6   Switching among Presbyterians, Disciples, Baptists, and Others

Present Denomination	Religion When Growing Up						
	Presby.	Christ. Ch. (Disciples)	White So. Baptists	Other	None	(N)	Net Gain or Loss
Presbyterian	54.1%	3.3%	2.1%	1.8%	2.8%		-9.2%
(N)	(570)	(11)	(47)	(310)	(18)	(956)	(-97)
Christian Church	0.9%	56.5%	0.5%	0.7%	2.0%		+3.0%
(N)	(9)	(191)	(11)	(124)	(13)	(348)	(+10)
So. Baptists	3.3%	3.6%	76.2%	1.7%	4.0%		-7.3%
(N)	(35)	(12)	(1,707)	(295)	(26)	(2,075)	(-164)
Other	34.5%	30.8%	18.2%	89.5%	48.5%		-3.6%
(N)	(363)	(104)	(407)	(15,505)	(316)	(16,695)	(-628)
None	7.2%	5.9%	3.0%	6.3%	42.7%		+135.0%
(N)	(76)	(20)	(67)	(1,089)	(278)	(1,530)	(+879)
(Total N)	(1,503)	(338)	(2,239)	(17,323)	(651)	(21,604)	

adults. This compares to only 54.1 percent of Presbyterians and 56.5 percent of Disciples. Also evident from Table 6 is the fact that Presbyterians and Disciples lose a larger proportion of their adherents to the ranks of the "nones" than do Baptists. Presbyterians lose 7.2 percent, Disciples lose 5.9 percent, and white Southern Baptists lose 3.0 percent. These data mirror findings in the Search Institute's ongoing study of "effective Christian education." In this study, which involved members drawn from the churches of six denominations, Southern Baptist youth were much more likely to see themselves as being active members at age twenty-one than were the youth in the other participating mainline denominations — including the Christian Church (Disciples of Christ) and the Presbyterian Church (USA).

On the other hand, white Southern Baptists are big losers in terms of net gains and losses through switching. A total of 2,239 respondents were raised Southern Baptist, whereas only 2,075 now claim to be Southern Baptist — a net loss of 7.3 percent. Presbyterians do even worse, losing 9.2 percent, while Disciples gain through the switching process, adding 3.0 percent. So even though the Christian Church/Disciples of Christ cluster is rather unstable, it more than makes up for its losses among those reared as Disciples through the switching process.

The "nones" are the biggest gainers, increasing a full 135 percent. It should be noted, however, that this gain is not as new or as dramatic as Roof and McKinney suggest in *American Mainline Religion*. It appears to be a dramatic change when compared to Stark and Glock's findings in *American Piety*, but it should be remembered that Stark and Glock were comparing *father's religion* to that of the respondent (rather than the respondent's religion when growing up). Data from the 1988 General Social Survey reveal that today, just as in the 1960s, the "none" category drops when father's religion is compared to that of the respondent. By comparing other surveys that used the same questions to measure switching, it can be determined that there was a rise in disaffiliation in the late 1960s and early 1970s, but the rise was not as dramatic as suggested by Roof and McKinney and most of the other literature on denominational switching.

Although I do not show the results here in tabular form, I replicated the analysis shown in Table 6 focusing on differences between younger respondents and older respondents. Presbyterians and Baptists fared better in terms of net gains and losses among older respondents (over 44). For the Baptists, the net loss was only reduced slightly, from 7.3 percent to 5.3 percent. For Presbyterians, however, controlling for age made a dramatic difference. Among younger respondents the net loss was 21.3 percent, but among older respondents the pattern was reversed to a gain of 3.5 percent. This is consistent with Roof and McKinney's finding that the net gains through switching among liberal denominations were produced by older respondents. Disciples, on the other hand, did better among the young. Among those under 45, Disciples had a net gain of 17.1 percent, whereas among older respondents Disciples had a net loss of 7.6 percent.

TABLE 7 Selected Characteristics of Switchers and Stayers

	Mean Age	Mean Education	Mean Occupational Prestige	Mean Level Worship Attendance	Mean Number of Children	(N)
Presbyterians						
No Change	47.2	13.1	43.9	3.4	1.7	(570)
From Other Denoms.	51.4	13.3	45.5	4.3	2.1	(368)
From Nonaffiliation	45.3	13.9	43.6	3.9	1.9	(18)
To Other Denominations	47.2	13.1	43.2	4.5	2.3	(407)
To Nonaffiliation	36.3	14.1	45.2	0.8	1.2	(76)
Christian Church (Disciples)						
No Change	48.1	11.7	39.4	3.7	2.0	(191)
From Other Denoms.	48.3	11.9	39.0	5.0	2.1	(144)
From Nonaffiliation	44.9	11.9	42.4	4.8	1.7	(13)
To Other Denominations	54.4	12.5	42.7	4.2	2.3	(127)
To Nonaffiliation	44.4	11.4	35.2	0.6	1.0	(20)
White Southern Baptists						
No Change	44.9	11.0	37.6	4.4	2.1	(1,705)
From Other Denoms.	48.3	11.3	38.8	4.9	2.5	(342)
From Nonaffiliation	45.5	10.0	36.0	5.0	2.5	(342)
To Other Denominations	46.7	11.6	40.8	4.9	2.4	(464)
To Nonaffiliation	37.6	10.6	36.2	1.1	1.3	(67)

The effort to separate "true Disciples" from independent Christian Church adherents may help clarify this odd picture. First, among this restricted set of Disciples, the level of stability remains about the same. Overall, Disciples are a rather unstable denomination in terms of switching. However, net gains through switching are reduced from +3.0 percent to +1.8 percent. Even more important is the fact that these net gains come from switching among older respondents rather than among younger respondents — reversing the pattern seen among the larger (unrefined) Disciples/Christian Church denominational cluster.

Further insight, and possibly further confusion, about switching and its impact on denominational growth is provided by Table 7. Here we see selected characteristics of stayers (those who did not switch denominations) and switchers among Presbyterians, Disciples, and white Southern Baptists. Disciples stayers and Presbyterian stayers tend to be somewhat older and less active church attendees than do Baptist stayers. As expected, Presbyterian stayers have the highest levels of education and occupational prestige, followed by Disciples and white Southern Baptists. Presbyterians have the smallest number of children among stayers.

Presbyterians, Disciples, and Baptists all tend to gain from other denominations' adherents who have somewhat more education than their stayers. However, only Presbyterians lose people who have the same level of education as those who join. The other two denominations both lose adherents who have more education than those who join. A similar effect is evident with respect to occupational prestige. Thus it would appear that a small status effect does exist, but it helps only the Presbyterians.

All three denominational clusters gain some of their "best" adherents from the ranks of the nonaffiliated. Although they are few in number, on average these converts attend church more than do the stayers. It is interesting to note that nonaffiliated individuals who join the white Southern Baptists tend to have less education and lower occupational prestige than do the Baptist stayers. A different pattern can be seen for Presbyterians and Disciples. This finding provides support for the notion that conservative denominations play a role in converting people from the lower rungs of the social ladder. Also interesting are the characteristics of those who leave the three groups to become nonaffiliated. Clearly, Presbyterians are losing high-status, highly educated individuals. These are the "up and outers" who have probably become too liberal and irreligious even for a high-status liberal denomination in which commitment levels tend to be relatively low. Among Disciples and white Southern Baptists, on the other hand, the people who switch to the nonaffiliated category tend to have lower average levels of education and occupational prestige.

All three denominational clusters tend to gain adherents from other denominations who have higher mean levels of worship attendance than do their stayers. This is consistent with earlier studies, which found that switchers tend to be "more religious" than stayers. It was somewhat surprising, however, to find that those who switched to the Christian Church/Disciples of Christ cluster had about the same average levels of worship attendance as those who switched to the Baptists. Worship attendance was measured using a nine point scale ranging from 0 (never attend) to 8 (attend several times a week). A mean level of 5.0 indicates that the average person switching into the Disciples from another denomination attends worship two to three times a month.

All three denominational clusters also lose adherents to other denominations who are more likely to attend church than their stayers. This should not hurt the Disciples, however, because they gain more committed adherents than they lose. Among the Presbyterians, on the other hand, the people who leave attend church more frequently than the people who join. For Baptists, the "quality" of those lost is the same as those who are gained from other denominations.

Differences in birth rates were somewhat smaller than expected. As noted earlier, Presbyterians had the smallest and Baptists had the largest average number of children. Further, those who switched into the Baptists from other denominations and from nonaffiliation tend to have more children than any other group (an average of 2.5 children). The pattern for Presbyterians and Disciples is nearly identical in this area. Both gain from other denominations adherents who have 2.1 children on average, and lose adherents who have 2.3 children. In terms of birth rate, Baptists fare better than either Presbyterians or Disciples, although the differences are not large. Still, having 0.4 more children per couple in a 14.8 million member denomination which tends to hold onto its adherents may explain a large proportion of the growth differential between Baptists and Presbyterians.

The effort to separate "true Disciples" from independent Christian Church adherents provides additional help in interpreting this table, but it does not answer all of the questions that might arise. For instance, it is instructive that the restricted set of Disciples is *older* in all categories except among those who switch from the Disciples to other denominations. The restricted set also tends to be more highly educated and to have higher occupational prestige than does the larger Christian Church/Disciples group. The restricted set still gains converts who are more committed than those it loses (although the magnitude of this trend is reduced), but it is important to note that *these converts are the oldest of any group* (a mean age of 55.5 years), and they are more likely to have joined many years ago.

CONCLUSIONS

The impact of switching on denominational trends is difficult to summarize, especially with regard to Disciples and Baptists. However, for Presbyterians it is much easier, because nearly all of the patterns are negative, which is consistent with their severe membership losses over the past two decades. They are unstable, their members are less committed on average, they have severe net losses though switching among younger respondents, they lose a large proportion of their members to the nonaffiliated category, and they have an aging membership with a low birth rate. It is no wonder that they are declining.

For Baptists and Disciples the picture is mixed. Baptists are denominationally stable, they have relatively active adherents, their birth rate is high, and their adherents are younger than Presbyterians and Disciples. On the other hand, Baptists experience rather serious net losses through switching. Apparently, a denomination can grow even when it loses more than it gains through switching and through evangelism — if it has a high enough birth rate, if enough of its adherents are in their child-bearing years, if it is able to hold on to enough of its adherents, and if a large enough proportion of its adherents actually join a church. Unfortunately, these data do not let us know which of these "ifs" are most important to denominational growth.

For the Christian Church, the pattern is even more difficult to interpret. This denominational cluster is very unstable, and its longtime adherents are less active and older on average than are Baptists. On the other hand, their birth rate is only slightly lower than that of the Baptists, and those they gain through switching tend to be active in the church. Further, they experience net gains through switching among the younger population. So why are Baptists growing while the Disciples are declining? There are several possible explanations. Stability may be more important to growth than patterns of net gains if a denomination has an active core membership and a reasonably high birth rate. But clearly part of the problem is that the Christian Church/Disciples cluster is a roughly even mix of people who identify with the Christian Church (Disciples of Christ), which is declining, and people affiliated with the independent Christian Churches, which are not experiencing membership losses. Thus, the switching patterns seen in Table 7 may accurately reflect a *denominational family* that as a whole is neither growing nor declining.

The effort to refine the Christian Church cluster only reinforces the above conclusion and gives additional insight into why the Disciples of Christ are in decline. First of all, the pattern of net gain is reduced and occurs solely among older respondents. Second, the average age of those who were reared as Disciples (and who remain) and those who switch in from other denominations is considerably older than the corresponding stayers and converts among Baptists and Presbyterians. So it would appear that most of the positives that were observed for Disciples turn into negatives when efforts are made to remove independent Christian Church adherents from the set.

Even though the link between switching and denominational growth is complex, one thing is clear from this research: the impact of social mobility on denominational switching is *slight*. Those who are mobile in social status are more likely to switch denominations, and among those who do switch denominations there is a tendency to switch "toward consistency" in social status. Still, the relationship has very little impact except among older Protestants who have seen large increases in social status. Of course, this is the group among which we would expect to find the greatest impact, and the relationship may be a legacy of a past era in which suburban religion and culture were more closely aligned than they are today. Denominational preference has become increasingly irrelevant to social status, and the evidence suggests that the relationship may never have been very strong.

This means that the membership declines that have been suffered by the Disciples of Christ cannot be attributed to upwardly mobile Disciples switching to higher-status denominations. The trend is simply too small to produce such an effect.

Patterns of Participation and Giving Related to Growth in Christian Church (Disciples of Christ) Congregations: Causes and Consequences

Eleanor Scott Meyers and Daniel V. A. Olson

National denominational bodies grow and decline in relationship to real growth and decline in local congregations. Thus the focus of this work is on the local church, specifically the causes and consequences of local congregational growth. Dean R. Hoge and David A. Roozen have provided a helpful cross-classification for categorizing the causes of congregational growth and decline.[1] These causes may be contextual (outside of the congregation) or institutional (internal to the congregation). Simultaneously, they may be either national or local in the scope of their influence. Other researchers have demonstrated the importance of local contextual factors (especially community demographics) in explaining local church growth.[2] In contrast, the findings we present in this essay focus on local institutional factors. While we recognize the potential importance of national and international factors and local contextual factors, our data force us to consider primarily local and institutional variables.

Using a national sample of approximately 400 Christian (Disciples of Christ) congregations, we found that in the period from 1978 to 1982 high levels of member involvement (as reflected in higher levels of per capita giving and higher church school participation rates) *preceded* increases in church size. However, growth itself appears to have lowered average levels of member involvement. If this is true, congregational growth may be a self-limiting process.

---

1. Hoge and Roozen, "Research on Factors Influencing Church Commitment," in *Understanding Church Growth and Decline: 1950-1978,* ed. Dean R. Hoge and David A. Roozen (New York: Pilgrim Press, 1979).
2. E.g., C. Kirk Hadaway, "The Demographic Environment and Church Membership Change," *Journal for the Scientific Study of Religion* 20 (1981): 77-89.

DATA SOURCES

The findings presented here are based on a reanalysis of data from an earlier study of the effects of different kinds of ministerial training (and other variables) on congregational loyalty to centralized denominational bureaucracies as reflected in giving to the denomination, making annual reports, and the like.[3]

Many of the variables used in this study come from the annual yearbooks of the Christian Church (Disciples of Christ). The earlier study used data from the yearbooks for 1978 through 1983 that were obtained in machine-readable form from DISCIPLEDATA. Because of the large number of Disciples churches (more than four thousand in the early 1980s), a one-tenth sample was drawn by starting at a randomly chosen church and taking every tenth church in the order listed in the yearbooks.

The earlier study collected additional information about each sampled church, including (among other measures) community location (urban versus rural), the racial group of the majority of members (in each church), and the median income for persons of that racial group in the surrounding county or metropolitan area. The data set also includes information on the seminaries attended by the ministers of each sampled church for each of the twelve years from 1971 through 1982. These data were collected through mailed surveys, phone interviews with knowledgeable informants, and published census reports.

Our reanalysis of these data is largely exploratory. We did not start with a hypothesis that determined the variables to be included in the study. Instead, like many secondary analyses, we began with an existing data set that contained some variables of interest. In our case, we were interested in congregational growth or decline. We then sought other study variables that might be associated with growth. The focus of our reanalysis on institutional rather than contextual variables is, therefore, not the result of any theoretical predisposition toward institutional factors; rather, it derives from the nature of the variables collected for the original study.

In order to measure congregational growth, we divided the number of participating members (i.e., official church members who either attend or give money to the church during the year) reported for a congregation in the 1983 yearbook (reporting figures for 1982) by the number of participating members in the 1979 yearbook (reporting figures for 1978). The resulting growth ratio equals 1 when there is no change, is greater than 1 for growing churches, and is less than 1 for declining churches. We chose the years 1979 and 1983 because the number of congregations filing annual reports to the denomination was higher in these years.

---

3. Eleanor Scott Meyers, "Professionalization and Centralization in the Free Church Tradition: The Political Economy of the Christian Church (Disciples of Christ)" (Ph.D. diss., University of Wisconsin-Madison, 1985).

Unfortunately, the growth ratio can only be calculated for some of the churches in the sample. There are 427 sampled churches in the 1979 yearbook data, but by 1983 sixteen of these churches were no longer in existence. More importantly, many Disciples churches fail to or choose not to submit annual reports to the denomination. Only 308 of the churches in the 1979 sample submitted reports; 326 filed reports in 1983. The yearbook staff carries forward participating membership figures from previous years for churches making no reports. However, since some churches make reports very infrequently, we chose to recode these cases to missing. No growth ratio could be calculated for churches that filed no reports for either 1979 or 1983. This eliminated all but 289 of the churches.

Thus the findings presented here regarding congregational growth are biased toward churches that make frequent reports. In other analyses we found that these tend to be churches whose members are predominantly white rather than black, churches located in the southeast region of the United States, and churches not undergoing an interim period between ministers. For other variables collected via surveys and informants (e.g., race), we have data for all or nearly all of the churches in the sample.

In preliminary analyses of the 427 sampled churches, we found that 46 percent are located in urban areas (standardized metropolitan statistical area as determined by the Bureau of Census), 90 percent are predominantly white, and all but 19 percent are located in the South East and South Central U.S. census region and in states bordering the Ohio River. We have no figures on the actual income of members, but we do have median income figures for the areas in which the churches are located. These figures suggest that Disciples churches are generally found in middle- to upper middle-class communities. The largest sampled church had about 4,000 official members and about 3,000 participating members. The smallest church had 7 official and participating members. The average sampled church had 287 official and 213 participating members in 1983. Average church school enrollment in this same year was only 63. The average annual budget for these churches was just over $75,000 in 1983.

As noted earlier, the study contains data on the seminary training (or lack of training) of the minister in each sampled church. Because the earlier study was interested in the professional linkages of ministers to the Disciples denomination, it classified the seminaries attended by church leaders into several groups. Leaders were first subdivided into those having seminary degrees and those without seminary degrees. Church leaders with seminary degrees were further subdivided according to where they received their training. Since leadership of a congregation may change frequently, a separate measure of the seminary training of the primary minister or church leader was made for each of the twelve years from 1971 through 1983. For each church we calculated the percentage of time (out of twelve possible years) in which it had leadership of each specific type.

We found among the sampled churches that the "average church" was without a minister 29 percent of the time and had a minister with no seminary training (an option in the Disciples denomination) 16 percent of the time. During those periods with seminary-trained ministers (55 percent of the time), 86 percent of the time these ministers had degrees either from one of the four Disciples seminaries or from other seminaries that are Disciples-related, often having a "Disciples House" on campus (e.g., the University of Chicago).

In looking at the years for which we have yearbook data, we found that, on average, churches made reports to the denomination in 4.4 out of the 6 years. The proportion of nonreporting churches and years approximately corresponds to the proportion of churches and years without a pastor. Regressions not described here show that some of the failure to report may have been due to administrative difficulties in making reports among churches with no pastor. It may also reflect that churches that choose to have no professional minister (an option among Disciples churches) also do not like to send reports to the denomination. Approximately 12 percent of the churches made no reports in any of the six yearbook years for which we have data.

PREDICTORS OF LOCAL CHURCH GROWTH

From the yearbook data we extracted three kinds of variables. For each church there are (1) variables taken from the 1979 yearbook (e.g., participating membership for 1978), (2) analogous variables taken from the 1983 yearbook (e.g., participating membership for 1982), and (3) the ratio of the value for 1983 divided by the value for 1979. We constructed similar change ratios for variables other than participating membership (e.g., change in per capita giving, etc.).

In the first phase of our analysis we use multiple regression to attempt to "predict" the change ratio for participating membership (growth). We limit ourselves to independent variables that are temporally prior to the dependent variable (the change ratio for participating membership — growth). The independent variables in these regressions are all taken from the 1979 yearbook or they are variables that did not change appreciably from 1979 to 1983 (e.g., race and urban/rural location), or they are variables whose values were largely determined prior to 1979 (the ministerial training variables). Thus, while we are not able to say with certainty that independent variables having large regression betas are the *causes* of growth or decline, we know at least that they are not the results of the growth we measured from 1979 to 1983.

Because of the exploratory nature of this analysis, we first present our findings and then we suggest several plausible explanations for our results. We are able to rule out some of these explanations through further analysis, but we are often left with one or several explanations that can be tested only through further research.

TABLE 1 Church Growth Related to Temporally Prior Variables

Variable	Coefficient	Standard Error	Standard Coefficient	Tolerance	T	P(2 Tail)
CONSTANT	0.994	0.089	0.000		11.202	0.000
ELITE	0.013	0.007	0.106	0.960	1.870	0.063
PDISI	-0.183	0.087	-0.120	0.950	-2.111	0.036
PNOSEM	-0.132	0.063	-0.124	0.880	-2.091	0.037
PCHSCH79	0.195	0.058	0.190	0.951	3.338	0.001
PCPTOT79	0.001	0.000	0.293	0.926	5.085	0.000
RACE	-0.325	0.080	-0.238	0.901	-4.077	0.000

DEP VAR: CHPTMEM
MULTIPLE R: .430
ADJUSTED SQUARED MULTIPLE R: .166

N: 272
SQUARED MULTIPLE R: .185
STANDARD ERROR OF ESTIMATE: 0.257

ANALYSIS OF VARIANCE

Source	Sum of Squares	DF	Mean Square	F-Ratio	P
REGRESSION	3.952	6	0.659	10.001	0.000
RESIDUAL	17.455	265	0.066		

We tried many regression equations in our attempt to predict growth rates. Table 1 shows one of our best preliminary regressions predicting church growth from temporally prior variables. The six independent variables used in this model account for 18.5 percent of the variation in church growth (CHPTMEM). These variables include: the proximity of a local church to Disciples college or seminary (ELITE); the proportion of years (out of twelve) that the congregation had ministerial leadership from individuals with a degree from a mainline, Disciples-related institution other than one of the four Disciples seminaries (PDISI), such as the University of Chicago or Vanderbilt; the proportion of years (out of twelve) that the congregation had ministerial leadership from individuals with no seminary training (PNOSEM); the proportion of participating members who were in church school in 1979 (PCHSCH79); per capita expenditures in 1979 (PCPTOT79); and congregations with predominately white membership (RACE).

According to Table 1, church growth is positively related to the per capita expenditures in 1979 (PCPTOT79). This variable is the total budget (expenses) divided by the number of participating members. Churches that spent more per member in 1979 were more likely to grow during the 1979 to 1983 time period. Among the standardized beta coefficients in Table 1, per capita spending is the largest, suggesting that it is the most important factor examined here. This is an important finding since, unlike community demographic variables, churches can work at changing their giving and spending patterns to affect planned change. This finding suggests that higher per capita spending *precedes* growth.

We separated the declining churches (those with growth ratios less than 1) from the growing churches (with ratios of 1 or more) and calculated the average per capita expenditures for each group in 1979. The growing churches spent $255 per participating member in 1979, while the declining churches spent only $212 per participating member; the churches that grew from 1979 to 1983 spent about 20 percent more per person in 1979 than did the churches that declined.

There are several possible explanations for these findings. The straight-forward explanation is that greater spending buys additional staff time and/or competency, better programs, and larger, more attractive facilities to attract and accommodate more people. Alternatively, it may be that high per capita spending simply measures the commitment and involvement of the congregation. The relationship with church growth may indicate, as Dean M. Kelley suggests, that high-commitment churches grow faster or decline less than low-commitment churches.[4] We have no independent measure of commitment to test this explanation.

It may be that per capita spending is only a reflection of church size. Large and resource-rich churches may spend less on maintenance and other fixed costs and thus be able to devote a larger percentage of their budget to outreach and programs that attract new members. However, the actual size of the budget in 1979 is not correlated with church growth. What seems to be important is the amount given per member regardless of whether the church (and its budget) is large or small. Moreover, in other analyses not shown here we found, as we expected, that large churches spend a lower proportion of their budgets on operating expenses and more on outreach to organizations outside the church, but the proportions spent on the three budget areas had no effect on growth from 1979 to 1983.

Finally, higher per capita spending may simply reflect greater member wealth, which may somehow be associated with church growth. This appears to be a weak explanation. First, it is well known that churches having wealthier members give a smaller *proportion* of their income to their church.[5] Second, the hypothesis that congregations with wealthy members would grow faster than less wealthy congregations appears to run counter to the general trend that high-growth, high-commitment denominations tend to have somewhat less wealthy, less educated, evangelical members.[6]

As in all such analyses, one must proceed with caution, since there may be other variables not included in the study that account for the observed relationship between per capita spending and growth. In other analyses not

4. Kelley, *Why Conservative Churches Are Growing* (New York: Harper & Row, 1972).
5. See, e.g., Rodney Stark and Charles Glock, *American Piety* (Berkeley and Los Angeles: University of California Press, 1968).
6. Stark and Glock, *American Piety;* Kelley, *Why Conservative Churches Are Growing;* Wade Clark Roof and William McKinney, *American Mainline Religion: Its Changing Shape and Future* (New Brunswick, N.J.: Rutgers University Press, 1987).

included here, we have attempted to account for any such spurious or indirect relationships arising from other variables included in our data. In these analyses we paid special attention to variables that are predictors of the independent variables used to predict growth in Table 1. These analyses suggest that per capita spending has a *direct* effect on growth.

Table 1 shows that the proportion of participating members who are in church school in 1979 (PCHSCH79) has a positive effect on church growth. Churches with proportionately large Sunday Schools in 1979 grew faster than other churches. The average church school participation rate for growing churches is 62 percent, compared to 46 percent in the declining churches.

It is interesting to consider what aspects of church school programs lead to growth. One would think that a church offering larger and (one assumes) more diverse programs would attract more people. But interestingly, the actual size of the church school in 1979 has little effect on growth. Again, it is the *proportion* of participating members who are involved that is important. This suggests that other factors underlie this finding. We identify three possibilities.

First, it may be that churches with high levels of church school participation are younger churches (in terms of the average age of the participants). High church school participation rates seem likely in churches where there are many children (who will be in the church school) and adults who attend church school because their children are in church school at the same time. (The yearbook includes both youth and adults in the count of church school members.) Young churches are more likely to be located in areas experiencing an influx of new residents (areas where younger couples can afford to buy homes). Thus it may be that the church growth is due to community growth rather than the proportion of members in the church school.

Second, some prior variable such as theological conservatism, not included in our data, may account for both growth and high church school involvement. For example, a highly committed, evangelistic congregation may be more active in its recruitment of new members. Unfortunately, our data do not include any measures of orthodoxy or commitment other than per capita expenses.

Third, another theory suggests that high church school involvement facilitates friendship among church members and allows members greater opportunities for fellowship. Other research suggests that fellowship, or the lack of it, is an important reason that churchgoers select a particular church.[7] Other research also suggests that church school participation is one of the major means whereby such fellowship ties develop.[8] Thus churches with high church school participation rates may tend to be churches that offer newcomers

---

7. Daniel V. A. Olson, "Networks of Religious Belonging in Five Baptist Congregations" (Ph.D. diss., University of Chicago, 1987); and "Church Friendships: Boon or Barrier to Church Growth?" *Journal for the Scientific Study of Religion* 28 (December 1989): 432-47.

8. Olson, "Networks of Religious Belonging in Five Baptist Congregations."

more fellowship opportunities and hence churches that grow more easily. Our data do not allow us to test whether such an explanation lies behind our finding.

The beta for RACE suggest that black Disciples churches grow faster than white Disciples churches. However, several caveats must be mentioned. First, there are only forty-five predominately black churches in the total sample. Of these, only thirteen made reports in both 1979 and 1983, and so we could calculate growth rates for only thirteen. The average increase for the thirteen churches, however, was 25 percent compared to a loss of about 1 percent among white churches reporting in both years. As noted above, churches experiencing growth may be more likely to make reports (due to added resources, pride, etc.). This tendency may be even greater among the black churches, where reporting rates are even lower than among white Disciples churches. So the calculated growth rates for reporting black churches may be quite a bit higher than the real average for all black Disciples churches. Despite the fact that there are only thirteen churches with valid data, and despite the fact that these thirteen may not be very representative, a 26 percent difference is very large. The matter deserves further investigation.

The ELITE variable, indicating a church location near one of the Disciples colleges or seminaries ("an elite training center"), appears to have a modest positive effect on church growth. It is difficult to know exactly why. Our guess is that this variable is strongly correlated with some other variable related to growth, but we do not know what that variable is. Some moderately strong correlations with region, income, and urban/rural differences are seen with the elite variable, but none of these variables is related to growth. It may be that areas around Disciples colleges and seminaries have higher concentrations of Disciples-raised persons in the general population. This could increase the potential for rapid growth, but one would not expect the effect to last after such areas became saturated with Disciples churches. Other factors may be that the increased Disciples visibility produced by these institutions and/or educational programs and leadership made available to the churches by these institutions encourages growth.

According to Table 1, having a minister trained at an independent Disciples-related institution other than one of the four Disciples seminaries (e.g., the University of Chicago or Vanderbilt) apparently depresses growth. If one assumes that such seminaries are theologically more liberal than other seminaries training Disciples leaders,[9] then it may be that the relative liberalism of the leaders and the churches that select them underlies this finding: more conservative churches grow more quickly. In analyses not included in this essay, we found evidence that churches with leaders trained in evangelical seminaries grow much faster than other Disciples churches. However, there were only seven churches in our sample that had evangel-

9. This is only an assumption, but it would seem to be supported by the work of James L. Guth and Helen Lee Turner on p. 385 in this volume.

ically trained ministers, and this is too small a number on which to base any conclusions.

Table 1 shows that churches with ministers having no professional training (an option among Disciples churches) are less likely to grow. Two kinds of explanations seem plausible. It may be that professional training better enables ministers to nurture growth, or it may be that churches that cannot afford or do not want professional leaders do not grow as well as other churches. This analysis cannot separate these classes of explanations.

In addition to the variables that are directly related to growth described above, there are a number of variables that have no *direct* relationship with growth even though one might think they would. These include church size, total budget, region, average income in the community, rapid turnover in church leadership, and urban/rural location. While some of these variables are correlated with growth, regression reveals that these relationships are either spurious or mediated by the variables having direct relationships to growth.

The most interesting of these is church size. There is a weak negative relationship between church size and growth (correlation equals -.1202). In 1979 the average size of churches that grew was 187, while declining churches averaged 279 participating members. However, this relationship disappears when one controls for church school participation rates and per capita giving. Large churches are less likely to grow because their participation and giving rates are lower, not because they are large. Large churches with high participation rates are just as likely to grow as small churches with similar participation rates.

In the regressions above, per capita spending in 1979 is the strongest predictor of growth. We explore this relationship further in Table 2 (p. 518). This table resembles Table 1 except that the category of per capita expenditures has been divided into three categories: operating expenses, including all local expenditures for salaries, programs, fuel bills, and so on (PCAPOP79); capital expenses, including maintenance and debt payment on buildings and equipment (PCPCAP79); and total outreach, including money sent to the Disciples denomination and other agencies (PCAPTO79).

Note that breaking down expenditures into three categories increases the amount of explained variation in growth to just over 20 percent. Table 2 suggests that the greatest effect on future growth comes from per capita spending on *operating expenses*. Unfortunately, our data do not allow us to determine which kinds of operating expenditures are most related to growth. Spending on capital expenses also has some positive effect. It may be that churches that build new additions or refurbish old buildings later experience increased growth. It is more likely, however, that it reflects the heavy capital expenditures of churches with new buildings in new, quickly growing communities. Per capita spending on outreach appears not to be related to future growth. Note that outreach does not include money for local church salaries

TABLE 2 Church Growth Related to Per Capita Spending

Variable	Coefficient	Standard Error	Standard Coefficient	Tolerance	T	P(2 Tail)
CONSTANT	0.985	0.088	0.000	.	11.174	0.000
ELITE	0.012	0.007	0.103	0.960	1.839	0.067
PDISI	-0.163	0.086	-0.107	0.942	-1.898	0.059
PNOSEM	-0.140	0.062	-0.131	0.878	-2.240	0.026
PCHSCH79	0.182	0.058	0.177	0.940	3.123	0.002
RACE	-0.316	0.079	-0.232	0.899	-3.997	0.000
PCAPOP79	0.001	0.000	0.297	0.809	4.867	0.000
PCPCAP79	0.001	0.000	0.154	0.985	2.780	0.006
PCAPTO79	-0.001	0.001	-0.083	0.816	-1.369	0.172

DEP VAR: CHPTMEM
MULTIPLE R: .454
ADJUSTED SQUARED MULTIPLE R: .182

N: 272
SQUARED MULTIPLE R: .206
STANDARD ERROR OF ESTIMATE: 0.254

ANALYSIS OF VARIANCE

Source	Sum of Squares	DF	Mean Square	F-Ratio	P
REGRESSION	4.411	8	0.551	8.531	0.000
RESIDUAL	16.997	263	0.065		

supporting either evangelistic or social programs but only money sent to other organizations including the Disciples denomination.

CONCLUSION

Throughout this essay we have been cautious about asserting causal relationships between variables. Despite these cautions, a likely pattern of events seems to emerge from our analysis. Churches that grew the most and declined the least between 1979 and 1983 were the churches that had higher participation rates and per capita spending in 1979. While per capita spending is not the same as per capita giving, the two variables are closely linked in most churches. It strikes us that both church school involvement and member giving are indicators of church commitment and that this commitment leads, in some way, to church growth. Though we suggest several possibilities, the mechanism of the commitment/growth connection cannot be ascertained from our data.

Ironically, our findings also suggest that growth may lead to decreasing rates of member involvement and giving. Several explanations are possible. It may be, as we suggest above, that the lower rates are due to the greater number of newcomers in growing churches, who are less likely to be as committed to church participation and giving as longtime members. However, it is also possible that growth alienates some of the longtime members, who then reduce their participation and giving.[10]

Whatever the cause of declining participation in growing churches, our findings suggest that church growth may be a self-limiting process. High levels of involvement lead to growth, which then lowers levels of involvement and thus lowers future growth. As mentioned earlier, we found in analyses not included in this essay that participation rates (reflected in church school participation rates and per capita expenditures) are lower in large churches than in small churches. Whether it is their past growth or something about large size itself that is responsible for lower rates of participation and giving, the evidence from large churches further suggests a self-limiting mechanism restraining growth.

This may be only one of several growth-restraining mechanisms at work in congregations. Lyle E. Schaller has suggested that physical plant limitations, especially seating and parking capacities, may have a similar function.[11] Other studies indicate that the formation of cliques may also limit congregational growth by limiting opportunities for fellowship.[12]

If our interpretation of these findings is correct, they suggest two strategies for church leaders interested in denominational growth or simply in increasing the number of churchgoers within a community. The first is to raise levels of participation and giving within each church. Our data suggest that church size is not itself a barrier to future growth, only the lower levels of participation and giving found in large churches. Of course, in saying this, we realize we are only restating the problem in terms of commitment levels rather than in terms of membership gains and losses. If we only knew how to raise commitment levels, membership gains would probably follow. What this study seems to suggest is that commitment to what is happening within the congregation — as made evident through increased levels of participation and giving — is importantly tied to church growth.

While our findings do not tell us how to raise church commitment, they do suggest that active church school programs may be one of the most important programmatic efforts leading to church growth. They also suggest that increased per capita giving precedes growth. Churches wanting to grow (whatever their size) may initially need to spend beyond their means to establish the programs or facilities that are the basis of future growth.

A second strategy for denominational growth may be to recognize the natural limitations on church size and growth and focus instead on new church development. Our data show that smaller churches have higher church school participation rates, higher per capita giving, and higher percentage growth. Such a strategy is premised on the assumption that there is something about

---

10. See Lyle E. Schaller, *Assimilating New Members* (Nashville: Abingdon Press, 1978).

11. Schaller, *Growing Pains* (Nashville: Abingdon Press, 1983).

12. Olson, "Church Friendships," substantiating a suggestion by Schaller in *Assimilating New Members.*

small size that increases participation. While there are a number of reasons for accepting this premise, it may also be true that some people avoid small churches for this very reason: they prefer the anonymity of large churches to the visibility of small churches, where high levels of participation and commitment may be expected. A reemphasis on new small churches, without removing resources from large churches, might avoid some of the natural limits to growth and leave the larger churches intact as a haven for those seeking a low-commitment membership.

These suggestions are somewhat speculative in that they go a bit beyond what our data actually reveal. Nevertheless, we think they suggest fruitful directions for further analysis.

Attrition and Retention among Christian Church (Disciples of Christ) Congregations in Three Metropolitan Regions: A Mail Survey of 1,149 Active and Inactive Members

Walter R. Schumm, Ruth C. Hatch, Jon Hevelone, and Kimberly R. Schumm

Membership attrition among most mainline Protestant denominations during the previous two decades is a widely recognized phenomenon.[1] W. J. Hartman reports the loss of nearly two million members from the United Methodist Church since 1964![2] The Christian Church (Disciples of Christ)

1. See Wade Clark Roof and William McKinney, *American Mainline Religion: Its Changing Shape and Future* (New Brunswick, N.J.: Rutgers University Press, 1987); C. Kirk Hadaway, *Growing off the Plateau: A Survey of the 1988 "Church on the Plateau" Survey* (Nashville: Research Services Department of the Sunday School Board of the Southern Baptist Convention, 1989); Dean M. Kelley, *Why Conservative Churches Are Growing*, 2d ed. (New York: Harper & Row, 1977); Peter L. Berger, "American Religion: Conservative Upsurge, Liberal Prospects," in *Liberal Protestantism: Realities and Possibilities*, ed. R. S. Michaelsen and Wade Clark Roof (New York: Pilgrim Press, 1986), pp. 19-36.

2. Hartman, "Factors Related to Church Growth and Decline," *Discipleship Trends* 5 (February 1987): 1-4.

We would like to express our appreciation to many who provided us with technical guidance and encouragement, including D. Newell Williams, C. Kirk Hadaway, Herb Miller, Warren Hartman, Paul Pallmeyer, Margaret Owen-Clark, David C. Downing, Colbert D. Cartwright, Robert E. Stewart, and the many pastors and congregation members who helped with or participated in the study. We also express our appreciation for the tireless efforts of Lori Nighswonger, Connie Fechter, Linda Frey, and Sigrid Vovk in their administrative and secretarial support of the project. —WALTER R. SCHUMM, RUTH C. HATCH, JON HEVELONE, and KIMBERLY R. SCHUMM

lost at least 30 percent of its membership between 1965 and 1985.[3] In order better to understand this phenomenon, we conducted a survey of current and former members of the Christian Church (Disciples of Christ). Our survey complements previous surveys that have sampled the entire Christian Church (Disciples of Christ) and new members.[4] Rather than focusing on who Disciples are or on the reasons individuals first become members as these earlier surveys did, we focused on why members decrease their involvement in their congregations, switch to other denominations, and become religiously inactive altogether. Since we surveyed current and former members within congregations, we also chose to investigate congregational growth and decline as a function of the same factors examined with respect to individual members.

Well over twenty explanations have been developed within secular academic circles for variations in church activity and growth. It became apparent to us in the early stages of the development of the survey that it would be impossible to thoroughly test each hypothesis about church activity or growth.[5] In fact, there are well over one hundred specific factors thought to be related to our dependent variables. All of these hypotheses can be identified as pointing to the influence of either contextual or institutional factors. The relative influence of local contextual factors versus local institutional factors has been debated for some time.[6] Contextual factors thought to be of importance include the affluence of the local community, presence of middle-class neighborhoods, absence of minorities, local population growth, and absence of competing congregations.[7] Contextual factors are usually not under the control of the local

3. R. D. Perrin, "American Religion in the Post-Aquarian Age: Values and Demographic Factors in Church Growth and Decline," *Journal for the Scientific Study of Religion* 28 (1989): 75-89; Herb Miller, "Notebook," *The Disciple*, October 1986, p. 8.

4. For the survey of the entire Church, see Ann Updegraff-Spleth and Charles Brackbill, *Report on Disciple Churchwide Survey* (Indianapolis: Christian Church [Disciples of Christ] Division of Homeland Ministries, 1986); for the survey of new members, see C. W. Sayre and Herb Miller, *The Christian Church (Disciples of Christ) New Members Study: A Final Report* (Indianapolis: Christian Church [Disciples of Christ] Division of the Homeland Ministries, 1985).

5. Regarding these hypotheses, see W. Arn and Donald McGavran, *How to Grow a Church* (Glendale, Cal.: Regal, 1973); Donald McGavran, *Understanding Church Growth* (Grand Rapids: William B. Eerdmans, 1970); Donald McGavran and W. C. Arn, *Ten Steps for Church Growth* (New York: Harper & Row, 1977); Donald McGavran and G. G. Hunter III, *Church Growth: Strategies That Work* (Nashville: Abingdon Press, 1980).

6. See, e.g., Dean R. Hoge and David A. Roozen, *Understanding Church Growth and Decline* (New York: Pilgrim Press, 1979); William McKinney and Dean R. Hoge, "Community and Congregational Factors in the Growth and Decline of Protestant Churches," *Journal for the Scientific Study of Religion* 22 (1983): 51-66; David A. Roozen, "Church Dropouts: Changing Patterns of Disengagement and Re-entry," *Review of Religious Research* 21 (1980): 427-50; E. L. Perry, J. H. Davis, R. T. Doyle, and J. E. Dyble, "Toward a Typology of Unchurched Protestants," *Review of Religious Research* 21 (1980): 388-404.

7. See R. W. Rathge and G. A. Goreham, "The Influence of Economic and Demographic Factors on Rural Church Viability," *Journal for the Scientific Study of Religion* 28 (1989): 59-74.

congregation, even though they may impact on the potential for that congregation's growth. Institutional factors concern things that can be changed by congregations or pastors (i.e., internal improvements). We decided to focus on a few of the most important hypotheses, placing more emphasis on institutional factors than on contextual factors.

1. In *Why Conservative Churches Are Growing,* Dean Kelley proposes that conservative church groups tend to experience more growth than liberal church groups because certain elements of conservatism foster more cohesion and evangelism. Kelley's hypothesis remains controversial even though it has been extensively researched.[8] One recent study claims that because liberal groups have become secularized they have presented a less potent spiritual message and hence have been in decline with respect to conservative denominations since 1776![9] However, having found minimal differences in overall membership declines among Disciples and more conservative sister denominations, L. C. Keene has challenged the Kelley hypothesis, at least with respect to the Christian Church (Disciples of Christ).[10]

2. Another explanation for church activity focuses on the importance of the pastor. Common sense as well as research supports the idea that the pastor plays a key role in church retention or attrition.[11] However, Hartman has suggested that the pastor may be less important in churches with less than 100 members and that leadership struggles in churches with 50 to 150

8. See R. W. Bibby, "Why Conservative Churches Really Are Growing: Kelley Revisited," *Journal for the Scientific Study of Religion* 17 (1978): 129-37; G. D. Bouma, "The Real Reason One Conservative Church Grew," *Review of Religious Research* 20 (1979): 127-37; Robert Wuthnow, "Religious Commitment and Conservatism: In Quest of an Elusive Relationship," in *Religion in Sociological Perspective,* ed. Charles Y. Glock (Belmont, Cal.: Wadsworth 1973); Dean R. Hoge and D. T. Polk, "A Test of Theories of Protestant Church Participation and Commitment," *Review of Religious Research* 21 (1980): 315-29; A. W. Black, "The Impact of Theological Orientation and of Breadth of Perspective on Church Members' Attitudes and Behaviors: Roof, Mol, and Kaill Revisited," *Journal for the Scientific Study of Religion* 24 (1985): 87-100; R. S. Warner, "Research Note: Visits to a Growing Evangelical and Declining Liberal Church in 1978," *Sociological Analysis* 44 (1983): 243-54; William McKinney and Dean R. Hoge, "Community and Congregational Factors in the Growth and Decline of Protestant Churches"; Hadaway, *Growing off the Plateau;* J. P. O'Hara, "A Research Note on the Sources of Adult Church Commitment among Those Who Were Regular Attenders during Childhood," *Review of Religious Research* 21 (1980): 462-67; M. K. Roberts and J. S. Davidson, "The Nature and Sources of Religious Involvement," *Review of Religious Research* 25 (1984): 334-50; J. P. Alston and W. A. McIntosh, "An Assessment of the Determinants of Religious Participation," *Sociological Quarterly* 20 (1979): 49-62.

9. R. Finke and R. Stark, "How the Upstart Sects Won America: 1776-1850," *Journal for the Scientific Study of Religion* 28 (1989): 27-44.

10. Keene, "Heirs of Stone and Campbell on the Pacific Slope: A Sociological Approach," in *Impact: Disciples of Christ on the Pacific Slope,* Forrest F. Reed Lectures, 9th series (Claremont, Cal.: School of Theology at Claremont, 1984).

11. Alston and McIntosh, "An Assessment of the Determinants of Religious Participation"; C. P. Wagner, *Your Church Can Grow* (Glendale, Cal.: Regal, 1976); Hadaway, *Growing off the Plateau.*

members may dampen their growth potential.[12] Perhaps for similar reasons, C. P. Wagner identifies 150 members as a minimum threshold for rapid growth by a congregation.[13]

3. Research has consistently supported the idea that a climate of love and acceptance, of belonging and meaning in a congregation, helps retain members.[14] Some research has supported the need for church members to be involved in small groups in order to prevent attrition.[15] Hartman goes so far as to say that members often drop out of a congregation if they don't become integrated into a small group of some type within two or three years after first joining a congregation.[16] F. R. Newbern proposes that people join a church to meet basic needs (he uses Maslow's hierarchy of physiological, safety, love, esteem, and self-actualization needs).[17] However, we are not aware of research that has attempted to correlate measures of those five needs with church member retention or attrition.

4. Another explanation involves the phenomenon of "transfer ecumenism."[18] According to this hypothesis, when people move away from their old congregation, they are likely to "shop around" for their next congregation. The tendency to shop around rather than automatically attend a local congregation affiliated with their denomination may be magnified when people perceive more variation in the characteristics of the congregations of their denomination. Even if they really liked the former congregation, they may not be sure that a congregation under the same denominational umbrella in the new location will be as compatible if they believe that congregations vary a great deal in characteristics such as friendliness, doctrinal views, worship styles, and the like. The more they fear significant differences between the former and the new congregation, the more they will be inclined to shop around for the "best" congregation, regardless of its denominational affiliation. The decentralized structure of the Christian Church (Disciples of Christ) and wide variations in values and beliefs among

12. Hartman, "Factors Related to Church Growth and Decline"; and "They Aren't All Alike," *Discipleship Trends,* February 1985, pp. 1-4.

13. Wagner, *Your Church Can Grow.*

14. D. B. McGaw, "Commitment and Religious Community: A Comparison of a Charismatic and Mainline Congregation," *Journal for the Scientific Study of Religion* 18 (1980): 146-63; Roberts and Davidson, "The Nature and Sources of Religious Involvement"; Warren J. Hartman, "Large Churches Are Complex," *Discipleship Trends,* October 1986, pp. 1-4; Hadaway, *Growing off the Plateau.*

15. R. L. Dudley and D. Cummings, "A Study of Factors Relating to Church Growth in the North American Division of Seventh-Day Adventists," *Review of Religious Research* 24 (1983): 322-33.

16. Hartman, "Large Churches Are Complex."

17. Newbern, "The Conflict of Goals in Church Membership" (D.Min. diss., School of Theology at Claremont, 1977); A. H. Maslow, "A Theory of Human Motivation," *Psychological Review* 50 (1943): 370-96.

18. See Herb Miller, "Notebook," *The Disciple,* August 1986, p. 49.

both laity and clergy may increase its local diversity and the impact of transfer ecumenism.[19]

5. *Internal structure* has also been tied to church growth and attrition. The size of the congregation and the average income and education of its members have been cited as important factors, though we think the research is not yet conclusive.[20]

6. *Localism* has also been cited as an explanation for church activity; in fact, the localism hypothesis has attracted a great deal of attention.[21] The idea is that a local (as opposed to cosmopolitan) orientation is congruent with the maintenance of religious plausibility structures. People who are involved in their community and thus tied to social networks that serve to make them accountable for their behavior should, according to the theory, find church attendance less of a hindrance to their personal lifestyle. One recent study found that frequent moving reduced friendship ties and church attendance.[22]

7. *Child-rearing* theory has also received some support. The idea is that couples, especially those with school-aged children, seek out congregations to gain assistance in socializing their children in prosocial, if not religious, values. Congregations that do not develop such programs for parents will (1) fail to attract the parents and (2) fail to retain the children when they grow up. Though the findings are not always consistent, there appears to be some support for this theory.[23]

8. *Evangelism* has also been cited as a cause of growth. Herb Miller reports that the primary reason by far for new members first attending a

19. On the variegated nature of the Disciples, see Keene, "Heirs of Stone and Campbell on the Pacific Slope"; Updegraff-Spleth and Brackbill, *Report on Disciple Churchwide Survey;* J. E. Craig and R. L. Friedly, "Who Are the Disciples of Christ?" in *Religions of America,* ed. L. Rosten (New York: Simon & Schuster, 1975), pp. 83-95; H. E. Quinley, "The Dilemma of an Activist Church: Protestant Religion in the Sixties and Seventies," *Journal for the Scientific Study of Religion* 13 (1974): 1-21.

20. See Wagner, *Your Church Can Grow;* Perrin, "American Religion in the Post-Aquarian Age"; Rathge and Goreham, "The Influence of Economic and Demographic Factors on Rural Church Viability"; Dudley and Cummings, "A Study of Factors Relating to Church Growth in the North American Division of Seventh-Day Adventists."

21. Wade Clark Roof, *Community and Commitment* (New York: Elsevier, 1978); Wade Clark Roof and R. B. Perkins, "On Conceptualizing Salience in Religious Commitment," *Journal for the Scientific Study of Religion* 14 (1975): 111-28; Black, "The Impact of Theological Orientation and of Breadth of Perspective on Church Members' Attitudes and Behaviors"; Wade Clark Roof and Dean R. Hoge, "Church Involvement in America: Social Factors Affecting Membership and Participation," *Review of Religious Research* 21 (1980): 405-26.

22. M. R. Welch and J. Baltzell, "Geographic Mobility, Social Integration, and Church Attendance," *Journal for the Scientific Study of Religion* 23 (1984): 75-91.

23. Dean R. Hoge and J. W. Carroll, "Determinants of Commitment and Participation in Suburban Protestant Churches," *Journal for the Scientific Study of Religion* 17 (1978): 107-27; Alston and McIntosh, "An Assessment of the Determinants of Religious Participation"; Roof and Hoge, "Church Involvement in America"; D. P. Mueller and P. W. Cooper, "Religious Interest and Involvement of Young Adults: A Research Note," *Review of Religious Research* 27 (1986): 245-54.

Disciples congregation was having been invited by a member.[24] With one exception, most scholars cite evangelism as a key factor in church growth, a necessary way of making up for ordinary attrition due to deaths, transfers, and so on.[25] C. Kirk Hadaway reports a large correlation (r = .56) between rapid growth and a pastor's rating of his congregation's success in evangelism.[26] Thus, our eighth hypothesis was that member attitudes toward inviting others to attend their local congregation's worship services would correlate with retention.

9. We derived a ninth hypothesis from conversations we had at the Christian Theological Seminary in December 1988; there, many pastors and representatives from minority congregations claimed to be doing well in evangelism and in growth and retention. Therefore, we added a test of minority versus Anglo congregational makeup to our hypotheses.

10. Some research suggests that *value structures* affect church retention and attrition. The hypothesis is that conservative moral values are associated with retention and growth.[27] The basic idea is that modern values in such areas as sexuality, divorce, and drugs are incompatible with traditional Christian virtues, and individuals who adopt such values will be more likely to reject church participation along with other conventional values.

11. R. S. Michaelson and Wade Clark Roof have suggested that role conflicts between church activity and job or family concerns may encourage members to become less active, if not drop out altogether, as a way of reducing the role conflict.[28]

12. A final hypothesis concerns the impact of regional differences on the Christian Church (Disciples of Christ).[29] Growth rates and other factors may vary from one region of the United States to another. Furthermore, region may interact with other factors in predicting retention or attrition. Our general concern here was how things might differ in the Los Angeles area compared to the basic heartland of the Christian Church (Disciples of Christ) in the Midwest and southern plains (e.g., Kansas City and Dallas/Fort Worth).

24. Herb Miller, "Notebook," *The Disciple,* May 1986, p. 49; and "Notebook," *The Disciple,* September 1986, p. 51; Sayre and Miller, *The Christian Church (Disciples of Christ) New Members Study.*

25. Dudley and Cummings, "A Study of Factors Relating to Church Growth in the North American Division of Seventh-Day Adventists"; Wagner, *Your Church Can Grow;* Hartman, "Factors Related to Church Growth and Decline"; Warren J. Hartman, "Small Yet Big," *Discipleship Trends,* April 1984, pp. 1-4. The exception is R. W. Bibby and M. B. Brinkerhoff, "Circulation of the Saints Revisited: A Longitudinal Look at Conservative Church Growth," *Journal for the Scientific Study of Religion* 22 (1983): 253-62.

26. Hadaway, *Growing off the Plateau,* p. 13.

27. Roof and Hoge, "Church Involvement in America"; Perry, Davis, Doyle, and Dyble, "Toward a Typology of Unchurched Protestants."

28. Michaelson and Roof, *Liberal Protestantism: Realities and Possibilities* (New York: Pilgrim Press, 1986).

29. See the essay by Roger W. Stump on pp. 445-68 in this volume.

METHODOLOGY

SURVEY PROCEDURES

We selected the Kansas City, Dallas/Fort Worth, and Los Angeles metropolitan areas for the study in an attempt to compare two traditionally strong Disciples regions with a region that had experienced higher rates of attrition in recent decades. The church response rate based on the initial mailed request was low. Those churches that did not respond were contacted by telephone. Member surveys were mailed between February and July 1989 from Manhattan, Kansas, to the three regions. We used D. A. Dillman's total design survey methodology, sending one letter with a replacement questionnaire and two postcards as follow-ups for those members who had not yet responded.[30] We revised the timing of the second postcard, however, sending it a week ahead of the second mailing rather than a week after, because we had the impression that many people might be willing to read a postcard but not to open an envelope that might appear to be a funding request from a university with which they were not associated. To deal with the latter problem, we added a note on the outside of the follow-up mailings to Dallas and Los Angeles stating what the material was for and requesting any recipients who had never been members of the Christian Church (Disciples of Christ) to refuse the envelope and check a blank space to indicate that they had never been members. We had a higher return of ineligibles in that category from the Los Angeles and Dallas/Fort Worth regions than from the Kansas City region.

The participation rate from all the churches was really quite excellent; those churches that declined were in most cases simply trying to protect the privacy of their members. In the end it was necessary to send packets to seven churches in Kansas City, twelve in Texas, and thirty-two in California in order to gain their participation (packets contained enough questionnaires and return envelopes to allow the churches to send them randomly, as we requested, to four percent of their membership—active and inactive). Final follow-up surveys were mailed to Texas and California in mid-July 1989. The cut-off date for analysis of the data presented in this report was 24 September 1989. Participation rates for congregations and members are presented in Tables 1 and 2, respectively (p. 528).

SAMPLE CHARACTERISTICS

The sample was approximately two-thirds women and one-third men. Ages of the respondents ranged from 18 to 98, with an average of 52.9 years.

---

30. Dillman, *Mail and Telephone Surveys: The Total Design Method* (New York: Wiley, 1978).

TABLE 1 Participation Rates for Christian Church (Disciples of Christ) Congregations in Three Metropolitan Regions

Categories	Kansas City	Dallas/Fort Worth	Los Angeles	Totals
Total Listed	80	44	92	217
Ineligibles[a]	14	2	15	23
Total Eligible Churches	66	42	77	185
Decline to Participate	5	1	3	9
Agreed to Participate at First;				
No Responses Received	2	3	8	13
Total Participating Churches	59	38	66	163
Participation Rate	89.4%	90.5%	85.7%	88.1%

a. Ineligible congregations included those that were too small (less than 60 to 75 participating members) and those that were closing down or were not members of the denomination.

TABLE 2 Participation Rates among Current and Former Church Members

Categories	Kansas City	Dallas/Fort Worth	Los Angeles	Totals
Total Members Contacted among Participating Churches	1,024[a]	638	720	2,382
Ineligible Members[b]	97	30	69	196
Deceased	1	1	3	5
Incorrect Address/Moved	82	13	12	107
Never a Church Member	6	5	20	31
Miscellaneous	8	11	34	53
Total Eligible Members	927	608	651	2,186
Members Declining to Participate	453	311	273	1,037
Returned Refusal Postcards	242	27	47	316
No Response Either Way	211	284	226	721
Members Responding[c]	474	297	378	1,149
Participation Rate	51.1%	48.8%	58.1%	52.6%

a. In order to improve the response from Kansas City, where she lives, Ruth Hatch tried to contact 173 people by telephone from among those who had not responded to the survey after the Kansas City mailings. She obtained the following results:

Telephone number not available	47	27.0%
Not at home (no answer)	38	21.8%
Refused to participate	26	14.9%
Already completed the survey	22	12.6%
Requested a replacement survey	19	10.9%
Too ill to participate (ineligible)	9	5.2%
Had moved away (ineligible)	9	5.2%
Had never been a member (ineligible)	4	2.3%
Had not lost survey, would still do it	3	1.7%

Since less than 13 percent of the people (22 individuals returned surveys in response to the time-consuming calls, the senior author terminated the telephone follow-ups.

b. Category included adolescents under age 18, elderly, and anyone otherwise unable to complete a questionnaire for medical reasons.

c. As of 7 November 1989.

Many (31.3%) of the respondents were age 65 or older, somewhat more than in a similar sampling of United Methodist Church members (21.3%).[31] However, there were more baby boomers, age 19 to 34 (28%), than in the United Methodist church (12.4%). Most of the subjects were married (66.5%) or remarried (6.9%), with smaller numbers never married (5.3%), widowed (11.9%), divorced (6.8%), separated (0.6%), or living together (1.1%). The average level of formal education was 14.5 years with a range of 2 to 25 years. The largest number of respondents had total pretax incomes in 1988 of $25,000 to $49,999 (41.5%), with 24.8 percent less than $25,000, 20.9 percent between $50,000 and $75,000, and 12.8 percent over $75,000. Not surprisingly, since we sampled metropolitan regions, most subjects were from large cities (45.2% from cities of over 250,000), but others were from medium size cities (30.0% — 50,000 to 250,000), small cities (14.3% — 10,000 to 49,999), small towns (6.4% — population of less than 10,000), and rural areas (4.1%). Though respondents had lived in their present neighborhoods from zero to 78 years, the average tenure was 20.2 years. Respondents had moved an average of 1.2 times within the previous ten years, though the range was from zero to fourteen. Respondents had been members of their specific Disciples congregation from zero to 76 years, averaging 18.7 years. Denominational tenure as a Christian Church (Disciples of Christ) member was longer, zero to 80 years, averaging 29.7 years. Of those who responded to the optional question about racial heritage, 93.1% were Caucasian, 2.6% were black, 1.7% Hispanic, with 1.1% Asian, 0.2% American Indian, and 1.3% other. The average age for first confession of faith in Christ was 14.5 years, but 59.5 percent had made their first confession of faith before they reached 13 years of age. While 27.9 percent said that they had a significant religious conversion experience, 22.2 percent were not sure and most (43.2%) said they had not. The average travel time to church was 14 minutes. Most subjects reported attending religious services or activities once a week (39.3%), with 26.7 percent attending more often, and 18.7 percent attending once to three times a month, with others (15.4%) attending less than once a month. Very few (3.2%) subjects gave no income each year for religious purposes, while others gave up to 4.9 percent (38.9%), between 5.0 and 9.9 percent (29.2%), 10 percent (13.8%), and over 10 percent (7.6%).

In terms of the breakdown by activity level, 66.3 percent described themselves as active, 22.1 percent as less active, 4.5 percent as having switched to another church, and 4.2 percent as having stopped attending church anywhere.

31. Warren J. Hartman, "Our Missing Generation," *Discipleship Trends*, August 1987, pp. 1-4.

MEASUREMENT

Dependent Variables

We assessed congregational growth or decline by a seven-point scale based on data from Disciples Yearbooks for 1984 and 1988.[32] If a congregation had grown by at least 50 percent in both participating membership and average worship attendance from 1984 to 1988, it was assigned a value of 7; a similar decline was assigned a value of 1. Gains or losses of 20 percent in both categories were assigned values of 6 and 2, respectively. Gains or losses of at least 10 percent were assigned values of 5 and 3. All other churches were assigned a value of 4 for congregational growth. Church growth was predicted not from individual data but from aggregate data — individual data averaged by congregation for all individuals reporting from that congregation. SPSS-X's (1989) AGGREGATE program was used to average the data by congregations.

At the individual level, we correlated three dependent variables with our independent variables. Church attendance and giving were used as indicators of current activity, the idea being that decreases in either would reflect initial steps toward attrition. A third variable was the respondent's self-description as active, less active than before, having switched to a different denomination, or as having altogether ceased attending church anywhere. The vast majority of respondents described themselves as active or less active, with only about ten percent saying they had switched churches or had dropped out.

Independent Variables

Most of the independent variables are presented in Tables 3 through 12 or in the description of sample characteristics. Many of the scales were designed specifically for this study, while others were adapted, with or without some modification, from previous research.

Table 3 presents the first twenty-three items in the survey, which respondents could identify as "not," "some," or "very" important to their satisfaction with their current or former Christian Church (Disciples of Christ) congregation. Table 4 presents the third set of items in the survey, twenty-two items about their satisfaction with their pastor, rated from "very dissatisfied" to "very satisfied" in five categories. Table 5 presents the second set of items in the survey, twenty items about their needs being fulfilled in their congregation, items based on Maslow's hierarchy of needs, with responses from "strongly agree" to "strongly disagree" in five categories. Items in Tables 4 and 5 are arranged in subsets determined by a principal axis factor analysis with varimax

---

32. *Yearbook and Directory of the Christian Church (Disciples of Christ)*, ed. S. L. Cox (Indianapolis: Office of the General Minister and President, 1984, 1989).

TABLE 3 Percentage Ratings of "Very Important" Reported for Twenty-Three Characteristics of Christian Church (Disciples of Christ) Congregations

Characteristic	Percent Responses as "Very Important"
1. The quality of the pastor's leadership	91.4
2. The Christian education of children	88.2
3. Having a meaningful worship experience in the church	81.4
4. Congregation's personal support, caring attitude	81.0
5. Activities for children and youth	80.2
6. Opportunities for personal Christian (spiritual) growth	73.8
7. Deep commitment of members to follow Christ	72.0
8. Weekly practice of communion (Lord's Supper)	71.0
9. Being able to sense God's Spirit at work in the church	70.4
10. The opportunity to serve others	65.4
11. Ministering to needy of community	62.9
12. The sharing of common values and beliefs with other church members	56.5
13. Having good friends in the church	54.3
14. Evangelistic emphasis (leading others to Christ)	50.3
15. A wide variety of programs	38.2
16. Loyalty to the denomination	32.1
17. Effective regional level leadership of the churches	23.3
18. Location in your local community/neighborhood	22.8
19. Lobbying for positive changes in society	19.8
20. A well-designed, attractive church building	17.6
21. An active foreign mission program	17.3
22. A unique denominational heritage/history	14.3
23. Charismatic gifts (tongues, etc.) are accepted	3.2

rotation, using a standard eigenvalue = 1.0 criterion for determining the number of factors extracted. The Maslow scales factored somewhat differently than we expected, but most of the items in the personal development, spiritual growth, belonging, acceptance, and physical needs subscales correspond to Maslow's self-actualization, esteem, love, and safety and physical needs, respectively. The items in Table 6 (p. 534) were placed immediately after the pastoral items (Table 4, p. 532) in the survey; these items were used to identify perceived local congregational priorities.

The next set of items in the survey are presented in Table 7 (p. 534) and were designed to test, along with the item responses in Table 8 (p. 535), the transfer ecumenism hypothesis. Respondents rated each of the eleven items in Table 7 with regard to similarity from one Disciples congregation to another on a six-point continuum from very similar to very dissimilar, while selecting one of six options from the item in Table 8.

Table 9 (p. 536) presents the items used to assess reasons that active church members gave for staying in the Christian Church (Disciples of Christ); items were rated in three categories from "not," "some," to "very" important. Inactive or less active members rated the items in Table 11 (p. 538) as having

TABLE 4   Percentage Ratings of "Very Satisfied" Reported for Twenty-Two Characteristics of Christian Church (Disciples of Christ) Ministers

Characteristic[a]	Percent Responses as "Very Satisfied"
Regular Services	
1. Preaching sermons	46.1
2. Leading worship	43.3
Pastoral Support	
1. Being friendly to everyone	52.1
2. Pastor's own moral life is above reproach	46.6
3. Visiting sick, lonely, grieving church members	45.0
4. Conducting special services (weddings, funerals, etc.)	36.2
5. Encouraging members when they are discouraged	32.3
6. Pastoral care for my family's needs	27.5
Pastoral Leadership/Administration	
1. Developing vision/goals for the future of the church	27.1
2. Promoting stewardship (including church budget)	22.9
3. Administrative role in the church	22.0
4. Making Christian (Disciples of Christ) doctrine clear	21.7
5. Encouraging development and use of many members' spiritual gifts	20.7
6. Teaching members how to live by spiritual values	20.3
7. Development of Christian education programs	18.8
8. Ability to feel angry about wrongs or injustice to others	16.3
9. Taking stands on social issues	15.4
10. Evangelistic outreach to non-Christians	14.6
11. Teaching members how to pray more effectively	12.5
Pastoral Counseling	
1. Doing pastoral counseling (individuals)	19.7
2. Doing marriage or family counseling	13.7
3. Doing premarital counseling (couples before marriage)	13.6

a. Items grouped by subsets determined by factor analysis, a statistical procedure that identifies groups of items with a common theme.

"no," "uncertain," "some," or "much" influence as reasons for becoming less active in the Christian Church (Disciples of Christ). Several of the items in Table 10 (p. 537) were used with permission from the Gallup survey of unchurched Americans (e.g., items 5, 8, 10, 11, 12, and 13).[33]

Table 11 presents data on theological beliefs of the respondents, as well as the coding used to create a four-item scale of theological conservatism. The majority of respondents endorsed moderate to conservative theological viewpoints. Theological conservatism was significantly correlated with agreement with the statement "My relationship with Christ is a vitally important part of my life" at $r = .40$ (which is a 16% overlap). However, many respondents who

33. O'Hara, "A Research Note on the Sources of Adult Church Commitment"; Roozen, "Church Dropouts"; *The Unchurched American* (Princeton: Gallup Organization, 1978).

TABLE 5   Ratings of "Strongly Agree" Reported for Twenty Items Evaluated by Respondents about Their Christian Church (Disciples of Christ) Congregation

Characteristic[a]	Percent Responses as "Strongly Agree"
Personal Development	
1. Church participation helps me develop deeper and more meaningful relationships with people	23.1
2. The church helps bring out the best qualities in my personality	20.8
Spiritual Growth	
1. The church helps me develop a more vital personal relationship with God	27.8
2. The church helps me find greater meaning/purpose in life	27.5
3. The church helps me appreciate how much God loves me	26.9
4. Church worship is exciting and meaningful to me	25.3
5. Through the church I am able to pray more often and more deeply than I have done before	20.1
Belonging	
1. I feel I am a valued member of at least one small group in the church (a class, a women's or men's group, a Bible study, an activity group, committee, etc.)	36.8
2. Some church members care enough about me to keep in touch	30.6
3. The church appreciates the work I do for the church	20.5
4. I feel my ideas are respected by church members	15.2
Acceptance	
1. Church people will help me if I have special needs (illness, death in the family, etc.)	43.9
2. Church people will pray for me if I share my personal needs and concerns	42.1
3. I feel loved and accepted by church members	38.2
Physical Needs	
1. I feel safe in the church and parking area(s)[b]	32.3
2. The church is usually comfortable (temperature, pews, light, sound, etc.)	23.2
3. Visitors who come to the church are very much impressed by the attractiveness and upkeep of the building(s)	17.6
4. The church offers free transportation to services	10.9

a. Items grouped by factor analysis, as in Table 4.
b. Correlated r = -.12 (p < .001) with urban versus rural residence.

espoused liberal theology also experienced Christ as a vitally important part of their life, which may suggest that the personal relationship is more essential to the Christian life than theology per se.[34] At the same time, fewer than 11 percent of all respondents denied that their relationship with Christ was a vitally important part of their life.

Table 12 (p. 539) presents the remaining independent variables. Church size was based on an average of participating membership and average Sunday

34. R. S. Warner, *New Wine in Old Wineskins: Evangelicals and Liberals in a Small-Town Church* (Berkeley and Los Angeles: University of California Press, 1988), p. 283.

TABLE 6   Percentage of Respondents Identifying Seven Characteristics as "Major Emphases" Practiced by Their Christian (Disciples of Christ) Congregation

Characteristic[a]	Percent Identifying as "Major Emphasis"[b]
1. Mission to the community	78.2
2. Cooperation with other major denominations	66.1
3. Encouragement of deep spiritual growth of members (discipleship, prayer)	63.8
4. Trying to lead others to Christ (evangelism)	49.6
5. Close cooperation with church's regional office	49.1
6. Using gifts of the Holy Spirit	19.7
7. Social action/policy (political issues: civil rights, refugees, Nicaragua, etc.)	16.9

a. Respondents could circle none, any, or all of the seven characteristics if they felt they were a major emphasis within their particular congregation.

b. There were few significant regional differences in emphases. The Kansas City region ranked "using gifts of the Holy Spirit" as having more emphasis than did the other two regions, whereas the Los Angeles region gave less emphasis to mission to the community and to evangelism than did the other two regions.

TABLE 7   Percentage of Respondents Describing Eleven Characteristics of Christian (Disciples of Christ) Churches as Being "Very Similar" from One Congregation to Another

Characteristic[a]	Percent Identifying as "Very Similar"[b]
1. Practice of weekly Holy Communion	40.6
2. Friendliness of congregation	16.9
3. Quality of worship experience in services	10.4
4. Opportunity for active small-group involvement by newcomers	10.3
5. Opportunity for members to grow spiritually in depth (discipleship)	10.1
6. Quality of Christian education for children	10.0
7. Emphasis on evangelism	9.5
8. Social action emphasis by pastor	7.8
9. Emphasis on unique denominational heritage of the Christian (Disciples of Christ) Church	7.7
10. Acceptance of charismatic movement	6.9
11. Income/education levels of average members	5.9

a. Respondents could circle six responses, 1 to 6, from very similar to very different. Percentages reflect those who circled 1 for most similar.

b. There were few significant regional differences. However, Los Angeles respondents reported less similarity regarding weekly Holy Communion (the Dallas/Fort Worth region had the most similarity), and the charismatic movement. The Dallas/Fort Worth region respondents had the most differences in income/education, while Kansas City region respondents had the fewest differences in income/education.

morning attendance, as taken from the 1988 Disciples Yearbook, coded into four levels: less than 100, 100 to 499, 500 to 999, and 1000 or more. Education and income, as well as number of moves in the previous ten years, length of residence in present neighborhood, and the child-rearing variables are de-

TABLE 8   Percentage and Average Ages of Respondents Selecting Various Attendance Options if "They Had to Move out of the Area"

Percentage Selecting Each Option

Options	Total	Kansas City	Dallas/ Fort Worth	Los Angeles	Average Age of Respondents
1. Attend the closest Christian Church (Disciples of Christ) congregation	26.3	24.7	24.3	30.1	60.8[a]
2. Attend the "best" Christian Church (Disciples of Christ) congregation	33.7	33.5	42.6	26.9	51.4
3. Attend the "best" church regardless of denomination	26.0	28.3	23.3	25.1	46.1
4. Visit church(es) occasionally without joining	5.9	7.2	4.7	5.1	52.0
5. Not go to church except for special occasions	1.2	2.1	0.3	0.8	45.1
6. Stop going to church at all	0.4	0.4	0.0	0.5	44.3

a. Overall differences in ages across the six options were statistically significant ($p < .001$) as evaluated through a one-way analysis of variance.

scribed in the previous section on sample characteristics. The first two items on localism are adopted or modified from studies by A. W. Black and J. P. O'Hara.[35] Cosmopolitan values were measured by the item "I prefer to think of myself as a 'citizen of the world' rather than confining my interests mainly to the community in which I live." Attitude toward voluntary community organizations (other than churches) was measured by an item "It is important to me to belong to voluntary community organizations other than the church."

The scales for intrinsic and extrinsic religiosity were shortened versions of I-E scales crafted by R. L. Gorsuch and G. D. Venable, each scale having five items in our survey.[36] Examples of intrinsic items are "I have often had a strong sense of God's presence" and "My religion is important to me because it answers many questions about the meaning of life." We used items 5, 7, 9, 11, and 12 from Gorsuch and Venable's "age universal" I-E scale to represent intrinsic religiosity and items 2, 4, 14, 17, and 20 to represent extrinsic religiosity. Examples of extrinsic items are "Although I am religious, I don't let it affect my daily life" and "I go to church mainly because I enjoy seeing people I know there." We added another single item not from the I-E scale to assess intrinsic religiosity: "My relationship with

35. Black, "The Impact of Theological Orientation and of Breadth of Perspective on Church Members' Attitudes and Behaviors"; O'Hara, "A Research Note on the Sources of Adult Church Commitment."

36. Gorsuch and Venable, "Development of an 'Age Universal' I-E Scale," *Journal for the Scientific Study of Religion* 22 (1983): 181-87.

TABLE 9 Percentages of Respondents Rating as "Very Important" Reasons Why They Continue to Be Members of Their Current Christian (Disciples of Christ) Congregation

Reason	Percent Responses of "Very Important"
1. Children and youth are highly valued in this church	60.8
2. Offers communion (Lord's Supper) weekly	60.8
3. I really like the pastor	54.6
4. I get along really well with church members	52.7
5. I like this denomination better than others	48.5
6. It is easy for newcomers to feel "like they belong"	47.7
7. Meets my needs for spiritual nurture and growth	47.6
8. The church promotes Christian values in the community and nation	45.6
9. My family belongs (spouse, children, parents)	44.7
10. I find I am encouraged by my experiences here	43.5
11. This church welcomes people from a wide variety of socioeconomic backgrounds	42.3
12. Meets my needs for some supportive friends	38.1
13. Church members share most of my beliefs and values	35.9
14. The church is large enough to offer a wide variety of good programs	34.6
15. This church is much involved in community service projects	32.5
16. The church is making progress toward recognized, important goals	32.1
17. It seems that prayers really get answered here	26.9
18. Overall, this church is simply better than its competition	23.9
19. It allows members to practice spiritual gifts freely	23.6
20. This church is near my home	21.1
21. Provides for special needs of my family (e.g., education for children, handicapped services)	19.6
22. This is the only church in which I have actively participated	17.6
23. I became a Christian here	15.6
24. Helps me become involved in political issues	2.3

Christ is a vitally important part of my life" because we wanted to assess a specifically Christian intrinsic orientation (the ten I-E items generalize to any faith that accepts God or the Bible). We performed a factor analysis on the eleven I-E items and found that they formed one primary factor; therefore, we combined the items to form a larger intrinsic scale (recoding the extrinsic items). In Tables 12, 13, and 17 the intrinsic religiosity variable refers to the eleven-item scale; the extrinsic religiosity variable refers to the five extrinsic items only.

Conservative moral values were measured by three items involving a desire for greater acceptance of sexual freedom, divorce, and marijuana usage in our society.[37] A brief evangelism scale of three items was used with items that assessed felt comfort with inviting "young couples or couples with chil-

---

37. These items were adapted from Roof and Hoge, "Church Involvement in America"; and P. E. Hammond and J. D. Hunter, "On Maintaining Plausibility: The Worldview of Evangelical College Students," *Journal for the Scientific Study of Religion* 23 (1984): 221-38.

TABLE 10   Percentages of Respondents Rating as "Having Much Influence" Reasons Why They Have Begun to Reduce Their Involvement in a Christian (Disciples of Christ) Congregation

Reason	Percent Responses of "Much Influence"[a]
1. I was unhappy with the church being run by the same small group all the time	7.5
2. I was unhappy with the way decisions were made	6.1
3. I was unhappy with the church's priorities	5.6
4. I was unhappy with the quality of worship	5.1
5. Poor health of myself or of my family	4.6
6. I was unhappy with the lack of spiritual help for my own or my family's spiritual development	4.3
7. I was unhappy with the lack of programs to meet the needs of my family	3.9
8. I found other interests and activities which led me to spend less and less time on church-related activities	3.9
9. I felt persons in the church didn't care enough about me to contact me when I was absent	3.8
10. I had specific problems with the pastor or staff	3.6
11. I had specific conflicts or problems with church members	1.9
12. Stress associated with my divorce or separation	1.7[b]
13. I felt my lifestyle was no longer compatible with the values of the church	1.2
14. Moral standards were not strict enough	1.1
15. Civil rights and/or social action issues upset me	1.1
16. Conflicts with my family about my church activities	1.0
17. The church didn't offer ways for me to help others	0.8
18. The church's teachings about biblical interpretation were too liberal	0.9
19. The church's teachings about God tended to discourage recognition and discussion of doubts	0.8
20. The church's teachings about biblical interpretation were too conservative	0.4
21. The church's teachings about moral standards were too strict or narrow	0.4
22. I felt my needs could be better met through religious television or radio	0.4
23. I no longer believed in Christ	0.3

a. Approximately 340 subjects who said they had reduced their involvement in the church responded to these items. Percentages shown reflect percent of all 1,141 subjects; to obtain percentages relative to the 340 subjects, multiply percentage figures by approximately 3.5.

b. Respondents were instructed to skip this item if they had not separated or divorced. Among those who did apparently separate or divorce, the percentage would have been between 10 and 12 percent indicating much influence, with another 10 to 12 percent indicating some influence in their decision to become less involved with the church.

dren," "people I know well," and "casual acquaintances" to church. Although the scale does not assess behavior, we thought that evangelistic behavior would be less on average when members did not feel comfortable about inviting others to their church.

All the items discussed here from localism through evangelism used "strongly disagree" to "strongly agree" responses in five categories. Minority churches were identified as such either by their pastors or by their regional or area minister (middle judicatory official).

TABLE 11 Theological Views of Members of the Christian Church (Disciples of Christ)

Subject Item	Percent Agreement	Coding[a]	Percent Intrinsic[b]
Bible			
Actual inspired Word of God, completely trustworthy, without any error (in the original documents) in statements or teachings	30.5	4	97.9
Inspired Word of God, accurate in its religious teachings, but it may not be accurate in matters of science, history, etc.	51.0	3	88.5
An ancient book of legends, history, and moral precepts recorded by men	9.7	1	7.0
Not sure	4.5	2	84.0
Jesus			
I am not sure Jesus existed	0.5	1	100.0[c]
Jesus was only a man, although an extraordinary one	0.9	2	77.8
Jesus was a great religious prophet/teacher, but not the Son of God	2.3	3	48.0
Jesus was the Son of God, both truly human and truly God	89.8	4	92.4
I can't decide	3.7	3	41.0
Miracles			
Really occurred as described in the Bible	71.3	4	94.8
Miraculous events occurred in Bible times but can be explained by science today	10.0	3	78.8
Miracles did not really occur in Bible times	1.2	2	67.7
I am not sure	14.4	3	72.4
Salvation			
People are accepted *only* through faith in Jesus Christ	33.5	4	95.4
People are accepted by faith in Jesus Christ, acted out in good behavior	14.0	4	93.1
People are accepted by their doing good works (behavior)	1.5	2	56.3
People of *all faiths* are accepted by God	42.8	3	85.1
I don't know	3.2	3	86.1

a. To form a four-item scale of conservative theological belief.

b. Percent who agreed or strongly agreed to the statement "My relationship with Christ is a vitally important part of my life."

c. Based on N = 5 cases.

The final independent variable was used only with the third of the sample that received an optional additional two-page questionnaire dealing with family strengths. Conflict between job/family and church activities was measured by three items, "If I were more involved in the church, it would take too much time away from my family or my own activities," "My job and/or family life take up enough time as is; I can't afford to give much more time to the church," and "Church activities don't present much of a time problem for me; I can do them and still have lots of time left over for myself and my family."

TABLE 12 **Predicting Congregational Growth and Individual Attendance and Giving from Seven Sets of Independent Variables**
(N = 163 Congregations, N = 1,145 People)

		PEARSON CORRELATION WITH		
Theory	Independent Variables	Attendance	Giving	Congregational Growth[a]
Internal Structure	Church size[b]	—	—	—
	Education	—	-.05*	—
	Income	—	-.10**	.20**
Localism	Cosmopolitan values	—	—	—
	Nonchurch voluntary organizations	—	—	—
	Number of moves in previous ten years	—	-.16***	—
	Length of residence in present neighborhood	—	.15***	-.14*
Child-rearing	Preschool children[c]	—	-.10***	—
	Elementary school age children	—	-.10***	—
	Teenage children	—	-.08**	—
Conservatism	Intrinsic religiosity	.22***	.33***	—
	Extrinsic religiosity	-.15***	-.23***	-.19**
	Relationship with Christ "vitally important"	.25***	.29***	.17*
	Conservative moral values	.09**	.16***	.14*
	Conservative theology	.16***	.15***	—
Evangelism	Evangelism comfort scale	.21***	.11***	—
Minority church growth	Minority churches versus[d] Anglo churches	.24**	.40***	.14*
Pastoral leadership	Regular services	.11***	—	—
	Pastoral support	.17***	.10***	—
	Leadership/Administration	—	—	—
	Counseling	.06*	.10***	—
Maslow Needs and Role Conflict	Physical Needs	-.07*	-.07*	-.17*
	Acceptance	.24***	.11***	—
	Belonging	.40***	.22***	—
	Valued small group member item	.46***	.24***	—
	Spiritual growth	.20***	.12***	—
	Personal development	.24***	.13***	—
	Job/Family/Church role conflict	-.13*	-.19***	—

a. Correlations between congregational growth and all other variables are based on SPSS-X AGGREGATE program, in which all independent variables represent either the average of that variable or a percentage of that variable for all respondents in each congregation (N = 163 congregations).
b. Since congregational size is a congregation characteristic rather than an individual characteristic, it was correlated with aggregate (average) attendance and giving in each congregation, as was done with the congregational growth correlations.
c. Number of preschool children, elementary school age children, and teenage children used for correlations with attendance and giving; percent of each congregation's respondents having each category of child was used for correlation with congregational growth.
d. Correlations with attendance and giving, as well as with congregational growth, were based on aggregate data on minority congregations rather than minority individuals.

*p < .05   **p < .01   ***p < .001

ANALYSIS

We used SPSS-X (1989) to perform all analyses. Pearson zero-order correlations were used in Tables 12, 13, and 14. Pearson correlations identify how much of a straight-line type of relationship exists between two variables. Multiplying a Pearson correlation times itself yields an estimate of how much overlap exists between two variables. For example, a correlation of .50 (r = .50) between two variables means that there is a .5 x .5 = .25 or 25 percent overlap between the two variables. For 4 = .28, the overlap is just over 3 percent. With a sample as large as ours, a correlation that is very small can still be statistically significant. The relative importance of small correlations can be determined by the significance level — p < .05, .01, or .001. Respectively, the latter figures mean that finding a correlation of a certain size would occur by chance alone less than fifty, ten, or one times out of a thousand.

We used one-way analyses of variance to compare average (mean) scores on a variable as a function of another variable in Tables 16 and 17. In those tables we compare active, less active, drop-out, and switcher members, a procedure that distinguished drop-outs from those who switched to another denomination (some scholars consider both groups to be switchers). The SPSS-X FACTOR routine was used to perform the factor analyses shown in Tables 4 and 5.

RESULTS

Descriptive results are presented in Tables 3 through 11. Table 3 presents results for factors seen as important to satisfaction with the congregation. The most important characteristics — the pastor, programs for children, and worship — mirror results found previously by C. W. Sayre and Herb Miller, as discussed by Miller.[38] The low ranking given to evangelism may contribute to Disciples attrition. Furthermore, denominational issues (loyalty, history) are also ranked fairly low. Indirectly, the rankings in Table 3 support the idea of transfer ecumenism inasmuch as people seem to be looking for characteristics that could be found in many Protestant (and even non-Protestant) congregations.

Table 4 is a report card on pastoral leadership. The congregations would appear to grade Disciples pastors well on leading worship services and pastoral support but not as well on leadership/administration and counseling. However, the latter low percentages of "very satisfied" may reflect unfamiliarity with the pastor's administrative or counseling roles. Even so, the perceived lack of leadership in vision/goals, Christian education, and evangelistic outreach among Disciples pastors may contribute to attrition.

38. Sayre and Miller, *The Christian Church (Disciples of Christ) New Members Study;* Miller, "Notebook," *The Disciple,* September 1986, p. 51.

TABLE 13   Regional Differences between Minority and Anglo Congregations

Correlation between Minority versus Anglo Type of Congregation and Other Variables	Total	Kansas City	Dallas/Fort Worth	Los Angeles
Number of minority congregations	24	3	7	14
Congregational growth	.14*	.23*	-.22†	.34**
Giving	.40***	.43**	.40**	.35**
Conservative values	.04	.04	-.08	.06
Intrinsic religiosity	.23***	.31**	.22†	.17
Conservative theology	.26***	.22†	.48***	.16
Evangelism	.28***	-.01	.28*	.35**
Attendance	.24**	.14	.40**	.17
Intrinsic religiosity (Christian item)	.27***	.27***	.24†	.32**

†p < .10   *p < .05   **p < .01   ***p < .001

TABLE 14   Correlations among Eleven Items Assessed for Similarity among Disciples Churches with Intentions to Attend "Best" Church Regardless of Denomination as Opposed to Attending "Best" or Closest Disciples' Church if Respondent Were to Move from Present Home Area

Items: Degree of Similarity among Disciples Churches on —	Kansas City	Dallas/Fort Worth	Los Angeles	Total[a]
Practice of weekly Holy Communion	-.19***	—	—	—
Friendliness of congregation	—	.17**	—	.08**
Quality of worship experience	.10*	.25***	—	.13***
Opportunity for active small-group involvement by newcomers	—	.12*	—	.06*
Opportunity for members to grow spiritually in depth	.15**	.18**	—	.11***
Quality of Christian education for children	.14**	.22***	.11*	.15***
Emphasis on unique denominational heritage	.15**	—	—	.07*
Acceptance of charismatic movement	.13*	—	—	—
Income/education levels of average members	.24***	.20***	—	.15***

a. Positive correlations indicate that the greater the perceived similarity among Disciples congregations, the more likely the respondent indicated that he or she would continue to attend a Christian Church (Disciples of Christ) congregation if moving to a new location away from his or her current Disciples congregation. Positive correlations support the transfer ecumenism hypothesis; negative correlations do not.

*p < .05   **p < .01   ***p < .001

Table 5 evaluates the need fulfillment provided within Disciples congregations. Members' needs for acceptance appear to be met fairly well, but not other needs. The rating for small-group involvement — which may seem low or high depending on the reader's perspective — is especially noteworthy in the context of its favorable impact on attendance and giving as shown in Table 12.

Table 6 presents results for the emphases that members identified as "major" within their congregations. Evangelism ranks in the middle of the emphases. Interestingly, correlating the aggregate score for evangelism here across congregations with church growth yields a significant, though small, result: r = .15 (p < .001). Thus, there is a slight tendency for congregations that emphasize evangelism to be growing more than those that don't (based on members' perceptions of emphasis on evangelism). Social action was not identified as a major emphasis by most respondents. This perception is consistent with the findings of Joseph E. Faulkner's study of the content of Disciples preaching in 1988 (pp. 416-39 in this volume).

Table 7 shows that many members believe that there is much similarity in the practice of weekly communion among Disciples congregations but that on other matters there is much more variation. The results in Table 7 do not tell us how members felt about each item. However, if they perceive little similarity from one congregation to another, it is likely that some congregations are perceived more favorably than others on the characteristics, a situation that favors transfer ecumenism.

Table 8 further reinforces Herb Miller's notions about transfer ecumenism.[39] Most members admit to having "shopped around" for either the best Disciples congregation or the best congregation of another denomination. Furthermore, younger members are more likely to "shop around" than are older members, a very important finding given the high percentage of elderly in Disciples congregations and the need to gain younger members to counteract losses among the elderly over time. The implication is that few congregations today can rely on denominational loyalty alone to pick up transfers; transfers must be sold on a congregation at their new location. The phenomenon appears to be important in each of the regions sampled, though slightly less important in Los Angeles than the other two regions.

Table 9 also reinforces the findings of Sayre and Miller about reasons people continue in congregations. It appears that few people stay in a congregation simply because they became Christians there first. Involvement in political issues runs dead last as a drawing card for retaining members. The hypothesis that quality relationships are very important to retention may be supported by the fact that items 1, 3, 4, 6, 9, and 12 are ranked in the top half of all of the items used. Similarly, unhappy relationships appear to be important in attrition, as shown in Table 10. Items 1, 9, 10, 11, and 12 — mostly in the top half of those used — concern relationships. The first two items may reflect

39. See Miller, "Notebook," *The Disciple,* August 1986, p. 49.

some sort of power struggle between respondents and congregational leadership. Crises of belief or doctrine rank low as reasons for reducing involvement in the congregation. Notably, attrition does not appear to be very much related to competition from radio and television ministries.

Table 11 illustrates the interrelationship between conservative theology and intrinsic religiosity, primarily to set the stage for Table 12, which presents results for most of our hypotheses. Results for localism and internal structure are not especially noteworthy in Table 12; church growth does seem to be higher in congregations whose members have higher incomes and have not lived very long in their present neighborhoods, which may reflect growth in growing suburban areas (i.e., areas that have new arrivals with higher incomes). Child-rearing theory is not supported, though children may represent a demand on family income that reduces giving slightly.

The test of the conservatism hypothesis yielded some very interesting results. Conservative theology and moral values were indeed related positively to attendance and giving, if not always church growth. However, intrinsic and extrinsic religiosity was related to attendance, giving, and church growth at least as much. We performed a follow-up analysis to compare the relative effects of intrinsic religiosity and conservatism. We found that controlling for intrinsic religiosity reduced the correlations between conservatism and the dependent variables much more than vice versa; when we controlled for conservatism, the correlations between intrinsic religiosity and the dependent variables remained stronger. The partial correlation between conservatism and attendance, controlling for intrinsic religiosity, was only .06 ($p < .05$). The same partial correlation for conservatism and giving, controlling for intrinsic religiosity, was .12 ($p < .001$). The partial correlation for conservative moral values and attendance was not significant, controlling for intrinsic religiosity. The partial correlation for conservative values and giving was actually negative, -.09 ($p < .01$), controlling for intrinsic religiosity — which suggests that those with conservative moral values may actually give less than those with more liberal values when both have similar levels of intrinsic religiosity. In contrast, controlling for both conservative theology and values, the partial correlations for intrinsic religiosity with attendance and giving were stronger, .17 ($p < .001$) and .25 ($p < .001$), respectively. These results imply that the critical factor is intrinsic religiosity rather than conservatism, even though they are related to each other.

Evangelism comfort was related to attendance and giving but not to church growth; feeling comfortable about inviting others may be a necessary but not sufficient condition for actually achieving success in evangelism.

Minority congregations appeared to be doing well in attendance, giving, and growth relative to Anglo congregations within the Christian Church (Disciples of Christ). Table 13 represents a further exploration of this finding. Minority congregations appear to be more conservative theologically, though not necessarily morally, as well as being more intrinsically religious and evangelistic. However, there is much regional variation in the characteristics of minority congregations relative to Anglo congregations, except in the area of giving, which is uniformly better — a notable result considering that giving may involve more sacrifice for generally lower-income minorities than for wealthier Anglo Disciples. Minority growth, evangelism, and intrinsic religiosity appear to be especially notable in the Los Angeles region.

Pastoral leadership variables did not predict the dependent variables as well as we had anticipated. Pastoral support had the strongest relationships, while pastoral administration had no effect at all. Following the suggestions of Wagner and Hartman mentioned before, we followed up our analysis of pastoral leadership by repeating the correlations only for those congregations with more than 100 members; however, the results obtained were no stronger for the larger congregations than for all congregations combined.

The strongest consistent results were obtained for the Maslow needs as predictors of attendance and giving. The strong correlation ($r = .46$) between small-group involvement and attendance was especially noteworthy. However, since the attendance item was worded broadly enough to include small-group activities, we did a follow-up analysis in which we subtracted 1 point from the attendance scores of all subjects who agreed with the small-group item (in order to rule out the possibility that the .46 relationship was an artifact of small-group involvement being counted twice, in both attendance and the small-group item). The resulting correlation was reduced to .23, but it was still very significant statistically ($p < .001$). Therefore, we hesitate to say that small-group involvement is the key to attendance, but it still seems very important relative to the other valid predictors.

The correlation between attendance and the four-item belonging needs scale was quite strong ($r = .40$); to control for the possible overlap between group membership and attendance, we deleted the group item from the belonging scale and correlated the remaining three-item scale with attendance. The resulting correlation was a bit smaller ($r = .32$) but still very significant ($p < .001$). Therefore, we do not think that the importance of belonging is an artifact of the small-group item.

However, the Maslow needs did not predict church growth. Again, having one's needs met may be a necessary but not sufficient condition for church growth; one response may be to sit back and enjoy rather than reaching out so others can have their needs met too. The negative relationship between growth and physical needs was interesting and may reflect research suggesting that growing churches often run out of space and overtax their facilities as membership growth exceeds the growth of the facility/building program.[40]

Job/family conflict appeared to be a significant factor in explaining reductions in attendance and giving.

---

40. Hadaway, *Growing off the Plateau;* Wagner, *Your Church Can Grow.*

TABLE 15   **Breakdown of Christian Church (Disciples of Christ) Switchers and Drop-outs by Denomination (N = 99)**

Category	Denomination	Total Number	Definite Switchers	Total	Switchers	Definite Switchers
					PERCENTAGES	
Drop-Outs[a]	NA	48	NA	48%	NA	NA
Switchers[b]		51				
	Roman Catholic	2	0	2%	NA	NA
	None Listed[c]	16	0	16%	NA	NA
	Liberal Protestant	5	1	5%	15%	18%
	Episcopalian	2	1			
	Presbyterian	2	0			
	Presbyterian/Methodist	1	0			
	Moderate Protestant	18	5	18%	55%	38%
	Lutheran	3	0			
	Methodist	6	2			
	Baptist/Methodist	1	0			
	Baptist	8	3			
	Conservative Protestant	10	7	10%	30%	54%
	Southern Baptist	1	0			
	Conservative Lutheran	1	1			
	Nondenominational	2	2			
	Charismatic	2	2			
	Independent Christian Church	1	1			
	Church of Christ	1	0			
	Nazarene	1	0			
	Assembly of God	1	1			

a. Those who indicated that they no longer attend any congregation.
b. Those who indicated that they were attending church elsewhere.
c. Those who indicated that they were attending church elsewhere but cited no further information about denominational affiliation.

Table 14 provides some support for the transfer ecumenism hypothesis, especially for Kansas City and Dallas/Fort Worth region members. Those who perceive more similarity among Disciples congregations are more likely to say they will attend the closest or "best" Disciples congregation in their location rather than seeking the best church in another denomination.

DROP-OUTS AND SWITCHERS

Table 15 presents a breakdown of the number of drop-outs and switchers who responded to our survey. Unfortunately, we did not ask the switchers what denomination they had transferred to; we did ask all subjects if they had ever been a member of another denomination. The best we can do is to assume that switchers would likely put down their present denomination, the one to which

TABLE 16   Comparisons among Active Members, Less-Active Members, Drop-outs, and Switchers on Socioeconomic Variables and Conservatism

Group	Mean Scores				
	Conservative Theology	Conservative Values	Class	Income	Education
Active members	14.23	12.68	3.17	2.21	14.45
Less-active members	14.06	12.41	3.13	2.28	14.67
Drop-outs	13.60	12.68	2.93	1.98	14.46
Switchers					
No denomination listed	14.17	12.24	3.06	2.41	14.61
Conservative Protestant	15.60	14.00	3.20	2.38	14.00
Baptist	15.13	14.00	3.25	2.57	12.75
Moderate Protestants	15.10	13.40	3.40	2.50	16.56
Liberal Protestants	12.75	10.50	3.40	2.20	16.00
F-test value	3.67	2.36	1.10	.92	2.08
Significance[a]	.0006	.0212	.3629	.4924	.0426

a. Significance test associated with overall comparison of all group mean scores. None of the tests between individual groups was significant at the .05 level by the Scheffe test. The results for class and income are not significant. The most significant results are for theology, values, and education in that order.

they had switched, since it would probably be more salient in their minds at the moment than any denomination they might have joined prior to being a Disciple. Some switchers did put down their present denomination in hand-written comments; their comments form the basis for the "definite switchers" column in Table 15. Our results contain an anomaly. Taken together, losses to nonaffiliation and liberal Protestant churches are greater than to other moderate or more conservative groups, a result that confirms the expectations of Roof and McKinney. However, among switchers per se, losses are greater to conservatives than to liberal groups, especially among definite switchers. Thus, if we look at both drop-outs and switchers, the picture is of losses to more liberal groups (nonaffiliated individuals are often assumed to be more liberal). But if we look at switchers only, and especially definite switchers, the picture is of losses to more conservative groups. The anomaly may reflect a loss of more committed individuals to conservative groups.[41]

To explore differences among the switchers and drop-outs further, we conducted a one-way analysis of variance among active members, less active members, drop-outs, and switchers, breaking the category of switchers down into those listing no denomination and those cited as Baptists, conservative Protestants, moderate Protestants, and liberal Protestants (Table 16). We kept Baptists separate because we were unable to distinguish between moderate (northern) baptists and conservative (southern) baptists. As might have been expected, we found liberal Protestants and drop-outs to be the most liberal

41. Roof and McKinney, *American Mainline Religion,* p. 177.

theologically, while conservative Protestant switchers were the most conservative. Baptists fell closer to the moderates than the conservatives theologically. A similar though less significant pattern held true for moral values, except that Baptists were more similar to conservative Protestants here than to liberal Protestants. Differences by social class or income were not significant. Moderate and liberal Protestants had the highest level of education, Baptists the lowest. The results refute the notion that drop-outs are leaving because of lifestyle issues, since their moral values scores are similar to active Disciples. Those switching to moderate or conservative groups may indeed be looking for more conservative moral and theological groups, since their scores are more conservative than active Disciples in both areas. Drop-outs have lower conservative theology scores than active Disciples but higher scores than switchers to liberal Protestant groups; thus, it is not clear why they drop out rather than switch to more liberal groups.

Table 17 (pp. 548-49) summarizes differences we found between actives, less actives, drop-outs, and switchers with respect to our basic hypotheses. Internal structure failed to differentiate the four groups. The localism hypothesis was not supported; in fact, those results that were significant came out opposite to what would have been expected. The child-rearing hypothesis received some support in that switchers had more children; perhaps they were switching to churches with better children's programs. The results for the conservatism hypothesis show that switchers are at least as committed intrinsically as actives, while drop-outs are much less committed. Switchers are more conservative morally and theologically. Switchers also reported perceiving less emphasis on evangelism, spiritual growth, and spiritual gifts than other members before they left, perhaps implying that they wanted more emphasis than they found in their Disciples congregations. Actives were the highest on evangelism, as might be expected. Minority congregations did not appear to' have fewer switchers or drop-outs than Anglo congregations; that finding, combined with their higher rates of growth, suggests that their growth comes from either evangelism or birth rate rather than a reduction in attrition. The results for pastoral leadership are much clearer here: switchers are much less satisfied with all aspects of pastoral leadership. Effective pastoral leadership may not cause growth, but it surely can cause attrition (see Tables 12 and 17).

Switchers appear to complain that their needs for spiritual growth and acceptance were not met, suggesting that they leave in search of groups that offer more acceptance and meet their spiritual needs better — needs that are often more conservative in nature. The loss of these switchers is especially regrettable because they tend not only to be highly committed but also to have more time on their hands to exercise their commitment; they equal actives in lack of perceived job/family versus church conflict.

Other factors help to describe switchers and drop-outs. Switchers are highly committed in terms of giving, devotions, and attendance. They are also the youngest, making them an especially unfortunate loss for a mainstream

TABLE 17   Comparing Active Members, Less-Active Members, Switchers, and Drop-outs on Key Variables

Theory	Independent Variables	Summary of Results[a]
Internal structure	Education	No significant differences (n.s.)
	Income	n.s.
	Size of church	n.s.
Localism	Cosmopolitan values	ACTIVES most cosmopolitan
	Nonchurch voluntary organizations	n.s.
	Number of moves	n.s.
	Length of residence in neighborhood	DROP-OUTS have longest tenure; SWITCHERS the shortest tenure
Child-rearing	% Preschool children	n.s. (SWITCHERS have more, though)
	% Elementary children	SWITCHERS have twice as many as any other group
	% Teen children	n.s. (SWITCHERS have more, though)
Conservatism	Intrinsic religiosity	ACTIVES and LESS ACTIVES have the highest scores, slightly higher than SWITCHERS, while DROP-OUTS have substantially lower scores
	Relationship with Christ "vitally important"	ACTIVES and SWITCHERS have highest scores, about equal to each other
	Liberal moral values	n.s. (SWITCHERS most conservative, though)
	Conservative theology	SWITCHERS have the highest scores, DROP-OUTS the lowest (least conservative)
	Perceived church emphasis on evangelism	SWITCHERS perceive the least emphasis
	Perceived church emphasis on spiritual growth	SWITCHERS perceive the least emphasis
	Perceived church emphasis on spiritual gifts	SWITCHERS perceived the least emphasis
Evangelism	Evangelism comfort scale	ACTIVES the highest
Minority church growth	Percent minorities	n.s.
Pastoral leadership	Regular services	SWITCHERS are the lowest
	Pastoral support	ACTIVES the highest; SWITCHERS the lowest
	Leadership/Administration	ACTIVES the highest; SWITCHERS the lowest
	Counseling	SWITCHERS especially low
Maslow needs and role conflict	Physical needs	n.s.
	Acceptance	SWITCHERS are very low
	Belonging	ACTIVES the highest
	Valued small-group member item	ACTIVES the highest
	Spiritual growth	SWITCHERS are very low
	Personal development	ACTIVES the highest
	Job/Family/Church conflict scale	LESS ACTIVES highest, ACTIVES and SWITCHERS lowest

a. ACTIVES, LESS ACTIVES, SWITCHERS, and DROP-OUTS were compared on the variables shown using one-way analysis of variance.

TABLE 17 (cont.)

Theory	Independent Variables	Summary of Results
Others	Travel time to church	DROP-OUTS have very long times (28.1 minutes compared to the next highest of 15.1 minutes)
	Giving	ACTIVES highest; SWITCHERS second highest; DROP-OUTS the lowest
	Personal devotions	SWITCHERS the highest
	Age	ACTIVES are the oldest (54.1 years); SWITCHERS the youngest (46.5 years)
	Attendance	ACTIVES highest; SWITCHERS next highest; DROP-OUTS the lowest

church that has been having a difficult time retaining young people. The drop-outs are notable for living far away from their congregation; why they don't join a closer congregation, even if not a Disciples congregation, is unknown.

REASONS GIVEN FOR SWITCHING

We found thirteen categories of reasons given by switchers for their decision to leave their Disciples congregation. Of the fifty-one switchers, ten gave no reasons. The other forty-one often gave more than one reason, but the categories occurred with approximately the following frequency:

Dissatisfaction with pastor	12
Wanted more meaningful or spiritual situation	9
Moved away (often no Disciples congregation in new area)	8
Wanted better relationships within congregation	8
Needs not being met	5
Lack of attention for children's needs	4
Too much social activism or political activity	3
Wanted a church with more young people	2
Drifted away upon growing up	1
Married into another denomination	1
Disliked charismatic practices within the congregation	1
Too much emphasis on money	1

The most frequent sources of dissatisfaction had to do with the minister. A few pastors were held in moral disrepute because of alleged dishonesty, immorality, drunkenness, and improper language. More often the minister was seen as an ineffective leader, as someone who played favorites or let too many needs go unmet within some groups in the congregation while putting his or her own needs first. It is possible that some congregations have too few ministers for their size so that needs go unmet despite their best efforts. The longest comment that we received on a pastor said a great deal:

> This minister did not meet our family's spiritual or personal needs and seems to have a great deal of difficulty ministering to this congregation. The minister's calling seems to be to higher things that deal with world issues. As a result, many of the needs of the membership go unattended. The sermons were hard to put into focus and relate to. . . . Administrative abilities are almost non-existent. Tasks were given to others without any guidance or leadership at all. This minister was very jealous of . . . personal time and had very little of it to give to emergencies that would develop.[42]

While our research has shown that liberal theology and intrinsic religiosity are not inevitably incompatible, some of the switchers seemed to see them as incompatible. Switchers complained of too little emphasis on the gifts of the Holy Spirit, a personal relationship with Jesus, and studying the Bible as the word of God. Two comments stood out:

> As a long-time member, I found the trend toward intellectualism which denied the miracles, even the resurrection and second coming to be extremely oppressive within the denomination as a whole.

> We were raised in a Disciple church and it broke our hearts to leave the denomination, but the liberalness was too much.

Some of the switchers had simply moved, often to a location in which there was no Disciples congregation, at least not within a reasonable drive. Some of those who moved were actually within thirty minutes or so of a Disciples congregation but apparently wanted to attend a neighborhood church rather than drive so far.

Several switchers mentioned poor relationships as a reason for leaving. In some cases, the switcher or members of the switcher's family had been rejected by other members. In other cases, the switcher simply never felt truly accepted. One reported that after trying to break into a congregation's social circles for two years, "I never stopped feeling like an outsider." In other cases, the congregation's power structure was a problem, often focusing on the role of the elders in the congregation. Here two comments stood out:

> Anyone who served on the board of elders who was not in the board president's social circle was totally ignored or put down and humiliated in front of everyone else.

> The pastor was railroaded out of the church by some of the elders. This was not done in accordance with the by-laws. I was told to blindly accept the wise elders' decision as they knew best.

42. We altered this response to obscure any identifying clues to the respondent's gender, age, region, etc.

We would affirm the danger of church power struggles with respect to attrition. While the pastor who is "railroaded out" may recover professionally — one such pastor eventually became chaplain of his state's senate — some members of the congregation may never return to any church in their disillusionment with the practice of the "gospel" by ostensibly spiritual, mature, and wise elders. The fallout may be especially bad if the elders adopt a nonempathetic attitude toward those who are feeling hurt and ignored, saying things like "The real problem is not what we did but your bad attitude and bitterness about it. A genuine — or at least a more mature — Christian would accept our decisions without complaint. If you prayed more, you would see things our way and not get so upset." It is difficult to describe the outrage one can feel when a natural response to a perceived injustice is characterized as a sin. If forced to accept a "gospel" that promotes gross injustice or leave a denomination, a layperson with any sense of integrity may well leave, as the only remaining way of effectively protesting the injustice.

Several switchers mentioned lack of attention to their needs and to programs for children. A couple mentioned politics:

> Emphasis on political issues more than spiritual.

> Repeated conflict with the minister and his lack of centering on Jesus Christ as the true leader of the church instead of politics.

While these comments enrich the results of the study and we think confirm many of the ideas discussed previously in our report, we do not think they lead to any completely new hypotheses about attrition among Disciples.

Overall results are summarized in Table 18 (p. 552). We do not rank the relative importance of each result but merely whether or not we found any evidence in favor of each major hypothesis. Our most consistent results showed up in the "giving" category (eight of the hypotheses received at least partial support). Regional effects and congregational growth received the least consistent results, with only two or three hypotheses receiving support.

IMPLICATIONS

Initially our results suggested that membership in a supportive small group was the best predictor of activity; even with controls, its Maslow subscale remained one of the strongest predictors. In general, we think that a focus on meeting needs can be a worthy objective for a congregation as long as the focus does not become too introverted (excluding concern for one's community and world) or too narrow (e.g., stressing emotional needs to the exclusion of spiritual needs or vice versa).

A second concern would be the extent to which a congregation fosters intrinsic religious commitment, which was one of the few variables to have

TABLE 18   Summary of Results: Support for Hypotheses

Hypothesis	Attendance	Giving	Congregational Growth	Activity Level	Regional Effect
Conservatism	YES	YES	NO	YES	NO
Intrinsic religiosity	YES	YES	?	YES	NO
Pastoral effectiveness	YES	YES	NO	YES	NO
Maslow's needs	YES	YES	NO	YES	NO
Transfer ecumenism	NA	NA	NA	YES[a]	YES
Internal structure	NO	YES	YES	NO	NO
Localism	NO	?	NO	NO	NO
Child-rearing	NO	NO	NO	YES	NO
Evangelism	YES	YES	NO[b]	YES	NO
Value structures	YES	YES	YES	NO	NO
Job/Family role conflict	YES	YES	NO	YES	NO

a. Hypothetical future activity (see Table 9).

b. However, aggregate scores on evangelism emphasis within congregations are correlated significantly, positively ($r = .15$) with congregational growth.

some relationship with almost all the dependent variables. In retrospect, the importance of intrinsic religiosity within a congregation is not so illogical. If a congregation is only existing to serve the purpose of a social club, why bother? There are too many competing organizations that may serve equally well as places to fellowship. In contrast, church congregations are one of the few places where one should be able to grow in faith in the context of a supportive group of fellow pilgrims. A congregation that becomes nothing but another social club may deserve to perish in the competition. While conservatism seemed related to attrition among Disciples, the deeper underlying frustration — possibly shared by liberals and conservatives alike in different ways — may be with the issue of whether the church is an echo or a challenge in society. That is, is the church as much a victim of secularization as other institutions?[43] The Disciples may be in a unique position to challenge secularization at both levels — in terms of both personal life and social justice — in a society that likes to hear comforting words in both areas. The problem is keeping a balance: too much emphasis on the personal can obscure God's concern for all peoples, while too much emphasis on social injustice can obscure the concern that God has for individuals. Perhaps one reason that minority congregations seem to be doing so well within Disciples is that they are able to maintain this balance better than their Anglo brothers and sisters.

It has been observed before that conservatives are important for keeping local congregations going since they are among the most active participants.[44] The key element here may not be conservatism per se but its relationship with intrinsic religiosity. Those who are willing to admit their need for spiritual

43. See Berger, "American Religion."
44. Roof, *Community and Commitment*, p. 296.

help may be among the intrinsically religious; as R. S. Warner comments, admitting one's needs is a great leveler.[45] A pastor would seem to be at a good starting point for helping intrinsically religious people grow spiritually if he or she can openly say, "I have spiritual needs; you have spiritual needs; we all have spiritual, emotional, and physical needs. The good news is that God through Christ and the Holy Spirit wants to meet these legitimate needs for all peoples."

Our findings with respect to the transfer ecumenism hypothesis merit careful consideration. Though we found this problem to be greater in some regions than others, and though it was not as much of a problem as some other things, it nonetheless serves to underscore the warning we have heard elsewhere, such as that of McKinney and Roof — "Liberal Protestants can no longer sit back and wait passively for people to come and join them."[46] Denominational loyalty, especially among the young, is low. We think that people shop around for a church that will meet their felt needs, which would mean that churches that do the best job of selling themselves as places to get needs met will retain and gain the most members. Young families with children may represent a special opportunity: they are likely to be looking for support in socializing their children in intrinsically religious, prosocial ways.

Our results confirm the importance of the pastor and others in church leadership positions within the local congregation. While the correlations between pastoral leadership and the dependent variables were not as strong as we might have expected, pastoral leadership was clearly a leading factor in the decisions of many switchers to leave their Disciples congregation.

In contrast, contextual factors such as localism and internal structure did not do as well in predicting many of the dependent variables. While our results do not deny the importance of contextual factors, they do point more toward the importance of institutional factors. Pastors and congregations are not helpless in reducing attrition or promoting growth. Our results leave us more encouraged about the future of the Christian Church (Disciples of Christ) and, by extension, other mainstream Protestant denominations than others have seemed to be.[47]

45. Warner, *New Wine in Old Wineskins*, p. 294.

46. William McKinney and Wade Clark Roof, "Liberal Protestantism: A Sociodemographic Perpsective," in *Liberal Protestantism: Realities and Possibilities,* ed. R. S. Michaelson and Wade Clark Roof (New York: Pilgrim Press, 1986), p. 50.

47. For some more pessimistic views, see Roof and McKinney, *American Mainline Religion;* Roof, *Community and Commitment;* Berger, "American Religion," p. 33; McKinney and Roof, "Liberal Protestantism," p. 48; D. M. Kelley, *Why Conservative Churches Are Growing* (New York: Harper & Row, 1972).

Working Group Response:
Ecology of Growth and Decline

Jeff Gill, Recorder

The working group on Ecology of Growth and Decline did not hear an early draft of the paper by Meyers and Olson because they were ill.

We looked at patterns of attrition and retention, the geography of religion, sociocultural development of religion in urban areas, and denominational switching as it relates to social mobility. We looked over charts, graphs, maps, and tables, and some of us learned what a Chi Square Analysis is. In short, we sifted through a large mass of data. It was far from dry. In fact, there was enough data to drown in. Our discussions on growth and decline tended to dive directly into the middle and come up for air looking for a direction in which to swim.

Our focus came from returning to the title of our working group — ecology of growth and decline. All of our presenters conducted their research looking at the Disciples of Christ as an organism, an entity with many parts, sharing certain characteristics. You might remember from high school biology that every organism is adapted to a particular environment. When the environment (or context) changes, an organism has three options: (1) it can go in search of the old, familiar environment in a new place — migration; (2) it can adapt to the new environment, change so that life continues to flourish under new conditions — adaptation; or (3) the organism can stay in the new environment without adapting — extinction.

Our presenters' papers all gave us insights into how the old, familiar, comfortable, white, English-speaking, male environments that the Disciples of Christ once flourished in are no longer as congenial.

To look at how we must adapt requires that we first know what we are adapting from. The Disciples Belt, the nine states on an arc between Ohio and Texas, is no longer the growth environment that it once was. The phenomenon of individuals switching denominations due to social mobility, long a suspected cause of attrition among mainline denominations, appears to cause negligible losses. Institutions of higher education that once nurtured the Disciples are now secular or, perhaps worse, have few Disciples.

Even before we began to look at possible adaptations, concern was expressed about our identity as a faith community. One clear area of consensus among those surveyed was that the Church must meet needs. They raised the question of what constitute *appropriate* needs and appropriate ways for the church to meet them. If we adapt just to meet needs, we might transform the Church into little more than another social service organization.

Again, we looked to our model for some focus. In different environments, ecological pressures create many different adaptations. In warm, wet areas, plants may have thin, large leaves; while in hot, dry climates plants will have small leaves with thick waxy coatings. But both are still plants. Despite their differences, they continue to share the characteristics of all plants in the way that, say, an armadillo does not.

As a church, we are called to proclaim the good news of God's love made manifest in Jesus Christ and to witness to that love in word and deed to all people. If anything we do as a church denies or prevents us from maintaining this gospel, then we are no longer a church. If we adapt in ways that deny the love of God or our freedom to tell the story of God's gracious care for God's creation, then we will no longer be Christ's church, as the armadillo is not a plant.

In fact, our group has agreed that any adaptation we attempt must be directed toward attempts to better maintain and proclaim the gospel — not toward institutional survival. The gospel must be our norm for appropriate change, not the survival of the Disciples of Christ.

Having said that, we felt more confident in pointing out particular adaptive responses that we feel will allow this denomination to continue to reach more people. In a highly mobile society, there are needs for the church to nurture among the new American gypsies of all socioeconomic groups. Adults as well as children are fearful in new communities, and they readily enter churches where invitations come freely and often. Family life is a part of contemporary life that is in need of nurture. Ministry to families as families, not just youth ministry, is a need that churches would do well to attend to. Those infamous sixty-four million baby boomers are showing a growing desire to develop their family life, and they see the church as a context in which they might be able to do so, but they give evidence of a Missouri skepticism as well: we will have to "show them." That ministry might simply take the form of bringing together families for a structured discussion within the church. Boomers don't want to be lectured. At the same time, they want some adhesive to reassemble their fragmented lives. There is even some data suggesting that younger people see the Disciples of Christ as an accepting church where they might be welcome as young people.

The character of family life in America entails two things more. Individuals have a larger need for a support system in terms of conversation, counseling, prayer, and simple mutual encouragement. This comes out of the survey material as a market preference for churches with a large and varied small-group life. It doesn't matter if it is Sarah's Circle, the men's softball team, the prayer group, or the property committee. There must be some small group for any individual who comes into the church. The small-group factor was a leading indicator in surveys for growth as well as for stability of membership. A related but separate characteristic for which people are searching is friend-ship. Did you talk with another member of your church between Sundays last week? If you did, your church is more likely to be growing, and you are likely to stay.

Individuals also want their church to meet their spiritual needs. They want the preaching and teaching they receive to help them find meaning and purpose in life and to bring them into a closer relationship with God. If they don't find this, they will look elsewhere.

Another significant factor identified was leadership, specifically pastoral leadership with a passion for the gospel and a vision for the church's mission. Individuals clearly rate this factor very highly. It also seems to be one of the clearest indicators for stability and growth, regardless of the environment in which a church is located. This should not be surprising, since leadership, be it lay leadership, pastoral leadership, or national leadership, is the agent of adaptation. Leaders must be sensitive to their environment, noting changes in needs and priorities. At the same time, leaders must also be able to articulate identity.

We looked at leadership recruitment. The Hispanic population of the U.S. is large and growing. Are we encouraging Hispanic students to go into the ministry?

Dare we ask if we are recruiting anybody at all to the ministry? Or are we just waiting for our leadership to walk in the seminary doors? How do we deal with those who are in seminary? Does seminary education prepare stu-dents to leave the office and the word processor behind and go out into communities of flux and change that are today's environment for ministry?

We cannot say on the basis of currently available material just why the church has proved itself so unable to adapt to the changes of the past few decades, but we can say with some confidence that pastors with a passion for the gospel and a vision for the church's mission will be the most effective agents for adaptation in the decades to come.

Perhaps the most exciting story we heard was of the Haitian and Hispanic Disciples in New York City — the Evangelical Crusade/Fishers of Men (a French-speaking Haitian church) and La Hermosa (a Hispanic congregation). It was exciting to hear about Philius Nicolas, pastor of the Fishers of Men who read about the restoration movement of Stone and Campbell. He inquired into the polity of modern-day Disciples and then brought a whole new perspective of worship and mission into the Disciples of Christ.

It was exciting to hear about La Hermosa and its work in the mission field of New York City. Again, to see that the Disciples balance of local independence and mainstream identity is appealing to a young, struggling, transitional group of lower-middle-class Hispanics.

In truth, we began to see how this seemingly radical adaptation — Disciples of Christ polity with a social group that is marginalized and largely disenfranchised — really takes us back to our historical roots. Stone and Campbell knew their frontier constituency well: young families struggling in adverse conditions to gain some stability, marginalized and largely disenfranchised. What we often call diversity may really be history. We have been more diverse than many of us seem to know, and today we are already more diverse than most of us realize. We need to understand that our denominational priority of "Dynamic Faith Communities" may have to mean "Adaptive Faith Communities." As an institution, the church at large needs to be able to adapt more quickly. To do so we will have to continue research into diversity and growth as they relate regionally and nationally.

Obviously, we can't ask every congregation to be all things to all people, but we must somehow understand how that diversity works on the larger level in multiple congregation areas. We must continue to embrace the diversity that has always been ours. Part of this is financial. How might financial structures be ordered to adapt more quickly? Part of it is structural, as in buildings. We need a sense of identity that will let Disciples be more willing to worship in gyms, in town halls, and in apartment complex "party" rooms.

Our prospects for growth, our adaptation to new environments, our journey together with a shared vision on a common mission sounds very much like a walk in the wilderness. We are called to be a pilgrim people, and we have to be able to travel light and fast when necessary. But no matter how spread out our band becomes, we have a common destination. When we get to that promised land, we may find that the destination looks remarkably familiar.

VIII. CONCLUSION

Future Prospects of the Christian Church (Disciples of Christ)

D. Newell Williams

The Christian Church (Disciples of Christ) might well be troubled regarding its future prospects.

1. Over the past century the Disciples have become successively alienated from sizable groups within the U.S. population and have thus been cut off from directly influencing the culture of a large number of contemporary Americans. In 1906 the federal census acknowledged the separation of the Churches of Christ from the Disciples of Christ. The members of this new church represented a predominantly rural and agrarian people located primarily in the South. As a result of this separation, the direct cultural influence of the Disciples was limited to people who were more identified with the urban and industrial bands of American society and culture than with the rural and agrarian bands of American culture and society. In 1927 an alternative to the Disciples' International Convention was established by conservative Disciples who refused to support organizations with liberals in positions of leadership (the North American Christian Convention). In 1971 adherents of this convention were disproportionately rural and suburban as compared to the Disciples. Though the Disciples have continued to have a direct influence on rural and suburban Americans, their direct cultural influence has been limited to liberals and conservatives who are willing to support organizations that include liberals as leaders. Though both of the Disciples divisions are related to major social developments in American history, their division itself can be credited to the failure of the Disciples to claim a basis for Christian union that would enable them to remain united despite emerging cleavages in American society and culture.

2. The Disciples have failed to appeal to the current generation of younger adults. This failure is related to the gap between the theological and moral views of Disciples ministers and active laity and the failure of the Disciples professional leadership to identify a distinctively Christian norm for

561

judging theological statements and moral action. The negative effects of these two factors, intensified by the general social and cultural polarization that occurred in the 1960s, has prevented Disciples from generating the increased commitment to the programs of their congregations necessary to appeal to the current generation of younger adults. As a result, Disciples have less direct influence on the culture of younger Americans than ever before in their history, and less influence than conservative Protestant denominations currently have.

3. Since 1971 the Disciples have suffered numerically as a result of the large concentration of their members in areas characterized by one or more of the following factors: low population growth, the presence of competing Independent Christian Churches, and unidentified contextual factors that have also limited the growth of the Presbyterians and United Methodists in the same areas.

On the basis of findings reported in this volume, one might easily predict that the Disciples can only continue to decline numerically and have progressively less influence on American culture. On the other hand, this study suggests that the Disciples' numerical decline and loss of influence on American culture is largely, though not completely, the result of weaknesses in their theology and institutional life. To be specific, the decline appears to be largely the result of their failure to identify a basis for Christian union that can overcome social and cultural division, the difference between the views of their ministers and active laity, and the failure of their professional leadership to identify a distinctively Christian norm for judging theological statements and moral action. Though the impact of contextual factors should not be underestimated, if the Disciples could successfully address their theological and institutional failings, they might be able to enlist and influence a broader range of contemporary Americans than is currently the case. In other words, if Disciples could remedy their theological and institutional failings, it does not appear that it would be impossible to reverse their numerical decline and loss of influence on American culture. In any event, unlike the geographical location of large numbers of Disciples, theological and institutional failings are factors that the Disciples can be expected to affect. Moreover, theological and institutional failings of the sort identified in this study should be of concern to a church even if its numbers and cultural influence remain on the rise.

It should be noted that the identification of a basis for Christian union is integrally related to the identification of a distinctively Christian norm for judging theological statements and moral action. That is, whatever a communion determines to be its distinctively Christian norm *will* be its basis for Christian union, and vice versa. It may also be noted that identifying a basis for Christian union that can overcome social and cultural division would go a long way toward helping to remedy the institutional problems associated with the gap between the views of Disciples ministers and active members. Thus, it is recommended that the first thing the Disciples should do in response to their current situation is identify a basis for Christian union capable of overcoming social and cultural division that can serve at the same time as a distinctively Christian norm for judging theological statements and moral action.

THE GOSPEL

For the Churches of Christ, Independent Christian Churches, and conservative Protestants generally, the basis of Christian union and a distinctively Christian norm is the Bible, received as the infallible word of God. This basis of Christian union and distinctively Christian norm cannot be adopted by the Disciples — at least not by liberal Disciples. Having accepted the application of the idea of development to history and the Bible, liberals will not accept the characterization of the Bible (or any book) as an infallible revelation from God (see p. 7 in this volume). Contrary to the conclusion of the late-nineteenth-century Disciples conservative J. W. McGarvey (see p. 111), belief with regard to such issues is *not* a matter of moral choice; it is a matter of credibility. In turn, standards of credibility are socially determined: what people can believe to be true is the result of their education. Thus, liberals *cannot* believe that the Bible is an infallible revelation from God. Moreover, the Disciples' first major division shows that the Bible received as the infallible word of God is *not* a basis for Christian union that can overcome social and cultural divisions.

Is there a basis for Christian union and a distinctively Christian norm for judging theological statements and moral action other than the Bible received as the infallible word of God? Of course! Furthermore, such a basis is identified and employed in the writings of the most prominent of the nineteenth-century Disciples leaders, Alexander Campbell. Campbell maintained that the basis of Christian union and the distinctively Christian norm is the gospel. Nor was this idea unique to him. Indeed, he publicly acknowledged that it had been taught by the great sixteenth-century reformer Martin Luther.[1]

Campbell identified the gospel, as distinct from the Bible as a whole, as the apostles' witness to the "facts" about Jesus Christ. Campbell defines a fact as a "deed" or "something done." For Campbell deeds disclose the character of the doer. In the case of Jesus Christ, the doer is God. Campbell summarized the deeds of God in Jesus Christ reported by the apostles as follows: "He died for our sins — he was buried in the grave — he rose from the dead for our justification — and is ascended to the skies to prepare mansions for his dis-

---

1. Campbell, *The Christian System* (Cincinnati: Standard Publishing, 1901), p. 153. Subsequent references to this volume will be made parenthetically in the text, using the abbreviation *CS*. For a discussion of the ideas of Luther and Calvin regarding the authority of the gospel in relation to the Scriptures, see Richard Robert Osmer, *A Teachable Spirit* (Louisville: Westminster/John Knox Press, 1990).

ciples." For Campbell the *meaning* of the facts about Jesus Christ reported by the apostles is that "God is love" (*CS,* pp. 90-91, 220-21).

According to Campbell, the message that God is love is the basis (he used the word *foundation*) for Christian union. Why? Because the message that God is love, received in faith, alone has the spiritual power to reconcile people to God and to one another. How did Campbell arrive at the conclusion that people are reconciled to God and one another only by faith in the message that God is love? Like other evangelical Protestants of his day, he believed that all people are sinners. Furthermore, like other evangelical Protestants of his day, he believed that as people become aware of their sin, they become convinced that God hates them because of it. Arguing that in the human realm hate begets hate, Campbell taught that people who believe that God hates them cannot love God. Hence, for Campbell, reason as well as Scripture and experience shows that it is only the message of God's unconditional love that can reconcile sinners to God. Only persons who are reconciled to God can be reconciled to one another. Thus, the message that God is love, received in faith, alone has the power to unite the church (*CS,* pp. 87-91, 220-21).

To be sure, Campbell sought the union of Christians through the restoration of the apostolic or ancient order of the church revealed in the New Testament. Nevertheless, he did not make restoration of the ancient order the basis of Christian union. Campbell's understanding of Christian union was not mechanical but dynamic. Union was the relationship with God and neighbor produced by faith in the gospel. He believed that "apostolic" practices such as weekly observance of the Lord's Supper and believer's immersion for the remission of sins were more effective in communicating the message that God is love than "modern" practices. Thus, restoration of the ancient order, which would further communication of the message that God is love, would lead to Christian union (*CS,* p. 204).[2]

For Campbell the gospel was also the distinctively Christian norm for judging theological statements and moral action. This can be seen in his well-known rules for interpreting the Bible. After listing historical, grammatical, and philological rules for interpreting Scripture, Campbell identifies knowledge of the gospel of God's unconditional love as *the* critical condition for the "salutary and sanctifying" knowledge of the Scriptures. Using the analogy of sight, Campbell argues that "There is a sound eye in reference to spiritual light, as well as in reference to material light. Now, while the philological principles and rules of interpretation enable many men to be skilful in biblical criticism, and in the interpretation of words and sentences, who neither

2. See William J. Richardson, "Alexander Campbell as an Advocate of Christian Union," in *Lectures in Honor of the Alexander Campbell Bicentennial, 1788-1988* (Nashville: Disciples of Christ Historical Society, 1988), pp. 110-18; see also William E. Tucker and Lester G. McAllister, *Journey in Faith: A History of the Christian Church (Disciples of Christ)* (St. Louis: Bethany Press, 1975), pp. 156-58; and Richard M. Tristano, *The Origins of the Restoration Movement: An Intellectual History* (Atlanta: Glenmary Research Center, 1988), pp. 118-24.

perceive nor admire the *things* represented by these words; the sound eye contemplates the things themselves, and is ravished with the moral scenes which the Bible unfolds." Campbell defines "moral *soundness* of vision" as "having the eyes of the understanding fixed solely on God himself, his approbation and complacent [unconditional] affection for us" (*CS*, pp. 4-5). He asserts that to interpret the Scriptures to the salvation of one's soul, one must study them with the intent to hear "the still small voice of God's philanthropy." To study the Bible with this intent is to come within "the understanding distance." Campbell asserts that all who come within the understanding distance will be able to understand God easily "in all matters of piety [religion] and morality." To remain outside of the understanding distance in one's study of the Bible is to fail to understand what God is saying in the Bible (*CS*, pp. 4-5). Thus, rather than making knowledge of the Bible received as the infallible word of God the key to one's interpretation of the meaning of the gospel, Campbell makes knowledge of the *meaning* of the gospel — the message of God's unconditional love — the key to one's interpretation of the meaning of the Bible regarding all matters of religion and morality.

How could Campbell identify knowledge of the meaning of the gospel, rather than some other aspect of biblical teaching, as *the* indispensable condition for truly perceiving and spiritually benefiting from what God is saying in the Bible? Very simply, Campbell was convinced that the message that God is love, received in faith, *alone* has the power to reconcile people to God and neighbor. Assuming, as Campbell did, that the Bible is a revelation from God, and that God's purpose in revelation is to restore human beings to right relationship with God and neighbor, it can only follow that faith in the message that God is love is *the* key to truly understanding and benefiting spiritually from study of the Scriptures. Thus, for Campbell, the gospel was the ultimate check on the interpretation of the Bible. Any interpretation of the Bible that denied or simply overlooked the message of God's unconditional love for sinners would hinder God's purpose in revelation.

Campbell's use of the gospel as the distinctively Christian norm for judging theological statements can be illustrated nowhere more clearly than in his most important essay on baptism, "Remission of Sins." Campbell, who identified his movement as the "current reformation," begins by affirming Luther's identification of the gospel as the measure of the church's teaching. "Luther said that the doctrine of justification, or forgiveness, was the test of a standing or falling church. If right in this, she could not be very far wrong in any thing else; but if wrong here, it was not easy to suppose her right in any thing. . . . We agree with him in this as well as in many other sentiments" (*CS*, p. 153). He then argues that the purpose of baptism is to provide believers with an *assurance* of the forgiveness of their sin — an interpretation of the purpose of baptism he believed to be fully in accord with the meaning of the gospel, which he refers to as "the doctrine of justification, or forgiveness" in his paraphrase of Luther quoted above. Proceeding in accord with the four standard theological canons of his day (sometimes referred to today as the "Methodist" quadrilateral), he grounds his argument in (1) Scripture (the statements and actions of the apostles in relation to persons who had been baptized), (2) reason (our human need for some action to assure us of the forgiveness of our sin), (3) experience (the reports of persons who had been baptized "for remission of sins"), and (4) tradition (statements from widely approved church histories, the writings of the Church Fathers, and several historic confessions regarding the purpose of baptism). Typically Protestant in his method, Campbell gives priority to the authority of Scripture. He uses the authorities of reason, experience, and tradition to confirm his interpretation of Scripture. However, in light of Campbell's rules for interpreting Scripture — and his paraphrase of Luther's statement regarding the test of a standing or falling church — it seems clear that he felt the ultimate norm for his position on the purpose of baptism was not a particular text or even all of the texts of the Bible but the conformity of his interpretation of the purpose of baptism to the meaning of the gospel.

How does the gospel function as a norm for judging moral action? For Campbell the fundamental moral standard is conformity to the implications of the gospel received in faith. In "Remission of Sins" he observes that the moral appeals of the apostles addressed to the first disciples were uniformly based on the disciples' understanding of themselves as persons who are accepted by God despite their sin. According to Campbell, the apostles exhorted the first disciples to forgive because God had forgiven them, to be just because God had justified them, to seek peace with all persons because God had made peace with them, to be benevolent toward all persons because God had been benevolent toward them, to live in dignity and purity because they had been adopted by God (*CS,* p. 160). Campbell affirmed the apostolic practice as a model for his own day.

It might be further asked how the standard of conformity to the implications of the gospel received in faith applies to specific moral issues. How is one to determine the dictates of peacemaking or justice or purity in regard to particular situations? Judging by examples of Campbell's ethical reflection, it is clear he believed that Christians need other norms, in addition to the norm of conformity to the implications of the message of God's unconditional love received in faith, in order to make appropriate moral decisions in regard to specific issues.

Examples of Campbell's moral thinking with regard to war, the role of women, and slavery illustrate the variety of norms he used to arrive at specific moral decisions. With regard to whether a Christian should participate in war, he looked to the teachings of Jesus.[3] His views on the role of women were influenced by his reading of Genesis 2, his perception of differences in the natural gifts of men and women, and a philosophy of knowledge that empha-

---

3. Campbell, "Address on War," in *Popular Lectures and Addresses* (Philadelphia: James Challen & Son, 1866), pp. 342-66.

sized the importance of nurture and education in the formation of "civilized" human beings.[4] In the case of American slavery, he relied heavily on social, economic, and psychological analysis of the contemporary situation. He denied that the message that God loves us despite our sin condemns the master-slave relationship in *all* situations. He acknowledged that the apostles had taught slaves to be obedient to their masters. Thus, he frankly admitted that the Bible is not *opposed* to the simple master-slave relationship. Nevertheless, he was convinced that the *American* institution of slavery was socially, economically, and psychologically destructive to both the slave and the slaveholder. Furthermore, he believed that slavery was in conflict with the "genius of the age" reflected in the various eighteenth- and early nineteenth-century human rights philosophies. Thus, despite what many nineteenth-century American Christians judged to be the Bible's support of American slavery, Campbell opposed American slavery and called on others to join him in supporting a succession of efforts aimed at ending slavery in America.[5]

Thus, Campbell did not believe that conformity to the fundamental implications of the gospel received in faith is the *only* norm that Christians need in order to make appropriate moral decisions in specific cases. The examples noted above show that he also referred to biblical teachings distinct from the gospel, philosophy, his own observations, and analysis of the contemporary situation. However, a careful reading of Campbell's treatment of moral issues shows that his ultimate moral norm was conformity to the fundamental implications of the gospel, no matter what other norms he might employ in arriving at a specific decision. For Campbell, the ultimate standards of moral action were justice, peace, benevolence, dignity. This explains how Campbell, who clearly gave serious attention to the specific moral injunctions of Scripture, could advocate ending the American institution of slavery with full knowledge of the biblical injunction directing slaves to obey their masters.

Is the gospel a basis of Christian union and a distinctively Christian norm that can overcome social and cultural diversity? It appears that it is. First, the message of God's unconditional love, received in faith, reconciles persons to God and neighbor. In his major treatise on the Lord's Supper, Campbell states that "each disciple, in handing the symbols to his fellow disciple, says, in effect . . . 'under Jesus the Messiah we are one. Mutually embraced in the Everlasting arms, I embrace you in mine; thy sorrows shall be my sorrows, and thy joys my joys. Joint debtors to the favor of God and the love of Jesus, we shall jointly suffer with him, that we may jointly reign with him" (*CS*, p. 273). Thus the gospel of God's gracious love for all overcomes social and cultural diversity by establishing a distinctively Christian basis of relationship.

---

4. Campbell, "Woman and Her Mission," in *Popular Lectures and Addresses,* pp. 213-29.
5. See Robert O. Fife, "In the Spirit of the Prophets: Alexander Campbell as a Social Thinker," in *Lectures in Honor of the Alexander Campbell Bicentennial, 1788-1988* (Nashville: Disciples of Christ Historical Society, 1988), pp. 19-24, 28-33.

Second, as Campbell demonstrated by his own practice, acceptance of the gospel as the distinctively Christian norm, while providing an ultimate norm for judging the apparent claims of all other authorities, does not require that one abandon other authorities. Thus, acceptance of the gospel as the basis for Christian unity and the distinctively Christian norm also overcomes social and cultural division by allowing the claims of various authorities, while providing a distinctively Christian norm for judging the apparent claims of all other authorities. For example, contemporary American Christians are divided over such issues as the role of women, homosexuality, and the possibility of salvation apart from a confession of faith in Jesus Christ. Identification of the gospel as the basis of Christian unity and the distinctively Christian norm does not rule out arguments for or against the authority of specific biblical teachings regarding such issues (no matter what those teachings are judged to be). Neither does it rule out arguments for or against the authority of philosophy, psychology, or the social sciences regarding these issues (regardless of the school of thought to which one subscribes). However, identification of the gospel as the basis of Christian unity and the distinctively Christian norm would provide American Christians with a distinctive measure by which they could judge their own conclusions and the conclusions of others regarding these and other issues. Currently, American Christians who differ on such matters tend either to avoid conversation with each other or to shout at each other; dialogue based on recognition of a common Christian norm is rare.

In light of the statement that liberals *cannot* adopt the Bible received as the infallible word of God as the basis for Christian union and their distinctively Christian norm, it might be asked whether liberals can accept the gospel as such a basis. This is a question that individual liberals must answer for themselves. It should be underscored, however, that Campbell did not ground the authority of the gospel on acceptance of the authority of the Bible. For Campbell, the authority of the gospel as a revelation from God is confirmed by its spiritual power to produce acts of love and courage in the lives of people who receive its message in faith (*CS*, pp. 223-24, 234-35, 256-57).[6] Thus, the question is whether liberals can accept the gospel as the basis for Christian union and as their distinctively Christian norm for judging theological statements and moral action on the same grounds advanced by Campbell or on other grounds external to the Bible.

Judging by the positions of at least two contemporary liberal Disciples theologians, the answer to this question is Yes. In a book published in 1965, H. Jackson Forstman identifies the understanding that one stands in relationship with God by virtue of God's sheer grace as the basis of genuine community and the norm for determining all matters related to the Christian life.[7] In this case, it

6. See also D. Newell Williams, "The Gospel as the Power of God to Salvation: Alexander Campbell and Experimental Religion," in *Lectures in Honor of the Alexander Campbell Bicentennial*, pp. 136-37.

7. Forstman, *Christian Faith and the Church* (St. Louis: Bethany Press, 1965).

seems that something like Campbell's notion of the effect of the gospel received in faith has been identified as the foundation for Christian unity and the norm for judging all matters pertaining to the Christian life. Clark M. Williamson has defined the distinctively Christian norm by which all theological statements and moral action are to be judged as "the good news that God graciously and freely offers the divine love to each and all (oneself included) and that this God who loves all the creatures therefore *commands* that justice be done to them."[8] In this case it appears that what Campbell called the gospel has been combined with what he understood to be an effect of receiving the gospel in faith (the doing of justice) to become the distinctively Christian norm for judging theological statements and moral action. Although there are significant differences in the ways these two theologians ground their positions, both affirm with Campbell the gospel as the basis of Christian union and the distinctively Christian norm for judging theological statements and moral action.

In light of the fact that most active Disciples laity are conservative, it might also be asked whether conservatives can accept the gospel as the basis for Christian union and the distinctively Christian norm. Of course, this is a question that individual conservatives must answer for themselves. Nevertheless, it should be noted that Campbell, who lived *before* the emergence of the social and intellectual issues that divided American Protestants into liberals and conservatives, identified the gospel, rather than the Bible received as the infallible word of God, as the basis of Christian union and the distinctively Christian norm. He did so on the basis of the spiritual power of the gospel received in faith to reconcile people to God. If conservatives are acquainted with the spiritual power of the gospel to reconcile persons to God, they, too, may well be able to claim the gospel (as distinguished from the Bible) received as the infallible word of God as the basis of Christian union and as the distinctively Christian norm for judging theological statements and moral action.

Would acceptance of the gospel as the basis of Christian union and the distinctively Christian norm mean that the church would no longer have need for the Bible? Certainly not! The Bible, both Old and New Testaments, discloses the gospel. Study of the Scriptures with, as Campbell put it, the right "intent" — the intent of hearing the "still small voice of God's philanthropy" — is a primary means of encountering the gospel. Campbell could not see how any Christian would grow in the Christian life who did not frequently engage — with the right intent — in the study of the Scriptures (*CS*, pp. 241-42). The Scriptures also contain the earliest interpretation of the meaning of the gospel (the New Testament) and the literature from which the earliest Christians interpreted the meaning of the gospel (the Old Testament). If, as is surely the case, Christians benefit from dialogue with contemporary Christians, they will just as surely benefit from dialogue with the earliest interpreters of the gospel

---

8. Williamson, "Preaching the Gospel: Some Theological Reflections," *Encounter* 49 (1988): 191-201.

and from study of the Scriptures by which the earliest Christians grasped the meaning of the gospel. To give up the spiritual companionship and guidance of the Scriptures would be to impoverish the Christian life for either liberal or conservative. To accept the gospel as the basis of Christian union and the distinctively Christian norm is not to reject the Bible but simply to recognize that the gospel created the church (and all Christian literature) and is, therefore, the ultimate norm of all things pertaining to the Christian life.

One might further ask whether the gospel is a *distinctively* Christian norm. Surely it is. It may not be a uniquely Christian norm. Many Christians have come to affirm that Judaism also teaches God's unconditional love for persons. Nevertheless, the message that God accepts us despite our sin, if not uniquely Christian, is distinctively Christian. Where else in contemporary American society does one hear this message proclaimed?

OVERCOMING THE GAP

Once the Disciples have begun to identify the gospel as a basis of Christian union that can overcome social and cultural division and serve at the same time as a distinctively Christian norm, they should attend to overcoming the negative effect that the gap between the views of their ministers and and active members has on the commitment to the congregational program. Surely it is not necessary that Disciples ministers and active members agree completely on all issues in order to support a common program. On the other hand, it does seem likely that some mutual understanding and appreciation of the different views of Disciples ministers and active members, if not some narrowing of differences on issues where they differ most widely, would facilitate increased commitment to the program of Disciples congregations. Even if Disciples identify a basis of Christian union capable of overcoming social and cultural division that can serve at the same time as a distinctively Christian norm, they cannot be expected to increase commitment to the program of their congregation unless they are convinced that their congregation promotes ideas and activities that are intellectually credible and morally responsible.

The difference in the views of Disciples ministers and active members appears to be rooted in differences in the types of education they have received. It is maintained, at least in part, by their failure to engage in serious and sustained dialogue regarding issues that divide them. Thus, the following recommendations are aimed at helping the Disciples to engage in discussion of theological and moral issues over which they differ.

1. Disciples need to recognize the importance of theology. Twentieth-century Disciples have claimed that their unity is based on their common confession that Jesus is the Christ. At the same time, they have been remarkably vague regarding the theological content of this affirmation. The underlying

message has been that all theological positions are acceptable as long as unity is maintained and there is some prospect of the denomination serving as a force for good in the world. Identification of the gospel as the basis for Christian union and the distinctively Christian norm would go a long way toward helping Disciples to recognize the importance of discussing issues theologically.

2. Liberal Disciples ministers need to be more forthright in discussing their theological and social positions and especially the arguments that have led them to accept those positions. This study shows that Disciples pastors are hesitant to address subjects on which they perceive a wide difference between their own views and those of the majority of their congregation. This study also shows that Disciples denominational leaders have been hesitant to address issues on which they perceive a wide difference between their own views and those of the majority of the constituency. Clearly there is reason for Disciples professional leaders to be hesitant with regard to frankly discussing their theological and social views with the Disciples constituency: Disciples congregations can fire their "teachers," and the regional and general organizations of the Disciples are dependent in significant measure on annual offerings. But if Disciples professional leaders do not address in a more forthright manner issues on which they differ with the active membership, it is hard to see how the denomination as a whole will be able to deal with the divisive issues. Thus, despite the risk to individual careers and denominational offerings, it is recommended that for the sake of stimulating dialogue within the denomination, Disciples ministers should become more forthright in discussing their theological and social positions.

3. Liberal Disciples ministers need to listen to conservatives. Differences in education amount to differences in experience. There is no reason to believe that the theology and practice of the Disciples would not be enhanced by the insights gained from a critical sharing of liberal and conservative perspectives.

4. Disciples academicians need to serve as teachers not only of Disciples ministers but of the broader Disciples constituency. This would allow them to share their insights with the Disciples laity directly, as they currently do with their ministerial students. It would also allow the broader Disciples constituency to respond directly to the academicians. Of course, if Disciples scholars are to teach the broader Disciples constituency, their services must be requested. While Boring and Perdue show that Disciples have had scholars who sought to serve as teachers of the Disciples laity, Toulouse (pp. 220-21) and Rowell and Seymour (p. 335, n. 51) suggest that Disciples denominational leaders have not always recognized the value of having academicians teach the church.

5. The Disciples need to free their pastors for sermon preparation. The weaknesses in recent Disciples preaching identified by Faulkner (failure to define theological terms, pointless illustrations, etc.) may be as much, if not more, a result of the limited amount of time Disciples ministers devote to the preparation of their sermons as it is a result of their qualifications as teachers. If the Disciples are to engage in serious and sustained dialogue regarding issues

that divide them, the laity must be able to discern what the issues are and why they are important. One strategy for freeing pastors to devote more time to the preparation of their sermons would be to designate someone, or even hire someone (!), to carry much of the routine administrative burden often shouldered by Disciples ministers (a first-rate administrative assistant/secretary might be the answer in some congregations). Revitalization of the Disciples office of elder could also help to relieve the primary teaching minister of the congregation of some of the pastoral support responsibilities often borne by Disciples ministers.[9] Revitalization of the Disciples office of deacon as an office of service to the congregation and the world would also allow Disciples ministers to devote more time to the preparation of their sermons. Also, quality pastoral counseling services need to be available, and pastors need to be encouraged to refer individuals and families who desire long-term counseling to such services and to other counseling services. All of these suggestions imply greater financial and time commitment of the laity.

Meyers and Olson have suggested that Disciples might want to focus on establishing new congregations based on their finding that during the period from 1978 to 1983, larger congregations — apparently as a result of lower levels of commitment to the program of the congregation — were less likely to grow than smaller congregations (pp. 519-20). In light of the need for Disciples ministers to devote more time to the preparation of their sermons, Disciples should be careful to provide sufficient support to new congregations to enable the kind of staffing necessary to allow the minister in new congregations (identified among Disciples by the title "pastor-developer") to devote adequate time to the preparation of sermons.

6. The Disciples need to address the "teachability" of their congregational education resources. This does not mean that Disciples congregational resources need to be "easy to teach." Rather, "teachability," as defined by Rowell and Seymour, has to do with how persons become open to engaging issues in the study of the Bible and theology and to doing critical reflection on ethical and social issues (p. 335).

7. The Disciples need to arrange for their pastors to have a direct role in congregational education. The pastor — often the only person in the congregation with a formal theological education — frequently contributes little to the educational program of the congregation. For many congregations, allowing the pastor to have a direct role in the educational program would require restructuring the educational program away from its Sunday morning concentration.[10]

8. The Disciples need to reconsider the role of higher education in their total educational program. Only a small percentage of Disciples attend Disciples-

9. See D. Newell Williams, "Elders as Assistant Ministers: A Call for Restructure of the Ministry in Congregations of the Christian Church (Disciples of Christ)," *Encounter* 48 (1987): 93-103.
10. See Wesner Fallaw, *Church Education for Tomorrow* (Philadelphia: Westminster Press, 1960).

related institutions of higher education. The curricula of Disciples-related undergraduate institutions have been secularized as they have sought students and funding from beyond the Disciples and accreditation from secular accrediting agencies. The following are some of the questions that the Disciples should consider in relation to the role of higher education in their total educational ministry: How might Disciples-related undergraduate schools attract more of the Disciples constituency? Should more of the students in Disciples schools be encouraged to take a less secularized course of study — a course of study more like the program in religion, psychology, and the social sciences that preministerial candidates are encouraged to complete? How might these institutions serve the educational needs of congregations in their area and at a distance? Should Disciples seminaries be encouraged to develop programs aimed at the laity? How might the Disciples impact *secular* institutions of higher education?

9. Disciples historians need to undertake a fresh appraisal of Disciples history. The last historian of the Disciples to attempt a comprehensive reappraisal of Disciples history was W. E. Garrison. As Gilpin has shown, Garrison's efforts "enabled him to account for the religious situation to which history had brought the Disciples of Christ in his own time and, usually implicitly, to suggest a line to march into the future" (p. 267). Disciples need just such a history today written from the perspective of their current situation. The basic orientation of the history that is needed is already evident. Whatever else they do, contemporary Disciples historians must demonstrate that the Disciples have a theological tradition, pay attention to it in relation to the larger Christian and especially Protestant tradition, and examine the important social and intellectual factors, including previous historiography, that have brought the Disciples to where they are today. It will be necessary to find categories for describing theological and/or religious continuities that are not immediately apparent in surveys of ecclesiastical conflict. This, along with a sympathetic attentiveness to strengths in the positions of all parties in Disciples controversies, could produce a history that would help contemporary Disciples of different theological and social views to understand and appreciate each other's positions, to recognize common ground, and to engage in dialogue regarding issues over which they differ.

THE DISCIPLES' MISSION

It might be suggested that there is an alternative way for the Disciples to identify a distinctively Christian norm and to overcome the negative impact on commitment to congregational program that results from the difference in the views of their ministers and active members: simply get rid of the liberal ministers and the Disciples educational institutions that produce them! Were that done, the Disciples would no longer have a gap between the theological and moral views of their ministers and active members. No doubt such action would also run off the smaller number of active *liberal* laity. On the face of it, this might seem to be a plausible suggestion. On closer inspection it proves unacceptable for two reasons.

First, it is clear that getting rid of the liberals and the Disciples educational institutions that produce them would be a violation of Disciples identity. The commitment to hold in fellowship persons of diverse views has been a hallmark of the Disciples since the days of Disciples founders, Stone and Campbell. Furthermore, this commitment is not simply a matter of denominational identity. Rather, it is rooted in the biblical concept of who Christians are and who they can become through faith in Jesus Christ: a reconciling community embracing humanity in all of its diversity (Gal. 3:28; Rom. 12:3-21; 1 Cor. 12–13; Eph. 4:1-16; Col. 3:11-15). A Roman Catholic scholar who is not overly impressed with the Disciples' track record regarding unity has, nevertheless, recently stated that the "genius" of the early Disciples movement was its perception of the *need* to balance "pluralism and authority, individual conscience and community, toleration and religious certitude."[11] Although the Disciples need to claim a distinctively Christian basis for unity, they would not be Disciples — or faithful to the biblical concept of the church — if they gave up their determination to be a people who accept diversity.

Second, for Disciples to repudiate their liberals and the Disciples educational institutions would be to miss a critical opportunity for distinctive service. The most rapidly growing "religious" sector in America is *not* the conservative churches but the nonaffiliated sector.[12] This sector is composed of highly educated younger adults who have theological and political views much closer to those of Disciples ministers and inactive members than to those of the currently active Disciples membership.[13] If the rapidly expanding nonaffiliated sector and the Disciples' own inactive members are to become active in the church, it seems unlikely that they will be drawn to congregations that identify themselves by their opposition to liberalism. To serve the religious needs of these people, the Disciples must continue to be a church that accepts diversity.

However, to serve the religious needs of the religiously nonaffiliated, inactive Disciples, and other Americans, the Disciples must do more than accept diversity. They must show that they represent positions that are theologically and morally plausible. Beyond this, they must speak a word that adds a quality to human existence not to be found outside of the Christian community. As Alexander Campbell and some contemporary Disciples have understood, this word is nothing other than the gospel of God's gracious love for all made known in the apostolic witness to Jesus Christ.

11. Tristano, *The Origins of the Restoration Movement*, p. 154.
12. Wade Clark Roof and William McKinney, *American Mainline Religion: Its Changing Shape and Future* (New Brunswick, N.J.: Rutgers University Press, 1987), pp. 149-85.
13. Roof and McKinney, *American Mainline Religion*, pp. 187-228.

Index

Abortion, 378-79, 407

Academic freedom: Disciples tradition of, 303-4

Ainslie, Peter, 178-79, 206-7, 239, 244, 248

American Baptists, 254-55, 486, 488

Ames, Edward Scribner, 120-25, 141-42

Anti-Catholicism, 134-37, 178, 184, 192

Anticommunism, 184-85, 192

Association of Disciples for Theological Discussion, 144

Athearn, Walter S., 323, 324

Baby boomers, 11, 391-92, 409-10. *See also* Numerical decline

Baird, George B., 199, 205, 207-8, 220, 221-22, 225-26

Baptism, 6, 8, 130, 565

Baptists. *See* American Baptists, Southern Baptist Convention

Barr, William, 155-56, 233-34

Bates, Miner Lee, 301, 309-10

Beazley, George G., 153-54, 190

Bethany Series, 325, 327

Bethelehem United Church, 474-77

Bible chairs, 306-8

Biblical scholarship, 30-34; of James Philip Hyatt, 87-106; of John William McGarvey, 36-65 *passim;* of Herbert Lockwood Willett, 36-65 *passim,* 72-87

Birth rate of Disciples, Presbyterians, and Southern Baptists, 396, 506-7; implications for evangelism, 410-11

Black congregations, 11-12, 516

Bowen, T. Hassell, 143-44

Bower, William Clayton, 274, 289, 290, 294, 297, 318-19, 324, 325

Brown, Kenneth I., 313, 316

Bureaucratization, 343-44; and career tracks of Disciples professional leaders, 347, 349, 350-58

Butler University, 300

Calhoun, Hall Laurie, 288-89, 290, 291

Campbell, Alexander: as interpreted by E. S. Ames, 122; as model theologian for contemporary Disciples, 563-70; on universal salvation, 53

Chicago-Lambeth Quadrilateral, 254

Christian, The (journal): support of ecumenical relations, 189-91; positions on Vietnam War, 187-88

Christian Board of Publication, 323

Christian Century, 82, 129-30

Christian Church (Disciples of Christ): An Interpretative Examination in Cultural Context, 153-54

Christian Churches: separation from Disciples, 5-11, 12, 257; impact on Disciples geographical distribution, 459-61, 467

Christian education. *See* Religious education

Christian Education: Shared Approaches (CE:SA) curriculum, 330-31.

Christian-Evangelist, The (journal): and anti-Catholicism, 178, 189; and anticommunism, 184-85; on denominationalism, 176-79, 185-87; on ecumenical relations, 178-80, 186-87; on progressive religious education, 323; on the Social Gospel, 182; on the United States, 172-76, 181-85

Christian Life Curriculum, 329-30

Christian Standard: on denominationalism, 176-79; on ecumenical relations, 178, 179-80; on the Philadelphia Plan, 251; opposition to progressive religious educa-